GENERAL MOTORS FULL-SIZE TRUCKS
1999-06 REPAIR MANUAL

CHILTON'S

Covers U.S. and Canadian models of
Chevrolet Silverado, GMC Sierra and
Sierra Denali Pick-ups (1999 thru 2006 and 2007 "Classic"
models), Chevrolet Suburban and Tahoe, GMC Yukon,
Yukon XL and Yukon Denali (2000 thru 2006),
Chevrolet Avalanche (2002 thru 2006)
Two- and four-wheel drive, gasoline engine versions

Does not include 1999 and 2000 C/K Classic, 1999 and 2000 Sierra Classic, or information specific to diesel engine models, 8.1L engine models, CNG models, hybrids, models equipped with rear-wheel steering or heavy-duty models

by Jeff Kibler, A.S.E.

CHILTON *Automotive Books*

PUBLISHED BY **HAYNES NORTH AMERICA, Inc.**

Manufactured in USA
© 2004, 2005, 2007 Haynes North America, Inc.
ISBN-10: 1-56392-686-5
ISBN-13: 978-1-56392-686-0
Library of Congress Control No. 2007931320

Haynes Publishing Group
Sparkford Nr Yeovil
Somerset BA22 7JJ England

Haynes North America, Inc
861 Lawrence Drive
Newbury Park
California 91320 USA

ABCDE
FGHIJ
2

6T12

Contents

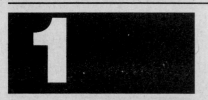

INTRODUCTORY PAGES

1

TUNE-UP AND ROUTINE MAINTENANCE – 1-1

2

V6 ENGINE – 2A-1
V8 ENGINES – 2B-1
GENERAL ENGINE OVERHAUL PROCEDURES – 2C-1

3

COOLING, HEATING AND AIR-CONDITIONING SYSTEMS – 3-1

4

FUEL AND EXHAUST SYSTEMS – 4-1

5

ENGINE ELECTRICAL SYSTEMS – 5-1

6

EMISSIONS AND ENGINE CONTROL SYSTEMS – 6-1

2000 Chevrolet Silverado pick-up

ACKNOWLEDGMENTS

Technical writers who contributed to this project include Eric Godfrey, Bob Henderson, Jay Storer, Larry Warren and Robert Maddox. Wiring diagrams originated by Valley Forge Technical Information Services.

About this manual

ITS PURPOSE

The purpose of this manual is to help you get the best value from your vehicle. It can do so in several ways. It can help you decide what work must be done, even if you choose to have it done by a dealer service department or a repair shop; it provides information and procedures for routine maintenance and servicing; and it offers diagnostic and repair procedures to follow when trouble occurs.

We hope you use the manual to tackle the work yourself. For many simpler jobs, doing it yourself may be quicker than arranging an appointment to get the vehicle into a shop and making the trips to leave it and pick it up. More importantly, a lot of money can be saved by avoiding the expense the shop must pass on to you to cover its labor and overhead costs. An added benefit is the sense of satisfaction and accomplishment that you feel after doing the job yourself.

USING THE MANUAL

The manual is divided into Chapters. Each Chapter is divided into numbered Sections. Each Section consists of consecutively numbered paragraphs.

At the beginning of each numbered Section you will be referred to any illustrations which apply to the procedures in that Section. The reference numbers used in illustration captions pinpoint the pertinent Section and the Step within that Section. That is, illustration 3.2 means the illustration refers to Section 3 and Step (or paragraph) 2 within that Section.

Procedures, once described in the text, are not normally repeated. When it's necessary to refer to another Chapter, the reference will be given as Chapter and Section number. Cross references given without use of the word "Chapter" apply to Sections and/or paragraphs in the same Chapter. For example, "see Section 8" means in the same Chapter.

References to the left or right side of the vehicle assume you are sitting in the driver's seat, facing forward.

Even though we have prepared this manual with extreme care, neither the publisher nor the author can accept responsibility for any errors in, or omissions from, the information given.

→NOTE

A *Note* provides information necessary to properly complete a procedure or information which will make the procedure easier to understand.

⁂ CAUTION

A *Caution* provides a special procedure or special steps which must be taken while completing the procedure where the Caution is found. Not heeding a Caution can result in damage to the assembly being worked on.

⁂ WARNING

A *Warning* provides a special procedure or special steps which must be taken while completing the procedure where the Warning is found. Not heeding a Warning can result in personal injury.

Introduction

The 1999 and later model year Silverado and Sierra models, while similar in appearance to earlier models, are a new design. Pick-ups are available as standard two-door bodies, or with a third (smaller) door behind the right passenger door, and an optional fourth door behind the driver's door on extended-cab models. The sport utility models, introduced in 2000, are all four-doors, with either a liftgate or optional twin doors at the rear. Engines are either V6 or V8, equipped with electronic, sequential multi-port fuel injection.

The chassis layout is conventional with the engine mounted at the front and the power being transmitted through either a four-speed automatic or five-speed manual transmission or driveshaft to the rear axle. On 4WD models a transfer case transmits the power to the front differential and then to the front wheels through independent driveaxles.

These models feature independent front suspension with coil springs (2WD pick-up models) or torsion bars (4WD pick-ups and all SUV models) and shock absorbers at the front. At the rear, all models have a solid rear axle supported by leaf springs and shock absorbers on pick-ups and 2500 series SUV models, and coil springs with shock absorbers on 1500 series SUV models.

The power-assisted steering is either rack-and-pinion (2WD 1500 pick-ups) or conventional recirculating ball type (all other models). The rack-and-pinion steering unit is mounted in front of the engine and the conventional steering box is located on the left-side frame rail.

Some 2002 and later models are equipped with an optional four-wheel steering system called Quadrasteer™. The system allows the driver to choose between several steering modes that can improve maneuverability under certain low-speed, high-speed or towing conditions.

Most models have a power assisted disc-type front and rear brake system with Anti-lock Brake System (ABS) standard. Some later models are equipped with rear drum brakes.

Vehicle identification numbers

VEHICLE IDENTIFICATION NUMBERS

Modifications are a continuing and unpublicized process in vehicle manufacturing. Since spare parts manuals and lists are compiled on a numerical basis, the individual vehicle numbers are essential to correctly identify the component required.

VEHICLE IDENTIFICATION NUMBER (VIN)

The Vehicle Identification Number (VIN), which appears on the Vehicle Certificate of Title and Registration, is also embossed on a gray plate located on the upper left (driver's side) corner of the dashboard, near the windshield (see illustration). The VIN tells you when and where a vehicle was manufactured, its country of origin, make, type, passenger safety system, line, series, body style, engine and assembly plant.

VIN ENGINE AND MODEL YEAR CODES

Two particularly important pieces of information found in the VIN are the engine code and the model year code. Counting from the left, the engine code letter designation is the 8th character and the model year code is the 10th character.

On the model years covered by this manual the engine codes are:

B... 5.3L V8 (L33)
N... 6.0L V8 (LQ9)
T... 5.3L V8 (LM7)
U... 6.0L V8 (LQ4)
V... 4.8L V8 (LR4)
W... 4.3L V6 (L35)
X... 4.3L V6 (LU3)
Z... 5.3L V8 (L59)

On the models covered by this manual the model year codes are:

X... 1999
Y... 2000
1... 2001

The VIN plate is visible from the outside of the vehicle, through the driver's side of the windshield

2... 2002
3... 2003
4... 2004
5... 2005
6... 2006
7... 2007

VEHICLE SAFETY CERTIFICATION LABEL

The Vehicle Safety Certification label is attached to the rear edge of the driver's door (see illustration). The label contains the name of the manufacturer, the month and year of production, the Gross Vehicle Weight Rating (GVWR), the Gross Axle Weight Rating (GAWR) and the certification statement. On most models, the label also includes the OEM tire sizes and pressures.

SERVICE PARTS IDENTIFICATION LABEL

Located on the inside of the glove compartment lid, this label contains information about the options on your vehicle and the paint and trim codes (see illustration). This information is important when ordering parts or when bodywork and repainting is done.

The Vehicle Safety Certification label is affixed to the drivers side door end or post

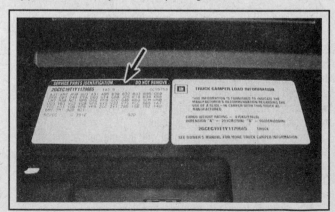

The Service Parts Identification label (arrow) contains information on options and trim/paint codes

On V8 engines the identification number (arrow) is located at the left rear of the engine (seen here from below)

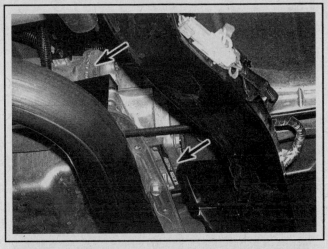

Typical automatic transmission identification number locations

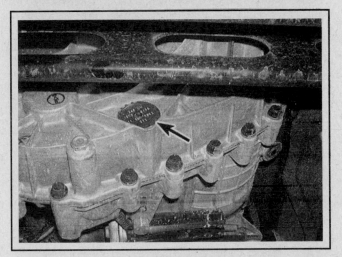

Location of the transfer case identification tag

ENGINE IDENTIFICATION NUMBER (EIN)

The V8 Engine Identification Number (EIN) is stamped into the rear of the engine block just below the left cylinder head (see illustration). On V6 engines the EIN is located either on the block below the left cylinder head or on the rear of the block near the right side cylinder head.

TRANSMISSION IDENTIFICATION NUMBER (TIN)

The manual Transmission Identification Number (TIN) is located on a tag or label on top of the left portion of the bellhousing area of the transmission. On automatic transmissions the TIN is stamped into the transmission case (see illustration).

TRANSFER CASE IDENTIFICATION LABEL

The transfer case identification information is on a tag affixed to the rear side of the case (see illustration).

Buying parts

Replacement parts are available from many sources, which generally fall into one of two categories - authorized dealer parts departments and independent retail auto parts stores. Our advice concerning these parts is as follows:

Retail auto parts stores: Good auto parts stores will stock frequently needed components which wear out relatively fast, such as clutch components, exhaust systems, brake parts, tune-up parts, etc. These stores often supply new or reconditioned parts on an exchange basis, which can save a considerable amount of money. Discount auto parts stores are often very good places to buy materials and parts needed for general vehicle maintenance such as oil, grease, filters, spark plugs, belts, touch-up paint, bulbs, etc. They also usually sell tools and general accessories, have convenient hours, charge lower prices and can often be found not far from home.

Authorized dealer parts department: This is the best source for parts which are unique to the vehicle and not generally available elsewhere (such as major engine parts, transmission parts, trim pieces, etc.).

Warranty information: If the vehicle is still covered under warranty, be sure that any replacement parts purchased - regardless of the source - do not invalidate the warranty!

To be sure of obtaining the correct parts, have engine and chassis numbers available and, if possible, take the old parts along for positive identification.

MAINTENANCE TECHNIQUES

There are a number of techniques involved in maintenance and repair that will be referred to throughout this manual. Application of these techniques will enable the home mechanic to be more efficient, better organized and capable of performing the various tasks properly, which will ensure that the repair job is thorough and complete.

Fasteners

Fasteners are nuts, bolts, studs and screws used to hold two or more parts together. There are a few things to keep in mind when working with fasteners. Almost all of them use a locking device of some type, either a lockwasher, locknut, locking tab or thread adhesive. All threaded fasteners should be clean and straight, with undamaged threads and undamaged corners on the hex head where the wrench fits. Develop the habit of replacing all damaged nuts and bolts with new ones. Special locknuts with nylon or fiber inserts can only be used once. If they are removed, they lose their locking ability and must be replaced with new ones.

Rusted nuts and bolts should be treated with a penetrating fluid to ease removal and prevent breakage. Some mechanics use turpentine in a spout-type oil can, which works quite well. After applying the rust penetrant, let it work for a few minutes before trying to loosen the nut or bolt. Badly rusted fasteners may have to be chiseled or sawed off or removed with a special nut breaker, available at tool stores.

If a bolt or stud breaks off in an assembly, it can be drilled and removed with a special tool commonly available for this purpose. Most automotive machine shops can perform this task, as well as other repair procedures, such as the repair of threaded holes that have been stripped out.

Flat washers and lockwashers, when removed from an assembly, should always be replaced exactly as removed. Replace any damaged washers with new ones. Never use a lockwasher on any soft metal surface (such as aluminum), thin sheet metal or plastic.

Fastener sizes

For a number of reasons, automobile manufacturers are making wider and wider use of metric fasteners. Therefore, it is important to be able to tell the difference between standard (sometimes called U.S. or SAE) and metric hardware, since they cannot be interchanged.

All bolts, whether standard or metric, are sized according to diameter, thread pitch and length. For example, a standard 1/2 - 13 x 1 bolt is 1/2 inch in diameter, has 13 threads per inch and is 1 inch long. An M12 - 1.75 x 25 metric bolt is 12 mm in diameter, has a thread pitch of 1.75 mm (the distance between threads) and is 25 mm long. The two bolts are nearly identical, and easily confused, but they are not interchangeable.

In addition to the differences in diameter, thread pitch and length, metric and standard bolts can also be distinguished by examining the bolt heads. To begin with, the distance across the flats on a standard bolt head is measured in inches, while the same dimension on a metric bolt is sized in millimeters (the same is true for nuts). As a result, a standard wrench should not be used on a metric bolt and a metric wrench should not be used on a standard bolt. Also, most standard bolts have slashes radiating out from the center of the head to denote the grade or strength of the bolt, which is an indication of the amount of torque that can be applied to it. The greater the number of slashes, the greater the strength of the bolt. Grades 0 through 5 are commonly used on automobiles. Metric bolts have a property class (grade) number, rather than a slash, molded into their heads to indicate bolt strength. In this case, the higher the number, the stronger the bolt. Property class numbers 8.8, 9.8 and 10.9 are commonly used on automobiles.

Strength markings can also be used to distinguish standard hex nuts from metric hex nuts. Many standard nuts have dots stamped into one side, while metric nuts are marked with a number. The greater the number of dots, or the higher the number, the greater the strength of the nut.

Metric studs are also marked on their ends according to property class (grade). Larger studs are numbered (the same as metric bolts), while smaller studs carry a geometric code to denote grade.

It should be noted that many fasteners, especially Grades 0 through 2, have no distinguishing marks on them. When such is the case, the only way to determine whether it is standard or metric is to measure the thread pitch or compare it to a known fastener of the same size.

Standard fasteners are often referred to as SAE, as opposed to metric. However, it should be noted that SAE technically refers to a non-metric fine thread fastener only. Coarse thread non-metric fasteners are referred to as USS sizes.

Since fasteners of the same size (both standard and metric) may have different strength ratings, be sure to reinstall any bolts, studs or nuts removed from your vehicle in their original locations. Also, when replacing a fastener with a new one, make sure that the new one has a strength rating equal to or greater than the original.

Tightening sequences and procedures

Most threaded fasteners should be tightened to a specific torque value (torque is the twisting force applied to a threaded component such as a nut or bolt). Overtightening the fastener can weaken it and cause it to break, while undertightening can cause it to eventually come loose. Bolts, screws and studs, depending on the material they are made of and their thread diameters, have specific torque values, many of which are noted in the Specifications at the end of each Chapter. Be sure to follow the torque recommendations closely. For fasteners not assigned a specific torque, a general torque value chart is presented here as a guide. These torque values are for dry (unlubricated) fasteners threaded into steel or cast iron (not aluminum). As was previously mentioned, the size and grade of a fastener determine the amount of torque that can safely be applied to it. The figures listed here are approximate for Grade 2 and Grade 3 fasteners. Higher grades can tolerate higher torque values.

Fasteners laid out in a pattern, such as cylinder head bolts, oil pan bolts, differential cover bolts, etc., must be loosened or tightened in sequence to avoid warping the component. This sequence will normally be shown in the appropriate Chapter. If a specific pattern is not given, the following procedures can be used to prevent warping.

Initially, the bolts or nuts should be assembled finger-tight only. Next, they should be tightened one full turn each, in a criss-cross or diagonal pattern. After each one has been tightened one full turn, return to the first one and tighten them all one-half turn, following the same pattern. Finally, tighten each of them one-quarter turn at a time until each fastener has been tightened to the proper torque. To loosen and remove the fasteners, the procedure would be reversed.

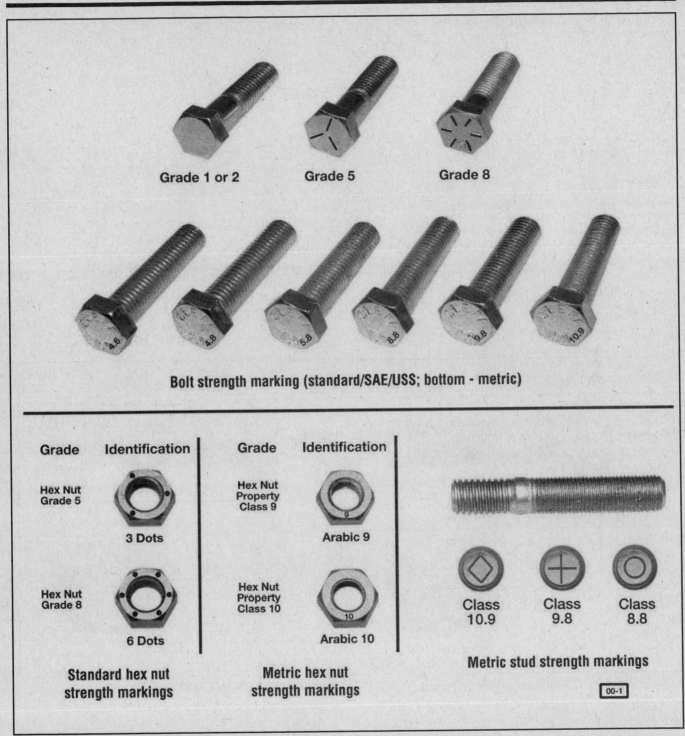

Grade 1 or 2   Grade 5   Grade 8

Bolt strength marking (standard/SAE/USS; bottom - metric)

Grade	Identification
Hex Nut Grade 5	3 Dots
Hex Nut Grade 8	6 Dots

Standard hex nut strength markings

Grade	Identification
Hex Nut Property Class 9	Arabic 9
Hex Nut Property Class 10	Arabic 10

Metric hex nut strength markings

Class 10.9   Class 9.8   Class 8.8

Metric stud strength markings

00-1

Component disassembly

Component disassembly should be done with care and purpose to help ensure that the parts go back together properly. Always keep track of the sequence in which parts are removed. Make note of special characteristics or marks on parts that can be installed more than one way, such as a grooved thrust washer on a shaft. It is a good idea to lay the disassembled parts out on a clean surface in the order that they were removed. It may also be helpful to make sketches or take instant photos of components before removal.

When removing fasteners from a component, keep track of their locations. Sometimes threading a bolt back in a part, or putting the washers and nut back on a stud, can prevent mix-ups later. If nuts and bolts cannot be returned to their original locations, they should be kept in a compartmented box or a series of small boxes. A cupcake or muffin tin is ideal for this purpose, since each cavity can hold the bolts and nuts from a particular area (i.e. oil pan bolts, valve cover bolts, engine mount bolts, etc.). A pan of this type is especially helpful when working on assemblies with very small parts, such as the carburetor, alternator,

Metric thread sizes

	Ft-lbs	Nm
M-6	6 to 9	9 to 12
M-8	14 to 21	19 to 28
M-10	28 to 40	38 to 54
M-12	50 to 71	68 to 96
M-14	80 to 140	109 to 154

Pipe thread sizes

1/8	5 to 8	7 to 10
1/4	12 to 18	17 to 24
3/8	22 to 33	30 to 44
1/2	25 to 35	34 to 47

U.S. thread sizes

1/4 - 20	6 to 9	9 to 12
5/16 - 18	12 to 18	17 to 24
5/16 - 24	14 to 20	19 to 27
3/8 - 16	22 to 32	30 to 43
3/8 - 24	27 to 38	37 to 51
7/16 - 14	40 to 55	55 to 74
7/16 - 20	40 to 60	55 to 81
1/2 - 13	55 to 80	75 to 108

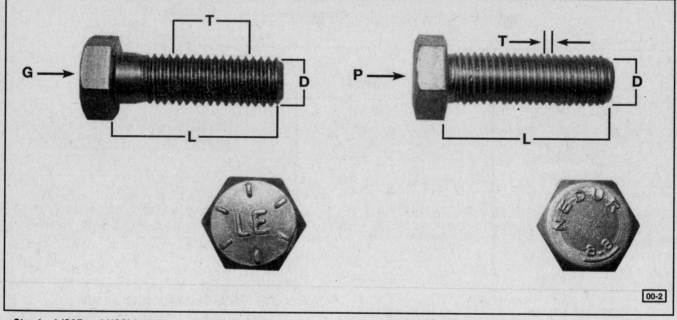

00-2

Standard (SAE and USS) bolt dimensions/grade marks

G   Grade marks (bolt strength)
L   Length (in inches)
T   Thread pitch (number of threads per inch)
D   Nominal diameter (in inches)

Metric bolt dimensions/grade marks

P   Property class (bolt strength)
L   Length (in millimeters)
T   Thread pitch (distance between threads in millimeters)
D   Diameter

valve train or interior dash and trim pieces. The cavities can be marked with paint or tape to identify the contents.

Whenever wiring looms, harnesses or connectors are separated, it is a good idea to identify the two halves with numbered pieces of masking tape so they can be easily reconnected.

Gasket sealing surfaces

Throughout any vehicle, gaskets are used to seal the mating surfaces between two parts and keep lubricants, fluids, vacuum or pressure contained in an assembly.

Many times these gaskets are coated with a liquid or paste-type gasket sealing compound before assembly. Age, heat and pressure can sometimes cause the two parts to stick together so tightly that they are very difficult to separate. Often, the assembly can be loosened by striking it with a soft-face hammer near the mating surfaces. A regular hammer can be used if a block of wood is placed between the hammer and the part. Do not hammer on cast parts or parts that could be easily damaged. With any particularly stubborn part, always recheck to make sure that every fastener has been removed.

Avoid using a screwdriver or bar to pry apart an assembly, as they

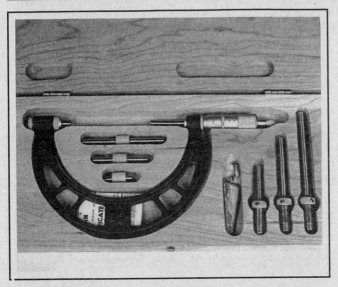

Micrometer set

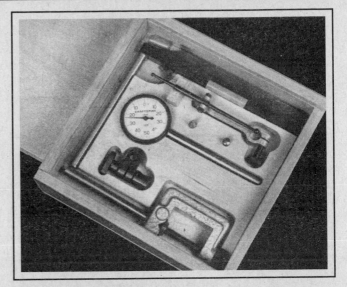

Dial indicator set

can easily mar the gasket sealing surfaces of the parts, which must remain smooth. If prying is absolutely necessary, use an old broom handle, but keep in mind that extra clean up will be necessary if the wood splinters.

After the parts are separated, the old gasket must be carefully scraped off and the gasket surfaces cleaned. Stubborn gasket material can be soaked with rust penetrant or treated with a special chemical to soften it so it can be easily scraped off.

✳✳CAUTION:

Never use gasket removal solutions or caustic chemicals on plastic or other composite components.

A scraper can be fashioned from a piece of copper tubing by flattening and sharpening one end. Copper is recommended because it is usually softer than the surfaces to be scraped, which reduces the chance of gouging the part. Some gaskets can be removed with a wire brush, but regardless of the method used, the mating surfaces must be left clean and smooth. If for some reason the gasket surface is gouged, then a gasket sealer thick enough to fill scratches will have to be used during reassembly of the components. For most applications, a non-drying (or semi-drying) gasket sealer should be used.

Hose removal tips

✳✳ WARNING:

If the vehicle is equipped with air conditioning, do not disconnect any of the A/C hoses without first having the system depressurized by a dealer service department or a service station.

Hose removal precautions closely parallel gasket removal precautions. Avoid scratching or gouging the surface that the hose mates against or the connection may leak. This is especially true for radiator hoses. Because of various chemical reactions, the rubber in hoses can bond itself to the metal spigot that the hose fits over. To remove a hose, first loosen the hose clamps that secure it to the spigot. Then, with slip-joint pliers, grab the hose at the clamp and rotate it around

the spigot. Work it back and forth until it is completely free, then pull it off. Silicone or other lubricants will ease removal if they can be applied between the hose and the outside of the spigot. Apply the same lubricant to the inside of the hose and the outside of the spigot to simplify installation.

As a last resort (and if the hose is to be replaced with a new one anyway), the rubber can be slit with a knife and the hose peeled from the spigot. If this must be done, be careful that the metal connection is not damaged.

If a hose clamp is broken or damaged, do not reuse it. Wire-type clamps usually weaken with age, so it is a good idea to replace them with screw-type clamps whenever a hose is removed.

TOOLS

A selection of good tools is a basic requirement for anyone who plans to maintain and repair his or her own vehicle. For the owner who has few tools, the initial investment might seem high, but when compared to the spiraling costs of professional auto maintenance and repair, it is a wise one.

To help the owner decide which tools are needed to perform the tasks detailed in this manual, the following tool lists are offered: *Maintenance and minor repair, Repair/overhaul and Special.*

The newcomer to practical mechanics should start off with the *maintenance and minor repair* tool kit, which is adequate for the simpler jobs performed on a vehicle. Then, as confidence and experience grow, the owner can tackle more difficult tasks, buying additional tools as they are needed. Eventually the basic kit will be expanded into the *repair and overhaul* tool set. Over a period of time, the experienced do-it-yourselfer will assemble a tool set complete enough for most repair and overhaul procedures and will add tools from the special category when it is felt that the expense is justified by the frequency of use.

Maintenance and minor repair tool kit

The tools in this list should be considered the minimum required for performance of routine maintenance, servicing and minor repair work. We recommend the purchase of combination wrenches (box-end and open-end combined in one wrench). While more expensive than open end wrenches, they offer the advantages of both types of wrench.

Combination wrench set (1/4-inch to 1 inch or 6 mm to 19 mm)

Adjustable wrench, 8 inch
Spark plug wrench with rubber insert
Spark plug gap adjusting tool
Feeler gauge set
Brake bleeder wrench
Standard screwdriver (5/16-inch x 6 inch)
Phillips screwdriver (No. 2 x 6 inch)
Combination pliers - 6 inch

Hacksaw and assortment of blades
Tire pressure gauge
Grease gun
Oil can
Fine emery cloth
Wire brush
Battery post and cable cleaning tool
Oil filter wrench

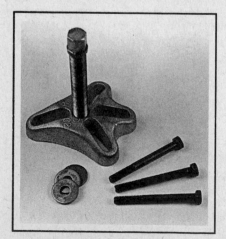

Dial caliper

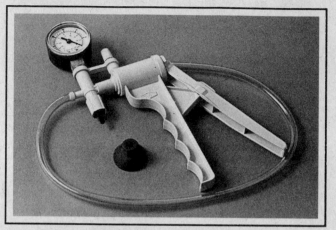

Hand-operated vacuum pump

Timing light

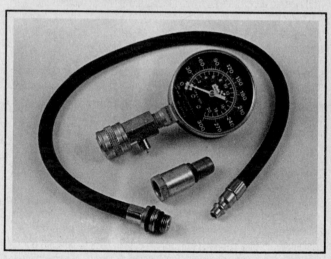

Compression gauge with spark plug hole adapter

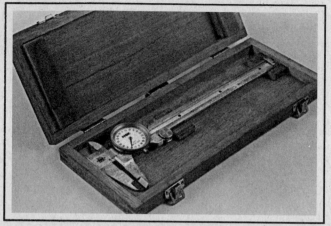

Damper/steering wheel puller

General purpose puller

Hydraulic lifter removal tool

Funnel (medium size)
Safety goggles
Jackstands (2)
Drain pan

➡**Note: If basic tune-ups are going to be part of routine maintenance, it will be necessary to purchase a good quality stroboscopic timing light and combination tachometer/dwell meter. Although they are included in the list of special tools, it is mentioned here because they are absolutely necessary for tuning most vehicles properly.**

Repair and overhaul tool set

These tools are essential for anyone who plans to perform major repairs and are in addition to those in the maintenance and minor repair tool kit. Included is a comprehensive set of sockets which, though expensive, are invaluable because of their versatility, especially when various extensions and drives are available. We recommend the 1/2-inch drive over the 3/8-inch drive. Although the larger drive is bulky and more expensive, it has the capacity of accepting a very wide range of large sockets. Ideally, however, the mechanic should have a 3/8-inch drive set and a 1/2-inch drive set.

Valve spring compressor

Valve spring compressor

Ridge reamer

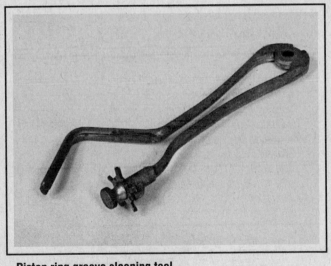

Piston ring groove cleaning tool

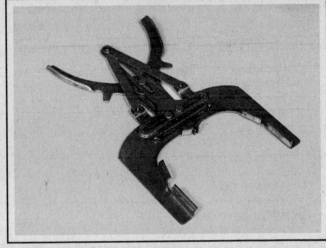

Ring removal/installation tool

Ring compressor

Cylinder hone

Brake hold-down spring tool

Torque angle gauge

Socket set(s)
Reversible ratchet
Extension - 10 inch
Universal joint
Torque wrench (same size drive as sockets)
Ball peen hammer - 8 ounce
Soft-face hammer (plastic/rubber)
Standard screwdriver (1/4-inch x 6 inch)
Standard screwdriver (stubby - 5/16-inch)
Phillips screwdriver (No. 3 x 8 inch)
Phillips screwdriver (stubby - No. 2)
Pliers - vise grip
Pliers - lineman's
Pliers - needle nose
Pliers - snap-ring (internal and external)
Cold chisel - 1/2-inch
Scribe
Scraper (made from flattened copper tubing)
Centerpunch
Pin punches (1/16, 1/8, 3/16-inch)
Steel rule/straightedge - 12 inch
Allen wrench set (1/8 to 3/8-inch or 4 mm to 10 mm)
A selection of files
Wire brush (large)
Jackstands (second set)
Jack (scissor or hydraulic type)

➡**Note: Another tool which is often useful is an electric drill with a chuck capacity of 3/8-inch and a set of good quality drill bits.**

Special tools

The tools in this list include those which are not used regularly, are expensive to buy, or which need to be used in accordance with their manufacturer's instructions. Unless these tools will be used frequently, it is not very economical to purchase many of them. A consideration would be to split the cost and use between yourself and a friend or friends. In addition, most of these tools can be obtained from a tool rental shop on a temporary basis.

This list primarily contains only those tools and instruments widely available to the public, and not those special tools produced by the vehicle manufacturer for distribution to dealer service departments. Occasionally, references to the manufacturer's special tools are included in the text of this manual. Generally, an alternative method of doing the

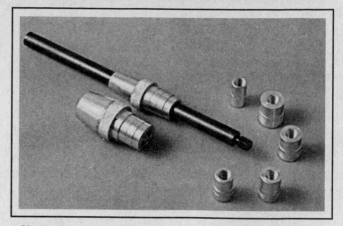

Clutch plate alignment tool

job without the special tool is offered. However, sometimes there is no alternative to their use. Where this is the case, and the tool cannot be purchased or borrowed, the work should be turned over to the dealer service department or an automotive repair shop.

Valve spring compressor
Piston ring groove cleaning tool
Piston ring compressor
Piston ring installation tool
Cylinder compression gauge
Cylinder ridge reamer
Cylinder surfacing hone
Cylinder bore gauge
Micrometers and/or dial calipers
Hydraulic lifter removal tool
Balljoint separator
Universal-type puller
Impact screwdriver
Dial indicator set
Stroboscopic timing light (inductive pick-up)
Hand operated vacuum/pressure pump
Tachometer/dwell meter
Universal electrical multimeter
Cable hoist
Brake spring removal and installation tools
Floor jack

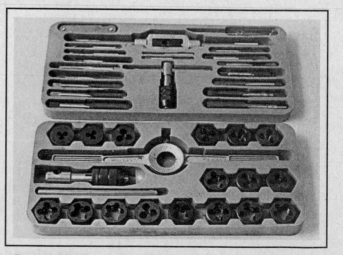

Tap and die set

Buying tools

For the do-it-yourselfer who is just starting to get involved in vehicle maintenance and repair, there are a number of options available when purchasing tools. If maintenance and minor repair is the extent of the work to be done, the purchase of individual tools is satisfactory. If, on the other hand, extensive work is planned, it would be a good idea to purchase a modest tool set from one of the large retail chain stores. A set can usually be bought at a substantial savings over the individual tool prices, and they often come with a tool box. As additional tools are needed, add-on sets, individual tools and a larger tool box can be purchased to expand the tool selection. Building a tool set gradually allows the cost of the tools to be spread over a longer period of time and gives the mechanic the freedom to choose only those tools that will actually be used.

Tool stores will often be the only source of some of the special tools that are needed, but regardless of where tools are bought, try to avoid cheap ones, especially when buying screwdrivers and sockets, because they won't last very long. The expense involved in replacing cheap tools will eventually be greater than the initial cost of quality tools.

Care and maintenance of tools

Good tools are expensive, so it makes sense to treat them with respect. Keep them clean and in usable condition and store them properly when not in use. Always wipe off any dirt, grease or metal chips before putting them away. Never leave tools lying around in the work area. Upon completion of a job, always check closely under the hood for tools that may have been left there so they won't get lost during a test drive.

Some tools, such as screwdrivers, pliers, wrenches and sockets, can be hung on a panel mounted on the garage or workshop wall, while others should be kept in a tool box or tray. Measuring instruments, gauges, meters, etc. must be carefully stored where they cannot be damaged by weather or impact from other tools.

When tools are used with care and stored properly, they will last a very long time. Even with the best of care, though, tools will wear out if used frequently. When a tool is damaged or worn out, replace it. Subsequent jobs will be safer and more enjoyable if you do.

HOW TO REPAIR DAMAGED THREADS

Sometimes, the internal threads of a nut or bolt hole can become stripped, usually from overtightening. Stripping threads is an all-too-common occurrence, especially when working with aluminum parts, because aluminum is so soft that it easily strips out.

Usually, external or internal threads are only partially stripped. After they've been cleaned up with a tap or die, they'll still work. Sometimes, however, threads are badly damaged. When this happens, you've got three choices:

1) *Drill and tap the hole to the next suitable oversize and install a larger diameter bolt, screw or stud.*

2) *Drill and tap the hole to accept a threaded plug, then drill and tap the plug to the original screw size. You can also buy a plug already threaded to the original size. Then you simply drill a hole to the specified size, then run the threaded plug into the hole with a bolt and jam nut. Once the plug is fully seated, remove the jam nut and bolt.*

3) *The third method uses a patented thread repair kit like Heli-Coil or Slimsert. These easy-to-use kits are designed to repair damaged threads in straight-through holes and blind holes. Both are available as kits which can handle a variety of sizes and thread patterns. Drill the hole, then tap it with the special included tap. Install the Heli-Coil and the hole is back to its original diameter and thread pitch.*

Regardless of which method you use, be sure to proceed calmly and carefully. A little impatience or carelessness during one of these relatively simple procedures can ruin your whole day's work and cost you a bundle if you wreck an expensive part.

WORKING FACILITIES

Not to be overlooked when discussing tools is the workshop. If anything more than routine maintenance is to be carried out, some sort of suitable work area is essential.

It is understood, and appreciated, that many home mechanics do not have a good workshop or garage available, and end up removing an engine or doing major repairs outside. It is recommended, however, that the overhaul or repair be completed under the cover of a roof.

A clean, flat workbench or table of comfortable working height is an absolute necessity. The workbench should be equipped with a vise that has a jaw opening of at least four inches.

As mentioned previously, some clean, dry storage space is also required for tools, as well as the lubricants, fluids, cleaning solvents, etc. which soon become necessary.

Sometimes waste oil and fluids, drained from the engine or cooling system during normal maintenance or repairs, present a disposal problem. To avoid pouring them on the ground or into a sewage system, pour the used fluids into large containers, seal them with caps and take them to an authorized disposal site or recycling center. Plastic jugs, such as old antifreeze containers, are ideal for this purpose.

Always keep a supply of old newspapers and clean rags available. Old towels are excellent for mopping up spills. Many mechanics use rolls of paper towels for most work because they are readily available and disposable. To help keep the area under the vehicle clean, a large cardboard box can be cut open and flattened to protect the garage or shop floor.

Whenever working over a painted surface, such as when leaning over a fender to service something under the hood, always cover it with an old blanket or bedspread to protect the finish. Vinyl covered pads, made especially for this purpose, are available at auto parts stores.

Jacking and towing

JACKING

The jack supplied with the vehicle should only be used for raising the vehicle when changing a tire or placing jackstands under the frame. NEVER work under the vehicle or start the engine when the vehicle supported only by a jack.

The vehicle should be parked on level ground with the wheels blocked, the parking brake applied and the transmission in Park (automatic) or Reverse (manual). If the vehicle is parked alongside the roadway, or in any other hazardous situation, turn on the emergency hazard flashers. If a tire is to be changed, loosen the lug nuts one-half turn before raising off the ground.

Place the jack under the vehicle in the indicated positions (see illustrations). Operate the jack with a slow, smooth motion until the wheel is raised off the ground. Remove the lug nuts, pull off the wheel, install the spare and thread the lug nuts back on with the beveled side facing

in. Tighten the lug nuts snugly, lower the vehicle until some weight is on the wheel, tighten them completely in a criss-cross pattern and remove the jack.

TOWING

Equipment specifically designed for towing should be used and attached to the main structural members of the vehicle. Optional tow hooks may be attached to the frame at both ends of the vehicle; they are intended for emergency use only, for rescuing a stranded vehicle. Do not use the tow hooks for highway towing. Stand clear when using tow straps or chains (they may break, causing serious injury.)

The manufacturer recommends that these vehicles be towed only by wheel-lift equipment or a flatbed car-carrier.

Safety is a major consideration when towing and all applicable state and local laws must be obeyed. In addition to a tow bar, a safety chain must be used for all towing.

Two-wheel drive vehicles with automatic transmission may be towed with the rear wheels on a towing dolly with no mileage restriction (at posted highway speeds). If the front wheels are on the dolly, speed should be no more than 35 mph for no more than 50 miles, or damage may be done to the automatic transmission.

Two-wheel drive vehicles with manual transmission can be towed 50 miles with the ignition lock in the Off position and the transmission in Neutral.

Four-wheel drive vehicles should be towed with the transfer case in Neutral. With the front end lifted, towing is not limited, but if the rear end is lifted and the front is on the ground, towing is restricted to a maximum of 50 miles distance.

If any vehicle is to be towed with the front wheels on the ground and the rear wheels raised, the ignition key must be turned to the OFF position to unlock the steering column and a steering wheel clamping device designed for towing must be used or damage to the steering column lock may occur.

Front jacking position for two-wheel drive pick-ups with the factory jack

Front jacking position with factory jack on all other Series

Rear jacking position - the axle must be secure in the jack head grooves

Booster battery (jump) starting

Observe these precautions when using a booster battery to start a vehicle:

a) *Before connecting the booster battery, make sure the ignition switch is in the Off position.*

b) *Turn off the lights, heater and other electrical loads.*

c) *Your eyes should be shielded. Safety goggles are a good idea.*

d) *Make sure the booster battery is the same voltage as the dead one in the vehicle.*

e) *The two vehicles MUST NOT TOUCH each other!*

f) *Make sure the transaxle is in Neutral (manual) or Park (automatic).*

g) *If the booster battery is not a maintenance-free type, remove the vent caps and lay a cloth over the vent holes.*

The main battery on these vehicles (some models have an optional second battery) is located in the left front corner of the engine compartment, where the battery cable connections are difficult to access with jumper cables. Due to the lack of accessibility, remote battery connections are provided inside the engine compartment for jump-starting (see illustration).

Connect the red jumper cable to the positive (+) terminals of each battery.

Connect one end of the black cable to the negative (-) terminal of the booster battery. The other end of this cable should be connected to a good ground on the engine block (see illustration). Make sure the cable will not come into contact with the fan, drivebelts or other moving parts of the engine.

Start the engine using the booster battery, then run the booster vehicle at a fast idle for a few minutes to instill some charge in the dead battery. Let the engine idle, then disconnect the jumper cables in the reverse order of connection. The vehicle with the dead battery may have to be driven for 20 minutes or more to sufficiently recharge the battery for independent starting.

On these vehicles it's easier to attach the battery jumper cables to these remote terminals, rather than the battery itself - open this red plastic cover (A) and connect the positive cable to the stud inside. Attach the negative booster cable clamp to the metal grounding ledge (B) below the alternator

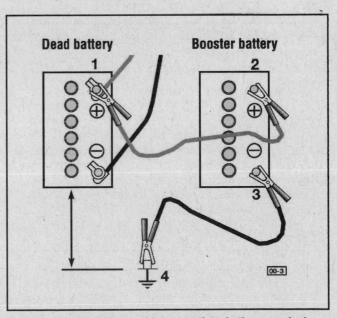

Make the booster battery cable connections in the numerical order shown (note that the negative cable of the booster battery is NOT attached to the negative terminal of the dead battery)

Anti-theft audio system

※※ WARNING:

Refer to the Warning and Caution in Chapter 5, Section 1 under "Battery disconnection" before proceeding with the following Steps.

GENERAL INFORMATION

1   Some of these models are equipped with THEFTLOCK audio systems, which include an anti-theft feature that will render the stereo inoperative if stolen. If the power source to the stereo is cut with the anti-theft feature activated, the stereo will be inoperative. Even if the power source is immediately re-connected, the stereo will not function.

2   If your vehicle is equipped with this anti-theft system, do not disconnect the battery, remove the stereo or disconnect related components unless you have either turned off the feature or have the individual ID (code) number for the stereo.

DISABLING THE ANTI-THEFT FEATURE

3   Press the stereo's 1 and 4 buttons at the same time for five seconds with the ignition on and the radio power off. The display will show SEC, indicating the unit is in the secure mode (anti-theft feature enabled).

4   Press the MN button. The display will show "000".

5   Press the MN button until the last two numbers are the same as your secret code.

6   Press HR until the first one or two numbers displayed match your code. The numbers will be displayed as entered.

7   Press AM/FM. If the display shows "_ _ _" you have successfully disabled the anti-theft feature. If SEC is displayed, the code you entered was incorrect and the anti-theft feature is still enabled.

UNLOCKING THE STEREO AFTER A POWER LOSS

8   When the power is restored to the stereo, the stereo won't turn on and LOC will appear on the display. Enter your ID code as follows, without pausing more than 15 seconds between Steps.

9   Turn the ignition switch to ON, but leave the stereo off.

10 Press the MN button. "000" should display.

11 Press the HR button to make the last two numbers match your code, then release the button.

12 Press the HR button until the first one or two numbers match your code.

13 Press AM/FM. SEC should appear, indicating the stereo is unlocked. If LOC appears, the numbers you entered were not correct and the stereo is still inoperative.

14 You should have the code written down in a secure place, for use in unlocking the THEFTLOCK feature.

➡**Note: When performing the above procedures, you are allowed only eight tries. After that, the system shuts down for an hour, with the radio displaying "INOP." At the end of that period, you have another three tries, after which you will have to bring the vehicle to your dealer for activation.**

CONVERSION FACTORS

LENGTH (distance)

Inches (in)	X	25.4	= Millimeters (mm)	X 0.0394	= Inches (in)
Feet (ft)	X	0.305	= Meters (m)	X 3.281	= Feet (ft)
Miles	X	1.609	= Kilometers (km)	X 0.621	= Miles

VOLUME (capacity)

Cubic inches (cu in; in³)	X	16.387	= Cubic centimeters (cc; cm³)	X 0.061	= Cubic inches (cu in; in³)
Imperial pints (Imp pt)	X	0.568	= Liters (l)	X 1.76	= Imperial pints (Imp pt)
Imperial quarts (Imp qt)	X	1.137	= Liters (l)	X 0.88	= Imperial quarts (Imp qt)
Imperial quarts (Imp qt)	X	1.201	= US quarts (US qt)	X 0.833	= Imperial quarts (Imp qt)
US quarts (US qt)	X	0.946	= Liters (l)	X 1.057	= US quarts (US qt)
Imperial gallons (Imp gal)	X	4.546	= Liters (l)	X 0.22	= Imperial gallons (Imp gal)
Imperial gallons (Imp gal)	X	1.201	= US gallons (US gal)	X 0.833	= Imperial gallons (Imp gal)
US gallons (US gal)	X	3.785	= Liters (l)	X 0.264	= US gallons (US gal)

MASS (weight)

Ounces (oz)	X	28.35	= Grams (g)	X 0.035	= Ounces (oz)
Pounds (lb)	X	0.454	= Kilograms (kg)	X 2.205	= Pounds (lb)

FORCE

Ounces-force (ozf; oz)	X	0.278	= Newtons (N)	X 3.6	= Ounces-force (ozf; oz)
Pounds-force (lbf; lb)	X	4.448	= Newtons (N)	X 0.225	= Pounds-force (lbf; lb)
Newtons (N)	X	0.1	= Kilograms-force (kgf; kg)	X 9.81	= Newtons (N)

PRESSURE

Pounds-force per square inch (psi; lbf/in^2; lb/in^2)	X	0.070	= Kilograms-force per square centimeter (kgf/cm^2; kg/cm^2)	X 14.223	= Pounds-force per square inch (psi; lbf/in^2; lb/in^2)
Pounds-force per square inch (psi; lbf/in^2; lb/in^2)	X	0.068	= Atmospheres (atm)	X 14.696	= Pounds-force per square inch (psi; lbf/in^2; lb/in^2)
Pounds-force per square inch (psi; lbf/in^2; lb/in^2)	X	0.069	= Bars	X 14.5	= Pounds-force per square inch (psi; lbf/in^2; lb/in^2)
Pounds-force per square inch (psi; lbf/in^2; lb/in^2)	X	6.895	= Kilopascals (kPa)	X 0.145	= Pounds-force per square inch (psi; lbf/in^2; lb/in^2)
Kilopascals (kPa)	X	0.01	= Kilograms-force per square centimeter (kgf/cm^2; kg/cm^2)	X 98.1	= Kilopascals (kPa)

TORQUE (moment of force)

Pounds-force inches (lbf in; lb in)	X	1.152	= Kilograms-force centimeter (kgf cm; kg cm)	X 0.868	= Pounds-force inches (lbf in; lb in)
Pounds-force inches (lbf in; lb in)	X	0.113	= Newton meters (Nm)	X 8.85	= Pounds-force inches (lbf in; lb in)
Pounds-force inches (lbf in; lb in)	X	0.083	= Pounds-force feet (lbf ft; lb ft)	X 12	= Pounds-force inches (lbf in; lb in)
Pounds-force feet (lbf ft; lb ft)	X	0.138	= Kilograms-force meters (kgf m; kg m)	X 7.233	= Pounds-force feet (lbf ft; lb ft)
Pounds-force feet (lbf ft; lb ft)	X	1.356	= Newton meters (Nm)	X 0.738	= Pounds-force feet (lbf ft; lb ft)
Newton meters (Nm)	X	0.102	= Kilograms-force meters (kgf m; kg m)	X 9.804	= Newton meters (Nm)

VACUUM

Inches mercury (in. Hg)	X	3.377	= Kilopascals (kPa)	X 0.2961	= Inches mercury
Inches mercury (in. Hg)	X	25.4	= Millimeters mercury (mm Hg)	X 0.0394	= Inches mercury

POWER

Horsepower (hp)	X	745.7	= Watts (W)	X 0.0013	= Horsepower (hp)

VELOCITY (speed)

Miles per hour (miles/hr; mph)	X	1.609	= Kilometers per hour (km/hr; kph)	X 0.621	= Miles per hour (miles/hr; mph)

FUEL CONSUMPTION *

Miles per gallon, Imperial (mpg)	X	0.354	= Kilometers per liter (km/l)	X 2.825	= Miles per gallon, Imperial (mpg)
Miles per gallon, US (mpg)	X	0.425	= Kilometers per liter (km/l)	X 2.352	= Miles per gallon, US (mpg)

TEMPERATURE

Degrees Fahrenheit = (°C x 1.8) + 32   Degrees Celsius (Degrees Centigrade; °C) = (°F − 32) x 0.56

It is common practice to convert from miles per gallon (mpg) to liters/100 kilometers (l/100km), where mpg (Imperial) x l/100 km = 282 and mpg (US) x l/100 km = 235

FRACTION/DECIMAL/MILLIMETER EQUIVALENTS

DECIMALS TO MILLIMETERS

Decimal	mm	Decimal	mm
0.001	0.0254	0.500	12.7000
0.002	0.0508	0.510	12.9540
0.003	0.0762	0.520	13.2080
0.004	0.1016	0.530	13.4620
0.005	0.1270	0.540	13.7160
0.006	0.1524	0.550	13.9700
0.007	0.1778	0.560	14.2240
0.008	0.2032	0.570	14.4780
0.009	0.2286	0.580	14.7320
0.010	0.2540	0.590	14.9860
0.020	0.5080	0.600	15.2400
0.030	0.7620	0.610	15.4940
0.040	1.0160	0.620	15.7480
0.050	1.2700	0.630	16.0020
0.060	1.5240	0.640	16.2560
0.070	1.7780	0.650	16.5100
0.080	2.0320	0.660	16.7640
0.090	2.2860	0.670	17.0180
0.100	2.5400	0.680	17.2720
0.110	2.7940	0.690	17.5260
0.120	3.0480	0.700	17.7800
0.130	3.3020	0.710	18.0340
0.140	3.5560	0.720	18.2880
0.150	3.8100	0.730	18.5420
0.160	4.0640	0.740	18.7960
0.170	4.3180	0.750	19.0500
0.180	4.5720	0.760	19.3040
0.190	4.8260	0.770	19.5580
0.200	5.0800	0.780	19.8120
0.210	5.3340	0.790	20.0660
0.220	5.5880	0.800	20.3200
0.230	5.8420	0.810	20.5740
0.240	6.0960	0.820	20.8280
0.250	6.3500	0.830	21.0820
0.260	6.6040	0.840	21.3360
0.270	6.8580	0.850	21.5900
0.280	7.1120	0.860	21.8440
0.290	7.3660	0.870	22.0980
0.300	7.6200	0.880	22.3520
0.310	7.8740	0.890	22.6060
0.320	8.1280	0.900	22.8600
0.330	8.3820	0.910	23.1140
0.340	8.6360	0.920	23.3680
0.350	8.8900	0.930	23.6220
0.360	9.1440	0.940	23.8760
0.370	9.3980	0.950	24.1300
0.380	9.6520	0.960	24.3840
0.390	9.9060	0.970	24.6380
0.400	10.1600	0.980	24.8920
0.410	10.4140	0.990	25.1460
0.420	10.6680	1.000	25.4000
0.430	10.9220		
0.440	11.1760		
0.450	11.4300		
0.460	11.6840		
0.470	11.9380		
0.480	12.1920		
0.490	12.4460		

FRACTIONS TO DECIMALS TO MILLIMETERS

Fraction	Decimal	mm	Fraction	Decimal	mm
1/64	0.0156	0.3969	33/64	0.5156	13.0969
1/32	0.0312	0.7938	17/32	0.5312	13.4938
3/64	0.0469	1.1906	35/64	0.5469	13.8906
1/16	0.0625	1.5875	9/16	0.5625	14.2875
5/64	0.0781	1.9844	37/64	0.5781	14.6844
3/32	0.0938	2.3812	19/32	0.5938	15.0812
7/64	0.1094	2.7781	39/64	0.6094	15.4781
1/8	0.1250	3.1750	5/8	0.6250	15.8750
9/64	0.1406	3.5719	41/64	0.6406	16.2719
5/32	0.1562	3.9688	21/32	0.6562	16.6688
11/64	0.1719	4.3656	43/64	0.6719	17.0656
3/16	0.1875	4.7625	11/16	0.6875	17.4625
13/64	0.2031	5.1594	45/64	0.7031	17.8594
7/32	0.2188	5.5562	23/32	0.7188	18.2562
15/64	0.2344	5.9531	47/64	0.7344	18.6531
1/4	0.2500	6.3500	3/4	0.7500	19.0500
17/64	0.2656	6.7469	49/64	0.7656	19.4469
9/32	0.2812	7.1438	25/32	0.7812	19.8438
19/64	0.2969	7.5406	51/64	0.7969	20.2406
5/16	0.3125	7.9375	13/16	0.8125	20.6375
21/64	0.3281	8.3344	53/64	0.8281	21.0344
11/32	0.3438	8.7312	27/32	0.8438	21.4312
23/64	0.3594	9.1281	55/64	0.8594	21.8281
3/8	0.3750	9.5250	7/8	0.8750	22.2250
25/64	0.3906	9.9219	57/64	0.8906	22.6219
13/32	0.4062	10.3188	29/32	0.9062	23.0188
27/64	0.4219	10.7156	59/64	0.9219	23.4156
7/16	0.4375	11.1125	15/16	0.9375	23.8125
29/64	0.4531	11.5094	61/64	0.9531	24.2094
15/32	0.4688	11.9062	31/32	0.9688	24.6062
31/64	0.4844	12.3031	63/64	0.9844	25.0031
1/2	0.5000	12.7000	1	1.0000	25.4000

Automotive chemicals and lubricants

A number of automotive chemicals and lubricants are available for use during vehicle maintenance and repair. They include a wide variety of products ranging from cleaning solvents and degreasers to lubricants and protective sprays for rubber, plastic and vinyl.

CLEANERS

Carburetor cleaner and choke cleaner is a strong solvent for gum, varnish and carbon. Most carburetor cleaners leave a dry-type lubricant film which will not harden or gum up. Because of this film it is not recommended for use on electrical components.

Brake system cleaner is used to remove brake dust, grease and brake fluid from the brake system, where clean surfaces are absolutely necessary. It leaves no residue and often eliminates brake squeal caused by contaminants.

Electrical cleaner removes oxidation, corrosion and carbon deposits from electrical contacts, restoring full current flow. It can also be used to clean spark plugs, carburetor jets, voltage regulators and other parts where an oil-free surface is desired.

Demoisturants remove water and moisture from electrical components such as alternators, voltage regulators, electrical connectors and fuse blocks. They are non-conductive and non-corrosive.

Degreasers are heavy-duty solvents used to remove grease from the outside of the engine and from chassis components. They can be sprayed or brushed on and, depending on the type, are rinsed off either with water or solvent.

LUBRICANTS

Motor oil is the lubricant formulated for use in engines. It normally contains a wide variety of additives to prevent corrosion and reduce foaming and wear. Motor oil comes in various weights (viscosity ratings) from 0 to 50. The recommended weight of the oil depends on the season, temperature and the demands on the engine. Light oil is used in cold climates and under light load conditions. Heavy oil is used in hot climates and where high loads are encountered. Multi-viscosity oils are designed to have characteristics of both light and heavy oils and are available in a number of weights from 0W-20 to 20W-50.

Gear oil is designed to be used in differentials, manual transmissions and other areas where high-temperature lubrication is required.

Chassis and wheel bearing grease is a heavy grease used where increased loads and friction are encountered, such as for wheel bearings, ball-joints, tie-rod ends and universal joints.

High-temperature wheel bearing grease is designed to withstand the extreme temperatures encountered by wheel bearings in disc brake equipped vehicles. It usually contains molybdenum disulfide (moly), which is a dry-type lubricant.

White grease is a heavy grease for metal-to-metal applications where water is a problem. White grease stays soft under both low and high temperatures (usually from -100 to +190-degrees F), and will not wash off or dilute in the presence of water.

Assembly lube is a special extreme pressure lubricant, usually containing moly, used to lubricate high-load parts (such as main and rod bearings and cam lobes) for initial start-up of a new engine. The assembly lube lubricates the parts without being squeezed out or washed away until the engine oiling system begins to function.

Silicone lubricants are used to protect rubber, plastic, vinyl and nylon parts.

Graphite lubricants are used where oils cannot be used due to contamination problems, such as in locks. The dry graphite will lubricate metal parts while remaining uncontaminated by dirt, water, oil or acids. It is electrically conductive and will not foul electrical contacts in locks such as the ignition switch.

Moly penetrants loosen and lubricate frozen, rusted and corroded fasteners and prevent future rusting or freezing.

Heat-sink grease is a special electrically non-conductive grease that is used for mounting electronic ignition modules where it is essential that heat is transferred away from the module.

SEALANTS

RTV sealant is one of the most widely used gasket compounds. Made from silicone, RTV is air curing, it seals, bonds, waterproofs, fills surface irregularities, remains flexible, doesn't shrink, is relatively easy to remove, and is used as a supplementary sealer with almost all low and medium temperature gaskets.

Anaerobic sealant is much like RTV in that it can be used either to seal gaskets or to form gaskets by itself. It remains flexible, is solvent resistant and fills surface imperfections. The difference between an anaerobic sealant and an RTV-type sealant is in the curing. RTV cures when exposed to air, while an anaerobic sealant cures only in the absence of air. This means that an anaerobic sealant cures only after the assembly of parts, sealing them together.

Thread and pipe sealant is used for sealing hydraulic and pneumatic fittings and vacuum lines. It is usually made from a Teflon compound, and comes in a spray, a paint-on liquid and as a wrap-around tape.

CHEMICALS

Anti-seize compound prevents seizing, galling, cold welding, rust and corrosion in fasteners. High-temperature anti-seize, usually made with copper and graphite lubricants, is used for exhaust system and exhaust manifold bolts.

Anaerobic locking compounds are used to keep fasteners from vibrating or working loose and cure only after installation, in the absence of air. Medium strength locking compound is used for small nuts, bolts and screws that may be removed later. High-strength locking compound is for large nuts, bolts and studs which aren't removed on a regular basis.

Oil additives range from viscosity index improvers to chemical treatments that claim to reduce internal engine friction. It should be noted that most oil manufacturers caution against using additives with their oils.

Gas additives perform several functions, depending on their chemical makeup. They usually contain solvents that help dissolve gum and varnish that build up on carburetor, fuel injection and intake parts. They also serve to break down carbon deposits that form on the inside surfaces of the combustion chambers. Some additives contain upper cylinder lubricants for valves and piston rings, and others contain chemicals to remove condensation from the gas tank.

MISCELLANEOUS

Brake fluid is specially formulated hydraulic fluid that can withstand the heat and pressure encountered in brake systems. Care must be taken so this fluid does not come in contact with painted surfaces or plastics. An opened container should always be resealed to prevent contamination by water or dirt.

Weatherstrip adhesive is used to bond weatherstripping around doors, windows and trunk lids. It is sometimes used to attach trim pieces.

Undercoating is a petroleum-based, tar-like substance that is designed to protect metal surfaces on the underside of the vehicle from corrosion. It also acts as a sound-deadening agent by insulating the bottom of the vehicle.

Waxes and polishes are used to help protect painted and plated surfaces from the weather. Different types of paint may require the use of different types of wax and polish. Some polishes utilize a chemical or abrasive cleaner to help remove the top layer of oxidized (dull) paint on older vehicles. In recent years many non-wax polishes that contain a wide variety of chemicals such as polymers and silicones have been introduced. These non-wax polishes are usually easier to apply and last longer than conventional waxes and polishes.

Safety first!

Regardless of how enthusiastic you may be about getting on with the job at hand, take the time to ensure that your safety is not jeopardized. A moment's lack of attention can result in an accident, as can failure to observe certain simple safety precautions. The possibility of an accident will always exist, and the following points should not be considered a comprehensive list of all dangers. Rather, they are intended to make you aware of the risks and to encourage a safety conscious approach to all work you carry out on your vehicle.

ESSENTIAL DOS AND DON'TS

DON'T rely on a jack when working under the vehicle. Always use approved jackstands to support the weight of the vehicle and place them under the recommended lift or support points.

DON'T attempt to loosen extremely tight fasteners (i.e. wheel lug nuts) while the vehicle is on a jack - it may fall.

DON'T start the engine without first making sure that the transmission is in Neutral (or Park where applicable) and the parking brake is set.

DON'T remove the radiator cap from a hot cooling system - let it cool or cover it with a cloth and release the pressure gradually.

DON'T attempt to drain the engine oil until you are sure it has cooled to the point that it will not burn you.

DON'T touch any part of the engine or exhaust system until it has cooled sufficiently to avoid burns.

DON'T siphon toxic liquids such as gasoline, antifreeze and brake fluid by mouth, or allow them to remain on your skin.

DON'T inhale brake lining dust - it is potentially hazardous (see Asbestos below).

DON'T allow spilled oil or grease to remain on the floor - wipe it up before someone slips on it.

DON'T use loose fitting wrenches or other tools which may slip and cause injury.

DON'T push on wrenches when loosening or tightening nuts or bolts. Always try to pull the wrench toward you. If the situation calls for pushing the wrench away, push with an open hand to avoid scraped knuckles if the wrench should slip.

DON'T attempt to lift a heavy component alone - get someone to help you.

DON'T rush or take unsafe shortcuts to finish a job.

DON'T allow children or animals in or around the vehicle while you are working on it.

DO wear eye protection when using power tools such as a drill, sander, bench grinder, etc. and when working under a vehicle.

DO keep loose clothing and long hair well out of the way of moving parts.

DO make sure that any hoist used has a safe working load rating adequate for the job.

DO get someone to check on you periodically when working alone on a vehicle.

DO carry out work in a logical sequence and make sure that everything is correctly assembled and tightened.

DO keep chemicals and fluids tightly capped and out of the reach of children and pets.

DO remember that your vehicle's safety affects that of yourself and others. If in doubt on any point, get professional advice.

STEERING, SUSPENSION AND BRAKES

These systems are essential to driving safety, so make sure you have a qualified shop or individual check your work. Also, compressed suspension springs can cause injury if released suddenly - be sure to use a spring compressor.

AIRBAGS

Airbags are explosive devices that can CAUSE injury if they deploy while you're working on the vehicle. Follow the manufacturer's instructions to disable the airbag whenever you're working in the vicinity of airbag components.

ASBESTOS

Certain friction, insulating, sealing, and other products - such as brake linings, brake bands, clutch linings, torque converters, gaskets, etc. - may contain asbestos or other hazardous friction material. Extreme care must be taken to avoid inhalation of dust from such products, since it is hazardous to health. If in doubt, assume that they do contain asbestos.

FIRE

Remember at all times that gasoline is highly flammable. Never smoke or have any kind of open flame around when working on a vehicle. But the risk does not end there. A spark caused by an electrical short circuit, by two metal surfaces contacting each other, or even by static electricity built up in your body under certain conditions, can ignite gasoline vapors, which in a confined space are highly explosive. Do not, under any circumstances, use gasoline for cleaning parts. Use an approved safety solvent.

Always disconnect the battery ground (-) cable at the battery before working on any part of the fuel system or electrical system. Never risk spilling fuel on a hot engine or exhaust component. It is strongly recommended that a fire extinguisher suitable for use on fuel and electrical fires be kept handy in the garage or workshop at all times. Never try to extinguish a fuel or electrical fire with water.

FUMES

Certain fumes are highly toxic and can quickly cause unconsciousness and even death if inhaled to any extent. Gasoline vapor falls into this category, as do the vapors from some cleaning solvents. Any draining or pouring of such volatile fluids should be done in a well ventilated area.

When using cleaning fluids and solvents, read the instructions on the container carefully. Never use materials from unmarked containers.

Never run the engine in an enclosed space, such as a garage. Exhaust fumes contain carbon monoxide, which is extremely poisonous. If you need to run the engine, always do so in the open air, or at least have the rear of the vehicle outside the work area.

THE BATTERY

Never create a spark or allow a bare light bulb near a battery. They normally give off a certain amount of hydrogen gas, which is highly explosive.

Always disconnect the battery ground (-) cable at the battery before working on the fuel or electrical systems.

If possible, loosen the filler caps or cover when charging the battery from an external source (this does not apply to sealed or maintenance-free batteries). Do not charge at an excessive rate or the battery may burst.

Take care when adding water to a non maintenance-free battery and when carrying a battery. The electrolyte, even when diluted, is very corrosive and should not be allowed to contact clothing or skin.

Always wear eye protection when cleaning the battery to prevent the caustic deposits from entering your eyes.

HOUSEHOLD CURRENT

When using an electric power tool, inspection light, etc., which operates on household current, always make sure that the tool is correctly connected to its plug and that, where necessary, it is properly grounded. Do not use such items in damp conditions and, again, do not create a spark or apply excessive heat in the vicinity of fuel or fuel vapor.

SECONDARY IGNITION SYSTEM VOLTAGE

A severe electric shock can result from touching certain parts of the ignition system (such as the spark plug wires) when the engine is running or being cranked, particularly if components are damp or the insulation is defective. In the case of an electronic ignition system, the secondary system voltage is much higher and could prove fatal.

HYDROFLUORIC ACID

This extremely corrosive acid is formed when certain types of synthetic rubber, found in some O-rings, oil seals, fuel hoses, etc. are exposed to temperatures above 750-degrees F (400-degrees C). The rubber changes into a charred or sticky substance containing the acid. *Once formed, the acid remains dangerous for years. If it gets onto the skin, it may be necessary to amputate the limb concerned.*

When dealing with a vehicle which has suffered a fire, or with components salvaged from such a vehicle, wear protective gloves and discard them after use.

Troubleshooting

CONTENTS

Section   Symptom

Engine

1   Engine will not rotate when attempting to start
2   Engine rotates but will not start
3   Starter motor operates without rotating engine
4   Engine hard to start when cold
5   Engine hard to start when hot
6   Starter motor noisy or excessively rough in engagement
7   Engine starts but stops immediately
8   Engine lopes while idling or idles erratically
9   Engine misses at idle speed
10   Engine misses throughout driving speed range
11   Engine stalls
12   Engine lacks power
13   Engine backfires
14   Pinging or knocking engine sounds during acceleration or uphill
15   Engine diesels (continues to run) after switching off

Engine electrical system

16   Battery will not hold a charge
17   Alternator light fails to go out.
18   Alternator light fails to come on when key is turned on

Fuel system

19   Excessive fuel consumption
20   Fuel leakage and/or fuel odor

Cooling system

21   Overheating
22   Overcooling
23   External coolant leakage
24   Internal coolant leakage
25   Coolant loss
26   Poor coolant circulation

Clutch

27   Fails to release (pedal pressed to the floor - shift lever does not move freely in and out of Reverse)
28   Clutch slips (engine speed increases with no increase in vehicle speed)
29   Grabbing (chattering) as clutch is engaged
30   Squeal or rumble with clutch fully engaged (pedal released)
31   Squeal or rumble with clutch fully disengaged (pedal depressed)
32   Clutch pedal stays on floor when disengaged

Manual transmission

33   Noisy in Neutral with engine running
34   Noisy in all gears
35   Noisy in one particular gear
36   Slips out of high gear
37   Difficulty in engaging gears
38   Oil leakage

Section   Symptom

Automatic transmission

39   General shift mechanism problems
40   Transmission will not downshift with accelerator pedal pressed to the floor
41   Transmission slips, shifts rough, is noisy or has no drive in forward or reverse gears
42   Fluid leakage

Transfer case

43   Transfer case is difficult to shift into the desired range
44   Transfer case noisy in all gears
45   Noisy or jumps out of four-wheel drive Low range
46   Lubricant leaks from the vent or output shaft seals

Driveshaft

47   Oil leak at front of driveshaft
48   Knock or clunk when the transmission is under initial load (just after transmission is put into gear)
49   Metallic grinding sound consistent with vehicle speed
50   Vibration

Axles

51   Noise
52   Vibration
53   Oil leakage

Driveaxles (4WD)

54   Clicking
55   Shudder on acceleration
56   Vibration on highway

Brakes

57   Vehicle pulls to one side during braking
58   Noise (high-pitched squeal with the brakes applied)
59   Excessive brake pedal travel
60   Brake pedal feels spongy when depressed
61   Excessive effort required to stop vehicle
62   Pedal travels to the floor with little resistance
63   Brake pedal pulsates during brake application

Suspension and steering systems

64   Vehicle pulls to one side
65   Shimmy, shake or vibration
66   Excessive pitching and/or rolling around corners or during braking
67   Excessively stiff steering
68   Excessive play in steering
69   Lack of power assistance
70   Excessive tire wear (not specific to one area)
71   Excessive tire wear on outside edge
72   Excessive tire wear on inside edge
73   Tire tread worn in one place

This section provides an easy reference guide to the more common problems that may occur during the operation of your vehicle. These problems and possible causes are grouped under various components or systems; i.e. Engine, Cooling System, etc., and also refer to the Chapter and/or Section that deals with the problem.

Remember that successful troubleshooting is not a mysterious black art practiced only by professional mechanics. It's simply the result of a bit of knowledge combined with an intelligent, systematic approach to the problem. Always work by a process of elimination, starting with the simplest solution and working through to the most complex - and never overlook the obvious. Anyone can forget to fill the gas tank or leave the lights on overnight, so don't assume that you are above such oversights.

Finally, always get clear in your mind why a problem has occurred and take steps to ensure that it doesn't happen again. If the electrical system fails because of a poor connection, check all other connections in the system to make sure that they don't fail as well. If a particular fuse continues to blow, find out why - don't just go on replacing fuses. Remember, failure of a small component can often be indicative of potential failure or incorrect functioning of a more important component or system.

ENGINE

1 Engine will not rotate when attempting to start

1 Battery terminal connections loose or corroded. Check the cable terminals at the battery. Tighten the cable or remove corrosion as necessary.
2 Battery discharged or faulty. If the cable connections are clean and tight on the battery posts, turn the key to the On position and switch on the headlights and/or windshield wipers. If they fail to function, the battery is discharged.
3 Automatic transmission not completely engaged in Park or Neutral or clutch pedal not completely depressed.
4 Broken, loose or disconnected wiring in the starting circuit. Inspect all wiring and connectors at the battery, starter solenoid and ignition switch.
5 Starter motor pinion jammed in flywheel ring gear. If manual transmission, place transmission in gear and rock the vehicle to manually turn the engine. Remove starter and inspect pinion and flywheel at earliest convenience (Chapter 5).
6 Starter solenoid faulty (Chapter 5).
7 Starter motor faulty (Chapter 5).
8 Ignition switch faulty (Chapter 12).

2 Engine rotates but will not start

1 Fuel tank empty, fuel filter plugged or fuel line restricted.
2 Fault in the fuel injection system (Chapter 4).
3 Battery discharged (engine rotates slowly). Check the operation of electrical components as described in the previous Section.
4 Battery terminal connections loose or corroded (see previous Section).
5 Fuel pump faulty (Chapter 4).
6 Excessive moisture on, or damage to, ignition components (see Chapter 5).
7 Worn, faulty or incorrectly gapped spark plugs (Chapter 1).
8 Broken, loose or disconnected wiring in the starting circuit (see previous Section).
9 Broken, loose or disconnected wires at the ignition coils (Chapter 5).

3 Starter motor operates without rotating engine

1 Starter pinion sticking. Remove the starter (Chapter 5) and inspect.
2 Starter pinion or flywheel teeth worn or broken. Remove the flywheel/driveplate access cover and inspect.

4 Engine hard to start when cold

1 Discharged or low battery. Check as described in Section 1.
2 Fault in the fuel or ignition systems (Chapters 4 and 5).
3 Injector(s) leaking (Chapter 4).
4 Distributor rotor carbon-tracked (Chapter 1).

5 Engine hard to start when hot

1 Air filter clogged (Chapter 1).
2 Fault in the fuel or ignition systems (Chapters 4 and 5).
3 Fuel not reaching the injectors (see Chapter 4).
4 Low cylinder compression (Chapter 2).
5 Malfunctioning EVAP system (Chapter 6).

6 Starter motor noisy or excessively rough in engagement

1 Pinion or flywheel gear teeth worn or broken. Remove the cover at the rear of the engine (if equipped) and inspect.
2 Starter motor mounting bolts loose or missing.

7 Engine starts but stops immediately

1 Loose or faulty electrical connections at the distributor (V6), coils or alternator.
2 Fault in the fuel or ignition systems (Chapters 4 and 5).
3 Vacuum leak at the gasket surfaces of the intake manifold or throttle body. Make sure all mounting bolts/nuts are tightened securely and all vacuum hoses connected to the manifold are positioned properly and in good condition.
4 Restricted intake or exhaust systems (Chapter 4).

8 Engine lopes while idling or idles erratically

1 Vacuum leakage. Check the mounting bolts/nuts at the throttle body and intake manifold for tightness. Make sure all vacuum hoses are connected and in good condition. Use a stethoscope or a length of fuel hose held against your ear to listen for vacuum leaks while the engine is running. A hissing sound will be heard. A soapy water solution will also detect leaks.
2 Fault in the fuel or ignition systems (Chapters 4 and 5).
3 Plugged PCV valve or hose (see Chapters 1 and 6).
4 Air filter clogged (Chapter 1).
5 Fuel pump not delivering sufficient fuel to the fuel injectors (see Chapter 4).
6 Leaking head gasket. Perform a compression check (Chapter 2C).
7 Camshaft lobes worn (Chapter 2).

9 Engine misses at idle speed

1 Spark plugs worn, fouled or not gapped properly (Chapter 1).
2 Fault in the fuel or ignition systems (Chapters 4 and 5).
3 Faulty spark plug wires (Chapter 1).
4 Vacuum leaks at intake manifold or hose connections. Check as described in Section 8.
5 Uneven or low cylinder compression. Check compression as described in Chapter 2C.

10 Engine misses throughout driving speed range

1 Fuel filter clogged and/or impurities in the fuel system (Chapter 1).

2 Faulty or incorrectly gapped spark plugs (Chapter 1).

3 Fault in the fuel or ignition systems (Chapters 4 and 5).

4 Defective spark plug wires (Chapter 1).

5 Faulty emissions system components (Chapter 6).

6 Low or uneven cylinder compression pressures. Remove the spark plugs and test the compression with a gauge (Chapter 2C).

8 Vacuum leaks at the throttle body, intake manifold or vacuum hoses (see Section 8).

11 Engine stalls

1 Fuel filter clogged and/or water and impurities in the fuel system (Chapter 1).

2 Fault in the fuel system or sensors (Chapters 4 and 6).

3 Faulty emissions system components (Chapter 6)

4 Faulty or incorrectly gapped spark plugs (Chapter 1). Also check the spark plug wires (Chapter 1).

5 Vacuum leak at the throttle body, intake manifold or vacuum hoses. Check as described in Section 8.

12 Engine lacks power

1 Fault in the fuel or ignition systems (Chapters 4 and 5).

2 Faulty or incorrectly gapped spark plugs (Chapter 1).

3 Faulty coils (Chapter 5).

4 Brakes binding (Chapter 1).

5 Automatic transmission fluid level incorrect (Chapter 1).

6 Clutch slipping (Chapter 8).

7 Fuel filter clogged and/or impurities in the fuel system (Chapter 1).

8 Emissions control system not functioning properly (Chapter 6).

9 Use of substandard fuel. Fill the tank with the proper fuel.

10 Low or uneven cylinder compression pressures. Test with a compression tester, which will detect leaking valves and/or a blown head gasket (Chapter 2).

11 Restriction in the intake or exhaust system (Chapter 4).

13 Engine backfires

1 Emissions system not functioning properly (Chapter 6).

2 Fault in the fuel or ignition systems (Chapters 4 and 5).

3 Faulty secondary ignition system (cracked spark plug insulator or faulty plug wires) (Chapters 1 and 5).

4 Fuel injection system not functioning properly (Chapter 4).

5 Vacuum leak at the throttle body, intake manifold or vacuum hoses. Check as described in Section 8.

6 Valves sticking (Chapter 2).

7 Crossed plug wires (Chapter 1).

14 Pinging or knocking engine sounds during acceleration or uphill

1 Incorrect grade of fuel. Fill the tank with fuel of the proper octane rating.

2 Fault in the fuel or ignition systems (Chapters 4 and 5).

3 Improper spark plugs. Check the plug type against the VECI label located in the engine compartment. Also check the plugs and wires for damage (Chapter 1).

4 Faulty emissions system (Chapter 6).

5 Vacuum leak. Check as described in Section 9.

15 Engine diesels (continues to run) after switching off

1 Idle speed too high (Chapter 4).

2 Fault in the fuel or ignition systems (Chapters 4 and 5).

3 Excessive engine operating temperature. Probable causes of this are a low coolant level (see Chapter 1), malfunctioning thermostat, clogged radiator or faulty water pump (see Chapter 3).

ENGINE ELECTRICAL SYSTEM

16 Battery will not hold a charge

1 Alternator drivebelt defective or not adjusted properly (Chapter 1).

2 Electrolyte level low or battery discharged (Chapter 1).

3 Battery terminals loose or corroded (Chapter 1).

4 Alternator not charging properly (Chapter 5).

5 Loose, broken or faulty wiring in the charging circuit (Chapter 5).

6 Short in the vehicle wiring causing a continuous drain on the battery (refer to Chapter 12 and the Wiring Diagrams).

7 Battery defective internally.

17 Alternator light fails to go out

1 Fault in the alternator or charging circuit (Chapter 5).

2 Alternator drivebelt defective or not properly adjusted (Chapter 1).

18 Alternator light fails to come on when key is turned on

1 Instrument cluster warning light bulb defective (Chapter 12).

2 Alternator faulty (Chapter 5).

3 Fault in the instrument cluster printed circuit, dashboard wiring or bulb holder (Chapter 12).

FUEL SYSTEM

19 Excessive fuel consumption

1 Dirty or clogged air filter element (Chapter 1).

2 Emissions system not functioning properly (Chapter 6).

3 Fault in the fuel or ignition systems (Chapters 4 and 5).

4 Low tire pressure or incorrect tire size (Chapter 1).

5 Restricted exhaust system (Chapter 4).

20 Fuel leakage and/or fuel odor

1 Leak in a fuel feed or vent line (Chapter 4).

2 Tank overfilled. Fill only to automatic shut-off.

3 Evaporative emissions system canister clogged (Chapter 6).

4 Vapor leaks from system lines or injectors (Chapter 4).

COOLING SYSTEM

21 Overheating

1 Insufficient coolant in the system (Chapter 1).

2 Water pump drivebelt defective or not adjusted properly (Chapter 1).

3 Radiator core blocked or radiator grille dirty and restricted (see Chapter 3).
4 Thermostat faulty (Chapter 3).
5 Fan blades broken or cracked (Chapter 3).
6 Surge tank cap not maintaining proper pressure. Have the cap pressure tested by a gas station or repair shop.
7 Fault in electrical circuit for cooling fans (Chapter 3).

22 Overcooling

1 Thermostat faulty (Chapter 3).
2 Inaccurate temperature gauge (Chapter 12).
3 Fault in electrical circuit for cooling fans (Chapter 3).

23 External coolant leakage

1 Deteriorated or damaged hoses or loose clamps. Replace hoses and/or tighten the clamps at the hose connections (Chapter 1).
2 Water pump seals defective. If this is the case, water will drip from the weep hole in the water pump body (Chapter 3).
3 Leakage from the radiator core or side tank(s). This will require the radiator to be professionally repaired (see Chapter 3 for removal procedures).
4 Engine drain plug(s) leaking (Chapter 1) or water jacket core plugs leaking (see Chapter 2C).
5 Leakage at the heater core. Signs of leakage should show up on interior carpeting (Chapter 3).

24 Internal coolant leakage

➡Note: Internal coolant leaks can usually be detected by examining the oil. Check the dipstick and inside of the valve cover for water deposits and an oil consistency like that of a milkshake.

1 Leaking cylinder head gasket. Have the cooling system pressure tested.
2 Cracked cylinder bore or cylinder head. Remove the head(s) and inspect (Chapter 2).
3 Leaking intake manifold gasket (Chapter 2).

25 Coolant loss

1 Too much coolant in the system (Chapter 1).
2 Coolant boiling away due to overheating (see Section 15).
3 External or internal leakage (see Sections 23 and 24).
4 Faulty surge tank cap. Have the cap pressure tested.

26 Poor coolant circulation

1 Inoperative water pump. A quick test is to pinch the top radiator hose closed with your hand while the engine is idling, then let it loose. You should feel the surge of coolant if the pump is working properly (see Chapter 1).
2 Restriction in the cooling system. Drain, flush and refill the system (Chapter 1). If necessary, remove the radiator (Chapter 3) and have it reverse flushed.
3 Water pump drivebelt defective or not adjusted properly (Chapter 1).
4 Thermostat sticking (Chapter 3).
5 Drivebelt incorrectly routed, causing the pump to turn backward (Chapter 1).

CLUTCH

27 Fails to release (pedal pressed to the floor - shift lever does not move freely in and out of Reverse)

1 Leak in the clutch hydraulic system. Check the master cylinder, slave cylinder and lines (Chapters 1 and 8).
2 Clutch plate warped or damaged (Chapter 8).
3 Broken release bearing (Chapter 8).

28 Clutch slips (engine speed increases with no increase in vehicle speed)

1 Clutch plate oil-soaked or lining worn. Remove clutch (Chapter 8) and inspect.
2 Clutch plate not seated. It may take 30 or 40 normal starts for a new one to seat.
3 Pressure plate worn (Chapter 8).

29 Grabbing (chattering) as clutch is engaged

1 Oil on clutch plate lining. Remove (Chapter 8) and inspect. Correct any leakage source.
2 Worn or loose engine or transmission mounts. These units move slightly when the clutch is released. Inspect the mounts and bolts (Chapter 2).
3 Worn splines on clutch plate hub. Remove the clutch components (Chapter 8) and inspect.
4 Warped pressure plate or flywheel. Remove the clutch components and inspect.

30 Squeal or rumble with clutch fully engaged (pedal released)

Release bearing binding on transmission bearing retainer. Remove clutch components (Chapter 8) and check slave cylinder and release bearing assembly. Remove any burrs or nicks; clean and relubricate before installing.

31 Squeal or rumble with clutch fully disengaged (pedal depressed)

1 Worn, defective or broken release bearing (Chapter 8).
2 Worn or broken pressure plate springs (or diaphragm fingers) (Chapter 8).

32 Clutch pedal stays on floor when disengaged

1 Release bearing binding, or a fault in the hydraulic system (Chapter 8).
2 Clutch master cylinder faulty (Chapter 8).

MANUAL TRANSMISSION

➡Note: All the following references are in Chapter 7A, unless noted.

33 Noisy in Neutral with engine running

1 Input shaft bearing worn.
2 Damaged main drive gear bearing.

3 Worn countershaft bearings.
4 Worn or damaged countershaft endplay shims.

34 Noisy in all gears

1 Any of the above causes, and/or:
2 Insufficient lubricant (see the checking procedures in Chapter 1).

35 Noisy in one particular gear

1 Worn, damaged or chipped gear teeth for that particular gear.
2 Worn or damaged synchronizer for that particular gear.

36 Slips out of high gear

1 Transmission loose on clutch housing.
2 Dirt between the transmission case and engine or misalignment of the transmission.

37 Difficulty in engaging gears

1 Clutch not releasing completely (see clutch adjustment in Chapter 1).
2 Loose or damaged shifter. Make a thorough inspection, replacing parts as necessary.

38 Oil leakage

1 Excessive amount of lubricant in the transmission (see Chapter 1 for correct checking procedures). Drain lubricant as required.
2 Transmission oil seal in need of replacement.

AUTOMATIC TRANSMISSION

→**Note: Due to the complexity of the automatic transmission, it's difficult for the home mechanic to properly diagnose and service this component. For problems other than the following, the vehicle should be taken to a dealer service department or a transmission shop.**

39 General shift mechanism problems

1 Chapter 7B deals with checking and adjusting the shift cable on automatic transmissions. Common problems that may be attributed to poorly adjusted cable are:

a) *Engine starting in gears other than Park or Neutral.*
b) *Indicator on shifter pointing to a gear other than the one actually being selected.*
c) *Vehicle moves when in Park.*

2 Refer to Chapter 7A to adjust the linkage.
3 Problem with the electronic shift solenoid. Check for Diagnostic Trouble Codes (Chapter 6).

40 Transmission will not downshift with accelerator pedal pressed to the floor

Transmission pressure control solenoid valve faulty. Check for Diagnostic Trouble Codes (Chapter 6).

41 Transmission slips, shifts rough, is noisy or has no drive in forward or reverse gears

1 Of the many probable causes for the above problems, the home mechanic should be concerned with only one possibility - fluid level.
2 Before taking the vehicle to a repair shop, check the level and condition of the fluid as described in Chapter 1. Correct fluid level as necessary or change the fluid and filter if needed. If the problem persists, have a professional diagnose the probable cause.
3 If the transmission shifts late and the shifts are harsh, suspect a faulty transmission pressure control solenoid valve. Check for Diagnostic Trouble Codes (Chapter 6).

42 Fluid leakage

1 Automatic transmission fluid is a deep red color. Fluid leaks should not be confused with engine oil, which can easily be blown by airflow to the transmission.
2 To pinpoint a leak, first remove all built-up dirt and grime from around the transmission. Degreasing agents and/or steam cleaning will achieve this. With the underside clean, drive the vehicle at low speeds so airflow will not blow the leak far from its source. Raise the vehicle and determine where the leak is coming from. Common areas of leakage are:

a) **Pan:** *Tighten the mounting bolts and/or replace the pan gasket as necessary (see Chapter 1).*
b) **Filler pipe:** *Replace the rubber seal where the pipe enters the transmission case.*
c) **Transmission oil lines:** *Tighten the connectors where the lines enter the transmission case and/or replace the lines.*
d) **Vent pipe:** *Transmission overfilled and/or water in fluid (see checking procedures, Chapter 1).*
e) **Speed sensor connector:** *Replace the O-ring where the vehicle speed sensor enters the transmission case (Chapter 6).*

TRANSFER CASE

43 Transfer case is difficult to shift into the desired range

1 Speed may be too great to permit engagement. Stop the vehicle and shift into the desired range.
2 Shift linkage loose, bent or binding. Check the linkage for damage or wear and replace or lubricate as necessary (Chapter 7C).
3 If the vehicle has been driven on a paved surface for some time, the driveline torque can make shifting difficult. Stop and shift into two-wheel drive on paved or hard surfaces.
4 Insufficient or incorrect grade of lubricant. Drain and refill the transfer case with the specified lubricant (Chapter 1).
5 Worn or damaged internal components. Disassembly and overhaul of the transfer case, by a qualified shop, may be necessary.
6 Fault in the electrical system of the front axle or automatic transfer case. Check for Diagnostic Trouble Codes (Chapter 6).

44 Transfer case noisy in all gears

Insufficient or incorrect grade of lubricant. Drain and refill (Chapter 1).

45 Noisy or jumps out of four-wheel drive Low range

1 Transfer case not fully engaged. Stop the vehicle, shift into Neutral and then engage 4L.
2 Shift linkage loose, worn or binding. Tighten, repair or lubricate linkage as necessary.

3   Shift fork cracked, inserts worn or fork binding on the rail. Disassemble and repair as necessary (Chapter 7C).

4   Fault in the electrical system of the front axle or automatic transfer case. Check for Diagnostic Trouble Codes (Chapter 6).

46   Lubricant leaks from the vent or output shaft seals

1   Transfer case is overfilled. Drain to the proper level (Chapter 1).

2   Vent is clogged or jammed closed. Clear or replace the vent.

3   Output shaft seal incorrectly installed or damaged. Replace the seal and check contact surfaces for nicks and scoring.

DRIVESHAFT

47   Oil leak at seal end of driveshaft

Defective transmission or transfer case oil seal. See Chapter 7 for replacement procedures. While this is done, check the splined yoke for burrs or a rough condition that may be damaging the seal. Burrs can be removed with crocus cloth or a fine whetstone.

48   Knock or clunk when the transmission is under initial load (just after transmission is put into gear)

1   Loose or disconnected rear suspension components. Check all mounting bolts, nuts and bushings (see Chapter 10).

2   Loose driveshaft bolts. Inspect all bolts and nuts and tighten them to the specified torque.

3   Worn or damaged universal joint bearings. Check for wear (see Chapter 8).

49   Metallic grinding sound consistent with vehicle speed

Pronounced wear in the universal joint bearings. Check as described in Chapter 8.

50   Vibration

➡Note: Before assuming that the driveshaft is at fault, make sure the tires are perfectly balanced and perform the following test.

1   Install a tachometer inside the vehicle to monitor engine speed as the vehicle is driven. Drive the vehicle and note the engine speed at which the vibration (roughness) is most pronounced. Now shift the transmission to a different gear and bring the engine speed to the same point.

2   If the vibration occurs at the same engine speed (rpm) regardless of which gear the transmission is in, the driveshaft is NOT at fault since the driveshaft speed varies.

3   If the vibration decreases or is eliminated when the transmission is in a different gear at the same engine speed, refer to the following probable causes.

4   Bent or dented driveshaft. Inspect and replace as necessary (see Chapter 8).

5   Undercoating or built-up dirt, etc. on the driveshaft. Clean the shaft thoroughly and recheck.

6   Worn universal joint bearings. Remove and inspect (see Chapter 8).

7   Driveshaft and/or companion flange out of balance. Check for

missing weights on the shaft. Remove the driveshaft (see Chapter 8) and reinstall 180-degrees from original position, then retest. Have the driveshaft professionally balanced if the problem persists.

AXLES

51   Noise

1   Road noise. No corrective procedures available.

2   Tire noise. Inspect tires and check tire pressures (Chapter 1).

3   Rear wheel bearings worn or damaged (Chapter 8).

52   Vibration

See probable causes under Driveshaft. Proceed under the guidelines listed for the driveshaft. If the problem persists, check the rear wheel bearings by raising the rear of the vehicle and spinning the rear wheels by hand. Listen for evidence of rough (noisy) bearings. Remove and inspect (see Chapter 8).

53   Oil leakage

1   Pinion seal damaged (see Chapter 8).

2   Axleshaft oil seals damaged (see Chapter 8).

3   Differential inspection cover leaking. Tighten the bolts or replace the gasket as required (see Chapter 8).

DRIVEAXLES (4WD)

54   Clicking noise on turns

Worn or damaged outboard CV joints (Chapter 8).

55   Shudder or vibration during acceleration

1   Excessive toe-in. Have alignment checked.

2   Incorrect spring heights (Chapter 10).

3   Worn or damaged inboard or outboard CV joints (Chapter 8).

4   Sticking inboard CV joint assembly (Chapter 8).

56   Vibration at highway speeds

1   Out-of-balance front wheels and/or tires (Chapters 1 and 10).

2   Out-of-round front tires (Chapters 1 and 10).

3   Worn CV joints (Chapter 8).

BRAKES

➡Note: Before assuming that a brake problem exists, make sure that the tires are in good condition and inflated properly (see Chapter 1), that the front-end alignment is correct and that the vehicle is not loaded with weight in an unequal manner.

57   Vehicle pulls to one side during braking

1   Defective, damaged or oil contaminated disc brake pads on one side. Inspect as described in Chapter 9.

2   Excessive wear of brake pad material or disc on one side. Inspect

and correct as necessary.

3   Loose or disconnected front suspension components. Inspect and tighten all bolts to the specified torque (Chapter 10).

4   Defective brake caliper assembly. Remove the caliper and inspect for a stuck piston or other damage (Chapter 9).

5   Inadequate lubrication of front brake caliper slide pins. Remove caliper and lubricate slide pins (Chapter 9).

58   Noise (high-pitched squeal with the brakes applied)

1   Disc brake pads worn out. The noise comes from the wear sensor rubbing against the disc (does not apply to all vehicles) or the actual pad backing plate itself if the material is completely worn away. Replace the pads with new ones immediately (Chapter 9). If the pad material has worn completely away, the brake discs should be inspected for damage as described in Chapter 9.

2   Linings contaminated with dirt or grease. Replace pads.

3   Incorrect linings. Replace with correct linings.

59   Excessive brake pedal travel

1   Partial brake system failure. Inspect the entire system (Chapter 9) and correct as required.

2   Insufficient fluid in the master cylinder. Check (Chapter 1), add fluid and bleed the system if necessary (Chapter 9).

60   Brake pedal feels spongy when depressed

1   Air in the hydraulic lines. Bleed the brake system (Chapter 9).

2   Faulty flexible hoses. Inspect all system hoses and lines. Replace parts as necessary.

3   Master cylinder mounting bolts/nuts loose.

4   Master cylinder defective (Chapter 9).

61   Excessive effort required to stop vehicle

1   Power brake booster not operating properly (see check in Chapter 1, repairs in Chapter 9).

2   Excessively worn pads. Inspect and replace if necessary (Chapter 9).

3   One or more caliper pistons seized or sticking. Inspect and rebuild as required (Chapter 9).

4   Brake pads contaminated with oil or grease. Inspect and replace as required (Chapter 9).

5   New pads installed and not yet seated. It will take a while for the new material to seat against the disc.

62   Pedal travels to the floor with little resistance

1   Little or no fluid in the master cylinder reservoir caused by leaking caliper piston(s), loose, damaged or disconnected brake lines. Inspect the entire system and correct as necessary.

2   Worn master cylinder seals (Chapter 9).

63   Brake pedal pulsates during brake application

1   Caliper improperly installed. Remove and inspect (Chapter 9).

2   Disc(s) defective. Remove (Chapter 9) and check for excessive lateral runout and parallelism. Have the disc(s) resurfaced or replace it with a new one.

SUSPENSION AND STEERING SYSTEMS

64   Vehicle pulls to one side

1   Tire pressures uneven or tires mismatched (Chapter 1).

2   Defective tire (Chapter 1).

3   Excessive wear in suspension or steering components (Chapter 10).

4   Front end in need of alignment.

5   Front brakes dragging. Inspect the brakes as described in Chapter 9.

65   Shimmy, shake or vibration

1   Tire or wheel out-of-balance or out-of-round. Have professionally balanced.

2   Loose, worn or out-of-adjustment front wheel bearings (Chapter 1).

3   Shock absorbers and/or suspension components worn or damaged (Chapter 10).

66   Excessive pitching and/or rolling around corners or during braking

1   Defective shock absorbers. Replace as a set (Chapter 10).

2   Broken or weak springs and/or suspension components. Inspect as described in Chapters 1 and 10.

67   Excessively stiff steering

1   Lack of fluid in power steering fluid reservoir (Chapter 1).

2   Incorrect tire pressures (Chapter 1).

3   Lack of lubrication at steering joints (see Chapter 1).

4   Front end out of alignment.

5   Lack of power assistance (see Section 69).

68   Excessive play in steering

1   Loose front wheel bearings (Chapters 1 and 10).

2   Excessive wear in suspension or steering components (Chapter 10).

3   Steering gearbox damaged or out of adjustment (Chapter 10).

69   Lack of power assistance

1   Steering pump drivebelt faulty or not adjusted properly (Chapter 1).

2   Fluid level low (Chapter 1).

3   Hoses or lines restricted. Inspect and replace parts as necessary.

4   Air in power steering system. Bleed the system (Chapter 10).

70   Excessive tire wear (not specific to one area)

1   Incorrect tire pressures (Chapter 1).

2   Tires out-of-balance. Have professionally balanced.

3   Wheels damaged. Inspect and replace as necessary.

4   Suspension or steering components excessively worn (Chapter 10).

71   Excessive tire wear on outside edge

1   Inflation pressures incorrect (Chapter 1).

2   Excessive speed in turns.

3   Front-end alignment incorrect. Have the front end professionally aligned.

4   Suspension arm bent or twisted (Chapter 10).

72   Excessive tire wear on inside edge

1   Inflation pressures incorrect (Chapter 1).

2   Front-end alignment incorrect. Have the front end professionally aligned.

3   Loose or damaged steering components (Chapter 10).

73   Tire tread worn in one place

1   Tires out-of-balance.

2   Damaged or buckled wheel. Inspect and replace if necessary.

3   Defective tire (Chapter 1).

Section

1

TUNE-UP
AND ROUTINE
MAINTENANCE

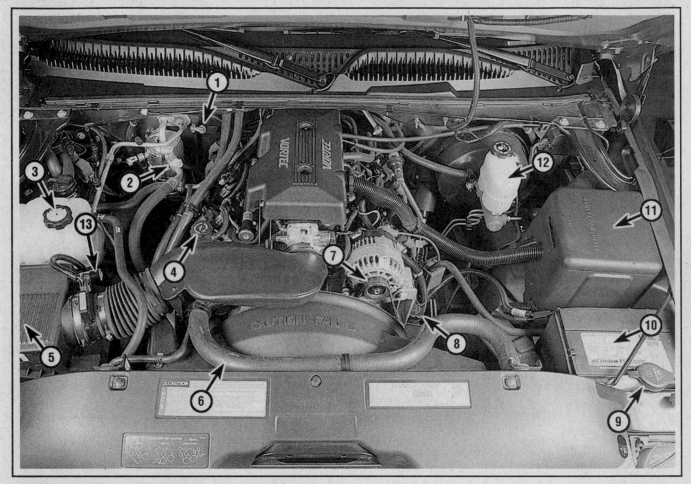

Engine compartment components (V8 shown, V6 similar)

1	Automatic transmission fluid dipstick	5	Air filter housing	9	Windshield washer fluid reservoir
2	Engine oil dipstick	6	Upper radiator hose	10	Battery
3	Surge tank pressure cap	7	Drivebelt	11	Underhood fuse/relay box
4	Oil filler cap	8	Power steering fluid reservoir	12	Brake fluid reservoir
				13	Air filter restriction indicator (2002)

Typical engine compartment underside components (V8, 2WD 1500 pick-up)

1	Balljoint	5	Exhaust pipe	8	Steering gear boot
2	Engine oil pan drain plug	6	Shock absorber (lower mount shown)	9	Stabilizer bar
3	Automatic transmission fluid drain plug	7	Tie-rod end	10	Lower control arm bushing
4	Engine oil filter				

Typical rear underside components

1	Shock absorber	3	Brake caliper	5	Fuel tank	7	Muffler
2	Leaf spring	4	Parking brake cables	6	Universal joint	8	Differential cover

1 Maintenance schedule

The following maintenance intervals are based on the assumption that the vehicle owner will be doing the maintenance or service work, as opposed to having a dealer service department do the work. These are the minimum maintenance intervals recommended by the factory for vehicles that are driven daily. If you wish to keep your vehicle in peak condition at all times, you may wish to perform some of these procedures even more often. Because frequent maintenance enhances the efficiency, performance and resale value of your car, we encourage you to do so. If you drive in dusty areas, tow a trailer, idle or drive at low speeds for extended periods or drive for short distances (less than four miles) in below freezing temperatures, shorter intervals are also recommended.

When the vehicle is new, follow the maintenance schedule to the letter, record the maintenance performed in your owners manual and keep all receipts to protect the new vehicle warranty. In many cases the initial maintenance check is done at no cost to the owner (check with your dealer service department for more information).

EVERY 250 MILES OR WEEKLY, WHICHEVER COMES FIRST

Check the engine oil level (Section 4)
Check the coolant level (Section 4)
Check the windshield washer fluid level (Section 4)
Check the brake and clutch fluid levels (Section 4)
Check the tires and tire pressures (Section 5)

EVERY 3000 MILES OR 3 MONTHS, WHICHEVER COMES FIRST

All items listed above, plus . . .
Check the power steering fluid level (Section 6)
Check the automatic transmission fluid level (Section 7)
Change the engine oil and filter (Section 8)

EVERY 6000 MILES OR 6 MONTHS, WHICHEVER COMES FIRST

All items listed above, plus . . .
Check the seat belts (Section 9)
Inspect the windshield wiper blades (Section 10)
Check and service the battery (Section 11)
Check the engine drivebelt (Section 12)
Inspect underhood hoses (Section 13)
Check the cooling system (Section 14)
Rotate the tires (Section 15)
Check the lubricant level in the front (4x4) and rear axles (Section 16)

EVERY 15,000 MILES OR 12 MONTHS, WHICHEVER COMES FIRST

All items listed above, plus . . .
Lubricate the chassis (Section 17)
Check the fuel system (Section 18)

Check the brake system (Section 19)*
Check the exhaust system (Section 20)
Check the manual transmission lubricant level (Section 21)
Check the transfer case lubricant level - 4WD (Section 22)
Replace the interior ventilation filter (Section 23)*

EVERY 30,000 MILES OR 30 MONTHS, WHICHEVER COMES FIRST

All items listed above, plus . . .
Change the brake fluid (Section 24)
Replace the air filter (Section 25)*
Replace the fuel filter (Section 26)
Replace the spark plugs (conventional, non-platinum or iridium) (Section 27)**
Service the cooling system (drain, flush and refill) (green-colored ethylene glycol anti-freeze only) (Section 28)
Check the steering, suspension and driveaxle boots (Section 29)
Change the automatic transmission fluid and filter (Section 30)**

EVERY 60,000 MILES OR 48 MONTHS, WHICHEVER COMES FIRST

Change the manual transmission lubricant (Section 31)
Change the transfer case lubricant (Section 32)
Inspect the Exhaust Gas Recirculation (EGR) valve (Section 33)
Change the differential lubricant (Section 34)**
Replace the Positive Crankcase Ventilation (PCV) valve (Section 35)

EVERY 100,000 MILES OR 60 MONTHS, WHICHEVER COMES FIRST

Inspect/replace the spark plug wires (Section 36)
Replace the spark plugs (platinum or iridium type) (Section 27)
Service the cooling system (drain, flush and refill) (orange-colored DEX-COOL anti-freeze only) (Section 28)

* *This item is affected by "severe" operating conditions, as described below. If the vehicle is operated under severe conditions, perform all maintenance indicated with an asterisk (*) at half the indicated intervals. Severe conditions exist if you mainly operate the vehicle . . .*

in dusty areas
towing a trailer
idling for extended periods
driving at low speeds when outside temperatures remain below freezing and most trips are less than four miles long

** *Perform this procedure at half the recommended interval if operated under one or more of the following conditions:*

in heavy city traffic where the outside temperature regularly reaches 90-degrees F or higher in hilly or mountainous terrain
frequent trailer towing
if the vehicle has been driven through deep water

2 Introduction

This Chapter is designed to help the home mechanic maintain the Chevrolet/GMC pickup or Tahoe/Yukon/Suburban vehicle with the goals of maximum performance, economy, safety and reliability in mind.

Included is a master maintenance schedule, followed by procedures dealing specifically with each item on the schedule. Visual checks, adjustments, component replacement and other helpful items are included. Refer to the accompanying illustrations of the engine compartment and the underside of the vehicle for the locations of various components.

Servicing your vehicle in accordance with the mileage/time maintenance schedule and the step-by-step procedures will result in a planned maintenance program that should produce a long and reliable service life. Keep in mind that it's a comprehensive plan, so maintaining some items but not others at the specified intervals will not produce the same results.

As you service your vehicle, you will discover that many of the procedures can - and should - be grouped together because of the nature of the particular procedure you're performing or because of the close proximity of two otherwise unrelated components to one another.

For example, if the vehicle is raised for chassis lubrication, you should inspect the exhaust, suspension, steering and fuel systems while you're under the vehicle. When you're rotating the tires, it makes good sense to check the brakes since the wheels are already removed. Finally, let's suppose you have to borrow or rent a torque wrench. Even if you only need it to tighten the spark plugs, you might as well check the torque of as many critical fasteners as time allows.

The first step in this maintenance program is to prepare yourself before the actual work begins. Read through all the procedures you're planning to do, then gather up all the parts and tools needed. If it looks like you might run into problems during a particular job, seek advice from a mechanic or an experienced do-it-yourselfer.

Owner's Manual and VECI label information

Your vehicle Owner's Manual was written for your year and model and contains very specific information on component locations, specifications, fuse ratings, part numbers, etc. The Owner's Manual is an important resource for the do-it-yourselfer to have; if one was not supplied with your vehicle, it can generally be ordered from a dealer parts department.

Among other important information, the Vehicle Emissions Control Information (VECI) label contains specifications and procedures for tune-up adjustments (if applicable) and spark plugs (see Chapter 6 for more information on the VECI label). The information on this label is the exact maintenance data recommended by the manufacturer. This data often varies by intended operating altitude, local emissions regulations, month of manufacture, etc.

This Chapter contains procedural details, safety information and more ambitious maintenance intervals than you might find in the manufacturer's literature. However, you may also find procedures and specifications in your Owner's Manual or VECI label that differ with what's printed here. In these cases, the Owner's Manual or VECI label can be considered correct, since it is specific to your particular vehicle.

3 Tune-up general information

The term tune-up is used in this manual to represent a combination of individual operations rather than one specific procedure that will maintain a gasoline engine in proper tune.

If, from the time the vehicle is new, the routine maintenance schedule is followed closely and frequent checks are made of fluid levels and high wear items, as suggested throughout this manual, the engine will be kept in relatively good running condition and the need for additional work will be minimized.

More likely than not, however, there may be times when the engine is running poorly due to lack of regular maintenance. This is even more likely if a used vehicle, which has not received regular and frequent maintenance checks, is purchased. In such cases, an engine tune-up will be needed outside of the regular routine maintenance intervals.

The first step in any tune-up or diagnostic procedure to help correct a poor running engine is a cylinder compression check. A compression check (see Chapter 2C) will help determine the condition of internal engine components and should be used as a guide for tune-up and repair procedures. If, for instance, the compression check indicates serious internal engine wear, a conventional tune-up won't improve the performance of the engine and would be a waste of time and money. Because of its importance, the compression check should be done by someone with the right equipment and the knowledge to use it properly.

The following procedures are those most often needed to bring a generally poor running engine back into a proper state of tune.

MINOR TUNE-UP

Check all engine related fluids (Section 4)
Clean, inspect and test the battery (Section 11)
Check and adjust the drivebelt (Section 12)
Check all underhood hoses (Section 13)
Check the cooling system (Section 14)
Check the air filter (Section 25)
Replace the spark plugs (Section 27)
Inspect the spark plug wires (Section 36)

MAJOR TUNE-UP

All items listed under Minor tune-up, plus . . .
Replace the air filter (Section 25)
Replace the spark plug wires (Section 36)
Check the ignition system (Chapter 5)
Check the charging system (Chapter 5)

4 Fluid level checks (every 250 miles or weekly)

➡️**Note: The following are fluid level checks to be done on a 250 mile or weekly basis. Additional fluid level checks can be found in specific maintenance procedures that follow. Regardless of intervals, be alert to fluid leaks under the vehicle, which would indicate a fault to be corrected immediately.**

1 Fluids are an essential part of the lubrication, cooling, brake, clutch and windshield washer systems. Because the fluids gradually become depleted and/or contaminated during normal operation of the vehicle, they must be periodically replenished. See *Recommended lubricants and fluids* at the end of this Chapter before adding fluid to any of the following components.

➡️**Note: The vehicle must be on level ground when fluid levels are checked.**

ENGINE OIL

▶ **Refer to illustrations 4.2, 4.4 and 4.6**

2 The engine oil level is checked with a dipstick that extends through a tube and into the oil pan at the bottom of the engine (see illustration).

3 The oil level should be checked before the vehicle has been driven, or about 5 minutes after the engine has been shut off. If the oil is checked immediately after driving the vehicle, some of the oil will remain in the upper engine components, resulting in an inaccurate reading on the dipstick.

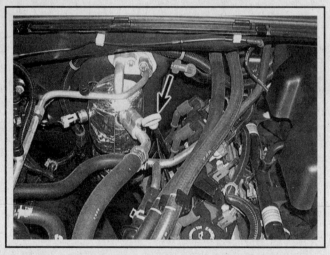

4.2 The engine oil dipstick (arrow) is clearly marked

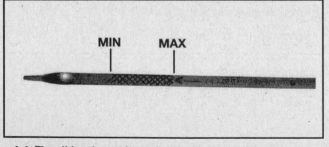

4.4 The oil level must be maintained between the marks at all times - it takes one quart of oil to raise the level from the MIN to MAX mark

4 Pull the dipstick out of the tube and wipe all the oil from the end with a clean rag or paper towel. Insert the clean dipstick all the way back into the tube, then pull it out again. Note the oil at the end of the dipstick. Add oil as necessary to keep the level between the MIN and MAX marks or within the SAFE zone on the dipstick (see illustration).

5 Do not overfill the engine by adding too much oil since this may result in oil-fouled spark plugs, oil leaks or oil seal failures.

6 Oil is added to the engine after unscrewing a cap from the valve cover (see illustration). A funnel may help to reduce spills.

7 Checking the oil level is an important preventive maintenance step. A consistently low oil level indicates oil leakage through damaged seals, defective gaskets or past worn rings or valve guides. If the oil looks milky or has water droplets in it, the cylinder head gasket(s) may be blown or the head(s) or block may be cracked. The engine should be checked immediately. The condition of the oil should also be checked. Whenever you check the oil level, slide your thumb and index finger up the dipstick before wiping off the oil. If you see small dirt or metal particles clinging to the dipstick, the oil should be changed (see Section 8).

ENGINE COOLANT

▶ **Refer to illustration 4.9**

✳✳ WARNING:

Do not allow antifreeze to come in contact with your skin or painted surfaces of the vehicle. Rinse off spills immediately with plenty of water. Antifreeze is highly toxic if ingested. Never leave antifreeze lying around in an open container or in puddles on the floor; children and pets are attracted by its sweet smell and may drink it. Check with local authorities on disposing of used anti-freeze. Many communities have collection centers that will see that antifreeze is disposed of safely.

➡️**Note: Non-toxic antifreeze is now manufactured and available at local auto parts stores, but even this type should be disposed of properly.**

4.6 Oil is added to the engine after unscrewing the oil filler cap (arrow) - always make sure the area around the opening is clean before removing the cap to prevent dirt from contaminating the engine

4.9 The coolant surge tank is located on the right side, near the air filter - keep the level near the Hot mark (arrow) or Cold mark on the side of the reservoir, depending on engine temperature

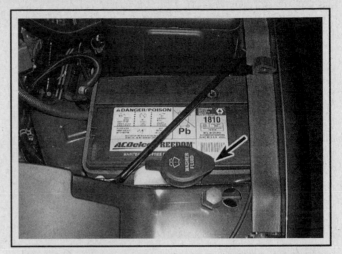

4.14 Flip open the cap (arrow) to check the fluid level in the windshield washer tank

ger, then remove the cap.

13 Check the condition of the coolant as well. It should be relatively clear. If it is brown or rust colored, the system should be drained, flushed and refilled. Even if the coolant appears to be normal, the corrosion inhibitors wear out, so it must be replaced at the specified intervals. If the system is filled with standard green coolant/water, it must be flushed and replaced more frequently than if the original "DEX-COOL" coolant is retained.

WINDSHIELD WASHER FLUID

▶ **Refer to illustration 4.14**

14 Fluid for the windshield washer system is located in a plastic reservoir in the left side of the engine compartment (see illustration).

15 In milder climates, plain water can be used in the reservoir, but it should be kept no more than 2/3 full to allow for expansion if the water freezes. In colder climates, use windshield washer system antifreeze, available at any auto parts store, to lower the freezing point of the fluid. Mix the antifreeze with water in accordance with the manufacturer's directions on the container.

> ❈❈ **CAUTION:**
>
> **Don't use cooling system antifreeze - it will damage the vehicle's paint.**

16 To help prevent icing in cold weather, warm the windshield with the defroster before using the washer.

BATTERY ELECTROLYTE

17 These vehicles are equipped with a battery which is permanently sealed (except for vent holes) and has no filler caps. Water doesn't have to be added to these batteries at any time. If a maintenance-type battery is installed, the caps on the top of the battery should be removed periodically to check for a low electrolyte level. This check is most critical during the warm summer months. Add only distilled water to any battery.

> ❈❈ **CAUTION:**
>
> **Never mix green-colored ethylene glycol anti-freeze and orange-colored "DEX-COOL" silicate-free coolant because doing so will destroy the efficiency of the "DEX-COOL" coolant which is designed to last for 100,000 miles or five years.**

8 All vehicles covered by this manual are equipped with a pressurized coolant surge tank, located at the right side of the engine compartment, and connected by hoses to the radiator and cooling system.

9 The coolant level in the surge tank should be checked regularly.

> ❈❈ **WARNING:**
>
> **Do not remove the pressure cap to check the coolant level when the engine is warm.**

The level of coolant in the surge tank varies with the temperature of the engine. When the engine is cold, the coolant level should be at or slightly above the COLD mark on the surge tank (see illustration). Once the engine has warmed up, the level should be at or near the HOT mark. If it isn't, add coolant to the surge tank. To add coolant simply twist open the cap and add a 50/50 mixture of ethylene glycol based green-colored antifreeze or orange-colored "DEX-COOL" silicate-free coolant and water (see the **Caution** at the beginning of this Section).

10 Drive the vehicle and recheck the coolant level. If only a small amount of coolant is required to bring the system up to the proper level, water can be used. However, repeated additions of water will dilute the antifreeze and water solution. In order to maintain the proper ratio of antifreeze and water, always top up the coolant level with the correct mixture. An empty plastic milk jug or bleach bottle makes an excellent container for mixing coolant. Do not use rust inhibitors or additives.

11 If the coolant level drops consistently, there may be a leak in the system. Inspect the radiator, hoses, filler cap, drain plugs and water pump (see Section 14). If no leaks are noted, have the pressure cap tested by a service station.

12 If you have to remove the pressure cap, wait until the engine has cooled completely, then wrap a thick cloth around the cap and slowly unscrew it. If coolant or steam escapes, let the engine cool down lon-

4.19 Never let the brake fluid level drop below the MIN mark (arrow)

BRAKE AND CLUTCH FLUID

▶ **Refer to illustration 4.19**

18 The brake master cylinder is mounted on the upper left of the engine compartment firewall. The clutch cylinder used on manual transmission models is mounted next to the master cylinder.

19 The translucent plastic reservoir allows the fluid inside to be checked without removing the cap (see illustration). Note that the clutch system is a sealed unit and it shouldn't be necessary to add fluid under most conditions (see Chapter 8 for more information). Be sure to

wipe the top of either reservoir cap with a clean rag to prevent contamination of the brake and/or clutch system before removing the cover.

20 When adding fluid, pour it carefully into the reservoir to avoid spilling it on surrounding painted surfaces. Be sure the specified fluid is used, since mixing different types of brake fluid can cause damage to the system. See Recommended lubricants and fluids at the end of this Chapter or your owner's manual.

✳✳ WARNING:

Brake fluid can harm your eyes and damage painted surfaces, so use extreme caution when handling or pouring it. Do not use brake fluid that has been standing open or is more than one year old. Brake fluid absorbs moisture from the air. Moisture in the system can cause a dangerous loss of brake performance.

21 At this time, the fluid and master cylinder can be inspected for contamination. The system should be drained and refilled if deposits, dirt particles or water droplets are seen in the fluid.

22 After filling the reservoir to the proper level, make sure the cover or cap is on tight to prevent fluid leakage.

23 The brake fluid level in the master cylinder will drop slightly as the pads at the front wheels wear down during normal operation. If the master cylinder requires repeated additions to keep it at the proper level, it's an indication of leakage in the brake system, which should be corrected immediately. Check all brake lines and connections (see Section 19 for more information).

24 If, upon checking the master cylinder fluid level, you discover one or both reservoirs empty or nearly empty, the brake system should be bled and thoroughly inspected (see Chapter 9).

5   Tire and tire pressure checks (every 250 miles or weekly)

▶ **Refer to illustrations 5.2, 5.3, 5.4a, 5.4b and 5.8**

1   Periodic inspection of the tires may spare you the inconvenience of being stranded with a flat tire. It can also provide you with vital information regarding possible problems in the steering and suspension systems before major damage occurs.

2   The original tires on this vehicle are equipped with 1/2-inch

wide wear bands that will appear when tread depth reaches 1/16-inch, at which point the tires can be considered worn out. Tread wear can be monitored with a simple, inexpensive device known as a tread depth indicator (see illustration).

3   Note any abnormal tread wear (see illustration). Tread pattern irregularities such as cupping, flat spots and more wear on one side than the other are indications of front end alignment and/or balance problems. If any of these conditions are noted, take the vehicle to a tire shop or service station to correct the problem.

4   Look closely for cuts, punctures and embedded nails or tacks. Sometimes a tire will hold air pressure for a short time or leak down very slowly after a nail has embedded itself in the tread. If a slow leak persists, check the valve stem core to make sure it's tight (see illustration). Examine the tread for an object that may have embedded itself in the tire or for a "plug" that may have begun to leak (radial tire punctures are repaired with a plug that's installed in a puncture). If a puncture is suspected, it can be easily verified by spraying a solution of soapy water onto the puncture area (see illustration). The soapy solution will bubble if there's a leak. Unless the puncture is unusually large, a tire shop or service station can usually repair the tire.

5   Carefully inspect the inner sidewall of each tire for evidence of brake fluid leakage. If you see any, inspect the brakes immediately.

6   Correct air pressure adds miles to the lifespan of the tires, improves mileage and enhances overall ride quality. Tire pressure cannot be accurately estimated by looking at a tire, especially if it's a

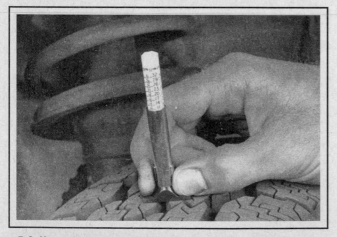

5.2 Use a tire tread depth indicator to monitor tire wear - they are available at auto parts stores and service stations and cost very little

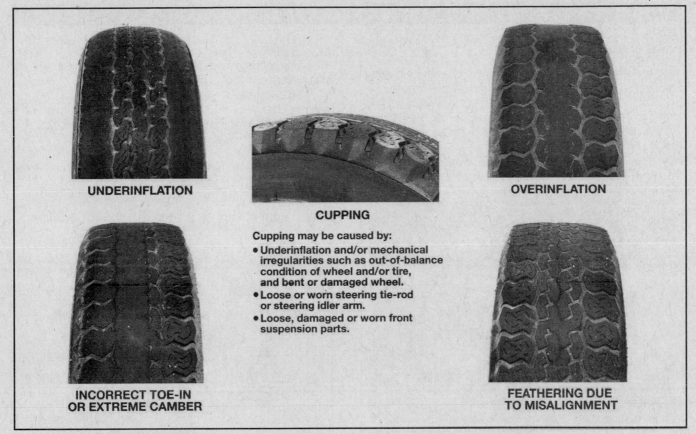

UNDERINFLATION

CUPPING

Cupping may be caused by:
- Underinflation and/or mechanical irregularities such as out-of-balance condition of wheel and/or tire, and bent or damaged wheel.
- Loose or worn steering tie-rod or steering idler arm.
- Loose, damaged or worn front suspension parts.

OVERINFLATION

INCORRECT TOE-IN OR EXTREME CAMBER

FEATHERING DUE TO MISALIGNMENT

5.3 This chart will help you determine the condition of the tires and the probable cause(s) of abnormal wear

radial. A tire pressure gauge is essential. Keep an accurate gauge in the vehicle. The pressure gauges attached to the nozzles of air hoses at gas stations are often inaccurate.

7   Always check tire pressure when the tires are cold. Cold, in this case, means the vehicle has not been driven over a mile in the three hours preceding a tire pressure check. A pressure rise of four to eight pounds is not uncommon once the tires are warm.

8   Unscrew the valve cap protruding from the wheel or hubcap and push the gauge firmly onto the valve stem (see illustration). Note the reading on the gauge and compare the figure to the recommended tire pressure shown on the placard on the driver's side door pillar. Be sure to reinstall the valve cap to keep dirt and moisture out of the valve stem mechanism. Check all four tires and, if necessary, add enough air to bring them up to the recommended pressure.

9   Don't forget to keep the spare tire inflated to the specified pressure (refer to your owner's manual or the tire sidewall).

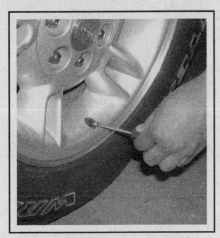

5.4a If a tire loses air on a steady basis, check the valve stem core first to make sure it's snug (special inexpensive wrenches are commonly available at auto parts stores)

5.4b If the valve stem core is tight, raise the corner of the vehicle with the low tire and spray a soapy water solution onto the tread as the tire is turned slowly - leaks will cause small bubbles to appear

5.8 To extend the life of the tires, check the air pressure at least once a week with an accurate gauge (don't forget the spare!)

6   Power steering fluid level check (every 3000 miles or 3 months)

▶ **Refer to illustrations 6.2 and 6.6**

1   Unlike manual steering, the power steering system relies on fluid which may, over a period of time, require replenishing.

2   On all models, the fluid reservoir for the power steering pump is located on the pump body at the front of the engine (see illustration).

3   For the check, the front wheels should be pointed straight ahead and the engine should be off.

4   Use a clean rag to wipe off the reservoir cap and the area around the cap. This will help prevent any foreign matter from entering the

reservoir during the check.

5   Twist off the cap and check the temperature of the fluid at the end of the dipstick with your finger.

6   Wipe off the fluid with a clean rag, reinsert the dipstick, then withdraw it and read the fluid level. The fluid should be at the proper level, depending on whether it was checked hot or cold (see illustration). Never allow the fluid level to drop below the lower mark on the dipstick.

7   If additional fluid is required, pour the specified type directly into the reservoir, using a funnel to prevent spills.

8   If the reservoir requires frequent fluid additions, all power steering hoses, hose connections, steering gear and the power steering pump should be carefully checked for leaks.

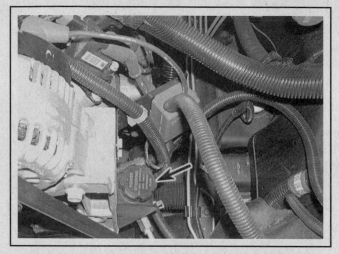

6.2 The power steering fluid dipstick on V6 and V8 models (arrow) is located in the power steering pump reservoir - turn the cap counterclockwise to remove it

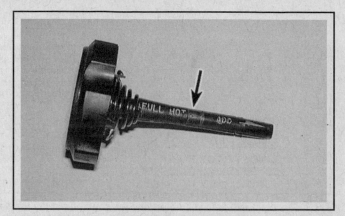

6.6 The power steering fluid dipstick has marks on it so the fluid can be checked hot (arrow) or cold

7   Automatic transmission fluid level check (every 3000 miles or 3 months)

7.3 The automatic transmission dipstick (arrow) is located at the right rear of the engine compartment - flip up the handle before pulling out the dipstick

▶ **Refer to illustrations 7.3 and 7.6**

1   The automatic transmission fluid level should be carefully maintained. Low fluid level can lead to slipping or loss of drive, while overfilling can cause foaming and loss of fluid.

2   With the parking brake set, start the engine, then move the shift lever through all the gear ranges, ending in Park. The fluid level must be checked with the vehicle level and the engine running at idle.

➡**Note: Incorrect fluid level readings will result if the vehicle has just been driven at high speeds for an extended period, in hot weather in city traffic, or if it has been pulling a trailer. If any of these conditions apply, wait until the fluid has cooled (about 30 minutes).**

3   With the transmission at normal operating temperature, remove the dipstick from the filler tube. The dipstick is located at the rear of the engine compartment on the passenger's side (see illustration).

4   Wipe the fluid from the dipstick with a clean rag and push it back into the filler tube until the cap seats.

5   Pull the dipstick out again and note the fluid level.

6   If the fluid is warm, the level should be between the two dimples (see illustration). If it's hot, the level should be in the crosshatched

area, near the MAX line. If additional fluid is required, add it directly into the tube using a funnel. It takes about one pint to raise the level from the bottom of the crosshatched area to the MAX line with a hot transmission, so add the fluid a little at a time and keep checking the level until it's correct.

7   The condition of the fluid should also be checked along with the level. If the fluid at the end of the dipstick is a dark reddish-brown color, or if it smells burned, it should be changed. If you are in doubt about the condition of the fluid, purchase some new fluid and compare the two for color and smell.

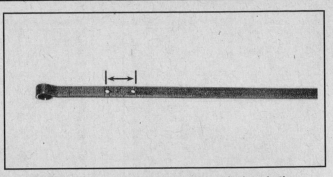

7.6 The automatic transmission fluid must be kept in the regions marked, depending on the fluid temperature

8   Engine oil and filter change (every 3000 miles or 3 months)

▶ **Refer to illustrations 8.3, 8.9, 8.14 and 8.18**

➡**Note: These vehicles are equipped with an oil life indicator system that illuminates a light or message on the instrument panel when the system deems it necessary to change the oil. A number of factors are taken into consideration to determine when the oil should be considered "worn out." Generally, this system will allow the vehicle to accumulate more miles between oil changes than the traditional 3000 mile interval, but we believe that frequent oil changes are "cheap insurance" and will prolong engine life. If you do decide not to change your oil every 3000 miles and rely on the oil life indicator instead, make sure you don't exceed 7,500 miles before the oil is changed, regardless of what the oil life indicator shows.**

1   Frequent oil changes are the most important preventive maintenance procedures that can be done by the home mechanic. As engine oil ages, it becomes diluted and contaminated, which leads to premature engine wear.

2   Although some sources recommend oil filter changes every other oil change, we feel that the minimal cost of an oil filter and the relative ease with which it is installed dictate that a new filter be installed every time the oil is changed.

3   Gather together all necessary tools and materials before beginning this procedure (see illustration).

4   You should have plenty of clean rags and newspapers handy to mop up any spills. Access to the under side of the vehicle may be improved if the vehicle can be lifted on a hoist, driven onto ramps or supported by jackstands.

✳✳ WARNING:

Do not work under a vehicle which is supported only by a bumper, hydraulic or scissors-type jack.

5   If this is your first oil change, familiarize yourself with the locations of the oil drain plug and the oil filter.

6   Warm the engine to normal operating temperature. If the new oil or any tools are needed, use this warm-up time to gather everything necessary for the job. The correct type of oil for your application can be found in Recommended lubricants and fluids at the end of this Chapter.

7   With the engine oil warm (warm engine oil will drain better and more built-up sludge will be removed with it), raise and support the vehicle. Make sure it's safely supported!

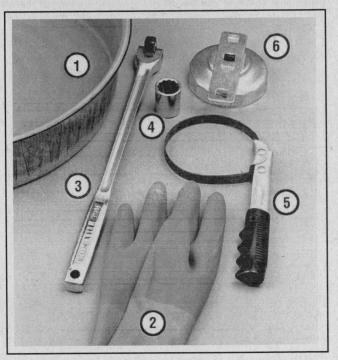

8.3   These tools are required when changing the engine oil and filter

1   *Drain pan* - It should be fairly shallow in depth, but wide to prevent spills
2   *Rubber gloves* - When removing the drain plug and filter, you will get oil on your hands (the gloves will prevent burns)
3   *Breaker bar* - Sometimes the oil drain plug is tight, and a long breaker bar is needed to loosen it
4   *Socket* - To be used with the breaker bar or a ratchet (must be the correct size to fit the drain plug - six-point preferred)
5   *Filter wrench* - This is a metal band-type wrench, which requires clearance around the filter to be effective
6   *Filter wrench* - This type fits on the bottom of the filter and can be turned with a ratchet or breaker bar (different-size wrenches are available for different types of filters)

8   Move all necessary tools, rags and newspapers under the vehicle. Set the drain pan under the drain plug. Keep in mind that the oil will initially flow from the pan with some force; position the pan accordingly.

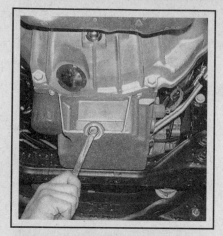

8.9 Use a proper size box-end wrench or socket to remove the oil drain plug and avoid rounding it off

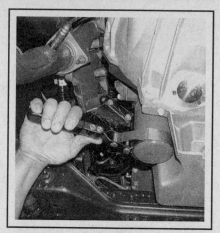

8.14 Since the oil filter is on very tight, you'll need a special wrench for removal - DO NOT use the wrench to tighten the new filter

8.18 Lubricate the oil filter gasket with clean engine oil before installing the filter on the engine

9 Being careful not to touch any of the hot exhaust components, use a wrench to remove the drain plug near the bottom of the oil pan (see illustration). Depending on how hot the oil is, you may want to wear gloves while unscrewing the plug the final few turns.

10 Allow the oil to drain into the pan. It may be necessary to move the pan as the oil flow slows to a trickle.

11 After all the oil has drained, wipe off the drain plug with a clean rag. Small metal particles may cling to the plug and would immediately contaminate the new oil.

12 Clean the area around the drain plug opening and reinstall the plug. Tighten the plug securely with the wrench. If a torque wrench is available, use it to tighten the plug to the torque listed in this Chapter's Specifications.

13 Move the drain pan into position under the oil filter.

14 Use the oil filter wrench to loosen the oil filter (see illustration).

15 Completely unscrew the old filter. Be careful: it's full of oil. Empty the oil inside the filter into the drain pan, then lower the filter.

16 Compare the old filter with the new one to make sure they're the same type.

17 Use a clean rag to remove all oil, dirt and sludge from the area where the oil filter mounts to the engine. Check the old filter to make sure the rubber gasket isn't stuck to the engine. If the gasket is stuck to the engine (use a flashlight if necessary), remove it.

18 Apply a light coat of clean oil to the rubber gasket on the new oil filter (see illustration).

19 Attach the new filter to the engine, following the tightening directions printed on the filter canister or packing box. Most filter manufacturers recommend against using a filter wrench due to the possibility of overtightening and damage to the seal.

20 Remove all tools, rags, etc. from under the vehicle, being careful not to spill the oil in the drain pan, then lower the vehicle.

21 Move to the engine compartment and locate the oil filler cap.

22 Pour the fresh oil through the filler opening. A funnel may be helpful.

23 Refer to the engine oil capacity in this Chapter's Specifications and add the proper amount of fresh oil into the engine. Wait a few minutes to allow the oil to drain into the pan, then check the level on the oil dipstick (see Section 4 if necessary). If the oil level is above the hatched area, start the engine and allow the new oil to circulate.

24 Run the engine for only about a minute and then shut it off. Immediately look under the vehicle and check for leaks at the oil pan drain plug and around the oil filter.

25 With the new oil circulated and the filter now completely full, recheck the level on the dipstick and add more oil as necessary.

26 During the first few trips after an oil change, make it a point to check frequently for leaks and proper oil level.

27 The old oil drained from the engine cannot be reused in its present state and should be disposed of. Check with your local auto parts store, disposal facility or environmental agency to see if they will accept the oil for recycling. After the oil has cooled it can be drained into a container (capped plastic jugs, topped bottles, milk cartons, etc.) for transport to one of these disposal sites. Don't dispose of the oil by pouring it on the ground or down a drain!

OIL LIFE MONITOR

28 The Oil Life Monitor is a function of the PCM that tracks engine operating temperature and rpm. If the PCM determines that your engine's oil has been used long enough, an indicator that shows "Change Engine Oil" will light on the instrument panel.

29 When you change your engine oil and filter, whether you change it at the interval recommended in this Chapter or only when the light comes on, you will have to reset the system to make the indicator go out.

30 To reset, switch the ignition key to Run (engine not running) and depress/let up the throttle pedal quickly three times. The light should flash for five seconds, to let you know the system is reset properly.

9 Seat belt check (every 6000 miles or 6 months)

1 Check seat belts, buckles, latch plates and guide loops for obvious damage and signs of wear.

2 Where the seat belt receptacle bolts to the floor of the vehicle, check that the bolts are secure.

3 See if the seat belt reminder light comes on when the key is turned to the Run or Start position. A chime should also sound.

10 Wiper blade inspection and replacement (every 6000 miles or 6 months)

▶ **Refer to illustration 10.3**

1   The windshield wiper blade elements should be checked periodically for cracks and deterioration.

2   Lift the wiper blade assembly away from the glass.

3   Press the release lever and slide the blade assembly out of the hook in the end of the wiper arm (see illustration).

4   Squeeze the two rubber prongs at the end of the blade element, then slide the element out of the frame.

➡**Note: These elements can be replaced by hand, without pliers.**

5   Compare the new element with the old for length, design, etc. Some replacement elements come in a three-piece design (two metal strips, one on either side of the rubber) that is held together by several small plastic sleeves. Keep the sleeves in place on this design until you start sliding the element into the frame. Remove each of the plastic sleeves as needed when they reach the frame.

6   Slide the new element into the frame, notched end last and secure the clips into the notches of the frame.

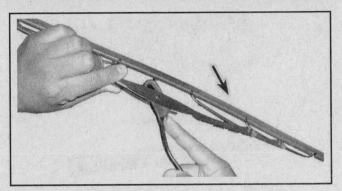

10.3 Depress the release lever (finger is on it here) and slide the wiper assembly down the wiper arm and out of the hook in the end of the arm

7   Reinstall the blade assembly on the arm, wet the windshield and test for proper operation.

11 Battery check, maintenance and charging (every 6000 miles or 6 months)

▶ **Refer to illustrations 11.1, 11.5, 11.7a, 11.7b and 11.7c**

❋❋ WARNING:

Refer to the Warning and Caution in Chapter 5, Section 1 under "Battery disconnection" before proceeding with the following Steps.

❋❋ WARNING:

Certain precautions must be followed when checking and servicing the battery. Hydrogen gas, which is highly flammable, is always present in the battery cells, so keep lighted tobacco and all other open flames and sparks away from the battery. The electrolyte inside the battery is actually dilute sulfuric acid, which will cause injury if splashed on your skin or in your eyes. It will also ruin clothes and painted surfaces. When removing the battery cables, always detach the negative cable first and hook it up last!

1   A routine preventive maintenance program for the battery in your vehicle is the only way to ensure quick and reliable starts. But before performing any battery maintenance, make sure that you have the proper equipment necessary to work safely around the battery (see illustration).

➡**Note: Some of the covered models have an auxiliary battery in addition to the standard battery. All of the following care and maintenance should be applied to both batteries.**

2   There are also several precautions that should be taken whenever battery maintenance is performed. Before servicing the battery, always turn the engine and all accessories off and disconnect the cable from the negative terminal of the battery.

3   The battery produces hydrogen gas, which is both flammable and explosive. Never create a spark, smoke or light a match around the battery. Always charge the battery in a ventilated area.

4   Electrolyte contains poisonous and corrosive sulfuric acid. Do not allow it to get in your eyes, on your skin or on your clothes. Never ingest it. Wear protective safety glasses when working near the battery. Keep children away from the battery.

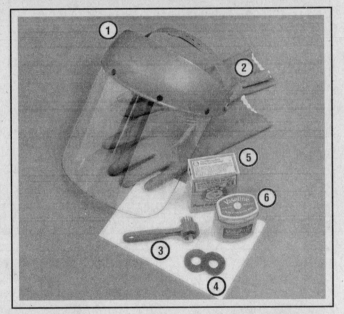

11.1 Tools and materials required for battery maintenance

1   *Face shield/safety goggles* - When removing corrosion with a brush, the acidic particles can easily fly up into your eyes

2   *Rubber gloves* - Another safety item to consider when servicing the battery - remember that's acid inside the battery!

3   *Battery terminal/cable cleaner* - This wire brush cleaning tool will remove all traces of corrosion from the battery posts and cable clamps

4   *Treated felt washers* - Placing one of these on each post, directly under the cable clamps, will help prevent corrosion

5   *Baking soda* - A solution of baking soda and water can be used to neutralize corrosion

6   *Petroleum jelly* - A layer of this on the battery posts will help prevent corrosion

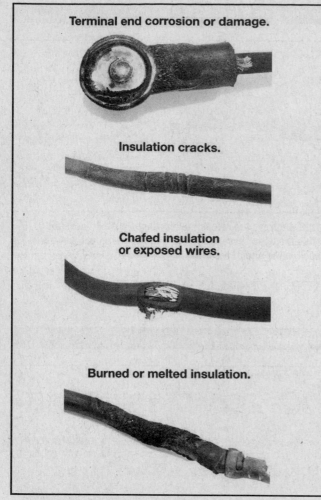

Terminal end corrosion or damage.

Insulation cracks.

Chafed insulation or exposed wires.

Burned or melted insulation.

11.5 Typical battery cable problems

5   Note the external condition of the battery. If the positive terminal and cable clamp on your vehicle's battery is equipped with a rubber protector, make sure that it's not torn or damaged. It should completely cover the terminal. Look for any corroded or loose connections, cracks in the case or cover or loose hold-down clamps. Also check the entire length of each cable for cracks and frayed conductors (see illustration).

6   If corrosion, which looks like white, fluffy deposits is evident, particularly around the terminals, the battery should be removed for cleaning. Loosen the cable bolts with a wrench, being careful to remove the ground cable first, and slide them off the terminals. Then disconnect the hold-down clamp bolt and nut, remove the clamp and lift the battery from the engine compartment.

7   Clean the cable ends thoroughly with a battery brush or a terminal cleaner and a solution of warm water and baking soda. Wash the terminals and the side of the battery case with the same solution but make sure that the solution doesn't get into the battery. When cleaning the cables, terminals and battery case, wear safety goggles and rubber gloves to prevent any solution from coming in contact with your eyes or hands. Wear old clothes too - even diluted, sulfuric acid splashed onto clothes will burn holes in them. If the terminals have been corroded, clean them up with a terminal cleaner (see illustrations). Thoroughly wash all cleaned areas with plain water.

8   Make sure that the battery tray is in good condition and the hold-down clamp bolts are tight. If the battery is removed from the tray, make sure no parts remain in the bottom of the tray when the battery is reinstalled. When reinstalling the hold-down clamp bolts, do not over-tighten them.

9   Any metal parts of the vehicle damaged by corrosion should be covered with a zinc-based primer, then painted.

10   Information on removing and installing the battery can be found in Chapter 5. Information on jump starting can be found at the front of this manual.

CHARGING

✳ WARNING:

When batteries are being charged, hydrogen gas, which is very explosive and flammable, is produced. Do not smoke or allow open flames near a charging or a recently charged battery. Wear eye protection when near the battery during charging. Also, make sure the charger is unplugged before connecting or disconnecting the battery from the charger.

11.7a A tool like this one (available at auto parts stores) is used to clean the side-terminal type battery-cable contact area

11.7b Use the brush side of the tool to finish the job

11.7c Regardless of the type of tool used on the battery and cables, a clean, shiny surface should be the result

➡**Note: The manufacturer recommends the battery be removed from the vehicle for charging because the gas that escapes during this procedure can damage the paint. Fast charging with the battery cables connected can result in damage to the electrical system.**

11 Slow-rate charging is the best way to restore a battery that's discharged to the point where it will not start the engine. It's also a good way to maintain the battery charge in a vehicle that's only driven a few miles between starts. Maintaining the battery charge is particularly important in the winter when the battery must work harder to start the engine and electrical accessories that drain the battery are in greater use.

12 It's best to use a one or two-amp battery charger (sometimes called a "trickle" charger). They are the safest and put the least strain on the battery. They are also the least expensive. For a faster charge, you can use a higher amperage charger, but don't use one rated more than 1/10th the amp/hour rating of the battery. Rapid boost charges that claim to restore the power of the battery in one to two hours are hardest on the battery and can damage batteries not in good condition. This type of charging should only be used in emergency situations.

13 The average time necessary to charge a battery should be listed in the instructions that come with the charger. As a general rule, a trickle charger will charge a battery in 12 to 16 hours.

14 Remove all the cell caps (if equipped) and cover the holes with a clean cloth to prevent spattering electrolyte. Disconnect the negative battery cable and hook the battery charger cable clamps up to the battery posts (positive to positive, negative to negative), then plug in the charger. Make sure it is set at 12-volts if it has a selector switch.

15 If you're using a charger with a rate higher than two amps, check the battery regularly during charging to make sure it doesn't overheat. If you're using a trickle charger, you can safely let the battery charge overnight after you've checked it regularly for the first couple of hours.

16 If the battery has removable cell caps, measure the specific gravity with a hydrometer every hour during the last few hours of the charging cycle. Hydrometers are available inexpensively from auto parts stores - follow the instructions that come with the hydrometer. Consider the battery charged when there's no change in the specific gravity reading for two hours and the electrolyte in the cells is gassing (bubbling) freely. The specific gravity reading from each cell should be very close to the others. If not, the battery probably has a bad cell(s).

17 Some batteries with sealed tops have built-in hydrometers on the top that indicate the state of charge by the color displayed in the hydrometer window. Normally, a bright-colored hydrometer indicates a full charge and a dark hydrometer indicates the battery still needs charging.

18 If the battery has a sealed top and no built-in hydrometer, you can hook up a digital voltmeter across the battery terminals to check the charge. A fully charged battery should read 12.5 volts or higher.

19 Further information on the battery and jump-starting can be found in Chapter 5 and at the front of this manual.

12 Drivebelt check, adjustment and replacement (every 6000 miles or 6 months)

▶ **Refer to illustrations 12.2, 12.4a, 12.4b, 12.5 and 12.7**

1 A serpentine drivebelt is located at the front of the engine and plays an important role in the overall operation of the engine and its components. Due to its function and material make up, the belt is prone to wear and should be periodically inspected. The serpentine belt drives the alternator, power steering pump, water pump and air conditioning compressor.

➡**Note: V6 models have one belt. V8 models have one main belt and a second, inner belt just for the air conditioning compressor (if equipped).**

2 With the engine off, open the hood and use your fingers (and a flashlight, if necessary), to move along the belt checking for cracks and separation of the belt plies. Also check for fraying and glazing, which gives the belt a shiny appearance (see illustration). Both sides of the belt should be inspected, which means you will have to twist the belt to check the underside.

3 Check the ribs on the underside of the belt. They should all be the same depth, with none of the surface uneven.

4 The tension of the belt is maintained by a spring-loaded tensioner assembly and isn't adjustable. The belt should be replaced when

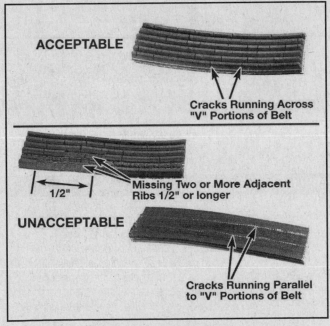

12.2 Check ribbed (serpentine) belts for signs of wear like these - if it looks worn, replace it

12.4a The indexing arrow (A) on the main belt's tensioner must remain between the marks (B) on the tensioner assembly (V8 shown, main belt)

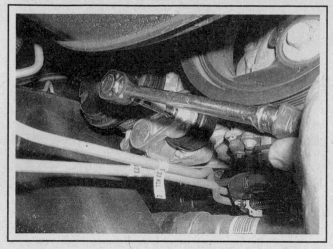

12.4b On V8 models with air conditioning, the inner belt tensioner (arrow) is best accessed from below - use a 3/8-inch-drive tool in the tensioner's square hole to rotate it for belt removal

12.5 Use a drivebelt tool to turn the tensioner bolt for belt removal - there may not be room for a standard socket and breaker bar

the indexing arrow is lined up with the indexing mark on the tensioner assembly (see illustrations).

5   To replace the belt, rotate the tensioner to release belt tension (see illustration).

6   Remove the belt from the tensioner and auxiliary components and slowly release the tensioner.

7   Route the new belt over the various pulleys, again rotating the tensioner to allow the belt to be installed, then release the belt tensioner.

➡Note: A drivebelt routing decal is located on the radiator support to help during drivebelt installation (see illustration).

TENSIONER REPLACEMENT

◆ **Refer to illustrations 12.8a and 12.8b**

8   To replace a tensioner that doesn't fall into the proper tension range, even with a new belt, or that exhibits binding or a worn-out pulley/bearing, remove the mounting bolts (see illustrations).

9   Installation is the reverse of the removal procedure.

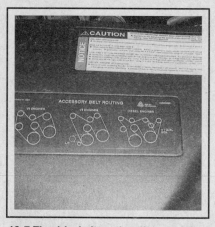

12.7 The drivebelt routing diagram is found on the radiator support (V8 shown)

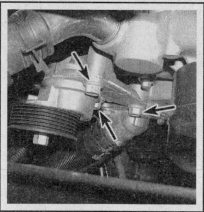

12.8a Main belt tensioner mounting bolts (arrows)

12.8b Mounting bolts (arrow) for V8 air-conditioning belt tensioner

13 Underhood hose check and replacement (every 6000 miles or 6 months)

GENERAL

❋❋ **CAUTION:**

Replacement of air conditioning hoses must be left to a dealer service department or air conditioning shop that has the equipment to depressurize the system safely and recover the refrigerant. Never remove air conditioning components or hoses until the system has been depressurized.

1   High temperatures in the engine compartment can cause the deterioration of the rubber and plastic hoses used for engine, accessory and emission systems operation. Periodic inspection should be made for cracks, loose clamps, material hardening and leaks. Information specific to the cooling system hoses can be found in Section 14.

2   Some, but not all, hoses are secured to their fittings with clamps. Where clamps are used, check to be sure they haven't lost their tension, allowing the hose to leak. If clamps aren't used, make sure the hose has not expanded and/or hardened where it slips over the fitting, allowing it to leak.

VACUUM HOSES

3   It's quite common for vacuum hoses, especially those in the emissions system, to be color-coded or identified by colored stripes molded into them. Various systems require hoses with different wall thickness, collapse resistance and temperature resistance. When replacing hoses, be sure the new ones are made of the same material.

4   Often the only effective way to check a hose is to remove it completely from the vehicle. If more than one hose is removed, be sure to label the hoses and fittings to ensure correct installation.

5   When checking vacuum hoses, be sure to include any plastic T-fittings in the check. Inspect the fittings for cracks and the hose where it fits over the fitting for distortion, which could cause leakage.

6   A small piece of vacuum hose (1/4-inch inside diameter) can be used as a stethoscope to detect vacuum leaks. Hold one end of the hose to your ear and probe around vacuum hoses and fittings, listening for the "hissing" sound characteristic of a vacuum leak.

✳✳ WARNING:

When probing with the vacuum hose stethoscope, be very careful not to come into contact with moving engine components such as the drivebelt, cooling fan, etc.

FUEL HOSE

✳✳ WARNING:

Gasoline is extremely flammable, so take extra precautions when you work on any part of the fuel system. Don't smoke or allow open flames or bare light bulbs near the work area, and don't work in a garage where a natural gas-type appliance (such as a water heater or clothes dryer) is present. Since gasoline is carcinogenic, wear latex gloves when there's a possibility of being exposed to fuel, and, if you spill any fuel on your skin, rinse it off immediately with soap and water. Mop up any spills immediately and do not store fuel-soaked rags where they could ignite. When you perform any kind of work on the fuel system, wear safety glasses and have a Class B type fire extinguisher on hand. The fuel system is under pressure, so if any lines must be disconnected, the pressure in the system must be relieved first (see Chapter 4 for more information).

7   Check all rubber fuel lines for deterioration and chafing. Check especially for cracks in areas where the hose bends and just before fittings, such as where a hose attaches to the fuel filter and fuel injection unit.

8   High quality fuel line, specifically designed for high-pressure fuel injection applications, must be used for fuel line replacement. Never, under any circumstances, use regular fuel line, unreinforced vacuum line, clear plastic tubing or water hose for fuel lines.

9   Spring-type (pinch) clamps are commonly used on fuel lines. These clamps often lose their tension over a period of time, and can be "sprung" during removal. Replace all spring-type clamps with screw clamps whenever a hose is replaced.

METAL LINES

10 Sections of metal line are routed along the frame, between the fuel tank and the engine. Check carefully to be sure the line has not been bent or crimped and no cracks have started in the line.

11 If a section of metal fuel line must be replaced, only seamless steel tubing should be used, since copper and aluminum tubing don't have the strength necessary to withstand normal engine vibration.

12 Check the metal brake lines where they enter the master cylinder and brake proportioning unit for cracks in the lines or loose fittings. Any sign of brake fluid leakage calls for an immediate and thorough inspection of the brake system.

14 Cooling system check (every 6000 miles or 6 months)

▶ Refer to illustration 14.4

✳✳ WARNING:

Wait until the engine is completely cool before beginning this procedure.

✳✳ CAUTION:

Never mix green-colored ethylene glycol anti-freeze and orange-colored "DEX-COOL" silicate-free coolant because doing so will destroy the efficiency of the "DEX-COOL" coolant which is designed to last for 100,000 miles or five years.

1   Many major engine failures can be attributed to a faulty cooling system. If the vehicle is equipped with an automatic transmission, the cooling system also cools the transmission fluid and thus plays an important role in prolonging transmission life.

2   The cooling system should be checked with the engine cold. Do this before the vehicle is driven for the day or after it has been shut off for at least three hours.

3   Remove the coolant pressure cap on the surge tank by slowly unscrewing it. If you hear any hissing sounds (indicating there is still pressure in the system), wait until it stops. Thoroughly clean the cap, inside and out, with clean water. Also clean the filler neck on the surge tank. All traces of corrosion should be removed. The coolant inside the surge tank should be relatively transparent. If it is rust colored, the system should be drained and refilled (see Section 28). If the coolant level is not up to the Cold mark, add additional antifreeze/coolant mixture (see Section 4).

4   Carefully check the large upper and lower radiator hoses along with any smaller diameter heater hoses that run from the engine to the firewall. Inspect each hose along its entire length, replacing any hose that is cracked, swollen or shows signs of deterioration. Cracks may become more apparent if the hose is squeezed (see illustration on next page).

5   Make sure all hose connections are tight. A leak in the cooling system will usually show up as white or rust-colored deposits on the areas adjoining the leak. If wire-type clamps are used at the ends of the hoses, it may be wise to replace them with more secure, screw-type clamps.

6   Use compressed air or a soft brush to remove bugs, leaves, etc. from the front of the radiator or air conditioning condenser. Be careful not to damage the delicate cooling fins or cut yourself on them.

7   Every other inspection, or at the first indication of cooling system problems, have the cap and system pressure tested. If you don't have a pressure tester, most gas stations and repair shops will do this for a minimal charge.

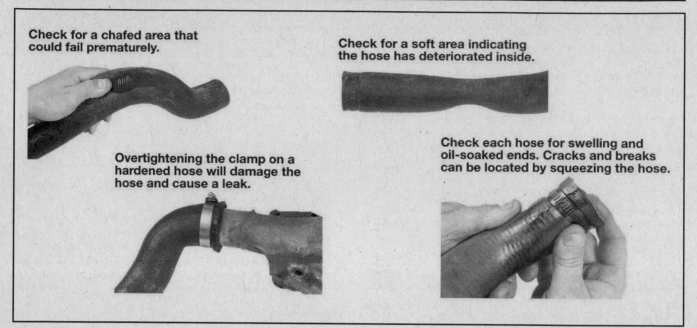

Check for a chafed area that could fail prematurely.

Check for a soft area indicating the hose has deteriorated inside.

Overtightening the clamp on a hardened hose will damage the hose and cause a leak.

Check each hose for swelling and oil-soaked ends. Cracks and breaks can be located by squeezing the hose.

14.4 Hoses, like drivebelts, have a habit of failing at the worst possible time - to prevent the inconvenience of a blown radiator or heater hose, inspect them carefully as shown here

OVERHEAT PROTECTION OPERATING MODE

8   Models with V8 engines have a system to protect the engine from damage caused by severe overheating. When the computer senses an overheat condition, an instrument panel warning light comes on that says "reduced power." In this mode, the computer switches the firing of the individual coils On and Off at each cylinder to allow cooling cycles between the firing cycles. The engine will have a dramatic loss of power, but will allow vehicle operation in an emergency.

9   If this light is On, find a safe place to get off the road as soon as possible, and allow the engine to cool thoroughly.

10 Check the coolant level and inspect for a split hose or other obvious signs of coolant leakage.

11 The engine oil will be ruined after this mode has operated, since unburned fuel will get into the oil. After fixing the overheating problem, change the oil and filter right away and reset the Oil Life Monitor (see Section 8).

15   Tire rotation (every 6000 miles or 6 months)

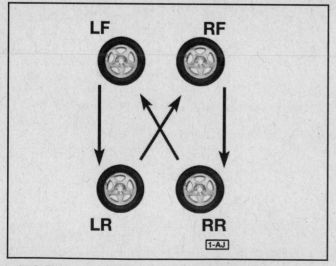

LF   RF

LR   RR

1-AJ

15.2 The recommended four-tire rotation pattern for non-directional radial tires

♦ **Refer to illustration 15.2**

1   The tires should be rotated at the specified intervals and whenever uneven wear is noticed.

2   Tires must be rotated in the recommended pattern (see illustration).

3   Refer to the information in Jacking and towing at the front of this manual for the proper procedures to follow when raising the vehicle and changing a tire. If the brakes are to be checked, don't apply the parking brake as stated. Make sure the tires are blocked to prevent the vehicle from rolling as it's raised.

4   Preferably, the entire vehicle should be raised at the same time. This can be done on a hoist or by jacking up each corner and then lowering the vehicle onto jackstands placed under the frame rails. Always use four jackstands and make sure the vehicle is safely supported.

5   After rotation, check and adjust the tire pressures as necessary. Tighten the lug nuts to the torque listed in this Chapter's Specifications.

16 Differential lubricant level check (every 6,000 miles or 6 months)

▶ **Refer to illustrations 16.2a and 16.2b**

➡**Note: 4WD vehicles have two differentials - one in the center of each axle. 2WD vehicles have one differential - in the center of the rear axle. On 4WD vehicles, be sure to check the lubricant level in both differentials.**

1   The filler plug on all front and most rear differentials is a threaded metal type. If the vehicle is raised to gain access to the plug, be sure to support it safely on jackstands - DO NOT crawl under the vehicle when it's supported only by the jack. Be sure the vehicle is level or the check may not be accurate.

2   Remove the plug from the filler hole in the differential housing or cover (see illustrations).

3   The lubricant level should be at the bottom of the filler hole If you're checking the rear differential and it is filled with synthetic lubricant, the level should be below the fill-plug opening by 1-5/8 inch on 1500 Series models, but no more than 3/8-inch lower than the hole on 2500 Series models. If not, use a pump or squeeze bottle to add the recommended lubricant until it just starts to run out of the opening. On some models a tag is located in the area of the plug which gives information regarding lubricant type.

4   Install the plug securely into the filler hole.

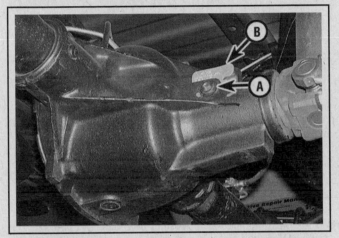

16.2a Remove the rear axle filler plug (A) to check the differential lubricant level - some models may have a tag with specific information about the required lubricant (B)

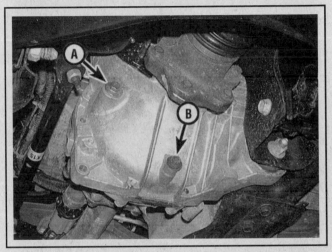

16.2b Remove the front (4WD) axle filler plug (A) to check the differential lubricant level - B is the drain plug

17 Chassis lubrication (every 15,000 miles or 12 months)

▶ **Refer to illustration 17.1, 17.2a and 17.2b**

1   Refer to Recommended lubricants and fluids at the end of this Chapter to obtain the necessary grease, etc. You'll also need a grease gun (see illustration). If a suspension component has no grease fitting

in place, this indicates the part is sealed and doesn't require periodic lubrication. Some components on 4WD models have fittings that aren't on 2WD versions, and vice versa. On 2002 models with Quadrasteer™ four-wheel steering option, lubricate the rear balljoints and rear steering components equipped with grease fittings.

17.1 Materials required for chassis and body lubrication

1   *Engine oil -* *Light engine oil in a can like this can be used for door and hood hinges*
2   *Graphite spray -* *Used to lubricate lock cylinders*
3   *Grease -* *Grease, in a variety of types and weights, is available for use in a grease gun. Check the Specifications for your requirements*
4   *Grease gun -* *A common grease gun, shown here with a detachable hose and nozzle, is needed for chassis lubrication. After use, clean it thoroughly!*

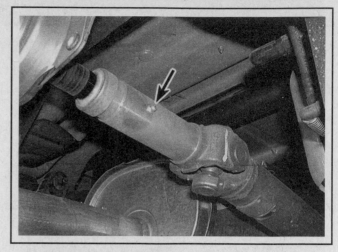

17.2a Wipe the dirt from the grease fittings before pushing the grease gun nozzle onto the fitting - lube the tie-rod end (A), the lower balljoint (B) and the upper balljoint (C)

17.2b On driveshafts with a sliding joint, lube the fitting (arrow) during chassis lubrication

2   Look under the vehicle and locate the grease fittings (see illustrations).

3   For easier access under the vehicle, raise it with a jack and place jackstands under the frame. Make sure it's safely supported by the stands. If the wheels are to be removed at this interval for tire rotation or brake inspection, loosen the lug nuts slightly while the vehicle is still on the ground.

4   Before beginning, force a little grease out of the nozzle to remove any dirt from the end of the gun. Wipe the nozzle clean with a rag.

5   With the grease gun and plenty of clean rags, crawl under the vehicle and begin lubricating the components.

6   Wipe one of the grease fittings clean and push the nozzle firmly over it. Pump the gun until the component is completely lubricated. On balljoints, stop pumping when the rubber seal is firm to the touch. Do not pump too much grease into the fitting as it could rupture the seal. For all other suspension and steering components, continue pumping grease into the fitting until it oozes out of the joint between the two components. If it escapes around the grease gun nozzle, the fitting is clogged or the nozzle is not completely seated on the fitting. Resecure the gun nozzle to the fitting and try again. If necessary, replace the fitting with a new one.

7   Wipe the excess grease from the components and the grease fitting. Repeat the procedure for the remaining fittings.

8   Clean the fitting and pump grease into the driveline universal joints until the grease can be seen coming out of the contact points. The other U-joints are sealed and do not require lubrication.

➡Note: Most replacement driveshaft U-joints aren't permanently sealed, and are sold with grease fittings. If your U-joints have been replaced, make sure you include them in your routine chassis lubrication.

9   Also clean and lubricate the parking brake cable guides and levers.

✳✳ CAUTION:

Do not use chassis lubrication on the brake cables themselves. The grease will cause the cable housings to deteriorate.

18 Fuel system check (every 15,000 miles or 12 months)

▶ **Refer to illustration 18.7**

✳✳ WARNING:

Gasoline is extremely flammable, so take extra precautions when you work on any part of the fuel system. Don't smoke or allow open flames or bare light bulbs near the work area, and don't work in a garage where a natural gas-type appliance (such as a water heater or clothes dryer) is present. Since gasoline is carcinogenic, wear latex gloves when there's a possibility of being exposed to fuel, and, if you spill any fuel on your skin, rinse it off immediately with soap and water. Mop up any spills immediately and do not store fuel-soaked rags where they could ignite. When you perform any kind of work on the fuel system, wear safety glasses and have a Class B type fire extinguisher on hand. The fuel system is under constant pressure, so, before any lines are disconnected, the fuel system pressure must be relieved (see Chapter 4).

1   If you smell gasoline while driving or after the vehicle has been sitting in the sun, inspect the fuel system immediately.

2   Remove the gas filler cap and inspect if for damage and corrosion. The gasket should have an unbroken sealing imprint. If the gasket is damaged or corroded, install a new cap.

3   Inspect the fuel feed and return lines for cracks. Make sure that the connections between the fuel lines and the fuel injection system are tight.

✳✳ WARNING:

Your vehicle is fuel injected, so you must relieve the fuel system pressure before servicing fuel system components. The fuel system pressure relief procedure is outlined in Chapter 4.

4   If the fuel injectors are visible, look for signs of fuel leakage (wet spots) around any of the injectors, they may need new O-rings (see

Chapter 4).

5   Since some components of the fuel system - the fuel tank and part of the fuel feed and return lines, for example - are underneath the vehicle, they can be inspected more easily with the vehicle raised on a hoist. If that's not possible, raise the vehicle and support it on jackstands.

6   With the vehicle raised and safely supported, inspect the gas tank and filler neck for punctures, cracks and other damage. The connection between the filler neck and the tank is particularly critical. Sometimes a rubber filler neck will leak because of loose clamps or deteriorated rubber. Inspect all fuel tank mounting brackets and straps to be sure that the tank is securely attached to the vehicle.

❋❋ WARNING:

Do not, under any circumstances, try to repair a fuel tank (except rubber components). A welding torch or any open flame can easily cause fuel vapors inside the tank to explode.

7   Carefully check all rubber hoses and metal lines leading away from the fuel tank (see illustration). Check for loose connections, deteriorated hoses, crimped lines and other damage. Repair or replace damaged sections as necessary (see Chapter 4).

8   The evaporative emissions control system can also be a source of fuel odors. The function of the system is to store fuel vapors from the fuel tank in a charcoal canister until they can be routed to the intake

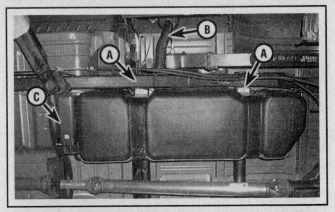

18.7 Inspect the fuel tank mounting straps (A), the various fuel and vapor lines (B indicates the filler hose), and the evaporative emissions canister (C)

manifold where they mix with incoming air before being burned in the combustion chambers.

9   The most common symptom of a faulty evaporative emissions system is a strong odor of fuel in the engine compartment. If a fuel odor has been detected, and you have already checked the areas described above, check the charcoal canister, located under the rear of the vehicle, and the hoses connected to it (see illustration 18.7).

19 Brake system check (every 15,000 miles or 12 months)

❋❋ WARNING:

The dust created by the brake system is harmful to your health. Never blow it out with compressed air and don't inhale any of it. An approved filtering mask should be worn when working on the brakes. Do not, under any circumstances, use petroleum-based solvents to clean brake parts. Use brake system cleaner only! Try to use non-asbestos replacement parts whenever possible.

➡Note: For detailed photographs of the brake system, refer to Chapter 9.

1   In addition to the specified intervals, the brakes should be inspected every time the wheels are removed or whenever a defect is suspected.

2   Any of the following symptoms could indicate a potential brake system defect: The vehicle pulls to one side when the brake pedal is depressed; the brakes make squealing or dragging noises when applied; brake pedal travel is excessive; the pedal pulsates; or brake fluid leaks, usually onto the inside of the tire or wheel.

3   Loosen the wheel lug nuts.

4   Raise the vehicle and place it securely on jackstands.

5   Remove the wheels (see Jacking and towing at the front of this book, or your owner's manual, if necessary).

DISC BRAKES

♦ Refer to illustrations 19.7a, 19.7b, 19.9 and 19.11

6   There are two pads (an outer and an inner) in each caliper. The

pads are visible with the wheels removed. The vehicles covered by this manual have disc brakes front and rear, with a mechanical, drum-type parking brake mechanism inside the rear discs.

7   Check the pad thickness by looking at each end of the caliper and through the inspection window in the caliper body (see illustrations). If the lining material is less than the thickness listed in this Chapter's Specifications, replace the pads.

19.7a With the wheel off, check the thickness of the inner pad (arrow) through the inspection hole (front caliper shown, rear caliper similar)

19.7b The outer pad (arrow) is more easily checked at the edge of the caliper

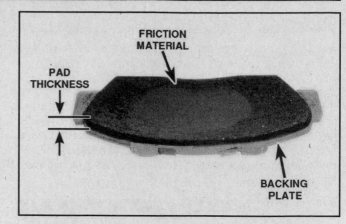

19.9 If a more precise measurement of pad thickness is necessary, remove the pads and measure the remaining friction material

➡Note: Keep in mind that the lining material is riveted or bonded to a metal backing plate and the metal portion is not included in this measurement.

8   If it is difficult to determine the exact thickness of the remaining pad material by the above method, or if you are at all concerned about the condition of the pads, remove the caliper(s), then remove the pads from the calipers for further inspection (refer to Chapter 9).

9   Once the pads are removed from the calipers, clean them with brake cleaner and re-measure them with a ruler or a vernier caliper (see illustration).

10 Measure the disc thickness with a micrometer to make sure that it still has service life remaining. If any disc is thinner than the specified minimum thickness, replace it (refer to Chapter 9). Even if the disc has service life remaining, check its condition. Look for scoring, gouging and burned spots. If these conditions exist, remove the disc and have it resurfaced (see Chapter 9).

11 Before installing the wheels, check all brake lines and hoses for damage, wear, deformation, cracks, corrosion, leakage, bends and twists, particularly in the vicinity of the rubber hoses at the calipers (see illustration). Check the clamps for tightness and the connections for leakage. Make sure that all hoses and lines are clear of sharp edges, moving parts and the exhaust system. If any of the above conditions are noted, repair, reroute or replace the lines and/or fittings as necessary (see Chapter 9).

BRAKE BOOSTER CHECK

12 Sit in the driver's seat and perform the following sequence of tests.

13 With the brake fully depressed, start the engine - the pedal should move down a little when the engine starts.

14 With the engine running, depress the brake pedal several times - the travel distance should not change.

19.11 Check along the brake hoses and at each fitting (arrows) for deterioration, cracks and leakage

15 Depress the brake, stop the engine and hold the pedal in for about 30 seconds - the pedal should neither sink nor rise.

16 Restart the engine, run it for about a minute and turn it off. Then firmly depress the brake several times - the pedal travel should decrease with each application.

17 If your brakes do not operate as described, the brake booster has failed. Refer to Chapter 9 for the replacement procedure.

PARKING BRAKE

18 One method of checking the parking brake is to park the vehicle on a steep hill with the parking brake set and the transmission in Neutral (be sure to stay in the vehicle for this check). If the parking brake cannot prevent the vehicle from rolling, it's in need of attention (see Chapter 9).

20 Exhaust system check (every 15,000 miles or 12 months)

▶ **Refer to illustrations 20.2a and 20.2b**

1   With the engine cold (at least three hours after the vehicle has been driven), check the complete exhaust system from the manifold to the end of the tailpipe. Be careful around the catalytic converter, which may be hot even after three hours. The inspection should be done with the vehicle on a hoist to permit unrestricted access. If a hoist isn't available, raise the vehicle and support it securely on jackstands.

2   Check the exhaust pipes and connections for signs of leakage and/or corrosion indicating a potential failure. Make sure that all brack-ets and hangers are in good condition and tight (see illustrations).

3   Inspect the underside of the body for holes, corrosion, open seams, etc. which may allow exhaust gasses to enter the passenger compartment. Seal all body openings with silicone sealant or body putty.

4   Rattles and other noises can often be traced to the exhaust system, especially the hangers, mounts and heat shields. Try to move the pipes, mufflers and catalytic converter. If the components can come in contact with the body or suspension parts, secure the exhaust system with new brackets and hangers.

20.2a Inspect the muffler (A) for signs of deterioration, and all hangers (B)

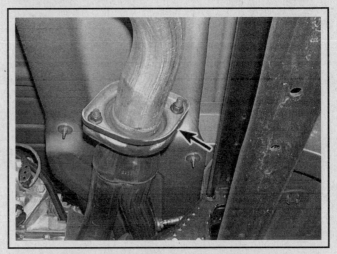

20.2b Inspect all flanged joints (arrow indicates front exhaust pipe joint) for signs of exhaust gas leakage

21 Manual transmission lubricant level check (every 15,000 miles or 12 months)

▶ **Refer to illustration 21.2**

1   The manual transmission has a filler plug which must be removed to check the lubricant level. If the vehicle is raised to gain access to the plug, be sure to support it safely on jackstands - DO NOT crawl under a vehicle that is supported only by a jack! Be sure the vehicle is level or the check may be inaccurate.

2   Using the appropriate wrench, unscrew the plug from the transmission (see illustration).

3   Use your little finger to reach inside the housing to feel the lubricant level. The level should be at or near the bottom of the plug hole. If it isn't, add the recommended lubricant through the plug hole with a syringe or squeeze bottle.

4   Install and tighten the plug. Check for leaks after the first few miles of driving.

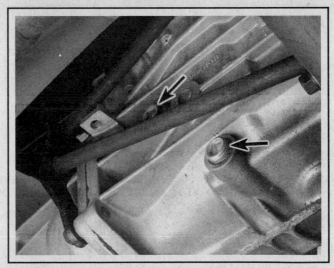

21.2 Manual transmission drain (on bottom) and fill plug (on passenger side) locations

22 Transfer case lubricant level check (4WD models) (every 15,000 miles or 12 months)

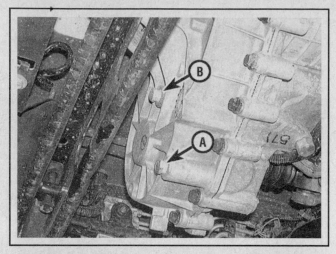

22.1 The drain plug (A) and fill plug (B) are on the rear cover of the transfer case

▶ **Refer to illustration 22.1**

1   The transfer case lubricant level is checked by removing the upper plug located at the rear of the case (see illustration).

2   After removing the plug, reach inside the hole. The lubricant level should be just at the bottom of the hole. If not, add the appropriate lubricant through the opening.

23 Interior ventilation filter replacement (every 15,000 miles or 12 months)

▶ **Refer to illustrations 23.2 and 23.3**

1   Some of these models are equipped with a pair of air filters under the dash that clean the air entering the vehicle through the ventilation system, as well as recirculated air.

2   Reach under the center of the instrument panel and remove the screw securing the cover, then pull down the access cover at the bot-tom-right of the housing surrounding the evaporator core (see illustration).

3   Slide the filters down out of the housing and replace with new ones at the specified interval (see illustration).

4   The remainder of the installation is the reverse of the removal procedure.

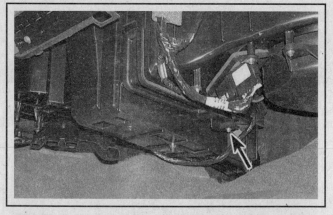

23.2 Remove the screw (arrow) and pull down the access door below the ventilation filters

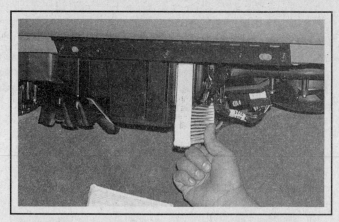

23.3 Slide the filters down out of the HVAC housing - when the first filter is pulled out, the second will come down

24 Brake fluid change (every 30,000 miles or 24 months)

✳✳ WARNING:

Brake fluid can harm your eyes and damage painted surfaces, so use extreme caution when handling or pouring it. Do not use brake fluid that has been standing open or is more than one year old. Brake fluid absorbs moisture from the air. Excess moisture can cause a dangerous loss of braking effectiveness.

1   At the specified intervals, the brake fluid should be drained and replaced. Since the brake fluid may drip or splash when pouring it, place plenty of rags around the master cylinder to protect any surrounding painted surfaces.

2   Before beginning work, purchase the specified brake fluid (see Recommended lubricants and fluids at the end of this Chapter).

3   Remove the cap from the master cylinder reservoir.

4   Using a hand suction pump or similar device, withdraw the fluid from the master cylinder reservoir.

5   Add new fluid to the master cylinder until it rises to the line indicated on the reservoir.

6   Bleed the brake system as described in Chapter 9 at all four brakes until new and uncontaminated fluid is expelled from the bleeder screw. Be sure to maintain the fluid level in the master cylinder as you perform the bleeding process. If you allow the master cylinder to run dry, air will enter the system.

7   Refill the master cylinder with fluid and check the operation of the brakes. The pedal should feel solid when depressed, with no sponginess.

> ✳✳ **WARNING:**
>
> **Do not operate the vehicle if you are in doubt about the effectiveness of the brake system.**

25 Air filter replacement (every 30,000 miles or 24 months)

▸ **Refer to illustrations 25.3a and 25.3b**

1   At the specified intervals, the air filter element should be replaced with a new one.

2   On all models, the air filter is housed in a black plastic box mounted on the inner fenderwell on the right side of the engine compartment. Attached to the box is a plastic gauge that measures the airflow through the filter and indicates when the filter should be changed. If you drive in conditions that are particularly dusty, the gauge may indicate the need for a filter change before the normally-recommended mileage interval.

3   Loosen the captive screws and pull the housing cover up, then lift the air filter element out of the housing (see illustrations). Wipe out the inside of the air filter housing with a clean rag.

4   While the cover is off, be careful not to drop anything down into the air filter housing.

5   Place the new filter element in the air filter housing. Make sure it seats properly in the groove of the housing.

6   Installation is the reverse of removal. After installing the new filter, push in on the top of the filter indicator to reset it.

25.3a Loosen the screws (A) and lift the air filter housing cover, (B) is the air filter condition indicator

25.3b Holding the cover up, slip out the filter element

26 Fuel filter replacement (every 30,000 miles or 30 months)

▸ **Refer to illustration 26.5**

> ✳✳ **WARNING:**
>
> **Gasoline is extremely flammable, so take extra precautions when you work on any part of the fuel system. Don't smoke or allow open flames or bare light bulbs near the work area, and don't work in a garage where a natural gas-type appliance (such as a water heater or clothes dryer) is present. Since gasoline is carcinogenic, wear latex gloves when there's a possibility of being exposed to fuel, and, if you spill any fuel on your skin, rinse it off immediately with soap and water. Mop up any spills immediately and do not store fuel-soaked rags where they could ignite. The fuel system is under constant pressure, so, if any fuel lines are to be disconnected, the fuel pressure in the system must be relieved first (see Chapter 4 for more information). When you perform any kind of work on the fuel system, wear safety glasses and have a Class B type fire extinguisher on hand.**

➡ **Note:** 2005 and later models are equipped with a non-replaceable fuel filter built into the fuel sender assembly.

1   Relieve the fuel system pressure (see Chapter 4).

2   Raise the vehicle and support it securely on jackstands.

3   The fuel filter is mounted to the right frame rail, near the fuel tank.

4   Use compressed air or carburetor cleaner to clean any dirt surrounding the fuel inlet and outlet line fittings.

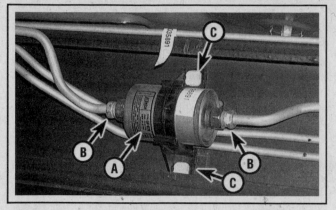

26.5 When changing the fuel filter (A), use a flare-nut wrench to disconnect the fittings (B) - remove the nuts on these carriage bolts (C) to remove the filter and bracket

5 There are screw-in fittings at each end of the filter, requiring two wrenches to loosen each fitting (see illustration).

➡**Note: Have spare rags or a small container to catch or wipe up extra gasoline that will spill from the filter assembly.**

6 Use an open end wrench to steady the hex on the filter and a flare-nut wrench to unscrew the fuel line nut, then separate the line from the filter. Using a flare-nut wrench will help to avoid rounding the corners off of the fuel line nuts.

7 Detach the fuel filter mounting bracket nuts and remove the fuel filter.

8 Installation is the reverse of removal.

27 Spark plug replacement (see maintenance schedule for service intervals)

▶ **Refer to illustrations 27.2, 27.5a, 27.5b, 27.6, 27.8, 27.9a, 27.9b and 27.10**

1 The spark plugs are threaded into the sides of the cylinder heads, adjacent to the exhaust ports.

2 In most cases, the tools necessary for spark plug replacement include a spark plug socket which fits onto a ratchet (spark plug sockets are padded inside to prevent damage to the porcelain insulators on the new plugs), various extensions and a gap gauge to check and adjust the gaps on the new plugs (see illustration). A special plug wire removal tool is available for separating the wire boots from the spark plugs, but it isn't absolutely necessary. A torque wrench should be used to tighten the new plugs.

➡**Note: The spark plugs on these models are 1/8-inch longer than standard plugs previously used. Make sure your spark plug socket doesn't bottom-out on the longer plugs, which could crack the insulators.**

3 The best approach when replacing the spark plugs is to purchase the new ones in advance, adjust them to the proper gap and replace them one at a time. When buying the new spark plugs, be sure to obtain the correct plug type for your particular engine. This information can be found in the factory owner's manual and the Specifications at the front of this Chapter.

4 Allow the engine to cool completely before attempting to remove any of the plugs. While you're waiting for the engine to cool, check the new plugs for defects and adjust the gaps.

5 The gap is checked by inserting the proper-thickness gauge between the electrodes at the tip of the plug (see illustration). The gap between the electrodes should be the same as the one specified on the Emissions Control Information label or in this Chapter's Specifications. The wire should just slide between the electrodes with a slight amount of drag. If the gap is incorrect, use the adjuster on the gauge body to bend the curved side electrode slightly until the proper gap is obtained

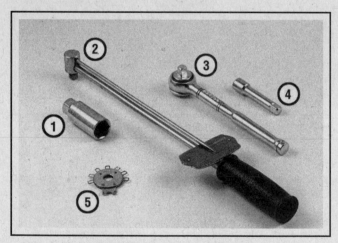

27.2 Tools required for changing spark plugs

1 *Spark plug socket* - This will have special padding inside to protect the spark plug's porcelain insulator
2 *Torque wrench* - Although not mandatory, using this tool is the best way to ensure the plugs are tightened properly
3 *Ratchet* - Standard hand tool to fit the spark plug socket
4 *Extension* - Depending on model and accessories, you may need special extensions and universal joints to reach one or more of the plugs
5 *Spark plug gap gauge* - This gauge for checking the gap comes in a variety of styles. Make sure the gap for your engine is included

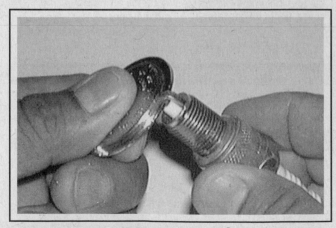

27.5a Spark plug manufacturers recommend using a tapered thickness gauge when checking the gap - slide the thin side into the gap and turn until the gauge just fills the gap, then read the thickness on the gauge - do not force the tool into the gap or use the tapered portion to widen a gap

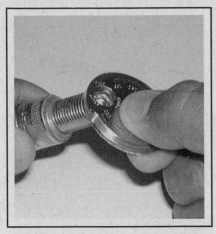

27.5b To change the gap, bend the side electrode only, using the adjuster hole in the tool, and be very careful not to crack or chip the porcelain insulator surrounding the center electrode

27.6 A tool like this one makes the job of removing the spark plug boot easier - twist it back-and-forth and pull only on the boot

27.8 Use a socket and extension to unscrew the spark plugs - various length extensions and perhaps a flex-joint may be required to reach some plugs

(see illustration). If the side electrode is not exactly over the center electrode, bend it with the adjuster until it is. Check for cracks in the porcelain insulator (if any are found, the plug should not be used).

➡**Note: Manufacturers recommend using a tapered thickness gauge when checking platinum-type spark plugs. Other types of gauges may scrape the thin platinum coating from the electrodes, thus dramatically shortening the life of the plugs.**

6   With the engine cool, remove the spark plug wire from one spark plug. Pull only on the boot at the end of the wire - do not pull on the wire. A plug wire removal tool should be used if available (see illustration).

7   If compressed air is available, use it to blow any dirt or foreign material away from the spark plug hole. The idea here is to eliminate the possibility of debris falling into the cylinder as the spark plug is removed.

8   Place the spark plug socket over the plug and remove it from the engine by turning it in a counterclockwise direction (see illustration).

9   Compare the spark plug with the illustration to get an indication of the general running condition of the engine. Before installing the new plugs, it is a good idea to apply a thin coat of anti-seize compound to the threads (see illustration).

10   Thread one of the new plugs into the hole until you can no

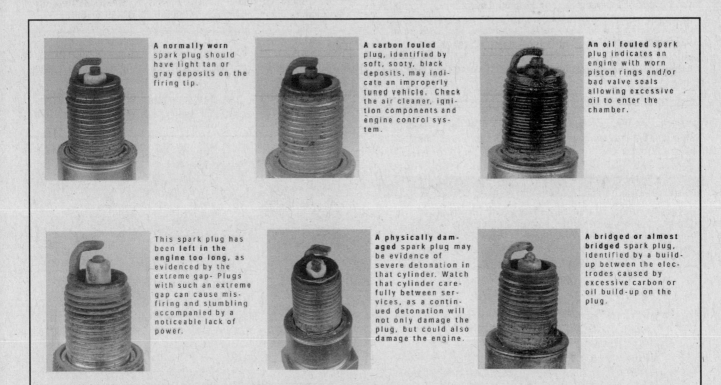

A **normally worn** spark plug should have light tan or gray deposits on the firing tip.

A **carbon fouled** plug, identified by soft, sooty, black deposits, may indicate an improperly tuned vehicle. Check the air cleaner, ignition components and engine control system.

An **oil fouled** spark plug indicates an engine with worn piston rings and/or bad valve seals allowing excessive oil to enter the chamber.

This spark plug has been **left in the engine too long**, as evidenced by the extreme gap- Plugs with such an extreme gap can cause misfiring and stumbling accompanied by a noticeable lack of power.

A **physically damaged** spark plug may be evidence of severe detonation in that cylinder. Watch that cylinder carefully between services, as a continued detonation will not only damage the plug, but could also damage the engine.

A **bridged** or almost **bridged** spark plug, identified by a build-up between the electrodes caused by excessive carbon or oil build-up on the plug.

27.9a Inspect the spark plug to determine engine running conditions

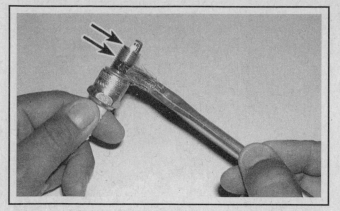

27.9b Apply a thin coat of anti-seize compound to the spark plug threads, being careful not to get any near the lower threads (arrows)

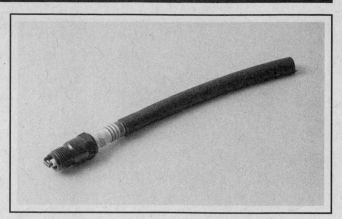

27.10 A length of snug-fitting rubber hose will save time and prevent damaged threads when installing the spark plugs

longer turn it with your fingers, then tighten it with a torque wrench (if available) or the ratchet. Where plugs are at the rear of the engine and harder to reach, it might be a good idea to slip a short length of rubber hose over the end of the plug to use as a tool to thread it into place (see illustration). The hose will grip the plug well enough to turn it, but

will start to slip if the plug begins to cross-thread in the hole - this will prevent damaged threads and the accompanying repair costs.

11 Attach the plug wire to the new spark plug, again using a twisting motion on the boot until it's seated on the spark plug.

12 Repeat the procedure for the remaining spark plugs, replacing them one at a time to prevent mixing up the spark plug wires.

28 Cooling system servicing (draining, flushing and refilling) (see maintenance schedule for interval)

✳✳ WARNING:

Do not allow antifreeze to come in contact with your skin or painted surfaces of the vehicle. Rinse off spills immediately with plenty of water. Antifreeze is highly toxic if ingested. Never leave antifreeze lying around in an open container or in puddles on the floor; children and pets are attracted by its sweet smell and may drink it. Check with local authorities on disposing of used antifreeze. Many communities have collection centers that will see that antifreeze is disposed of safely. Antifreeze is flammable under certain conditions - be sure to read the precautions on the container.

➡Note: Non-toxic coolant is available at local auto parts stores. Although the coolant is non-toxic when fresh, proper disposal is still required.

✳✳ CAUTION:

Never mix green-colored ethylene glycol anti-freeze and orange-colored "DEX-COOL" silicate-free coolant because doing so will destroy the efficiency of the "DEX-COOL" coolant, which is designed to last for 100,000 miles or five years.

DRAINING

◗ **Refer to illustrations 28.3 and 28.4**

1 Periodically, the cooling system should be drained, flushed and refilled to replenish the antifreeze mixture and prevent formation of rust and corrosion, which can impair the performance of the cooling system and cause engine damage. When the cooling system is serviced, all hoses and the surge tank cap should be checked and replaced if necessary.

2 Apply the parking brake and block the wheels.

✳✳ WARNING:

If the vehicle has just been driven, wait several hours to allow the engine to cool down before beginning this procedure.

3 Move a large container under the radiator drain to catch the coolant. The drain valve is located on the lower left side of the radiator (see illustration).

➡Note: Some models may not be equipped with a drain valve. Disconnect the lower radiator hose to drain the cooling system.

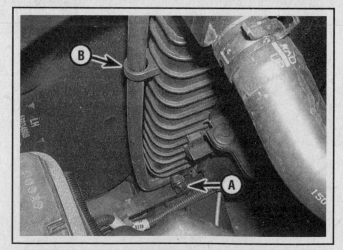

28.3 The radiator drain valve (A) is located at the left corner of the radiator - before draining, pull the rubber drain hose out of its support (B) and aim it down into your drain pan

28.4 Cylinder block drain (arrow, this one is a block heater, not a standard plug) - there is one on each side of the block

Remove the drain hose from its support and direct it into the container, then open the drain fitting (a pair of pliers may be required to turn it). Remove the surge tank cap.

4   After coolant stops flowing out of the radiator, move the container under the engine block drain plugs - there's one on each side of the block (see illustration). Remove the plugs and allow the coolant in the block to drain.

➡Note: Frequently, the coolant will not drain from the block after the plug is removed. This is due to a rust layer that has built up behind the plug. Insert a Phillips screwdriver into the hole to break the rust barrier.

5   While the coolant is draining, check the condition of the radiator hoses, heater hoses and clamps (refer to Section 14 if necessary).

6   Replace any damaged clamps or hoses. Reinstall the drain plugs and tighten them securely, using Permatex #2 sealant on the threads of the plugs.

FLUSHING

♦ **Refer to illustration 28.9**

7   Once the system is completely drained, remove the thermostat from the engine (see Chapter 3). Then reinstall the thermostat housing without the thermostat. This will allow the system to be thoroughly flushed.

8   Reinstall the lower radiator hose and tighten the radiator drain plug. Turn your heating system controls to Hot, so that the heater core will be flushed at the same time as the rest of the cooling system.

9   Disconnect the upper radiator hose, then place a garden hose in the upper radiator inlet and flush the system until the water runs clear at the upper radiator hose (see illustration).

10 In severe cases of contamination or clogging of the radiator, remove the radiator (see Chapter 3) and have a radiator repair facility clean and repair it if necessary.

11 Many deposits can be removed by the chemical action of a cleaner available at auto parts stores. Follow the procedure outlined in the manufacturer's instructions.

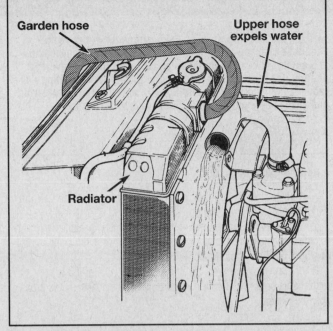

28.9 With the thermostat removed, disconnect the upper radiator hose and flush the radiator and engine block with a garden hose

➡Note: When the coolant is regularly drained and the system refilled with the correct antifreeze/water mixture, there should be no need to use chemical cleaners or descalers.

REFILLING

12 To refill the system, install the thermostat and reconnect any radiator hoses.

13 Place the heater temperature control in the maximum heat position.

14 Be sure to use the proper coolant listed in this Chapter's Specifications. Slowly fill the surge tank with the recommended mixture of antifreeze and water to the FILL COLD mark.

15 With the surge tank cap off, start the engine and let it idle for about a minute.

16 Install the cap on the surge tank, but don't tighten it down (pressure must be able to escape). Raise the engine speed to approximately 3000 rpm in 30-second cycles until the engine reaches normal operating temperature and the thermostat opens.

17 Turn the engine off and remove the surge tank cap. If there is any hissing noise coming from the tank, wait until it stops then remove the cap.

18 Start the engine and let it idle for one minute. Add coolant to the tank until the level is 1/2-inch above the FILL COLD mark, repeat Step 16, then turn the engine off.

19 Add coolant as necessary to bring the level to 1/2-inch above the FILL COLD mark on the tank. Install the surge tank cap securely.

20 Check the cooling system for leaks.

29 Suspension, steering and driveaxle boot check (every 30,000 miles or 30 months)

➡Note: The steering linkage and suspension components should be checked periodically. Worn or damaged suspension and steering linkage components can result in excessive and abnormal tire wear, poor ride quality and vehicle handling and reduced fuel economy. For detailed illustrations of the steering and suspension components, refer to Chapter 10.

SHOCK ABSORBER CHECK

▶ **Refer to illustration 29.6**

1 Park the vehicle on level ground, turn the engine off and set the parking brake. Check the tire pressures.

2 Push down at one corner of the vehicle, then release it while noting the movement of the body. It should stop moving and come to rest in a level position within one or two bounces.

3 If the vehicle continues to move up-and-down or if it fails to return to its original position, a worn or weak shock absorber is probably the reason.

29.6 Check for signs of fluid leakage at this point (arrow) on shock absorbers (front shock shown)

4 Repeat the above check at each of the three remaining corners of the vehicle.

5 Raise the vehicle and support it securely on jackstands.

6 Check the shock absorbers for evidence of fluid leakage (see illustration). A light film of fluid is no cause for concern. Make sure that any fluid noted is from the shocks and not from some other source. If leakage is noted, replace the shocks as a set.

7 Check the shocks to be sure that they are securely mounted and undamaged. Check the upper mounts for damage and wear. If damage or wear is noted, replace the shocks as a set (front or rear).

8 If the shocks must be replaced, refer to Chapter 10 for the procedure.

STEERING AND SUSPENSION CHECK

▶ **Refer to illustrations 29.9a, 29.9b, 29.9c, 29.9d and 29.11**

9 Visually inspect the steering and suspension components (front and rear) for damage and distortion. Look for damaged seals, boots and bushings and leaks of any kind. Examine the bushings where the control arms meet the chassis (see illustrations).

10 Clean the lower end of the steering knuckle. Have an assistant grasp the lower edge of the tire and move the wheel in-and-out while you look for movement at the steering knuckle-to-control arm balljoint. If there is any movement the suspension balljoint(s) must be replaced.

11 Grasp each front tire at the front and rear edges, push in at the front, pull out at the rear and feel for play in the steering system components. If any freeplay is noted, check the idler arm and the tie-rod ends for looseness (see illustration).

12 Additional steering and suspension system information and illustrations can be found in Chapter 10.

DRIVEAXLE BOOT CHECK (4WD MODELS)

▶ **Refer to illustration 29.14**

13 The driveaxle boots are very important because they prevent dirt, water and foreign material from entering and damaging the constant velocity (CV) joints. Oil and grease can cause the boot material to dete-

29.9a Examine the mounting points (arrows) for the upper . . .

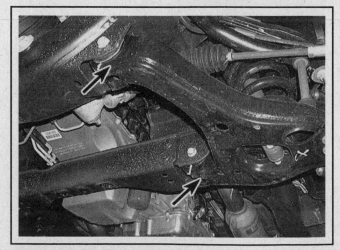

29.9b . . . and lower control arms on the front suspension (arrows)

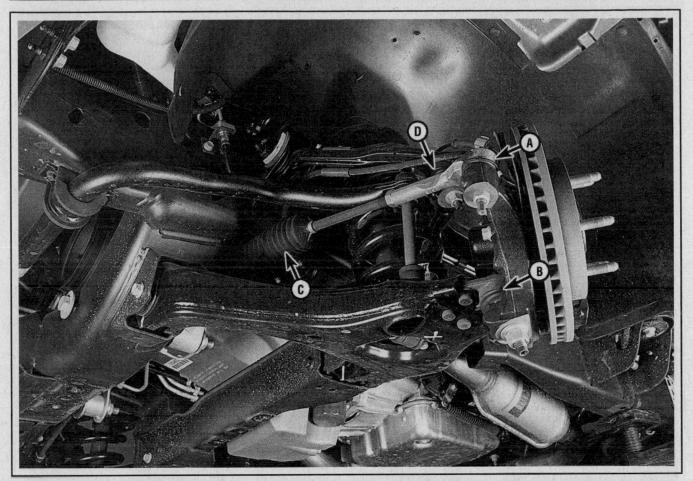

29.9c Inspect the tie-rod ends (A), the lower balljoints (B), the steering gear boots (C), (2WD 1500 pick-ups) and the upper balljoints (D)

riorate prematurely, so it's a good idea to wash the boots with soap and water. Because it constantly pivots back and forth following the steering action of the front hub, the outer CV boot wears out sooner and should be inspected regularly.

14 Inspect the boots for tears and cracks as well as loose clamps (see illustration). If there is any evidence of cracks or leaking lubricant, they must be replaced as described in Chapter 8.

29.9d On 2WD 1500 pick-up models, Inspect the steering gear boots (shown) for signs of cracking or lubricant leakage

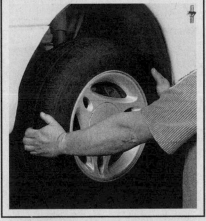

29.11 With the steering wheel in the locked position and the vehicle raised, grasp the front tire as shown and try to move it back-and-forth - if any play is noted, check the steering gear mounts and tie-rod ends for looseness

29.14 Inspect the inner and outer driveaxle boots on 4WD models for loose clamps, cracks or signs of leaking lubricant (inner boot shown)

30 Automatic transmission fluid and filter change (every 30,000 miles or 30 months)

♦ **Refer to illustrations 30.5, 30.6, 30.7, 30.11, 30.12 and 30.13**

1   At the specified intervals, the transmission fluid should be drained and replaced. Since the fluid will remain hot long after driving, perform this procedure only after the engine has cooled down completely.

2   Before beginning work, purchase the specified transmission fluid (see Recommended lubricants and fluids at the end of this Chapter) and a new filter and pan gasket.

3   Other tools necessary for this job include a floor jack, jackstands to support the vehicle in a raised position, a drain pan capable of holding at least eight quarts, newspapers and clean rags.

4   Raise the vehicle and support it securely on jackstands.

5   Place the drain pan underneath the transmission pan. Remove the drain plug and allow the fluid to drain until it barely comes out, then reinsert the drain plug (see illustration).

6   To access the pan bolts on the right side of the vehicle, remove the heat shield next to the catalytic converter (see illustration).

7   On the driver's side of the transmission, the shift linkage must be removed to access the pan bolts (see illustration).

8   Remove the transmission pan mounting bolts, then carefully pry the transmission pan loose with a screwdriver.

❋❋ WARNING:

There is still some transmission fluid in the pan.

9   Carefully clean the gasket surface of the transmission to remove all traces of the old gasket and sealant.

10 Clean the pan with solvent and dry it with compressed air, if available.

➡**Note: Some models are equipped with magnets in the transmission pan to catch metal debris. Clean the magnet thoroughly. A small amount of metal material is normal at the magnet. If there is considerable debris, consult a dealer or transmission specialist.**

11 Remove the filter from the valve body inside the transmission (see illustration).

30.5 Drain the transmission fluid pan by removing the drain plug (arrow)

30.6 Remove the two bolts (arrows) and the heat shield at the right side of the transmission

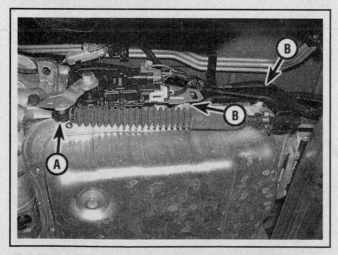

30.7 Disconnect the shift cable end from the ball-stud (A), then remove the two bolts securing the shift cable bracket to the transmission (B) (this allows room to access the oil pan bolts)

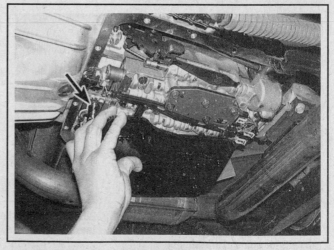

30.11 Remove the filter from the transmission by pulling it straight down

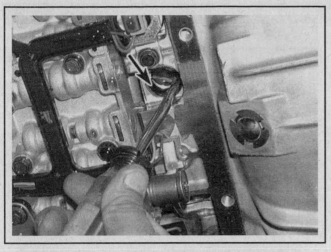

30.12 Use a seal removal tool to remove the transmission filter seal (arrow) from the valve body, then replace it with a new seal - be careful not to scratch the aluminum cavity

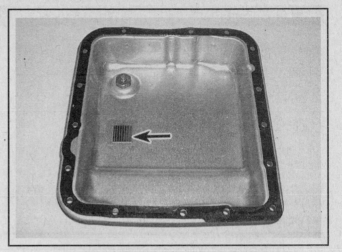

30.13 Clean the transmission pan, position the magnet (arrow) back in place, and install the new pan gasket

➡Note: Be very careful not to gouge the delicate aluminum gasket surface on the valve body.

12 Install a new seal and filter. On many replacement filters, the seal is attached to the filter to simplify installation (see illustration).

13 Make sure the gasket surface on the transmission pan is clean, then install a new gasket on the pan (see illustration). Put the pan in place against the transmission and install all of the bolts. Working around the pan, tighten each bolt a little at a time to the torque listed in this Chapter's Specifications.

14 Reinstall the components removed for access to the pan bolts.

15 Lower the vehicle and add approximately 4 quarts of the speci-

fied type of automatic transmission fluid through the filler tube (see Section 7).

16 With the transmission in Park and the parking brake set, run the engine at a fast idle, but don't race it.

17 Move the gear selector through each range and back to Park, then let the engine idle for a few minutes. Check the fluid level. It will probably be low. Add enough fluid to bring the level to the proper mark on the dipstick. Be careful not to overfill.

18 Check under the vehicle for leaks during the first few trips. Check the fluid level again when the transmission is hot (see Section 7).

31 Manual transmission lubricant change (every 60,000 miles or 48 months)

1 This procedure should be performed after the vehicle has been driven so the lubricant will be warm and therefore will flow out of the transmission more easily. Raise the vehicle and support it securely on jackstands.

2 Move a drain pan, rags, newspapers and wrenches under the transmission.

3 Remove the transmission drain plug at the bottom of the case and allow the lubricant to drain into the pan (see Section 21).

4 After the lubricant has drained completely, reinstall the plug and

tighten it securely.

5 Remove the fill plug from the side of the transmission case. Using a hand pump, syringe or squeeze bottle, fill the transmission with the specified lubricant until it just reaches the bottom edge of the hole. Reinstall the fill plug and tighten it securely.

6 Lower the vehicle.

7 Drive the vehicle for a short distance, then check the drain and fill plugs for leakage.

32 Transfer case lubricant change (4WD models) (every 60,000 miles or 48 months)

1 This procedure should be performed after the vehicle has been driven so the lubricant will be warm and therefore will flow out of the transfer case more easily.

2 Raise the vehicle and support it securely on jackstands.

3 Remove the filler plug from the case (see illustration 22.1).

4 Remove the drain plug from the lower part of the case and allow the lubricant to drain completely.

5 After the case is completely drained, carefully clean and install

the drain plug. Tighten the plug securely.

6 Fill the case with the specified lubricant until it is level with the lower edge of the filler hole.

7 Install the filler plug and tighten it securely.

8 Drive the vehicle for a short distance and recheck the lubricant level. In some instances a small amount of additional lubricant will have to be added.

33 Exhaust Gas Recirculation (EGR) valve inspection (every 60,000 miles or 48 months)

1 The factory recommends having the EGR valve checked at the specified interval.

CLEANING

▶ **Refer to illustrations 33.2 and 33.3**

2 Disconnect the electrical connector, then remove the two bolts and take the EGR valve off for examination (see illustration).

✷✷ WARNING:

The engine should be cool for this procedure.

3 Look closely at the pintle on the bottom of the valve (see illustration). Look for accumulated deposits on the pintle and its seat. Clean the area with a soft cloth.

✷✷ CAUTION:

Do not use any chemicals or wire brushes to clean the EGR.

4 Use the eraser end of a pencil to push the pintle in and out of the EGR valve. If the pintle doesn't move freely, replace the EGR valve.

TROUBLESHOOTING

5 Symptoms of an EGR valve that is flowing too much exhaust gas include: stalling, surging, and misfiring at idle.

6 Symptoms of an EGR valve that is not flowing enough exhaust gas include: poor fuel economy, overheating and detonation.

7 If any of these symptoms are present, it's suggested that the vehicle be checked at your dealership or repair facility with a scan tool, to look for trouble codes that relate to the EGR operation.

33.2 Disconnect the EGR valve electrical connector (A) and remove the two mounting bolts (B)

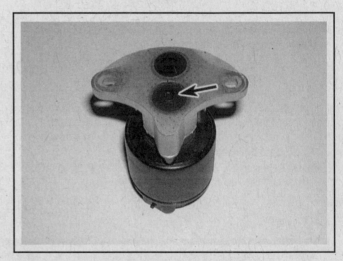

33.3 Use a cloth to clean the pintle and seat area (arrow) of the EGR valve

34 Differential lubricant change (every 60,000 miles or 48 months)

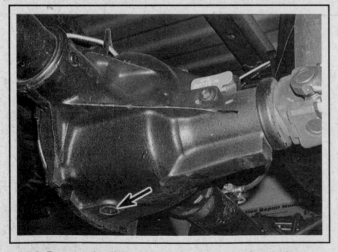

34.3 Remove the differential drain plug (arrow) to drain the lubricant

▶ **Refer to illustration 34.3**

1 This procedure should be performed after the vehicle has been driven, so the lubricant will be warm and therefore will flow out of the differential more easily.

2 Raise the vehicle and support it securely on jackstands. You'll be draining the lubricant by removing the drain plug, so move a drain pan, rags, newspapers and wrenches under the vehicle.

3 Remove the plug and allow the lubricant to drain into the pan, then clean and reinstall the drain plug (see illustration).

➡**Note: On differentials not equipped with a drain plug, the differential cover must be removed to drain the lubricant.**

4 Use a hand pump, syringe or squeeze bottle to fill the differential housing with the specified lubricant until it's level with the bottom of the fill-plug hole. If using synthetic axle lubricant, the level should be below the fill-plug opening by 5/8-inch to 1 5/8-inch on 1500 Series models, but no more than 3/8-inch lower than the hole on 2500 Series models.

➡**Note: On some models with limited-slip differentials, a different lubricant or additive may be required.**

35 Positive Crankcase Ventilation (PCV) valve replacement (every 60,000 miles or 48 months)

▶ Refer to illustration 35.2

1   The PCV valve is located in the valve cover on all engines.

2   With the engine idling at normal operating temperature, pull the valve (with hose attached) from the rubber grommet in the cover (see illustration).

3   Place your finger over the valve opening. If there's no vacuum at the valve, check for a plugged hose, manifold port, or the valve itself. Replace any plugged or deteriorated hoses.

4   Turn off the engine and shake the PCV valve, listening for a rattle. If the valve doesn't rattle, replace it with a new one.

5   To replace the valve, pull it from the end of the hose, noting its installed position.

6   When purchasing a replacement PCV valve, make sure it's for your particular vehicle and engine size. Compare the old valve with the new one to make sure they're the same.

7   Push the valve into the end of the hose until it's seated.

8   Inspect the rubber grommet for damage and hardening. Replace it with a new one if necessary.

9   Push the PCV valve and hose securely into position.

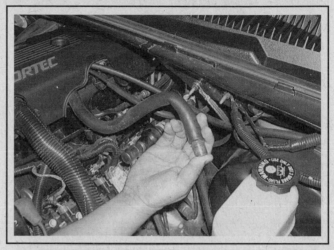

35.2 The PCV valve (arrow, V8 engine shown) is located at the rear of the left valve cover - pull it out and check for vacuum with your finger

36 Spark plug wires, distributor cap and rotor check and replacement (every 100,000 miles or 60 months)

SPARK PLUG WIRES

▶ Refer to illustration 36.6

1   The spark plug wires should be checked at the recommended intervals and whenever new spark plugs are installed in the engine. V6 engines have spark plug wires that go from the plugs all the way to the distributor, while V8 engines have individual coils for each cylinder (no distributor is used) and short plug wires from each coil to the corresponding spark plug.

2   Begin this procedure by making a visual check of the spark plug wires while the engine is running. In a darkened garage (make sure there is adequate ventilation) start the engine and observe each plug wire. Be careful not to come into contact with any moving engine parts. If there is a break in the wire, you will see arcing or a small spark at the damaged area. If arcing is noticed, make a note to obtain new wires, then allow the engine to cool and check the distributor cap and rotor.

3   Disconnect the plug wire from one spark plug (with the engine off). To do this, grab the rubber boot, twist slightly and pull the wire free. Do not pull on the wire itself, only on the rubber boot. A boot-pulling tool is helpful (see illustration 27.6).

4   Check inside the boot for corrosion, which will look like a white crusty powder. Push the wire and boot back onto the end of the spark plug. It should be a tight fit on the plug. If it isn't, remove the wire and use a pair of pliers to carefully crimp the metal connector inside the boot until it fits securely on the end of the spark plug.

5   Using a clean rag, wipe the entire length of the wire to remove any built-up dirt and grease. Once the wire is clean, check for holes, burned areas, cracks and other damage. Don't bend the wire excessively or the conductor inside might break.

6   Disconnect the wire from the distributor cap (V6 engines) or coil (V8 engines). Pull the wire straight out of the cap. Pull only on the rubber boot during removal (see illustration). Check for corrosion and a

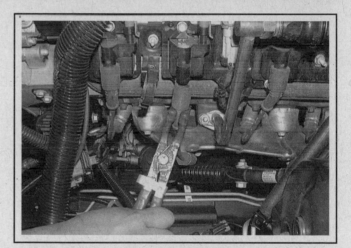

36.6 Use a spark plug boot pulling tool to remove each end of a spark plug wire (V8 shown) - never pull on the wire itself

tight fit in the same manner as the spark plug end. Reattach the wire to the distributor cap or individual coil.

7   Check the remaining spark plug wires one at a time, making sure they are securely fastened at both ends when the check is complete.

8   If new spark plug wires are required, purchase a new set for your specific engine model. Wire sets are available pre-cut, with the rubber boots already installed. Remove and replace the wires one at a time to avoid mix-ups in the firing order. The wire routing is extremely important, so be sure to note exactly how each wire is situated before removing it. On V6 engines, release the ignition wire loom clamps to exchange the wires, then snap the clamps back in place on the new wires. On V8 engines, there are two designs of plug wires, and the lengths are different. Compare your old ones to the new ones to insure obtaining the correct replacements.

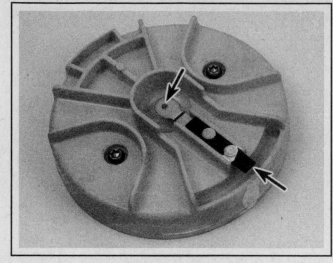

36.10 The ignition rotor should be checked for wear and corrosion (if in doubt about its condition, buy a new one)

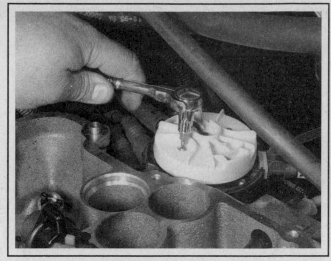

36.11 Remove the two screws to remove the rotor from the distributor - a Torx bit on a 1/4-inch drive ratchet is used here

DISTRIBUTOR CAP AND ROTOR (V6 ENGINES ONLY)

▶ **Refer to illustrations 36.10, 36.11 and 36.13**

9   Remove the distributor cap screws. Pull up on the cap, with the wires attached, to separate it from the distributor, then position it to one side.

36.13 Inspect the inside of the cap for corrosion, carbon tracks and wear (check the outside of the cap for carbon tracks, too)

10 The rotor is now visible on the end of the distributor shaft. Check it carefully for cracks and carbon tracks. Make sure the center terminal spring tension is adequate and look for corrosion and wear on the rotor tip (see illustration). If in doubt about its condition, replace it with a new one.

11 If replacement is required, remove the two screws, then detach the rotor from the shaft and install a new one (see illustration).

12 The rotor is indexed to the shaft so it can only be installed one way. It has an internal key that must line up with a slot in the end of the shaft (or vice versa).

13 Check the distributor cap for carbon tracks, cracks and other damage. Closely examine the terminals on the inside of the cap for excessive corrosion and damage (see illustration). Slight deposits are normal. Again, if in doubt about the condition of the cap, replace it with a new one. Be sure to apply a small dab of silicone dielectric grease to each terminal before installing the cap. Also, make sure the carbon brush (center terminal) is correctly installed in the cap - a wide gap between the brush and rotor will result in rotor burn-through and/or damage to the distributor cap.

14 To replace the cap, simply separate it from the distributor and transfer the spark plug wires, one at a time, to the new cap. Be very careful not to mix up the wires!

15 Reattach the cap to the distributor, then install the screws to hold it in place.

➡**Note: The original screws are coated to prevent loosening under vibration. The factory recommends using new screws for the cap and rotor. If you reuse the original screws, use a mild thread-locking coating on them.**

Specifications

Recommended lubricants and fluids

➡Note: Listed here are manufacturer recommendations at the time this manual was written. Manufacturers occasionally upgrade their fluid and lubricant specifications, so check with your local auto parts store for current recommendations.

Engine oil	API "certified for gasoline engines"
Viscosity	See accompanying chart
Fuel	Unleaded gasoline, 87 octane minimum
Automatic transmission fluid	DEXRON III automatic transmission fluid (2006 and later models require DEXRON VI)
Manual transmission lubricant	
NV 3500	Synchromesh transmission fluid or equivalent
NV 4500	Syn-torq synthetic transmission fluid or equivalent
ZF S6-650	Trans-Synd synthetic transmission fluid or equivalent
Manual transfer case	
New Venture 261 NP2	DEXRON III automatic transmission fluid (2006 and later models require DEXRON VI)
Automatic transfer case	
New Venture 236 NP8, New Venture 246-NP8,	GM Auto Trak II transfer case fluid
All others	DEXRON-III automatic transmission fluid (2006 and later models require DEXRON VI)
Differential	
Front	
Selectable 4WD	SAE 80W90 GL-5 gear oil
Full-time 4WD	SAE 75W90 synthetic gear oil
Rear	SAE 75W90 synthetic gear oil
Quadrasteer rear axle	GM synthetic axle lubricant
Power steering fluid	GM power steering fluid
Brake hydraulic fluid	DOT 3 brake fluid

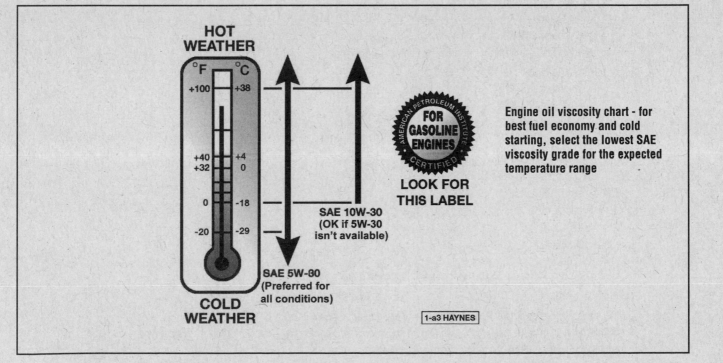

HOT WEATHER

°F   °C

+100   +38

+40   +4
+32   0

0   -18

-20   -29

SAE 10W-30 (OK if 5W-30 isn't available)

SAE 5W-30 (Preferred for all conditions)

COLD WEATHER

FOR GASOLINE ENGINES — AMERICAN PETROLEUM INSTITUTE CERTIFIED

LOOK FOR THIS LABEL

Engine oil viscosity chart - for best fuel economy and cold starting, select the lowest SAE viscosity grade for the expected temperature range

1-a3 HAYNES

Recommended lubricants and fluids (continued)

Clutch hydraulic fluid	
5-speed transmission	DOT 3 brake fluid
6-speed transmission	GM clutch hydraulic fluid
Engine coolant	50/50 mixture of DEX-COOL coolant and demineralized water
Parking brake mechanism grease	White lithium-based grease NLGI no. 2
Chassis lubrication grease	NLGI Grade 2 LB or GC-LB chassis grease
Hood, door and trunk hinge lubricant	Lubriplate, lubricant aerosol spray
Door hinge and check spring grease	NLGI no. 2 multi-purpose grease or equivalent
Key lock cylinder lubricant	Graphite spray
Hood latch assembly lubricant	NLGI no. 2 multi-purpose grease or equivalent
Door latch lubricant	NLGI no. 2 multi-purpose grease or equivalent

Capacities*

Engine oil (including filter)	
V6 engine	4.5 quarts
V8 engine	6.0 quarts
Manual transmission	
New Venture 3500	2.2 quarts
New Venture 4500	4.0 quarts
ZF S6-650	6.3 quarts
Automatic transmission	
Fluid and filter change	
4L60-E/4L65-E	5.0 quarts
4L80-E/4L85-E	7.7 quarts
From dry, including torque converter	
4L60-E/4L65-E	11.2 quarts
4L80-E/4L85-E	13.5 quarts
Transfer case	
New Venture 246-NP8	
1999 through 2001	2.4 quarts
2002 and later	2.0 quarts
New Venture 236-NP8	2.0 quarts
New Venture 149-NP	2.4 quarts
New Venture 263-NP1	2.0 quarts
New Venture 149-NP3	2.2 quarts
New Venture 261-NP2	
1999 through 2001	2.3 quarts
2002 and later	2.0 quarts
Borg Warner 4481-NR3	1.5 quarts
Borg Warner 4482-NR4	1.5 quarts
Cooling system**	
V6 engine	13.0 qts
V8 engine	
4.8L and 5.3L	16.7 qts
6.0L	
Yukon Denali, Yukon XL Denali	19.0 qts
All others	16.8 qts

*All capacities approximate. Add as necessary to bring to appropriate level.

**Cooling system capacities vary depending on engine/transmission package, radiator and A/C system type. Add coolant as necessary to bring to appropriate level.

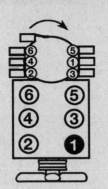

V6 engine cylinder numbering and distributor rotation diagram

V8 engine cylinder numbering diagram

24046-1SPECS

Brakes

Disc brake pad wear limit	3/32 inch
Drum brake shoe wear limit	1/16 inch
Parking brake shoe wear limit	1/16 inch

Ignition system

Spark plug type
    1999

V6 engine	AC Delco 41-932 or equivalent
V8 engine	AC Delco 41-952 or equivalent

    2000

V6 engine	AC Delco 41-932 or equivalent
V8 engine	AC Delco 41-952 or equivalent

    2001

V6 engine	AC Delco 41-932 or equivalent
V8 engine	NGK PZTR-5A15 or equivalent

    2002

V6 engine	AC Delco 41-932 or equivalent
V8 engine	NGK PZTR-5A15 or equivalent

    2003

V6 engine	AC Delco 41-932 or equivalent
V8 engine	AC Delco 41-974 or equivalent

    2004 through 2005

V6 engine	AC Delco 41-932 or equivalent
V8 engine	AC Delco 41-985 or equivalent

    2006 and later

V6 engine	AC Delco 41-932 or equivalent
V8 engine	AC Delco 25171803 or equivalent

Spark plug gap

V6 engine	0.060 inch
V8 engine	
1999 through 2003	0.060 inch
2004 and later	0.040 inch

Firing order

V6 engine	1-6-5-4-3-2
V8 engine	1-8-7-2-6-5-4-3

Torque specifications	Ft-lbs (unless otherwise indicated)
Spark plugs	132 in-lbs
Wheel lug nuts	140
Automatic transmission	
4L60-E/4L65-E	
Pan bolts	97 in-lbs
Drain plug	156 in-lbs
4L80-E/4L85-E	
Pan bolts	
2004 and 2005 models	18
All others	97 in-lbs
Drain plug	156 in-lbs
Drivebelt tensioner/idler pulley	
Drivebelt tension belt	37
Idler pulley bolt	37
Air conditioning drivebelt	
tensioner bolt (V8 engines)	37
Engine oil drain plug	18
Manual transmission fill and drain plugs	
New Venture 3500	22
New Venture 4500	27
ZF S6-650	26
Transfer case drain/fill plug	15
Differential drain and fill plugs	
Front differential	24
Rear differential	
1999	45
2000 and 2001	24
2002 and later	
Drain plug	
9.75 inch ring gear	20
All except 9.75 inch ring gear	24
Fill plug	
9.75 inch ring gear	15
All except 9.75 inch ring gear	24

2A

4.3L V6 ENGINE

1 General information

This Part of Chapter 2 is devoted to in-vehicle repair procedures for the 4.3L V6 engine. These engines utilize cast-iron blocks with six cylinders arranged in a "V" shape at a 90-degree angle between the two banks. The overhead valve cast iron cylinder heads are equipped with integral valve guides and seats. Hydraulic roller lifters actuate the valves through tubular pushrods and rocker arms. A balance shaft has been incorporated into this engine to smooth power pulsations. The balance shaft is located directly above the camshaft in the engine block and is driven off the camshaft. The oil pump is mounted to the rear main cap and is driven by the distributor and the oil pump driveshaft.

To positively identify this engine, locate the Vehicle Identification Number (VIN) on the left front corner of the instrument panel. The VIN is visible from the outside of the vehicle through the windshield. The eighth character in the sequence is the engine designation:

W = 4.3 liter V6 engine (L35)
X = 4.3 liter V6 engine (LU3)

All information concerning engine removal and installation and engine block and cylinder head overhaul can be found in Part C of this Chapter. The following repair procedures are based on the assumption that the engine is installed in the vehicle. If the engine has been removed from the vehicle and mounted on a stand, many of the steps outlined in this Part of Chapter 2 will not apply.

The Specifications included in this Part of Chapter 2 apply only to the procedures contained in this Part. Part C of Chapter 2 contains the Specifications necessary for cylinder head and engine block rebuilding.

2 Repair operations possible with the engine in the vehicle

Many major repair operations can be accomplished without removing the engine from the vehicle.

Clean the engine compartment and the exterior of the engine with some type of pressure washer before any work is done. It will make the job easier and help keep dirt out of the internal areas of the engine.

Remove the hood, if necessary, to improve access to the engine as repairs are performed (see Chapter 11 if necessary).

If vacuum, exhaust, oil or coolant leaks develop, indicating a need for gasket or seal replacement, the repairs can generally be made with the engine in the vehicle. The intake and exhaust manifold gaskets, timing chain cover gasket, oil pan gasket, crankshaft oil seals and cylinder head gaskets are all accessible with the engine in place.

Exterior engine components, such as the intake and exhaust manifolds, the oil pan and oil pump, the water pump, the starter motor, the alternator, the distributor and the fuel system components can be removed for repair with the engine in place.

Since the cylinder heads can be removed without pulling the engine, valve component servicing can also be accomplished with the engine in the vehicle. Replacement of the timing chain and sprockets is also possible with the engine in the vehicle.

3 Top Dead Center (TDC) - locating

▶ **Refer to illustration 3.7**

1   Top Dead Center (TDC) is the highest point in the cylinder that each piston reaches as it travels up the cylinder bore. Each piston reaches TDC on the compression stroke and again on the exhaust stroke, but TDC generally refers to piston position on the compression stroke.

2   Positioning the piston(s) at TDC is an essential part of many procedures such as distributor and timing chain/sprocket removal.

3   Before beginning this procedure, be sure to place the transmission in Neutral and apply the parking brake or block the rear wheels. Also, disable the ignition system by disconnecting the coil wire from the distributor and grounding it to the engine block, then remove the spark plugs (see Chapter 1).

4   In order to bring any piston to TDC, the crankshaft must be turned using one of the methods outlined below. When looking at the front of the engine, normal crankshaft rotation is clockwise.

a) *The preferred method is to turn the crankshaft with a socket and ratchet attached to the bolt threaded into the front of the crankshaft. Apply pressure on the bolt in a clockwise direction only. Never turn the bolt counterclockwise.*

b) *A remote starter switch, which may save some time, can also be used. Follow the instructions included with the switch. Once the piston is close to TDC, use a socket and ratchet as described in the previous paragraph.*

c) *If an assistant is available to turn the ignition switch to the Start position in short bursts, you can get the piston close to TDC without a remote starter switch. Make sure your assistant is out of the vehicle, away from the ignition switch, then use a socket and ratchet as described in Paragraph (a) to complete the procedure.*

5   Place your finger partially over the number one spark plug hole

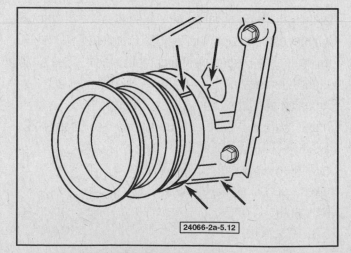

24066-2a-5.12

3.6 After compression is felt at the number one cylinder, align the timing marks on the vibration damper with the timing marks on the front cover

and rotate the crankshaft using one of the methods described above until air pressure is felt at the spark plug hole. Air pressure at the spark plug hole indicates that the cylinder has started the compression stroke. Once the compression stroke has begun, TDC for the number one cylinder is obtained when the piston reaches the top of the cylinder on the compression stroke.

6   To bring the piston to the top of the cylinder, continue to turn the crankshaft until the timing marks on the vibration damper align with the timing marks on the front cover (see illustration).

7   If you go past TDC, rotate the crankshaft counterclockwise until the piston is approximately one inch below TDC, then slowly rotate the crankshaft clockwise again until TDC is reached.

8   After the number one piston has been positioned at TDC on the compression stroke, TDC for any of the remaining pistons can be located by turning the crankshaft 120-degrees (1/3-turn) at a time and following the firing order.

4   Valve covers - removal and installation

REMOVAL

1   Disconnect the cable from the negative terminal of the battery.

✳✳ CAUTION:

On models equipped with the Theftlock audio system, be sure the lockout feature is turned off before performing any procedure which requires disconnecting the battery (see the front of this manual).

2   Remove the air cleaner assembly and air intake duct (see Chapter 4).
3   Remove the secondary air injection crossover pipe, then remove the air injection check valve and pipe assembly from the exhaust manifold on the side from which you wish to remove the valve cover (see Chapter 6). If both valve covers are being removed, both air injection check valves and pipe assemblies must be removed.

Right side

▶ **Refer to illustration 4.7**

4   Remove the heater hose bracket bolt and move the heater hoses aside without disconnecting them.
5   Unclip and lay aside the wiring harness.
6   Disconnect the spark plug wires from their clips and remove the spark plug wires from the spark plugs (see Chapter 1). Be sure each plug wire is labeled before removal to ensure correct reinstallation.
7   Remove the three valve cover bolts, then detach the cover from the cylinder head (see illustration).

➡**Note: If the cover is stuck to the cylinder head, bump one end with a block of wood and a hammer to jar it loose. If that doesn't work, try to slip a flexible putty knife between the cylinder head and cover to break the gasket seal. Don't pry at the cover-to-head joint or damage to the sealing surfaces may occur (leading to oil leaks in the future).**

Left side

▶ **Refer to illustration 4.11**

8   Remove the nuts and bolts securing the engine wiring harness to the upper intake manifold and to the positive battery cable junction block bracket. Disconnect the connector from the engine coolant temperature sensor and position the engine wiring harness aside.
9   Remove the vacuum hose from the power brake booster.
10 Disconnect the spark plug wires from their clips and remove the spark plug wires from the spark plugs (see Chapter 1). Be sure each plug wire is labeled before removal to ensure correct reinstallation.
11 Disconnect the PCV valve and the oil filler tube from the valve cover (see illustration).

➡**Note: On 2002 models, the PCV valve is located on the left side of the intake manifold, not on the valve cover.**

12 Remove the three valve cover bolts, then detach the cover from the cylinder head.

➡**Note: If the cover is stuck to the cylinder head, bump one end with a block of wood and a hammer to jar it loose. If that doesn't work, try to slip a flexible putty knife between the cylinder head and cover to break the gasket seal. Don't pry at the cover-to-head joint or damage to the sealing surfaces may occur (leading to oil leaks in the future).**

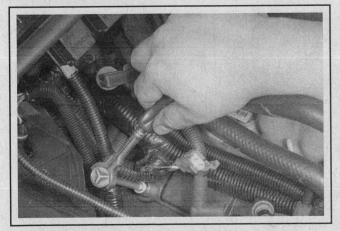

4.7 Remove the three retaining bolts from the center of the valve cover

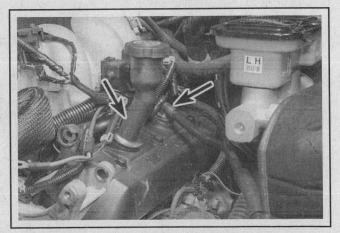

4.11 The PCV valve (right arrow) and hose must be disconnected and moved for left valve cover removal - the oil filler tube (left arrow) easily twists out of the valve cover

INSTALLATION

13 The mating surfaces of each cylinder head and valve cover must be perfectly clean when the covers are installed. Use a gasket scraper to remove all traces of sealant and old gasket material, then clean the mating surfaces with lacquer thinner or acetone. If there's sealant or oil on the mating surfaces when the cover is installed, oil leaks may develop.

14 Clean the mounting bolt threads with a die to remove any corrosion and restore damaged threads. Make sure the threaded holes in the cylinder head are clean - run a tap into them to remove corrosion and restore damaged threads.

15 The gaskets should be mated to the covers before the covers are installed. Apply a thin coat of RTV sealant to the cover flange, then position the gasket inside the cover lip and allow the sealant to set up so the gasket adheres to the cover.

16 Install new valve cover bolt grommets to the valve cover and carefully position the cover(s) on the cylinder head and install the bolts.

17 Tighten the bolts in three or four steps to the torque listed in this Chapter's Specifications.

18 The remaining installation steps are the reverse of removal.

19 Start the engine and check carefully for oil leaks as the engine warms up.

5 Rocker arms and pushrods - removal, inspection and installation

REMOVAL

▶ **Refer to illustration 5.4**

➡**Note: 2001 and later 4.3L V6 engines have roller rocker arms mounted with bolts, rather than the stud/ball/nut mounting on earlier models.**

1 Detach the valve cover(s) from the cylinder head(s) (see Section 4).

2 Beginning at the front of one cylinder head, loosen and remove the rocker arm stud nuts. Store them separately in marked containers to ensure that they will be reinstalled in their original locations.

➡**Note: If the pushrods are the only items being removed, loosen each nut just enough to allow the rocker arms to be rotated to the side so the pushrods can be lifted out.**

3 Lift off the rocker arms and pivot balls and store them in the marked containers with the nuts (they must be reinstalled in their original locations).

4 Remove the pushrods and store them separately to make sure they don't get mixed up during installation (see illustration).

INSPECTION

5 Check each rocker arm for wear, cracks and other damage, especially where the pushrods and valve stems contact the rocker arm faces.

6 Make sure the hole at the pushrod end of each rocker arm is open.

7 Check each rocker arm pivot area for wear, cracks and galling. If the rocker arms are worn or damaged, replace them with new ones and use new pivot balls as well. On 2001 and later models, check the roller bearings in the rocker arm for free rotation.

8 Inspect the pushrods for cracks and excessive wear at the ends. Roll each pushrod across a piece of plate glass to see if it's bent (if it wobbles, it's bent).

INSTALLATION

▶ **Refer to illustrations 5.10, 5.11 and 5.12**

9 Lubricate the lower end of each pushrod with clean engine oil or moly-base grease and install them in their original locations. Make sure each pushrod seats completely in the lifter.

10 Apply moly-base grease to the ends of the valve stems and the upper ends of the pushrods before positioning the rocker arms over the studs (see illustration).

11 Set the rocker arms in place, then install the pivot balls and nuts. Apply moly-base grease to the pivot balls to prevent damage to the mating surfaces before engine oil pressure builds up (see illustration).

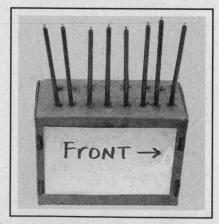

5.4 A perforated cardboard box can be used to store the pushrods to ensure that they're installed in their original positions - note the label indicating the front of the engine

5.10 Lube the ends of the pushrods and the valve stems with moly-base grease prior to installation of the rocker arms

5.11 Moly-base grease applied to the pivot balls will ensure adequate lubrication until oil pressure builds up when the engine is started

Be sure to install each nut with the flat side against the pivot ball.

➡Note: On 2001 and later models, lubricate the roller bearings in the rocker arms with clean engine oil. If the rocker arm supports (below the rocker arms) were removed, make sure to reinstall them with the cast-in arrows pointing UP (away from the cylinder head) before installing the rocker arms.

12 Rotate the crankshaft so that the second timing mark on the vibration damper is 60-degrees before TDC (see illustration). This is a neutral position in the engine rotation and will allow less valve spring tension as the rocker arms are tightened. Tighten the rockerarm nuts to the torque listed in this Chapter's Specifications.

13 The remainder of the installation is the reverse of removal.

14 Start the engine and check for valve cover leaks and valvetrain noise.

5.12 Before tightening the rocker arm nuts, position the crankshaft so that the 2nd timing mark is 60 degrees before TDC

---

6 Valve springs, retainers and seals - replacement

♦ Refer to illustrations 6.5, 6.7a, 6.7b, 6.13a, 6.13b and 6.15

➡Note: Broken valve springs and defective valve stem seals can be replaced without removing the cylinder heads. Two special tools and a compressed air source are normally required to perform this operation, so read through this Section carefully and rent or buy the tools before beginning the job.

1 Remove the valve cover from the cylinder head (see Section 4). If all of the valve stem seals are being replaced, remove both valve covers.

2 Remove the spark plug from the cylinder which has the defective component. If all of the valve stem seals are being replaced, all of the spark plugs should be removed.

3 Turn the crankshaft until the piston in the affected cylinder is at top dead center on the compression stroke (see Section 3). If you are replacing all of the valve stem seals, begin with cylinder number 1 and work on the valves for one cylinder at a time. Move from cylinder-to-cylinder following the firing order sequence (1-6-5-4-3-2). Each cylinder in the firing order is 120-degrees of crankshaft rotation (clockwise) from the previous one.

4 Remove the nut, pivot ball and rocker arm for the valve with the defective part and pull out the pushrod (see Section 5). If all the valve stem seals are being replaced, all of the rocker arms and pushrods should be removed.

5 Thread an adapter into the spark plug hole (see illustration) and connect an air hose from a compressed air source to it. Most auto parts stores can supply the air hose adapter.

➡Note: Many cylinder compression gauges utilize a screw-in fitting that may work with your air hose quick-disconnect fitting.

6 Apply 90 to 100 psi of compressed air to the cylinder. The valves should be held in place by the air pressure.

✳✳ WARNING:

If the cylinder isn't exactly at TDC, air pressure may cause the engine to rotate. Do not leave a socket or wrench on the vibration damper bolt; damage or personal injury may result.

7 Stuff shop rags into the cylinder head holes to prevent parts and

6.5 Use compressed air to hold the valve closed when the springs are removed - the air hose adapter (arrow) threads into the spark plug hole and accepts the hose from the compressor

6.7a Once the spring is depressed, the keepers can be removed with a small magnet or needle-nose pliers (a magnet is preferred to prevent dropping the keepers)

6.7b Lever-type valve spring compressors use the rocker arm stud and nut as a pivot point to apply leverage to the valve spring - it is usually less expensive than the type that grips the spring coils

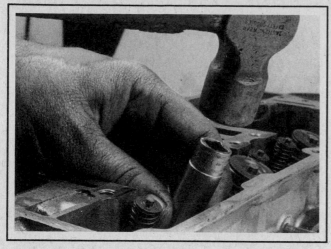

6.13a Using a deep socket and hammer, gently tap the new seals onto the valve guide to the specified depth

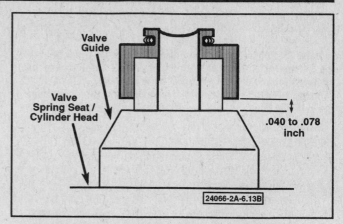

6.13b Valve seal installation depth - don't bottom the seal against the valve guide

tools from falling into the engine, then use a valve spring compressor to compress the valve spring and the valve spring retainer. Remove the keepers with small needle-nose pliers or a magnet (see illustration).

➡**Note: A couple of different types of tools are available for compressing the valve springs with the cylinder head in place. One type grips the lower spring coils and presses on the retainer as the knob is turned, while the other type utilizes the rocker arm stud and nut for leverage (see illustration). Both types work very well, although the lever type is usually less expensive.**

8   Remove the spring retainer or rotator and valve spring assembly (on some models there is both an inner and outer valve spring for each valve - the inner is called a spring damper), then remove the valve stem seal from the valve guide.

➡**Note: If air pressure fails to hold the valve in the closed position during this operation, the valve face and/or seat is probably damaged. If so, the cylinder head will have to be removed for additional repair operations.**

9   Wrap a rubber band or tape around the top of the valve stem so the valve won't fall into the combustion chamber, then release the air pressure.

10 Inspect the valve stem for damage. Rotate the valve in the guide and check the end for eccentric movement, which would indicate that

the valve is bent.

11 Move the valve up-and-down in the guide and make sure it does not bind. If the valve stem binds, either the valve is bent or the guide is damaged. In either case, the cylinder head will have to be removed for repair.

12 Reapply air pressure to the cylinder to retain the valve in the closed position, then remove the tape or rubber band from the valve stem.

13 Lubricate the valve stems with engine oil and install the new valve stem seals. Using the stem of the valves as a guide, slide the seals down to the top of each valve guide, then use a hammer and a deep socket or seal installation tool to gently tap each seal into place until it's positioned to the specified depth (see illustrations).

❈ CAUTION:

Intake and exhaust seals are color coded - do not mix them up. Intake seals are typically white or off-white in color, while exhaust valve stem seals are brown with a white stripe. Don't twist or cock the seals during installation or they won't seal properly on the valve stems. Make sure the garter spring is still in place around the top of the seal.

14 Install the valve spring and damper (if equipped) over the valve, with the more closely-wound spring coils toward the cylinder head.

15 Install the valve spring retainer or rotator.

➡**Note: Rotators are used on the exhaust valves only.**

Compress the valve springs and carefully position the valve stem keepers in the groove. Apply a small dab of grease to the inside of each keeper to hold it in place (see illustration).

16 Disconnect the air hose and remove the adapter from the spark plug hole.

17 Repeat the above procedure on the remaining cylinders, following the firing order sequence (see the Specifications). Bring each piston to top dead center on the compression stroke before applying air pressure.

18 Install the rocker arm(s) and pushrod(s) (see Section 5).

19 Install the valve cover(s) (see Section 4).

20 Install the spark plug(s) and hook up the wire(s).

21 Start and run the engine, then check for oil leaks and unusual sounds coming from the valve cover area.

6.15 Apply a small dab of grease to each keeper as shown here before installation - it will hold them in place on the valve stem as the spring is released

7 Intake manifold - removal and installation

➡**Note: The upper and lower intake manifolds can be removed as a unit, by removing only the lower intake manifold bolts. For repairs or inspection of the fuel-meter body or injectors, refer to Chapter 4 for removal of the upper intake plenum.**

REMOVAL

1 Disconnect the cable from the negative terminal of the battery.

✳✳ CAUTION:

On models equipped with the Theftlock audio system, be sure the lockout feature is turned off before performing any procedure which requires disconnecting the battery (see the front of this manual).

2 Refer to Chapter 4 and relieve the fuel system pressure, then remove the air intake duct and detach the throttle cable and the cruise control cable from the throttle body.

3 Drain the cooling system and remove the drivebelt (see Chapter 1).

4 Remove the secondary air injection crossover pipe (see Chapter 6).

5 Label and disconnect the hoses and electrical connectors attached to the intake manifold and throttle body. Also disconnect the electrical connectors from the A/C compressor and the alternator.

6 Remove the ground strap from the rear of the right cylinder head.

7 Remove the wiring harness brackets from the studs on the intake manifold and set the wiring harness aside.

8 Remove the upper radiator hose from the intake manifold. Remove the coolant bypass hose from the intake manifold and the water pump. Remove the heater hose support bracket from the alternator bracket and detach the heater hoses from the engine (see Chapter 3).

9 Remove the spark plug wires (see Chapter 1) and the distributor (see Chapter 5).

10 Refer to Chapter 6 and remove the EGR pipe from the intake manifold and the exhaust manifold.

11 Disconnect the fuel feed and return lines at the rear of the intake manifold (see Chapter 4).

12 Loosen the retaining nut securing the side of the power steering pump to the power steering pump rear bracket, then remove the lower nut securing the front of the pump to the rear bracket.

13 Remove the bolts and nuts securing the power steering pump mounting bracket to the front of the engine and slide the bracket forward with the A/C compressor attached. This will allow access to the front intake manifold bolt on the driver's side.

14 Loosen the intake lower manifold mounting bolts in 1/4-turn increments in the reverse order of the tightening sequence until they can be removed by hand (see illustration 7.23). The manifold will probably be stuck to the cylinder heads and force may be required to break the gasket seal. A pry bar can be positioned to pry up a casting projection at the front of the manifold to break the bond made by the gasket.

✳✳ CAUTION:

Do not pry between the block and manifold or the heads and manifold or damage to the gasket sealing surfaces may result and vacuum leaks could develop.

15 Remove the intake manifold (see illustration). As the manifold is lifted from the engine, be sure to check for and disconnect anything still attached to the manifold.

INSTALLATION

◆ **Refer to illustrations 7.16, 7.17, 7.18, 7.20 and 7.23**

➡**Note: The mating surfaces of the cylinder heads, block and manifold must be perfectly clean when the manifold is installed. Gasket removal solvents in aerosol cans are available at most auto parts stores and may be helpful when removing old gasket material that is stuck to the heads and manifold. Be sure to follow the directions printed on the container.**

16 Use a gasket scraper to remove all traces of sealant and old gasket material, then clean the mating surfaces with lacquer thinner or acetone. If there's old sealant or oil on the mating surfaces when the manifold is installed, oil or vacuum leaks may develop. When working on the cylinder heads and block, cover the lifter valley with shop rags to keep debris out of the engine (see illustration). Use a vacuum cleaner to remove any gasket material that falls into the intake ports in the cylinder heads.

17 Use a tap of the correct size to chase the threads in the bolt

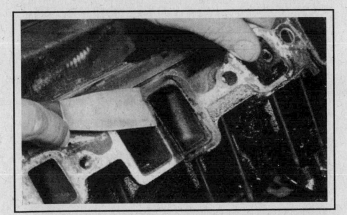

7.16 After covering the lifter valley, use a gasket scraper to remove all traces of sealant and old gasket material from the cylinder head and manifold mating surfaces

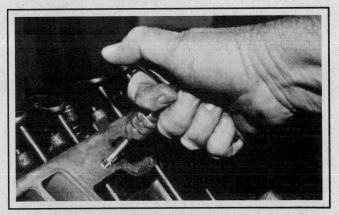

7.17 The bolt hole threads must be clean and dry to ensure accurate torque readings when the manifold mounting bolts are installed

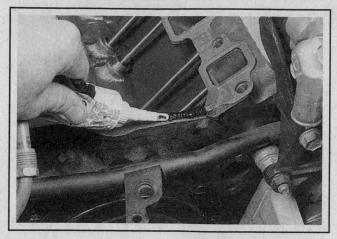

7.18 Apply a 3/16-inch bead of RTV sealant to the front and rear manifold mating surfaces of the engine block - be sure the beads extend up the cylinder heads 1/2-inch on each side.

7.20 Be sure the gaskets are installed with the marks UP!

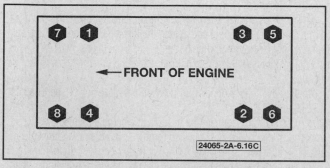

7.23 Lower intake manifold bolt tightening sequence

holes, then use compressed air (if available) to remove the debris from the holes (see illustration).

❋❋ WARNING:

Wear safety glasses or a face shield to protect your eyes when using compressed air! Remove excessive carbon deposits and corrosion from the exhaust, EGR and coolant passages in the cylinder heads and manifold.

18 Apply a 3/16-inch wide bead of RTV sealant to the front and rear manifold mating surfaces of the block (see illustration). Make sure the beads extend up the cylinder heads 1/2-inch on each side.

19 If the new manifold gaskets do not come equipped with a rubber sealing ring around the coolant passages, apply a thin coat of RTV sealant around the coolant passage holes on the cylinder head side of the new intake manifold gaskets.

➡Note: **Factory replacement gaskets come equipped with a rubber sealant ring around the coolant passages and do not require extra RTV sealant around the coolant passages.**

20 Position the gaskets on the cylinder heads, with the ears at each end overlapping the bead of RTV sealant on the cylinder head. The upper side of each gasket should have a THIS SIDE UP label stamped into it to ensure correct installation (see illustration).

21 Make sure all intake port openings, coolant passage holes and bolt holes are aligned correctly. Some gaskets may have small tabs which must be bent over until they're flush with the rear surface of each

cylinder head.

22 Carefully set the manifold in place while the sealant is still wet.

❋❋ CAUTION:

Don't disturb the gaskets and don't move the manifold fore-and-aft after it contacts the sealant on the block.

23 Following the recommended sequence, install the bolts (with thread-locking compound on the bolts) and tighten them to the torque listed in this Chapter's Specifications (see illustration). Work up to the final torque in three stages.

24 The remaining installation steps are the reverse of removal. If the upper intake manifold was removed, refer to Chapter 4 for installation. Start the engine and check carefully for oil and coolant leaks at the intake manifold joints.

8 Exhaust manifolds - removal and installation

REMOLD

▶ **Refer to illustrations 8.4, 8.8 and 8.12**

❋❋ WARNING:

Use caution when working around the exhaust manifolds, the sheetmetal heat shields can be sharp on the edges. Also, the engine should be cold when this procedure is followed.

1 Disconnect the cable from the negative terminal of the battery.

❋❋ CAUTION:

On models equipped with the Theftlock audio system, be sure the lockout feature is turned off before performing any procedure which requires disconnecting the battery (see the front of this manual).

2 Raise the vehicle and support it securely on jackstands.

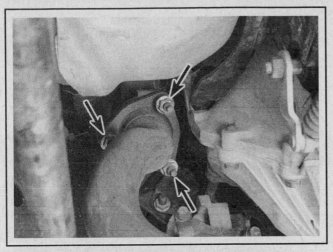

8.4 Access the exhaust pipe bolts/nuts from underneath the vehicle - on some models it may be easier to remove the wheel and work through the fenderwell opening

3   Working under the vehicle, apply penetrating oil to the exhaust pipe-to-manifold studs and nuts (they're usually rusty).

4   Remove the nuts retaining the exhaust pipe(s) to the manifold(s) (see illustration).

Right side manifold

5   Remove the air cleaner assembly (see Chapter 4).

6   Remove the secondary air injection pipe (if equipped) from the exhaust manifold (see Chapter 6).

7   Detach the spark plug wires from the plugs, then remove the plug wire retaining bracket from the cylinder head and position them out of the way.

8   Remove the oil dipstick, unbolt the dipstick tube bracket and move the dipstick tube (see illustration).

9   Bend the lock tabs back (if equipped), then remove the mounting bolts and separate the exhaust manifold from the cylinder head. Remove the heat shields from the manifold after the bolts are removed.

Left side manifold

10 Remove the secondary air injection pipe (if equipped) from the exhaust manifold (see Chapter 6).

11 Detach the spark plug wires from the plugs, then remove the plug wire retaining bracket from the cylinder head and position them out of the way.

12 Disconnect the EGR pipe from the exhaust manifold (see illustration).

13 Disconnect the electrical connector from the Engine Coolant Temperature (ECT) sensor (see Chapter 6).

14 Bend the lock tabs back (if equipped), then remove the mounting bolts and separate the exhaust manifold from the cylinder head. Remove the heat shields from the manifold after the bolts are removed.

8.8 Right exhaust manifold mounting bolts and the oil dipstick tube mounting bolt (A)

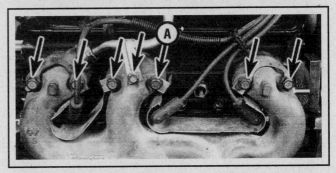

8.12 Left exhaust manifold mounting bolts and the EGR tube mounting nut (A)

INSTALLATION

15 Check the manifold for cracks and make sure the bolt threads are clean and undamaged. The manifold and cylinder head mating surfaces must be clean before the manifolds are reinstalled - use a gasket scraper to remove all carbon deposits.

16 Position the manifold on a bench and install the heat shields, bolts and gaskets onto the manifold. Retaining tabs surrounding the gasket bolt holes will hold the assembly together as the manifold is installed. Place the manifold on the cylinder head install the mounting bolts finger tight.

17 When tightening the mounting bolts, work from the center to the ends and be sure to use a torque wrench. Tighten the bolts in two steps to the torque listed in this Chapter's Specifications. If equipped bend the locking tabs back against the bolt heads.

18 The remaining installation steps are the reverse of removal.

19 Start the engine and check for exhaust leaks.

9   Cylinder heads - removal and installation

➡Note: The engine must be completely cool when the cylinder heads are removed. Failure to allow the engine to cool off could result in cylinder head warpage. When cool, refer to Chapter 1 and drain the cooling system.

REMOVAL

1   Remove the intake manifold (see Section 7), and exhaust manifolds (see Section 8).

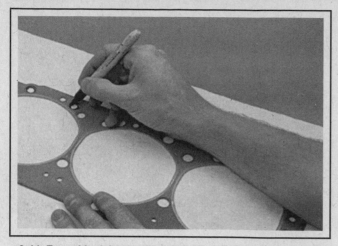

9.11 To avoid mixing up the cylinder head bolts, use a new gasket to transfer the bolt hole pattern to a piece of cardboard, then punch holes to accept the bolts

2   Remove the valve covers (see Section 4).
3   Remove the pushrods (see Section 5).
4   Remove the engine cooling fan (see Chapter 3).

Right cylinder head

5   Remove the alternator (see Chapter 5)
6   Remove the alternator mounting bracket from the cylinder head.

Left cylinder head

7   Remove the engine ground wire and electrical harness at the rear of the cylinder head.

8   Unbolt the air conditioning compressor from the engine and set it aside without disconnecting the refrigerant lines (see Chapter 3). If the vehicle is not equipped with air conditioning it will be necessary to remove the drivebelt idler pulley from the accessory mounting bracket.

9   Unbolt and lay aside the power steering pump, without disconnecting the power steering hoses (see Chapter 10).

10   Remove the accessory mounting brackets from the left cylinder head.

Both cylinder heads

▶ **Refer to illustration 9.11**

11   Using a new cylinder head gasket, outline the cylinders and bolt pattern on a piece of cardboard (see illustration). Be sure to indicate the front of the engine for reference. Punch holes at the bolt locations.

12   Loosen the cylinder head bolts in 1/4-turn increments until they can be removed by hand. Work from bolt-to-bolt in a pattern that's the reverse of the tightening sequence shown in illustration 9.22.

➡**Note: Don't overlook the row of bolts on the lower edge of each cylinder head, near the spark plug holes. Store the bolts in the cardboard holder as they're removed; this will ensure that the bolts are reinstalled in their original holes.**

13   Lift the cylinder head(s) off the engine. If resistance is felt, DO NOT pry between the cylinder head and block as damage to the mating surfaces will result. To dislodge the cylinder head, place a block of wood against the end of it and strike the wood block with a hammer. Store the cylinder heads on wood blocks to prevent damage to the gasket sealing surfaces.

14   Cylinder head disassembly and inspection procedures are covered in detail in Chapter 2, Part C.

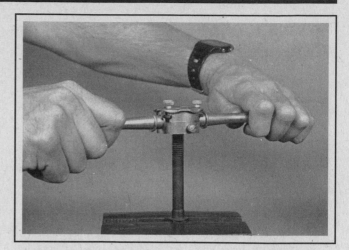

9.18 A die should be used to remove sealant and corrosion from the cylinder head bolt threads prior to installation

INSTALLATION

▶ **Refer to illustrations 9.18, 9.19a, 9.19b, 9.21 and 9.22**

15   The mating surfaces of the cylinder heads and block must be perfectly clean when the cylinder heads are installed.

16   Use a gasket scraper to remove all traces of carbon and old gasket material, then clean the mating surfaces with lacquer thinner or acetone. If there's oil on the mating surfaces when the cylinder heads are installed, the gaskets may not seal correctly and leaks may develop. When working on the block, cover the lifter valley with shop rags to keep debris out of the engine. Use a vacuum cleaner to remove any debris that falls into the cylinders.

17   Check the block and cylinder head mating surfaces for nicks, deep scratches and other damage. If damage is slight, it can be removed with a file - if it's excessive, machining may be the only alternative.

18   Use a tap of the correct size to chase the threads in the cylinder head bolt holes. Mount each bolt in a vise and run a die down the threads to remove corrosion and restore the threads (see illustration). Dirt, corrosion, sealant and damaged threads will affect torque readings.

19   Position the new gaskets over the dowel pins in the block (see illustrations).

9.19a Locating dowels (arrows) are used to position the cylinder head gaskets on the block

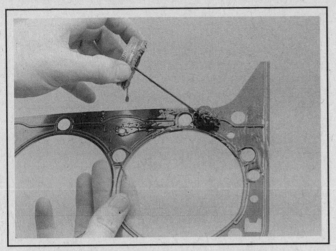

9.19b Steel gaskets should be coated with a sealant such as K&W Copper Coat before installation - composite gaskets do not use sealant

➡ Note: If a steel gasket is used, apply a thin, even coat of a sealant such as K&W Copper Coat to both sides prior to installation (see illustration).

❋❋ WARNING:

Composition-type gaskets are used on some engines, with a thin, sheetmetal core. Be very careful when handling because the edges may be very sharp. Composition gaskets do not require sealant.

20 Carefully position the cylinder heads on the block without disturbing the gaskets.

21 Before installing the cylinder head bolts, coat the threads with a non-hardening sealant such as Permatex no. 2 (see illustration).

22 Install the bolts in their original locations and tighten them finger tight. Follow the recommended sequence and tighten the bolts in

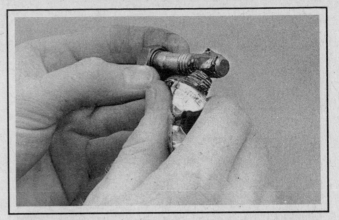

9.21 The cylinder head bolts MUST be coated with a non-hardening sealant (such as Permatex no. 2) before they're installed - coolant will leak past the bolts if this isn't done

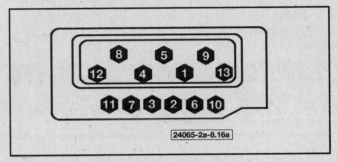

`24065-2a-8.16a`

9.22 Cylinder head bolt TIGHTENING sequence

several steps to the torque and angle of rotation listed in this Chapter's Specifications (see illustration).

23 The remaining installation steps are the reverse of removal.

24 Change the engine oil and filter (see Chapter 1), then start the engine and check carefully for oil and coolant leaks.

10 Vibration damper and pulley - removal and installation

▶ Refer to illustrations 10.3, 10.5 and 10.6

1 Disconnect the cable from the negative terminal of the battery.

❋❋ CAUTION:

On models equipped with the Theftlock audio system, be sure the lockout feature is turned off before performing any procedure which requires disconnecting the battery (see the front of this manual).

2 Refer to Chapter 3 and remove the fan shroud and the engine cooling fan, then refer to Chapter 1 and remove the engine drivebelt.

3 Remove the bolts and separate the crankshaft pulley from the vibration damper (see illustration).

4 Remove the large vibration damper-to-crankshaft bolt. To keep the crankshaft from turning, remove the starter (see Chapter 5) and have an assistant wedge a large screwdriver against the ring gear teeth.

10.3 Remove the crankshaft pulley bolts and separate the pulley from the vibration damper

10.5 Use a bolt-on-type puller to remove the vibration damper

10.6 The pulley keyway must be aligned with the Woodruff key (arrow) in the crankshaft nose

5   Using the proper puller (commonly available from auto parts stores), detach the vibration damper from the crankshaft (see illustration).

⁂ CAUTION:

Do not use a puller with jaws that grip the outer edge of the damper. The puller must be the type that utilizes bolts to apply force to the center of the damper hub only.

Be careful not to lose the Woodruff key.

⁂ CAUTION:

Insert a short bolt somewhat smaller than the damper bolt into the crankshaft for the tip of the tool to push against, to avoid damage to the threads in the crankshaft.

6   Make sure the Woodruff key is in place, then position the vibration damper on the crankshaft and slide it on as far as it will go. Use a small dab of RTV sealant on the keyway of the damper before installation. Note that the slot (keyway) in the hub must be aligned with the Woodruff key in the end of the crankshaft (see illustration).

7   Using a vibration damper installation tool, press the damper onto the crankshaft. Note that the crankshaft bolt can also be used to press the crankshaft balancer into position, but when doing so, use a liberal amount of clean engine oil on the bolt threads to prevent galling. Make sure the raised crown of the damper bolt washer is away from the crankshaft.

8   Tighten the crankshaft bolt to the torque listed in this Chapter's Specifications.

9   The remaining installation steps are the reverse of removal.

11 Crankshaft front oil seal - replacement

▸ **Refer to illustrations 11.2, 11.3, 11.5 and 11.6**

1   Remove the crankshaft pulley and vibration damper (see Section 10).

2   Note how the seal is installed - the new one must be installed to the same depth and facing the same way. Carefully pry the oil seal out of the cover with a seal puller or a large screwdriver (see illustration).

⁂ CAUTION:

Be careful not to scratch, gouge or distort the area that the seal fits into or an oil leak will develop. Wrap electrician's tape around the tip of the screwdriver to avoid damage to the crankshaft.

3   If the seal is being replaced with the timing chain cover removed, support the cover on top of two blocks of wood and drive the seal out from the backside with a hammer and punch (see illustration).

⁂ CAUTION:

Be careful not to scratch, gouge or distort the area that the seal fits into or a leak will develop.

11.2 If you're replacing the seal with the timing chain cover installed, pry it out with a seal removal tool or a large screwdriver

4   Clean the seal bore to remove any old seal material and corrosion. Position the new seal in the bore with the seal lip (usually the side

with the spring) facing IN (toward the engine). A small amount of oil applied to the outer edge of the new seal will make installation easier.

5   Drive the seal into the bore with a seal driver or a large socket and hammer until it's completely seated (see illustration). Select a socket that's the same outside diameter as the seal and make sure the new seal is pressed into place until it bottoms against the cover flange.

6   Check the surface of the damper that the oil seal rides on. If the surface has been grooved from long-time contact with the seal, a press-on sleeve may be available to renew the sealing surface (see illustra-

tion). This sleeve is pressed into place with a hammer and a block of wood and is commonly available from auto parts stores.

7   Lubricate the seal lips with engine oil and reinstall the vibration damper. Use a vibration damper installation tool to press the damper onto the crankshaft.

8   Install the vibration damper-to-crankshaft bolt and tighten it to the torque listed in this Chapter's Specifications. Install the crankshaft pulley and tighten the bolts to the torque listed in this Chapter's Specifications.

9   The remainder of installation is the reverse of the removal.

11.3 If you're replacing the seal with the timing chain cover removed, drive the old seal out from the inside with a hammer and punch or a screwdriver while supporting the cover near the seal bore,

11.5 Use a seal driver or large socket to drive the new seal into the cover

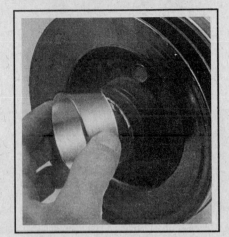

11.6 If the sealing surface of the damper hub has a wear groove from contact with the seal, repair sleeves are available at most auto parts stores

12 Timing chain and sprockets - removal and installation

❈❈ WARNING:

Wait until the engine is completely cool before beginning this procedure.

REMOVAL

◆ Refer to illustrations 12.5, 12.8 and 12.9

1   Disconnect the cable from the negative terminal of the battery.

❈❈ CAUTION:

On models equipped with the Theftlock audio system, be sure the lockout feature is turned off before performing any procedure which requires disconnecting the battery (see the front of this manual). Drain the cooling system (see Chapter 1).

2   Refer to Chapter 3 and remove the upper and lower fan shrouds, drivebelt, cooling fan and water pump.

3   Position the number four piston at TDC on the compression stroke (see Section 3).

❈❈ CAUTION:

Once this has been done, DO NOT turn the crankshaft until the timing chain and sprockets have been reinstalled!

4   Refer to Section 10 and remove the drivebelt pulley and the vibration damper.

5   Remove the crankshaft position sensor and the nut retaining the wiring harness to the front cover (see illustration).

6   Remove the oil pan (see Section 14).

7   Remove the cover bolts and separate the timing chain cover from the block. It may be stuck - if so, use a putty knife or screwdriver to break the gasket seal.

12.5 Remove the crankshaft position sensor (lower arrow) and remove the nut (upper arrow) retaining the wiring harness to the cover stud

12.8 Before removing the sprockets or chain, remove the reluctor ring from the crankshaft

12.9 Remove the three bolts from the end of the camshaft and remove the camshaft sprocket and chain as an assembly

12.12 Before installing the camshaft sprocket, make sure the timing marks on the balance shaft gears are properly aligned (arrows)

➡**Note: This engine uses a timing chain cover that is made of a composite material, which is not reusable. It is recommended to replace the front cover and the oil seal rather than try to reseal it and have it leak later.**

8   Remove the crankshaft position sensor reluctor ring just inside the front cover (see illustration). Measure the timing chain freeplay. If it is more than 5/8 inch, the chain and both sprockets should be replaced.

9   Remove the three bolts from the end of the camshaft, then detach the camshaft sprocket and chain as an assembly (see illustration).

➡**Note: The balance shaft drive gear will stay attached to the camshaft and the driven gear will stay attached to the balance shaft.**

If replacement of the timing chain is necessary, remove the sprocket on the crankshaft with a two- or three-jaw puller, but be careful not to damage the threads in the end of the crankshaft.

INSTALLATION

◆ **Refer to illustrations 12.12 and 12.13**

10   Use a gasket scraper to remove all traces of old gasket material and sealant from the engine block. Clean the block sealing surfaces with lacquer thinner or acetone.

11   If a new timing chain is being installed, be sure to align the keyway in the crankshaft sprocket with the Woodruff key in the end of the crankshaft. Press the sprocket onto the crankshaft with the vibration damper bolt, a large socket and some washers, or tap it gently into place until it's completely seated.

❊❊ **CAUTION:**

If resistance is encountered, DO NOT hammer the sprocket onto the crankshaft. It may eventually move onto the shaft, but it may be cracked in the process and fail later, causing extensive engine damage.

---

12   Before installing the timing chain and camshaft sprocket, align the balance shaft gears (see illustration). The camshaft should be posi-

tioned with the balance shaft drive gear timing mark at 12 o'clock and the driven gear mark at 6 o'clock.

13   Position the crankshaft so the sprocket timing mark is in the 12 o'clock position. Loop the chain over the camshaft sprocket, mesh the chain with the crankshaft sprocket and position the camshaft sprocket on the camshaft with the timing mark in the 6 o'clock position. When correctly installed, the marks on the sprockets will be aligned as shown (see illustration).

➡**Note: The number four piston will be at TDC on the compression stroke with the sprockets aligned as shown.**

14   Apply a non-hardening thread locking compound to the camshaft sprocket bolt threads, then install and tighten them to the torque listed in this Chapter's Specifications. Lubricate the chain with clean engine oil.

15   Install the crankshaft position sensor reluctor ring. Be sure to install the reluctor with the dished side facing OUT!

16   Apply a thin layer of RTV sealant to the engine block sealing surface, then position a **new** front cover and oil seal assembly on the engine block (the dowel pins and sealant will hold it in place).

➡**Note: Composite covers do not have a gasket, they use**

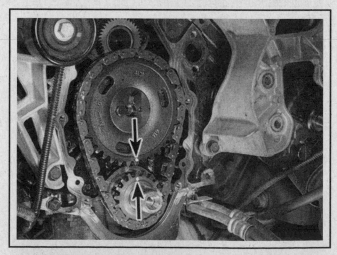

12.13 Position the timing marks on the camshaft and crankshaft sprockets in the 6 and 12 o'clock positions, respectively. When aligned as shown the number four piston is at TDC on the compression stroke

sealant only. Always purchase a New front cover and oil seal assembly to avoid sealing problems caused by the distortion of prying the old cover off.

17 Install the cover retaining bolts and tighten them to the torque listed in this Chapter's Specifications.

18 Refer to the appropriate Sections and install the oil pan, vibration damper and the crankshaft position sensor. Be sure to use a new O-ring on the crankshaft position sensor.

19 The remaining installation steps are the reverse of removal.

13 Camshaft and lifters - removal and installation

➡Note: *The camshaft should always be thoroughly inspected before installation and camshaft endplay should always be checked prior to camshaft removal. Refer to Chapter 2C for the camshaft inspection procedures.*

REMOVAL

▶ **Refer to illustrations 13.2, 13.4 and 13.5**

1 Refer to the appropriate Sections and remove the intake manifold, the rocker arms, the pushrods, the timing chain, camshaft sprocket and the balance shaft drive gear. The balance shaft drive gear can easily be removed after the camshaft sprocket and timing chain are removed. The fan shrouds, fan, radiator and condenser should be removed as well (see Chapter 3).

2 Before removing the lifters, arrange to store them in a clearly labeled box to ensure that they're reinstalled in their original locations. Remove the lifter retainer (see illustration). Remove the lifters and store them where they won't get dirty. DO NOT attempt to withdraw the camshaft with the lifters in place.

3 There are several ways to extract the lifters from the bores. A special tool designed to grip and remove lifters is manufactured by many tool companies and is widely available, but it may not be required in every case. On newer engines, without a lot of varnish buildup, the lifters can often be removed with a small magnet or even with your fingers. A machinist's scribe with a bent end can be used to pull the lifters out by positioning the point under the retainer ring in the top of each lifter.

✳✳ CAUTION:

Don't use pliers to remove the lifters unless you intend to replace them with new ones (along with the camshaft). The pliers will damage the precision machined and hardened lifters, rendering them useless.

4 Remove the two Torx bolts and the camshaft retainer plate, noting which direction faces the block (see illustration).

5 Thread three 6-inch long, 5/16-18 bolts into the camshaft sprocket bolt holes to use as a "handle" when removing the camshaft from the block (see illustration).

6 Carefully pull the camshaft out. Support the cam near the block so the lobes don't nick or gouge the bearings as it's withdrawn.

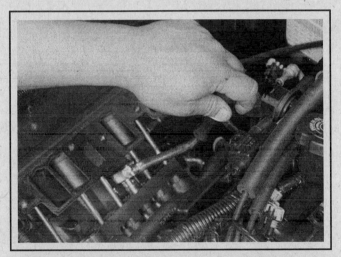

13.2 The roller lifters are held in place by a retainer - remove the four retainer bolts and remove the retainer

13.4 Remove the Torx bolts and take off the camshaft retainer plate, noting which side faces the block

13.5 Thread three long bolts into the camshaft to use as a handle - pull the camshaft straight out, without nicking the bearings

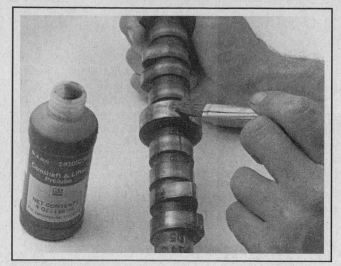

13.7 Lubricate the camshaft journals and lobes with camshaft and lifter assembly lube before installation to provide initial lubrication

INSTALLATION

▶ **Refer to illustration 13.7**

7 Lubricate the camshaft bearing journals and cam lobes with camshaft and lifter assembly lube (see illustration).

8 Slide the camshaft into the engine. Support the cam near the block and be careful not to scrape or nick the bearings.

9 Turn the camshaft until the dowel pin is in the 3 o'clock position, install the camshaft thrust plate, then tighten the bolts to the torque listed in this Chapter's Specifications.

10 Install the balance shaft drive gear over the camshaft, aligning the dowel pin. Make sure the balance shaft timing marks are properly aligned (see illustration 12.12).

11 Install the timing chain and sprockets (see Section 12).

12 Lubricate the lifters with clean engine oil and install them in the block. If the original lifters are being reinstalled, be sure to return them to their original locations. If a new camshaft is being installed, install new lifters as well.

13 The remaining installation steps are the reverse of removal.

14 Before starting and running the engine, change the oil and install a new oil filter (see Chapter 1).

14 Oil pan - removal and installation

▶ **Refer to illustrations 14.16a and 14.16b**

REMOVAL

1 Disconnect the cable from the negative terminal of the battery.

✳✳ **CAUTION:**

On models equipped with a Delco Loc II audio system, be sure the lockout feature is turned off before performing any procedure which requires disconnecting the battery.

2 Raise the vehicle and support it securely on jackstands, then refer to Chapter 1 and drain the engine oil and remove the oil filter.

3 Remove the oil pan skid plate if equipped.

4 Remove the lower control arm crossmember from below the oil pan.

5 On 4WD vehicles remove the front differential carrier (see Chapter 8).

6 Disconnect the front exhaust Y pipe from the engine and the exhaust system and remove it from the vehicle. This step is not absolutely necessary, but it will help facilitate removal of the oil pan.

7 Remove the starter motor (see Chapter 5). Also remove the plastic bellhousing covers (see illustrations 8.8a and 8.8b in Chapter 7B).

8 Remove the battery cable bracket from the front of the oil pan and the bracket on the passenger side of the oil pan securing the transmission oil cooler lines (if equipped) and the starter motor wiring.

9 Disconnect the electrical connector from the oil level sensor.

10 Remove the transmission-to-oil pan bolts (see Chapter 7). On 2001 and later models, remove the four bolts and the frame crossbar.

11 Remove the access plugs covering the nuts at the rear of the oil pan.

12 Remove all the oil pan bolts, then lower the pan from the engine. The pan will probably stick to the engine, so strike the pan with a rubber mallet until it breaks the gasket seal.

✳✳ **CAUTION:**

Before using force on the oil pan, be sure all the bolts have been removed. Carefully slide the oil pan out, to the rear.

INSTALLATION

13 Wash out the oil pan with solvent.

14 Thoroughly clean the mounting surfaces of the oil pan and engine block of old gasket material and sealer. Wipe the gasket surfaces clean with a rag soaked in lacquer thinner or acetone.

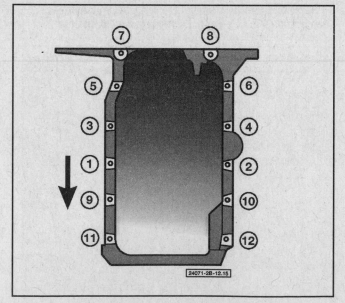

14.16a Bolt tightening sequence for the cast aluminum oil pan

➡Note: On models with a low-oil-level sensor, remove the sensor and install a new sensor upon assembly.

15 Apply a 3/16-inch wide, one inch long bead of RTV sealant to the corners where the front cover meets the block and at the rear where the rear main cap meets the block. Then attach the new gasket to the pan, install the pan and tighten the bolts/studs finger-tight.

16 The alignment of the rear face of the aluminum pan to the rear of the block is important. Measure between the rear face of the pan and the front face of the transmission bellhousing with feeler gauges. Clearance should ideally be flush, but up to 0.011-inch is allowable. If the clearance is OK, tighten the pan bolts/studs in sequence to the torque listed in this Chapter's Specifications (see illustrations).

17 The remainder of installation is the reverse of removal.

18 Add the proper type and quantity of oil (see Chapter 1), start the engine and check for leaks before placing the vehicle back in service.

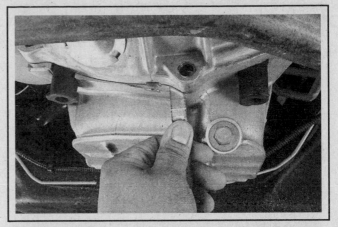

14.16b Before tightening the oil pan bolts, measure the gap between the bellhousing and the oil pan in three places - if the gap is greater than 0.011 the oil pan will have to move towards the bellhousing - ideally the oil pan should be flush with the bellhousing

15 Oil pump - removal and installation

1 Remove the oil pan (see Section 14).

2 While supporting the oil pump, remove the pump-to-rear main bearing cap bolt.

3 Lower the pump and remove it along with the pump driveshaft.

4 If a new oil pump is installed, make sure the pump driveshaft is mated with the shaft inside the pump and a new driveshaft retainer is used.

5 Position the pump over the dowel pins on the rear main cap and make sure the slot in the upper end of the driveshaft is aligned with the tang on the lower end of the distributor shaft. The distributor drives the oil pump, so it is absolutely essential that the components mate properly. Also note that no gasket is used between the oil pump and the rear main cap.

6 Install the mounting bolt and tighten it to the torque listed in this Chapter's Specifications.

7 Install the oil pan and refill the engine with fresh oil. The remainder of assembly is the reverse of the disassembly procedures.

16 Flywheel/driveplate - removal and installation

REMOVAL

▶ **Refer to illustration 16.2**

1 Raise the vehicle and support it securely on jackstands, then refer to Chapter 7 and remove the transmission. If the vehicle is equipped with a manual transmission, remove the clutch components (see Chapter 8).

2 Mark the relationship between the flywheel/driveplate and the crankshaft with a marker or similar device, then remove the bolts that secure the flywheel/driveplate to the crankshaft (see illustration). If the crankshaft turns, wedge a screwdriver in the ring gear teeth to jam the flywheel/driveplate.

➡Note: If there is a retaining ring between the bolts and the driveplate, note which side faces the driveplate when removing it.

3 Remove the flywheel/driveplate from the crankshaft. Since the flywheel/driveplate is fairly heavy, be sure to support it while removing the last bolt.

16.2 Before removing the flywheel or driveplate, mark its relationship to the crankshaft

✳✳ CAUTION:

When removing a flywheel, wear gloves to protect your fingers - the edges of the ring gear teeth may be sharp.

4 Clean the flywheel/driveplate to remove grease and oil. Inspect the surface for cracks, and check for cracked and broken ring gear teeth. Lay the driveplate on a flat surface to check for warpage.

5 Clean and inspect the mating surfaces of the flywheel/driveplate and the crankshaft. If the rear main oil seal is leaking, replace it before reinstalling the driveplate (see Section 17).

INSTALLATION

6 Position the flywheel/driveplate against the crankshaft. Be sure to align the marks made during removal. Note that some engines have an alignment dowel or staggered bolt holes to ensure correct installation. Before installing the bolts, apply thread locking compound to the threads and place the retaining ring (if equipped) in position on the flywheel/driveplate.

➡️**Note: If you're installing a new flywheel on a V6 engine with a manual transmission, be sure to remove the weights from the old flywheel and install them in the new flywheel in the exact positions from which they were removed from the old flywheel.**

7 Wedge a screwdriver through the ring gear teeth to keep the flywheel/driveplate from turning as you tighten the bolts to the torque listed in this Chapter's Specifications. On vehicles equipped with automatic transmissions, if the front pump seal/O-ring leaking, now would be a very good time to replace it.

8 The remainder of installation is the reverse of the removal procedure.

17 Rear main oil seal - replacement

17.4 Carefully pry the old seal out

Refer to illustration 17.4

1 Remove the transmission (see Chapter 7).
2 Remove the flywheel/driveplate (see Section 16).
3 Inspect the oil seal, as well as the oil pan and engine block surface for signs of leakage. Sometimes an oil pan gasket leak can appear to be a rear oil seal leak.
4 Pry the oil seal from the block with a screwdriver (see illustration). Be careful not to nick or scratch the crankshaft or the seal bore. Thoroughly clean the seal bore in the block with a shop towel. Remove all traces of oil and dirt.
5 Lubricate the seal surface on the crankshaft with a very small amount engine oil. Install the seal over the end of the crankshaft (make sure the lips of the seal point toward the engine) and carefully tap it into place. A special aftermarket tool may be available at your local auto parts store. The tool just fits the diameter of the seal and, used with a hammer, drives the seal in.

➡️**Note: Do not drive it in any further than the original seal was installed.**

6 Install the flywheel/driveplate (see Section 16).
7 Install the transmission (see Chapter 7).

18 Engine mounts - check and replacement

The engine mount replacement for V6 engines is identical to the engine mount replacement procedure for the V8 engines. Refer to Chapter 2 Part B for the procedure and use the torque figures in this Chapter's Specifications.

Specifications

General

Displacement	262 cubic inches (4.3 liters)
Bore and stroke	4.012 x 3.480 inches
Cylinder numbers	
Left bank	1-3-5
Right bank	2-4-6
Firing order	1-6-5-4-3-2
Distributor rotation (viewed from above)	Clockwise

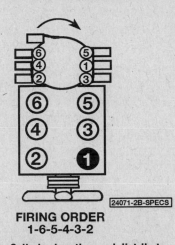

**FIRING ORDER
1-6-5-4-3-2**

**Cylinder location and distributor
rotation diagram**

Camshaft

Journal diameter	1.8677 to 1.8696 inch
Endplay	0.0010 to 0.0090 inch
Lobe lift	
1999 through 2004 models	
Intake	0.274 to 0.278 inch
Exhaust	0.283 to 0.287 inch
2005 models	
Intake	0.270 inch
Exhaust	0.279 inch
Runout	
1999 through 2004 models	0.0026 inch
2005 models	0.0039 inch

Torque specifications — Ft-lbs (unless otherwise indicated)

Camshaft retainer bolt	106 in-lbs
Camshaft sprocket bolt	18
Crankshaft pulley bolts	43
Cylinder head bolts (in sequence - see illustration 9.22)	
Step 1 (all bolts)	22
Step 2	
Long bolts	Tighten an additional 75 degrees
Medium length bolts	Tighten an additional 65 degrees
Short bolts	Tighten an additional 55 degrees
Driveplate-to-crankshaft bolts	74
Flywheel-to-crankshaft bolts	74
Upper intake manifold stud	
Step 1	44 in-lbs
Step 2	80 in-lbs
Lifter retainer bolts	144 in-lbs
Lower intake manifold bolts	
Step 1	27 in-lbs
Step 2	106 in-lbs
Step 3	132 in-lbs
Exhaust manifold bolt/stud	
Step 1	132 in-lbs
Step 2	22

Torque specifications (continued)   Ft-lbs (unless otherwise indicated)

Oil pan mounting bolt/nut	18
Oil pan baffle bolt	106 in-lbs
Oil pump mounting bolt	66
Rocker arm ballstud (2000 and earlier models)	35
Rocker arm nut(s) (2000 and earlier models)	18
Rocker arm bolts (2001 and later)	22
Valve cover-to-cylinder head bolts	106 in-lbs
Timing chain cover-to-block bolts	106 in-lbs
Vibration damper bolt	70

2B

V8 ENGINES

Section

Reference to other Chapters

1 General information

This Part of Chapter 2 is devoted to in-vehicle repair procedures for the 4.8L, 5.3L and 6.0L V8 engines. These engines utilize cast-iron blocks with eight cylinders arranged in a "V" shape at a 90-degree angle between the two banks. All V8 cylinder heads utilize an overhead valve arrangement. The 4.8L and 5.3L engines use aluminum cylinder heads with pressed-in valve guides and hardened valve seats, while 6.0L V8 engines use cast iron cylinder heads with integral valve guides and pressed-in valve seats. Hydraulic roller lifters actuate the valves through tubular pushrods and rocker arms. The oil pump is mounted at the front of the engine behind the timing chain cover and is driven by the crankshaft.

To positively identify these engines, locate the Vehicle Identification Number (VIN) on the left front corner of the instrument panel. The VIN is visible from the outside of the vehicle through the windshield. The eighth character in the sequence is the engine designation:

V = 4.8 liter V8 engine
B, T, Z = 5.3 liter V8 engine
U, N = 6.0 liter V8 engine

All information concerning engine removal and installation and engine block and cylinder head overhaul can be found in Part C of this Chapter. The following repair procedures are based on the assumption that the engine is installed in the vehicle. If the engine has been removed from the vehicle and mounted on a stand, many of the steps outlined in this Part of Chapter 2 will not apply.

The Specifications included in this Part of Chapter 2 apply only to the procedures contained in this Part. Part C of Chapter 2 contains the Specifications necessary for cylinder head and engine block rebuilding.

2 Repair operations possible with the engine in the vehicle

Many major repair operations can be accomplished without removing the engine from the vehicle.

Clean the engine compartment and the exterior of the engine with some type of pressure washer before any work is done. A clean engine will make the job easier and will help keep dirt out of the internal areas of the engine.

Depending on the components involved, it may be a good idea to remove the hood to improve access to the engine as repairs are performed (refer to Chapter 11 if necessary).

If oil or coolant leaks develop, indicating a need for gasket or seal replacement, the repairs can generally be made with the engine in the vehicle. The oil pan gasket, the cylinder head gaskets, intake and exhaust manifold gaskets, timing chain cover gaskets and the crankshaft oil seals are all accessible with the engine in place.

Exterior engine components, such as the water pump, the starter motor, the alternator, the distributor and the fuel injection components, as well as the intake and exhaust manifolds, can be removed for repair with the engine in place.

Since the cylinder heads can be removed without removing the engine, valve component servicing can also be accomplished with the engine in the vehicle.

Replacement of, repairs to or inspection of the timing chain and sprockets and the oil pump are all possible with the engine in place.

In extreme cases caused by a lack of necessary equipment, repair or replacement of piston rings, pistons, connecting rods and rod bearings is possible with the engine in the vehicle. However, this practice is not recommended because of the cleaning and preparation work that must be done to the components involved.

3 Top Dead Center (TDC) for number one piston - locating

◆ **Refer to illustration 3.6**

1 Top Dead Center (TDC) is the highest point in the cylinder that each piston reaches as it travels up the cylinder bore. Each piston reaches TDC on the compression stroke and again on the exhaust stroke, but TDC generally refers to piston position on the compression stroke.

2 Positioning the piston(s) at TDC is an essential part of many procedures such as distributor and timing chain/sprocket removal.

3 Before beginning this procedure, be sure to place the transmission in Neutral and apply the parking brake or block the rear wheels. Also, disable the ignition system by disconnecting the primary electrical connectors at the ignition coil packs, then remove the spark plugs (see Chapter 1).

4 In order to bring any piston to TDC, the crankshaft must be turned using one of the methods outlined below. When looking at the front of the engine, normal crankshaft rotation is clockwise.

a) *The preferred method is to turn the crankshaft with a socket and ratchet attached to the bolt threaded into the front of the crank-shaft. Apply pressure on the bolt in a clockwise direction only. Never turn the bolt counterclockwise.*

b) *A remote starter switch, which may save some time, can also be used. Follow the instructions included with the switch. Once the piston is close to TDC, use a socket and ratchet as described in the previous paragraph.*

c) *If an assistant is available to turn the ignition switch to the Start position in short bursts, you can get the piston close to TDC without a remote starter switch. Make sure your assistant is out of the vehicle, away from the ignition switch, then use a socket and ratchet as described in Paragraph (a) to complete the procedure.*

5 Place your finger partially over the number one spark plug hole and rotate the crankshaft using one of the methods described above until air pressure is felt at the spark plug hole. Air pressure at the spark plug hole indicates that the cylinder has started the compression stroke. Once the compression stroke has begun, TDC for the number one cylinder is obtained when the piston reaches the top of the cylinder

on the compression stroke.

6   To bring the piston to the top of the cylinder, insert a long screwdriver into the number one spark plug hole until it touches the top of the piston.

➡Note: Make sure to wrap the tip of the screwdriver with tape to avoid scratching the top of the piston and the cylinder walls.

Use the screwdriver (as a feeler gauge) to tell where the top of the piston is located in the cylinder while slowly rotating the crankshaft (see illustration). As the piston rises the screwdriver will be pushed out. The point at which the screwdriver stops moving outward is TDC.

➡Note: Always hold the screwdriver upright while the engine is being rotated so that the screwdriver will not get wedged as the piston travels upward.

7   If you go past TDC, rotate the crankshaft counterclockwise until the piston is approximately one inch below TDC, then slowly rotate the crankshaft clockwise again until TDC is reached.

8   After the number one piston has been positioned at TDC on the compression stroke, TDC for any of the remaining pistons can be located by turning the crankshaft 90-degrees (1/4 turn) at a time and following the firing order.

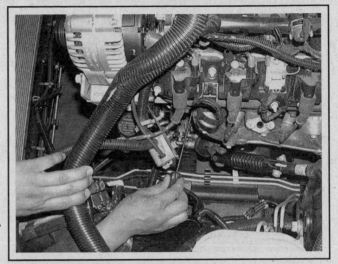

3.6 A long screwdriver inserted in the number one spark plug hole can be used to determine the highest point reached by that piston - make sure to wrap the tip of the screwdriver with tape to avoid scratching the top of the piston or the cylinder walls

4   Valve covers - removal and installation

REMOVAL

♦ Refer to illustrations 4.4 and 4.12

1   Disconnect the cable from the negative terminal of the battery.

❉❉ CAUTION:

On models equipped with the Theftlock audio system, be sure the lockout feature is turned off before performing any procedure which requires disconnecting the battery (see the front of this manual).

2   On models so equipped, remove the secondary air injection crossover pipe, then remove the air injection check valve and pipe assembly from the exhaust manifold on the side from which you wish to remove the valve cover (see Chapter 6). If both valve covers are being removed, both air injection check valves and pipe assemblies must be removed.

➡Note: On some later models you must first remove the plastic engine cover. It is secured with a single bolt.

Right side

3   Remove the filter housing (see Chapter 4).

4   Remove the heater hose bracket bolt and move the heater hoses aside without disconnecting them (see illustration).

5   Disconnect the electrical connectors from the ignition coils and the EGR valve. Unclip the wiring harness from the ignition coil bracket and lay it aside.

6   Remove the ignition coils from the valve cover (see Chapter 5). Be sure each plug wire is labeled before removal to ensure correct reinstallation.

7   Remove the valve cover bolts, then detach the cover from the cylinder head.

➡Note: If the cover is stuck to the cylinder head, bump one end with a block of wood and a hammer to jar it loose. If that

4.4 Detach or lay aside the following components for valve cover removal - 2000 Silverado shown

A   Secondary Air Injection crossover pipe
B   Ignition coils (passenger side)
C   Heater hoses
D   EGR valve
E   Secondary Air Injection check valve and pipe assembly (driver side)
F   Wiring harness
G   Ignition coils (driver side)
H   Power brake booster hose

doesn't work, try to slip a flexible putty knife between the cylinder head and cover to break the gasket seal. Don't pry at the cover-to-head joint or damage to the sealing surfaces may occur (leading to oil leaks in the future).

Left side

8   Detach the clips securing the engine wiring harness to the valve

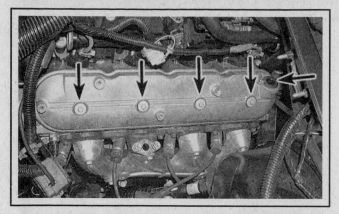

4.12 Valve cover mounting bolts (arrows) - arrow to the far right indicates location of the PCV valve (left valve cover shown)

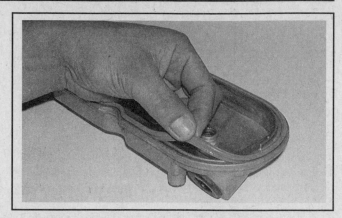

4.15 Position the new gasket in the valve cover lip

cover and to positive battery cable junction block bracket and position the engine wiring harness aside.

9   Remove the power brake booster vacuum hose from the power brake booster.

10 Remove the ignition coils from the valve cover (see Chapter 5). Be sure each plug wire is labeled before removal to ensure correct reinstallation.

11 Disconnect the PCV valve from the valve cover.

12 Remove the valve cover bolts (see illustration), then detach the cover from the cylinder head.

➡Note: If the cover is stuck to the cylinder head, bump one end with a block of wood and a hammer to jar it loose. If that doesn't work, try to slip a flexible putty knife between the cylinder head and cover to break the gasket seal. Don't pry at the cover-to-head joint or damage to the sealing surfaces may occur (leading to oil leaks in the future).

INSTALLATION

▶ **Refer to illustration 4.15**

13 The mating surfaces of each cylinder head and valve cover must be perfectly clean when the covers are installed. Use a gasket scraper

to remove all traces of sealant and old gasket material, then clean the mating surfaces with lacquer thinner or acetone. If there's sealant or oil on the mating surfaces when the cover is installed, oil leaks may develop.

14 Clean the mounting bolt threads with a die to remove any corrosion and restore damaged threads. Make sure the threaded holes in the cylinder head are clean - run a tap into them to remove corrosion and restore damaged threads.

15 The gaskets should be mated to the covers before the covers are installed. Position the gasket inside the cover lip (see illustration). If the gasket will not stay in place in the cover lip, apply a thin coat of RTV sealant to the cover flange, then and allow the sealant to set up so the gasket adheres to the cover.

16 Inspect the valve cover bolt grommets for damage. If the grommets aren't damaged they can be reused. Carefully position the valve cover(s) on the cylinder head and install the bolts and grommets. On 2001 and later models, remove the oil filler tube and replace it with a new one.

17 Tighten the bolts in three or four steps to the torque listed in this Chapter's Specifications.

18 The remaining installation steps are the reverse of removal.

19 Start the engine and check carefully for oil leaks as the engine warms up.

5   Rocker arms and pushrods - removal, inspection and installation

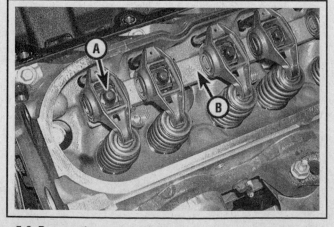

5.2 Remove the mounting bolts (A) and rocker arms, then remove the pivot support pedestal (B)

REMOVAL

▶ **Refer to illustrations 5.2 and 5.3**

1   Refer to Section 4 and detach the valve covers from the cylinder heads.

2   Loosen the rocker arm pivot bolts one at a time and detach the rocker arms and bolts, then detach the pivot support pedestal (see illustration). Keep track of the rocker arm positions, since they must be returned to the same locations. Store each set of rocker components separately in a marked plastic bag to ensure that they're reinstalled in their original locations.

3   Remove the pushrods and store them separately to make sure they don't get mixed up during installation (see illustration).

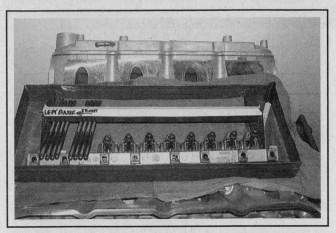

5.3 Store the pushrods and rocker arms in order to ensure they are reinstalled in their original locations - note the arrow indicating the front of the engine

INSPECTION

▶ **Refer to illustration 5.4**

4   Check each rocker arm for wear, cracks and other damage, especially where the pushrods and valve stems contact the rocker arm (see illustration).

5   Check the pivot bearings for binding and roughness. If the bearings are worn or damaged, replacement of the entire rocker arm will be necessary.

➡**Note: Keep in mind that there is no valve adjustment on these engines, so excessive wear or damage in the valve train can easily result in excessive valve clearance, which in turn will cause valve noise when the engine is running. Also check the rocker arm pivot support pedestal for cracks and other obvious damage.**

6   Make sure the hole at the pushrod end of each rocker arm is open.

7   Inspect the pushrods for cracks and excessive wear at the ends, also check that the oil hole running through each pushrod is not clogged. Roll each pushrod across a piece of plate glass to see if it's bent (if it wobbles, it's bent).

INSTALLATION

▶ **Refer to illustration 5.9**

8   Lubricate the lower end of each pushrod with clean engine oil or engine assembly lube and install them in their original locations. Make sure each pushrod seats completely in the lifter socket.

9   Apply engine assembly lube to the ends of the valve stems and to the upper ends of the pushrods to prevent damage to the mating surfaces on initial start-up (see illustration). Also apply clean engine oil to the pivot shaft and bearing of each rocker arm and install the rocker arms loosely in their original locations. DO NOT tighten the bolts at this time!

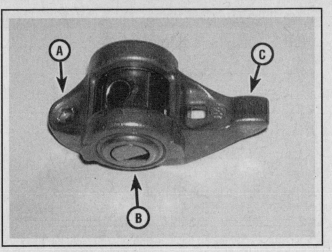

5.4 Rocker arm wear points

A   *Pushrod socket*   C   *Valve stem contact point*
B   *Pivot bearings*

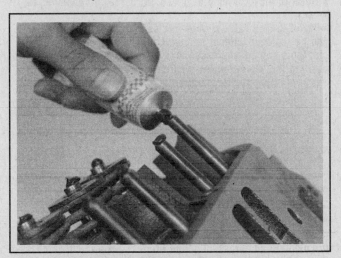

5.9 Lubricate the pushrod ends and the valve stems with engine assembly lube before installing the rocker arms

10 Rotate the crankshaft until the number one piston is at TDC (see Section 3). With the number one piston is at TDC, tighten the intake valve rocker arms for the Number 1, 3, 4, and 5 cylinders and the exhaust rocker arms for the Number 1, 2, 7, and 8 cylinders. Tighten each of the specified rocker arm bolts to the torque listed in this Chapter's Specifications.

11 Rotate the crankshaft 360 degrees. Tighten the intake valve rocker arms for the Number 2, 6, 7, and 8 cylinders and the exhaust rocker arms for the Number 3, 4, 5, and 6 cylinders. Tighten each of the rocker arm bolts to the torque listed in this Chapter's Specifications.

12 Refer to Section 4 and install the valve covers. Start the engine, listen for unusual valve train noses and check for oil leaks at the valve cover gaskets.

6 Valve springs, retainers and seals - replacement

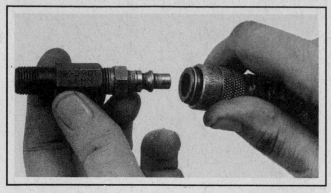

6.5 This is what the air hose adapter that fits into the spark plug hole looks like - they're commonly available from auto parts stores

▸ Refer to illustrations 6.5, 6.8, 6.10, 6.15a, 6.15b and 6.19

➡**Note: Broken valve springs and defective valve stem seals can be replaced without removing the cylinder head. Two special tools and a compressed air source are normally required to perform this operation, so read through this Section carefully and rent or buy the tools before beginning the job.**

1 Remove the spark plugs (see Chapter 1).

2 Remove the valve covers (see Section 4).

3 Rotate the crankshaft until the number one piston is at top dead center on the compression stroke (see Section 3).

4 Remove the rocker arms for the number 1 piston.

5 Thread an adapter into the spark plug hole and connect an air hose from a compressed air source to it (see illustration). Most auto parts stores can supply the air hose adapter.

➡**Note: Many cylinder compression gauges utilize a screw-in fitting that may work with your air hose quick-disconnect fitting. If a cylinder compression gauge fitting is used it will be necessary to remove the schrader valve from the end of the fitting before using it in this procedure.**

6 Apply compressed air to the cylinder. The valves should be held in place by the air pressure.

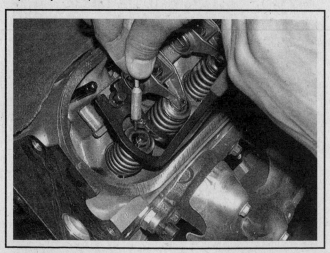

6.8 Once the spring is depressed, the keepers can be removed with a small magnet or needle-nose pliers (a magnet is preferred to prevent dropping the keepers)

✳✳ WARNING:

If the cylinder isn't exactly at TDC, air pressure may force the piston down, causing the engine to quickly rotate. DO NOT leave a wrench on the crankshaft balancer bolt or you may be injured by the tool.

7 Stuff shop rags into the cylinder head holes around the valves to prevent parts and tools from falling into the engine.

8 Using a socket and a hammer gently tap on the top of each valve spring retainer several times (this will break the seal between the valve keeper and the spring retainer and allow the keeper to separate from the valve spring retainer as the valve spring is compressed), then use a valve-spring compressor to compress the spring. Remove the keepers with small needle-nose pliers or a magnet (see illustration).

➡**Note: Several different types of tools are available for compressing the valve springs with the head in place. One type grips the lower spring coils and presses on the retainer as the knob is turned, while the lever-type shown here utilizes the rocker arm bolt for leverage. Both types work very well, although the lever type is usually less expensive.**

9 Remove the valve spring and retainer.

➡**Note: If air pressure fails to retain the valve in the closed position during this operation, the valve face or seat may be damaged. If so, the cylinder head will have to be removed for repair.**

10 Remove the old valve stem seals, noting differences between the intake and exhaust seals (see illustration).

11 Wrap a rubber band or tape around the top of the valve stem so the valve won't fall into the combustion chamber, then release the air pressure.

12 Inspect the valve stem for damage. Rotate the valve in the guide and check the end for eccentric movement, which would indicate that the valve is bent.

13 Move the valve up-and-down in the guide and make sure it does not bind. If the valve stem binds, either the valve is bent or the guide is damaged. In either case, the head will have to be removed for repair.

14 Reapply air pressure to the cylinder to retain the valve in the

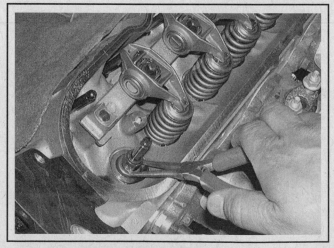

6.10 Use a pair of needle nose pliers to remove the valve seals

6.15a Be sure to install the seals on the correct valve stems

1   Intake valve seal
2   Exhaust valve seal

6.15b Install the intake and exhaust valve seals to the specified depth - measure from the spring seat to the top edge of the valve seal

0.712
to
0.752

6.19 Apply small dab of grease to each keeper as shown here before installation - it'll hold them in place on the valve stem as the spring is released

closed position, then remove the tape or rubber band from the valve stem.

15 If you're working on an exhaust valve, install the new exhaust valve seal on the valve stem and press it down over the valve guide to the specified depth. Don't force the seal against the top of the guide (see illustrations).

➡**Note: On aluminum heads be sure take this measurement from the steel spring seat to the top edge of the intake and exhaust valve seals, not from the aluminum seat on the head!**

16 If you're working on an intake valve, install a new intake valve stem seal over the valve stem and press it down over the valve guide to the specified depth. Don't force the intake valve seal against the top of the guide.

✳✳ **CAUTION:**

Do not install an exhaust valve seal on an intake valve, as high oil consumption will result.

17 Install the spring and retainer in position over the valve.

18 Compress the valve spring assembly only enough to install the keepers in the valve stem.

19 Position the keepers in the valve stem groove. Apply a small dab of grease to the inside of each keeper to hold it in place if necessary (see illustration). Remove the pressure from the spring tool and make sure the keepers are seated.

20 Disconnect the air hose and remove the adapter from the spark plug hole.

21 Repeat the above procedure on the remaining cylinders, following the firing order sequence (see this Chapter's Specifications). Bring each piston to top dead center on the compression stroke before applying air pressure (see Section 3).

22 Reinstall the rocker arm assemblies and the valve covers (see Sections 4 and 5).

23 Start the engine, then check for oil leaks and unusual sounds coming from the valve cover area. Allow the engine to idle for at least five minutes before revving the engine.

7 Intake manifold - removal and installation

✳✳ **WARNING:**

Wait until the engine is completely cool before starting this procedure.

REMOVAL

▶ **Refer to illustrations 7.3, 7.7a, 7.7b, 7.8a, 7.8b and 7.8c**

1   Disconnect the cable from the negative terminal of the battery.

✳✳ **CAUTION:**

On models equipped with the Theftlock audio system, be sure the lockout feature is turned off before performing any procedure which requires disconnecting the battery (see the front of this manual).

2   Clamp off the coolant hoses leading to the throttle body.

3   Remove the filter housing and the intake manifold cover (see illustration). Relieve the fuel system pressure (see Chapter 4).

7.3 Typical intake manifold cover retaining screws (arrows)

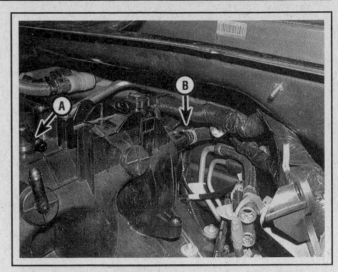

7.7a Disconnect the coolant hoses (A) and the crankcase breather hose (B) from the throttle body, then squeeze the retainer on the EVAP solenoid vent tube (C) and remove it from the top of the intake manifold

7.7b Detach the PCV hose (A) and the power brake booster vacuum hose (B) from the rear of the intake - PCV hose already removed in this photo

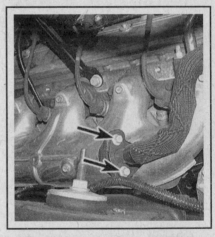

7.8a EGR pipe to intake manifold mounting bolts (arrows)

7.8b EGR valve mounting bracket to cylinder head mounting bolts (arrows)

7.8c EGR pipe to exhaust manifold mounting bolts (arrows)

4   Disconnect the accelerator linkage (see Chapter 4) and, if equipped, the cruise control linkage.

5   Disconnect the electrical connectors from the fuel injectors, EGR valve, EVAP solenoid, the MAP sensor and from the sensors on the throttle body. Label each connector clearly to aid in the reassembly process. Detach the large wiring harness bracket from the stud on the top of the intake manifold and lay the harness aside. Remove the MAP sensor if necessary for clearance.

6   Remove the fuel rails and injectors as an assembly (see Chapter 4). The two fuel rails can be pulled straight up with the injectors still attached, but it will take some force to dislodge the injectors from the intake manifold.

➡Note: This Step is not absolutely necessary but it will help prevent subsequent damage to the fuel injectors as the intake manifold is removed. Normally, the intake manifold is removed with the fuel injectors, fuel rails, and throttle body attached.

7   Disconnect any vacuum hoses attached to the intake manifold or throttle body such as the power brake booster, the PCV and the EVAP purge control solenoid. Also disconnect the coolant hoses from the throttle body (see illustrations). Remove the EVAP canister if necessary.

8   Remove the EGR valve and pipe assembly from the engine (see illustrations) if it interferes with intake manifold removal.

9   Disconnect any remaining electrical connectors or vacuum hoses connected to the intake manifold or throttle body.

10   Loosen the intake manifold mounting bolts in 1/4-turn increments in the reverse order of the tightening sequence until they can be removed by hand (see illustration 7.16). The manifold will probably be stuck to the cylinder heads and force may be required to break the gasket seal. A pry bar can be positioned between the front of the manifold and the valley tray to break the bond made by the gasket.

✳✳ CAUTION:

Do not pry between the manifold and the heads or damage to the gasket sealing surfaces may result and vacuum leaks could develop. Also, don't use too much force - the manifold is made of a plastic composite and could crack.

11   Remove the intake manifold. As the manifold is lifted from the engine, be sure to check for and disconnect anything still attached to the manifold.

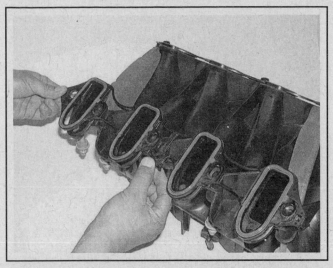

7.14 Align the tabs on the intake gaskets with the tabs on the manifold and snap the gasket into place

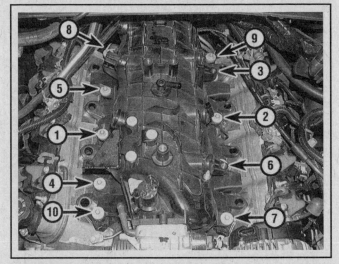

7.16 Intake manifold bolt tightening sequence - all V8 engines

INSTALLATION

▶ **Refer to illustrations 7.14 and 7.16**

➡**Note: The mating surfaces of the cylinder heads, block and manifold must be perfectly clean when the manifold is installed.**

12 Carefully remove all traces of old gasket material. Note that the intake manifold is made of a composite material and the cylinder heads on 4.8L and 5.3L engines are made of aluminum, therefore aggressive scraping is not suggested and will damage the sealing surfaces. After the gasket surfaces are cleaned and free of any gasket material wipe the mating surfaces with a cloth saturated with safety solvent. If there is old sealant or oil on the mating surfaces when the manifold is installed, oil or vacuum leaks may develop. Use a vacuum cleaner to remove any gasket material that falls into the intake ports in the heads.

13 Use a tap of the correct size to chase the threads in the bolt holes, then use compressed air (if available) to remove the debris from the holes.

⁕⁕ WARNING:

Wear safety glasses or a face shield to protect your eyes when using compressed air.

14 Position the new gaskets on the intake manifold (see illustration). Note that the gaskets are equipped with installation tabs that must snap into place on the intake manifold. The words "Manifold Side" may appear on the gasket, If so, this will ensure proper installation. Make sure the gaskets snap into place and all intake port openings align.

15 Carefully set the manifold in place.

16 Apply medium-strength threadlocking compound to the threads of the bolts. Install the bolts and tighten them following the recommended sequence (see illustration) to the torque listed in this Chapter's Specifications. Do not overtighten the bolts or gasket leaks may develop.

17 The remaining installation steps are the reverse of removal. Check the coolant level, adding as necessary (see Chapter 1). Start the engine and check carefully for vacuum leaks at the intake manifold joints.

8   Exhaust manifolds - removal and installation

REMOVAL

▶ **Refer to illustrations 8.4, 8.8 and 8.9**

⁕⁕ WARNING:

Use caution when working around the exhaust manifolds - the sheetmetal heat shields can be sharp on the edges. Also, the engine should be cold when this procedure is followed.

1   Disconnect the cable from the negative terminal of the battery.

⁕⁕ CAUTION:

On models equipped with the Theftlock audio system, be sure the lockout feature is turned off before performing any procedure which requires disconnecting the battery (see the front of this manual).

2   Raise the vehicle and support it securely on jackstands.

3   Working under the vehicle, apply penetrating oil to the exhaust pipe-to-manifold studs and nuts (they're usually rusty). Disconnect the electrical connector for oxygen sensor.

4   Remove the nuts retaining the exhaust pipe(s) to the manifold(s)

8.4 Remove the exhaust pipe-to-manifold nuts

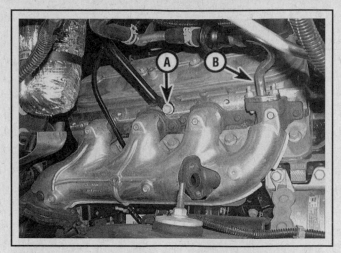

8.8 Remove the oil dipstick tube mounting bolt (A) and tube - (B) indicates the secondary air injection check valve and pipe assembly on the right manifold

(see illustration). Note that both exhaust manifolds are more easily accessed with the front tires and the inner fenderwells removed, but it's not absolutely necessary (see Chapter 11).

5 Detach the spark plug wires and remove the spark plugs from the side being worked on (see Chapter 1), If both manifolds are being removed, detach all the spark plug wires and remove all the spark plugs.

6 Remove the secondary air injection pipe (if equipped) from the exhaust manifold being removed (see Chapter 6).

Right side manifold

7 On early models, remove the air cleaner assembly if it interferes (see Chapter 4).

8 The oil dipstick tube also must be removed from early models (see illustration).

9 If the vehicle has the EGR valve attached to the exhaust manifold, it must be removed along with the EGR pipe (see illustrations 7.8a, 7.8b and 7.8c). Remove the mounting bolts and separate the exhaust manifold from the cylinder head (see illustration). Remove the heat shields from the manifold after the manifold has been removed.

Left side manifold

10 Disconnect the electrical connector from the Engine Coolant Temperature (ECT) sensor (see Chapter 6).

11 Remove the mounting bolts and separate the exhaust manifold from the cylinder head. Remove the heat shields from the manifold after the manifold has been removed.

INSTALLATION

12 Check the manifold for cracks and make sure the bolt threads are clean and undamaged. The manifold and cylinder head mating surfaces must be clean before the manifolds are reinstalled - use a gasket scraper to remove all carbon deposits and gasket material.

➡Note: The cylinder heads on 4.8L and 5.3L engines are made of aluminum, therefore aggressive scraping is not suggested and will damage the sealing surfaces.

13 Install the heat shields, then install the bolts and gaskets onto

8.9 Exhaust manifold fastener locations (right side shown, left side similar)

the manifold. Retaining tabs surrounding the gasket bolt holes should hold the assembly together as the manifold is installed.

14 Starting at the fourth thread, apply a 1/4-inch wide band of medium-strength threadlocking compound to the threads of the bolts.

➡Note: The manufacturer recommends not applying threadlocking compound on the first three threads.

15 Place the manifold on the cylinder head and install the mounting bolts finger tight.

16 When tightening the mounting bolts, work from the center to the ends and be sure to use a torque wrench. Tighten the bolts in two steps to the torque listed in this Chapter's Specifications. If required, bend the exposed end of the exhaust manifold gasket back against the cylinder head.

17 The remaining installation steps are the reverse of removal. Always use new O-rings and gaskets on the EGR valve and pipe assembly.

18 Start the engine and check for exhaust leaks.

9 Cylinder heads - removal and installation

➡Note: It will be necessary to purchase a new set of 11 mm head bolts before or during this procedure.

REMOVAL

▶ **Refer to illustrations 9.2, 9.6 and 9.8**

1 Disconnect the cable from the negative terminal of the battery and drain the cooling system (see Chapter 1).

❋❋ CAUTION:

On models equipped with the Theftlock audio system, be sure the lockout feature is turned off before performing any procedure which requires disconnecting the battery (see the front of this manual).

2 Remove the intake manifold (see Section 7) and the coolant pipe (see illustration).

3 Detach both exhaust manifolds from the cylinder heads (see Section 8). It is not necessary to disconnect the manifolds from the exhaust pipes.

4 Remove the valve covers (see Section 4).

5 Remove the rocker arms and pushrods (see Section 5).

❋❋ CAUTION:

Again, as mentioned in Section 5, keep all the parts in order so they are reinstalled in the same location.

6 Disconnect the wiring from the back of the alternator, then remove the power steering pump/alternator mounting bracket from the engine. Lay the bracket aside (with the components attached), without disconnecting the lines from the steering pump (see illustration).

7 Loosen the head bolts in 1/4-turn increments in the reverse order of the tightening sequence (see illustration 9.17) until they can be removed by hand.

➡Note: There will be different length and size head bolts for different locations. Make a note of the different sizes and lengths and where they go when removing the bolts to ensure correct installation of the new bolts.

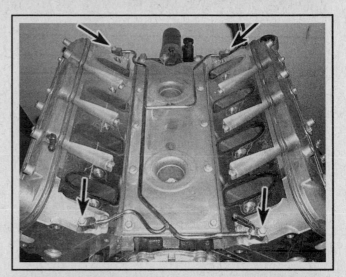

9.2 The coolant pipe is retained by two bolts at the front and two bolts at the rear of the cylinder heads (arrows)

8 Lift the heads off the engine. If resistance is felt, do not pry between the head and block as damage to the mating surfaces will result. To dislodge the head, place a pry bar or long screwdriver into the intake port and carefully pry the head off the engine (see illustration). Store the heads on blocks of wood to prevent damage to the gasket sealing surfaces.

9 Cylinder head disassembly and inspection procedures are covered in detail in Chapter 2, Part C.

INSTALLATION

▶ **Refer to illustrations 9.14, 9.17 and 9.18**

10 The mating surfaces of the cylinder heads and block must be perfectly clean when the heads are installed. Gasket removal solvents are available at auto parts stores and may prove helpful.

11 Use a gasket scraper to remove all traces of carbon and old gasket material, then wipe the mating surfaces with a cloth saturated with lacquer thinner or acetone.

9.6 Alternator/power steering pump mounting bracket bolts (arrows) - remove the bolts and lay the bracket aside with the components attached

9.8 Using a prybar inserted into an intake port to break the head loose - do not use excessive force or damage to the head may result

9.14 Position the head gasket over the dowels at each end of the cylinder head with the mark (arrow) facing the front of the vehicle

9.17 Cylinder head bolt tightening sequence - all V8 engines

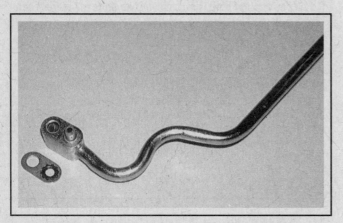

9.18 Be sure to use new gaskets at each cylinder head-to-coolant pipe joint - position the O-ring seal over the coolant pipe nipple

➡**Note: The cylinder heads on 4.8L and 5.3L engines are made of aluminum, therefore aggressive scraping is not suggested and will damage the sealing surfaces.**

If there is oil on the mating surfaces when the heads are installed, the gaskets may not seal correctly and leaks may develop. When working on the block, use a vacuum cleaner to remove any debris that falls into the cylinders.

12 Check the block and head mating surfaces for nicks, deep scratches and other damage. If damage is slight, it can be removed with emery cloth. If it is excessive, machining may be the only alternative.

13 Use a tap of the correct size to chase the threads in the head bolt holes in the block. If a tap is not available, spray a liberal amount of brake cleaner into each hole. Use compressed air (if available) to remove the debris from the holes.

✳ WARNING:

Wear safety glasses or a face shield to protect your eyes when using compressed air.

All cylinder head bolts should be replaced with **new** bolts

14 Position the new gaskets over the dowels in the block (see illustration).

15 Carefully position the heads on the block without disturbing the gaskets.

16 Before installing the 8mm head bolts, coat the threads with a medium-strength threadlocking compound. Then install the **new** 8mm head bolts (bolts 11 through 15).

17 Install **new** 11 mm head bolts (bolts 1 through 10) and tighten them finger tight. Following the recommended sequence (see illustration), tighten the bolts in four steps to the torque listed in this Chapter's Specifications.

✳ WARNING:

DO NOT reuse head bolts - always replace them with new ones.

18 Install the coolant pipe, using new gaskets, onto the cylinder heads (see illustration). Tighten the bolts to the torque listed in this Chapter's Specifications.

19 The remaining installation steps are the reverse of removal.

20 Add coolant and change the oil and filter (see Chapter 1). Start the engine and check for proper operation and coolant or oil leaks.

10 Crankshaft balancer - removal and installation

▶ Refer to illustrations 10.5, 10.6 and 10.9

➡Note: This procedure requires a special balancer installation tool that is available through specialized tool manufacturers only and a new crankshaft balancer bolt. Read through the entire procedure and obtain the tool and materials before proceeding.

1   Disconnect the cable from the negative terminal of the battery.

✳✳ CAUTION:

On models equipped with the Theftlock audio system, be sure the lockout feature is turned off before performing any procedure which requires disconnecting the battery (see the front of this manual).

2   Raise the front of the vehicle and support it securely on jackstands. Then apply the parking brake.
3   Remove the drivebelt (see Chapter 1) and the cooling fan (see Chapter 3).
4   Working under the vehicle, remove the stone shield from below the engine (if equipped).
5   Use a strap wrench around the crankshaft pulley to hold it while using a breaker bar and socket to remove the crankshaft pulley center bolt (see illustration).
6   Pull the balancer off the crankshaft with a puller (see illustration).

✳✳ CAUTION:

The jaws of the puller must only contact the hub of the balancer - not the outer ring.

➡Note: A long Allen-head bolt should be inserted into the crankshaft nose for the puller's tapered tip to push against to prevent damage to the crankshaft threads.

10.5 Use strap wrench to hold the crankshaft balancer while removing the center bolt (a chain-type wrench may be used if you wrap a section of old drivebelt or rag around the balancer first)

7   Position the crankshaft pulley/balancer on the crankshaft and slide it on as far as it will go. Note that the slot (keyway) in the hub must be aligned with the Woodruff key in the end of the crankshaft.
8   Using the specialized crankshaft balancer installation tool, press the crankshaft pulley/balancer onto the crankshaft.
9   Install the old crankshaft balancer bolt and tighten the crankshaft bolt to 240 ft-lbs. Remove the old bolt and measure the distance from the snout of the crankshaft to the balancer hub (see illustration). When properly installed, the balancer hub should extend 3/32 to 11/64-inch past the crankshaft snout. If the measurement is incorrect, reinstall the balancer installation tool and press the balancer on the crankshaft until the measurement is correct.
10   Install a **new** crankshaft balancer bolt and tighten it in two steps to the torque and angle of rotation listed in this Chapter's Specifications.
11   The remaining installation steps are the reverse of removal.

10.6 The use of a three jaw puller will be necessary to remove the crankshaft balancer - always place the puller jaws around the hub, not the outer ring

10.9 Before the new crankshaft bolt is installed and tightened, the balancer must be measured for proper installation - when properly installed, the balancer hub should extend 3/32 to 11/64-inch past the crankshaft snout

11 Crankshaft front oil seal - removal and installation

▶ **Refer to illustrations 11.2, 11.4 and 11.5**

1 Remove the crankshaft balancer (see Section 10).

2 Note how the seal is installed - the new one must be installed to the same depth and facing the same way. Carefully pry the oil seal out of the cover with a seal puller or a large screwdriver (see illustration). Be very careful not to distort the cover or scratch the crankshaft! Wrap electrician's tape around the tip of the screwdriver to avoid damage to the crankshaft.

3 If the seal is being replaced with the timing chain cover removed, support the cover on top of two blocks of wood and drive the seal out from the backside with a hammer and punch.

✳✳ CAUTION:

Be careful not to scratch, gouge or distort the area that the seal fits into or a leak will develop.

4 Apply clean engine oil or multi-purpose grease to the outer edge of the new seal, then install it in the cover with the lip (spring side) facing IN. Drive the seal into place (see illustration) with a large socket and a hammer (if a large socket isn't available, a piece of pipe will also work). Make sure the seal enters the bore squarely and stop when the front face is at the proper depth.

5 Check the surface on the balancer hub that the oil seal rides on. If the surface has been grooved from long-time contact with the seal, a press-on sleeve may be available to renew the sealing surface (see illustration). This sleeve is pressed into place with a hammer and a block of wood and is commonly available at auto parts stores for various applications.

6 Lubricate the balancer hub with clean engine oil and reinstall the crankshaft balancer as described in Section 10.

7 The remainder of installation is the reverse of the removal.

11.2 Carefully pry the old seal out of the timing chain cover - don't damage the crankshaft in the process

11.4 Drive the new seal into place with a large socket and hammer

11.5 If the sealing surface of the pulley hub has a wear groove from contact with the seal, repair sleeves are available at most auto parts stores

12 Timing chain - removal, inspection and installation

12.6 Timing chain cover mounting bolts (arrows)

REMOVAL AND INSPECTION

▶ **Refer to illustrations 12.6, 12.9 and 12.12**

1 Disconnect the cable from the negative terminal of the battery.

✳✳ CAUTION:

On models equipped with the Theftlock audio system, be sure the lockout feature is turned off before performing any procedure which requires disconnecting the battery (see the front of this manual).

2 Refer to Chapter 1 and drain the cooling system and engine oil.

3 Refer to Chapter 3 and remove the upper and lower fan shrouds, drivebelt, cooling fan and water pump.

4 Remove the crankshaft balancer (see Section 10).

5 Remove the oil pan (see Section 14).

6 Remove the timing chain cover mounting bolts and separate the

timing chain cover from the block (see illustration). The cover may be stuck; if so, use a putty knife to break the gasket seal. Since the cover is made of aluminum it can easily be damaged, so DO NOT attempt to pry it off.

7   Remove the oil pick-up tube and the oil pump (see Section 15).

8   Measure the timing chain freeplay. If it is more than 5/8 inch, the chain and both sprockets should be replaced.

9   Loosen the camshaft sprocket bolts one turn, then screw the crankshaft balancer bolt into the end of the crankshaft and rotate the crankshaft in the normal direction of rotation (clockwise) until the timing marks align (see illustration). Verify that the number one piston is at TDC.

10   Remove the three bolts from the end of the camshaft, then detach the camshaft sprocket and chain as an assembly.

11   Inspect the camshaft and crankshaft sprockets for damage or wear.

12   If replacement of the timing chain is necessary, remove the sprocket on the crankshaft with a two-or three-jaw puller, but be careful not to damage the threads in the end of the crankshaft (see illustration).

INSTALLATION

▸ **Refer to illustrations 12.15, 12.19 and 12.20**

➡**Note: Timing chains must be replaced as a set with the camshaft and crankshaft sprockets. Never put a new chain on old sprockets.**

13   Use a gasket scraper to remove all traces of old gasket material and sealant from the cover and engine block.

14   Align the crankshaft sprocket with the Woodruff key and press the sprocket onto the crankshaft (if removed) with the vibration damper bolt, a large socket and some washers or tap it gently into place until it is completely seated.

❉❉ CAUTION:

If resistance is encountered, do not hammer the sprocket onto the crankshaft. It may eventually move onto the shaft, but it may be cracked in the process and fail later, causing extensive engine damage.

12.9 Timing chain alignment marks (arrows) - when properly aligned, the crankshaft gear should be in the 12 o'clock position, the camshaft gear should be in the 6 o'clock position and the number one piston should be at TDC

15   Loop the new chain over the camshaft sprocket, then turn the sprocket until the timing mark is at the bottom (see illustration). Mesh the chain with the crankshaft sprocket and position the camshaft sprocket on the end of the camshaft. If necessary, turn the camshaft so the dowel in the camshaft fits into the hole in the sprocket with the timing mark in the 6 o'clock position (see illustration 12.9). When the chain is installed, the timing marks MUST align as shown.

16   Apply a thread locking compound to the camshaft sprocket bolt threads and tighten the bolts to the torque listed in this Chapter's Specifications.

17   Lubricate the chain with clean engine oil.

18   Install the oil pump and the oil pick up tube onto the engine (see Section 15). Now would be a good time to replace the crankshaft front oil seal (see Section 11).

19   Install the timing chain cover on the engine loosely using a new gasket (see illustration).

20   Align the timing chain cover as follows:

   a)   Install the crankshaft balancer on the engine as described in Sec-

12.12   The sprocket on the crankshaft can be removed with a two or three-jaw puller

12.15   Slip the chain and camshaft sprocket in place over the crankshaft sprocket with the camshaft sprocket timing mark (arrow) at the bottom

12.19   Install the front cover with a new gasket onto the engine block LOOSELY - the cover must be aligned properly before final installation

tion 10. This Step will align the front oil seal with the balancer hub.

b) *Place a straightedge on the engine block oil pan rail. Measure the distance on each side of the block from the oil pan rail to the timing chain cover with a feeler gauge (see illustration). This Step measures the difference between the sealing surface of the oil pan and the sealing surface of the timing chain cover in relationship to each other.*

c) *Tilt the front timing cover as necessary to achieve an even measurement on each side. This Step properly aligns the front timing cover to oil pan sealing surfaces. Typically 0.000 to 0.020 inch is an acceptable tolerance.*

➡**Note: Ideally the timing chain cover should be flush with the oil pan rail, but because of the differences in seal thickness, this may not always be obtainable. That is why there is a tolerance of 0.000 to 0.020 inch. Always let the front seal center itself around the crankshaft balancer hub and tilt the cover from side to side to even up the measurement at both oil pan rails. Never push downward on the front timing cover in an attempt to make the oil pan sealing surface flush, as this will distort the front oil seal and eventually lead to an oil leak!**

d) *With the timing chain cover properly aligned, tighten the cover bolts to the torque listed in this Chapter's Specifications.*

21 Apply a thin layer of RTV sealant to the areas where the timing chain cover and cylinder block meet, then install the oil pan as

described in Section 14.

22 The remaining installation steps are the reverse of removal.

23 Add coolant and oil to the engine (see Chapter 1). Run the engine and check for oil and coolant leaks.

12.20 With the crankshaft balancer in place and the front cover bolts installed LOOSELY, measure the distance between the oil pan rail and the front cover sealing surface on each side (arrows) - then adjust the cover so the measurements are even on both sides before tightening the cover bolts

13 Camshaft and lifters - removal and installation

➡**Note 1: The camshaft should always be thoroughly inspected before installation and camshaft endplay should always be checked prior to camshaft removal. Refer to Chapter 2C for the camshaft and lifter inspection procedures.**

➡**Note 2: If the camshaft is being replaced, always install new lifters as well. Do not use old lifters on a new camshaft.**

REMOVAL

▶ **Refer to illustrations 13.2a, 13.2b and 13.4**

1 Refer to the appropriate Sections and remove the intake mani-

fold, valve covers, rocker arms, pushrods, timing chain and the cylinder heads. Also remove the radiator and air conditioning condenser (see Chapter 3) and the camshaft position sensor (see Chapter 6).

2 Before removing the lifters, arrange to store them in a clearly labeled box to ensure that they're reinstalled in their original locations. Remove the lifter retainers and lifters and store them where they won't get dirty (see illustrations). DO NOT attempt to withdraw the camshaft with the lifters in place.

3 If the lifters are built up with gum and varnish they may not come out with the retainer. If so, there are several ways to extract the lifters from the bores. A special tool designed to grip and remove lifters

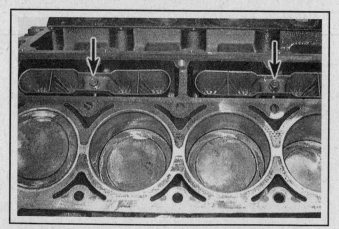

13.2a The roller lifters are held in place by retainers - remove the retainer bolts and remove the retainers and the lifters as an assembly - note that each retainer houses four individual lifters and they must be installed back in their original locations if they're going to be reused

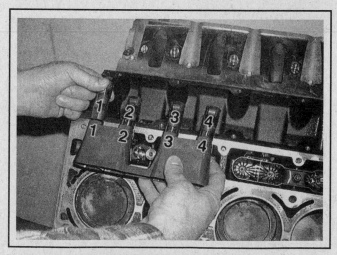

13.2b Once the lifters and retainers are removed from the block they can be marked (for location and installation purposes) and inspected

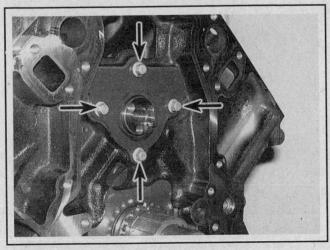

13.4 Remove the bolts (arrows) and take off the camshaft retainer plate, noting which side faces the block

is manufactured by many tool companies and is widely available, but it may not be required in every case. On newer engines without a lot of varnish buildup, the lifters can often be removed with a small magnet or even with your fingers. A machinist's scribe with a bent end can be used to pull the lifters out by positioning the point under the retainer ring in the top of each lifter.

> ❈❈ **CAUTION:**
>
> **Don't use pliers to remove the lifters unless you intend to replace them with new ones. The pliers will damage the precision machined and hardened lifters, rendering them useless.**

4   Remove the bolts and the camshaft retainer plate, noting which direction faces the block (see illustration).

5   Thread three 6-inch long bolts into the camshaft sprocket bolt holes to use as a "handle" when removing the camshaft from the block.

6   Carefully pull the camshaft out. Support the cam near the block so the lobes don't nick or gouge the bearings as it's withdrawn.

14 Oil pan - removal and installation

REMOVAL

▶ **Refer to illustrations 14.4 and 14.8**

1   Disconnect the cable from the negative terminal of the battery.

> ❈❈ **CAUTION:**
>
> **On models equipped with a Delco Loc II audio system, be sure the lockout feature is turned off before performing any procedure which requires disconnecting the battery.**

2   Raise the vehicle and support it securely on jackstands, then refer to Chapter 1 and drain the engine oil and remove the oil filter.

3   Remove the oil pan skid plate, if equipped.

4   Remove the lower control arm crossmember from below the oil pan, if equipped (see illustration).

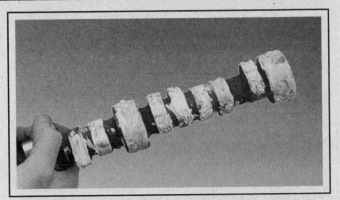

13.7 Be sure to apply camshaft assembly lube to the cam lobes and bearing journals before installing the camshaft

INSTALLATION

▶ **Refer to illustration 13.7**

7   Lubricate the camshaft bearing journals and cam lobes with camshaft and lifter assembly lube (see illustration).

8   Slide the camshaft into the engine. Support the cam near the block and be careful not to scrape or nick the bearings.

9   Turn the camshaft until the dowel pin is in the 3 o'clock position, and install the camshaft thrust plate, tighten the bolts to the torque listed in this Chapter's Specifications. Make sure the gasket surface on the camshaft thrust plate and the engine block are free from oil and dirt.

10   Install the timing chain and sprockets (see Section 12). Also install the camshaft position sensor using a new O-ring (see Chapter 6).

11   Lubricate the lifters with clean engine oil and install them in the lifter retainers. Be sure to align the flats on the lifters with the flats in the lifter retainers. Install the retainer and lifters into the engine block as an assembly. If the original lifters are being reinstalled, be sure to return them to their original locations. If a new camshaft is being installed, install new lifters as well. Tighten the lifter retainer bolts to the torque listed in this Chapter's Specifications.

12   The remaining installation steps are the reverse of removal.

13   Before starting and running the engine, change the oil and install a new oil filter (see Chapter 1).

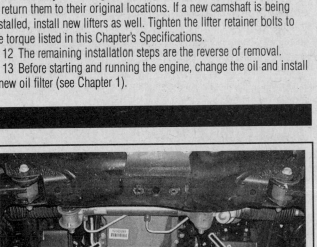

14.4 Remove the bolts (arrows) and the lower control arm support crossmember

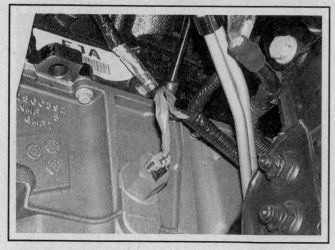

14.8 The oil level sensor is located on the passenger side of the oil pan

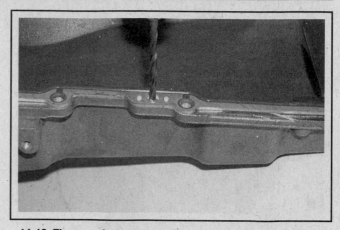

14.13 The manufacturer uses rivets to hold the gasket to the oil pan during assembly - carefully drill them out (it isn't necessary to rivet the new gasket to the oil pan)

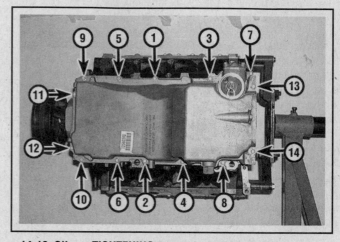

14.16 Oil pan TIGHTENING sequence - all V8 engines

5   On 4WD vehicles, unbolt and lower the front differential carrier with a floorjack (see Chapter 8).

6   Disconnect the front exhaust Y pipe from the engine and the exhaust system and remove it from the vehicle. This step is not absolutely necessary, but it will help facilitate removal of the oil pan.

7   Remove the starter motor (see Chapter 5). Also remove the plastic bellhousing covers (see illustrations 8.8a and 8.8b in Chapter 7B).

8   Remove the wiring harness bracket from the front of the oil pan and the bracket on the passenger side of the oil pan securing the transmission oil cooler lines (if equipped) and the starter motor wiring. Also disconnect the electrical connector from the oil level sensor (see illustration).

9   Remove the transmission to oil pan bolts (see Chapter 7).

10 If the vehicle is equipped with an engine oil cooler, remove the engine oil cooler lines and adapter from the driver's side of the oil pan.

11 Remove the access plugs covering the nuts at the rear of the oil pan (if equipped). On 2001 and later models with a 4L80-E automatic transmission, remove the converter cover bolts, and on models with the 4L60-E automatic, remove the stud and bolt on the right side.

12 Remove all the oil pan bolts, then lower the pan from the engine. The pan will probably stick to the engine, so strike the pan with a rubber mallet until it breaks the gasket seal.

✳✳ CAUTION:

Before using force on the oil pan, be sure all the bolts have been removed. Carefully slide the oil pan down and out, to the rear.

INSTALLATION

▸ **Refer to illustrations 14.13 and 14.16**

13 Drill out the rivets securing the oil pan gasket to the oil pan and remove the old gasket (see illustration). Wash out the oil pan with solvent.

14 Thoroughly clean the mounting surfaces of the oil pan and engine block of old gasket material and sealer. Wipe the gasket surfaces clean with a rag soaked in lacquer thinner, acetone or brake system cleaner.

15 Apply a 3/16-inch wide, one inch long bead of RTV sealant to the corners of the block where the front cover and the rear cover meet the

engine block. Then attach the new gasket to the pan, install the pan and tighten the bolts finger-tight. Be sure the oil gallery passages in the pan and the gasket are aligned properly.

➡**Note: Oil pan gasket rivets do not need to be installed on assembly.**

16 The alignment of the rear face of the aluminum pan to the rear of the block is important. Measure between the rear face of the pan and the front face of the transmission bellhousing with feeler gauges. Clearance should ideally be flush, but a gap of up to 0.010-inch is allowable. If the clearance is OK, tighten the pan bolts/studs in sequence to the torque listed in this Chapter's Specifications (see illustration). If the clearance is not acceptable, install the two lower oil pan-to-bellhousing bolts and tighten them finger tight. This should draw the oil pan flush with the bellhousing.

✳✳ CAUTION:

The rear of the oil pan should never protrude rearward of the bellhousing plane of the block.

17 The remainder of installation is the reverse of removal. Tighten the bolts to the torque listed in this Chapter's Specifications.

18 Add the proper type and quantity of oil (see Chapter 1), start the engine and check for leaks before placing the vehicle back in service.

15 Oil pump - removal, inspection and installation

REMOVAL

▶ **Refer to illustrations 15.2a, 15.2b and 15.3**

1   Refer to the Section 12, Steps 1 through 6 and remove the timing chain cover.

2   Remove the oil pump pick-up tube mounting nuts and bolts and lower the pick-up tube and screen assembly from the vehicle (see illustrations).

3   Remove the oil pump retaining bolts and slide the pump off the end of the crankshaft (see illustration).

INSPECTION

▶ **Refer to illustration 15.4**

4   Remove the oil pump cover and withdraw the rotors from the pump body (see illustration). Clean the components with solvent, dry them thoroughly and inspect for any obvious damage. Also check the bolt holes for damaged threads and the splined surfaces on the crankshaft sprocket for any apparent damage. If any of the components are scored, scratched or worn, replace the entire oil pump assembly. There are no serviceable parts currently available.

INSTALLATION

▶ **Refer to illustration 15.8**

5   Prime the pump by pouring clean motor oil into the pick-up tube hole, while turning the pump by hand.

6   Position the oil pump over the end of the crankshaft and align the teeth on the crank-shaft sprocket with the teeth on the oil pump drive gear. Making sure the pump is fully seated against the block.

7   Install the oil pump mounting bolts and tighten them to the torque listed in this Chapter's Specifications.

8   Install a new O-ring on the oil pump pick-up tube, then fasten it to the oil pump and the engine block main studs (see illustration).

❋❋ **CAUTION:**

Be absolutely certain that the pick-up tube-to-oil pump bolts are properly tightened so that no air can be sucked into the oiling system at this connection.

15.2a Oil pick-up tube-to-main stud retaining nuts (arrows)

15.2b Remove the bolt (arrow) securing the oil pick-up tube to the oil pump and remove it from the engine

9   Install and align the timing chain cover, then install the oil pan. Refer to Sections 12 and 14 for the installation procedures.

10 The remainder of installation is the reverse of removal.

11 Add oil and coolant as necessary. Run the engine and check for oil and coolant leaks. Also check the oil pressure as described in Chapter 2C.

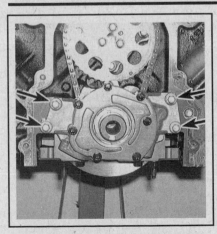

15.3 Oil pump mounting bolts (arrows)

15.4 Oil pump cover-to-oil pump housing mounting bolts (arrows)

15.8 Always install a new O-ring on the oil pump pick up tube

16 Flywheel/driveplate - removal and installation

The flywheel/driveplate replacement for V8 engines is identical to the flywheel/driveplate replacement procedure for the V6 engines. Refer to Chapter 2 Part A for the procedure and use the torque figures in this Chapter's Specifications.

➡ **Note:** *If the spacer between the driveplate and the crankshaft must be removed and it's stuck, insert bolts (M11 bolts, 1.5 mm long) into the two threaded holes in the spacer. Tightening the bolts will force the spacer off the crankshaft.*

17 Rear main oil seal - replacement

◆ **Refer to illustrations 17.3 and 17.4**

➡ **Note:** *If you're installing a new rear seal during a complete engine overhaul, refer to the procedure in Chapter 2C.*

1 Remove the transmission (see Chapter 7).
2 Remove the flywheel/driveplate (see Section 16).
3 Pry the oil seal from the rear cover with a screwdriver (see illustration). Be careful not to nick or scratch the crankshaft or the seal bore. Be sure to note how far it's recessed into the housing bore before removal so the new seal can be installed to the same depth. Thoroughly clean the seal bore in the block with a shop towel. Remove all traces of oil and dirt.

4 Lubricate the outside diameter of the seal and install the seal over the end of the crankshaft. Make sure the lip of the seal points toward the engine. Preferably, a seal installation tool (available at most auto parts store) should be used to press the new seal back into place. If the proper seal installation tool is unavailable, use a large socket, section of pipe or a blunt tool and carefully drive the new seal squarely into the seal bore and flush with the rear cover (see illustration).

5 Install the flywheel/driveplate (see Section 16).
6 Install the transmission (see Chapter 7).

17.3 Carefully pry the old seal out with a screwdriver at the notches provided in the rear cover

17.4 The rear oil seal can be pressed into place with a seal installation tool, a section of pipe or a blunt object shown here - in any case be sure the seal is installed squarely into the seal bore and flush with the rear cover

18 Engine mounts - check and replacement

1 Engine mounts seldom require attention, but broken or deteriorated mounts should be replaced immediately or the added strain placed on the driveline components may cause damage.

CHECK

2 During the check, the engine must be raised slightly to remove the weight from the mounts.
3 Raise the vehicle and support it securely on jackstands, then position the jack under the engine oil pan. Place a large block of wood between the jack head and the oil pan, then carefully raise the engine just enough to take the weight off the mounts. Do not use the jack to support the entire weight of the engine.
4 Check the mounts to see if the rubber is cracked, hardened or separated from the metal plates. Sometimes the rubber will split right down the center. Rubber preservative or WD-40 can be applied to the mounts to slow deterioration.

5 Check for relative movement between the mount plates and the engine or frame (use a large screwdriver or prybar to attempt to move the mounts). If movement is noted, check the tightness of the mount fasteners first before condemning the mounts. Usually when engine mounts are broken, they are very obvious as the engine will easily move away from the mount when pried or under load.

REPLACEMENT

◆ **Refer to illustrations 18.7a, 18.7b and 18.9**

6 Disconnect the cable from the negative terminal of the battery, then raise the vehicle and support it securely on jackstands.

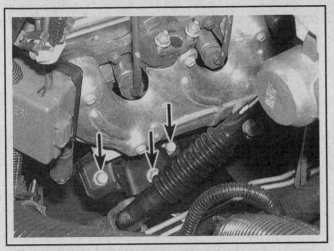

18.7a Driver's side engine mount-to-frame bracket bolts (arrows)

18.7b Passenger side engine mount-to-frame bracket bolts (arrows)

✳✳ CAUTION:

On models equipped with the Theftlock audio system, be sure the lockout feature is turned off before performing any procedure which requires disconnecting the battery (see the front of this manual).

7   Working in the engine compartment remove the engine mount-to-frame bracket bolts. There are three bolts on each side securing the mounts to the frame bracket (see illustrations).

8   Attach an engine hoist to the top of the engine for lifting; do not use a jack under the oil pan to support the entire weight of the engine or the oil pump pick-up could be damaged.

➡Note: If a hoist is not available, casting lugs on each side of the engine block can be used to support the entire weight of the engine while the engine mounts are being replaced.

9   Raise the engine slightly until the engine mount can be unbolted from the block. Unbolt the mount from the engine block and remove it from the vehicle (see illustration).

10   Installation is the reverse of removal. Use non-hardening thread-locking compound on the mount bolts and be sure to tighten them to the torque listed in this Chapter's Specifications.

18.9 Engine mount-to-engine block mounting bolts (arrows)

Specifications

General

Displacement

4.8L	293 cubic inches
5.3L	325 cubic inches
6.0L	364 cubic inches

Bore and stroke

4.8L	3.779 x 3.268 inches
5.3L	3.779 x 3.622 inches
6.0L	4.001 x 3.622 inches

Cylinder numbers (front-to-rear)

Left (driver's) side	1-3-5-7
Right side	2-4-6-8
Firing order	1-8-7-2-6-5-4-3

Cylinder compression pressure

Minimum	100 psi
Maximum variation between cylinders	25 percent from the highest reading

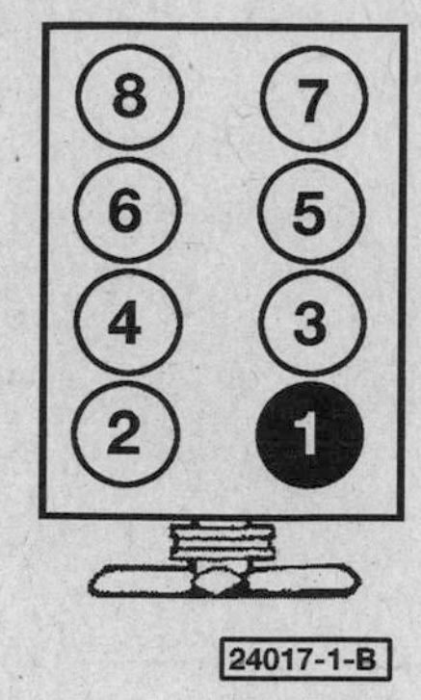

Cylinder numbering - V8 engines

24017-1-B

Camshaft

Journal diameters	2.164 to 2.166 inches
Camshaft endplay	0.001 to 0. 012 inch

Lobe Lift

1999 and 2000 (all)

Intake	0.268 inch
Exhaust	0.274 inch

2001

Intake	0.274 inch
Exhaust	0.281 inch

2002 and later models

4.8L and 5.3L engines

Intake	0.268 inch
Exhaust	0.274 inch

6.0L engines

Intake	0.274 inch
Exhaust	0.281 inch

Torque specifications*   Ft-lbs (unless otherwise indicated)

Camshaft sprocket bolts	26
Camshaft retainer bolts	18
Crankshaft balancer bolt	
Step one (use old bolt)	240
Step two (use new bolt)	37
Step three (use new bolt)	Tighten an additional 140 degrees
Cylinder head bolts (in sequence - see illustration 9.17)	
1999 through 2003 models	
Step 1	
All 11 mm bolts	22
Step 2	
All 11 mm bolts	Tighten an additional 90 degrees
Step 3	
11 mm bolts (1 through 8)	Tighten an additional 90 degrees
11 mm bolts (9 and 10)	Tighten an additional 50 degrees
Step 4	
All 8 mm bolts (11 through 15)	22
2004 and later models	
Design I (equipped with two different length	
11mm bolts; 3.94 inch and 6.1 inch)	
Step 1	
All 11 mm bolts	22
Step 2	
All 11 mm bolts	Tighten an additional 90 degrees
Step 3	
11 mm bolts (1 through 8)	Tighten an additional 90 degrees
11 mm bolts (9 and 10)	Tighten an additional 50 degrees
Step 4	
All 8 mm bolts (11 through 15)	22
Design II (equipped with one length	
11mm bolt; 3.94 inch)	
Step 1	
All 11 mm bolts (1 through 10)	22
Step 2	
All 11 mm bolts (1 through 10)	Tighten an additional 90 degrees
Step 3	
All 11 mm bolts (1 through 10)	Tighten an additional 70 degrees
Step 4	
All 8 mm bolts (11 through 15)	22
Engine mount retaining bolts	37
Exhaust manifold bolts	
Step one	132 in-lbs
Step two	18
Exhaust manifold heat shield bolt	80 in-lbs
Exhaust pipe flange nuts	20 to 25
Flywheel/driveplate bolts	
Step one	15
Step two	37
Step three	74

Intake manifold bolts	
Step one	44 in-lbs
Step two	89 in-lbs
Oil pan baffle bolts	106 in-lbs
Oil pan drain plug	18
Oil pan rear access plugs	80 in-lbs
Oil pan bolts	
Step 1 (to engine and front cover)	18
Step 2 (to rear cover)	106 in-lbs
Step 3 (bellhousing, converter cover and	
transmission bolts)	37
Oil pump cover bolts	106 in-lbs
Oil pump mounting bolts	18
Rocker arm bolts	22
Front timing chain cover bolts	18
Valve cover bolts	106 in-lbs
Vapor vent pipe bolts	106 in-lbs

*Note: Refer to Part C for additional specifications.

2C

GENERAL ENGINE OVERHAUL PROCEDURES

1 General information - engine overhaul

Included in this portion of Chapter 2 are the general overhaul procedures for the cylinder head(s) and internal engine components.

The information ranges from advice concerning preparation for an overhaul and the purchase of replacement parts to detailed, step-by-step procedures covering removal and installation of internal engine components and the inspection of parts.

The following Sections have been written based on the assumption that the engine has been removed from the vehicle. For information concerning in-vehicle engine repair, as well as removal and installation of the external components necessary for the overhaul, see Sections 5 and 7, and Chapters 2A and 2B.

The Specifications included in this Part are only those necessary for the inspection and overhaul procedures which follow. Refer to Parts A or B for additional Specifications.

It's not always easy to determine when, or if, an engine should be completely overhauled, as a number of factors must be considered.

High mileage is not necessarily an indication that an overhaul is needed, while low mileage doesn't preclude the need for an overhaul. Frequency of servicing is probably the most important consideration. An engine that's had regular and frequent oil and filter changes, as well as other required maintenance, will most likely give many thousands of miles of reliable service. Conversely, a neglected engine may require an overhaul very early in its life.

Excessive oil consumption is an indication that piston rings, valve seals and/or valve guides are in need of attention. Make sure that oil leaks aren't responsible before deciding that the rings and/or guides are bad. Perform a cylinder compression check to determine the extent of the work required (see Section 3).

Check the oil pressure with a gauge installed in place of the oil pressure sending unit (see Section 2) and compare it to the Specifications. If it's extremely low, the bearings and/or oil pump are probably worn out. Also check the vacuum readings under various conditions (see Section 4).

Loss of power, rough running, knocking or metallic engine noises, excessive valve train noise and high fuel consumption rates may also point to the need for an overhaul, especially if they're all present at the same time. If a complete tune-up doesn't remedy the situation, major mechanical work is the only solution.

An engine overhaul involves restoring the internal parts to the specifications of a new engine. During an overhaul, the piston rings are replaced and the cylinder walls are reconditioned (rebored and/or honed). If a rebore is done by an automotive machine shop, new oversize pistons will also be installed. The main bearings, connecting rod bearings and camshaft bearings are generally replaced with new ones and, if necessary, the crankshaft may be reground to restore the journals. Generally, the valves are serviced as well, since they're usually in less-than-perfect condition at this point.

While the engine is being overhauled, other components, such as the distributor, starter and alternator, can be rebuilt as well. The end result should be a like new engine that will give many thousands of trouble free miles.

➡**Note: Critical cooling system components such as the hoses, drivebelts, thermostat and water pump MUST be replaced with new parts when an engine is overhauled.**

There are engine rebuilders who will not guarantee their work if the radiator hasn't been professionally cleaned at the time of a rebuilt-engine installation. The radiator should be checked carefully to ensure that it isn't clogged or leaking (see Chapter 3). Also, we don't recommend overhauling the oil pump - always install a new one when an engine is rebuilt.

Before beginning the engine overhaul, read through the entire procedure to familiarize yourself with the scope and requirements of the job. Overhauling an engine isn't difficult if you have the right equipment and follow the instructions carefully, but it is time-consuming. Plan on the vehicle being tied up for a minimum of two weeks, especially if parts must be taken to an automotive machine shop for repair or reconditioning. Check on availability of parts and make sure that any necessary special tools and equipment are obtained in advance.

Most work can be done with typical hand tools, although a number of precision measuring tools are required for inspecting parts to determine if they must be replaced. Often an automotive machine shop will handle the inspection of parts and offer advice concerning reconditioning and replacement.

➡**Note: Always wait until the engine has been completely disassembled and all components, especially the engine block, have been inspected before deciding what service and repair operations must be performed by an automotive machine shop.**

Since the block's condition will be the major factor to consider when determining whether to overhaul the original engine or buy a rebuilt one, never purchase parts or have machine work done on other components until the block has been thoroughly inspected. As a general rule, time is the primary cost of an overhaul, so it doesn't pay to install worn or substandard parts.

As a final note, to ensure maximum life and minimum trouble from a rebuilt engine, everything must be assembled with care in a spotlessly-clean environment.

2 Oil pressure check

▶ **Refer to illustrations 2.2a, 2.2b and 2.5**

1 Low engine oil pressure can be a sign of an engine in need of rebuilding. A "low oil pressure" indicator (often called an "idiot light") is not a test of the oiling system. Such indicators only come on when the oil pressure is dangerously low. Even an original pressure gauge in the instrument panel is only a relative indication, although it's much better for driver information than a warning light. An accurate test can only be performed with a mechanical (not electrical) oil pressure gauge. When used in conjunction with an accurate tachometer, the engine's oil pressure performance can be compared to the manufacturer's Specifications for that year and model.

2 Locate the oil pressure indicator sending unit behind the rear of the intake manifold (see illustrations).

2.2a Oil pressure sending unit location - V6 engine

2.2b Oil pressure sending unit location - V8 engines

3   Remove the oil pressure sending unit and install a fitting which will allow you to directly connect your hand-held, mechanical oil pressure gauge. Use Teflon tape or sealant on the threads of the adapter and the fitting on the end of your gauge's hose.

4   Connect an accurate tachometer to the engine, according to the tachometer manufacturer's instructions.

5   Check the oil pressure with the engine running (full operating temperature) at the specified engine speed, and compare it to this Chapter's Specifications (see illustration). If it's extremely low, the bearings and/or oil pump are probably worn out.

2.5 Check the oil pressure with the engine running (full operating temperature) at the specified engine speed and compare it to this Chapter's Specifications

3   Compression check

▶ **Refer to illustration 3.6**

1   A compression check will tell you what mechanical condition the upper end (pistons, rings, valves, head gaskets) of your engine is in. Specifically, it can tell you if the compression is down due to leakage caused by worn piston rings, defective valves and seats or a blown head gasket.

➡**Note: The engine must be at normal operating temperature and the battery must be fully charged for this check.**

2   Begin by cleaning the area around the spark plugs before you remove them (compressed air should be used, if available). The idea is to prevent dirt from getting into the cylinders as the compression check is being done.

3   Remove all of the spark plugs from the engine (see Chapter 1).

4   Block the throttle wide open.

5   Disable the ignition system by disconnecting the primary electrical connectors at the ignition coil packs (V8 engines) or by disconnecting the primary (low voltage) electrical connectors from the distributor (V6 engines). The fuel pump circuit should also be disabled by removing the fuel pump relay (it's located in the underhood fuse/relay box - see Chapter 12).

6   Install the compression gauge in the number one spark plug hole (see illustration).

7   Crank the engine over at least seven compression strokes and

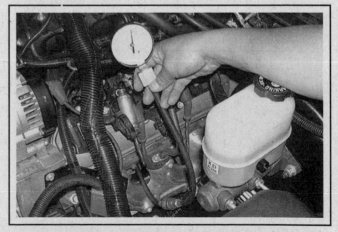

3.6 A compression gauge with a threaded fitting for the spark plug hole is preferred over the type that requires hand pressure to maintain the seal

watch the gauge. The compression should build up quickly in a healthy engine. Low compression on the first stroke, followed by gradually increasing pressure on successive strokes, indicates worn piston rings. A low compression reading on the first stroke, which doesn't build up during successive strokes, indicates leaking valves or a blown head gasket (a cracked head could also be the cause). Deposits on the undersides of the valve heads can also cause low compression. Record the highest gauge reading obtained.

8   Repeat the procedure for the remaining cylinders and compare the results to this Chapter's Specifications.

9   Add some engine oil (about three squirts from a plunger-type oil can) to each cylinder, through the spark plug hole, and repeat the test.

10   If the compression increases after the oil is added, the piston rings are definitely worn. If the compression doesn't increase significantly, the leakage is occurring at the valves or head gasket. Leakage past the valves may be caused by burned valve seats and/or faces or warped, cracked or bent valves.

11   If two adjacent cylinders have equally-low compression, there's a strong possibility that the head gasket between them is blown. The appearance of coolant in the combustion chambers or the crankcase would verify this condition.

12   If one cylinder is slightly lower than the others, and the engine has a rough idle, a worn lobe on the camshaft could be the cause.

13   If the compression is unusually high, the combustion chambers are probably coated with carbon deposits. If that's the case, the cylinder head(s) should be removed and decarbonized.

14   If compression is way down or varies greatly between cylinders, it would be a good idea to have a leak-down test performed by an automotive repair shop. This test will pinpoint exactly where the leakage is occurring and how severe it is.

4   Vacuum gauge diagnostic checks

▶ **Refer to illustrations 4.4 and 4.6**

1   A vacuum gauge provides valuable information about the condition of internal engine components. You can check for worn rings or cylinder walls, leaking head or intake manifold gaskets, restricted exhaust, stuck or burned valves, weak valve springs, improper ignition or valve timing and ignition problems.

2   Unfortunately, vacuum gauge readings are easy to misinterpret, so they should be used in conjunction with other tests to confirm the diagnosis.

3   Both the absolute readings and the rate of needle movement are important for accurate interpretation. Most gauges measure vacuum in inches of mercury (in-Hg). The following references to vacuum assume the diagnosis is being performed at sea level. As elevation increases (or atmospheric pressure decreases), the reading will decrease. For every 1,000 foot increase in elevation above approximately 2000 feet, the gauge readings will decrease about one inch of mercury.

4   Connect the vacuum gauge directly to intake manifold vacuum, not to ported (throttle body) vacuum (see illustration). Be sure no hoses are left disconnected during the test or false readings will result.

5   Before you begin the test, allow the engine to warm up completely. Block the wheels and set the parking brake. With the transmission in Park or Neutral, start the engine and allow it to run at normal idle speed.

6   Read the vacuum gauge; an average, healthy engine should normally produce about 17 to 22 inches of vacuum with a fairly steady needle (see illustration). Refer to the following vacuum gauge readings and what they indicate about the engine's condition:

a)   A low steady reading usually indicates a leaking gasket between the intake manifold and throttle body, a leaky vacuum hose, late ignition timing or incorrect camshaft timing. Check ignition timing with a timing light and eliminate all other possible causes, utilizing the tests provided in this Chapter before you remove the timing chain cover to check the timing marks.

b)   If the reading is three to eight inches below normal and it fluctuates at that low reading, suspect an intake manifold gasket leak at an intake port or a faulty fuel injector.

c)   If the needle has regular drops of about two-to-four inches at a steady rate, the valves are probably leaking. Perform a compression check or leak-down test to confirm this.

d)   An irregular drop or down-flick of the needle can be caused by a sticking valve or an ignition misfire. Perform a compression check or leak-down test and read the spark plugs.

e)   A rapid vibration of about four inches Hg vibration at idle combined with exhaust smoke indicates worn valve guides. Perform a leak-down test to confirm this. If the rapid vibration occurs with an increase in engine speed, check for a leaking intake manifold gasket or head gasket, weak valve springs, burned valves or ignition misfire.

f)   A slight fluctuation, say one inch up and down, may mean ignition problems. Check all the usual tune-up items and, if necessary, run the engine on an ignition analyzer.

g)   If there is a large fluctuation, perform a compression or leak-down test to look for a weak or dead cylinder or a blown head gasket.

h)   If the needle moves slowly through a wide range, check for a clogged PCV system, incorrect idle fuel mixture, carburetor/throttle body or intake manifold gasket leaks.

i)   Check for a slow return after revving the engine by quickly snapping the throttle open until the engine reaches about 2,500 rpm

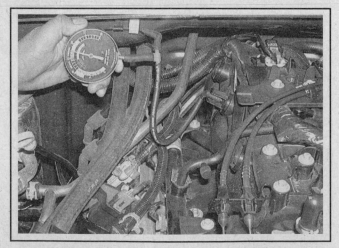

4.4 An inexpensive vacuum gauge can tell you a lot about an engine's condition

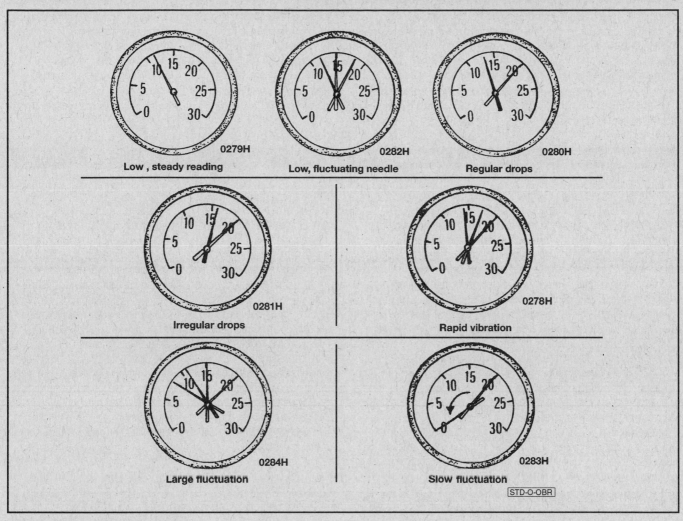

4.6 Typical vacuum gauge readings

and let it shut. Normally the reading should drop to near zero, rise above normal idle reading (about 5 in.-Hg over) and then return to the previous idle reading. If the vacuum returns slowly and doesn't peak when the throttle is snapped shut, the rings

may be worn. If there is a long delay, look for a restricted exhaust system (often the muffler or catalytic converter). An easy way to check this is to temporarily disconnect the exhaust ahead of the suspected part and re-test.

5   Engine rebuilding alternatives

The do-it-yourselfer is faced with a number of options when performing an engine overhaul. The decision to replace the engine block, piston/connecting rod assemblies and crankshaft depends on a number of factors, with the number one consideration being the condition of the block. Other considerations are cost, access to machine shop facilities, parts availability, time required to complete the project and the extent of prior mechanical experience on the part of the do-it-yourselfer.

Some of the rebuilding alternatives include:

Individual parts - If the inspection procedures reveal that the engine block and most engine components are in reusable condition, purchasing individual parts may be the most economical alternative. The block, crankshaft and piston/connecting rod assemblies should all be inspected carefully. Even if the block shows little wear, the cylinder bores should be surface-honed.

Crankshaft kit - This rebuild package consists of a reground crankshaft and a matched set of pistons and connecting rods. The pistons will already be installed on the connecting rods. Piston rings and the necessary bearings will be included in the kit. These kits are commonly available for standard cylinder bores, as well as for engine blocks which have been bored to a regular oversize.

Short block - A short block consists of an engine block with renewed crankshaft and piston/connecting rod assemblies already installed. All new bearings are incorporated and all clearances will be correct. The existing cylinder head(s), camshaft, valve train components and external parts can be bolted to the short block with little or no machine shop work necessary.

Long block - A long block consists of a short block plus an oil pump, oil pan, cylinder heads, valve covers, camshaft and valve train components, timing sprockets, timing chain and timing cover. All components are installed with new bearings, seals and gaskets incorporated throughout. The installation of manifolds and external parts is all that is necessary.

Used engine assembly - While overhaul provides the best assurance of a like-new engine, used engines available from wrecking yards and importers are often a very simple and economical solution. Many used engines come with warranties, but always give any engine a thorough diagnostic check-out before purchase. Check compression, vacuum and also for signs of oil leakage. If possible, have the seller run the engine, ether in the vehicle or on a test stand so you can be sure it runs smoothly with no knocking or other noises.

Give careful thought to which alternative is best for you and discuss the situation with local automotive machine shops, auto parts dealers or parts store countermen before ordering or purchasing replacement parts.

6   Engine removal - methods and precautions

If you've decided that an engine must be removed for overhaul or major repair work, several preliminary steps should be taken.

Locating a suitable place to work is extremely important. Adequate work space, along with storage space for the vehicle, will be needed. If a shop or garage isn't available, at the very least a flat, level, clean work surface made of concrete or asphalt is required.

Cleaning the engine compartment and engine before beginning the removal procedure will help keep your tools and your hands clean.

An engine hoist or A-frame will also be necessary. Make sure the equipment is rated in excess of the combined weight of the engine and accessories. Safety is of primary importance, considering the potential hazards involved in lifting the engine out of the vehicle.

If the engine is being removed by a novice, a helper should be available. Advice and aid from someone more experienced would also be helpful. There are many instances when one person cannot simultaneously perform all of the operations required when lifting the engine out of the vehicle.

Plan the operation ahead of time. Arrange for or obtain all of the tools and equipment you'll need prior to beginning the job. Some of the equipment necessary to perform engine removal and installation safely and with relative ease are (in addition to an engine hoist) a heavy duty floor jack, complete sets of wrenches and sockets as described in the front of this manual, wooden blocks and plenty of rags and cleaning solvent for mopping up spilled oil, coolant and gasoline. If the hoist must be rented, make sure that you arrange for it in advance and perform all of the operations possible without it beforehand. This will save you money and time.

Plan for the vehicle to be out of use for quite a while. A machine shop will be required to perform some of the work which the do-it-yourselfer can't accomplish without special equipment. These shops often have a busy schedule, so it would be a good idea to consult them before removing the engine in order to accurately estimate the amount of time required to rebuild or repair components that may need work.

Always be extremely careful when removing and installing the engine. Serious injury can result from careless actions. Plan ahead, take your time and a job of this nature, although major, can be accomplished successfully.

7   Engine - removal and installation

✳✳ WARNING 1:

The air conditioning system is under high pressure. Do not loosen any hose fittings or remove any components until after the system has been discharged. Air conditioning refrigerant should be properly discharged into an EPA-approved recov-ery/ recycling unit at a dealer service department or an automotive air conditioning repair facility. Always wear eye protection when disconnecting air conditioning system fittings.

✳✳ WARNING 2:

Gasoline is extremely flammable, so take extra precautions when you work on any part of the fuel system. Don't smoke or allow open flames or bare light bulbs near the work area, and don't work in a garage where a natural gas-type appliance (such as a water heater or a clothes dryer) is present. Since gasoline is carcinogenic, wear latex gloves when there's a possibility of being exposed to fuel, and, if you spill any fuel on your skin, rinse it off immediately with soap and water. Mop up any spills immediately and do not store fuel-soaked rags where they could ignite. The fuel system is under constant pressure, so, if any fuel lines are to be disconnected, the fuel pressure in the system must be relieved first (see Chapter 4 for more information). When you perform any kind of work on the fuel system, wear safety glasses and have a Class B type fire extinguisher on hand.

✳✳ WARNING 3:

The models covered by this manual are equipped with airbags. Always disable the airbag system before working in the vicinity of any airbag system components to avoid the possibility of accidental deployment of the airbag(s), which could cause personal injury (see Chapter 12).

REMOVAL

◆ **Refer to illustrations 7.5a, 7.5b, 7.5c, 7.12, 7.15, 7.22 and 7.27**

1   If the vehicle is equipped with air conditioning, have the system discharged and the refrigerant recovered by an air conditioning specialist.

2   Refer to Chapter 4 and relieve the fuel system pressure, then disconnect the cable from the negative terminal of the battery.

✳✳ CAUTION:

On models equipped with the Theftlock audio system, be sure the lockout feature is turned off before performing any procedure which requires disconnecting the battery (see the front of this manual).

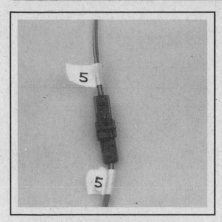

7.5a Label both ends of each wire before unplugging the connector

7.5b Don't forget to disconnect the electrical connections (arrows) at the rear of the block . . .

7.5c . . . and the ground straps (arrow) at the firewall

3   Cover the fenders and cowl and remove the hood (see Chapter 11). Special pads are available to protect the fenders, but an old bedspread or blanket will also work.

➡**Note: As an alternative to removing the hood, the side bolt in each hood hinge can be removed and installed in the lower hole of the hinge, which will secure the hood in an upright position. Have an assistant help hold the hood during this procedure.**

4   Remove the air cleaner assembly (see Chapter 4). Drain the cooling system (see Chapter 1).

5   Label the vacuum lines, emissions system hoses, wiring connectors, ground strap and fuel lines, to ensure correct reinstallation, then detach them (see illustrations). If there's any possibility of confusion, make a sketch of the engine compartment and clearly label the lines, hoses and wires. Detach the wiring harness brackets from the intake manifold and set the engine wiring harness aside.

6   Label and detach all coolant hoses from the engine.

7   Remove the drivebelt(s) (see Chapter 1). On V6 engines, remove the distributor cap and spark plug wires to avoid contact with the firewall as the engine is lifted from the vehicle.

8   Remove the cooling fan, shroud and radiator (see Chapter 3).

9   Remove the intake manifold cover If equipped. Disconnect the throttle linkage and the cruise control cable, (if equipped) from the throttle body (see Chapter 4).

10   Disconnect the fuel lines running from the engine to the chassis

(see Chapter 4). Plug or cap all open fittings/lines. Remove the secondary air injection pipe, if equipped, from the intake manifold and the exhaust manifolds (see Chapter 6).

11 On air-conditioned vehicles, disconnect the refrigerant lines from the compressor (see the Warning at the beginning of this Section). Plug all the hoses to avoid contamination of the A/C system and set the hoses aside. On V8 engines, unbolt the compressor from the compressor mounting bracket on the side of the block and remove It from the engine compartment (see Chapter 3).

12 On power steering equipped vehicles, disconnect the power steering pump lines and unbolt the rear of the power steering pump from the engine. Detach the power steering pump/air conditioning compressor bracket (V6 engines) or the power steering pump/alternator bracket (V8 engines) from the front of the engine (see illustration). Make sure the pump is kept in an upright position after being removed from the engine compartment. On V6 engines, this Step will remove the power steering pump, the power steering pump bracket and the air conditioning compressor. On V8 engines, this Step will remove the power steering pump, the power steering pump bracket and the alternator.

13 Raise the front of the vehicle and support it securely on jackstands. Working under the vehicle, drain the engine oil (see Chapter 1).

14 Unbolt the exhaust system from the exhaust manifolds.

15 On models with rack-and-pinion steering, remove the bolts securing the steering gear to the frame and lower the steering gear,

7.12 Alternator/power steering pump mounting bracket bolts (arrows) (V8 engine shown, V6 engine similar except that the A/C compressor is mounted where the alternator is on V8 engines)

7.15 Lowering the steering gear on 2WD 1500 pick-up models will allow clearance for the oil pan as the engine is moved forward to clear the cowl

7.22 On V8 engines, it will be necessary to attach the sling or chain to the cylinder heads

7.27 Pull the engine forward as far as possible to clear the transmission and the cowl, then lift the engine high enough to clear the body

allowing it to hang by the tie-rods (see illustration). This Step will allow clearance for the oil pan as the engine is moved forward to clear the cowl.

16 Remove the oil pan skid plates if equipped. Remove the lower control arm crossmember from below the oil pan (see illustration 14.4 in Chapter 2B).

17 Remove the starter motor (see Chapter 5).

18 Remove the transmission inspection cover and the bellhousing covers from the bellhousing (see illustrations 8.8a and 8.8b in Chapter 7B). If you're working on a vehicle with an automatic transmission, refer to Chapter 7B and remove the torque converter-to-driveplate fasteners.

19 Remove the wiring harness bracket from the front of the oil pan and the bracket on the passenger side of the oil pan securing the transmission oil cooler lines (if equipped) and the starter motor wiring. Disconnect the electrical connector from the oil level sensor and the crankshaft position sensor. Also disconnect the engine block heater if equipped.

20 If the vehicle is equipped with an engine oil cooler, remove the engine oil cooler lines and adapter from the driver's side of the oil pan.

21 Support the transmission with a jack. Position a block of wood between the jack and transmission to prevent damage to the transmission. Special transmission jacks with safety chains are available - use one if possible.

22 Attach an engine sling or a length of chain to the lifting brackets on the engine.

✳✳ CAUTION:

DO NOT lift the engine by the intake manifold. Lift the engine by the block or the cylinder head only.

➡Note: V8 engines are not equipped with lifting brackets. On these engines it will be necessary to attach a sling to the exhaust manifold bolts or directly to the cylinder heads (see illustration).

23 Roll the hoist into position and connect the sling to it. Take up the slack in the sling or chain, but don't lift the engine.

✳✳ WARNING:

DO NOT place any part of your body under the engine when it's supported only by a hoist or other lifting device.

24 Remove the transmission-to-engine block bolts.

25 Remove the engine mount-to-frame bolts (see Chapter 2A or 2B for engine mount removal procedures).

26 Recheck to be sure nothing is still connecting the engine to the transmission or vehicle. Disconnect anything still remaining.

27 Raise the engine slightly. Carefully work it forward to separate it from the transmission. If you're working on a vehicle with an automatic transmission, be sure the torque converter stays in the transmission (clamp a pair of vise-grips to the housing to keep the converter from sliding out). If you're working on a vehicle with a manual transmission, the input shaft must be completely disengaged from the clutch. Slowly raise the engine out of the engine compartment (see illustration). Check carefully to make sure nothing is hanging up.

28 Remove the flywheel/driveplate and mount the engine on an engine stand.

INSTALLATION

29 Install the flywheel/driveplate on the engine (see Chapter 2A or 2B). Check the engine and transmission mounts. If they're worn or damaged, replace them.

30 If you're working on a vehicle with a manual transmission, install the clutch and pressure plate onto the flywheel (see Chapter 7A). Now is a good time to install a new clutch.

31 Carefully lower the engine into the engine compartment - make sure the engine mounts line up.

32 If you're working on a vehicle with an automatic transmission, guide the torque converter into the crankshaft following the procedure outlined in Chapter 7B.

33 If you're working on a vehicle with a manual transmission, apply a dab of high-temperature grease to the input shaft and guide it into the crankshaft pilot bearing until the bellhousing is flush with the engine block.

➡Note: It may be necessary to place the transmission into first gear, then turn the output shaft on the transmission until the teeth on the input shaft align with the teeth on the clutch disc.

34 Install the transmission-to-engine bolts and tighten them securely.

✳✳ CAUTION:

DO NOT use the bolts to force the transmission and engine together!

35 Reinstall the remaining components in the reverse order of removal.

⁜ CAUTION:

On 2001 and later models, the throttle linkage should be replaced with a new one when the engine is reinstalled.

36 Add coolant, oil, power steering and transmission fluid as needed.

37 Run the engine and check for leaks and proper operation of all accessories, then install the hood and test drive the vehicle.

38 Have the air conditioning system recharged and leak tested.

8 Engine overhaul - disassembly sequence

1 It's much easier to disassemble and work on the engine if it's mounted on a portable engine stand. A stand can often be rented quite cheaply from an equipment rental yard. Before the engine is mounted on a stand, the flywheel/driveplate should be removed from the engine.

2 If a stand isn't available, it's possible to disassemble the engine with it blocked up on the floor. Be extra careful not to tip or drop the engine when working without a stand.

3 If you're going to obtain a rebuilt engine, all external components must come off first to be transferred to the replacement engine, just as they will if you're doing a complete engine overhaul yourself. These include:

Alternator and brackets
Emissions control components
Distributor, spark plug wires and spark plugs (V6 engines)
Ignition coils, spark plug wires and spark plugs (V8 engines)
Thermostat and housing cover
Water pump
Fuel injection components
Intake/exhaust manifold(s)
Oil filter
Engine mounts
Clutch and flywheel/driveplate

➡Note: **When removing the external components from the engine, pay close attention to details that may be helpful or important during installation. Note the installed position of gaskets, seals, spacers, pins, brackets, washers, bolts and other small items.**

4 If you're obtaining a short block, which consists of the engine block, crankshaft, pistons and connecting rods all assembled, then the cylinder head(s), oil pan and oil pump will have to be removed as well. See *Engine rebuilding alternatives* for additional information regarding the different possibilities to be considered.

5 If you're planning a complete overhaul, the engine must be disassembled and the internal components removed in the following order:

Valve cover(s)
Intake and exhaust manifolds
Rocker arms and pushrods
Cylinder head(s)
Valve lifters
Oil pan
Oil pump (V6 engines)
Timing chain cover
Oil pump (V8 engines)
Timing chain and sprockets
Camshaft
Balance shaft (V6 engines)
Piston/connecting rod assemblies
Rear main oil seal retainer
Crankshaft and main bearings

6 Before beginning the disassembly and overhaul procedures, make sure the following items are available. Also, refer to Section 23 for a list of tools and materials needed for engine reassembly.

Common hand tools
Small cardboard boxes or plastic bags for storing parts
Gasket scraper
Ridge reamer
Crankshaft balancer puller
Micrometers
Telescoping gauges
Dial-indicator set
Valve spring compressor
Cylinder surfacing hone
Piston ring groove-cleaning tool
Electric drill motor
Tap and die set
Wire brushes
Oil gallery brushes
Cleaning solvent

9 Cylinder head - disassembly

▶ **Refer to illustrations 9.2, 9.3 and 9.4**

➡Note: **New and rebuilt cylinder heads are commonly available for most engines at dealerships and auto parts stores. Due to the fact that some specialized tools are necessary for the disassembly and inspection procedures, and some parts may not be readily available, it may be more practical and economical for the home mechanic to purchase replacement head(s) rather than taking the time to disassemble, inspect and recondition the original(s).**

1 Cylinder head disassembly involves removal of the intake and exhaust valves and related components. If they're still in place, remove the rocker arm bolts, pivots and rocker arms from the cylinder head. Label the parts or store them separately so they can be reinstalled in their original locations.

2 Before the valves are removed, arrange to label and store them,

9.2 A small plastic bag, with an appropriate label, can be used to store the valve train components so they can be kept together and reinstalled in the correct guide

9.3 Use a valve spring compressor to compress the spring, then remove the keepers with a magnet or needle-nose pliers

9.4 If the valve won't pull through the guide, deburr the edge of the stem and the area around the top of the keeper groove with a file

along with their related components, so they can be kept separate and reinstalled in the same valve guides they were removed from (see illustration).

3   Compress the springs on the first valve with a spring compressor and remove the keepers (see illustration). Carefully release the valve spring compressor and remove the retainer, the spring and the spring seat (if used).

4   Pull the valve out of the head, then remove the oil seal from the guide. If the valve binds in the guide (won't pull through), push it back into the head and deburr the area around the keeper groove with a fine file or whetstone (see illustration).

5   Repeat the procedure for the remaining valves. Remember to keep all the parts for each valve together so they can be reinstalled in the same locations.

6   Once the valves and related components have been removed and stored in an organized manner, the head should be thoroughly cleaned and inspected. If a complete engine overhaul is being done, finish the engine disassembly procedures before beginning the cylinder head cleaning and inspection process.

10 Cylinder head - cleaning and inspection

CLEANING

▶ **Refer to illustrations 10.12, 10.14, 10.15, 10.16, 10.17 and 10.18**

1   Thorough cleaning of the cylinder head(s) and related valve train components, followed by a detailed inspection, will enable you to decide how much valve service work must be done during the engine overhaul.

➡**Note: If the engine was severely overheated, the cylinder head is probably warped (see Step 12).**

2   Scrape all traces of old gasket material and sealing compound off the head gasket, intake manifold and exhaust manifold sealing surfaces. Be very careful not to gouge the cylinder head. Special gasket removal solvents that soften gaskets and make removal much easier are available at auto parts stores.

3   Remove all built up scale from the coolant passages.

4   Run a stiff wire brush through the various holes to remove deposits that may have formed in them.

5   Run an appropriate size tap into each of the threaded holes to remove corrosion and thread sealant that may be present. If compressed air is available, use it to clear the holes of debris produced by this operation.

✳ WARNING:

Wear eye protection when using compressed air!

6   Clean the rocker arm pivot bolt threads (V8 engines) or studs (V6 engines) with a wire brush.

7   Clean the cylinder head with solvent and dry it thoroughly. Compressed air will speed the drying process and ensure that all holes and recessed areas are clean.

➡**Note: Decarbonizing chemicals are available and may prove very useful when cleaning cylinder heads and valve train components. They are very caustic and should be used with caution. Be sure to follow the instructions on the container.**

8   Clean the rocker arms, pivot balls or fulcrums, nuts or bolts and pushrods with solvent and dry them thoroughly (don't mix them up during the cleaning process). Compressed air will speed the drying process and can be used to clean out the oil passages.

9   Clean all the valve springs, spring seats, keepers and retainers (or rotators) with solvent and dry them thoroughly. Do the components from one valve at a time to avoid mixing up the parts.

10   Scrape off any heavy deposits that may have formed on the valves, then use a motorized wire brush to remove deposits from the valve heads and stems. Again, make sure the valves don't get mixed up.

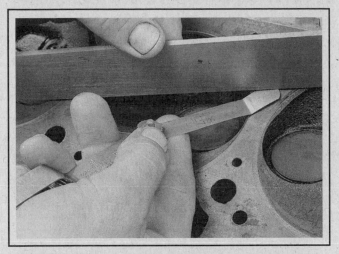

10.12 Check the cylinder head surface for warpage by trying to slip a feeler gauge under the straightedge - see the Specifications for the maximum warpage and use a feeler gauge of that size

INSPECTION

➡ **Note: Be sure to perform all of the following inspection procedures before concluding that machine shop work is required. Make a list of the items that need attention.**

Cylinder head

11 Inspect the head very carefully for cracks, evidence of coolant leakage and other damage. If cracks are found, check with an automotive machine shop concerning repair. If repair isn't possible, a new cylinder head must be obtained.

12 Using a straightedge and feeler gauge, check the head gasket mating surface for warpage (see illustration). If the warpage exceeds the specified limit, it can be resurfaced at an automotive machine shop.

➡ **Note: If the cylinder heads are resurfaced, the intake manifold flanges may also require machining.**

13 Examine the valve seats in each of the combustion chambers. If they're pitted, cracked or burned, the head will require valve service that's beyond the scope of the home mechanic.

14 Check the valve stem-to-guide clearance by measuring the lateral movement of the valve stem with a dial indicator attached securely to the head (see illustration). The valve must be in the guide and approximately 1/16-inch off the seat. The total valve stem movement indicated by the gauge needle must be divided by two to obtain the actual clearance. After this is done, if there's still some doubt regarding the condition of the valve guides, they should be checked by an automotive machine shop (the cost should be minimal). If the clearance is excessive, the machine shop will have to install new valve guides in the head(s).

Valves

15 Carefully inspect each valve for uneven wear, deformation, cracks, pits and burned areas (see illustration). Check the valve stem for scuffing and galling and the neck for cracks. Rotate the valve and check for any obvious indication that it's bent. Look for pits and excessive wear on the end of the stem. The presence of any of these conditions indicates the need for valve service by an automotive machine shop.

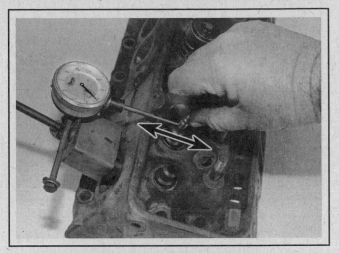

10.14 A dial indicator can be used to determine the valve stem-to-guide clearance - move the stem as indicated by the arrows

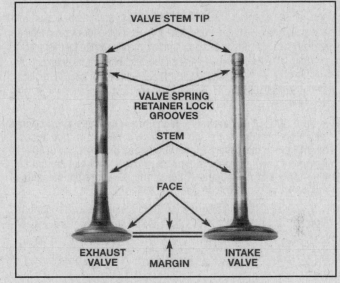

10.15 Check for valve wear at the points shown here

16 Measure the margin width on each valve (see illustration). Any valve with a margin narrower than that listed in this Chapter's Specifications will have to be replaced with a new one.

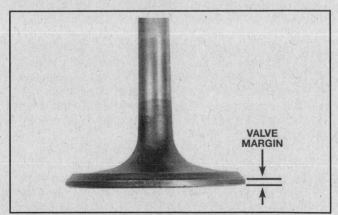

10.16 Valve margin width must be as specified - if no margin exists, the valve cannot be reused

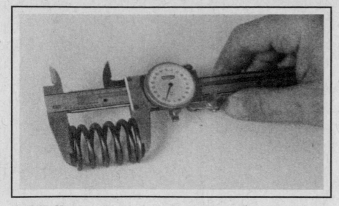

10.17 Measure the length of each valve spring with a dial or vernier caliper

Valve components

17 Check each valve spring for wear (on the ends) and pits. Measure the free length and compare it to this Chapter's Specifications (see illustration). Any springs that are shorter than specified have sagged and should not be reused. The tension of all springs should be checked with a special fixture before deciding that they're suitable for use in a rebuilt engine (take the springs to an automotive machine shop for this check).

18 Stand each spring on a flat surface and check it for squareness (see illustration). If any of the springs are distorted or sagged, replace all of them with new parts. Springs that aren't square can cause accelerated guide wear.

➡**Note: V8 engines are equipped with conical type valve springs which are smaller at the top. On these models it will be necessary to place the square along both sides of the spring (180 degrees apart) and note the measurements between the top of the spring and the square. if the spring is square the measurement will be the same on both sides.**

19 Check the spring retainers (or rotators) and keepers for obvious wear and cracks. Any questionable parts should be replaced with new ones, as extensive damage will occur if they fail during engine operation.

10.18 Check each spring for squareness

Rocker arm components

20 Check the rocker arm faces (the areas that contact the pushrod ends and valve stems) for pits, wear, galling, score marks and rough spots. Check the rocker arm pivot contact areas and pivots as well. Look for cracks in each rocker arm and nut or bolt. On V8 engines check the pivot bearings for binding and roughness.

21 Inspect the pushrod ends for scuffing and excessive wear. Roll each pushrod on a flat surface, like a piece of plate glass, to determine if it's bent.

22 Check the rocker arm bolt holes or stud threads in the cylinder heads for damaged threads and secure installation.

23 Any damaged or excessively worn parts must be replaced with new ones.

24 If the inspection process indicates that the valve components are in generally poor condition and worn beyond the limits specified, which is usually the case in an engine that's being overhauled, reassemble the valves in the cylinder head and refer to Section 11 for valve servicing recommendations.

11 Valves - servicing

1 Because of the complex nature of the job and the special tools and equipment needed, servicing of the valves, the valve seats and the valve guides, commonly known as a valve job, should be done by a professional.

2 The home mechanic can remove and disassemble the head(s), do the initial cleaning and inspection, then reassemble and deliver it (or them) to an automotive machine shop for the actual service work. Doing the inspection will enable you to see what condition the head and valvetrain components are in and will ensure that you know what work and new parts are required when dealing with an automotive machine shop.

3 The automotive machine shop, will remove the valves and springs, recondition or replace the valves and valve seats, recondition the valve guides, check and replace the valve springs, spring retainers or rotators and keepers (as necessary), replace the valve seals with new ones, reassemble the valve components and make sure the installed spring height is correct. The cylinder head gasket surface will also be resurfaced if it's warped. On V6 and V8 engines, both heads must be surfaced the same amount, and if more than .020-inch is taken off, the bottom and sides of the intake manifold must also be machined so that all passage and holes still line up properly. Note that some cylinder heads have a minimum resurfacing height (similar to a brake rotor or drum). If they're resurfaced past the minimum height they'll have to be replaced. Measure the height of the heads and check them against Specifications at the end of this Chapter to be sure. This information will tell you the maximum amount of material that can be machined off the deck surface of the cylinder head. Be sure to give this information to your machine shop, don't assume they already know.

4 After the valve job has been performed by a professional, the head will be in like-new condition. When the head is returned, be sure to clean it again before installation on the engine to remove any metal particles and abrasive grit that may still be present from the valve service or head resurfacing operations. Use compressed air, if available, to blow out all the oil holes, bolt holes and coolant passages.

12 Cylinder head - reassembly

▶ **Refer to illustrations 12.6, 12.7 and 12.9**

1   Regardless of whether or not the head was sent to an automotive repair shop for valve servicing, make sure it's clean before beginning reassembly.

2   If the head was sent out for valve servicing, the valves and related components will already be in place. Begin the reassembly procedure with Step 8.

3   Beginning at one end of the head, lubricate and install the first valve. Apply moly-base grease or clean engine oil to the valve stem.

4   Install the spring seat and shims, if originally installed, before the valve seals.

5   install a new valve stem seal over the valve stem and press it down over the valve guide to the specified depth using hand pressure (see illustrations 6.13b in Chapter 2A and 6.15b in Chapter 2B). Don't force the valve seal against the top of the guide.

✳✳ CAUTION:

Intake and exhaust valves on these models require different seals. Do not install an exhaust valve seal on an intake valve, as high oil consumption will result. Exhaust valve seals are typically brown in color and intake valve seals are typically black in color.

Do not hammer on the seals or they could be driven down too far and subsequently leak. Don't twist or cock the seals during installation or they won't seal properly on the valve stems. Many seal sets come with a plastic installer that slides over the top of the valve stem to keep the valve seal from catching in the valve keeper groove.

6   The valve components (see illustration) may be installed in the following order:

Valves
Valve spring seat (aluminum cylinder heads)
Valve stem seals
Valve spring shims (if any)
Valve springs
Retainers or rotators
Keepers

7   Compress the springs with a valve spring compressor and carefully install the keepers in the groove, then slowly release the compressor and make sure the keepers seat properly. Apply a small dab of

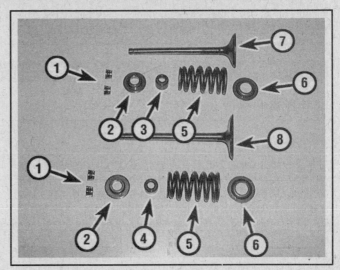

12.6 Valves and related components (V8 engine shown, V6 similar)

1	Valve keeper	6	Valve spring seat
2	Retainer		(aluminum heads)
3	Exhaust valve seal	7	Exhaust valve
4	Intake valve seal	8	Intake valve
5	Valve spring		

grease to each keeper to hold it in place if necessary (see illustration). Tap the valve stem tips with a plastic hammer to seat the keepers, if necessary.

8   Repeat the procedure for the remaining valves. Be sure to return the components to their original locations - don't mix them up!

9   Check the installed valve spring height with a ruler graduated in 1/32-inch increments or a dial caliper (see illustration). If the head was sent out for service work, the installed height should be correct (but don't automatically assume it is). The measurement is taken from the top of each spring seat or top shim to the bottom of the retainer. If the height is greater than specified in this Chapter, shims can be added under the springs to correct it.

12.7 Apply a small dab of grease to each keeper as shown here before installation - it will hold them in place on the valve stem as the spring is released

12.9 Be sure to check the valve spring installed height (the distance from the top of the seat/shims to the top of the shield or the bottom of the retainer)

13 Camshaft, lifters and bearings - removal and inspection

REMOVAL

▶ **Refer to illustrations 13.1a and 13.1b**

1 Refer to Chapter 2A (V6 engine) or 2B (V8 engines) for the camshaft and lifter removal procedure. Disregard the Steps that do not apply, since the engine is already removed from the vehicle. On V8 engines it will be necessary to remove the engine valley cover. Remove the bolts and detach the cover from the engine block. Be sure to install a new gasket and knock sensor oil seals upon installation (see illustrations). It is assumed that the cylinder heads and the coolant vapor vent tube is already removed at this point.

INSPECTION

Camshaft lobe lift check

▶ **Refer to illustrations 13.3, 13.9a and 13.9b**

2 The first and easiest method to check camshaft lobe lift is through the use of a dial indicator with the camshaft installed in the engine block and the rocker arms and spark plugs removed.

➡**Note: The following method can also be used if the cylinder heads and or pushrods have been removed by simply mounting the dial indicator on the deck surface of the engine block and placing the plunger against the top surface of the lifter on the cylinder you're checking.**

3 Beginning with the number one cylinder, mount a dial indicator on the engine and position the plunger against the top surface of the pushrod or lifter. Position the number one cylinder at TDC on the compression stroke (see Section 3, in Chapter 2A or 2B). The plunger should be directly above and in line with the pushrod (see illustration).

4 Zero the dial indicator, then very slowly turn the crankshaft in the normal direction of rotation (clockwise) until the indicator needle stops and begins to move in the opposite direction. The point at which it stops indicates maximum cam lobe lift.

5 Record this figure for future reference, then reposition the piston at TDC on the compression stroke again.

6 Move the dial indicator to the other number one cylinder pushrod or lifter and repeat the check. Be sure to record the results for each valve.

7 Repeat the check for the remaining valves. Since each piston must be at TDC on the compression stroke for this procedure, work from cylinder-to-cylinder following the firing order sequence.

8 The second method for measuring camshaft lobe lift is obtained through the use of a micrometer with the camshaft removed from the engine block.

9 Using this method, measure the camshaft lobe height and the base circle (see illustrations). The difference between the two measurements is the lobe lift (lobe height - base circle = lobe lift). Record this figure for future reference and repeat the check on the remaining camshaft lobes.

10 Apply moly-base grease to the rocker arm faces and the pivots, then install the rocker arms and pivots on the cylinder heads. Tighten the bolts or nuts finger-tight.

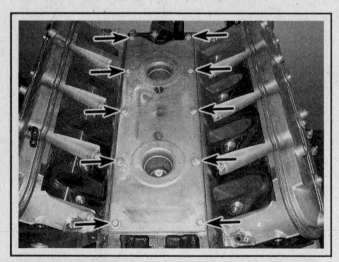

13.1a Valley cover mounting bolts - V8 engine

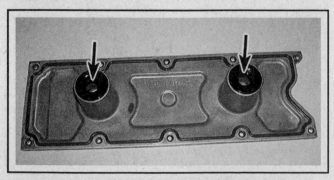

13.1b Be sure to replace the valley cover gasket and the knock sensor oil seals (arrows) upon installation

13.3 Checking camshaft lobe lift with the camshaft installed in the engine - always make sure the dial indicator plunger is directly in-line with the pushrod or lifter

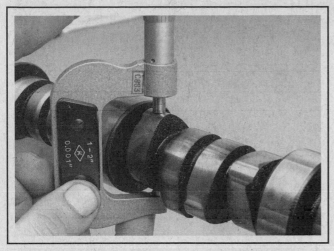

13.9a If the camshaft is removed from the engine, lobe lift can be obtained by measuring camshaft lobe height . . .

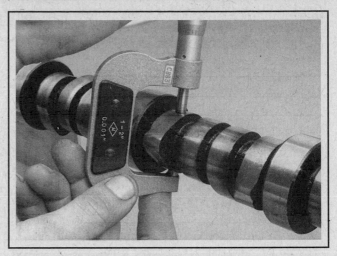

13.9b . . . and by measuring the camshaft base circle - the difference between the two measurements equals lobe lift

10 After the lobe lift check is complete, compare the results to the Specifications listed in Chapter 2A (V6 engine) or 2B (V8 engines). If the lobe lift is 0.002 inch less than specified, cam lobe wear has occurred and a new camshaft should be installed.

Bearing journals, lobes and bearings

▶ **Refer to illustration 13.12**

11 After the camshaft has been removed from the engine, cleaned with solvent and dried, inspect the bearing journals for uneven wear, pitting and evidence of seizure. If the journals are damaged, the bearing inserts in the block are probably damaged as well. Both the camshaft and bearings will have to be replaced.

➡**Note: Camshaft bearing replacement requires special tools and expertise that place it beyond the scope of the average home mechanic. The tools for bearing removal and installation are available at stores that carry automotive tools, possibly even found at a tool rental business. It is advisable though, if the bearings are bad and the procedure is beyond your ability, take the engine block to an automotive machine shop to ensure that the job is done correctly.**

12 Measure the bearing journals with a micrometer to determine if they are excessively worn or out-of-round (see illustration).

13 Check the camshaft lobes for heat discoloration, score marks, chipped areas, pitting and uneven wear. If the lobes are in good condition and if the lobe lift measurements recorded earlier are as specified, the camshaft can be reused.

LIFTERS

▶ **Refer to illustrations 13.14 and 13.15**

14 Clean the lifters with solvent and dry them thoroughly without mixing them up. Check each lifter wall and pushrod seat and for score marks and uneven wear (see illustration). If the lifter walls are damaged or worn (which is not very likely), inspect the lifter bores in the engine block as well. If the pushrod seats are worn, check the pushrod ends.

15 Check the rollers carefully for wear and damage and make sure they turn freely without excessive play (see illustration).

16 Used roller lifters can not be reinstalled with a new camshaft, but the original camshaft can be used if new lifters are installed. Always use new lifters when installing a new camshaft.

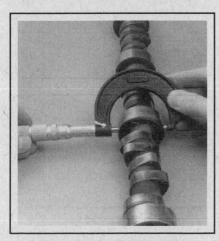

13.12 Check the diameter of each camshaft bearing journal to pinpoint excessive wear and out-of-round conditions

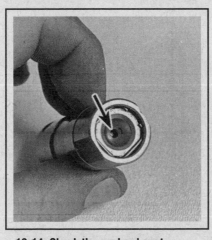

13.14 Check the pushrod seat (arrow) in the top of each lifter for wear

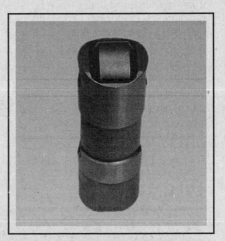

13.15 The roller on hydraulic roller lifters must turn freely - check for wear and excessive play as well

14 Balance shaft and bearings (V6 engines) - removal and inspection

REMOVAL

♦ **Refer to illustrations 14.1 and 14.2**

➡**Note: If the balance shaft is to be removed, the balance shaft gear bolt should be removed before the timing chain is removed, so that the shaft is held while the bolt is loosened.**

1   Remove the two bolts and the balance shaft retainer at the front of the block (see illustration).

2   The balance shaft front bearing fits tightly into the block; use a slide-hammer threaded into the front of the balance shaft to knock it out (see illustration).

14.1 Remove the two Torx bolts and the balance shaft retainer on V6 engines

INSPECTION

3   Inspect the balance shaft and measure the rear bearing journal diameter in the same manner as the camshaft. If the journal diameter doesn't fall within the values listed in this Chapter's Specifications, replace the balance shaft, bearing and bushing as a set. The balance shaft rides in a bearing at the front of the block and a bushing at the rear.

4   The rear bushing is similar to a camshaft bearing, pressed into the rear of the block. It must be installed by a machine shop with the proper tools, to the proper depth and with the oil hole aligned.

5   Inspect the balance shaft drive gear (the one behind the camshaft gear), and the balance shaft driven gear (bolted to the front of the balance shaft) for signs of wear, pitting, broken teeth or rough operation. As with the balance shaft and its bearings, the two balance shaft gears are serviced only as a set.

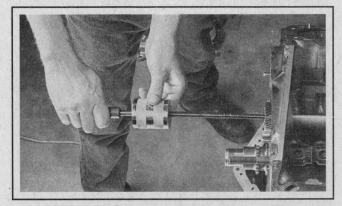

14.2 A small slide-hammer must be threaded into the front of the balance shaft to pull the balance shaft and front bearing out of the block

15 Pistons/connecting rods - removal

♦ **Refer to illustrations 15.1, 15.3, 15.4 and 15.6**

➡**Note: Prior to removing the piston/connecting rod assemblies, remove the cylinder head(s), the oil pan, the oil pump and the crankshaft windage tray if equipped by referring to the appropriate Sections in Chapter 2A or 2B.**

15.1 A ridge reamer is required to remove the ridge from the top of each cylinder - do this before removing the pistons!

1   Use your fingernail to feel if a ridge has formed at the upper limit of ring travel (about 1/4-inch down from the top of each cylinder). If carbon deposits or cylinder wear have produced ridges, they must be completely removed with a special tool (see illustration). Follow the manufacturer's instructions provided with the tool. Failure to remove the ridges before attempting to remove the piston/connecting rod assemblies may result in piston breakage.

2   After the cylinder ridges have been removed, turn the engine upside-down so the crankshaft is facing up.

3   Before the connecting rods are removed, check the endplay with feeler gauges. Slide them between the first connecting rod and the crankshaft throw until the play is removed (see illustration). The endplay is equal to the thickness of the feeler gauge(s). If the endplay exceeds the service limit, new connecting rods will be required. If new rods (or a new crankshaft) are installed, the endplay may fall under the specified minimum (if it does, the rods will have to be machined to restore it - consult an automotive machine shop for advice if necessary). Repeat the procedure for the remaining connecting rods.

4   Check the connecting rods and caps for identification marks (see illustration). If they aren't plainly marked, use a small center punch to make the appropriate number of indentations on each rod and cap (1, 2, 3, etc., depending on the engine type and cylinder they're associated with).

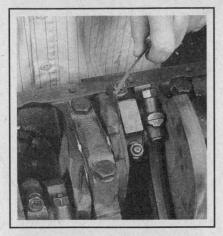

15.3 Check the connecting rod side clearance (endplay) with a feeler gauge as shown here between the rod and the crankshaft journal

15.4 The connecting rods should be marked with the corresponding cylinder number at the parting line of each rod and cap

15.6 To prevent damage to the crankshaft journals and cylinder walls, slip sections of rubber hose over the rod bolts before removing the piston/rod assemblies

5 Loosen each of the connecting rod cap nuts 1/2-turn at a time until they can be removed by hand. Remove the number one connecting rod cap and bearing insert. Don't drop the bearing insert out of the cap.

6 Slip a short length of plastic or rubber hose over each connecting rod cap bolt to protect the crankshaft journal and cylinder wall as the piston is removed (see illustration).

➡Note: On V8 engines the rod bolts are removed with the caps, so it may be helpful to make a set of connecting rod guides. Find several bolts that fit the rods at your local hardware store, or purchase a couple of new rod bolts. Cut the heads of the bolts off with a hacksaw or similar tool and slip a short length of hose over the end of each bolt to make a pair connecting rod guides. Screw the guides into the connecting rods during removal and installation of the piston/connecting rod from the engine block.

7 Remove the bearing insert and push the connecting rod/piston assembly out through the top of the engine. Use a wooden hammer handle to push on the upper bearing surface in the connecting rod (DO NOT tap on the connecting rod bolt). If resistance is felt, double-check to make sure that all of the ridge was removed from the cylinder.

8 Repeat the procedure for the remaining cylinders.

9 After removal, reassemble the connecting rod caps and bearing inserts in their respective connecting rods and install the cap nuts finger tight. Leaving the old bearing inserts in place until reassembly will help prevent the connecting rod bearing surfaces from being accidentally nicked or gouged.

10 Don't separate the pistons from the connecting rods (see Section 20 for additional information).

16 Crankshaft - removal

▶ Refer to illustrations 16.1a, 16.1b, 16.3, 16.4a and 16.4b

➡Note: The crankshaft can be removed only after the engine has been removed from the vehicle. It's assumed that the flywheel or driveplate, vibration damper, timing chain, oil pan, oil pump, windage tray and piston/connecting rod assemblies have already been removed.

1 Before the crankshaft can be withdrawn from the engine, the rear main oil seal retainer must be removed (see illustration) and the crankshaft endplay must be checked. Mount a dial indicator with the stem in line with the crankshaft and touching one of the crank throws or the nose of the crank (see illustration).

16.1a Rear main oil seal retainer mounting bolts - V8 engine shown

16.1b Checking the crankshaft endplay with a dial indicator

2   Push the crankshaft all the way to the rear and zero the dial indicator. Next, pry the crankshaft to the front as far as possible and check the reading on the dial indicator. The distance that it moves is the endplay. If it's greater than specified, check the crankshaft thrust surfaces for wear. If no wear is evident, new main bearings should correct the endplay.

3   If a dial indicator isn't available, feeler gauges can be used. Gently pry or push the crankshaft all the way to the front of the engine. Slip feeler gauges between the crankshaft and the front face of the thrust main bearing to determine the clearance (see illustration).

4   Check the main bearing caps to see if they're marked to indicate their locations. They should be numbered consecutively from the front of the engine to the rear (see illustration). If they aren't, mark them with number-stamping dies or a center punch (see illustration). Main bearing caps often have a cast-in arrow, which points to the front of the engine. If not, mark a paint arrow before removing the main caps. Loosen the main bearing cap bolts 1/4-turn at a time each, until they can be removed by hand. Note if any stud bolts are used and make sure they're returned to their original locations when the crankshaft is reinstalled.

5   Gently tap the caps with a soft-face hammer, then separate them from the engine block. If necessary, use the bolts as levers to remove the caps. Try not to drop the bearing inserts if they come out with the caps.

6   Carefully lift the crankshaft out of the engine. It may be a good idea to have an assistant available, since the crankshaft is quite heavy. With the upper bearing inserts in place in the engine block and the lower bearing inserts in place in the main bearing caps, return the caps to their respective locations on the engine block and tighten the bolts finger tight.

16.3 Checking crankshaft endplay with a feeler gauge

16.4a Main bearing caps are typically marked to indicate their locations (arrows) - they should be numbered consecutively from the front of the engine to the rear

16.4b If the main cap numbers aren't marked or they're not visible, mark the caps with a number stamp or a center punch

17   Engine block - cleaning

▶ **Refer to illustrations 17.1a, 17.1b, 17.4, 17.8 and 17.10**

1   Most engine core plugs are corroded firmly in place on an engine that has been in service for years. Use a small punch at the edge of the plug and carefully drive that edge in with a hammer (see illustration). Drive one edge in only far enough for the opposite side to protrude far enough to grab it with pliers and pull out (see illustration).

✳ CAUTION:

The core plugs (also known as freeze or soft plugs) may be difficult or impossible to retrieve if they're driven completely into the block coolant passages.

2   Using a gasket scraper, remove all traces of gasket material from the engine block. Be very careful not to nick or gouge the gasket sealing surfaces.

3   Remove the main bearing caps and separate the bearing inserts from the caps and the engine block. Tag the bearings, indicating which cylinder they were removed from and whether they were in the cap or the block, then set them aside.

4   Remove all of the threaded oil gallery plugs from the block (see illustration). The plugs are usually very tight - they may have to be drilled out and the holes retapped. Use new plugs when the engine is reassembled.

5   The engine should be taken to an automotive machine shop to be steam cleaned or hot tanked, although with patience it can be

17.1a The core plugs should be removed carefully by tapping in one side . . .

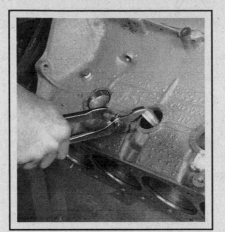

17.1b . . . then pulling out the opposite side with locking pliers

17.4 Removal of all the oil gallery plugs (arrow) will allow a more thorough cleaning of debris from the internal oil passages of the engine block

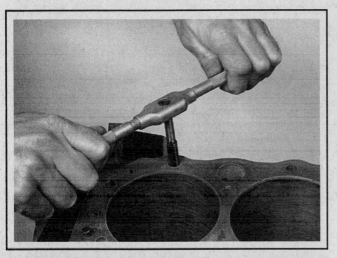

17.8 All bolts in the block, particularly the main bearing cap and head bolt holes, should be cleaned with the proper-sized tap

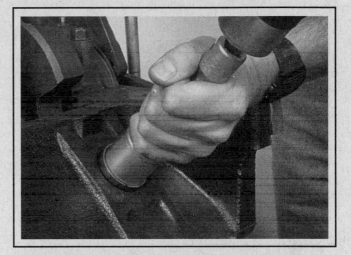

17.10 A large socket on an extension can be used to drive the new core plugs into the block - go slowly and stop when the plug is evenly flush with the block

cleaned at home.

6   After the block is returned, clean all oil holes and oil galleries one more time. Brushes specifically designed for this purpose are available at most auto parts stores. Flush the passages with warm water until the water runs clear, dry the block thoroughly and wipe all machined surfaces with a light, rust-preventive oil. If you have access to compressed air, use it to speed the drying process and to blow out all the oil holes and galleries.

> ⚘ **WARNING:**
>
> **Wear eye protection when using compressed air!**

7   If the block isn't extremely dirty or sludged up, you can do an adequate cleaning job with hot soapy water and a stiff brush. Take plenty of time and do a thorough job. Regardless of the cleaning method used, be sure to clean all oil holes and galleries very thoroughly, dry the block completely and coat all machined surfaces with light oil.

8   The threaded holes in the block must be clean to ensure accurate torque readings during reassembly. Run the proper size tap into each of the holes to remove rust, corrosion, thread sealant or sludge and

restore damaged threads (see illustration). If possible, use compressed air to clear the holes of debris produced by this operation.

> ⚘ **WARNING:**
>
> **Wear eye protection when using compressed air!**

Now is a good time to clean the threads on the head bolts and the main bearing cap bolts as well.

9   Reinstall the main bearing caps and tighten the bolts finger tight.

10   After coating the sealing surfaces of the new core plugs with core plug sealant, install them in the engine block (see illustration). Make sure they're driven in straight and seated properly or leakage could result. Special tools are available for this purpose, but a large socket, with an outside diameter that will just slip into the core plug, a 1/2-inch drive extension and a hammer will work just as well.

11   Apply non-hardening sealant (such as Permatex no. 2 or Teflon pipe sealant) to the new oil gallery plugs and thread them into the holes in the block. Make sure they're tightened securely.

12   If the engine isn't going to be reassembled right away, cover it with a large plastic trash bag to keep it clean.

18 Engine block - inspection

▶ **Refer to illustrations 18.4a, 18.4b and 18.4c**

1 Before the block is inspected, it should be cleaned as described in Section 17.

2 Visually check the block for cracks, rust and corrosion. Look for stripped threads in the threaded holes. It's also a good idea to have the block checked for hidden cracks by an automotive machine shop that has the special equipment to do this type of work. If defects are found, have the block repaired, if possible, or replaced.

3 Check the cylinder bores for scuffing and scoring.

4 Measure the diameter of each cylinder at the top (just under the ridge area), center and bottom of the cylinder bore, parallel to the crankshaft axis (see illustrations).

5 Next, measure each cylinder's diameter at the same three locations across the crankshaft axis. Compare the results to this Chapter's Specifications.

6 If the required precision measuring tools aren't available, the piston-to-cylinder clearances can be obtained, though not quite as accurately, using feeler-gauge stock. Feeler gauge stock comes in 12-inch lengths and various thicknesses and is generally available at auto parts stores.

7 To check the clearance, select a feeler gauge and slip it into the cylinder along with the matching piston. The piston must be positioned exactly as it normally would be. The feeler gauge must be between the piston and cylinder on one of the thrust faces (90-degrees to the piston-pin bore).

8 The piston should slip through the cylinder (with the feeler gauge in place) with moderate pressure.

9 If it falls through or slides through easily, the clearance is excessive and a new piston will be required. If the piston binds at the lower end of the cylinder and is loose toward the top, the cylinder is tapered. If tight spots are encountered as the piston/feeler gauge is rotated in the cylinder, the cylinder is out-of-round.

10 Repeat the procedure for the remaining pistons and cylinders.

11 If the cylinder walls are badly scuffed or scored, or if they're out-of-round or tapered beyond the limits given in the specifications, have the engine block rebored and honed at an automotive machine shop. If a rebore is done, oversize pistons and rings will be required.

12 If the cylinders are in reasonably-good condition and not worn to the outside of the limits, and if the piston-to-cylinder clearances can be maintained properly, then they don't have to be rebored. Honing is all that's necessary (see Section 19).

13 Using a precision straightedge and feeler gauge, check the block deck (the surface that mates with the cylinder head) for distortion and compare the results to this Chapter's Specifications.

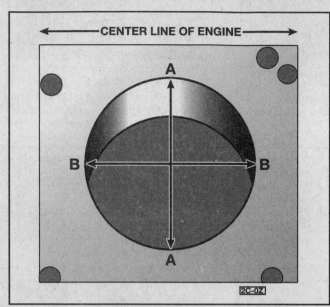

CENTER LINE OF ENGINE

2C-0Z

18.4a Measure the diameter of each cylinder at point A and at point B in three places, just under the wear ridge, at the center of the bore and at the bottom of the bore - out-of-round is the difference in diameter between point A and B at any place in the cylinder - taper is the difference in diameter between the top and the bottom of the cylinder

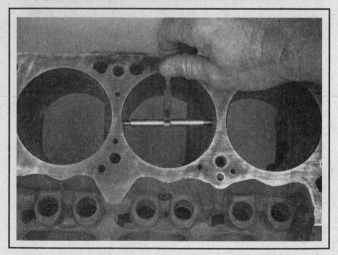

18.4b The ability to "feel" when the telescoping gauge is at the correct point will be developed over time, so work slowly and repeat the check until you're satisfied the bore measurement is accurate

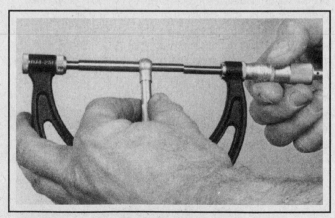

18.4c The gauge is then measured with a micrometer to determine the bore size

19 Cylinder honing

♦ Refer to illustrations 19.3a and 19.3b

1   Prior to engine reassembly, the cylinder bores must be honed so the new piston rings will seat correctly and provide the best possible combustion-chamber seal.

➡Note: If you don't have the tools or don't want to tackle the honing operation, most automotive machine shops will do it for a reasonable fee.

2   Before honing the cylinders, install the main bearing caps and tighten the bolts to the torque listed in this Chapter's Specifications.

3   Two types of cylinder hones are commonly available - the flex hone or "bottle brush" type and the more traditional surfacing hone with spring-loaded stones. Both will do the job, but for the less experienced mechanic the "bottle brush" hone will probably be easier to use. You'll also need some kerosene or honing oil, rags and an electric drill motor. Proceed as follows:

a) *Mount the hone in the drill motor, compress the stones (if applicable) and slip it into the first cylinder (see illustration). Be sure to wear safety goggles or a face shield!*

b) *Lubricate the cylinder with plenty of honing oil or kerosene, turn on the drill and move the hone up-and-down in the cylinder at a pace that will produce a fine crosshatch pattern on the cylinder walls. Ideally, the crosshatch lines should intersect at approximately a 60-degree angle (see illustration). Be sure to use plenty of lubricant and don't take off any more material than is absolutely necessary to produce the desired finish*

➡Note: Piston ring manufacturers may specify a smaller crosshatch angle than the traditional 60-degrees - read and follow any Instructions included with the new rings.

c) *Don't withdraw the hone from the cylinder while it's running. Instead, shut off the drill and continue moving the hone up-and-down in the cylinder until it comes to a complete stop, then compress the stones and withdraw the hone. If you're using a "bottle brush" type hone, stop the drill motor, then turn the chuck in the normal direction of rotation while withdrawing the hone from the cylinder.*

d) *Wipe the oil out of the cylinder and repeat the procedure for the remaining cylinders.*

4   After the honing job is complete, chamfer the top edges of the cylinder bores with a small file so the rings won't catch when the pistons are installed. Be very careful not to nick the cylinder walls with the end of the file.

5   The entire engine block must be washed again very thoroughly with warm, soapy water to remove all traces of the abrasive grit produced during the honing operation.

➡Note: The bores can be considered clean when a lint-free white cloth - dampened with clean engine oil - used to wipe them out doesn't pick up any more honing residue, which will show up as gray areas on the cloth. Be sure to run a brush through all oil holes and galleries and flush them with running water.

19.3a A "bottle brush" hone is the easiest type of hone to use

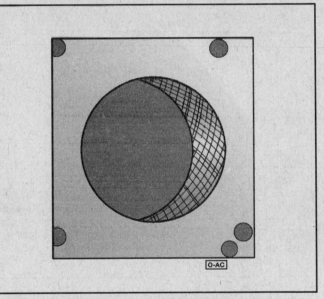

19.3b The cylinder hone should leave a smooth, crosshatch pattern with the lines intersecting at approximately a 60-degree angle

6   After rinsing, dry the block and apply a coat of light rust preventive oil to all machined surfaces. Wrap the block in a plastic trash bag to keep it clean and set it aside until reassembly.

20 Pistons/connecting rods - inspection

▶ **Refer to illustrations 20.4a, 20.4b, 20.10 and 20.11**

1 Before the inspection process can be carried out, the piston/connecting rod assemblies must be cleaned and the original piston rings removed from the pistons.

➡ **Note: Always use new piston rings when the engine is reassembled.**

2 Using a piston ring installation tool, carefully remove the rings from the pistons. Be careful not to nick or gouge the pistons in the process.

3 Scrape all traces of carbon from the top of the piston. A handheld wire brush or a piece of fine emery cloth can be used once the majority of the deposits have been scraped away. Do not, under any circumstances, use a wire brush mounted in a drill motor to remove deposits from the pistons. The piston material is soft and may be eroded away by the wire brush.

4 Use a piston-ring groove cleaning tool to remove carbon deposits from the ring grooves. If a tool isn't available, a piece broken off the old ring will do the job. Be very careful to remove only the carbon

deposits - don't remove any metal and do not nick or scratch the sides of the ring grooves (see illustrations).

5 Once the deposits have been removed, clean the piston/rod assemblies with solvent and dry them with compressed air (if available). Make sure the oil return holes in the back sides of the ring grooves are clear.

6 If the pistons and cylinder walls aren't damaged or worn excessively, and if the engine block is not rebored, new pistons won't be necessary. Normal piston wear appears as even vertical wear on the piston thrust surfaces and slight looseness of the top ring in its groove. New piston rings, however, should always be used when an engine is rebuilt.

7 Carefully inspect each piston for cracks around the skirt, at the pin bosses and at the ring lands.

8 Look for scoring and scuffing on the thrust faces of the skirt, holes in the piston crown and burned areas at the edge of the crown. If the skirt is scored or scuffed, the engine may have been suffering from overheating and/or abnormal combustion, which caused excessively high operating temperatures. Such pistons should be replaced. The cooling and lubrication systems should be checked thoroughly. A hole in the piston crown is an indication that abnormal combustion (preignition) was occurring. Burned areas at the edge of the piston crown are usually evidence of spark knock (detonation). If any of the above problems exist, the causes must be corrected or the damage will occur again. The causes may include intake air leaks, incorrect fuel/air mixture and incorrect ignition timing.

9 Corrosion of the piston, in the form of small pits, indicates that coolant is leaking into the combustion chamber and/or the crankcase. Again, the cause must be corrected or the problem may persist in the rebuilt engine.

10 Measure the piston ring side clearance by laying a new piston ring in each ring groove and slipping a feeler gauge in beside it (see illustration). Check the clearance at three or four locations around each groove. Be sure to use the correct ring for each groove - they are different. If the side clearance is greater than specified, new pistons will have to be used.

11 Check the piston-to-bore clearance by measuring the bore (see Section 18) and the piston diameter. Make sure the pistons and bores are correctly matched. Measure the piston across the skirt, at a 90-degree angle to piston pin and at the specified height (see illustration).

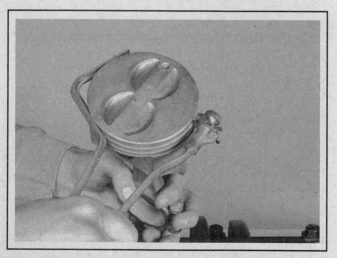

20.4a The piston ring grooves can be cleaned with a special tool, as shown here . . .

20.4b . . . or a section of a broken ring

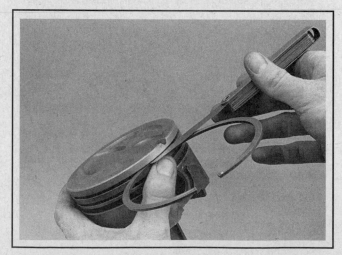

20.10 Check the ring side clearance with a feeler gauge at several points around the groove

Subtract the piston diameter from the bore diameter to obtain the clearance. If it's greater than specified, the block will have to be rebored and new pistons and rings installed.

12 Check the piston-to-rod clearance by twisting the piston and rod in opposite directions. Any noticeable play indicates excessive wear, which must be corrected. The piston/connecting rod assemblies should be taken to an automotive machine shop to have the pistons and rods resized and new pins installed.

13 If the pistons must be removed from the connecting rods for any reason, they should be taken to an automotive machine shop. While they are there, have the connecting rods checked for bend and twist, since automotive machine shops have special equipment for this purpose.

➡Note: Unless new pistons and/or connecting rods must be installed, do not disassemble the pistons and connecting rods.

14 Check the connecting rods for cracks and other damage. Temporarily remove the rod caps, lift out the old bearing inserts, wipe the rod and cap bearing surfaces clean and inspect them for nicks, gouges and scratches. After checking the rods, replace the old bearings, slip the caps into place and tighten the nuts finger tight.

➡Note: If the engine is being rebuilt because of a connecting rod knock, be sure to install new or reconditioned connecting rods.

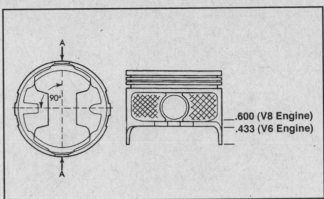

20.11 Measure the piston diameter at a 90-degree angle (A) to the piston pin and at the specified height from the bottom of the skirt

21 Crankshaft - inspection

▶ **Refer to illustrations 21.3, 21.4, 21.6 and 21.8**

1 Check the main and connecting rod bearing journals for uneven wear, scoring, pits and cracks.

2 Rub a penny across each journal several times. If a journal picks up copper from the penny, it's too rough and must be reground.

3 Remove all burrs from the crankshaft oil holes with a stone, file or scraper (see illustration).

4 Clean the crankshaft with solvent and dry it with compressed air (if available). Be sure to clean the oil holes with a stiff brush and flush them with solvent (see illustration).

5 Check the rest of the crankshaft for cracks and other damage. It should be magnafluxed to reveal hidden cracks - an automotive machine shop will handle the procedure. Also on V8 engines, check the crankshaft reluctor ring teeth for obvious damage and be sure to inspect the crankshaft rear oil gallery plug for proper installation and leakage.

6 Using a micrometer, measure the diameter of the main and connecting rod journals and compare the results to the specifications (see illustration). By measuring the diameter at a number of points around each journal's circumference, you'll be able to determine whether or not the journal is out-of-round. Take the measurement at each end of the journal, near the crank throws, to determine if the journal is tapered.

7 If the crankshaft journals are damaged, tapered, out-of-round or worn beyond the limits given in the specifications, have the crankshaft reground by an automotive machine shop. Be sure to use the correct-size bearing inserts if the crankshaft is reconditioned.

8 Check the oil seal journal at rear of the crankshaft for wear and

21.3 The oil holes should be chamfered so sharp edges don't gouge or scratch the new bearings

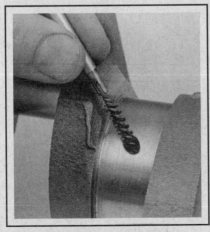

21.4 Use a wire or stiff plastic bristle brush to clean the oil passages in the crankshaft

21.6 Measure the diameter of each crankshaft journal at several points to detect taper and out-of-round conditions

damage (see illustration). If the seal has worn a groove in the journal, or if it's nicked or scratched, the new seal may leak when the engine is reassembled. In some cases, an automotive machine shop may be able to repair the journal by pressing on a thin sleeve. If repair isn't feasible, a new or different crankshaft should be installed.

9   Refer to Section 22 and examine the main and rod bearing inserts.

21.8 If the rear seal has worn a groove in the crankshaft journal, or if the seal contact surfaces are nicked or scratched, the new seal will leak

22 Main and connecting rod bearings - inspection

▶ **Refer to illustration 22.1**

1   Even though the main and connecting rod bearings should be replaced with new ones during the engine overhaul, the old bearings should be retained for close examination, as they may reveal valuable information about the condition of the engine (see illustration).

2   Bearing failure occurs because of lack of lubrication, the presence of dirt or other foreign particles, overloading the engine and corrosion. Regardless of the cause of bearing failure, it must be corrected before the engine is reassembled to prevent it from happening again.

3   When examining the bearings, remove them from the engine block, the main bearing caps, the connecting rods and the rod caps and lay them out on a clean surface in the same general position as their location in the engine. This will enable you to match any bearing problems with the corresponding crankshaft journal.

4   Dirt and other foreign particles get into the engine in a variety of ways. It may be left in the engine during assembly, or it may pass through filters or the PCV system. It may get into the oil, and from there into the bearings. Metal chips from machining operations and normal engine wear are often present. Abrasives are sometimes left in engine components after reconditioning, especially when parts are not thoroughly cleaned using the proper cleaning methods. Whatever the source, these foreign objects often end up embedded in the soft bearing material and are easily recognized. Large particles will not embed in the bearing and will score or gouge the bearing and journal. The best prevention for this cause of bearing failure is to clean all parts thoroughly and keep everything spotlessly clean during engine assembly. Frequent and regular engine oil and filter changes are also recommended.

5   Lack of lubrication (or lubrication breakdown) has a number of

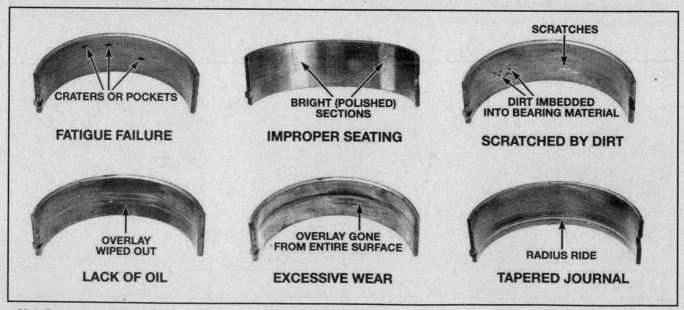

22.1 Typical bearing failures

interrelated causes. Excessive heat (which thins the oil), overloading (which squeezes the oil from the bearing face) and oil leakage or throw off (from excessive bearing clearances, worn oil pump or high engine speeds) all contribute to lubrication breakdown. Blocked oil passages, which usually are the result of misaligned oil holes in a bearing shell, will also oil starve a bearing and destroy it. When lack of lubrication is the cause of bearing failure, the bearing material is wiped or extruded from the steel backing of the bearing. Temperatures may increase to the point where the steel backing turns blue from overheating.

6   Driving habits can have a definite effect on bearing life. Low speed operation in too high a gear (lugging the engine) puts very high loads on bearings, which tends to squeeze out the oil film. These loads cause the bearings to flex, which produces fine cracks in the bearing face (fatigue failure). Eventually the bearing material will loosen in pieces and tear away from the steel backing. Short-trip driving leads to corrosion of bearings because insufficient engine heat is produced to drive off the condensed water and corrosive gases. These products collect in the engine oil, forming acid and sludge. As the oil is carried to the engine bearings, the acid attacks and corrodes the bearing material.

7   Incorrect bearing installation during engine assembly will lead to bearing failure as well. Tight-fitting bearings leave insufficient bearing oil clearance and will result in oil starvation. Dirt or foreign particles trapped behind a bearing insert result in high spots on the bearing which lead to failure.

23   Engine overhaul - reassembly sequence

1   Before beginning engine reassembly, make sure you have all the necessary new parts, gaskets and seals as well as the following items on hand:

Common hand tools
3/8-inch and 1/2-inch-drive torque wrenches
Piston ring installation tool
Piston ring compressor
Crankshaft balancer installation tool
Short lengths of rubber or plastic hose to fit over connecting rod bolts
Plastigage
Feeler gauges
A fine-tooth file
New engine oil
Engine assembly lube or moly-base grease
Gasket sealant
Thread locking compound

2   In order to save time and avoid problems, engine reassembly must be done in the following general order:

New camshaft bearings (must be done by automotive machine shop)
Piston rings
Crankshaft and main bearings
Piston/connecting rod assemblies
Camshaft and lifters
Balance shaft and gears (V6 engines)
Timing chain and sprockets
Windage tray (if equipped)
Oil pump and pick up tube
Front timing chain cover
Engine valley cover (V8 engines)
Cylinder head(s), pushrods and rocker arms
Rear main oil seal and retainer
Oil pan
Intake and exhaust manifolds
Rocker arm cover(s)
Flywheel/driveplate

24   Piston rings - installation

▶ **Refer to illustrations 24.3, 24.4, 24.5, 24.9a, 24.9b and 24.12**

1   Before installing the new piston rings, the ring end gaps must be checked. It's assumed that the piston ring side clearance has been checked and verified correct (see Section 20).

2   Lay out the piston/connecting rod assemblies and the new ring sets so the ring sets will be matched with the same piston and cylinder during the end gap measurement and engine assembly.

3   Insert the top (number one) ring into the first cylinder and square it up with the cylinder walls by pushing it in with the top of the piston (see illustration). The ring should be near the bottom of the cylinder, at the lower limit of ring travel.

24.3   When checking piston ring end gap, the ring must be square in the cylinder bore - use a piston to push it down approximately two inches from the bottom of the bore

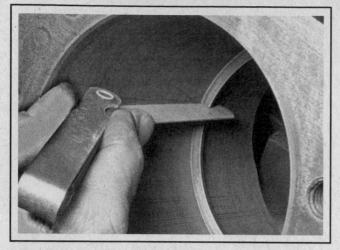

24.4 With the ring square in the cylinder, measure the end gap with feeler gauges

24.5 If the end gap is too small, clamp a fine file in a vise and file ring ends a little at a time and re-measure in the bore - file from the outside of the ring inward only

4   To measure the end gap, slip feeler gauges between the ends of the ring until a gauge equal to the gap width is found (see illustration). The feeler gauge should slide between the ring ends with a slight amount of drag. Compare the measurement to the Specifications. If the gap is larger or smaller than specified, double-check to make sure you have the correct rings before proceeding.

5   If the gap is too small, it must be enlarged or the ring ends may come in contact with each other during engine operation, which can cause serious damage to the engine. The end gap can be increased by filing the ring ends very carefully with a fine file. Mount the file in a vise equipped with soft jaws, slip the ring over the file with the ends contacting the file face and slowly move the ring to remove material from the ends. When performing this operation, file only from the outside in (see illustration). The ring ends must be filed squarely, and any tiny burrs on the end should be removed before final ring installation.

6   Excess end gap isn't critical unless it's greater than 0.040-inch. Again, double-check to make sure you have the correct rings for your engine.

7   Repeat the procedure for each ring that will be installed in the first cylinder and for each ring in the remaining cylinders. Remember to keep rings, pistons and cylinders matched up.

8   Once the ring end gaps have been checked/corrected, the rings can be installed on the pistons.

9   The oil control ring (lowest one on the piston) is usually installed first. It's normally composed of three separate components. Slip the spacer/expander into the groove (see illustration). If an anti-rotation tang is used, make sure it's inserted into the drilled hole in the ring groove. Next, install the lower side rail. Don't use a piston ring installation tool on the oil ring side rails, as they may be damaged. Instead, place one end of the side rail into the groove between the spacer/expander and the ring land, hold it firmly in place and slide a finger around the piston while pushing the rail into the groove (see illustration). Next, install the upper side rail in the same manner.

10 After the three oil ring components have been installed, check to make sure that both the upper and lower side rails can be turned smoothly in the ring groove and that the expander ends are butted together.

11 The number two (middle) ring is installed next. It's usually stamped with a mark which must face up, toward the top of the piston.

✽✽ CAUTION:

Always follow the instructions printed on the ring package or box - different manufacturers may require different approaches. Do not mix up the top and middle rings, as they have different cross sections.

12 Use a piston ring installation tool and make sure the identifica-

24.9a Installing the spacer/expander in the oil control ring groove

24.9b Slip the oil ring side rails in by hand - do not use a ring expander

24.12 Install the compression rings using a ring-expander tool like this one - note that the mark (arrow) on the ring should face UP

tion mark is facing the top of the piston, then slip the ring into the middle groove on the piston (see illustration). Don't expand the ring any more than necessary to slide it over the piston.

13 Install the number one (top) ring in the same manner. Making

sure that the dot or mark (if equipped) is facing up. Be careful not to confuse the number one and number two rings. Always check the instructions with the ring set your are using.

14 Repeat the procedure for the remaining pistons and rings.

25 Crankshaft - installation and main bearing oil clearance check

1 Crankshaft installation is the first major step in engine reassembly. It's assumed at this point that the engine block and crankshaft have been cleaned, inspected and repaired or reconditioned.

2 Position the engine with the bottom facing up.

3 Remove the main bearing cap bolts and lift out the caps. Lay the caps out in the proper order to ensure correct installation.

4 If they're still in place, remove the old bearing inserts from the block and the main bearing caps. Wipe the main bearing surfaces of the block and caps with a clean, lint free cloth. They must be kept spotlessly clean!

MAIN BEARING OIL CLEARANCE CHECK

▶ **Refer to illustrations 25.9, 25.11 and 25.13**

5 Clean the back sides of the new main bearing inserts and lay the bearing half with the oil groove in each main bearing saddle in the block. Lay the other bearing half from each bearing set in the corresponding main bearing cap. Make sure the tab on each bearing insert fits into the recess in the block or cap. Also, the oil holes in the block must line up with the oil holes in the bearing insert.

❋❋ CAUTION:

Do not hammer the bearings into place and don't nick or gouge the bearing faces. No lubrication should be used at this time.

6 Clean the faces of the bearings in the block and the crankshaft main bearing journals with a clean, lint-free cloth. Check or clean the oil holes in the crankshaft, as any dirt here can go only one way

- straight through the new bearings.

7 Once you're certain the crankshaft is clean, carefully lay it in position in the main bearings.

8 Before the crankshaft can be permanently installed, the main bearing oil clearance must be checked.

9 Trim several pieces of the appropriate-size Plastigage (they must be slightly shorter than the width of the main bearings) and place one piece on each crankshaft main bearing journal, parallel with the journal axis (see illustration).

10 Clean the faces of the bearings in the caps and install the caps in their respective positions (don't mix them up) with the arrows pointing toward the front of the engine. Don't disturb the Plastigage. Apply a light coat of oil to the bolt threads and the under sides of the bolt heads, then install them.

11 On V6 engines, tighten the main bearing cap bolts, starting in the center and working towards the ends, in two steps, to the torque listed in this Chapter's Specifications. Don't rotate the crankshaft at any time during this operation!

➡**Note: On V8 engines, the main bearing tightening procedure requires five steps. First tighten the inner bolts (bolts 1 through 10) in two steps to the torque and angle of rotation listed in this Chapter's Specifications, then tighten the outer bolts (bolts 11 through 20) in two steps to the torque and angle of rotation listed in this Chapter's Specifications (see illustration). The fifth step is tightening the side bolts, but DO NOT use the new side bolts during the oil clearance check as this will damage the O-ring on the new side bolts.**

12 Remove the bolts and carefully lift off the main bearing caps. Keep them in order. Don't disturb the Plastigage or rotate the crankshaft. If any of the main bearing caps are difficult to remove, tap them gently from side-to-side with a soft-face hammer to loosen them.

25.9 Lay the Plastigage strips (arrow) on the main bearing journals, parallel to the crankshaft centerline

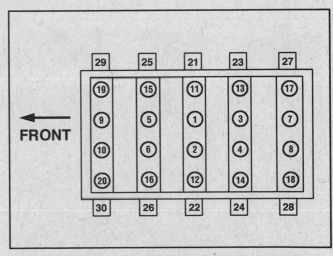

25.11 Main bearing cap TIGHTENING sequence - V8 engines

25.13 Compare the width of the crushed Plastigage to the scale on the envelope, taking the measurement at the widest point of the Plastigage

13 Compare the width of the crushed Plastigage on each journal to the scale printed on the Plastigage envelope to obtain the main bearing oil clearance (see illustration). Check the Specifications to make sure it's correct.

➡**Note: Make sure you are using the correct scale, both metric and standard ones are included in the package.**

14 If the clearance is not as specified, the bearing inserts may be the wrong size (which means different ones will be required). Before deciding that different inserts are needed, make sure that no dirt or oil was between the bearing inserts and the caps or block when the clearance was measured. If the Plastigage is noticeably wider at one end than the other, the journal may be tapered.

15 Carefully scrape all traces of the Plastigage material off the main bearing journals and/or the bearing faces. Don't nick or scratch the bearing faces (a plastic credit card edge does the job).

FINAL CRANKSHAFT INSTALLATION

16 Carefully lift the crankshaft out of the engine. Clean the bearing faces in the block, then apply a thin, uniform layer of engine assembly lube to each of the bearing surfaces.

17 Make sure the crankshaft journals are clean, then lay the crankshaft back in place in the block. Clean the faces of the bearings in the caps, then apply lubricant to them. Install all the caps in their respective positions.

18 Apply a light coat of oil to the bolt threads and the under sides of the bolt heads, then install them finger tight.

19 Pry the crankshaft slightly back and forth in the block to seat the thrust bearings. Tighten all main bearing cap bolts as described in Step 11 to specifications. On V8 engines, install new main bearing cap side bolts and tighten the bolts to the torque listed in this Chapter's Specifications. Be sure to tighten both side bolts on a main bearing cap before proceeding to the next cap and always install new side bolts or oil leaks may develop.

20 Check the crankshaft endplay with a feeler gauge or a dial indicator as described in Section 16. The endplay should be correct if the crankshaft thrust faces aren't worn or damaged and new bearings have been installed.

21 On manual transmission models, install a new pilot bearing in the end of the crankshaft (see Chapter 8).

22 Rotate the crankshaft a number of times by hand to check for any obvious binding.

26 Balance shaft (V6 engines) - installation

▶ **Refer to illustrations 26.2 and 26.6**

➡**Note: The balance shaft is installed after the camshaft. Refer to the camshaft installation procedures in Part B of this Chapter.**

1 Lubricate the balance shaft bearing journals with clean engine oil or engine assembly lube.

2 Slide the balance shaft into the engine. Support the balance shaft near the block and be careful not to scrape or nick the rear bearing.

Using a bearing driver or large socket, gently drive the shaft into the block until the front bearing is seated (see illustration).

3 Install the balance shaft retainer and two bolts and tighten them to the torque listed in this Chapter's Specifications (see illustration 14.1).

4 Install the balance shaft driven gear and tighten the bolt to the torque listed in Chapter Specifications.

26.2 Drive the balance shaft and front bearing into the block until the bearing retainer can be bolted in place

26.6 Position the balance shaft drive and driven gears with the timing marks aligned as shown

5   Rotate the camshaft so that, with the balance shaft drive gear temporarily installed, the timing mark is straight up at the 12 o'clock position. Remove the drive gear.

6   Rotate the balance shaft until the timing mark on the driven gear is facing straight down at the 6 o'clock position. Reinstall the balance shaft drive gear to the camshaft and make sure both balance shaft gears are aligned (see illustration).

7   Install the timing chain, sprockets and cover (see Part A of this Chapter).

27 Rear main oil seal and housing - installation

▶ **Refer to illustrations 27.7 and 27.9**

1   All engines covered by this manual are equipped with a one-piece rear main seal and a seal housing that bolts to the rear of the engine block. Although the rear main seal housings on V6 and V8 engines differ in appearance, seal installation is essentially the same with the exception of installing the seal housing onto the engine block. V6 engines use alignment dowels on the rear of the block to automatically center the seal housing over the end of the crankshaft. V8 engines are not equipped with alignment dowels on the rear of the block and therefore must be aligned manually prior to tightening of the rear seal housing.

2   The crankshaft must be installed first and the main bearing caps bolted in place, then the new seal should be installed in the housing and the housing bolted to the block .

3   Before installing the crankshaft, check the seal contact surface very carefully for scratches and nicks that could damage the new seal lip and cause oil leaks. If the crankshaft is damaged, the only alternative is a new or different crankshaft.

4   The old seal can be removed from the housing by inserting a large screwdriver into the three notches provided and prying it out (see Chapter 2A or 2B).

5   Be sure to note how far it's recessed into the housing bore before removing it; the new seal will have to be recessed an equal amount. Be very careful not to scratch or otherwise damage the bore in the housing or oil leaks could develop.

6   Make sure the housing is clean, then apply a thin coat of engine oil to the outer edge of the new seal. The seal must be pressed squarely into the housing bore, so hammering it into place is not recommended. If you don't have access to a press, sandwich the housing and seal between two smooth pieces of wood and press the seal into place with the jaws of a large vise. The pieces of wood must be thick enough to distribute the force evenly around the entire circumference of the seal. Work slowly and make sure the seal enters the bore squarely.

7   On V6 engines, make sure the dowel pins are in place before installing the housing. Lubricate the seal lips with small amount of clean engine oil and slide the rear seal/housing over the rear of the crankshaft (see illustration). Be sure to use a new gasket between the rear seal housing to the engine block - no sealant is required.

V6 ENGINE

8   Tighten the bolts a little at a time until the seal housing is fully seated against the engine block, then tighten them to the torque listed in this Chapter's Specifications.

V8 ENGINES

9   Install the rear seal housing retaining bolts on the engine loosely and align the rear housing as follows:

a) *Place a straightedge on the engine block oil pan rail. Measure the distance on each side of the block from the oil pan rail to the rear housing with a feeler gauge (see illustration). This Step measures the difference between the sealing surface of the oil pan and the sealing surface of the rear seal housing in relationship to each other.*

b) *Tilt the rear seal housing as necessary to achieve an even measurement on each side. This Step properly aligns the rear seal housing to oil pan sealing surfaces. Typically 0.000 to 0.020 inch is an acceptable tolerance.*

27.7 On these engines it will be necessary to install the new seal in the housing first, then install a new gasket and the seal housing on the block - be sure to lubricate the seal lip and carefully work the seal over the crankshaft with blunt tool

27.9 With the rear seal housing in place and the bolts installed LOOSELY, measure the distance between the oil pan rail and the seal housing on each side (arrows) - then adjust the housing so the measurements are even on both sides before tightening the cover bolts

→Note: Ideally the rear seal housing should be flush with the oil pan rail, but because of the differences in seal thickness, this may not always be obtainable. That is why there is a tolerance of 0.000 to 0.020 inch. Always let the rear seal center itself around the crankshaft and tilt the cover from side-to-side to even up the measurement at both oil pan rails. Never push downward on the rear seal housing in an attempt to make the oil pan sealing surface flush, as this will distort the rear oil seal and eventually lead to an oil leak!

c) With the rear seal housing properly aligned, tighten the housing bolts to the torque listed in this Chapter's Specifications.

28 Pistons/connecting rods - installation and rod bearing oil clearance check

▶ Refer to illustrations 28.1a, 28.1b, 28.3, 28.5, 28.9, 28.11, 28.13, 28.15 and 28.17

1 Before installing the piston/connecting rod assemblies, the cylinder walls must be perfectly clean, the top edge of each cylinder must be chamfered, and the crankshaft must be in place. If new pistons or connecting rods were installed, check the orientation of the connecting rod to the piston for correct installation by the machine shop. On V6 engines, the left bank connecting rod flanges must face the front of the engine and the right bank connecting rod flanges must face the rear of the engine, with the mark on the top of the pistons facing the front of the engine (see illustration). You should have three pistons with the connecting rod flanges and the mark on the pistons aligned on the same side (these are the left bank pistons) and three pistons with the connecting rod flanges opposite the mark on the pistons (these are the right bank pistons). On V8 engines, the flat side of the connecting rods and the marks on the top of each piston must all face the front of the engine (see illustration). So, the pistons and connecting rod assemblies can be installed in either the right or left bank if new rods were installed.

2 Remove the cap from the end of the number one connecting rod (refer to the marks made during removal). Remove the original bearing inserts and wipe the bearing surfaces of the connecting rod and cap with a clean, lint-free cloth. They must be kept spotlessly clean.

CONNECTING ROD BEARING OIL CLEARANCE CHECK

3 Clean the back side of the new upper bearing insert, then lay it in place in the connecting rod. Make sure the tab on the bearing fits into the recess in the rod (see illustration). Don't hammer the bearing insert into place and be very careful not to nick or gouge the bearing face. Don't lubricate the bearing at this time.

4 Clean the back side of the other bearing insert and install it in the rod cap. Again, make sure the tab on the bearing fits into the recess in the cap, and don't apply any lubricant. It's critically important that the mating surfaces of the bearing and connecting rod are perfectly clean and oil free when they're assembled.

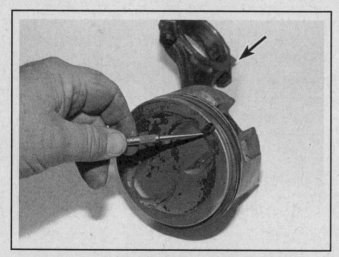

28.1a On V6 engines, the flanges on the rod (arrow) must be positioned correctly with the notch on the piston to have proper oiling of the cylinder walls - left bank piston shown, right bank pistons are opposite

28.1b On V8 engines, the flat side of the rods (arrow) and the notch in the top of the piston must face the front of the engine

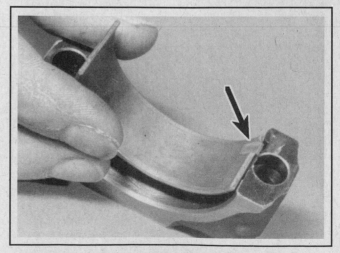

28.3 Make sure the bearing tang fits securely into the notch on the rod cap

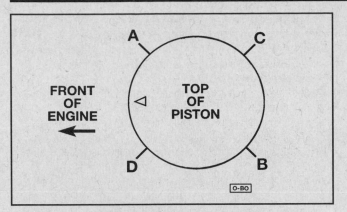

28.5 Position the piston ring gaps as shown here before installing the piston/connecting rod assembly into the engine

A   Top compression ring gap
B   Second compression ring and oil ring spacer gap
C   Upper oil ring rail gap
D   Lower oil ring rail gap

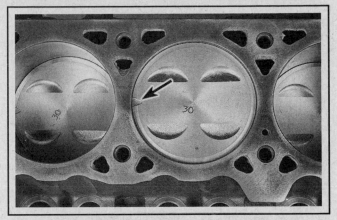

28.9 The notch (arrow) on the pistons must face forward

5   Position the piston ring gaps at intervals around the piston (see illustration).

6   Slip a section of plastic or rubber hose over each connecting rod cap bolt. On V8 engines install the connecting rod guides that were fabricated previously.

7   Lubricate the piston and rings with clean engine oil and attach a piston ring compressor to the piston. Leave the skirt protruding about 1/4-inch to guide the piston into the cylinder. The rings must be compressed until they're flush with the piston.

8   Rotate the crankshaft until the number one connecting rod journal is at BDC (bottom dead center) and apply a coat of engine oil to the cylinder walls.

9   With the arrow or notch on top of the piston (see illustration) facing the front of the engine, gently insert the piston/connecting rod assembly into the number one cylinder bore and rest the bottom edge of the ring compressor on the engine block.

10 Tap the top edge of the ring compressor to make sure it's contacting the block around its entire circumference.

11 Gently tap on the top of the piston with the end of a wooden or plastic hammer handle (see illustration) while guiding the end of the connecting rod into place on the crankshaft journal. The piston rings

may try to pop out of the ring compressor just before entering the cylinder bore, so keep some downward pressure on the ring compressor. Work slowly, and if any resistance is felt as the piston enters the cylinder, stop immediately. Find out what's hanging up and fix it before proceeding. Do not, for any reason, force the piston into the cylinder - you might break a ring and/or the piston.

12 Once the piston/connecting rod assembly is installed, the connecting rod bearing oil clearance must be checked before the rod cap is permanently bolted in place.

13 Cut a piece of the appropriate size Plastigage slightly shorter than the width of the connecting rod bearing and lay it in place on the number one connecting rod journal, parallel with the journal axis (see illustration).

14 Clean the connecting rod cap bearing face, remove the protective hoses from the connecting rod bolts and install the rod cap. Make sure the mating mark on the cap is on the same side as the mark on the connecting rod.

15 Install the nuts or bolts and tighten them in two steps, to the torque and angle of rotation listed in this Chapter's Specifications (see illustration).

➤**Note: Use a thin-wall socket to avoid erroneous torque readings that can result if the socket is wedged between the rod cap and nut. If the socket tends to wedge itself between the nut and the cap, lift up on it slightly until it no longer contacts the cap. Do not rotate the crankshaft at any time during this operation.**

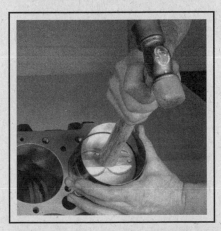

28.11 Drive the piston in gently with the end of a wooden hammer handle - go evenly and stop if you feel an obstruction

28.13 Lay the Plastigage strips on each rod bearing journal, parallel to the crankshaft centerline

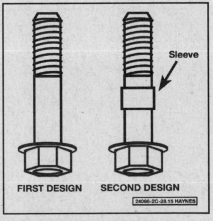

28.15 Connecting rod bolt design features

28.17 Measure the width of the crushed Plastigage to determine the rod bearing oil clearance and compare it to the Specifications

16 Remove the nuts or bolts and detach the rod cap, being very careful not to disturb the Plastigage.

17 Compare the width of the crushed Plastigage to the scale printed on the Plastigage envelope to obtain the oil clearance (see illustration). Compare it to the Specifications to make sure the clearance is correct.

18 If the clearance is not as specified, the bearing inserts may be the wrong size (which means different ones will be required). Before deciding that different inserts are needed, make sure that no dirt or oil was between the bearing inserts and the connecting rod or cap when the clearance was measured. Also, recheck the journal diameter. If the Plastigage was wider at one end than the other, the journal may be tapered, in which case the crankshaft needs to be machined.

FINAL CONNECTING ROD INSTALLATION

19 Carefully scrape all traces of the Plastigage material off the rod journal and/or bearing face. Be very careful not to scratch the bearing - use your fingernail or the edge of a credit card.

20 Make sure the bearing faces are perfectly clean, then apply a uniform layer of clean moly-base grease or engine assembly lube to both of them. You'll have to push the piston into the cylinder to expose the face of the bearing insert in the connecting rod - be sure to slip the protective hoses over the rod bolts first.

21 Slide the connecting rod back into place on the journal, remove the protective hoses from the rod cap bolts or the connecting rod guides, install the rod cap and tighten the nuts or bolts in two steps, to the torque and angle of rotation listed in this Chapter's Specifications.

22 Repeat the entire procedure for the remaining pistons/connecting rods.

23 The important points to remember are:

a) *Keep the back sides of the bearing inserts and the insides of the connecting rods and caps perfectly clean when assembling them.*
b) *Make sure you have the correct piston/rod assembly for each cylinder.*
c) *The notch or mark on the piston must face the front of the engine.*
d) *Stagger the ring end gaps (see illustration 28.5).*
e) *Lubricate the cylinder walls with clean oil.*
f) *Lubricate the bearing faces when installing the rod caps after the oil clearance has been checked.*

24 After all the piston/connecting rod assemblies have been properly installed, rotate the crankshaft a number of times by hand to check for any obvious binding.

25 As a final step, the connecting rod side clearance must be checked. Refer to Section-15 for this procedure.

26 Compare the measured side clearance to the Specifications to make sure it's correct. If it was correct before disassembly and the original crankshaft and rods were reinstalled, it should still be right. If new rods or a new crankshaft were installed, the side clearance may be inadequate. If so, the rods will have to be removed and taken to an automotive machine shop for resizing.

27 The remainder of the engine assembly work is in attaching the cylinder heads, valvetrain, front cover, water pump, flywheel, intake and exhaust manifolds and accessories, all of which are covered in Chapter-2A or 2B.

29 Initial start-up and break-in after overhaul

✳✳ WARNING:

Have a fire extinguisher handy when starting the engine for the first time.

1   Once the engine has been installed in the vehicle, double-check the engine oil and coolant levels.

2   With the spark plugs out of the engine and the ignition and fuel systems disabled (see Section 3), crank the engine until oil pressure registers on the gauge or the light goes out.

3   Install the spark plugs, connect the plug wires and restore the ignition and fuel system functions.

4   Start the engine. It may take a few moments for the fuel system to build up pressure, but the engine should start without a great deal of effort.

➡**Note: If backfiring occurs through the throttle body, recheck the valve timing and, on V6 engines, the distributor installation.**

5   After the engine starts, it should be allowed to warm up to normal operating temperature. Do not allow the engine to exceed a fast idle until the hydraulic lifters pump up and become quiet again (usually about five minutes).

6   While the engine is warming up, make a thorough check for fuel, oil and coolant leaks. If a new camshaft and lifters have been installed during the overhaul, the engine should run at a fast idle for 15 minutes after the lifters pump up and become quiet (keep an eye on the temperature gauge and don't allow the engine to overheat) to "break in" the cam and lifters.

7   Shut the engine off and recheck the engine oil and coolant levels.

8   Drive the vehicle to an area with minimum traffic, accelerate from 30 to 50 mph, then allow the vehicle to slow to 30 mph with the throttle closed. Repeat the procedure 10 or 12 times. This will load the piston rings and cause them to seat properly against the cylinder walls. Check again for oil and coolant leaks.

9   Drive the vehicle gently for the first 500 miles (no sustained high speeds) and keep a constant check on the oil level. It is not unusual for an engine to use oil during the break-in period.

10 At approximately 500 to 600 miles, change the oil and filter.

11 For the next few hundred miles, drive the vehicle normally. Do not pamper it or abuse it.

12 After 2000 miles, change the oil and filter again and consider the engine broken in.

V6 and V8 engines

General

Displacement

4.3L V6	262 cubic inches
4.8L V8	293 cubic inches
5.3L V8	325 cubic inches
6.0L V8	364 cubic inches

Cylinder compression pressure

Minimum	100 psi
Maximum variation between cylinders	25 percent from highest reading

Oil pressure (minimum)

1000 rpm	6 psi
2000 rpm	18 psi
4000 rpm	24 psi

Engine block

Bore diameter

4.3L V6	4.007 to 4.0017 inches
4.8L V8	3.779 to 3.780 inches
5.3L V8	3.779 to 3.780 inches
6.0L V8	4.0007 to 4.0014 inches
Taper (maximum)	0.001 inch
Out-of-round (maximum)	0.002 inch
Deck (head gasket surface) warpage limit	0.003 inch per 6 inches

Lifter bore diameter

V6 engine	not available
V8 engines	0.843 to 0.844 inch

Cylinder head and valves

Head warpage limit	0.003 inch per 6 inches

Valve margin (minimum)

V6 engine	0.031 inch
V8 engines	0.050 inch
Valve face angle (intake and exhaust)	45-degrees
Valve seat angle (intake and exhaust)	46-degrees

Valve seat width

V6 engine

Intake	0.035 to 0.060 inch
Exhaust	0.065 to 0.098 inch

V8 engines

Intake	0.040 to 0.060 inch
Exhaust	0.070 to 0.080 inch

Valve stem-to-guide clearance service limit

V6 engine	0.0037 inch

V8 engine

Intake	0.0037 inch

Exhaust

1999 and 2000	0.0041 inch
2001 and later	0.0037 inch

Valve spring free length

V6 engine	2.02 inches
V8 engines	2.08 inches

Cylinder head and valves (continued)

Valve spring installed height
  V6 engine   1.670 to 1.700 inches
  V6 engines   1.8 inches

Camshaft

Journal diameters
  V6 engine   1.8677 to 1.8696 inches
  V8 engines   2.164 to 2.166 inches
Journal taper and out-of-round (maximum,
  all engines)   0.001 inch
Lobe lift
  V6 engines
    1999 through 2004 models
      Intake   0.274 to 0.278 inch
      Exhaust   0.283 to 0.287 inch
    2005 and later models
      Intake   0.270 inch
      Exhaust   0.279 inch
  V8 engines
    1999 and 2000
      Intake   0.268 inch
      Exhaust   0.274 inch
    2001
      Intake   0.274 inch
      Exhaust   0.281 inch
    2002 and later models
      4.8L and 5.3L engines
        Intake   0.268 inch
        Exhaust   0.274 inch
      6.0L engines
        Intake   0.274 inch
        Exhaust   0.281 inch
Runout
  V6 engines
    1999 through 2004 models   0.0026 inch
    2005 and later models   0.0039 inch
  V8 engines   0.0020 inch
Endplay
  V6 engine   0.001 to 0.009 inch
  V8 engines   0.001 to 0.012 inch

Crankshaft and connecting rods

Rod journal diameter
  V6 engine   2.2487 to 2.2497 inches
  V8 engines   2.0990 to 2.100 inches
Rod journal taper (maximum)
  V6 engine   0.001 inch
  V8 engines   0.0008 inch
Rod journal out-of-round (maximum)
  V6 engine   0.001 inch
  V8 engines   0.0004 inch
Rod bearing oil clearance
  Desired
    V6 engine   0.0015 to 0.0031 inch
    V8 engines   0.0009 to 0.0025 inch

Allowable
    V6 engine   0.0010 to 0.0031 inch
    V8 engines   0.0009 to 0.003 inch
Connecting rod side clearance (endplay)
    V6 engine   0.006 to 0.017 inch
    V8 engines   0.00043 to 0.020 inch
Main bearing journal diameter
    V6 engine
        Journal number 1   2.4488 to 2.4495 inches
        Journal numbers 2 and 3   2.4485 to 2.4494 inches
        Journal number 4   2.4480 to 2.4489 inches
    V8 engines   2.558 to 2.559 inches
Main bearing journal taper (maximum)
    V6 engine   0.0003 inch
    V8 engines   0.0008 inch
Main bearing journal out-of-round (maximum)
    V6 engine   0.0010 inch
    V8 engines   0.0003 inch
Main bearing oil clearance
    V6 engine
        Journal 1   0.0008 to 0.0020 inch
        Journals 2, 3 and 4   0.0011 to 0.0023 inch
    V8 engines   0.0008 to 0.0021 inch
Crankshaft endplay
    V6 engine   0.002 to 0.008 inch
    V8 engines   0.0015 to 0.0078 inch

Pistons and rings

Piston-to-bore clearance
    V6 engine
        Production
            1999 to 2005   0.0007 to 0.0024 inch
            2006 and later   0.0005 to 0.0009 inch
        Service limit
            1999 to 2005   0.0029 inch
            2006 and later   0.0010 inch
    V8 engines
        2006 and later
            4.8L and 5.3L engines   -0.0014 to +0.0006 inch
            6.0L engines   -0.0009 to +0.0012 inch
        Service limit
            1999 through 2001   0.0028 inch
            2002
                4.8L, 5.3L, 6.0L LQ4 engines   0.0032 inch
                6.0L LQ9 engine   0.0031 inch
            2003 through 2005   0.0028 inch
            2006 through 2007
                4.8L, 5.3L, 6.0L LQ4 engines   0.0028 inch
                6.0L LQ9 engine   0.0031 inch
Piston ring end gap
    V6 engines
        Top compression ring
            Production   0.010 to 0.016 inch
            Service limit
               1999 through 2001   0.019 inch
               2002 and later   0.020 inch

V6 engines (continued)
    Second compression ring
        Production
            1999 through 2001 .... 0.018 to 0.026 inch
            2002 and later .... 0.015 to 0.023 inch
        Service limit .... 0.031 inch
    Oil ring
        Production .... 0.010 to 0.029 inch
        Service limit .... 0.035 inch
V8 engines
    Top compression ring
        Production
            1999 through 2002
                4.8L and 5.3L engines .... 0.010 to 0.016 inch
                6.0L engines .... 0.012 to 0.020 inch
            2003 and later
                4.8L and 5.3L engines .... 0.009 to 0.017 inch
                6.0L engines .... 0.012 to 0.020 inch
        Service limit
            4.8L and 5.3L engines .... 0.020 inch
            6.0L engines .... 0.023 inch
    Second compression ring
        Production
            1999 and 2000 .... 0.017 to 0.025 inch
            2001 .... 0.007 to 0.027 inch
            2002 and later
                4.8L and 5.3L engines .... 0.017 to 0.027 inch
                6.0L engines .... 0.020 to 0.030 inch
        Service limit
            1999 through 2002
                4.8L and 5.3L engines .... 0.028 inch
                6.0L engines .... 0.033 inch
            2003 and later
                4.8L and 5.3L engines .... 0.030 inch
                6.0L engines .... 0.033 inch
    Oil ring
        Production
            4.8L and 5.3L engines .... 0.007 to 0.029 inch
            6.0L engines .... 0.012 to 0.034 inch
        Service limit
            4.8L and 5.3L engines .... 0.032 inch
            6.0L engines .... 0.037 inch
Piston ring-to-groove clearance
    V6 engines
        Top compression ring
            Production .... 0.0012 to 0.0027 inch
            Maximum .... 0.0033 inch
        Second compression ring
            Production
                1999 through 2002 .... 0.0015 to 0.0031 inch
                2003 and later .... 0.0030 to 0.0110 inch
            Maximum .... 0.0033 inch
        Oil ring
            Production
                1999 through 2002 .... 0.0018 to 0.0037 inch
                2003 and later .... 0.0018 to 0.0077 inch

Maximum
    1999 through 2002   0.0039 inch
    2003 and later   0.0079 inch

V8 engines
  Top compression ring
    Production
      1999 through 2001   0.0016 to 0.0031 inch
      2002 and later
        4.8L and 5.3L engines   0.0016 to 0.0034 inch
        6.0L engines   0.0014 to 0.0031 inch
    Maximum
      1999 through 2001   0.0033 inch
      2002 and later
        4.8L and 5.3L engines   0.0034 inch
        6.0L engines   0.0031 inch
  Second compression ring
    Production
      2003 and later 6.0L engines   0.0013 to 0.0030 inch
      All other engines   0.0016 to 0.0031 inch
    Maximum
      1999 through 2002 except
        6.0L engines   0.0033 inch
      6.0L and all 2003 and later engines   0.0031 inch
  Oil ring
    Production
      1999 through 2001   0.0004 to 0.0080 inch
      2002 and later   0.0005 to 0.0078 inch
    Maximum
      1999 through 2001   0.0080 inch
      2002 and later   0.0078 inch

Balance shaft (V6 engine only)
  Rear bearing journal diameter   1.4994 to 1.5000 inches
  Rear bearing journal oil clearance   1.0020 to 1.0035 inch

Torque specifications*   **Ft-lbs (unless otherwise indicated)**

Main bearing cap bolts
  V6 engine
    Step one   15
    Step two   Turn an additional 73 degrees
  V8 engines (in sequence - (see illustration 25.11)
    1999 through 2002
      Inner bolts (1 through 10)
        Step 1   15
        Step 2   Tighten an additional 80-degrees
      Outer stud nuts (11 through 20)
        Step 1   15
        Step 2   Tighten an additional 50-degrees
      Side bolts (21 through 30)   18
    2003 and later
      Inner bolts (1 through 10)
        Step 1   15
        Step 2   Tighten an additional 80-degrees

Torque specifications*   Ft-lbs (unless otherwise indicated)

2003 and later (continued)	
Outer stud nuts (11 through 20)	
Step 1	15
Step 2	Tighten an additional 51-degrees
Side bolts (21 through 30)	18
Connecting rod cap bolts or nuts	
V6 engine	
1999 through 2005 and 2006 with forged connecting rods	
Step 1	20
Step 2	Tighten an additional 70-degrees
2006 with powdered metal connecting rods and later	
Step 1	15
Step 2	Tighten an additional 100-degrees
V8 engines (first design) (see illustration 28.15)	
Step one	15
Step two	Turn an additional 60 degrees
V8 engines (second design) (see illustration 28.15)	
Step one	15
Step two	Turn an additional 75 degrees
Crankshaft rear oil seal housing bolts	
V6 engine	106 in-lbs
V8 engines	18
Engine valley cover bolts	18
Windage tray nuts (V8 engines)	18

* Note: Refer to Part B for additional torque specifications.

Section

3

COOLING, HEATING AND AIR CONDITIONING SYSTEMS

1 General information

All vehicles covered by this manual employ a pressurized engine cooling system with thermostatically controlled coolant circulation. Coolant is drawn from the radiator by an impeller-type water pump mounted at the front of the block. The coolant is then circulated through the engine block, the cylinder heads and, on V6 engines, the intake manifold before it's redirected back into the radiator.

A wax pellet type thermostat is located in the thermostat housing on the engine. During warm up, the closed thermostat prevents coolant from circulating through the radiator. When the engine reaches normal operating temperature, the thermostat opens and allows hot coolant to travel through the radiator, where it is cooled before returning to the engine.

The cooling system is pressurized by the surge tank cap, which contains a blow-off pressure valve and a vacuum atmospheric valve. By maintaining higher atmospheric pressure, it increases the boiling point of the coolant. If the coolant temperature goes above this increased boiling point, the extra pressure in the system forces the cap valve off its seat and allows excess pressure to escape the system.

The surge tank serves as both the point at which fresh coolant is added to the cooling system to maintain the proper fluid level and as the point where coolant is circulated to allow air to bubble out of the system.

V8 engines are equipped with a Overheat Protection Mode operating system to protect the engine from damage caused by severe overheating. When the computer senses an overheat condition, an instrument panel warning light comes on that says "reduced power." In this mode, the computer switches the firing of the individual coils On and Off at each cylinder to allow cooling cycles between the firing cycles. The engine will have a dramatic loss of power, but will allow vehicle operation in an emergency. If this light is On, find a safe place to get off the road as soon as possible, and allow the engine to cool thoroughly. Check the coolant level and inspect for a split hose or other obvious signs of coolant leakage. The engine oil will be ruined after this mode has operated, since unburned fuel will get into the oil. After fixing the overheating problem, change the oil and filter right away and reset the Oil Life Monitor (see Chapter 1).

The heating system works by directing air through the heater core mounted in the dash and then to the interior of the vehicle by a system of ducts. Rear heating systems are equipped with separate heater core located at the rear of the vehicle. Temperature is controlled by mixing heated air with fresh air, using a system of doors in the ducts, and a blower motor.

Air conditioning is an optional accessory, consisting of an evaporator core located under the dash, a condenser in front of the radiator, an accumulator in the engine compartment and a belt-driven compressor mounted at the front of the engine. Rear air conditioning systems are equipped with a separate evaporator core located at the rear of the vehicle.

2 Antifreeze - general information

▶ Refer to illustration 2.4

※※ WARNING:

Do not allow antifreeze to come in contact with your skin or painted surfaces of the vehicle. Rinse off spills immediately with plenty of water. Antifreeze is highly toxic if ingested. Never leave antifreeze lying around in an open container or in puddles on the floor; children and pets are attracted by it's sweet smell and may drink it. Check with local authorities about disposing of used antifreeze. Many communities have collection centers which will see that antifreeze is disposed of safely. Never dump used anti-freeze on the ground or pour it into drains.

※※ CAUTION:

The manufacturer recommends using only DEX-COOL coolant for these systems. DEX-COOL is a long-lasting coolant designed for 100,000 miles or 5 years. Never mix green-colored ethylene glycol anti-freeze and orange-colored "DEX-COOL" silicate-free coolant because doing so will destroy the efficiency of the "DEX-COOL".

The cooling system should be filled with a water/ethylene glycol based antifreeze solution which will prevent freezing down to at least -20-degrees F (even lower in cold climates). It also provides protection against corrosion and increases the coolant boiling point.

The cooling system should be drained, flushed and refilled at least every other year (see Chapter 1). The use of antifreeze solutions for periods of longer than two years is likely to cause damage and encourage the formation of rust and scale in the system. However, these models are filled with a new, long-life "Dex-Cool" coolant, which the manufacturer claims is good for five years.

Before adding antifreeze, check all hose connections, because antifreeze tends to leak through very minute openings. Engines don't normally consume coolant, so if the level goes down, find the cause and correct it.

The exact mixture of antifreeze to water which you should use depends on the relative weather conditions. The mixture should contain at least 50-percent antifreeze, but should never contain more than 70-percent antifreeze. Consult the mixture ratio chart on the antifreeze container before adding coolant. Hydrometers are available at most auto parts stores to test the coolant (see illustration). Always use antifreeze which meets the vehicle manufacturer's specifications.

2.4 An inexpensive hydrometer can be used to test the condition of your coolant

3 Thermostat - check and replacement

CHECK

1 Before assuming the thermostat is to blame for a cooling system problem, check the coolant level, drivebelt tension (see Chapter 1) and temperature gauge (or light) operation.

2 If the engine seems to be taking a long time to warm up (based on heater output or temperature gauge operation), the thermostat is probably stuck open. Replace the thermostat with a new one.

3 If the engine runs hot, use your hand to check the temperature of the upper radiator hose. If the hose isn't hot, but the engine is, the thermostat is probably stuck closed, preventing the coolant inside the engine from escaping to the radiator. Replace the thermostat.

➡Note: The thermostat and housing on V8 engines is located on the inlet side (before the water pump), therefore this check will not work on V8 engines.

4 If the upper radiator hose is hot, it means the coolant is flowing and the thermostat is open. Consult the *Troubleshooting* Section at the front of this manual for cooling system diagnosis.

REPLACEMENT

V6 engines

▸ **Refer to illustrations 3.10 and 3.12**

5 Disconnect the cable from the negative terminal of the battery.

6 Remove the air filter housing and air intake duct (see Chapter 4).

7 Follow the upper radiator hose to the engine to locate the thermostat housing cover. The thermostat is located at the end of the lower intake manifold at the front of the engine.

8 Loosen the hose clamp, then detach the radiator hose from the thermostat housing cover. If the hose sticks, grasp it near the end with a pair of adjustable pliers and twist it to break the seal, then pull it off. If the hose is old or deteriorated, cut it off and install a new one.

9 If the outer surface of the cover fitting that mates with the hose is deteriorated (corroded, pitted, etc.) it may be damaged further by hose removal. If it is, the thermostat housing cover will have to be replaced.

10 Remove the bolts/nuts and detach the thermostat cover (see illustration). If the cover is stuck, tap it with a soft-face hammer to jar it loose. Be prepared for some coolant to spill as the gasket seal is broken.

11 Note how it's installed (which end is facing up), then remove the thermostat.

12 If a paper gasket was used, use a scraper or putty knife to remove all traces of old gasket material and sealant from the mating surfaces.

➡Note: Most of these models do not have a traditional gasket, but rather a rubber ring around the thermostat. If so, replace this ring and install the thermostat into the intake manifold without gasket sealant (see illustration).

13 Install the thermostat into the intake manifold and make sure the correct end faces out - the spring is directed toward the engine.

14 If a traditional paper gasket was used, apply a thin coat of RTV sealant to both sides of the new gasket and position it on the engine, over the thermostat, and make sure the gasket holes line up with the bolt holes in the housing.

15 Reattach the thermostat housing cover to the intake manifold and tighten the bolts to the torque listed in this Chapter's Specifications.

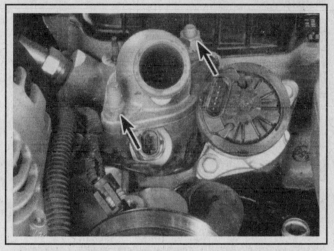

3.10 Thermostat housing cover bolts (arrows) - V6 engines

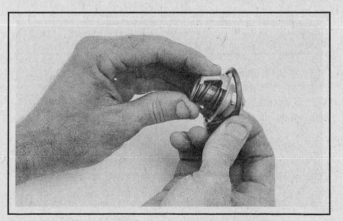

3.12 Install a new rubber seal around the thermostat

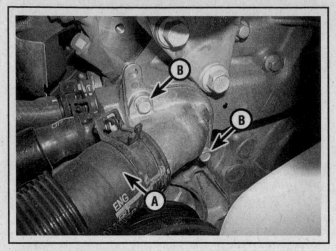

3.18a On V8 engines, remove the lower radiator hose (A) and the thermostat housing bolts (B)

3.18b Thermostat and housing assembly - V8 engines

V8 engines

▶ **Refer to illustrations 3.18a and 3.18b**

16 Drain the cooling system (see Chapter 1).

17 Remove the air intake duct and resonator. Removing the air filter housing will give you a little more working room, but it isn't absolutely necessary (see Chapter 4).

18 Disconnect the lower radiator hose and remove the thermostat housing cover from the engine (see illustration).

→**Note: The thermostat, the thermostat housing and the O-ring seal are pre-assembled at the factory as a single unit and must be replaced as a unit as well (see illustration).**

19 Clean the sealing surfaces on the water pump housing.

20 Place the thermostat housing onto the water pump housing and install the bolts. Tighten the bolts to the torque listed in this Chapter's Specifications

All engines

21 The remaining steps are the reverse of the removal procedure. Now would be a good time to check and replace the hoses and clamps (see Chapter 1).

22 Refer to Chapter 1 and refill the cooling system, then run the engine and check carefully for leaks.

23 Repeat steps 1 through 4 to be sure the repairs corrected the previous problem(s).

4 Engine cooling fans and clutch - check and replacement

❄ WARNING:

Keep hands, tools and clothing away from the fan. To avoid injury or damage DO NOT operate the engine with a damaged fan. Do not attempt to repair fan blades - replace a damaged fan with a new one.

CHECK

1 All V6 and V8 engines are equipped with thermostatically controlled fan clutches.

2 Begin the clutch check with a lukewarm engine (start it when cold and let it run for two minutes only).

3 Remove the key from the ignition switch for safety purposes.

4 Turn the fan blades and note the resistance. There should be moderate resistance, depending on temperature.

5 Drive the vehicle until the engine is warmed up. Shut it off and remove the key.

6 Turn the fan blades and again note the resistance. There should

be a noticeable increase in resistance.

7 If the fan clutch fails this check or is locked up solid, replacement is indicated. If excessive fluid is leaking from the hub or lateral play over 1/4-inch is noted, replace the fan clutch.

❄ WARNING:

8 If the fan is damaged in any way, don't attempt to repair it. Replace the fan with a new one.

REPLACEMENT

▶ **Refer to illustrations 4.10, 4.11 and 4.12**

9 Remove the air filter housing assembly and intake duct (see Chapter 4).

10 Detach any hoses attached to the upper fan shroud and position them aside. Remove the upper fan shroud (see illustration). It's only necessary to remove the upper portion for many service operations.

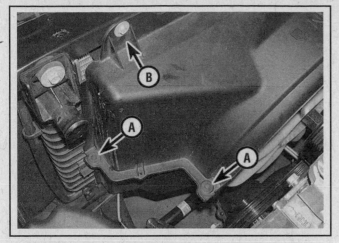

4.10 With the hoses removed, detach the retaining clips (A) and the bolts (B) on each side to remove the upper fan shroud

4.11 Loosening the fan clutch retaining nut while holding the pulley with a strap wrench

11 Use a large wrench to remove the fan clutch retaining nut and detach the fan clutch assembly from the engine. The drive belt should keep the pulley from turning as the fan nut is loosened. If the water pump pulley slips on the belt it will be necessary to remove the drivebelt(s) (see Chapter 1) and use a strap wrench to hold the pulley (see Illustration).

12 Remove the fasteners securing the fan to the fan clutch (see illustration).

13 Installation is the reverse of removal. Be sure to tighten all fasteners to the torques listed in this Chapter's Specifications.

4.12 Fan retaining bolts (arrows)

5   Radiator and coolant surge tank - removal and installation

⁂ WARNING:

The engine must be completely cool when this procedure is performed.

RADIATOR

▶ Refer to illustrations 5.2, 5.3, 5.4 and 5.8

➡Note: The vehicles covered by this manual use spring type radiator hose clamps. If you decide to reuse them, make sure that the hose is installed on a connection that is clean and dry. Don't try to reuse these clamps on aftermarket hoses. Replace them with conventional worm drive type clamps.

1 Disconnect the cable from the negative terminal of the battery.

⁂ CAUTION:

On models equipped with the Theftlock audio system, be sure the lockout feature is turned off before performing any procedure which requires disconnecting the battery (see the front of this manual).

2 Drain the cooling system as described in Chapter 1, then disconnect upper radiator hose from the radiator and the upper fan shroud and position it aside (see illustration). Remove the air intake duct and resonator.

5.2 Detach the upper radiator hose (arrow) from the radiator and the upper fan shroud, then position it aside

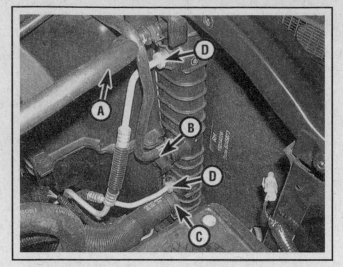

5.3 Remove the following components from the right side of the radiator

A	Coolant recovery hose	C	Lower radiator hose
B	Coolant vent pipe hose (if equipped)	D	Automatic transmission cooler lines (if equipped)

3   Disconnect the coolant surge tank hose, the vent pipe hose (if equipped) and the lower radiator hose from the radiator (see illustration).

4   If equipped with an automatic transmission, disconnect the transmission cooler lines from the right side of the radiator (see illustration). To disconnect the lines from the radiator, simply unsnap the plastic collar from the quick-connect fitting, then pry off the quick-connect fitting retaining clip and remove the lines. Plug the ends of the lines to prevent fluid from leaking out after you disconnect them. Have a drip pan ready to catch any spills. Always be sure to inspect the O-rings on the cooler lines before reinstallation.

➡**Note: Do not remove the clips by pulling straight out. Hold one side in with your fingers while using a pick (with a bent tip) to pull the other side out, then rotate the clip off. Install clips the same way, not straight on.**

5   If equipped with an engine oil cooler, disconnect the lines on the opposite side of the radiator, as described in the previous step. Also disconnect the engine oil cooler lines from the lower fan shroud.

6   Unbolt and remove the upper fan shroud and the engine cooling fan (see Section 4).

7   Detach the lower fan shroud, by pulling straight up and releasing it from the retaining tabs on the radiator.

8   Remove the radiator mounting bolts and lift the radiator from the engine compartment (see illustration).

9   Prior to installation of the radiator, replace any damaged radiator hoses and hose clamps.

10 Radiator installation is the reverse of removal. When installing the radiator, make sure that the radiator seats properly in the lower saddles and that the upper brackets are secure. Install the cooler line retaining clips onto the quick connect fitting before installing the lines, then snap the cooler lines into place on the quick connect fittings. Be sure to reinstall the plastic collars on the quick connect fittings as they lock the retaining clip in place.

11 After installation, refill the cooling system (see Chapter 1), then check the engine oil and automatic transmission fluid levels.

5.4 Unsnap the plastic collar, then pry off the retaining clip from the quick-connect fitting to disconnect the transmission and engine oil cooler lines

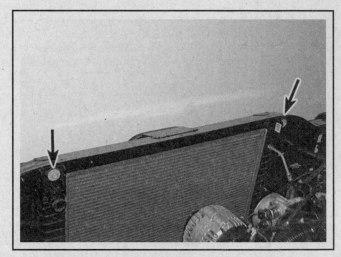

5.8 Radiator mounting bolts (arrows)

COOLANT SURGE TANK

▶ **Refer to illustration 5.15**

12 Disconnect the cable from the negative terminal of the battery.

✳✳ CAUTION:

On models equipped with the Theftlock audio system, be sure the lockout feature is turned off before performing any procedure which requires disconnecting the battery (see the front of this manual).

13 Drain the cooling system as described in Chapter 1 until the surge tank is empty. Refer to the coolant **Warning** in Section 2.

14 Remove the air filter housing (see Chapter 4).

15 Detach the coolant hoses from the surge tank. Unscrew the mounting bolt and nut, then lift the surge tank from the notch on the

inner fenderwell and disconnect the coolant level sensor connector (see illustration).

16   Remove the surge tank from the engine compartment.

17   Prior to installation make sure the reservoir is clean and free of debris which could be drawn into the radiator (wash it with soapy water and a brush if necessary, then rinse thoroughly).

18   Installation is the reverse of removal. Refill the cooling system (see Chapter 1) and check for leaks.

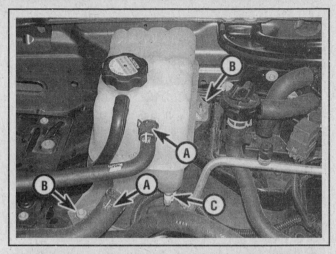

5.15   Remove the coolant hoses (A) and the mounting bolts (B), then lift the surge tank from the notch on the inner fenderwell and disconnect the coolant level sensor connector (C)

6   Water pump - check and replacement

✳✳ WARNING:

Wait until the engine is completely cool before starting this procedure.

CHECK

▶ **Refer to illustration 6.2**

1   Water pump failure can cause overheating and serious damage to the engine. There are three ways to check the operation of the water pump while it is installed on the engine. If any one of the following quick-checks indicates water pump problems, it should be replaced immediately.

2   A seal protects the water pump impeller shaft bearing from contamination by engine coolant. If this seal fails, a weep hole in the water pump snout will leak coolant (see illustration) (an inspection mirror can be used to look at the underside of the pump if the hole isn't on top). If the weep hole is leaking, shaft bearing failure will follow. Replace the water pump immediately.

3   The water pump impeller shaft bearing can also prematurely wear out. When the bearing wears out, it emits a high-pitched squealing sound. If such a noise is coming from the water pump during engine operation, the shaft bearing has failed - replace the water pump immediately.

➡ **Note: Do not confuse belt noise with bearing noise.**

4   To identify excessive bearing wear, remove the drivebelt (see Chapter 1), grasp the water pump pulley and try to force it up-and-down or from side-to-side. If the pulley can be moved either horizontally or vertically, the bearing is nearing the end of its service life. Replace the water pump.

5   It is possible for a water pump to be bad, even if it doesn't howl or leak water. Sometimes the fins on the back of the impeller can corrode away until the pump is no longer effective. The only way to check for this is to remove the pump for examination.

6.2   The weep hole (arrow) is located on the bottom of the water pump (V8 engine shown, V6 engine similar)

REPLACEMENT

▶ **Refer to illustrations 6.11, 6.12a and 6.12b**

6   Disconnect the cable from the negative terminal of the battery.

✳✳ CAUTION:

On models equipped with the Theftlock audio system, be sure the lockout feature is turned off before performing any procedure which requires disconnecting the battery (see the front of this manual).

7   Drain the coolant (see Chapter 1). Remove the air intake duct and resonator.

8   Remove the upper radiator shroud and fan/clutch assembly (see Section 4). On V6 engines, loosen the water pump pulley bolts a few

6.11 Heater hose-to-water pump housing connections - V8 engines

6.12a Water pump mounting bolts (arrows) - V6 engine

turns while the drivebelt is still installed on the engine.

9   Remove the serpentine belt (see Chapter 1).

10   On V6 engines, remove the water pump pulley, detach the lower radiator hose, the heater hose and the coolant by-pass hose from the water pump.

➡**Note: To detach the pulley on V6 engines, you will need a strap wrench or two-pin spanner to hold the pulley while the bolts are removed.**

11   On V8 engines, remove the lower radiator hose and the thermostat housing (see Section 3). Also remove the upper radiator hose and the heater hoses from the water pump housing (see illustration).

12   Unbolt the water pump (see illustrations). It may be necessary to tap the pump with a soft-face hammer to break the gasket seal. Inspect the pump's impeller blades on the backside for corrosion. If any fins are missing or badly corroded, replace the pump with a new one.

13   Clean the sealing surfaces of all gasket material on both the water pump and block. Wipe the mating surfaces with a rag saturated with lacquer thinner or acetone.

14   Apply a thin layer of RTV sealant to both sides of the new gasket and install the gasket on the water pump.

15   Place the water pump in position and install the bolts finger tight. Use caution to ensure that the gasket doesn't slip out of position. Tighten the bolts to the torque listed in this Chapter's Specifications.

➡**Note: On V6 engines, use RTV sealant on the water pump bolt threads.**

16   The remainder of the installation procedure is the reverse of removal.

6.12b Water pump mounting bolt locations (arrows) - V8 engines

➡**Note: If a new water pump in installed on a V8 engine, a new thermostat/housing assembly must be installed also.**

17   Add coolant to the specified level (see Chapter-1), start the engine and check for the proper coolant level. Be sure to bleed the cooling system of air as described in Chapter-1. Also check for coolant leaks around the water pump and hoses.

---

7   Coolant temperature gauge sending unit - check and replacement

CHECK

1   The coolant temperature indicator system is composed of a temperature gauge or warning light mounted in the dash and a coolant temperature sensor mounted on the engine. This coolant temperature sensor doubles as an information sensor for the fuel and emissions systems (see Chapter 6) and as a sending unit for the temperature gauge.

2   If an overheating indication occurs, check the coolant level in the system and then make sure the wiring between the gauge and the sending unit is secure and all fuses are intact.

3   Check the operation of the coolant temperature sensor (see

Chapter 6). If the sensor is defective, replace it with a new part of the same specification.

4   If the coolant temperature sensor is good, have the temperature gauge checked by a dealer service department. This test will require a scan tool to access the information as it is processed by the On Board computer.

REPLACEMENT

5   Refer to Chapter 6 for the engine coolant temperature sensor replacement procedure.

8   Blower motor and circuit - check

▶ **Refer to illustrations 8.3 and 8.5**

✳ WARNING:

These models have airbags. Always disable the airbag system before working in the vicinity of any airbag system component to avoid the possibility of accidental deployment of the airbag, which could cause personal injury (see Chapter 12).

➡**Note:** This procedure applies to the front blower motor and circuit on all models covered by this manual. Some models are equipped with rear auxiliary heating and air conditioning systems which can't be tested using conventional equipment. Due to the use of an integrated electronic control module that can only be tested with specialized equipment it will be necessary to take these vehicles to dealer service department or other qualified repair shop.

1   Check the fuse (marked HVAC) and all connections in the circuit for looseness and corrosion. Make sure the battery is fully charged.

➡**Note 1:** The heater/blower relay is located on the blower motor housing in the passenger compartment on 1999 through 2002 models and in the fuse/relay center in the engine compartment on 2003 and later models. The HVAC fuse is located in the fuse/relay panel under the left side of the dash (see Chapter 12).

➡**Note 2:** The auxiliary cooling fan fuses are located in the fuse/relay block next to the large fuse/relay center in the engine compartment.

2   With the transmission in Park (or Neutral on manual transmission equipped vehicles), set the parking brake securely and turn the ignition switch to the Run position. It isn't necessary to start the vehicle.

3   Remove the heater/air conditioning assembly cover (below the glove box) for access to the blower motor, then remove the blower motor cover (see illustration) (see Section 9).

· 4   Disconnect the blower motor connector, then hook one side of the blower motor terminals to a chassis ground and the other to a fused source of battery voltage. If the blower doesn't operate, it is faulty.

5   To check the blower resistor, use an ohmmeter to test for continuity between the blower feed terminal (purple wire) on the blower motor pigtail connector and terminals A, B, C and D on the blower resistor (see illustration). There should be continuity at all four terminals with varied resistance between them.

6   If the blower motor works in every position except HIGH, the blower high relay is probably defective and must be replaced. Since the blower resistor/relay is assembled as a single unit it will be necessary to replace the entire unit.

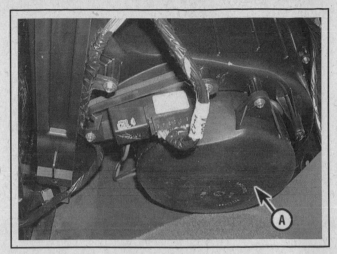

8.3   Remove the blower motor cover (A)

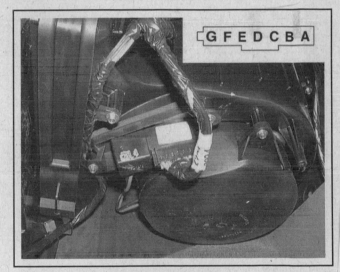

8.5   Blower motor resistor terminal guide

A	Medium 1 speed output terminal
B	Low speed output terminal
C	Medium 3 speed output terminal
D	Medium 2 speed output terminal
E	Ground terminal
F	High speed output terminal
G	Fused battery feed terminal

9 Blower motor - removal and installation

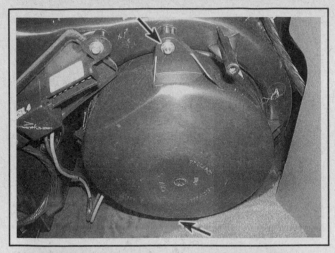

9.3 Remove the screws (arrows) retaining the blower motor cover

9.5 Pull down on the blower motor retaining tab (arrow) and rotate the fan assembly counterclockwise to remove it from the vehicle

✳✳ WARNING:

These models have airbags. Always disable the airbag system before working in the vicinity of any airbag system component to avoid the possibility of accidental deployment of the airbag, which could cause personal injury (see Chapter 12).

FRONT BLOWER MOTOR (ALL MODELS)

▶ **Refer to illustrations 9.3 and 9.5**

1　Remove the heater/air conditioning assembly cover.

2　Disconnect the electrical connector from the blower resistor (see Section 8).

3　Remove the blower motor cover (see illustration).

4　Disconnect the electrical connector from the blower motor.

5　Pull down the retaining tab and rotate the blower motor counterclockwise (see illustration) to remove it.

6　If you're replacing the blower motor with a new one, remove the fan from the blower motor. The fan is pressed onto the blower motor shaft and can be pried off with two screwdrivers.

7　Install the fan onto the new motor and install the blower motor into the heater housing.

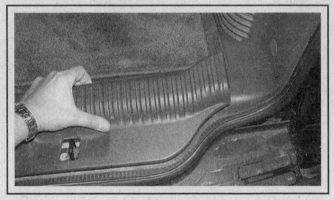

9.8a Remove the rear door sill plate

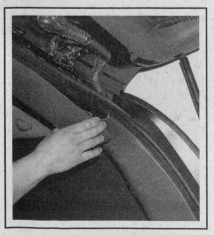

9.8b Remove the headliner trim panel

9.8c Pry off the rear door pillar trim panel and disconnect the electrical connectors (if equipped) from the rear of the panel

9.8d Pry off the right rear door pillar trim panel and position it aside without removing the rear safety belt

9.8e Remove the screw (arrow) at the front of the panel

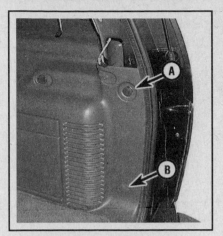

9.8f The rear of the trim panel is secured by the cargo net hook (A), which must be unscrewed, and a retaining clip (B)

9.8g Lift the right rear quarter trim panel up and away, then disconnect the electrical connectors from the rear of the panel and remove it from the vehicle

REAR AUXILIARY BLOWER MOTOR

▶ **Refer to illustrations 9.8a, 9.8b, 9.8c, 9.8d, 9.8e, 9.8f, 9.8g and 9.10**

8   Remove the right rear quarter trim panel (see illustrations).

9   Disconnect the electrical connector from the blower motor.

10 Detach the cooling hose and remove the blower motor retaining screws (see illustration).

11 Pull the blower motor straight out to remove it.

12 If you're replacing the blower motor with a new one, remove the fan from the blower motor. The fan is pressed onto the blower motor shaft and can be pried off with two screwdrivers.

13 Install the fan onto the new motor and install the blower motor into the heater housing.

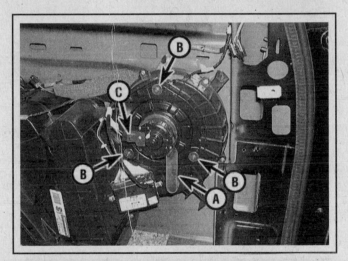

9.10 Rear auxiliary blower motor mounting details

A Blower motor cooling hose	B Mounting screws
	C Electrical connector

10 Heater and air conditioning control assembly - removal and installation

1   Disconnect the cable from the negative terminal of the battery

FRONT HEATER CONTROLS (ALL MODELS)

▶ **Refer to illustrations 10.4a and 10.4b**

2   Remove the main instrument panel bezel to allow access to the heater/air conditioning control mounting screws (see Chapter 11).

3   Remove the radio (see Chapter 12). On models so equipped, remove the passenger airbag On/Off switch from the instrument panel.

4   Release the control assembly retaining tabs and pull the unit from the dash (see illustrations on next page). It can be pulled out just far enough to allow disconnecting the electrical connections and control cables (if equipped) from the control head. Use a small screwdriver to release the clips.

5   To install the control assembly, reverse the removal procedure.

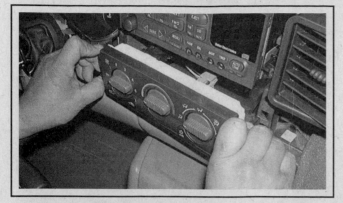

10.4a Pinch the retaining tabs and pull the control assembly outward . . .

REAR AUXILIARY HEATER CONTROLS

▶ **Refer to illustrations 10.6 and 10.7**

6   Using a small screwdriver pry out the rear control panel(s) (see illustration).

7   Pull the control head downward from the overhead console, disconnect the electrical connections and remove it from the vehicle (see illustration). Use a small screwdriver to release the clips.

8   To install the control assembly, reverse the removal procedure. Be sure the control head snaps securely into place on the overhead console.

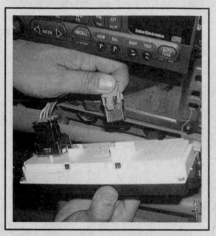

10.4b . . . disconnect the electrical connectors (and the control cables, if equipped)

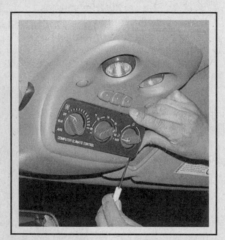

10.6 Pry the rear control assembly outward from the overhead console

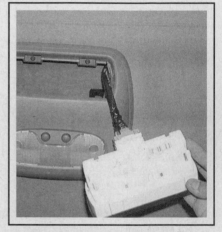

10.7 Disconnect the electrical connectors and remove it from the vehicle

11 Heater core - removal and installation

※※ WARNING 1:

These models have airbags. Always disable the airbag system before working in the vicinity of any airbag system component to avoid the possibility of accidental deployment of the airbag, which could cause personal injury (see Chapter 12).

※※ WARNING 2:

The air conditioning system is under high pressure. DO NOT loosen any fittings or remove any components until after the system has been discharged. Air conditioning refrigerant must be properly discharged into an EPA-approved container at a dealership service department or an automotive air conditioning facility. Always wear eye protection when disconnecting air conditioning system fittings.

※※ WARNING 3:

Wait until the engine is completely cool before beginning the procedure.

1   Have the air conditioning system discharged by a dealership service department or an automotive air conditioning facility (see **Warning** above).

2   Disconnect the cable at the negative terminal of the battery.

※※ CAUTION:

On models equipped with the Theftlock audio system, be sure the lockout feature is turned off before performing any procedure which requires disconnecting the battery (see the front of this manual).

FRONT HEATER CORE (ALL MODELS)

▶ **Refer to illustrations 11.3, 11.4, 11.7, 11.9, 11.10a and 11.10b**

3   Drain the cooling system (see Chapter 1). Remove the air conditioning lines from the evaporator core fittings at the firewall (see illustration). Be sure to plug each refrigerant line to avoid contamination of

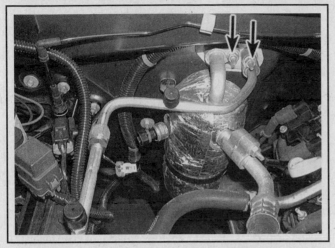

11.3 Have the air conditioning system discharged by a dealership service department or an automotive air conditioning facility, then remove the air conditioning lines (arrows) from the evaporator core fittings at the firewall

11.4 Disconnect the heater core hoses (arrows) at the engine compartment firewall

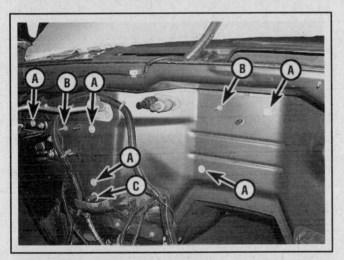

11.7 Heater/air conditioning unit mounting details

A	Mounting bolts
B	Mounting nuts
C	Drain tube

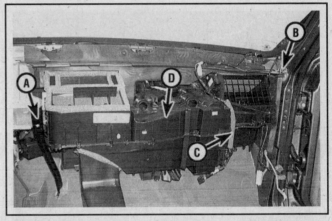

11.9 Remove the center support brace (A), ground strap (B), the electrical connectors (C) and the heating/air conditioning unit (D)

the air conditioning system.

4   Disconnect the heater hoses at the heater core inlet and outlet on the engine side of the firewall (passenger side) (see illustration) and plug the open fittings. If the hoses are stuck to the pipes, cut them off and replace them with new ones upon installation.

5   From the inside of the vehicle, remove the heater/air conditioning assembly cover from below the glove box.

6   Remove the instrument panel from the passenger compartment. Refer to Chapter 11 and read through the entire instrument panel removal procedure before attempting to remove it. The instrument panel removal procedure is quite lengthy and can be particularly difficult for a beginner. Once the instrument panel is removed from the vehicle, the heating /air conditioning unit can be removed from the vehicle and set on a workbench.

7   Working in the engine compartment, remove the fasteners securing the heating/air conditioning unit to the firewall (see illustration).

8   Disconnect the drain tube from the heater/air conditioning unit.

9   Working back inside the passenger compartment, remove the

center support brace, the electrical connections and any ground straps, then remove the heating/air conditioning unit from the vehicle (see illustration). Follow the remaining steps to remove the heater core from the heating/air conditioning unit.

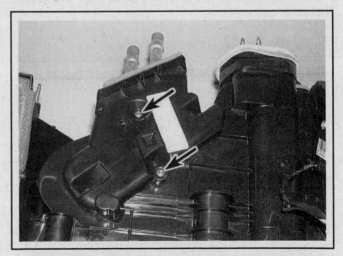

11.10a Remove the heater core cover screws (arrows)

11.10b Carefully slide the heater core out of the heater/air conditioning unit

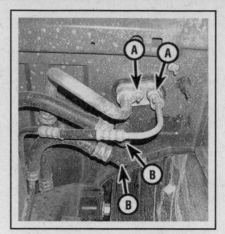

11.15 Raise the vehicle and support it securely on jackstands to access the rear air conditioning lines (A) and the rear heater hoses (B)

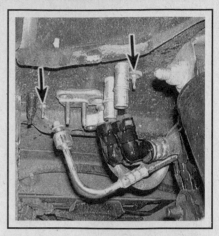

11.16 Rear heating/air conditioning unit lower mounting nuts (arrows)

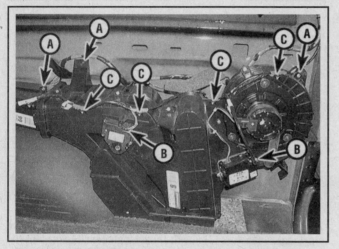

11.18 Rear heating/air conditioning unit mounting details

A Mounting screws	C Wiring harness retainers
B Electrical connectors	

10 Remove the heater core cover and slide the heater core out carefully (see illustrations).

11 Installation is the reverse of removal.

➡**Note: When reinstalling the heater core, make sure any original insulating/sealing materials are in place around the heater core pipes and around the core.**

12 Refill the cooling system (see Chapter 1). Have the air conditioning system charged by the shop that discharged it.

13 Start the engine and check for proper operation.

REAR AUXILIARY HEATER CORE

▶ **Refer to illustrations 11.15, 11.16, 11.18, 11.19a, 11.19b, 11.19c, 11.19d and 11.20**

14 Remove the air conditioning lines from the rear evaporator core fittings on the floorboard. Be sure to plug each refrigerant line to avoid contamination of the air conditioning system.

15 Clamp off the heater hoses leading to the rear heater core, then disconnect the hoses from the inlet and outlet fittings (see illustration)

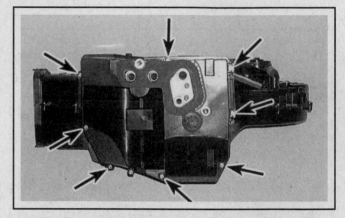

11.19a Remove the rear heater core cover screws (arrows)

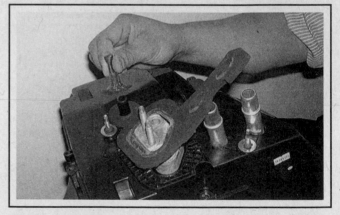

11.19b Detach the cover-to-floor pan gasket and the drain tube

and plug the open fittings. Pinch the tabs to release the quick-connect fittings.

16 Remove the rear heating/air conditioning unit lower mounting nuts (see illustration).

17 From the inside of the vehicle, remove the right rear quarter trim panel as described in Section 9, Step 8.

18 Remove the electrical connections and wiring harness retaining straps straps, then detach the rear heating/air conditioning unit mount-

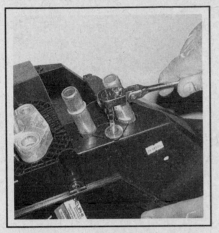

11.19c Detach the cover retaining stud . . .

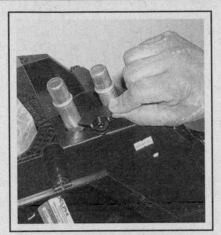

11.19d . . . and the cover retaining tab, then remove the rear heater core cover

11.20 Detach the heater core clamp (arrow) and remove the heater core from the housing

ing screws and remove it from the vehicle (see illustration).

➡**Note: It is not necessary to remove the air duct from the vehicle.**

Follow the remaining steps to remove the heater core from the rear heating/air conditioning unit.

19 Remove the heater core cover (see illustrations).

20 Remove the heater core retaining clamp and slide the heater core out of the rear heating and air conditioning unit (see illustration).

21 Installation is the reverse of removal.

➡**Note: When reinstalling the heater core, make sure any original insulating/sealing materials are in place around the heater core pipes and around the core.**

22 Check the coolant level, adding coolant as necessary (see Chapter 1). Have the air conditioning system charged by the shop that discharged it.

23 Start the engine and check for proper operation. Recheck the coolant level.

12 Air conditioning and heating system - check and maintenance

AIR CONDITIONING SYSTEM

➤ **Refer to illustration 12.1**

❋❋ **WARNING:**

The air conditioning system is under high pressure. Do not loosen any hose fittings or remove any components until after the system has been discharged. Air conditioning refrigerant must be properly discharged into an EPA-approved recov-ery/recycling unit at a dealer service department or an automotive air conditioning repair facility. Always wear eye protection when disconnecting air conditioning system fittings.

❋❋ **CAUTION 1:**

All models covered by this manual use environmentally friendly R-134a. This refrigerant (and its appropriate refrigerant oils) are not compatible R-12 refrigerant system components and must never be mixed or the components will be damaged.

❋❋ **CAUTION 2:**

When replacing entire components, additional refrigerant oil should be added equal to the amount that is removed with the component being replaced. Be sure to read the can before adding any oil to the system, to make sure it is compatible with the R-134a system.

1 The following maintenance checks should be performed on a regular basis to ensure that the air conditioning continues to operate at peak efficiency.

  a) *Inspect the condition of the compressor drivebelt. If it is worn or deteriorated, replace it (see Chapter 1).*

  b) *Check the drivebelt tension and, if necessary, adjust it (see Chapter 1).*

  c) *Inspect the system hoses. Look for cracks, bubbles, hardening*

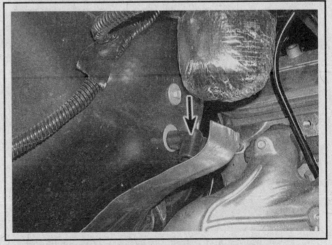

12.1 Check that the evaporator housing drain tube (arrow) at the firewall is clear of any blockage - the view here is from the right fenderwell

and deterioration. Inspect the hoses and all fittings for oil bubbles or seepage. If there is any evidence of wear, damage or leakage, replace the hose(s).

d) Inspect the condenser fins for leaves, bugs and any other foreign material that may have embedded itself in the fins. Use a "fin comb" or compressed air to remove debris from the condenser.

e) Make sure the system has the correct refrigerant charge.

f) If you hear water sloshing around in the dash area or have water dripping on the carpet, check the evaporator housing drain tube (see illustration) and insert a piece of wire into the opening to check for blockage.

2   It's a good idea to operate the system for about ten minutes at least once a month. This is particularly important during the winter months because long term non-use can cause hardening, and subsequent failure, of the seals. Note that using the Defrost function operates the compressor.

3   If the air conditioning system is not working properly, proceed to Step 6 and perform the general checks outlined below.

4   Because of the complexity of the air conditioning system and the special equipment necessary to service it, in-depth troubleshooting and repairs beyond checking the refrigerant charge and the compressor clutch operation are not included in this manual. However, simple checks and component replacement procedures are provided in this Chapter.

5   The most common cause of poor cooling is simply a low system refrigerant charge. If a noticeable drop in system cooling ability occurs, one of the following quick checks will help you determine whether the refrigerant level is low. Should the system lose its cooling ability, the following procedure will help you pinpoint the cause.

Check

▶ **Refer to illustration 12.9**

6   Warm the engine up to normal operating temperature.

7   Place the air conditioning temperature selector at the coldest setting and put the blower at the highest setting. Open the doors (to make sure the air conditioning system doesn't cycle off as soon as it cools the passenger compartment).

8   After the system reaches operating temperature, feel the two pipes connected to the evaporator at the firewall.

9   The pipe (thinner tubing) leading from the expansion (orifice)

12.9 Insert a thermometer in the center duct while operating the air conditioning system - the output air should be 35-40 degrees F less than the ambient temperature, depending on humidity (but not lower than 40-degrees F)

tube (see illustration 16.2) to the evaporator should be cold, and the evaporator outlet line (the thicker tubing that leads back to the compressor) should be slightly warmer (about 3 to 10 degrees F warmer). If the evaporator outlet is considerably warmer than the inlet, or if the evaporator inlet isn't cold, the system needs a charge. Insert a thermometer in the center air distribution duct (see illustration) while operating the air conditioning system at its maximum setting - the temperature of the output air should be 35 to 40 degrees F below the ambient air temperature (down to approximately 40 degrees F). If the ambient (outside) air temperature is very high, say 110 degrees F, the duct air temperature may be as high as 60 degrees F, but generally the air conditioning is 35 to 40 degrees F cooler than the ambient air.

10 If the air isn't as cold as it used to be, the system probably needs a charge.

11 If the air warm and the system doesn't seem to be operating properly check the operation of the compressor clutch.

12 Have an assistant switch the air conditioning On while you observe the front of the compressor. The clutch will make an audible click and the center of the clutch should rotate. If it doesn't, shut the engine off and disconnect the air conditioning system pressure switch (see illustration 12.22). Bridge the terminals of the connector with a jumper wire and turn the air conditioning On again. If it works now, the system pressure is too high or too low. Have your system tested by a dealer service department or air conditioning shop.

13 If the clutch still didn't operate, check the appropriate fuses. Inspect the fuses in the interior fuse panel.

14 Remove the compressor clutch (A/C) relay from the engine compartment relay panel and test it (see Chapter 12). With the relay out and the ignition On, check for battery power at two of the relay terminals (refer to the wiring diagrams for wire color designations to determine which terminals to check). There should be battery power with the key On, at the terminals for the relay control and power circuits.

15 Using a jumper wire, connect the terminals in the relay box from the relay power circuit to the terminal that leads to the compressor clutch (refer to the wiring diagrams for wire color designations to determine which terminals to connect). Listen for the clutch to click as you make the connection. If the clutch doesn't respond, disconnect the clutch connector at the compressor and check for battery voltage at the compressor clutch connector. Check for continuity to ground on the black wire terminal of the compressor clutch connector. If power and ground are available and the clutch doesn't operate when connected, the compressor clutch is defective.

16 If the compressor clutch, relay and related circuits are good and the system is fully charged with refrigerant and the compressor does not operate under normal conditions, have the PCM and related circuits checked by a dealer service department or other properly equipped repair facility.

17 Further inspection or testing of the system is beyond the scope of the home mechanic and should be left to a professional.

Adding refrigerant

▶ **Refer to illustrations 12.18, 12.21 and 12.22**

❉❉ CAUTION:

Make sure any refrigerant, refrigerant oil or replacement component your purchase is designated as compatible with environmentally friendly R-134a systems.

18 Purchase an R-134a automotive charging kit at an auto parts store (see illustration). A charging kit includes a 12-ounce can of

refrigerant, a tap valve and a short section of hose that can be attached between the tap valve and the system low side service valve.

❄ WARNING:

Never add more than one can of refrigerant to the system (you could overfill the system).

19 Hook up the charging kit by following the manufacturer's instructions.

❄ WARNING:

DO NOT hook the charging kit hose to the system high side! The fittings on the charging kit are designed to fit only on the low side of the system.

20 Back off the valve handle on the charging kit and screw the kit onto the refrigerant can, making sure first that the O-ring or rubber seal inside the threaded portion of the kit is in place.

❄ WARNING:

Wear protective eyewear when dealing with pressurized refrigerant cans.

21 Remove the dust cap from the low-side charging port and attach the quick-connect fitting on the kit hose (see illustration).
22 Warm up the engine and turn on the air conditioning. Keep the charging kit hose away from the fan and other moving parts.

➡**Note 1: The charging process requires the compressor to be running. If the clutch cycles off, you can put the air conditioning switch on High and leave the car doors open to keep the clutch on and compressor working.**

➡**Note 2: The compressor can be kept on during the charging by removing the connector from the low-pressure switch (combination high-limit and low-limit switch on some models) and bridging it with a paper clip or jumper wire during the procedure (see illustration).**

23 Turn the valve handle on the kit until the stem pierces the can, then back the handle out to release the refrigerant. You should be able to hear the rush of gas. Add refrigerant to the low side of the system, keeping the can upright at all times, but shaking it occasionally. Allow stabilization time between each addition.

➡**Note: The charging process will go faster if you wrap the can with a hot-water-soaked shop rag to keep the can from freezing up.**

24 If you have an accurate thermometer, you can place it in the center air conditioning duct inside the vehicle and keep track of the output air temperature (see illustration 12.9). A charged system that is working properly should cool down to approximately 40-degrees F. If the ambient (outside) air temperature is very high, say 110 degrees F, the duct air temperature may be as high as 60 degrees F, but generally the air conditioning is 30-40 degrees F cooler than the ambient air.
25 When the can is empty, turn the valve handle to the closed position and release the connection from the low-side port. Replace the dust cap.
26 Remove the charging kit from the can and store the kit for future use with the piercing valve in the UP position, to prevent inadvertently piercing the can on the next use.

HEATING SYSTEMS

27 If the carpet under the heater core is damp, or if antifreeze vapor or steam is coming through the vents, the heater core is leaking. Remove it (see Section 12) and install a new unit (most radiator shops will not repair a leaking heater core).
28 If the air coming out of the heater vents isn't hot, the problem could stem from any of the following causes:

a) *The thermostat is stuck open, preventing the engine coolant from warming up enough to carry heat to the heater core. Replace the thermostat (see Section 3).*

b) *There is a blockage in the system, preventing the flow of coolant through the heater core. Feel both heater hoses at the firewall. They should be hot. If one of them is cold, there is an obstruction in one of the hoses or in the heater core, or the heater control valve is shut. Detach the hoses and back flush the heater core with a water hose. If the heater core is clear but circulation is*

12.18 A basic charging kit for 134a systems is available at most auto parts stores - it must say 134a (not R-12) and so must the can of refrigerant

12.21 Attach the refrigerant kit to the low-side charging port (arrow) - it's near the accumulator - the cap should be marked with an "L"

12.22 The air conditioning pressure switch (arrow) is located on the accumulator - if the compressor will not stay engaged, disconnect the connector and bridge the terminals (on the harness side) with a jumper wire during the charging procedure

impeded, remove the two hoses and flush them out with a water hose.

c) *If flushing fails to remove the blockage from the heater core, the core must be replaced (see Section 11).*

ELIMINATING AIR CONDITIONING ODORS

▶ **Refer to illustration 12.32**

29 Unpleasant odors that often develop in air conditioning systems are caused by the growth of a fungus, usually on the surface of the evaporator core. The warm, humid environment there is a perfect breeding ground for mildew to develop.

30 The evaporator core on most vehicles is difficult to access, and factory dealerships have a lengthy, expensive process for eliminating the fungus by opening up the evaporator case and using a powerful disinfectant and rinse on the core until the fungus is gone. You can service your own system at home, but it takes something much stronger than basic household germ-killers or deodorizers.

31 Aerosol disinfectants for automotive air conditioning systems are available in most auto parts stores, but remember when shopping for them that the most effective treatments are also the most expensive. The basic procedure for using these sprays is to start by running the system in the RECIRC mode for ten minutes with the blower on its highest speed. Use the highest heat mode to dry out the system and keep the compressor from engaging by disconnecting the wiring connector at the compressor (see Section 14).

32 The disinfectant can usually comes with a long spray hose. Remove the passenger compartment air filter, point the nozzle inside the hole and to the left towards the evaporator core, and spray according to the manufacturer's recommendations (see illustration). Try to cover the whole surface of the evaporator core, by aiming the spray up, down and sideways. Follow the manufacturer's recommendations for the length of spray and waiting time between applications. The manufacturer recommends running the engine for 20 minutes while repeating the procedure

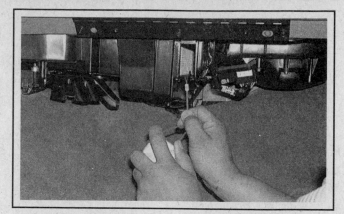

12.32 With the passenger compartment air filter removed, spray the disinfectant at the evaporator core

in Step 30 to dry the evaporator core again.

33 Once the evaporator has been cleaned, the best way to prevent the mildew from coming back again is to make sure your evaporator housing drain tube is clear (see illustration 12.1).

AUTOMATIC HEATING AND AIR CONDITIONING SYSTEMS

34 Some models are equipped with an optional automatic climate control system. This system has its own computer that receives inputs from various sensors in the heating and air conditioning system. This computer, like the PCM, has self diagnostic capabilities to help pinpoint problems or faults within the system. Vehicles equipped with automatic heating and air conditioning systems are very complex and considered beyond the scope of the home mechanic. Vehicles equipped with automatic heating and air conditioning systems should be taken to dealer service department or other qualified facility for repair.

13 Air conditioning accumulator/drier - removal and installation

REMOVAL

▶ **Refer to illustration 13.2**

✳✳ WARNING:

The air conditioning system is under high pressure. DO NOT loosen any fittings or remove any components until after the system has been discharged. Air conditioning refrigerant must be properly discharged into an EPA-approved container at a dealership service department or an automotive air conditioning repair facility. Always wear eye protection when disconnecting air conditioning system fittings.

1 Have the air conditioning system discharged (see Warning above). Disconnect the cable from the negative terminal of the battery.

✳✳ CAUTION:

On models equipped with the Theftlock audio system, be sure the lockout feature is turned off before performing any procedure which requires disconnecting the battery (see the front of this manual).

2 Disconnect the refrigerant inlet and outlet lines (see illustration). Loosen each nut and remove the fittings from the retaining stud(s). Cap or plug the open lines immediately to prevent the entry of dirt or moisture.

3 Disconnect the electrical connector from the pressure cycling switch.

4 Loosen the clamp bolt on the mounting bracket and slide the accumulator/drier assembly up and out of the engine compartment.

INSTALLATION

5   If you are replacing the accumulator/drier with a new one, add one ounce of fresh refrigerant oil to the new unit (oil must be R-134a compatible).

6   Place the new accumulator/drier into position in the bracket.

7   Install the inlet and outlet lines, using clean refrigerant oil on the new O-rings. Tighten the mounting bolt securely.

8   Connect the cable to the negative terminal of the battery.

9   Have the system evacuated, recharged and leak tested by a dealership service department or an automotive air conditioning repair facility.

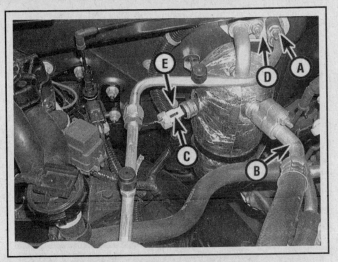

13.2 Accumulator mounting details

A   *Evaporator line fitting nut*
B   *Compressor hose*
C   *Pressure cycling switch*

D   *Accumulator line fitting nut*
E   *Mounting bracket bolt*

14 Air conditioning compressor - removal and installation

REMOVAL

♦ **Refer to illustrations 14.6a and 14.6b**

✳✳ WARNING:

The air conditioning system is under high pressure. **DO NOT loosen any fittings or remove any components until after the system has been discharged. Air conditioning refrigerant must be properly discharged into an EPA-approved container at a dealership service department or an automotive air conditioning repair facility. Always wear eye protection when disconnecting air conditioning system fittings.**

➡ **Note 1:** The accumulator/drier (see Section 13) should be replaced whenever the compressor is replaced.

➡ **Note 2:** Whenever the compressor is replaced because of internal damage, the expansion (orifice) tube should also be replaced (see Section 16).

1   Have the air conditioning system discharged (see Warning above). Disconnect the cable from the negative terminal of the battery.

✳✳ CAUTION:

On models equipped with the Theftlock audio system, be sure the lockout feature is turned off before performing any procedure which requires disconnecting the battery (see the front of this manual).

2   Clean the compressor thoroughly around the refrigerant line fittings.

3   Remove the serpentine drivebelt (see Chapter 1).

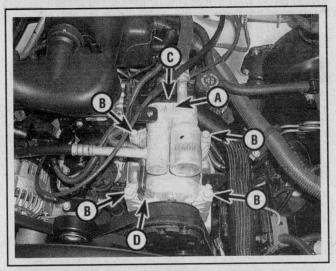

14.6a Air conditioning compressor mounting details - V6 engine

A   *Refrigerant line mounting bolt*
B   *Compressor mounting bolts*
C   *High pressure cycling switch electrical connector*
D   *Compressor clutch electrical connector*

4   On V8 engines, loosen the right front wheel lug nuts. Raise the vehicle and support it securely on jackstands. Remove the plastic inner fenderwell. On V6 engines detach the accelerator cable bracket.

5   Disconnect the electrical connector(s) from the air conditioning compressor.

6   Disconnect the suction and discharge lines from the compressor. Both lines are mounted to the compressor with a manifold secured by one bolt. Plug the open fittings to prevent the entry of dirt and

moisture, and discard the seals between the plate and compressor (see illustrations).

7   Remove the compressor mounting bolts. Detach the compressor

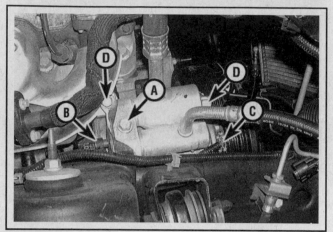

14.6b Air conditioning compressor mounting details - V8 engines

   A   *Refrigerant line mounting bolt*
   B   *High pressure cycling switch electrical connector*
   C   *Compressor clutch electrical connector*
   D   *Compressor mounting bolts (lower two bolts not visible)*

15 Air conditioning condenser - removal and installation

♦ **Refer to illustrations 15.4 and 15.5**

✳✳ WARNING:

The air conditioning system is under high pressure. DO NOT loosen any fittings or remove any components until after the system has been discharged. Air conditioning refrigerant must be properly discharged into an EPA-approved container at a dealership service department or an automotive air conditioning repair facility. Always wear eye protection when disconnecting air conditioning system fittings.

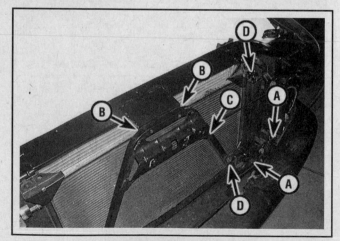

15.4 Hood latch support brace mounting details

   A   *Lower mounting bolts*
   B   *Upper mounting bolts*
   C   *Hood latch support brace*
   D   *Power steering cooler mounting bolts*

from the mounting bracket and remove the compressor from the engine compartment.

INSTALLATION

8   If a new compressor is being installed, pour the oil from the old compressor into a graduated container and add that exact amount of new refrigerant oil to the new compressor. Also follow any directions included with the new compressor.

➡**Note: Some replacement compressors come with refrigerant oil in them. Follow the directions with the compressor regarding the draining of excess oil prior to installation.**

✳✳ CAUTION:

The oil used must be labeled as compatible with R-134a refrigerant systems.

9   Installation is the reverse of the disassembly. When installing the line fitting bolt to the compressor, use new seals lubricated with clean refrigerant oil, and tighten the bolt securely.

10 Reconnect the cable to the negative terminal of the battery.

11 Have the system evacuated, recharged and leak tested by a dealership service department or an automotive air conditioning repair facility.

➡**Note: The accumulator/drier should be replaced if the condenser was damaged, causing the system to be open for some time (see Section 13).**

1   Have the air conditioning system discharged (if equipped) at a dealer service department or service station.

2   Disconnect the cable from the negative terminal of the battery.

✳✳ CAUTION:

On models equipped with the Theftlock audio system, be sure the lockout feature is turned off before performing any procedure which requires disconnecting the battery (see the front of this manual).

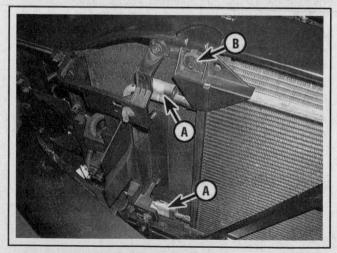

15.5 Disconnect the refrigerant lines (A) and the condenser mounting bolt (B) on the passenger side

3   On 1999 and 2000 models, refer to Chapter 11 and remove the radiator grille, then refer to Chapter 12 and remove the headlight housings. On 2001 and later models, remove the radiator (see Section 5).

4   On 1999 and 2000 models, remove the hood latch release cable from the hood latch (see Chapter 11). Remove the power steering cooler (if equipped) and the hood latch support brace from the vehicle (see illustration).

5   Disconnect the refrigerant lines from the condenser and the remaining condenser mounting bolt (see illustration). Plug the open ends of the condenser and the disconnected refrigerant lines to prevent entry of dirt or moisture. Remove the condenser from the vehicle.

6   Inspect the rubber insulator pads (on the lower crossmember) on which the radiator sits. Replace them if they're dried or cracked.

7   If the original condenser will be reinstalled, store it with the line fittings on top to prevent oil from draining out. If a new condenser is being installed, pour one ounce of R-134a-compatible refrigerant oil into it prior to installation.

8   Reinstall the components in the reverse order of removal. Be sure the rubber pads are in place under the condenser.

9   Have the system evacuated, recharged and leak tested by the shop that discharged it.

16 Air conditioning expansion (orifice) tube - removal and installation

▶ **Refer to illustrations 16.2 and 16.5**

✳✳ WARNING:

The air conditioning system is under high pressure. DO NOT loosen any fittings or remove any components until after the system has been discharged. Air conditioning refrigerant must be properly discharged into an EPA-approved container at a dealership service department or an automotive air conditioning repair facility. Always wear eye protection when disconnecting air conditioning system fittings.

1   Have the air conditioning system discharged and the refrigerant recovered (see **Warning** above). Disconnect the cable from the negative terminal of the battery.

✳✳ CAUTION:

On models equipped with the Theftlock audio system, be sure the lockout feature is turned off before performing any procedure which requires disconnecting the battery (see the front of this manual).

2   Open the the hood and locate the expansion orifice tube fitting (see illustration).

3   Hold the stationary fitting (on the line coming from the condenser) with one wrench, then loosen the other fitting with another wrench.

4   The expansion tube is a tube with a fixed-diameter orifice and a mesh filter at each end. When you separate the pipe at the fitting you will see one end of the orifice tube inside the pipe leading to the evaporator. Use needle-nose pliers to remove the orifice tube.

5   The orifice tube acts to meter the refrigerant, changing it from a high-pressure liquid to a low-pressure gas. It is possible to reuse the orifice tube if (see illustration):

   a) *The screens aren't plugged with grit or foreign material*
   b) *Neither screen is torn*
   c) *The plastic housing over the screens is intact*
   d) *The brass orifice inside the plastic housing is unrestricted*

6   Installation is the reverse of removal. Be sure to insert the expansion tube with the shorter end In flrst, toward the evaporator

✳✳ CAUTION:

Always use a new O-ring when installing the expansion (orifice) tube.

7   Reconnect the refrigerant line and tighten the fitting securely, then have the system evacuated, recharged and leak-tested by the shop that discharged it.

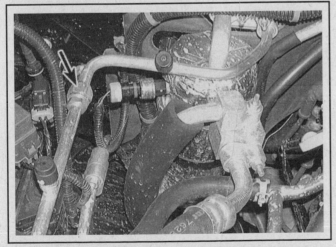

16.2 The expansion tube fitting (arrow) is located on the small line leading to the evaporator core

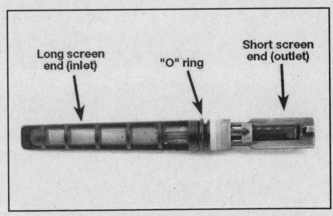

16.5 The expansion tube is equipped with a tapered mesh screen that must be cleaned and must not have any holes or damage

Specifications

General

Coolant capacity	See Chapter 1
Coolant reservoir pressure cap rating	15 psi
Refrigerant type	R-134a
Refrigerant capacity	
1999 and 2000	
Standard (front A/C only)	2.0 pounds
With rear air conditioning	2.5 pounds
2001 and 2002	
Standard (front A/C only)	1.8 pounds
With rear air conditioning	
Tahoe/Yukon	2.7 pounds
All others	3.0 pounds
2003 and later	
Standard (front A/C only)	1.6 pounds
With rear air conditioning	
Tahoe/Yukon	2.7 pounds
All others	3.0 pounds

Torque specifications

	Ft-lbs (unless otherwise indicated)
Engine cooling fan-to-fan clutch bolts	17
Engine cooling fan clutch nut	41
Thermostat housing nuts/bolts	
V6 engine	168 in-lbs
V8 engines	132 in-lbs
Water pump attaching bolts	
V6 engine	33
V8 engines	
Step one	132 in-lbs
Step two	22
Water pump pulley bolts	
V6 engine	18
V8 engines (if applicable)	
Step one	89 in-lbs
Step two	18

Section

Reference to other Chapters

4

FUEL AND EXHAUST SYSTEMS

1.1a Typical fuel system components - V6 engine

1 Throttle body
2 Accelerator cable
3 Fuel meter body and injectors (under upper intake manifold plenum)
4 Fuel pump relay (inside Underhood Electrical Center)
5 Air filter housing
6 Air intake duct and resonator

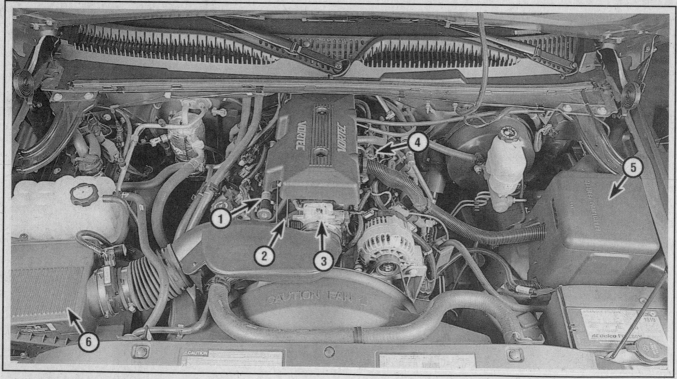

1.1b Typical fuel system components - V8 engines

1 Fuel rail and injectors
2 Accelerator cable
3 Throttle body
4 Fuel pressure regulator
5 Fuel pump relay (inside Underhood Electrical Center)
6 Air filter housing

1   General information

▶ Refer to illustrations 1.1a and 1.1b

✳✳ WARNING:

Gasoline is extremely flammable, so take extra precautions when you work on any part of the fuel system. Don't smoke or allow open flames or bare light bulbs near the work area, and don't work in a garage where a gas-type appliance (such as a water heater or a clothes dryer) is present. Since gasoline is carcinogenic, wear latex gloves when there's a possibility of being exposed to fuel, and, if you spill any fuel on your skin, rinse it off immediately with soap and water. Mop up any spills immediately and do not store fuel-soaked rags where they could ignite. The fuel system is under constant pressure, so, if any fuel lines are to be disconnected, the fuel pressure in the system must be relieved first. When you perform any kind of work on the fuel system, wear safety glasses and have a Class B type fire extinguisher on hand.

All models covered by this manual are equipped with Sequential Fuel Injection (SFI) (see illustrations). SFI systems use timed impulses to sequentially inject the fuel directly into the intake ports of each cylinder in the same sequence as the firing order. The Powertrain Control Module (PCM) controls the injectors. The PCM monitors various engine parameters and delivers the correct amount of fuel, in firing order sequence, into the intake ports. For more information about the fuel injection system, see Section 11.

The fuel pump is located in the roof of the fuel tank and protrudes down into the fuel inside the fuel tank. You must lower the fuel tank before you can remove the fuel pump from the fuel tank. The fuel level sending unit is an integral component of the fuel pump and it must be accessed in the same manner.

Models equipped with dual fuel tanks are equipped with a secondary fuel pump. The secondary fuel pump is mounted on the frame near the secondary fuel tank. This pump is activated by the PCM and sends fuel from the secondary tank into the primary tank when the fuel level in the primary tank falls below two gallons of the secondary tank. Once the primary fuel tank is low, it will empty all the fuel from the secondary tank.

There are two different types of fuel pressure regulation systems. 1999 through 2003 V8 models and 2004 and earlier V6 engines are equipped with a return-type fuel system. Fuel pressure is regulated at the throttle body (V6 models) or fuel rail (V8 models) by a fuel pressure regulator. Excess fuel is returned to the fuel tank by way of the fuel return line. 2004 and later V8 models and 2005 and later V6 models are equipped with a returnless fuel system. Fuel pressure is regulated at the fuel pump in the fuel tank by a fuel pressure regulator. Excess fuel is returned directly to the tank without extra lines or hoses.

There are two fuel filters. A nylon mesh fuel "sock" or strainer is located at the lower (inlet) end of the fuel pump/fuel level sending unit. The strainer is an extended-life part and does not need to be replaced at scheduled maintenance intervals. It should only be replaced if it becomes clogged with sediment. The main fuel filter, which looks like a small metal canister, is located under the vehicle, between the fuel tank and the engine compartment. It must be replaced at the specified service interval (see Chapter 1).

The exhaust system consists of the two exhaust manifolds and, on most models, two catalytic converters, exhaust pipes and mufflers. All of these components are replaceable. For further information regarding the catalytic converters, refer to Chapter 6.

2   Fuel pressure relief procedure

▶ Refer to illustration 2.3

✳✳ WARNING:

See the Warning in Section 1.

1   Remove the fuel filler cap. This will relieve any pressure that has built-up in the tank.
2   Locate the fuse and relay box in the engine compartment (see Section 3 in Chapter 12).
3   Remove the fuel pump relay (see illustration) from the engine compartment fuse and relay box. You can locate any relay by looking at the relay guide printed on the underside of the fuse box cover.
4   Turn the ignition key to START and crank over the engine for several seconds. It will either start momentarily and immediately stall, or it won't start at all.
5   Turn the ignition key to the OFF position.
6   Disconnect the cable from the negative terminal of the battery before beginning work on the fuel system.
7   After all work on the fuel system has been completed, install the fuel pump relay. The CHECK ENGINE light or SERVICE ENGINE SOON light might come on during operation because the engine was cranked with the fuel pump relay unplugged. The light will probably go out after a period of normal operation. If it doesn't, you'll have to clear the Diagnostic Trouble Code (DTC) with a generic scan tool (see Chapter 6) or

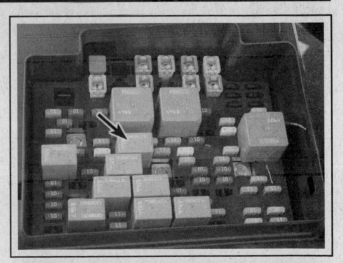

2.3 To depressurize the fuel system, remove the fuel pump relay, which is located inside the fuse and relay box in the engine compartment (this is the relay location on a Silverado model with a 4.3L V6) (be sure to check the underside of the fuse box cover for the relay location on your model)

have the DTC cleared by a dealer service department or other qualified repair shop.

3   Fuel pump/fuel pressure - check

⁂ WARNING:

See the Warning in Section 1.

PRELIMINARY CHECK

1   The fuel pump is located inside the fuel tank, which muffles its sound when the engine is running. But you can actually hear the fuel pump. Sit inside the vehicle with the windows closed, turn the ignition key to ON (not START) and listen carefully for the soft whirring sound made by the fuel pump as it's briefly turned on by the PCM to pressurize the fuel system prior to starting the engine. You will only hear a soft whirring sound for a second or two, but that sound tells you that the pump is working. If you can't hear the pump from inside the vehicle, remove the fuel filler cap, depress the spring-loaded door inside the fuel filler neck, then have an assistant turn the ignition switch to ON while you listen for the sound of the pump operating for a couple of seconds. If the pump does not come on when the ignition key is turned to ON, check the fuel pump fuse and relay both of which are located in the engine compartment fuse and relay box. If the fuse and relay are okay, check the wiring back to the fuel pump. If the fuse, relay and wiring are okay, the fuel pump is probably defective. If the pump runs continuously with the ignition key in its ON position, the Powertrain Control Module (PCM) is probably defective. Have the PCM checked by a dealer service department or other qualified repair shop.

PRESSURE CHECK

2   Relieve the fuel system pressure (see Section 2).

1999 through 2003 V8 models/2005 and later V6 models

▶ Refer to illustrations 3.3a, 3.3b and 3.3c

➡Note: In order to perform the fuel pressure test, you will need a fuel pressure gauge capable of measuring high fuel pressure. The fuel gauge must be equipped with the proper fitting required to attach it to the test port. To test the fuel pressure regulator, a fuel shut off valve must be installed in the fuel return line with the necessary adapters.

3   Remove the cap from the fuel pressure test port and attach a fuel pressure gauge (see illustration). The test port is located on the fuel

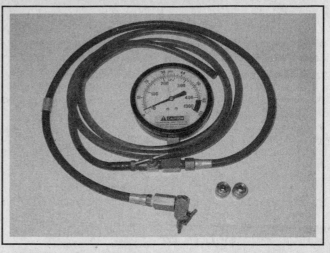

3.3a To check the fuel pressure, you'll need a fuel pressure gauge capable of reading the fuel pressure within the specified operating system pressure, a hose to connect the gauge to the fuel pressure test port and an adapter suitable for connecting the hose to the Schrader valve type test port

supply line on 4.3L V6 engines and the fuel rail on 4.8L, 5.3L and 6.0L V8 engines.

4   Turn the ignition key ON (engine not running). The fuel pump should run for approximately two seconds then shut off. Note the pressure indicated on the gauge and compare your reading with the pressure listed in this Chapter's Specifications. Cycle the ignition key On and Off several times, if necessary, to obtain the highest reading.

5   If the fuel pressure is lower than specified, turn the ignition key Off and relieve the fuel system pressure. Install a fuel shut-off valve in the fuel return line and close the valve.

⁂ CAUTION:

Do not pinch the flexible fuel line shut or damage to the fuel line may occur.

Turn the ignition key On and note the fuel pressure.

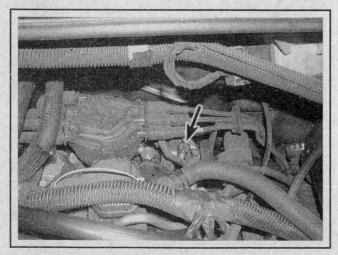

3.3b Fuel pressure test port location - V6 models

3.3c Fuel pressure test port location - V8 models

Do not allow the fuel pressure to rise above 75 psi or damage to the fuel pressure regulator may occur. If the fuel pressure is now above the specified pressure, replace the fuel pressure regulator (see Section 14).

If the fuel pressure is still lower than specified, check the fuel lines and the fuel filter for restrictions. If no restriction is found, remove the fuel pump module (see Section 7) and check the fuel strainer for restrictions, check the fuel flex pipe for leaks and check the fuel pump wiring for high resistance. If no problems are found, replace the fuel pump.

6   If the fuel pressure recorded in Step 4 is higher than specified, check the fuel return line for restrictions. If no restrictions are found, replace the fuel pressure regulator (see Section 14).

7   If the fuel pressure is within specifications, start the engine.

Make sure the fuel pressure gauge hose is positioned away from the engine drivebelt before starting the engine.

With the engine running, the fuel pressure should be 3 to 10 psi below the pressure recorded in Step 4. If it isn't, remove the vacuum hose from the fuel pressure regulator and verify there is 12 to 14 in-Hg of vacuum present at the hose. If vacuum is not present at the hose, check the hose for a restriction or a leak. If vacuum is present, reconnect the hose to the fuel pressure regulator. If the fuel pressure regulator does not decrease the fuel pressure with vacuum applied, replace the fuel pressure regulator.

➡ Note: On V6 models, the fuel pressure regulator cannot be accessed without some disassembly. Therefore the fuel pressure regulator vacuum check cannot be performed.

8   Turn the engine off and monitor the fuel pressure for five minutes. The fuel pressure should not drop more than 5 psi within five minutes. If it does, there is a leak in the fuel line, a fuel injector is leaking or the fuel pump module check valve is defective.

2004 and later V8 models/2005 and later V6 models

➡ Note: In order to perform the fuel pressure test, you will need a fuel pressure gauge capable of measuring high fuel pressure. You'll also need suitable fittings or adapters to attach it to the fuel rail. A dealer service department or other qualified shop should have a diagnostic scan tool that will give a more accurate graph of the performance of the fuel supply system as the engine is running.

9   For this check, you'll need to obtain a fuel pressure gauge with a hose and an adapter suitable for connecting it to the Schrader valve type test port on the fuel feed line or fuel rail (see illustration 3.3a).

10   The test port is located on the fuel supply rail (see illustration 3.3b or 3.3c).

11   Unscrew the threaded cap from the test port and connect the fuel pressure gauge hose to the test port.

12   Turn the ignition key ON (engine not running) and check the pressure on the gauge, comparing your reading with the pressure listed in this Chapter's Specifications.

13   If the fuel pressure is not within specifications, check the following:

a) If the pressure is lower than specified, check for a restriction in the fuel system (that includes the inlet strainer and the fuel filter). If there is no restriction, the fuel pressure regulator or the fuel pump could be defective.

b) If the fuel pressure is higher than specified, replace the fuel pressure regulator (see Section 14).

---

4   Fuel lines and fittings - repair and replacement

▶ Refer to illustration 4.2

Gasoline is extremely flammable, so take extra precautions when you work on any part of the fuel system. See the Warning in Section 2.

Before disconnecting any fuel line fittings, relieve the fuel system pressure (see Section 2) and equalize tank pressure by removing the fuel filler cap. This procedure will merely relieve the increased pressure necessary for the engine to run - remember that fuel will still be present in the system components, so you should be ready for fuel spills when disconnecting fuel line fittings.

1   Always relieve the fuel pressure (see Section 2) before servicing fuel lines or fittings, then disconnect the cable from the negative battery terminal before proceeding.

2   The fuel supply and return lines run from the fuel tank to the fuel meter body on V6 engines or to the fuel rail on V8 engines (1999 through 2003 models). The Evaporative Emission Control (EVAP) system vapor lines connect the fuel tank to the EVAP canister and connect the canister to the canister purge solenoid on the intake manifold. The fuel and EVAP lines are secured to the underbody with small plastic brackets that are attached to the underside of the vehicle (see illustration). To detach the lines from these brackets, spread the clips of the bracket apart and pull the line out.

3   Whenever you're working under the vehicle, be sure to inspect all fuel and EVAP lines for leaks, kinks, dents and other damage. Always replace a damaged fuel or EVAP line immediately. Leaking fuel and

4.2 The fuel lines (and EVAP lines) are secured to the underside of the vehicle by small plastic clips. This one is typical

EVAP lines will result in loss of fuel and excessive air pollution (the leaking raw fuel emits unburned hydrocarbon vapors into the atmosphere).

4 If you find signs of dirt in the lines during disassembly, disconnect all lines and blow them out with compressed air. Inspect the fuel strainer on the lower end of the fuel pump for damage and deterioration. And inspect the fuel filter (see Chapter 1).

STEEL TUBING

5 Because fuel lines used on fuel-injected vehicles are under fairly high pressure, it is critical that they be replaced with lines of equivalent specification. Never use copper or aluminum tubing to replace steel tubing. These materials cannot withstand normal vehicle vibration.

6 Some steel fuel lines have threaded fittings. When loosening these fittings to service or replace components:

a) Hold the stationary fitting with one wrench while loosening or tightening the tubing nut with another.

b) If you're going to replace one of these fittings, use original equipment parts or parts that meet original equipment standards.

PLASTIC TUBING

7 Some of the fuel and EVAP lines on the vehicles covered in this manual are plastic. If you ever have to replace a plastic line, use only plastic tubing meeting original equipment standards.

❄ CAUTION:

When removing or installing plastic fuel line tubing, be careful not to bend or twist it too much, which can damage it. And damaged fuel lines MUST be replaced! Also, be aware that the plastic fuel tubing is NOT heat resistant, so keep it away from excessive heat. Nor is it acid-proof, so don't wipe it off with a shop rag that has been used to wipe off battery electrolyte. If you accidentally spill or wipe electrolyte on plastic fuel tubing, replace the tubing.

FLEXIBLE HOSES

❄ WARNING:

Use only original equipment replacement hoses or their equivalent. Unapproved hoses might fail when subjected to the high operating pressures of the fuel system.

8 Don't route fuel hoses within four inches of exhaust system components or within ten inches of a catalytic converter. Make sure that no flexible hoses are installed directly against the vehicle, particularly in places where there is any vibration. If allowed to touch some vibrating part of the vehicle, a hose can easily become chafed and it might start leaking. A good rule of thumb is to maintain a minimum of 1/4-inch clearance around a hose (or metal line) to prevent contact with the vehicle underbody.

FUEL LINE AND EVAP LINE FITTINGS

9 The vehicles covered in this manual use two kinds of fuel line quick-connect fittings (metal or plastic) for most connections at the fuel pump, the fuel tank, under the vehicle and in the engine compartment. (A third type of plastic quick-connect fitting is used only at the EVAP canister and on the vent hose connection at the fuel tank for the

4.12 Pull the end of the retainer off the fuel line, then disengage the other end from the female side of the fitting

EVAP canister vent solenoid.)

10 The procedure for releasing each type of fuel line fitting is different. But a few rules of thumb apply to all fittings:

1) Inspect the fitting for dirt. If the fitting is dirty, clean it off before disassembling it. The seals in the fitting will stick to the fuel line as they age. Twist the fitting on the line, then push and pull the fitting until it moves freely.

2) Always disconnect all fuel line fittings from a fuel system component before removing the component.

3) When disconnecting a quick-connect fitting, inspect the condition of the retainer before reconnecting the fitting. The best strategy with respect to retainers is to simply replace the retainer every time that you disconnect the fitting.

4) When you disconnect a fitting with an O-ring inside, inspect the O-ring before reconnecting the fitting. Fuel line fittings are under the same pressure as the rest of the fuel system, so to avoid leaks (and fires!) make VERY SURE that the O-ring is good condition. Even better, simply replace it.

5) In most cases, the fitting itself is a non-removable part of the fuel line, so you might have to replace an entire fuel line if a fitting is damaged or defective.

Metal collar quick-connect fittings

Disconnection

▶ **Refer to illustrations 4.12, 4.13a and 4.13b**

➡ **Note: You'll need a special tool set (available at most auto parts stores) to disconnect these fittings.**

11 Relieve the fuel system pressure (see Section 2).

12 Pull off the clip end of the retainer, then remove it from the fitting (see illustration).

13 Using a fuel line separator tool of the proper size (available at most auto parts stores), insert the tool into the female side of the fitting, then push it into the fitting to release the locking tabs and pull the fitting apart (see illustrations).

Reconnection

▶ **Refer to illustrations 4.14 and 4.17**

14 Inspect the O-ring (see illustration). If it's dried out, cracked, torn or otherwise deteriorated, replace it.

15 Apply a few drops of clean engine oil to the male pipe end.

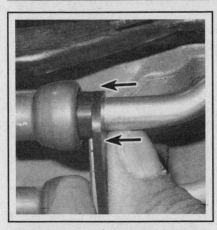

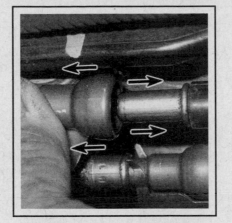

4.13a Insert the fuel line separator tool into the female side of the fitting, push it into the fitting until it releases the locking tabs inside the fitting . . .

4.13b . . . then pull the lines apart

4.14 Inspect the O-ring inside the female side of the fitting; if it's cracked, torn or deteriorated, replace it

16 Push both sides of the fitting together until the retaining tabs snap into place. Pull on both sides of the fitting to verify that it's securely connected.

17 Install the retainer, making sure it clips into place (see illustration).

18 Start the engine and check for fuel leaks.

Plastic collar quick-connect fittings

Disconnection

▶ Refer to illustrations 4.19a and 4.19b

19 To release this type of quick-connect fitting, depress the tabs of the retainer (see illustration). Once the retainer is released, continue pressing on the tabs while pulling the two fuel lines apart (see illustration).

20 Remove and discard the old retainer from the male side of the fitting.

21 Remove and discard the indicator ring from the male side of the fitting.

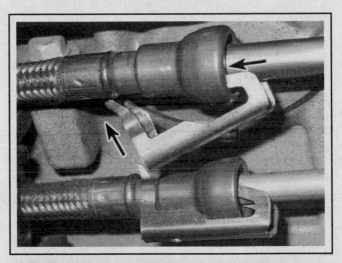

4.17 To install a retainer, insert the hooked end into the female side of the fitting, then push the clip end onto the fuel line until it snaps into place

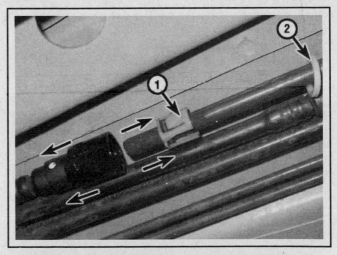

4.19a To release a plastic quick-connect fitting, depress the tabs on the retainer with a small screwdriver, then continue pressing on them . . .

4.19b . . . until the two fuel lines are disconnected, then remove and discard the old retainer (1) and the indicator ring (2) (the indicator ring is used only during factory assembly; there is no need to reinstall it)

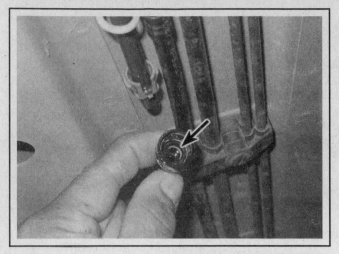

4.22 Inspect the O-ring inside the female side of the fitting; if it's cracked, torn or deteriorated, replace it

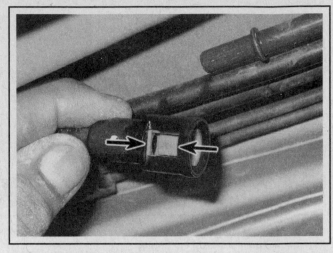

4.23 Install a new retainer in the female side of the fitting; make sure that the release tabs are aligned with the windows in the connector

Reconnection

▶Refer to illustrations 4.22 and 4.23

22 Inspect the O-ring inside the female side of the fitting (see illustration). If it's dried out, cracked, torn or deteriorated, replace it.

23 Insert a new retainer in the female side of the fitting. Make sure that the release tabs are aligned with the "windows" of the connector (see illustration).

24 Apply a few drops of engine oil to the tip of the male fuel line.

25 Push both sides of the fitting together until the retainer release tabs snap into place.

26 Pull on both sides of the fitting to verify that it's securely connected.

27 Start the engine and check for fuel leaks.

5 Fuel tank - removal and installation

▶ Refer to illustrations 5.5, 5.9, 5.10, 5.11 and 5.12

✳✳ WARNING:

See the *Warning* in Section 1.

➡Note: If necessary, clean the fuel tank and areas surrounding the fuel lines and hoses to prevent contaminating the fuel system.

1 Remove the fuel tank filler cap to relieve fuel tank pressure.
2 Relieve the fuel system pressure (see Section 2).
3 Disconnect the cable from the negative battery terminal.

✳✳ CAUTION:

On models equipped with the Theftlock audio system, be sure the lockout feature is turned off before performing any procedure which requires disconnecting the battery (see the front of this manual).

4 Using a siphoning kit (available at most auto parts stores), siphon the fuel into an approved gasoline container.

✳✳ WARNING:

Do not start the siphoning action by mouth!

5 On pick-up models, open the fuel filler door and remove the screws retaining the fuel filler tube flange to the body housing (see illustration).

6 Raise the vehicle and support it securely on jackstands. On models so equipped, remove the bolts and the shield over the fuel tank.

7 On pick-up models, remove the fuel filler pipe ground strap from the body.

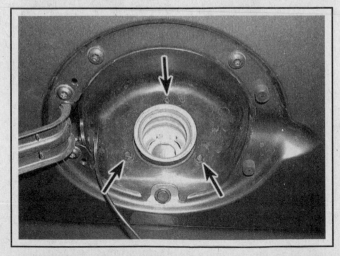

5.5 On pick-up models, remove the fuel filler pipe retaining screws (arrows)

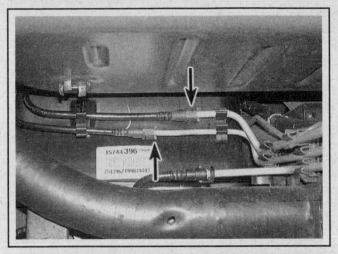

5.9 Disconnect the fuel supply and return lines (arrows)

5.10 On SUV models, loosen the hose clamps and disconnect the fuel filler and vent hoses (arrows) from the fuel tank

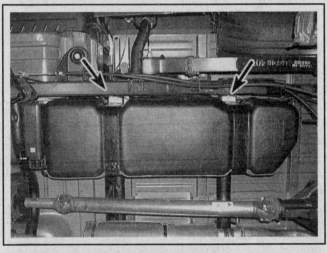

5.11 Remove the fuel tank strap bolts (arrows) and remove the straps

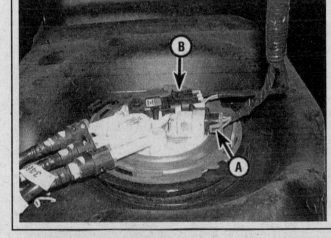

5.12 Lower the fuel tank and disconnect the fuel pump/fuel level sending unit (A) and fuel tank pressure sensor (B) electrical connectors from the fuel pump module

8 Remove the EVAP canister (see Chapter 6).
9 Disconnect the fuel supply and return lines (see Section 4) (see illustration).
10 On SUV models, loosen the hose clamps and disconnect the fuel filler and vent hoses from the fuel tank (see illustration).
11 Position a transmission jack under the fuel tank and support the tank. Remove the fuel tank strap bolts and remove the straps (see illustration).

12 Lower the tank slightly and disconnect the electrical connectors from the fuel pump module (see illustration).
13 Lower the jack and remove the tank from the vehicle.
14 On pick-up models, loosen the hose clamps and disconnect the fuel filler hose from the fuel tank.
15 Installation is the reverse of removal.

6 Fuel tank cleaning and repair - general information

1 The fuel tanks installed in the vehicles covered by this manual are not repairable. If the fuel tank becomes damaged, it must be replaced.
2 Cleaning the fuel tank (due to fuel contamination) should be performed by a professional with the proper training to carry out this critical and potentially dangerous work. Even after cleaning and flush-ing, explosive fumes may remain inside the fuel tank.
3 If the fuel tank is removed from the vehicle, it should not be placed in an area where sparks or open flames could ignite the fumes coming out of the tank. Be especially careful inside a garage where a natural gas-type appliance is located.

7 Fuel pump module - removal and installation

▶ **Refer to illustrations 7.5 and 7.6**

1   Relieve the fuel system pressure (see Section 2).
2   Disconnect the cable from the negative battery terminal.

✳✳ **CAUTION:**

On models equipped with the Theftlock audio system, be sure the lockout feature is turned off before performing any procedure which requires disconnecting the battery (see the front of this manual).

3   Remove the fuel tank from the vehicle (see Section 5).
4   Disconnect the fuel lines and EVAP line from the fuel pump module.
5   While prying the locking tab out, rotate the fuel pump module retaining ring counterclockwise until it's loose (see illustration).

6   Remove the fuel pump module from the tank (see illustration). Angle the assembly slightly to avoid damaging the fuel level sending unit float.

✳✳ **WARNING:**

Some fuel may remain in the module reservoir and spill as the module is removed. Have several shop towels ready and a drain pan nearby to place the module in.

7   The electric fuel pump is not serviced separately. In the event of failure, the complete assembly must be replaced. Transfer the fuel pressure sensor and fuel level sending unit to the new fuel pump module assembly, if necessary (see Section 8).
8   Clean the fuel tank sealing surface and install a new seal on the fuel pump module.
9   Install the fuel pump module, aligning the fuel line fittings with the fuel lines.
10   Press the fuel pump module down until seated and install the retaining ring. Make sure the retaining ring is fully seated and the locking tab is engaged with the slot.
11   The remainder of installation is the reverse of removal.

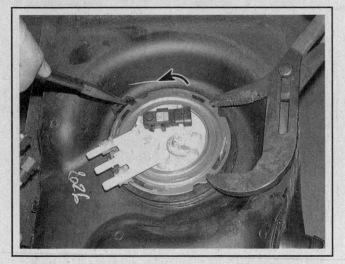

7.5 Release the locking tab and loosen the fuel pump module retaining ring by rotating it counterclockwise

7.6 Carefully remove the fuel pump module from the tank and drain the fuel from the reservoir

8 Fuel level sending unit - replacement

REPLACEMENT

▶ **Refer to illustrations 8.2, 8.3 and 8.4**

1   Remove the fuel tank and the fuel pump module (see Sections 5 and 7).

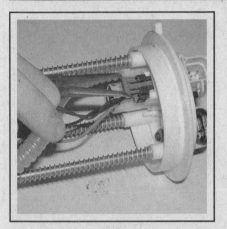

8.2 Disconnect the fuel pump/ fuel level sending unit electrical connector from the fuel pump module

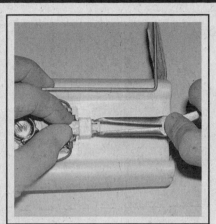

8.3 Remove the sending unit retaining clip

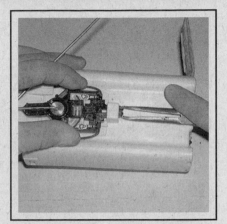

8.4 Pinch the tabs together and remove the fuel level sending unit from module

2   Disconnect the fuel level sending unit electrical connector from the module cover (see illustration).

3   Remove the sending unit retaining clip (see illustration).

4   Pinch the tabs together and slide the fuel level sending unit off

the module (see illustration). Note the routing of the wiring for installation.

5   Installation is the reverse of removal.

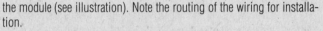

9   Air filter housing - removal and installation

▶ **Refer to illustrations 9.2, 9.3, 9.4 and 9.5**

1   Disconnect the electrical connector from the mass airflow sensor.

2   Loosen the air intake duct hose clamp and separate the air intake duct from the mass airflow sensor (see illustration on next page). Remove the mass airflow sensor (see Chapter 6).

❋❋ CAUTION:

Handle the mass airflow sensor carefully, damage to the sensor will effect the operation of the fuel injection system.

3   Loosen the screws and remove the cover and the air filter element (see illustration).

9.2 Loosen the hose clamp (arrow) and disconnect the air intake duct from the MAF sensor

9.3 Loosen the screws (arrows) and remove the air filter housing cover

9.4 Grasp the air filter housing and pull the studs out of the mounting grommets

9.5 On V6 models, remove the wing nut (arrow) and tilt the resonator forward to detach the clip from the throttle body

4   Grasp the housing and pull it straight up to detach the housing studs from the mounting adapter grommets (see illustration). Remove the assembly from the engine compartment.

5   If necessary, loosen the hose clamps, detach the fasteners and separate the air intake duct and resonator assembly from the throttle body (see illustration).

6   Installation is the reverse of removal.

10 Accelerator cable/Throttle Actuator Control (TAC) system - replacement

▶ **Refer to illustrations 10.4, 10.5a, 10.5b and 10.6**

➡ **Note: All engines use a conventional accelerator cable except for some 2001 and later 4.8L, 5.3L and 6.0L V8 engines equipped with the Throttle Actuator Control (TAC) system.**

1   Disconnect the cable from the negative battery terminal.

❋❋ CAUTION:

On models equipped with the Theftlock audio system, be sure the lockout feature is turned off before performing any procedure which requires disconnecting the battery (see the front of this manual).

ACCELERATOR CABLE

2   On V6 models, remove the air intake duct and resonator from the throttle body. On V8 models, remove the intake manifold cover.

3   Detach the cruise control cable from the throttle lever.

4   Rotate the throttle lever and separate the accelerator cable end from the throttle lever (see illustration).

5   Depress the locking tabs on the cable housing and push the cable housing through the bracket. Detach the cable from the cable routing retainers (see illustrations).

6   Remove the trim panel from under the dash and detach the cable from the accelerator pedal (see illustration).

10.4 Rotate the throttle lever and pass the cable through the slot in the throttle lever

10.5a Depress the locking tabs and remove the cable from the bracket

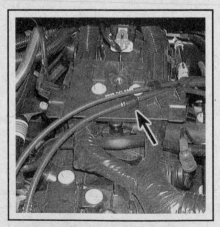

10.5b Detach the cable from the cable routing retainers

7 Depress the locking tabs on the cable housing and push the cable through the firewall and into the engine compartment.

8 Remove the cable from the engine compartment.

9 Installation is the reverse of removal.

THROTTLE CONTROL ACTUATOR (TAC) SYSTEM

10 Later models with 4.8L, 5.3L and 6.0L V8 engines are equipped with the Throttle Actuator Control (TAC) system, which is an all-electronic (no accelerator cable) throttle control system. Instead of an accelerator cable, which provides a direct mechanical link between the position of the accelerator pedal and the position of the throttle plate inside the throttle body, TAC-equipped vehicles use a pair of Accelerator Pedal Position (APP) sensors at the accelerator pedal assembly to monitor the angle of the accelerator pedal. Refer to Chapter 6 for more information on the accelerator pedal sensor.

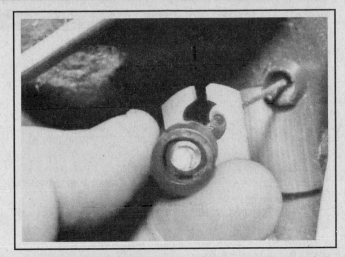

10.6 Pull the accelerator cable retainer out of the pedal and slide the cable through the slot

11 Fuel injection system - general information

The Sequential Multi Port Fuel Injection (SFI) system consists of three sub-systems: air intake, engine control and fuel delivery. The system uses a Powertrain Control Module (PCM) along with the sensors (coolant temperature sensor, throttle position sensor, mass airflow sensor, oxygen sensor, etc.) to determine the proper air/fuel ratio under all operating conditions.

The fuel injection system and the engine control system are closely linked in function and design. For additional information, refer to Chapter 6.

AIR INTAKE SYSTEM

The air intake system consists of the air filter, the air intake ducts, the throttle body, the air intake plenum (V6) and the intake manifold.

When the engine is idling, the air/fuel ratio is controlled by the idle air control system, which consists of the Powertrain Control Module (PCM) and the idle air control valve. This idle air control regulates the amount of airflow past the throttle plate and into the intake manifold, thus increasing or decreasing the engine idle speed. The PCM receives information from the sensors (vehicle speed, coolant temperature, air conditioning, power steering mode etc.) and adjusts the idle according to the demands of the engine and driver. Refer to Chapter 6 for information on the idle air control valve.

EMISSIONS AND ENGINE CONTROL SYSTEM

The emissions and engine control system is described in detail in Chapter 6.

FUEL DELIVERY SYSTEM

➡**Note: 2005 and later models use a Returnless Fuel System. This system uses a fuel pulse damper instead of a fuel pressure regulator, and has no fuel return lines to the fuel tank.**

The fuel delivery system consists of these components: the fuel pump, the fuel pressure regulator, the fuel meter body (V6) or fuel rail (V8) and the fuel injectors.

The fuel pump is an electric type. Fuel is drawn through an inlet screen into the pump, flows through the one-way valve, passes through the fuel filter and is delivered to the fuel meter body/fuel rail and injectors. The pressure regulator maintains a constant fuel pressure to the injectors. Excess fuel is routed back to the fuel tank through the fuel pressure regulator.

The injectors are solenoid-actuated pintle types consisting of a solenoid, plunger, needle valve and housing. When current is applied to the solenoid coil, the needle valve raises and pressurized fuel sprays out the nozzle. The injection quantity is determined by the length of time the valve is open (the length of time during which current is supplied to the solenoid coils).

On V6 models, the injectors are housed in a central fuel meter body located under the upper intake manifold (plenum). Six individual poppet nozzles are connected to the fuel injectors with nylon tubes. The injectors, tubes and poppet nozzles are serviced as an assembly. V8 models use a more conventional fuel rail/injector assembly.

The fuel pump relay is located in the engine compartment electrical center. The PCM controls the relay by supplying battery voltage to the relay coil. When energized, the fuel pump relay connects battery voltage to the fuel pump. If the PCM senses there is NO signal from the camshaft or crankshaft sensors (as with the engine not running or cranking), the PCM will de-energize the relay.

12 Fuel injection system - check

▶ Refer to illustrations 12.7, 12.8 and 12.9

➡Note: The following procedure is based on the assumption that the fuel pressure is adequate (see Section 3).

1 Check all electrical connectors that are related to the system. Check the ground wire connections for tightness. Loose connectors and poor grounds can cause many problems that resemble more serious malfunctions.

2 Check to see that the battery is fully charged, as the control unit and sensors depend on an accurate supply voltage in order to properly meter the fuel.

3 Check the air filter element - a dirty or partially blocked filter will severely impede performance and economy (see Chapter 1).

4 Check the related fuses. If a blown fuse is found, replace it and see if it blows again. If it does, search for a wire shorted to ground in the harness.

5 Check the air intake duct from the air filter housing to the throttle body for leaks, which will result in an excessively lean mixture. Also check the condition of all vacuum hoses connected to the intake manifold and/or throttle body.

6 Remove the air intake duct from the throttle body and check for dirt, carbon or other residue build-up on the throttle bore and throttle plate. If it's dirty, clean it with carburetor cleaner spray, a toothbrush and a shop towel.

❇ CAUTION:

Do not use a solvent containing Methyl Ethyl Ketone or damage to the throttle body may occur.

7 On V8 models, start the engine and place an automotive stethoscope against each injector, one at a time, and listen for a clicking sound, indicating operation (see illustration). If you don't have a stethoscope, place the tip of a screwdriver against the injector and listen through the handle.

8 On V8 models, disconnect the injector electrical connectors and measure the resistance of each injector (see illustration). Compare the

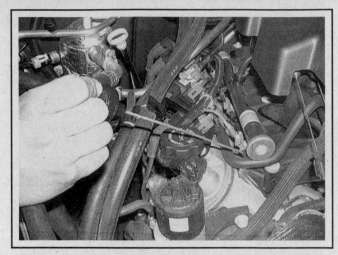

12.7 On V8 models, use a stethoscope to determine if the injectors are working properly - they should make a steady clicking sound that rises and falls with engine speed changes

measurements with the resistance values listed in this Chapter's Specifications.

➡Note: On V6 models, disconnect the fuel injector harness main connector at the fuel meter body and perform the tests there. Refer to the wiring diagrams at the end of Chapter 12 to determine the terminals for testing by wire color.

9 On V8 models, install an injector test light ("noid" light) into each injector electrical connector, one at a time (see illustration). Crank the engine over. Confirm that the light flashes evenly on each connector. This tests the PCM control of the injectors. If the light does not flash, have the PCM checked at a dealer service department or other properly equipped repair facility.

➡Note: On V6 models, disconnect the fuel injector harness main connector at the fuel meter body and perform the tests there. Refer to the wiring diagrams at the end of Chapter 12 to determine the terminals for testing by wire color.

12.8 Measure the resistance of each injector across the two terminals of the injector

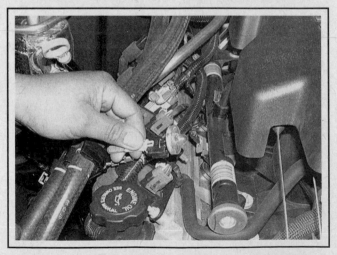

12.9 Install the "noid" light (available at most auto parts stores) into each injector electrical connector and confirm that it blinks when the engine is cranking

13 Throttle body - removal and installation

▶ Refer to illustrations 13.8a and 13.8b

Wait until the engine is completely cool before beginning this procedure.

On models equipped with the Theftlock audio system, be sure the lockout feature is turned off before performing any procedure which requires disconnecting the battery (see the front of this manual).

1 Disconnect the cable from the negative battery terminal.

2 On V8 models, partially drain the cooling system (see Chapter 1).
3 Remove the air intake duct and resonator.
4 Disconnect the electrical connectors from the throttle body.
5 Label and detach the vacuum hoses from the throttle body.
6 Detach the accelerator cable (see Section 10) and if equipped, the cruise control cable. On V6 models, remove the accelerator cable brackets.

➡Note: Some 2001 and later models are equipped with Electronic Throttle Control (ETC). On these models, there is no throttle cable, just electrical harness connectors at the throttle body and accelerator pedal, which is equipped with an Accelerator Pedal Position (APP) sensor.

7 On V8 models, detach the coolant hoses from the throttle body.
8 Remove the mounting bolts/nuts and remove the throttle body and gasket (see illustrations).
9 Remove all traces of old gasket material from the throttle body and intake manifold and install a new gasket.

Do not use solvent or a sharp tool to clean the throttle body gasket surface or damage to the throttle body may occur.

10 Install the throttle body and tighten the bolts to the torque listed in this Chapter's Specifications.
11 The remainder of installation is the reverse of removal.

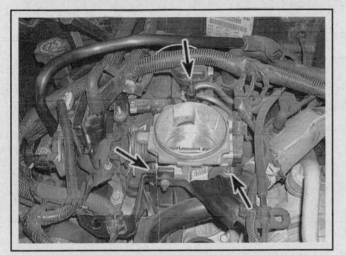

13.8a Throttle body mounting bolts (arrows) - V6 models

13.8b Throttle body mounting nuts (arrows) - early V8 models

14 Fuel pressure regulator - replacement

▶ Refer to illustrations 14.5a, 14.5b and 14.6

See the *Warning* in Section 1.

On models equipped with the Theftlock audio system, be sure the lockout feature is turned off before performing any procedure which requires disconnecting the battery (see the front of this manual).

1 Relieve the fuel system pressure (see Section 2).
2 Disconnect the cable from the negative battery terminal.

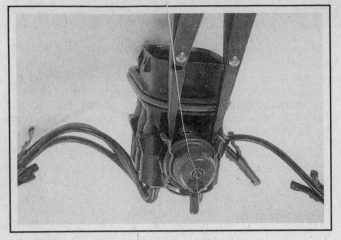

14.5a Remove the fuel pressure regulator retaining clip - 2004 and earlier V6 models

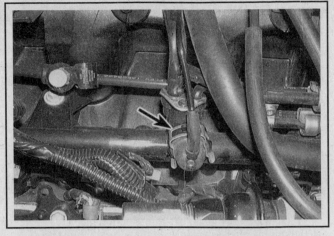

14.5b Remove the fuel pressure regulator retaining clip - 2003 and earlier V8 models

1999 THROUGH 2003 V8 MODELS/1999 THROUGH 2004 V6 MODELS

▶ Refer to illustrations 14.5a, 14.5b and 14.6

❋❋ WARNING:

See the Warning in Section 1.

3 On V6 models, remove the upper intake manifold for access to the fuel meter body (see Section 15).

4 On V8 models, remove the intake manifold cover and detach the vacuum hose from the port on the regulator.

5 Remove the pressure regulator retaining clip and detach the fuel pressure regulator (see illustrations).

❋❋ CAUTION:

On 2002 models, there are three different calibrations of regulators. If replacing a regulator, bring your old unit (and its retaining clip) to the parts store or dealership to ensure you get the right regulator and matching retaining clip.

6 Be sure to replace all O-ring seals, lubricating them with a light film of engine oil (see illustration).

➥Note: The small O-ring may remain in the fuel meter body or fuel rail.

7 Check the filter disc for contamination and clean or replace it as necessary.

8 The remainder of installation is the reverse of removal.

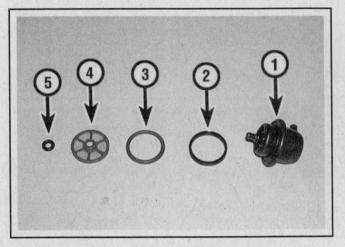

14.6 Fuel pressure regulator components

1 Fuel pressure regulator	4 Filter disc
2 Back-up ring	5 Small O-ring
3 Large O-ring	

2004 AND LATER V8 MODELS/2005 V6 MODELS

9 Remove the fuel pump module (see Section 7).

10 Remove the fuel level sending unit (see Section 8).

11 Replace the fuel pump module (fuel pulse damper/fuel pump) as a complete unit.

12 The remainder of installation is the reverse of removal.

---

15 Fuel meter body and injectors (V6 models) - removal and installation

❋❋ WARNING:

See the *Warning* in Section 1.

➥Note: When replacing components of the fuel meter body/injector assembly, refer to the identification numbers on the fuel meter body and injectors. Fuel injectors are calibrated with different flow rates and must not be interchanged with injectors from a different application.

REMOVAL

▶ Refer to illustrations 15.3, 15.4a, 15.4b, 15.5, 15.6, 15.7a, 15.7b, 15.8 and 15.9

1 Relieve the fuel system pressure (see Section 2).

2 Disconnect the cable from the negative battery terminal.

15.3 Remove the retaining clip and disconnect the electrical connector from the fuel meter body

> ※ **CAUTION:**
>
> On models equipped with the Theftlock audio system, be sure the lockout feature is turned off before performing any procedure which requires disconnecting the battery (see the front of this manual).

3 Remove the retaining clip and disconnect the electrical connector from the fuel meter body (see illustration).

4 Disconnect the fuel supply and return lines from the fittings at the rear of the engine (see illustration). Remove the bracket bolt. Loosen the nuts attaching the fuel lines to the fuel meter body and remove the lines (see illustration).

5 Remove the throttle body (see Section 13) and the accelerator control cable bracket. Remove the ignition coil/module assembly (see Chapter 5). Remove the EVAP purge valve (see Chapter 6). Remove the remaining mounting studs and carefully remove the upper intake manifold (see illustration).

> ※ **CAUTION:**
>
> Do not clean the composite upper intake manifold with solvent.

15.5 Upper intake manifold bolt locations (arrows) (upper intake manifold removed for clarity)

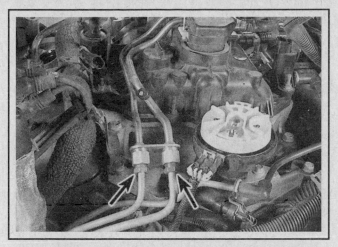

15.4a Disconnect the fuel supply and return lines from the fittings (arrows)

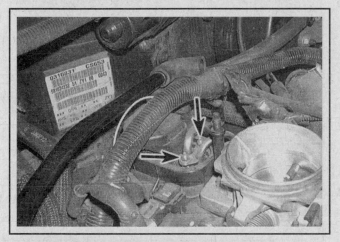

15.4b Remove the fuel line nuts and retainers (arrows) and remove the fuel lines from the fuel meter body

6 Detach the poppet nozzles by squeezing the tabs together and pulling the nozzle straight out of the intake manifold (see illustration).

➡Note: Apply a numbered tag to each nozzle or line with the corresponding cylinder number.

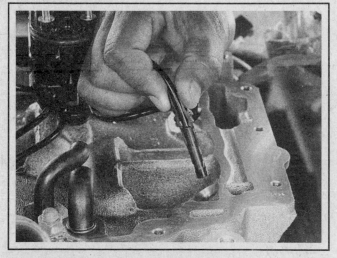

15.6 Squeeze the tabs and pull the poppet nozzle out of the intake manifold

15.7a Using two tools (arrows), pry the locking tabs away from the fuel meter body . . .

15.7b . . . and remove the fuel meter body along with the fuel lines and poppet nozzles from the intake manifold

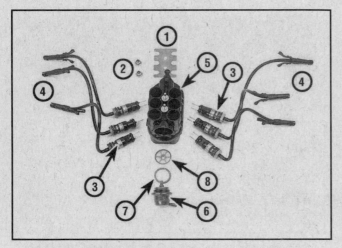

15.8 Fuel meter body components

1	Fuel injector hold-down plate	6	Fuel pressure regulator
2	Nuts		(2004 and earlier models)/
3	Fuel injectors		fuel pulse damper (2005 and
4	Poppet nozzles		later models)
5	Fuel meter body	7	O-ring
		8	Filter screen

15.9 To remove an injector from the fuel meter body, pull on the tube fitting while pushing the injector out

7   Pry the bracket locking tabs away from the fuel meter body and pull the assembly off the bracket (see illustrations). Place the assembly on a clean work bench.

8   Remove the fuel injector hold-down plate nuts and remove the plate from the fuel meter body (see illustration).

9   While pulling down on the injector tube fitting, push the injector out of the fuel meter body with a dull screwdriver (see illustration). Be careful not to damage the electrical terminals.

✳✳ CAUTION:

Do not attempt to remove the fuel line or poppet nozzle from the injector. They are serviced as a complete assembly.

INSTALLATION

10 Replace the injector O-rings. Apply a light coat of clean engine oil to the O-rings and press the injector into the fuel meter body until seated. Make sure the electrical terminals are properly aligned and the fuel tubes and nozzles are properly routed.

11 Install the injector hold-down plate and nuts.

12 Install the fuel meter body onto the intake manifold bracket. Install the poppet nozzles into the intake manifold, snapping them into place. Gently pull up on the fuel tube to ensure the nozzles are properly seated.

13 Inspect the fuel meter body and upper intake manifold seals for damage. Install new seals, if necessary. Install the upper intake manifold. Apply thread locking compound to the upper intake manifold bolts and tighten the bolts to the torque listed in this Chapter's Specifications. Install the EVAP purge valve and ignition coil/module assembly.

14 Inspect the fuel line O-rings and retainers for damage. Replace the O-rings and retainers, if necessary. Install the fuel lines onto the fuel meter body. Apply thread locking compound to the fuel line bracket bolt and install the bracket.

15 Inspect the throttle body seal for damage. Replace the seal, if necessary and install the throttle body (see Section 13).

16 The remainder of installation is the reverse of removal.

17 After the fuel meter body/injector assembly installation is complete, turn the ignition switch to On, but don't operate the starter (this activates the fuel pump for about two seconds, which builds up fuel pressure in the fuel lines and the fuel meter body). Cycle the ignition On and Off several times, then check the fuel lines and fuel meter body for fuel leakage.

16 Fuel rail and injectors (V8 models) - removal and installation

WARNING:

See the *Warning* in Section 1.

Note 1: E-85 models (ethanol, 85 percent) are equipped with a special design fuel rail. The fuel rail crossover pipe should NOT be detached from either fuel rail. Additionally, injector O-rings and retaining clips are not available separately; if an O-ring or clip needs replacing, the injector must be replaced.

Note 2: When replacing components of the fuel rail/injector assembly, refer to the identification numbers on the fuel rail and injectors. Fuel injectors are calibrated with different flow rates and must not be interchanged with injectors from a different application.

REMOVAL

Refer to illustrations 16.6, 16.7, 16.8, 16.9a and 16.9b

1 Relieve the fuel pressure (see Section 2).
2 Disconnect the cable from the negative battery terminal.

CAUTION:

On models equipped with the Theftlock audio system, be sure the lockout feature is turned off before performing any procedure which requires disconnecting the battery (see the front of this manual).

3 Remove the air intake duct and resonator (see Section 9). Remove the upper intake manifold cover and the cover mounting bracket.
4 Disconnect the accelerator cable and cruise control cable from the throttle body. Detach the cables from the bracket and position the cables aside.
5 Disconnect any electrical connectors that will interfere with fuel rail removal. Detach the upper engine wiring harness from the retainers and position the wiring harness aside.
6 Disconnect the fuel injector electrical connectors (see illustration).

Note: Apply a numbered tag to each connector with the corresponding cylinder number.

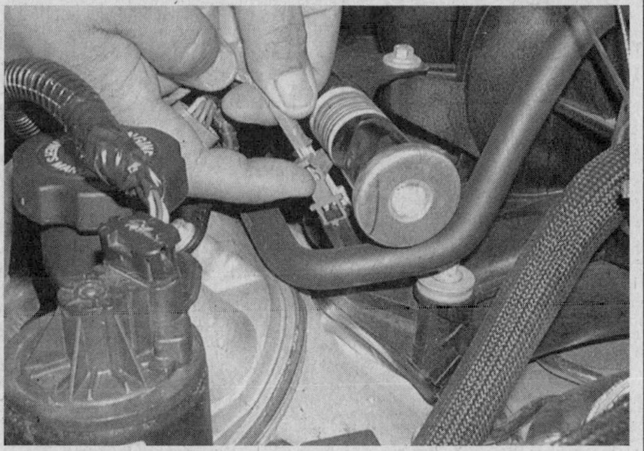

16.6 Pull the retainer up, push in on the tab and disconnect the electrical connector from the fuel injector

CAUTION:

On some models, the injector connectors are equipped with Connector Position Assurance (CPA) clips. Use only your fingers to release these clips, as pliers will damage them.

7 Disconnect the fuel supply and return lines from the fuel rail (see illustration). Disconnect the vacuum line from the fuel pressure regulator.
8 Clean any debris from around the injectors. Remove the fuel rail mounting bolts (see illustration). Loosen (but do not remove) the crossover tube retaining screw at the right (passenger) side fuel rail. Gently rock the fuel rail and injectors to loosen the injectors. Remove the fuel rail and fuel injectors as an assembly.
9 Remove the retaining clip and remove the injector(s) from the fuel rail assembly (see illustrations). Remove and discard the O-rings and seals.

Note: Whether you're replacing an injector or a leaking O-ring, it's a good idea to remove all the injectors from the fuel rail and replace all the O-rings (except on VIN Z [E-85 models], since the O-rings aren't available separately).

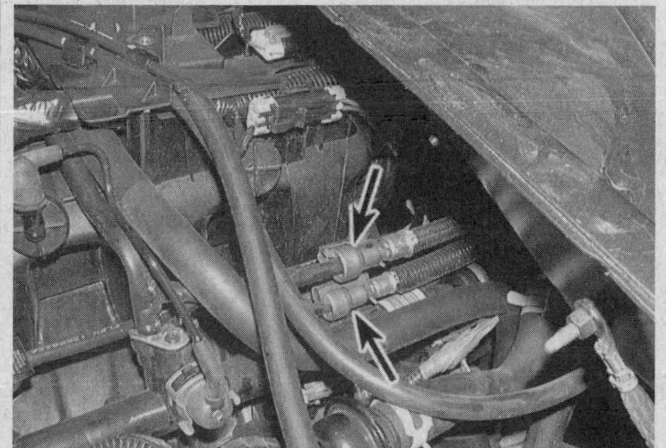

16.7 Using the proper fuel line disconnect tool, disconnect the fuel supply and return lines (arrows) from the fuel rail pipes

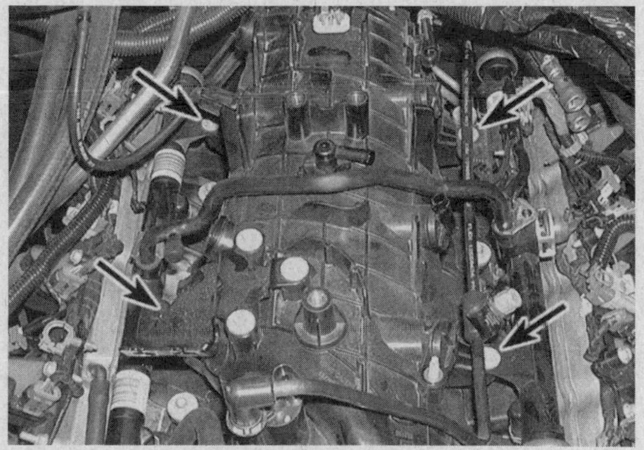

16.8 Remove the fuel rail mounting bolts (arrows)

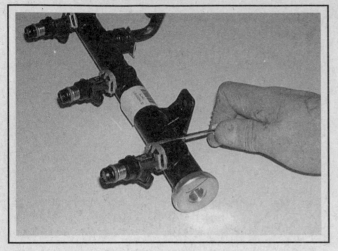

16.9a Remove the fuel injector retaining clip . . .

16.9b . . . and pry the injector out the fuel rail with a forked tool

INSTALLATION

10 Coat the new O-rings with clean engine oil and install them on the injector(s), then insert each injector into its corresponding bore in the fuel rail. Install the injector retaining clip.

11 Install the injector and fuel rail assembly on the intake manifold and fully seat the injectors. Apply thread locking compound to the fuel rail mounting bolts and tighten them to the torque listed in this Chapter's Specifications. Tighten the crossover tube retainer screw at the right fuel rail.

12 Connect the fuel supply and return lines and make sure they're securely installed.

13 Connect the electrical connectors to each injector, referring to the numbered tags.

14 The remainder of installation is the reverse of removal.

15 After the fuel rail/injector assembly installation is complete, turn the ignition switch to On, but don't operate the starter (this activates the fuel pump for about two seconds, which builds up fuel pressure in the fuel lines and the fuel rail). Cycle the ignition On and Off several times, then check the fuel lines, fuel rail and injectors for fuel leakage.

17 Exhaust system servicing - general information

✳✳ WARNING:

Inspection and repair of exhaust system components should be done only after enough time has elapsed after driving the vehicle to allow the system components to cool completely. Also, when working under the vehicle, make sure it is securely supported on jackstands.

1 The exhaust system consists of the exhaust manifolds, catalytic converters, muffler, resonators, the tailpipe and all connecting pipes, brackets, hangers and clamps. The exhaust system is attached to the body with mounting brackets and rubber hangers. If any of the parts are improperly installed, excessive noise and vibration will be transmitted to the body.

MUFFLER AND PIPES

▶ **Refer to illustrations 17.2a and 17.2b**

2 Conduct regular inspections of the exhaust system to keep it safe and quiet. Look for any damaged or bent parts, open seams, holes, loose connections, excessive corrosion or other defects which could allow exhaust fumes to enter the vehicle (see illustrations). Also check the catalytic converter when you inspect the exhaust system (see below). Deteriorated exhaust system components should not be repaired; they should be replaced with new parts.

3 If the exhaust system components are extremely corroded or rusted together, welding equipment will probably be required to remove them. The convenient way to accomplish this is to have a muffler repair shop remove the corroded sections with a cutting torch. If, however, you want to save money by doing it yourself (and you don't have a welding outfit with a cutting torch), simply cut off the old components with a hacksaw. If you have compressed air, special pneumatic cutting chisels can also be used. If you do decide to tackle the job at home, be sure to wear safety goggles to protect your eyes from metal chips and work gloves to protect your hands.

4 Here are some simple guidelines to follow when repairing the exhaust system:

   a) *Work from the back to the front when removing exhaust system components.*

   b) *Apply penetrating oil to the exhaust system component fasteners to make them easier to remove.*

   c) *Use new gaskets, hangers and clamps when installing exhaust systems components.*

   d) *Apply anti-seize compound to the threads of all exhaust system fasteners during reassembly.*

   e) *Be sure to allow sufficient clearance between newly installed parts and all points on the underbody to avoid overheating the floor pan and possibly damaging the interior carpet and insulation. Pay particularly close attention to the catalytic converter and heat shield.*

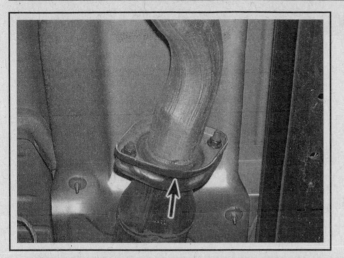

17.2a Inspect the exhaust system connections for leakage (arrow)

17.2b Inspect the rubber hangers for damage

CATALYTIC CONVERTER

❊❊ WARNING:

The converter gets very hot during operation. Make sure it has cooled down before you touch it.

➡ **Note: See Chapter 6 for additional information on the catalytic converter.**

5   Periodically inspect the heat shield for cracks, dents and loose or missing fasteners.

6   Inspect the converter for cracks or other damage.

7   If the catalytic converter requires replacement, refer to Chapter 6.

Specifications

Fuel pressure (key ON, engine OFF)	
V6 engines	60 to 66 psi
V8 engines	
VIN Z (E-85 [ethanol, 85-percent])	48 to 54 psi
All others	55 to 62 psi
Fuel injector resistance (approximate)	
V6 engine	not available
V8 engine	
1999 through 2002	11.4 to 12.6 ohms
2003 and later	11 to 14 ohms

Torque specifications — Ft-lbs (unless otherwise indicated)

Fuel rail mounting bolts (V8 engines)	89 in-lbs
Fuel tank mounting strap bolts	30
Throttle body mounting bolts	
V6 engine	
1999 and 2000	18
2001 and later	80 in-lbs
V8 engine	
1999 through 2002	97 in-lbs
2003 and later	89 in-lbs
Upper intake manifold bolts (V6 engine)	
Step 1	44 in-lbs
Step 2	80 in-lbs

5

ENGINE ELECTRICAL SYSTEMS

Section

Reference to other Chapters

1   General information and precautions

GENERAL INFORMATION

♦ **Refer to illustrations 1.1a and 1.1b**

The engine electrical systems include all ignition, charging and starting components (see illustrations). Because of their engine-related functions,

these components are discussed separately from body electrical devices such as the lights, instruments, etc. (which are included in Chapter 12).

PRECAUTIONS

Always observe the following precautions when working on the

1.1a Typical engine electrical system components - V6 engine

1	Ignition coil and ignition control module	3	Battery	5	Remote positive jumper terminal
2	Underhood Electrical Center	4	Battery cable	6	Alternator

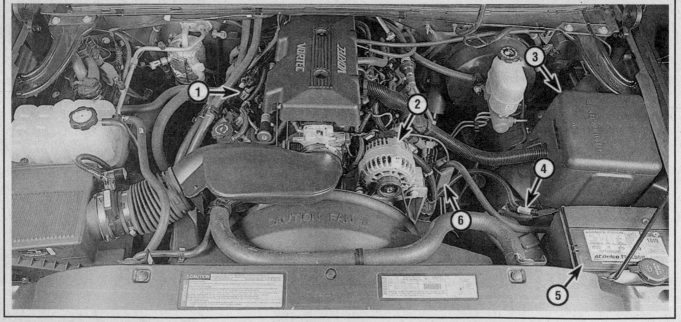

1.1b Typical engine electrical system components - V8 engines

1	Ignition coil (1 of 8)	3	Underhood electrical center	5	Battery
2	Alternator	4	Battery cable	6	Remote positive jumper terminal

electrical system:

a) Be extremely careful when servicing engine electrical components. They are easily damaged if checked, connected or handled improperly.

b) Never leave the ignition switched on for long periods of time when the engine is not running.

c) Never disconnect the battery cables while the engine is running.

d) Maintain correct polarity when connecting battery cables from another vehicle during jump starting - see the "Booster battery (jump) starting" section at the front of this manual.

e) Always disconnect the negative battery cable before working on the electrical system.

It's also a good idea to review the safety-related information regarding the engine electrical systems located in the "Safety first!" section at the front of this manual, before beginning any operation included in this Chapter.

BATTERY DISCONNECTION

WARNING:

On 2006 and later models with OnStar, make absolutely sure the ignition key is in the Off position and Retained Accessory Power (RAP) has been depleted before disconnecting the cable from the negative battery terminal. Also, never remove the OnStar fuse with the ignition key in any position other than Off. If these precautions are not taken, the OnStar system's back-up battery will be activated, and remain activated, until it goes dead. If this happens, the OnStar system will not function as it should in the event that the main vehicle battery power is cut off (as might happen during a collision).

CAUTION:

On models equipped with the Theftlock audio system, be sure the lockout feature is turned off before performing any procedure which requires disconnecting the battery (see the front of this manual).

Several systems on the vehicle require battery power to be available at all times, either to ensure their continued operation (such as the clock) or to maintain control unit memories (such as that in the engine management system's Powertrain Control Module) which would be wiped out if the battery were to be disconnected. Therefore, whenever the battery is to be disconnected, first note the following to ensure that there are no unforeseen consequences of this action:

a) First, on any vehicle with power door locks, it is a wise precaution to remove the key from the ignition and to keep it with you, so that it does not get locked inside if the power door locks should engage accidentally when the battery is reconnected!

b) The engine management system's PCM will lose the information stored in its memory when the battery is disconnected. This includes idling and operating values, and any fault codes detected (see Chapter 6). Whenever the battery is disconnected, the information relating to idle speed control and other operating values will have to be re-programmed into the unit's memory. The PCM does this by itself, but until then, there may be surging, hesitation, erratic idle and a generally inferior level of performance. To allow the PCM to relearn these values, start the engine and run it as close to idle speed as possible until it reaches its normal operating temperature, then run it for approximately two minutes at 1200 rpm. Next, drive the vehicle as far as necessary - approximately 5 miles of varied driving conditions is usually sufficient - to complete the relearning process.

Devices known as "memory-savers" can be used to avoid some of the above problems. Precise details vary according to the device used. Typically, it is plugged into the cigarette lighter, and is connected by its own wires to a spare battery; the vehicle's own battery is then disconnected from the electrical system, leaving the "memory-saver" to pass sufficient current to maintain audio unit security codes and PCM memory values, and also to run permanently live circuits such as the clock, all the while isolating the battery in the event of a short-circuit occurring while work is carried out.

WARNING:

Some of these devices allow a considerable amount of current to pass, which can mean that many of the vehicle's systems are still operational when the main battery is disconnected. If a "memory-saver" is used, ensure that the circuit concerned is actually "dead" before carrying out any work on it!

To disconnect the battery for service procedures requiring power to be cut from the vehicle, first open the driver's door to disable Retained Accessory Power (RAP), then loosen the cable end bolt and disconnect the cable from the negative battery terminal. Isolate the cable end to prevent it from coming into accidental contact with the battery terminal.

2 Battery - emergency jump starting

Refer to the *Booster battery (jump) starting* procedure at the front of this manual.

3 Battery - check and replacement

WARNING:

Hydrogen gas is produced by the battery, so keep open flames and lighted cigarettes away from it at all times. Always wear eye protection when working around a battery. Rinse off spilled electrolyte immediately with large amounts of water.

CHECK

Refer to illustrations 3.2 and 3.3

1 The battery's surface charge must be removed before accurate voltage measurements can be made. Turn On the high beams for ten

seconds, then turn them Off, let the vehicle stand for two minutes. Remove the battery from the vehicle (see Steps 4 through 10).

2   Check the battery state of charge. Visually inspect the indicator eye on the top of the battery, if the indicator eye is clear, charge the battery as described in Chapter 1. Next perform an open voltage circuit test using a digital voltmeter (see illustration). With the engine and

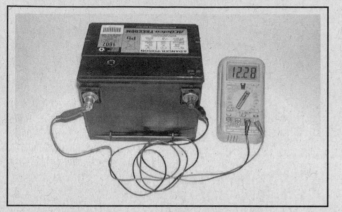

3.2 To test the open circuit voltage of the battery, connect a voltmeter to the battery - a fully charged battery should measure at least 12.4 volts (depending on outside air temperature)

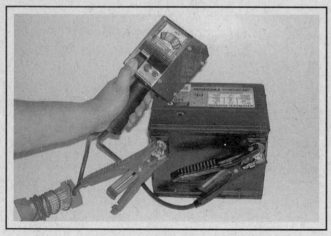

3.3 Connect a battery load tester to the battery and check the battery condition under load following the tool manufacturers instructions

all accessories Off, connect the negative probe of the voltmeter to the negative terminal of the battery and the positive probe to the positive terminal of the battery. The battery voltage should be 12.4 volts or more. If the battery is less than the specified voltage, charge the battery before proceeding to the next test. Do not proceed with the battery load test unless the battery charge is correct.

3   Perform a battery load test. An accurate check of the battery condition can only be performed with a load tester (available at most auto parts stores). This test evaluates the ability of the battery to operate the starter and other accessories during periods of heavy amperage draw (load). Install a special battery load testing tool onto the terminals (see illustration). Load test the battery according to the tool manufacturer's instructions. This tool utilizes a carbon pile to increase the load demand (amperage draw) on the battery. Maintain the load on the battery for 15 seconds or less and observe that the battery voltage does not drop below 9.6 volts. If the battery condition is weak or defective, the tool will indicate this condition immediately.

➡**Note: Cold temperatures will cause the minimum voltage requirements to drop slightly. Follow the chart given in the tool manufacturer's instructions to compensate for cold climates. Minimum load voltage for freezing temperatures (32 degrees F) should be approximately 9.1 volts.**

REPLACEMENT

▶ **Refer to illustrations 3.6 and 3.8**

❋❋ **WARNING:**

Refer to the Warning and Caution in Chapter 5, Section 1 under "Battery disconnection" before proceeding with the following Steps.

❋❋ **CAUTION:**

On models equipped with the Theftlock audio system, be sure the lockout feature is turned off before performing any procedure which requires disconnecting the battery (see the front of this manual).

4   Disconnect the cable from the negative battery terminal.
5   Disconnect the positive battery cable.
6   Remove the fender brace. Remove the battery retainer bolt and retainer (see illustration).

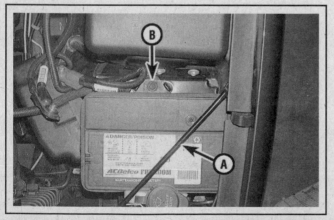

3.6 Before removing the battery, remove the fender brace (A), then remove the battery retainer (B) and lift out the battery

3.8 Inspect the tray, retainer brackets and related fasteners for corrosion or damage - if necessary, remove the bolts (arrows) and the battery tray

7 Remove the battery and place it on a workbench. Remove the battery insulator.

➡**Note: Battery handling tools are available at most auto parts stores for a reasonable price. They make it easier to remove and carry the battery.**

8 While the battery is removed, inspect the tray, retainer brackets and related fasteners for corrosion or damage (see illustration).

9 If corrosion is evident, remove the battery tray and use a baking soda/water solution to clean the corroded area to prevent further oxidation. Repaint the area as necessary using rust resistant paint.

10 Clean and service the battery and cables (see Chapter 1).

11 If you are replacing the battery, make sure you purchase one that is identical to yours, with the same dimensions, amperage rating, cold cranking amps rating, etc. Make sure it is fully charged prior to installation in the vehicle.

12 Installation is the reverse of removal. Connect the positive cable first and the negative cable last.

13 After connecting the cables to the battery, apply a light coating of petroleum jelly or grease to the connections to help prevent corrosion.

4 Battery cables - replacement

▶ **Refer to illustrations 4.4a, 4.4b, 4.4c, 4.4d and 4.4e**

✳✳ WARNING:

Refer to the Warning and Caution in Chapter 5, Section 1 under "Battery disconnection" before proceeding with the following Steps.

✳✳ CAUTION:

On models equipped with the Theftlock audio system, be sure the lockout feature is turned off before performing any procedure which requires disconnecting the battery (see the front of this manual).

1 Periodically Inspect the entire length of each battery cable for damage, cracked or burned insulation and corrosion. Poor battery cable connections can cause starting problems and decreased engine performance.

2 Check the cable-to-terminal connections at the ends of the cables for cracks, loose wire strands and corrosion. The presence of white, fluffy deposits under the insulation at the cable terminal connection is a sign that the cable is corroded and should be replaced. Check the terminals for distortion, missing mounting bolts and corrosion.

3 When removing the cables, always disconnect the negative cable

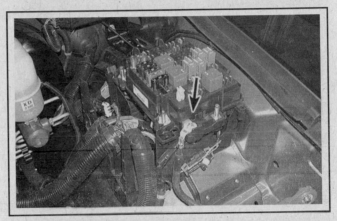

4.4a One branch of the positive cable is connected to the underhood electrical center

first and hook it up last or the battery may be shorted by the tool used to loosen the cable clamps. Even if only the positive cable is being replaced, be sure to disconnect the negative cable first (see Chapter 1 for further information regarding battery cable maintenance).

4 Disconnect the old cables from the battery, then disconnect them at the opposite end. Detach the cables from the starter solenoid, underhood electrical center and ground terminals, as necessary (see

4.4b Remove the nut (arrow) and disconnect the positive cable from the remote positive jumper terminal (do this only after disconnecting the cable from the negative terminal of the battery)

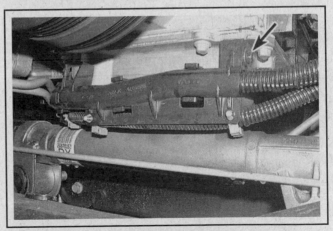

4.4c On V8 models, remove the bolt (arrow) and slide the positive cable retainer toward the drivers side of the vehicle to detach the retainer from the engine - release the clips and detach the wiring harness from the retainer

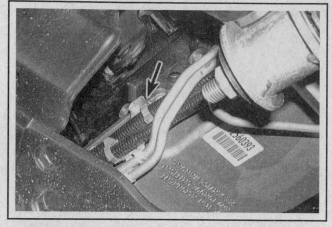

4.4d Release the clip and detach the positive cable from the retainer - this type retainer can be found at various points along the entire length of the cable

4.4e The negative cable is fastened to the engine block

illustrations). Note the routing of each cable to ensure correct installation. The positive cable is retained by clips and/or tape to the main wiring harness, the oil pan and the power steering pump. It is easiest to access these areas by first raising the vehicle and placing it securely on jackstands.

5   If you are replacing either or both of the battery cables, take them with you when buying new cables. It is vitally important that you replace the cables with identical parts. Cables have characteristics that make them easy to identify: positive cables are usually red and larger in cross-section; ground cables are usually black and smaller in cross-section.

6   Clean the threads of the starter solenoid or ground connection with a wire brush to remove rust and corrosion. Apply a light coat of battery terminal corrosion inhibitor or petroleum jelly to the threads to prevent future corrosion.

7   Attach the cable to the terminal and tighten the mounting nut/bolt securely.

8   Before connecting a new cable to the battery, make sure that it reaches the battery without having to be stretched.

5   Ignition system - general information

V6 models are equipped with a distributor-type electronic ignition system. The ignition system consists of the battery, distributor, ignition coil, ignition control module, spark plug wires, spark plugs, camshaft position sensor, crankshaft position sensor and the Powertrain Control Module (PCM).

V8 models are equipped with a distributorless ignition system. The ignition system consists of the battery, eight ignition coils (one per cylinder), spark plug wires, spark plugs, camshaft position sensor, crankshaft position sensor and the Powertrain Control Module (PCM).

On all models, the PCM controls the ignition timing and spark advance characteristics for the engine. The ignition timing is not adjustable.

The crankshaft position sensor produces a signal voltage to indicate crankshaft position and crankshaft speed. This signal is used by the Powertrain Control Module (PCM) to control the ignition system and ignition timing.

The camshaft position sensor operation is similar to a crankshaft position sensor, but produces only one pulse per camshaft revolution. The camshaft position sensor signal is not essential to engine operation. The PCM uses the camshaft position sensor signal for fuel synchronization and misfire detection.

The ignition system is also equipped with a knock sensor to detect detonation, or spark knock (usually caused by the use of sub-standard fuel). The system uses a knock sensor in conjunction with the Powertrain Control Module (PCM) to control spark timing. If a knock signal is received, the PCM will retard the timing until the knock is eliminated. The knock sensor system allows the engine to use maximum spark advance without spark knock, which improves driveability and fuel economy.

6   Ignition system - check

▶ **Refer to illustrations 6.4, 6.10a, 6.10b, 6.11, 6.14 and 6.15**

✳✳ WARNING 1:

Because of the high voltage generated by the ignition system, extreme care should be taken whenever an operation is performed involving ignition components. This not only includes the ignition coil, but related components and test equipment.

✳✳ WARNING 2:

The following procedure requires the engine to be cranked during testing, make sure the meter leads, loose clothing, long hair, etc. are away from the moving parts of the engine (drivebelt, cooling fan, etc.) before cranking the engine.

1   Before proceeding with the ignition system, check the following items:

a) Make sure the battery cable clamps, where they connect to the battery, are clean and tight.

b) Test the condition of the battery (see Section 3). If it does not pass all the tests, replace it with a new battery.

c) Check the ignition coil and ignition control module external wiring and connections.

d) Check the related fuses inside the underhood electrical center (see Chapter 12). If they're burned, determine the cause and repair the circuit.

2   If the engine turns over but won't start or has a severe misfire, make sure there is sufficient secondary ignition voltage to fire the spark plugs.

3   Disable the fuel system by removing the fuel pump relay from the underhood electrical center (see Chapter 12).

4   Disconnect a spark plug wire from one of the spark plugs and attach a calibrated ignition system tester (available at most auto parts stores) to the spark plug boot. Connect the clip on the tester to a bolt or metal bracket on the engine (see illustration). Crank the engine and watch the end of the tester to see if bright blue, well-defined sparks occur (weak spark or intermittent spark is the same as no spark).

5   If spark occurs, sufficient voltage is reaching the plug to fire it. Repeat the check at the remaining spark plug wires to verify that the distributor cap, rotor, spark plug wires, ignition coil(s) and control systems are functioning properly. If the ignition system is operating properly the problem lies elsewhere; i.e. a mechanical or fuel system problem. However, the spark plugs may be fouled, so remove and check them as described in Chapter 1.

6   If no spark occurs at one or more wires, remove the suspected spark plug wire from the ignition coil and check the terminals at both ends for damage. Connect an ohmmeter to the ends of the spark plug wire and check the wire for an open or high resistance. If the spark plug wire resistance is greater than 30 K-ohms, replace the wire.

7   If the engine won't start due to no spark or misfires severely, proceed with the ignition system check according to engine type as follows:

V6 MODELS

8   Disconnect the ignition coil wire from the distributor cap, connect the calibrated ignition tester to the coil wire, crank the engine and check for spark (see illustration 6.4). If adequate sparks occur at the coil wire, remove the distributor cap and check the distributor cap and rotor as described in Chapter 1. Replace the defective parts as necessary. Crank the engine while watching the distributor rotor. If the rotor does not turn, the distributor gear is stripped or the distributor shaft, timing chain/gears or camshaft are broken or damaged.

9   If no spark occurs at the coil wire, use an ohmmeter to check the resistance of the coil wire. Coil wire resistance should be approximately 1000 ohms per inch. Replace the coil wire if defective.

10 Disconnect the electrical connector from the ignition coil and from the ignition control module. Turn the ignition key On and check for battery voltage at the pink wire terminal of each harness connector (see illustrations). Also check for continuity to battery ground at the black

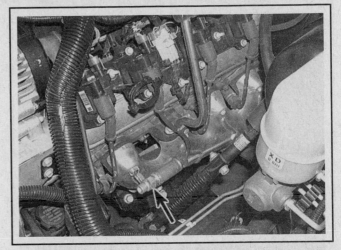

6.4 To use a calibrated ignition tester; disconnect a spark plug wire, connect the tester to the spark plug boot and clip the tester (arrow) to a convenient ground - crank the engine over, if there's enough power to fire the plug, bright blue sparks will be visible between the electrode tip and the tester body (weak spark or intermittent spark are the same as no spark)

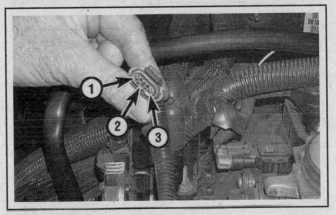

6.10a Ignition coil harness connector terminal identification

1	12-volt supply	3	Coil driver (from ignition
2	Not used		control module)

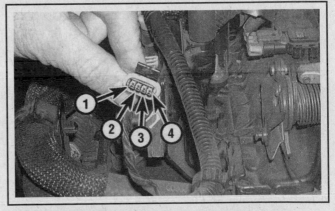

6.10b Ignition control module harness connector terminal identification

1	Ignition coil driver	3	Ignition timing control
2	Ground		(from PCM)
		4	12-volt supply

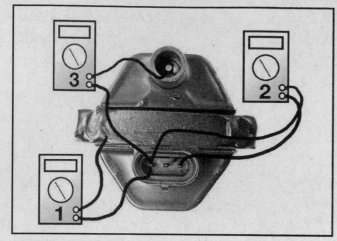

6.11 To check the primary and secondary resistance of the V6 ignition coil, perform the three tests as shown - replace the ignition coil if your measurements are not as specified

1 *The ohmmeter should read infinite resistance between the primary terminals and the core*
2 *The primary resistance should be approximately 0.1 ohm*
3 *The secondary resistance should be between 5,000 to 25,000 ohms*

wire terminal of the ignition module harness connector. If battery voltage is not available at the ignition coil and/or ignition module, check the circuits from the underhood electrical center to the coil or module (don't forget to check the fuses first).

11 Using an ohmmeter, check the primary and secondary resistance of the ignition coil (see illustration). Replace the ignition coil if defective.

12 If the previous checks are correct, check the trigger signal from the ignition control module. Reconnect the electrical connector to the ignition control module. Attach the lead of a test light to the positive battery terminal and touch the probe of the test light to the white/black wire terminal at the ignition coil connector. Crank the engine. The test light should blink with the engine cranking if a trigger signal is present. If a trigger signal is not present, disconnect the electrical connector from the ignition control module and connect the positive probe of a voltmeter to the white wire terminal of the harness connector. Connect the negative lead to a good engine ground point and set the meter on the AC volts scale. Crank the engine. Approximately 1.0 to 4.0 volts should be indicated, if not, check the crankshaft position sensor (see Chapter 6). If the crankshaft position sensor is good, check the related circuits for continuity. If the circuits are good, have the PCM checked by a dealer service department or other qualified repair shop.

➡**Note: Refer to the wiring diagrams at the end of Chapter 12 for wire color identification for testing and additional information on the circuits.**

13 If the 1.0 to 4.0 volts ignition control signal was present at the ignition control module connector, but no trigger signal was present at the ignition coil connector, check the white/black wire for continuity between the ignition module connector and the ignition coil connector. If the circuit is good, replace the ignition control module.

V8 MODELS

14 Check for battery voltage to the ignition coils from the ignition switch. Attach a 12 volt test light to the battery negative (-) terminal or other good ground. Disconnect the electrical connector from one of the ignition coils and check for power at the pink wire terminal (see illus-

6.14 Disconnect an ignition coil electrical connector (arrow) and check for battery power at the pink wire terminal of the connector

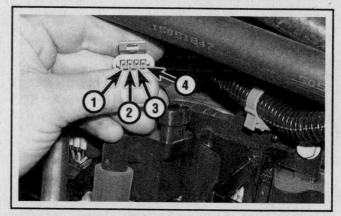

6.15 Using a test light connected to the positive battery terminal, check for a trigger signal at the ignition control terminal (1999 and 2000 models)

1 *12-volt supply*
2 *Ignition control (from PCM)*
3 *Reference low*
4 *Ground*

tration). Battery voltage should be available with the ignition key On. If there is no battery voltage present, check the wiring and/or circuit between the underhood electrical center and ignition coil connector (don't forget to check the fuses). Also check the black wire terminal for continuity to battery ground. If there is battery voltage at the coil, but there is no spark from the coil, the coil, crankshaft position sensor, PCM or wiring are likely culprits.

15 On 1999 and 2000 models, check for a trigger signal from the PCM. Attach the lead of a test light to the positive battery terminal and touch the probe of the test light to the ignition control circuit terminal (see illustration). Crank the engine. The test light should blink with the engine cranking if a trigger signal is present. Check each coil, if necessary. If a trigger signal is present at the coil, the power and ground circuits are good and there is no spark, replace the ignition coil. If a trigger signal is not present, check the crankshaft position sensor (see Chapter 6). If the crankshaft position sensor is good, check the circuits from the coil to the PCM. If the circuits are good, have the PCM checked by a dealer service department or other qualified repair shop.

➡**Note: Refer to the wiring diagrams at the end of Chapter 12 for wire color identification for testing and additional information on the circuits.**

7   Ignition coil and ignition control module (V6 models) - removal and installation

1   Disconnect the cable from the negative battery terminal.

✳ CAUTION:

On models equipped with the Theftlock audio system, be sure the lockout feature is turned off before performing any procedure which requires disconnecting the battery (see the front of this manual).

2   Remove the air intake duct and resonator from the throttle body (see Chapter 4).

IGNITION COIL

▶ **Refer to illustration 7.4**

3   Disconnect the electrical connectors from the ignition coil and ignition control module. Detach the coil wire from the ignition coil high-tension terminal.

4   Remove the ignition coil/module bracket mounting bolts and remove the assembly from the engine (see illustration). Remove the ignition control module from the bracket.

5   Place the assembly on a workbench. Using the appropriate size drill, drill out the center of the rivets retaining the coil to the bracket. Use a drift punch to punch out the rivets and remove the coil from the bracket.

6   Attach the ignition coil to the bracket using new screws.

➥**Note: Screws are provided with a new ignition coil.**

Attach the ignition module to the bracket.

7   Install the assembly on the engine and connect the electrical connectors and coil wire.

IGNITION CONTROL MODULE

▶ **Refer to Illustration 7.10**

8   The ignition control module can be removed without removing the coil bracket from the engine.

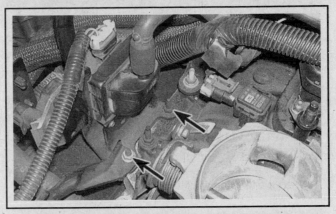

7.4 Remove the ignition coil/module bracket mounting bolts (arrows)

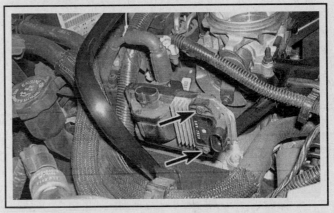

7.10 Ignition control module mounting screws (arrows)

9   Disconnect the electrical connector from the ignition control module.

10 Remove the mounting screws and remove the ignition control module from the bracket (see illustration).

11 Installation is the reverse of removal.

8   Ignition coils (V8 models) - removal and installation

▶ **Refer to illustrations 8.3 and 8.4**

1   Disconnect the cable from the negative battery terminal.

✳ CAUTION:

On models equipped with the Theftlock audio system, be sure the lockout feature is turned off before performing any procedure which requires disconnecting the battery (see the front of this manual).

2   The ignition coils may be removed from each cylinder bank as a complete assembly or removed from the mounting bracket individually.

3   If removing the complete assembly, disconnect the ignition coils main electrical connector. Disconnect the spark plug wires from the spark plugs. Remove the ignition coil bracket mounting nuts/bolts and remove the assembly from the engine (see illustration).

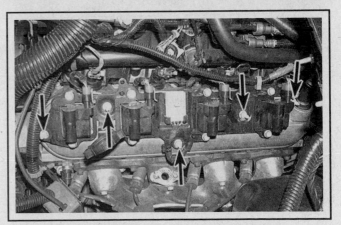

8.3 Remove the ignition coil bracket bolts (arrows)

8.4 Remove the ignition coil mounting screws (arrows)

4   If removing an individual coil, disconnect the spark plug wire from the coil. Remove the ignition coil mounting screws and remove the ignition coil from the bracket (see illustration).

5   Installation is the reverse of removal.

➡**Note: There are two different coil manufacturers, and the coils, plug wires and coil mounting brackets are not interchangeable. If you are replacing one or more coils, take the old coil with you for identification at the auto parts store.**

9   Distributor (V6 models) - removal and installation

REMOVAL

▶ **Refer to illustrations 9.6 and 9.7**

1   Disconnect the cable from the negative battery terminal.

✳ CAUTION:

On models equipped with the Theftlock audio system, be sure the lockout feature is turned off before performing any procedure which requires disconnecting the battery (see the front of this manual).

2   Remove the air intake duct and resonator assembly from the throttle body (see Chapter 4).

3   Position the engine with the number one cylinder at TDC on the compression stroke (see Chapter 2A).

4   Disconnect the electrical connector from the distributor.

5   Disconnect the coil wire from the distributor cap. Label and detach the spark plug wires from the spark plugs. Detach the spark plug wire retainers from the studs and brackets. Loosen the distributor cap mounting screws, remove the cap from the distributor and position the cap (with the spark plug wires attached) aside.

6   The distributor rotor should be pointing at the alignment mark; if necessary apply a paint mark on the edge of the distributor body directly below the rotor tip and in line with it (see illustration).

7   Mark the position of the distributor base to the engine to ensure the distributor can be re-installed in exactly the same position as originally installed (see illustration).

8   Remove the distributor hold-down bolt and pull out the distributor. Remove and discard the O-ring.

INSTALLATION

9   If the crankshaft has been moved while the distributor is out, the number one piston must be repositioned at TDC. This can be done by feeling for compression pressure at the number one spark plug hole as the crankshaft is rotated. Once compression is felt, continue rotating the crankshaft until the mark on the crankshaft damper is aligned with the TDC mark on the timing indicator (see Chapter 2A).

10 Install a new O-ring on the distributor housing.

11 Turn the rotor until it points approximately 42-degrees counterclockwise from the mark made in Step 6.

➡**Note: Make sure the oil pump drive gear is properly aligned with the tab on the distributor shaft. If necessary use a long screwdriver to turn the oil pump drive shaft.**

9.6 Apply a paint mark on the edge of the distributor body directly below the rotor tip and in line with it

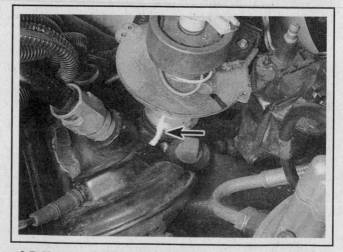

9.7 Mark the position of the distributor base to the engine

12 Insert the distributor into the engine block. As the distributor gear engages the camshaft the rotor will rotate clockwise and when fully seated, the rotor must align with the mark made in Step 6. Rotate the distributor base until the marks made in Step 7 align.

✳✳ CAUTION:

The distributor must be installed the same position as originally installed. Make sure the spark plug wire terminals are perpen- dicular to the engine centerline and the rotor remains aligned with the alignment mark. If the distributor is installed incorrectly, the engine will run poorly, the SERVICE ENGINE SOON light will illuminate and a diagnostic trouble code will set (see Chapter 6).

13 Install the distributor hold-down clamp and tighten the bolt to the torque listed in this Chapter's Specifications.
14 The remainder of installation is the reverse of removal.

10 Charging system - general information and precautions

The main components of the charging system are an alternator (with an integral voltage regulator), the battery and the wiring connecting the components. The components work together to supply electrical power for the electrical system and maintain the battery in a charged condition. The alternator is driven by the drivebelt at the front of the engine.

All models are equipped with either a model AD-230 or AD-244 alternator. AD type alternators should be considered non-serviceable and, if defective, exchanged as cores for new or rebuilt units. An identification number and amperage rating is stamped on the alternator housing. Refer to these numbers to obtain the correct replacement alternator, if necessary.

The purpose of the voltage regulator is to limit the alternator voltage output to a preset value. This prevents power surges and circuit overloads during peak voltage output. On all models with which this manual is concerned, the voltage regulator is integral with the alternator.

The charging system doesn't ordinarily require periodic maintenance. However, the drivebelt, battery and wires and connections should be inspected at the intervals outlined in Chapter 1.

The instrument panel warning light should come on when the ignition key is turned to START, then go off immediately after the engine has started. If the warning light stays on or comes on when the engine is running, a charging system problem has occurred (see Section 9).

Be very careful when making electrical circuit connections to a vehicle equipped with an alternator and note the following:

a) *When reconnecting wires to the alternator from the battery, be sure to note the polarity.*
b) *Before using arc welding equipment to repair any part of the vehicle, disconnect the wires from the alternator and the battery terminals.*

✳✳ CAUTION:

On models equipped with the Theftlock audio system, be sure the lockout feature is turned off before performing any procedure which requires disconnecting the battery (see the front of this manual).

c) *Never start the engine with a battery charger connected.*
d) *Always disconnect both battery leads before using a battery charger.*
e) *The alternator is turned by an engine drivebelt which could cause serious injury if your hands, hair or clothes become entangled in it with the engine running.*
f) *Because the alternator is connected directly to the battery, it could arc or cause a fire if overloaded or shorted out.*
g) *Wrap a plastic bag over the alternator and secure it with rubber bands before steam cleaning the engine.*

11 Charging system - check

▶ **Refer to illustration 11.2**

➡ **Note: These vehicles are equipped with an On-Board Diagnostic (OBD) system that is useful for detecting charging system problems. Refer to Chapter 6 for the list of diagnostic codes and procedures for obtaining the codes.**

1 If a malfunction occurs in the charging circuit, do not immediately assume that the alternator is causing the problem. First check the following items:

a) *The battery cables where they connect to the battery. Make sure the connections are clean and tight.*
b) *The battery electrolyte specific gravity (by observing the charge indicator on the battery). If it is low, charge the battery.*
c) *Check the external alternator wiring and connections.*
d) *Check the drivebelt condition and tension (see Chapter 1).*
e) *Check the alternator mounting bolts for tightness.*
f) *Run the engine and check the alternator for abnormal noise.*

2 Connect a voltmeter to the positive and negative battery terminals (see illustration). Check the battery voltage with the engine off.

11.2 To measure battery voltage, attach the voltmeter leads to the battery terminals (engine OFF) - to measure charging voltage, start the engine

It should be approximately 12.4 to 12.6 volts, if the battery is fully charged.

3   Start the engine and check the battery voltage again. It should now be greater than the voltage recorded in Step 2, but not more than 14.7 volts.

4   If the indicated voltage reading is less or more than the specified charging voltage, have the charging system checked at a dealer service department or other properly equipped repair facility.

➡**Note: Many auto parts stores will bench test an alternator off the vehicle. Refer to your local auto parts store regarding their policy, many will perform this service free of charge.**

12 Alternator - removal and installation

▶ **Refer to illustrations 12.3, 12.4a and 12.4b**

1   Disconnect the cable from the negative battery terminal.

✻✻ CAUTION:

On models equipped with the Theftlock audio system, be sure the lockout feature is turned off before performing any procedure which requires disconnecting the battery (see the front of this manual).

2   Remove the drivebelt (see Chapter 1).

3   Disconnect the output wire and the electrical connector from the alternator (see illustration).

4   Remove the mounting bolts and remove the alternator from the engine (see illustrations).

5   If you are replacing the alternator, take the old one with you when purchasing a replacement unit. Make sure the new/rebuilt unit looks identical to the old alternator. Look at the terminals - they should be the same in number, size and location as the terminals on the old alternator. Finally, look at the identification numbers - they will be stamped into the housing. Make sure the numbers are the same on both alternators.

6   Many new/rebuilt alternators do not have a pulley installed, so you may have to switch the pulley from the old unit to the new/rebuilt one. When buying an alternator, find out the shop's policy regarding pulleys; some shops will perform this service free of charge.

7   Installation is the reverse of removal. Tighten the mounting bolts to the torque listed in this Chapter's Specifications.

8   Install the drivebelt (see Chapter 1).

9   Check the charging voltage to verify proper operation of the alternator (see Section 11).

12.3 Remove the nut and wire terminal from the output terminal (A) and disconnect the alternator electrical connector (B)

12.4a Remove the alternator mounting bolts (arrows)

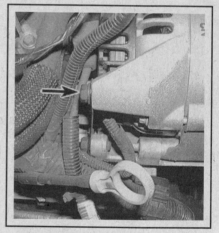

12.4b On V6 models, also remove the bracket bolt (if equipped) at the rear of the alternator (arrow)

13 Starting system - general information and precautions

The starter motor assembly is a permanent magnet, planetary gear drive starter motor. The starter motor assembly is serviced as a complete unit. If any component of the starter motor fails, including the solenoid, the entire assembly must be replaced.

The sole function of the starting system is to turn over the engine quickly enough to allow it to start. The starting system consists of the battery, starter motor assembly and the wiring connecting the components.

When the ignition key is turned to the START position, the starter solenoid is actuated through the starter control circuit. The starter solenoid then connects the battery to the starter motor. The battery supplies the electrical energy to the starter motor, which does the actual work of cranking the engine.

Always observe the following precautions when working on the starting system:

a) *Excessive cranking of the starter motor can overheat it and cause serious damage. Never operate the starter motor for more than 15 seconds at a time without pausing to allow it to cool for at least two minutes.*

b) *The starter is connected directly to the battery and could arc or cause a fire if mishandled, overloaded or shorted.*

c) *Always detach the cable from the negative terminal of the battery before working on the starting system.*

14 Starter motor and circuit - check

▶ **Refer to illustration 14.4**

1 If a malfunction occurs in the starting circuit, do not immediately assume that the starter is causing the problem. First, check the following items:

  a) *Make sure the battery cable clamps, where they connect to the battery, are clean and tight.*
  b) *Check the condition of the battery cables (see Section 4). Replace any defective battery cables with new parts.*
  c) *Test the condition of the battery (see Section 3). If it does not pass all the tests, replace it with a new battery.*
  d) *Check the starter motor wiring and connections.*
  e) *Check the starter motor mounting bolts for tightness.*
  f) *Check the related fuses in the engine compartment fuse box (see Chapter 12). If they're blown, determine the cause and repair the circuit.*
  g) *Check the ignition switch circuit for correct operation (see Chapter 12).*
  h) *Check the starter relay (located in the underhood electrical center) for proper operation (see Chapter 12).*
  i) *Check the operation of the clutch start switch (manual transmission) or the Park/Neutral position switch (automatic transmission) (see Chapter 8 or 7B). These systems must operate correctly to provide battery voltage to the starter relay.*

2 If the starter does not activate when the ignition switch is turned to the start position, check for battery voltage to the starter solenoid. This will determine if the solenoid is receiving the correct voltage from the starter relay. Install a 12-volt test light or a voltmeter to the starter solenoid terminal (purple wire). While an assistant turns the ignition switch to the start position, observe the test light or voltmeter. The test light should shine brightly or battery voltage should be indicated on the voltmeter. If voltage is not available to the starter solenoid, refer to the wiring diagrams in Chapter 12 and check the fuses, ignition switch, starter relay and related wiring in series with the starting system. If

voltage is available but there is no movement from the starter motor, remove the starter from the engine (see Section 15) and bench test the starter (see Step 4).

3 If the starter turns over slowly, check the starter cranking voltage and the current draw from the battery. This test must be performed with the starter assembly on the engine. Crank the engine over (for 10 seconds or less) and observe the battery voltage. It should not drop below 8.5 volts. Also, observe the current draw using an amp meter. Typically a starter amperage draw should not exceed 350 amps. If the starter motor amperage draw is excessive, have it tested by a dealer service department or other qualified repair shop. There are several conditions that may affect the starter cranking potential. The battery must be in good condition and the battery cold-cranking rating must not be under-rated for the particular application. Be sure to check the battery specifications carefully. The battery terminals and cables must be clean and not corroded. Also, in cases of extreme cold temperatures, make sure the battery and/or engine block is warmed before performing the tests.

4 If the starter is receiving voltage but does not activate, remove and check the starter motor assembly on the bench. Most likely the starter motor or solenoid is defective. In some rare cases, the engine may be seized so be sure to try and rotate the crankshaft pulley (see Chapter 2A or 2B) before proceeding. With the starter assembly mounted in a vise on the bench, install one jumper cable from the positive terminal of a test battery to the B+ terminal on the starter. Install another jumper cable from the negative terminal of the battery to the body of the starter (see illustration). Install a starter switch and apply battery voltage to the solenoid S terminal (for 10 seconds or less) and observe the solenoid plunger, shift lever and overrunning clutch extend and rotate the pinion drive. If the pinion drive extends but does not rotate, the solenoid is operating but the starter motor is defective. If there is no movement but the solenoid clicks, the solenoid and/or the starter motor is defective. If the solenoid plunger extends and rotates the pinion drive, the starter assembly is operating properly.

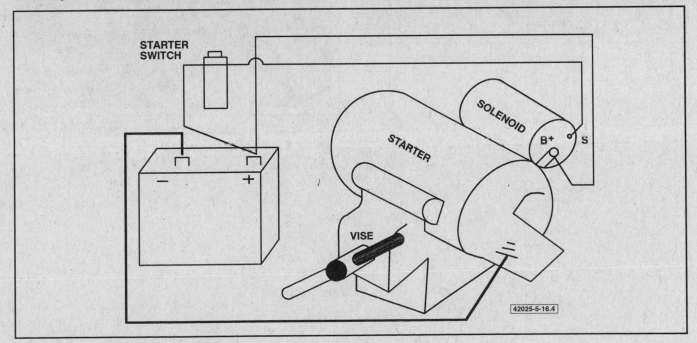

14.4 Starter motor bench testing details

15 Starter motor - removal and installation

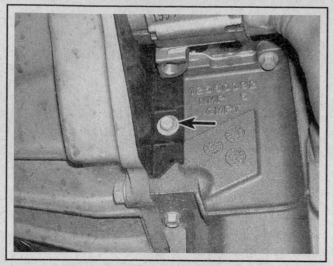

15.4 On V8 models, remove the transmission bellhousing cover bolt (arrow)

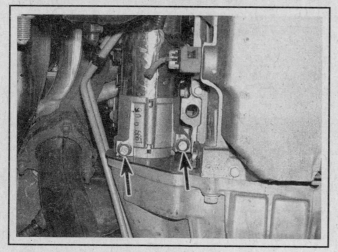

15.5 Remove the starter mounting bolts (arrows)

▶ **Refer to illustrations 15.4, 15.5 and 15.8**

1   Disconnect the cable from the negative battery terminal.

✳✳ CAUTION:

On models equipped with the Theftlock audio system, be sure the lockout feature is turned off before performing any procedure which requires disconnecting the battery (see the front of this manual).

2   Raise the vehicle and support it securely on jackstands.
3   Remove the splash shield, if equipped.
4   On V8 models, remove the starter solenoid shield and the transmission bellhousing cover bolt (see illustration). Disconnect the oil level sensor electrical connector.
5   Remove the starter mounting bolts (see illustration).
6   On V8 models, move the starter forward and remove the transmission bellhousing cover.
7   Carefully lower the starter. If necessary, detach the transmission cooler lines from the retainers at the oil pan and carefully position the lines aside - do not bend or kink the lines.
8   Disconnect the wires from the terminals on the starter motor solenoid (see illustration) and remove the starter from the vehicle.
9   Installation is the reverse of removal.

15.8 Remove the nuts and disconnect the battery cable (A) and the solenoid terminal (B) from the starter motor

Specifications

General

Battery voltage	
Engine off	12.0 to 12.6 volts
Engine running	13.5 to 14.7 volts

Torque specifications	Ft-lbs (unless otherwise indicated)
Alternator mounting bolts	
V6 engine	
Front mounting bolts	37
Rear bracket bolt	
Through 2001	18
2002	30
V8 engines	37
Distributor hold-down bolt (V6)	18
Starter mounting bolts	
V6 engine	32
V8 engines	37

Notes

Section

6

EMISSIONS AND ENGINE CONTROL SYSTEMS

1.1a *Typical emission and engine control system components - V6 models*

1	Throttle Position Sensor (TPS)	5	Vehicle Emissions Control Information (VECI) label
2	Idle Air Control (IAC) valve	6	Mass Airflow (MAF) sensor/Intake Air Temperature (IAT) sensor
3	Positive Crankcase Ventilation (PCV) valve	7	Secondary Air Injection (AIR) pump
4	Exhaust Gas Recirculation (EGR) valve		

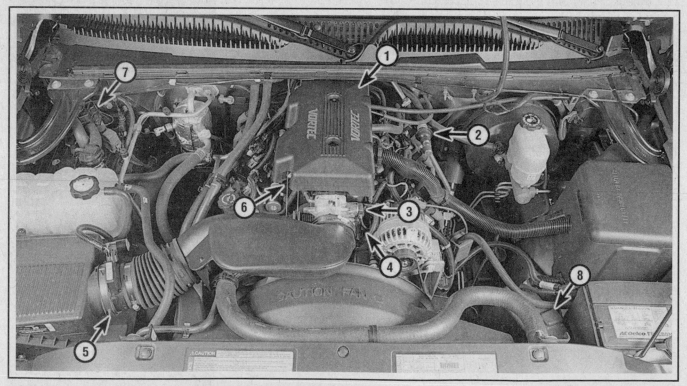

1.1b Typical emission and engine control system components - V8 models

1	Manifold Absolute Pressure (MAP) sensor (under cover)	5	Mass Airflow (MAF) sensor/Intake Air Temperature (IAT) sensor
2	Secondary Air Injection (AIR) check valve	6	Evaporative emissions system (EVAP) purge valve
3	Idle Air Control (IAC) valve	7	Secondary Air Injection (AIR) pump
4	Throttle Position Sensor (TPS)	8	Powertrain Control Module (PCM)

1 General information

▶ **Refer to illustrations 1.1a, 1.1b and 1.6**

To prevent pollution of the atmosphere from incompletely burned and evaporating gases, and to maintain good driveability and fuel economy, a number of emission control systems are incorporated (see illustrations). They include the:

Electronic engine control system
Crankcase ventilation system
Exhaust gas recirculation system
Evaporative emissions control system
Secondary air injection system
Catalytic converter

All of these systems are linked, directly or indirectly, to the emission control system.

The Sections in this Chapter include general descriptions,

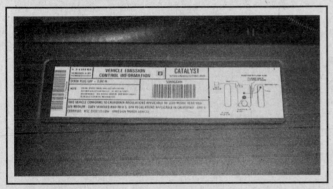

1.6 The Vehicle Emission Control Information (VECI) label is located in the engine compartment and contains information on the emission devices on your vehicle, vacuum line routing, etc.

checking procedures within the scope of the home mechanic (when possible) and component replacement procedures for each of the systems listed above.

Before assuming that an emissions control system is malfunctioning, check the fuel and ignition systems carefully. The diagnosis of some emission control devices requires specialized tools, equipment and training. If checking and servicing become too difficult or if a procedure is beyond your ability, consult a dealer service department or other properly equipped repair facility. Remember, the most frequent cause of emissions problems is simply a loose or broken vacuum hose or wire, so always check the hose and wiring connections first.

This doesn't mean, however, that emission control systems are particularly difficult to maintain and repair. You can quickly and easily perform many checks and do most of the regular maintenance at home with common tune-up and hand tools.

➡**Note: Because of a Federally mandated warranty which covers the emission control system components, check with your dealer about warranty coverage before working on any emissions-related systems. Once the warranty has expired, you may wish to perform some of the component checks and/or replacement procedures in this Chapter to save money.**

Pay close attention to any special precautions outlined in this Chapter. It should be noted that the illustrations of the various systems may not exactly match the system installed on the vehicle you're working on because of changes made by the manufacturer during production or from year-to-year.

A Vehicle Emissions Control Information (VECI) label is located in the engine compartment (see illustration). This label contains important emissions specifications and adjustment information, as well as a vacuum hose schematic with emissions components identified. When servicing the engine or emissions systems, the VECI label in your particular vehicle should always be checked for up-to-date information.

2 On-Board Diagnostic (OBD) system and trouble codes

DIAGNOSTIC TOOL INFORMATION

▶ **Refer to illustrations 2.1 and 2.2**

1 A digital multimeter is necessary for checking fuel injection and emission related components (see illustration). A digital volt-ohmmeter is preferred over the older style analog multimeter for several reasons. The analog multimeter cannot display the volts-ohms or amps measurement in hundredths and thousandths increments. When working with electronic circuits which are often very low voltage, this accurate reading is most important. Another good reason for the digital multimeter is the high impedance circuit. The digital multimeter is equipped with a high resistance internal circuitry (10 million ohms). Because a voltmeter is hooked up in parallel with the circuit when testing, it is vital that none of the voltage being measured should be allowed to travel the parallel path set up by the meter itself. This dilemma does not show itself when measuring larger amounts of voltage (9 to 12 volt circuits) but if you are measuring a low voltage circuit such as the oxygen sensor signal voltage, a fraction of a volt may be a significant amount when diagnosing a problem. However, there are several exceptions where using an analog voltmeter may be necessary to test certain sensors.

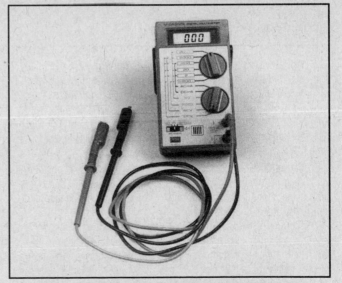

2.1 Digital multimeters can be used for testing all types of circuits; because of their high impedance, they are much more accurate than analog meters for measuring low-voltage computer circuits

2   Hand-held scanners are the most powerful and versatile tools for analyzing engine management systems used on later model vehicles (see illustration). Each brand scan tool must be examined carefully to match the year, make and model of the vehicle you are working on. Often interchangeable cartridges are available to access the particular manufacturer (Ford, GM, Chrysler, etc.). Some manufacturers will specify by continent (Asia, Europe, USA, etc.).

3   With the arrival of the Federally mandated emission control system (OBD-II), a specially designed scanner has been developed. Several tool manufacturers have released OBD-II scan tools for the home mechanic.

ON-BOARD DIAGNOSTIC SYSTEM GENERAL DESCRIPTION

4   All models described in this manual are equipped with the second generation On-Board Diagnostic (OBD-II) system. The system consists of an onboard computer, known as the Powertrain Control Module (PCM), information sensors and output actuators.

5   The information sensors monitor various functions of the engine and send data to the PCM. Based on the data and the information programmed into the computer's memory, the PCM generates output signals to control various engine functions via control relays, solenoids and other output actuators. The PCM is specifically calibrated to optimize the emissions, fuel economy and driveability of the vehicle.

➡**Note: On 2001 and later models, the PCM has an additional function called "torque management." With this function, The PCM reduces engine torque under certain driving conditions, such as heavy acceleration, loss of traction in one axle (4WD), or shifting under full throttle. The PCM adjusts the torque load by retarding the ignition timing and/or shutting off some fuel injectors.**

6   Because of a Federally mandated warranty which covers the emissions system components and because any owner-induced damage to the PCM, the sensors and/or the control devices may void the warranty, it isn't a good idea to attempt diagnosis or replacement of the system components while the vehicle is under warranty. Take the vehicle to a dealer service department if the PCM or a system component malfunctions.

INFORMATION SENSORS

7   **Accelerator pedal position (APP) sensor** - The APP sensor is an integral component of the accelerator pedal assembly. It is used only on later V8 models that have an electronically-controlled throttle system with no cable. It provides the PCM with a variable voltage signal that is proportional to the angle of the accelerator pedal. The PCM uses this datum to control the position of the throttle plate inside the throttle body via the throttle actuator control module.

8   **Camshaft Position (CMP) sensor** - The camshaft position sensor provides information on camshaft position. The PCM uses this information, along with the crankshaft position sensor information, to control fuel injection synchronization.

9   **Crankshaft Position (CKP) sensor** - The crankshaft position sensor senses crankshaft position (TDC) during each engine revolution. The PCM uses this information to control ignition timing and fuel injection synchronization.

10   **Engine Coolant Temperature (ECT) sensor** - The engine coolant temperature sensor senses engine coolant temperature. The PCM uses this information to control fuel injection duration and ignition timing.

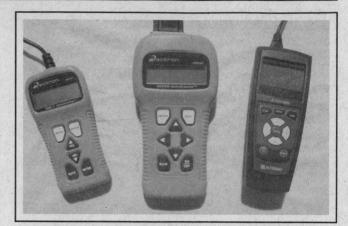

2.2 Scanners like these from Actron and AutoXray are powerful diagnostic aids - programmed with comprehensive diagnostic information, they can tell you just about anything you want to know about your engine management system

11   **Intake Air Temperature (IAT) sensor** - The intake air temperature senses the temperature of the air entering the intake manifold. The PCM uses this information to control fuel injection duration.

12   **Knock Sensor (KS)** - The knock sensor is a piezoelectric element that detects the sound of engine detonation, or "pinging". The PCM uses the input signal from the knock sensor to recognize detonation and retard spark advance to avoid engine damage.

13   **Manifold Absolute Pressure (MAP) sensor** - The manifold absolute pressure monitors intake manifold pressure and ambient barometric pressure. The PCM uses this input signal to determine engine load and adjusts fuel injection duration accordingly.

14   **Mass Airflow (MAF) sensor** - The mass airflow sensor measures the amount of air passing through the sensor body and ultimately entering the engine. The PCM uses this information to control fuel delivery.

15   **Oxygen (O2) sensor** - The oxygen sensors generate a voltage signal that varies with the varying oxygen content of the exhaust gas. The PCM uses this information to determine if the fuel system is running rich or lean and make adjustments accordingly.

16   **Throttle Position Sensor (TPS)** - The throttle position sensor senses throttle movement and position. This signal enables the PCM to determine when the throttle is closed, in a cruise position, or wide open. The PCM uses this information to control fuel delivery and ignition timing.

17   **Vehicle Speed Sensor (VSS)** - The vehicle speed sensor provides information to the PCM to indicate vehicle speed.

18   **Miscellaneous PCM inputs** - In addition to the various sensors, the PCM monitors various switches and circuits to determine vehicle operating conditions. The switches and circuits include:

   a) *Air conditioning system*
   b) *Battery voltage*
   c) *Brake On/Off switch*
   d) *Cruise control system*
   e) *EGR valve position*
   f) *Engine oil level and pressure*
   g) *EVAP system*
   h) *Fuel level and fuel tank pressure*
   i) *Ignition switch*
   j) *Park/neutral position switch*
   k) *Sensor signal and ground circuits*
   l) *Transmission controls*

OUTPUT ACTUATORS

19 **Air conditioning clutch relay** - The PCM controls the operation of the air conditioning compressor clutch with the air conditioning clutch relay.

20 **Service Engine Soon light** - The PCM will illuminate the Service Engine Soon light if a malfunction in the electronic engine control system occurs.

21 **Cruise control module** - The cruise control system operation is controlled by the PCM.

22 **Engine cooling fan relay** - The engine cooling fan is controlled by the PCM according to information received from the engine coolant temperature sensor.

23 **EGR valve** - The electronic EGR valve is controlled by the PCM. Ideal EGR flow is determined by the PCM and the EGR valve pintle position is adjusted accordingly.

24 **EVAP canister purge and vent valve solenoids** - The evaporative emission canister purge and vent valve solenoids are operated by the PCM to purge the fuel vapor canister and route fuel vapor to the intake manifold for combustion.

25 **Secondary Air Injection (AIR) pump and vacuum valve/solenoid** - The PCM operates the secondary air injection pump and opens the vacuum valve to inject fresh air into the exhaust stream, lower emission levels under certain operating conditions.

26 **Fuel injectors** - The PCM opens the fuel injectors individually in firing order sequence. The PCM also controls the time the injector is held open (pulse width). The pulse width of the injector (measured in milliseconds) determines the amount of fuel delivered. For more information on the fuel delivery system and the fuel injectors, including injector replacement, refer to Chapter 4.

27 **Fuel pump relay** - The fuel pump relay is activated by the PCM with the ignition switch in the Start or Run position. When the ignition switch is turned on, the relay is activated to supply initial line pressure to the system. For more information on fuel pump check and replacement, refer to Chapter 4.

28 **Idle Air Control valve (IAC)** - The idle air control valve controls the amount of air allowed to bypass the throttle plate when the throttle valve is closed or at idle position. The more air allowed to bypass the throttle plate, the higher the idle speed. The idle air control valve opening and the resulting idle speed is controlled by the PCM.

29 **Ignition coils/control module** - The PCM controls ignition timing through the ignition coils/control module depending on engine operation conditions. Refer to Chapter 5 for more information on the ignition coil(s) or ignition control module.

30 **Throttle actuator control module** - The throttle actuator control module receives information from the PCM and translates it into an electrical signal that is sent to the throttle body. All throttle setting from cold idle to full acceleration are governed in this way. This system is only used on later V8 models.

OBTAINING DIAGNOSTIC TROUBLE CODES

▶ **Refer to illustration 2.32**

➡**Note: The diagnostic trouble codes on all models can only be extracted from the Powertrain Control Module (PCM) using a specialized scan tool. Have the vehicle diagnosed by a dealer service department or other qualified automotive repair facility if the proper scan tool is not available.**

31 The PCM will illuminate the SERVICE ENGINE SOON light (also known as the Malfunction Indicator Lamp) on the dash if it recognizes a fault in the system. The light will remain illuminated until the problem

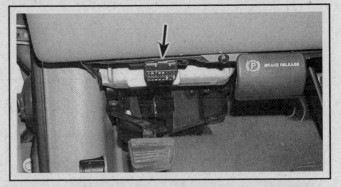

2.30 The diagnostic connector is typically located under the instrument panel

is repaired and the code is cleared or the PCM does not detect any malfunction for several consecutive drive cycles.

32 The diagnostic codes for the On-Board Diagnostic (OBD) system can only be extracted from the PCM using a scan tool. The scan tool is programmed to interface with the OBD system by plugging into the diagnostic connector (see illustration). When used, the scan tool has the ability to diagnose in-depth driveability problems and it allows freeze frame data to be retrieved from the PCM stored memory. Freeze frame data is an OBD II PCM feature that records all related sensor and actuator activity on the PCM data stream whenever an engine control or emissions fault is detected and a trouble code is set. This ability to look at the circuit conditions and values when the malfunction occurs provides a valuable tool when trying to diagnose intermittent driveability problems. If the tool is not available and intermittent driveability problems exist, have the vehicle checked at a dealer service department or other qualified repair shop.

CLEARING DIAGNOSTIC TROUBLE CODES

33 After the system has been repaired, the codes must be cleared from the PCM memory. The preferred method is with a scan tool, but the codes can be cleared by disconnecting battery power from the PCM for a minimum of thirty seconds. Battery power can be disconnected from the PCM by removing the PCM fuse, disconnecting the PCM power connector near the positive battery terminal (if equipped) or by disconnecting the negative battery cable from the battery.

✳✳ CAUTION:

On models equipped with the Theftlock audio system, be sure the lockout feature is turned off before performing any procedure which requires disconnecting the battery (see the front of this manual).

34 Always clear the codes from the PCM before starting the engine after a new electronic emission control component is installed onto the engine. The PCM stores the operating parameters of each sensor. The PCM may set a trouble code if a new sensor is allowed to operate before the parameters from the old sensor have been erased.

DIAGNOSTIC TROUBLE CODE IDENTIFICATION

35 The accompanying list of diagnostic trouble codes is a compilation of all the codes that may be encountered using a generic scan tool. Additional trouble codes may be obtainable with the use of the manufacturer specific scan tool. Not all codes pertain to all models and not all codes will illuminate the Service Engine Soon light when set. All models require a scan tool to access the diagnostic trouble codes.

OBD-II DIAGNOSTIC TROUBLE CODES (DTCS)

➡**Note: Not all trouble codes apply to all models.**

Code	Possible cause
P0030	HO2S heater control circuit bank 1 sensor 1
P0036	HO2S heater control circuit bank 1 sensor 2
P0050	HO2S heater control circuit bank 2 sensor 1
P0053	Heated O2 sensor resistance out of range (left cylinder bank, sensor 1)
P0054	Heated O2 sensor resistance out of range (left cylinder bank, sensor 2)
P0056	HO2S heater control circuit bank 2 sensor 2
P0059	Heated O2 sensor resistance out of range (right cylinder bank, sensor 2)
P0060	Heated O2 sensor resistance out of range (right cylinder bank, sensor 1)
P0068	MAF sensor circuit, difference between actual air flow and predicted speed density greater than expected
P0101	Mass Air Flow (MAF) sensor performance
P0102	Mass Air Flow (MAF) sensor circuit, low input
P0103	Mass Air Flow (MAF) sensor circuit, high input
P0106	Manifold Absolute Pressure (MAP) sensor signal out of range
P0107	Manifold Absolute Pressure (MAP) sensor circuit, voltage too low
P0108	Manifold Absolute Pressure (MAP) sensor circuit, voltage too high
P0112	Intake Air Temperature (IAT) sensor circuit, voltage too low (temperature too high)
P0113	Intake Air Temperature (IAT) sensor circuit, voltage too high (temperature too low)
P0116	Temperature difference between ECT and IAT sensors not within calibrated range
P0117	Engine Coolant Temperature (ECT) sensor circuit, voltage too low (temperature too high)
P0118	Engine Coolant Temperature (ECT) sensor circuit, voltage too high (temperature too low)
P0120	Throttle Position (TP) sensor No. 1 signal or reference voltage out of range (models with TAC)
P0121	Throttle Position (TP) sensor signal, voltage out of range
P0122	Throttle Position (TP) sensor circuit, voltage too low
P0123	Throttle Position (TP) sensor circuit, voltage too high
P0125	Engine Coolant Temperature (ECT) sensor takes too long to reach closed-loop temperature
P0128	Engine Coolant Temperature (ECT) sensor does not meet minimum thermostat regulating temperature
P0131	Upstream oxygen sensor (left cylinder bank), circuit voltage too low
P0132	Upstream oxygen sensor (left cylinder bank), circuit voltage too high
P0133	Upstream oxygen sensor (left cylinder bank), slow response
P0134	Upstream oxygen sensor (left cylinder bank) circuit, insufficient activity
P0135	Upstream oxygen sensor (left cylinder bank), heater performance
P0136	Downstream oxygen sensor (left cylinder bank) circuit, signal out of range
P0137	Downstream oxygen sensor (left cylinder bank) circuit, low voltage
P0138	Downstream oxygen sensor (left cylinder bank) circuit, high voltage
P0140	Downstream oxygen sensor (left cylinder bank) circuit, insufficient activity

Code	Possible cause
P0141	Downstream oxygen sensor (left cylinder bank) circuit, heater performance
P0143	Downstream oxygen sensor (left cylinder bank) circuit, low voltage
P0144	Downstream oxygen sensor (left cylinder bank) circuit, high voltage
P0146	Downstream oxygen sensor (left cylinder bank) circuit, insufficient activity
P0147	Downstream oxygen sensor (left cylinder bank), heater performance
P0151	Upstream oxygen sensor (right cylinder bank) circuit voltage too low
P0152	Upstream oxygen sensor (right cylinder bank), circuit voltage too high
P0153	Upstream oxygen sensor (right cylinder bank), slow response
P0154	Upstream oxygen sensor (right cylinder bank) circuit, insufficient activity
P0155	Upstream oxygen sensor (right cylinder bank), heater performance
P0156	Downstream oxygen sensor (right cylinder bank) circuit, signal out of range
P0157	Downstream oxygen sensor (right cylinder bank) circuit, low voltage
P0158	Downstream oxygen sensor (right cylinder bank) circuit, high voltage
P0160	Downstream oxygen sensor (right cylinder bank) circuit, insufficient activity
P0161	Downstream oxygen sensor (right cylinder bank), heater performance
P0169	Ambient fuel temperature high (E-85 fuel models)
P0171	Fuel trim system lean at upstream oxygen sensor (left cylinder bank)
P0172	Fuel trim system rich at upstream oxygen sensor (left cylinder bank)
P0174	Fuel trim system lean at upstream oxygen sensor (right cylinder bank)
P0175	Fuel trim system rich at upstream oxygen sensor (right cylinder bank)
P0178	Fuel Composition sensor frequency out of range (E 85 fuel models)
P0179	Fuel Composition sensor detects contaminated fuel (E 85 fuel models)
P0200	Fuel injector control circuit, incorrect voltage
P0218	Transmission fluid temperature high
P0220	Throttle Position (TP) sensor No. 2 signal or reference voltage outside normal range (models with TAC)
P0230	Fuel pump relay control circuit, commanded state of driver and actual state of control circuit don't match
P0300	Engine misfire detected
P0315	Crankshaft Position (CKP) system variation values not stored in PCM memory
P0325	Knock sensor circuit malfunction
P0327	Knock sensor signal frequency outside normal range
P0332	Knock sensor signal frequency outside normal range
P0335	No signal from Crankshaft Position (CKP) sensor for more than three seconds
P0336	Crankshaft Position (CKP) sensor signal incorrect for more than three seconds
P0337	Crankshaft Position (CKP) sensor circuit, low duty cycle
P0338	Crankshaft Position (CKP) sensor circuit, high duty cycle
P0339	Crankshaft Position (CKP) sensor circuit intermittent
P0340	Camshaft Position (CMP) sensor circuit
P0341	Camshaft Position (CMP) sensor signal not present or mismatch with CKP signal

OBD-II DIAGNOSTIC TROUBLE CODES (DTCS)

➡ **Note: Not all trouble codes apply to all models.**

Code	Possible cause
P0342	Camshaft Position (CMP) signal constantly low
P0343	Camshaft Position (CMP) signal constantly high
P0351	Ignition Control (IC) circuit out of range (coil 1)
P0352	Ignition Control (IC) circuit out of range (coil 2)
P0353	Ignition Control (IC) circuit out of range (coil 3)
P0354	Ignition Control (IC) circuit out of range (coil 4)
P0355	Ignition Control (IC) circuit out of range (coil 5)
P0356	Ignition Control (IC) circuit out of range (coil 6)
P0357	Ignition Control (IC) circuit out of range (coil 7)
P0358	Ignition Control (IC) circuit out of range (coil 8)
P0401	Exhaust Gas Recirculation (EGR) system, insufficient flow
P0404	Exhaust Gas Recirculation (EGR) system, open position performance
P0405	Exhaust Gas Recirculation (EGR) position sensor circuit, low voltage
P0410	Secondary Air Injection (AIR) system
P0418	Secondary air injection pump relay control system
P0420	Catalyst system (left cylinder bank), low efficiency (4.3L V6)
P0420	Oxygen storage ability of catalyst (left cylinder bank) below calibrated threshold (4.8L, 5.3L or 6.0L V8)
P0430	Catalyst system (right cylinder bank), low efficiency (4.3L V6)
P0430	Oxygen storage ability of catalyst (right cylinder bank) below calibrated threshold (4.8L, 5.3L or 6.0L V8)
P0440	Evaporative Emission (EVAP) system
P0442	Evaporative Emission (EVAP) control system, small leak detected
P0443	Evaporative Emission (EVAP) canister purge solenoid valve, incorrect voltage at driver
P0446	Evaporative Emission (EVAP) vent system performance
P0449	Evaporative Emission (EVAP) canister vent solenoid valve, incorrect voltage at driver
P0451	Fuel tank pressure sensor malfunction
P0452	Fuel tank pressure sensor circuit, low voltage
P0453	Fuel tank pressure sensor circuit, high voltage
P0454	Fuel tank pressure sensor detects problem with PCM diagnosis
P0455	Evaporative Emission (EVAP) system unable to reach calibrated vacuum level
P0461	Fuel level sensor performance
P0462	Fuel level sensor circuit, voltage too low
P0463	Fuel level sensor circuit, voltage too high
P0496	Evaporative Emission (EVAP) system, excessive (intake manifold) vacuum present
P0500	Vehicle Speed Sensor (VSS) circuit
P0502	Vehicle speed sensor circuit low output

Code	Possible cause
P0503	Vehicle speed sensor signal intermittent
P0506	Idle speed performance lower than expected or out of range
P0507	Idle speed performance higher than expected or out of range
P0562	System voltage low
P0563	System voltage high
P0601	PCM failure
P0602	PCM not programmed
P0603	PCM long-term memory reset
P0604	PCM Random Access Memory (RAM)
P0605	PCM Read-Only Memory (ROM)
P0607	PCM malfunction
P0608	Vehicle speed sensor output circuit
P0641	5-volt reference circuit to TP sensor, oil pressure sensor, MAP sensor or EGR valve out of range
P0650	Incorrect voltage on the Malfunction Indicator Light (MIL) control circuit
P0651	5-volt reference circuit for Fuel Tank Pressure (FTP) sensor out of range
P0654	Tachometer control circuit
P0704	Clutch start switch circuit
P0705	Transmission range sensor (Park/Neutral position switch), circuit malfunction
P0706	Transmission range sensor (Park/Neutral position switch) performance
P0711	Transmission fluid temperature sensor circuit out-of-range
P0712	Transmission fluid temperature sensor circuit low input
P0713	Transmission fluid temperature sensor circuit high input
P0716	Input speed sensor circuit out-of-range
P0717	Input speed sensor circuit no signal
P0719	Torque converter clutch brake switch circuit low
P0724	Torque converter clutch brake switch circuit high
P0730	Incorrect gear ratio
P0740	Torque converter clutch enable solenoid circuit
P0741	Torque converter clutch system stuck off
P0742	Torque converter clutch system stuck on
P0748	Pressure control solenoid valve circuit
P0751	1-2 shift solenoid performance
P0752	1-2 shift solenoid (4L60-E)
P0753	1-2 shift solenoid circuit
P0756	2-3 shift solenoid performance
P0758	2-3 shift solenoid circuit
P0785	2-3 shift solenoid circuit

OBD-II DIAGNOSTIC TROUBLE CODES (DTCS)

➡**Note: Not all trouble codes apply to all models.**

Code	Possible cause
P1106	Manifold absolute pressure sensor circuit intermittent high voltage
P1107	Manifold absolute pressure sensor circuit intermittent low voltage
P1111	Intake air temperature sensor circuit intermittent high voltage
P1112	Intake air temperature sensor circuit intermittent low voltage
P1114	Engine coolant temperature sensor circuit intermittent low voltage
P1115	Engine coolant temperature sensor circuit intermittent high voltage
P1121	Throttle position sensor circuit intermittent high voltage
P1122	Throttle position sensor circuit intermittent low voltage
P1125	Accelerator pedal position sensor malfunction
P1133	Oxygen sensor insufficient switching (pre-converter sensor, left bank)
P1134	Oxygen sensor transition time ratio (pre-converter sensor, left bank)
P1153	Oxygen sensor insufficient switching (pre-converter sensor, right bank)
P1154	Oxygen sensor transition time ratio (pre-converter sensor, right bank)
P1220	Throttle position sensor out of range
P1221	Throttle position sensor, discrepancy between two sensors
P1258	Engine coolant over temperature
P1275	Accelerator pedal position sensor, voltage
P1276	Accelerator pedal position sensor, discrepancy between the sensors
P1280	Accelerator pedal position sensor, disagreement between sensors 1 and 2
P1281	Accelerator pedal position sensor, disagreement between sensors 1 and 2, and 2 and 3
P1285	Accelerator pedal position sensor, sensor 3 voltage out of range
P1286	Accelerator pedal position sensor, disagreement between sensors 3 and 1, and 3 and 2
P1336	Crankshaft position sensor system variation not learned
P1345	Crankshaft position sensor/Camshaft position sensor correlation
P1351	Ignition control circuit high voltage
P1361	Ignition control circuit low voltage
P1380	Electronic brake control module rough road sensing error
P1381	No serial data from electronic brake control module
P1404	EGR valve closed pintle position
P1415	Secondary air injection system malfunction, left bank
P1416	Secondary air injection system malfunction, right bank
P1441	EVAP system flow during non-purge
P1508	Idle speed too low
P1509	Idle speed too high
P1514	MAF sensor, predicted airflow different than detected
P1515	TPS, difference between actual and detected throttle position

Code	Possible cause
P1516	TPS, sensor out of range
P1517	Throttle actuator control, failed internal data test
P1518	Throttle actuator control, invalid or missing data
P1600	PCM malfunction
P1621	PCM memory performance
P1626	Serial data communication failure with vehicle theft deterent controller (no password)
P1627	PCM malfunction
P1631	Theft deterent password incorrect
P1635	5-volt reference circuit
P1637	Alternator L terminal circuit
P1639	5-volt reference circuit
P1680	PCM malfunction
P1681	PCM malfunction
P1683	PCM flash memory performance
P1810	Transmission pressure switch assembly malfunction
P1860	Torque converter clutch pulse width modulator solenoid circuit
P1870	Transmission slipping
P1875	Four-wheel drive low switch circuit
P2101	Control module throttle actuator position performance malfunction
P2108	Control module throttle actuator position performance malfunction
P2120	Accelerator pedal position sensor 1 malfunction
P2121	Accelerator pedal position sensor 1 malfunction
P2125	Accelerator pedal position sensor 2 malfunction
P2135	Throttle position sensor malfunction
P2138	Accelerator pedal position sensors 1 and 2 malfunction
P2636	Fuel pump malfunction
P2A01	HO2S performance bank 1 sensor 2
P2A04	HO2S performance bank 2 sensor 2
U0107	No communication with throttle actuator control module

3 Powertrain Control Module (PCM) - removal and installation

▶ Refer to illustrations 3.2, 3.3 and 3.4

✳✳ CAUTION:

Avoid static electricity damage to the Powertrain Control Module (PCM) by grounding yourself to the body of the vehicle before touching the PCM and using a special anti-static pad to store the PCM on, once it is removed.

➡ Note 1: Anytime the PCM is replaced with a new unit the PCM must be reprogrammed by a dealership service department with special equipment. A crankshaft position sensor variation relearn procedure and a vehicle anti-theft system password relearn procedure must be performed, as well. The following procedure pertains to removal and installation of the original PCM only. If the PCM must be replaced with a new unit, take the vehicle to a dealership service department.

3.2 Remove the PCM cover

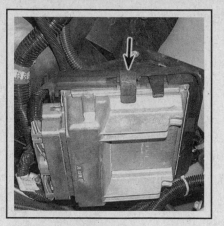

3.3 Detach the latch (arrow) and remove the PCM from the mounting bracket

3.4 Loosen the retaining bolts and disconnect the electrical connectors from the PCM

➡Note 2: Anytime the battery is disconnected, stored operating parameters may be lost from the PCM causing the engine to run rough for awhile while the PCM relearns the information.

1   Disconnect the cable from the negative battery terminal.

❈❈ CAUTION:

On models equipped with the Theftlock audio system, be sure the lockout feature is turned off before performing any procedure which requires disconnecting the battery (see the front of this manual).

2   Remove the protective cover from the PCM (see illustration).
3   Detach the PCM retainer latch and remove the PCM from the bracket (see illustration).
4   Unscrew the bolts and carefully disconnect the electrical connectors from the PCM (see illustration).
5   Installation is the reverse of removal.

4   Throttle Position Sensor (TPS) - replacement

◆ **Refer to illustrations 4.1a, 4.1b and 4.4**

1   The Throttle Position Sensor (TPS) is a variable potentiometer connected to the end of the throttle shaft on the throttle body (see illustrations). By monitoring the output voltage from the TPS, the PCM can determine fuel delivery based on throttle valve angle (driver demand). A broken or loose TPS can cause intermittent bursts of fuel from the injectors and an unstable idle because the PCM thinks the throttle is moving.

2   On V8 models, remove the alternator (see Chapter 5). On V6 models, remove the air intake duct and resonator (see Chapter 4).
3   Disconnect the electrical connector from the TPS.
4   Remove the TPS mounting screws and remove the TPS from the throttle body (see illustration).
5   Install a new O-ring on the TPS. With the throttle in the closed position, align the TPS with the throttle shaft and install the TPS. Tighten the screws securely.
6   The remainder of installation is the reverse of removal.

4.1a Throttle Position Sensor (TPS) location - V6 models

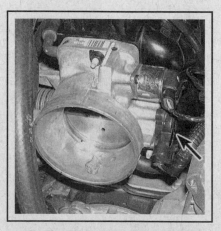

4.1b Throttle Position Sensor (TPS) location - V8 models

4.4 Remove the TPS mounting screws (arrows)

5   Manifold Absolute Pressure (MAP) sensor - replacement

▶ **Refer to illustration 5.1a, 5.1b and 5.4**

1   The Manifold Absolute Pressure (MAP) sensor monitors the intake manifold pressure changes resulting from changes in engine load and speed and converts the information into a voltage output (see illustrations). The PCM receives information as a varying voltage signal from closed throttle (high vacuum) to wide open throttle (low vacuum). The PCM uses the MAP sensor to control fuel delivery and ignition timing.

2   On V6 models, remove the intake air duct and resonator. On V8 models, remove the intake manifold cover.
3   Disconnect the electrical connector from the MAP sensor.
4   Detach the retaining clips and withdraw the MAP sensor from the upper intake manifold (see illustration). Replace the MAP sensor seal in the upper intake manifold.
5   Installation is the reverse of removal.

5.1a MAP sensor location - V6 models

5.1b MAP sensor location - V8 models

5.4 Detach the clips (arrows) and remove the MAP sensor from the upper intake manifold

6   Mass Airflow (MAF) sensor - replacement

▶ **Refer to illustrations 6.1 and 6.4**

1   The Mass Airflow Sensor (MAF) is located on the air filter housing (see illustration). The MAF sensor measures the amount of air passing through the sensor body and ultimately entering the engine through the throttle body. The PCM uses this information to control fuel delivery - the more air entering the engine (acceleration), the more fuel required.
2   Disconnect the electrical connector from the MAF sensor.
3   Loosen the hose clamp securing the air intake duct to the MAF

sensor and remove the duct.
4   Loosen the hose clamp retaining the MAF sensor to the air filter cover and remove the sensor (see illustration).

✳ CAUTION:

Handle the MAF sensor with care. Damage to this sensor will affect the operation of the entire fuel injection system.

5   Installation is the reverse of removal.

6.1 The Mass Airflow (MAF) sensor is attached to the air filter housing

6.4 Loosen the hose clamps (arrows) and remove the Mass Airflow sensor

7   Intake Air Temperature (IAT) sensor - replacement

1   The Intake Air Temperature (IAT) sensor is a thermistor (a resistor which varies the value of its resistance in accordance with temperature changes). The change in the resistance values will directly affect the voltage signal from the sensor to the PCM. As the sensor temperature INCREASES, the resistance values will DECREASE. As the sensor tem- perature DECREASES, the resistance values will INCREASE.

2   The IAT is part of the MAF sensor. Replace the MAF/IAT sensor as described in Section 6.

3   Installation is the reverse of removal.

8   Engine Coolant Temperature (ECT) sensor - replacement

▶ **Refer to illustration 8.1a and 8.1b**

❊❊ WARNING:

Wait until the engine is completely cool before beginning this procedure.

1   The Engine Coolant Temperature (ECT) sensor is a thermistor (a resistor which varies the value of its resistance in accordance with temperature changes) (see illustrations). The change in the resistance values will directly affect the voltage signal from the sensor to the PCM. As the sensor temperature INCREASES, the resistance values will DECREASE. As the sensor temperature DECREASES, the resistance values will INCREASE.

2   Drain the cooling system (see Chapter 1).

3   Disconnect the electrical connector from the sensor and carefully unscrew the sensor.

4   Before installing the new sensor, wrap the threads with Teflon sealing tape to prevent leakage and thread corrosion.

5   Installation is the reverse of removal.

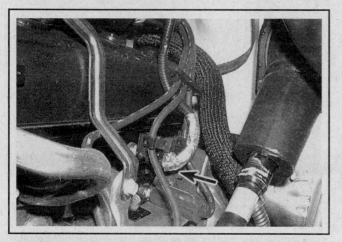

8.1a Engine Coolant Temperature sensor location - V6 models

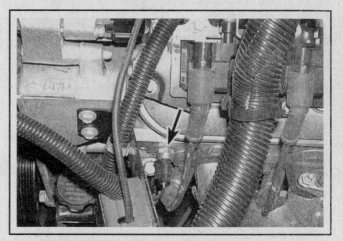

8.1b Engine Coolant Temperature sensor location - V8 models

9   Crankshaft Position (CKP) sensor - replacement

▶ **Refer to illustration 9.1a, 9.1b and 9.6**

1   The Crankshaft Position (CKP) sensor provides the PCM with a crankshaft position signal (see illustrations). The PCM uses the signal to determine the spark sequence (firing order) for each cylinder. The PCM also uses the signal to precisely control ignition timing and calculate engine speed (RPM). The signal is used by the Onboard Diagnostic system for misfire detection. The crankshaft position sensor is triggered by slots cut into a reluctor ring on the crankshaft. The sensor tip is positioned approximately 0.050 inch from the reluctor ring. As the notches pass the sensor the magnetic field is altered, producing a pulsating voltage. The ignition system will not operate if the PCM does not receive a crankshaft position sensor input.

➡Note: Anytime a crankshaft position sensor is disturbed, A Crankshaft Position Sensor Variation Learning Procedure should be performed or a false misfire diagnostic trouble code may be set. If after replacing the sensor, a false diagnostic trouble code is set, take the vehicle to a dealership service department for the procedure.

2   Disconnect the cable from the negative battery terminal.

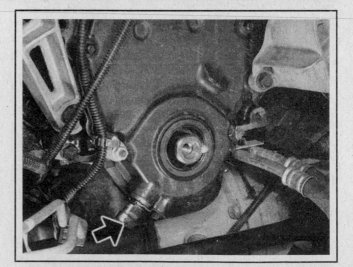

9.1a Crankshaft Position (CKP) sensor location - V6 models

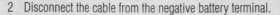

9.1b Crankshaft Position (CKP) sensor location - V8 models (starter removed for clarity)

9.6 Remove the mounting bolt (arrow) and withdraw the crankshaft position sensor

✳ CAUTION:

On models equipped with the Theftlock audio system, be sure the lockout feature is turned off before performing any procedure which requires disconnecting the battery (see the front of this manual).

3   Raise the vehicle and support it securely on jackstands.

4   Remove the skid plate, if equipped. On V8 models, remove the starter (see Chapter 5).

5   Disconnect the electrical connector from the sensor.

6   Remove the crankshaft position sensor mounting bolt and remove the sensor (see illustration).

7   Installation is the reverse of removal.

10 Camshaft Position (CMP) sensor - replacement

▶ **Refer to illustrations 10.1a and 10.1b**

1   The camshaft position sensor (see illustrations) is very similar in operation to the crankshaft position sensor, but it produces a signal pulse only once every two crankshaft revolutions, corresponding to cylinder number one Top Dead Center. The camshaft position sensor, in conjunction with the crankshaft position sensor, determines the timing for the fuel injection on each cylinder.

V6 MODELS

▶ **Refer to illustration 10.5**

2   Disconnect the cable from the negative battery terminal.

✳ CAUTION:

On models equipped with the Theftlock audio system, be sure the lockout feature is turned off before performing any procedure which requires disconnecting the battery (see the front of this manual).

3   Remove the distributor cap and rotor (see Chapter 1).

4   Disconnect the electrical connector from the camshaft position sensor.

5   Using a breaker bar and socket on the crankshaft pulley bolt, rotate the engine until the square slot in the reluctor aligns with the

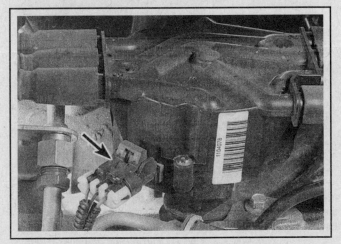

10.1a Camshaft position sensor location - V6 models

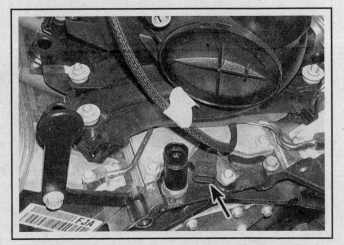

10.1b Camshaft position sensor location - V8 models

camshaft position sensor (see illustration).

6 Remove the camshaft position sensor mounting screws and remove the sensor from the distributor.

7 Installation is the reverse of removal. Apply thread locking compound to the camshaft position sensor, rotor and distributor cap screws before installing them.

V8 MODELS

8 Disconnect the electrical connector from the sensor (see illustration 10.1b).

9 Remove the camshaft position sensor mounting bolt and withdraw the sensor from the engine block.

10 Installation is the reverse of removal.

10.5 To remove the camshaft position sensor on V6 models, rotate the crankshaft until the square slot in the reluctor (arrow) aligns with the camshaft position sensor

11 Oxygen sensor - replacement

▶ **Refer to illustration 11.1, 11.2 and 11.9**

➡**Note: All models are equipped with four oxygen sensors; two pre-converter oxygen sensors and two post-converter oxygen sensors.**

1 An oxygen sensor, in effect, measures the oxygen remaining in the exhaust gas after the combustion process. The leftover oxygen in the exhaust reacts with the elements inside the oxygen sensor to produce a voltage output that varies from 0.1 volt (high oxygen, lean mixture) to 0.9 volt (low oxygen, rich mixture). The pre-converter oxygen sensor is mounted in the exhaust system before the catalytic converter. The PCM monitors the varying voltage signal from the pre-converter oxygen sensor continuously to determine the required fuel injector pulse width, controlling the engine air/fuel ratio (see illustration). A mixture ratio of 14.7 parts air to 1 part fuel is the ideal ratio for gasoline fuel to minimize exhaust emissions, as well as the best combination of

fuel economy and engine performance. Based on oxygen sensor signals, the PCM tries to maintain this air/fuel ratio of 14.7:1 at all times.

2 The post-converter oxygen sensor (mounted in the exhaust system after the catalytic converter) has no effect on PCM control of the air/fuel ratio (see illustration). However, the post-converter sensor is identical to the pre-converter sensor and operates in the same way. The PCM uses the post-converter signal to monitor the efficiency of the catalytic converter. A post-converter oxygen sensor will produce a slower fluctuating voltage signal that reflects the lower oxygen content in the post-catalyst exhaust.

3 An oxygen sensor produces no voltage when it is below its normal operating temperature of about 600-degrees F. During this warm-up period, the PCM operates in an open-loop fuel control mode. It does not use the oxygen sensor signal as a feedback indication of residual oxygen in the exhaust. Instead, the PCM controls fuel metering based on the inputs of other sensors and its own programs. All oxygen

11.1 The pre-converter oxygen sensor is located in the exhaust pipe before the catalytic converter

11.2 The post-converter oxygen sensor is located in the exhaust pipe after the catalytic converter

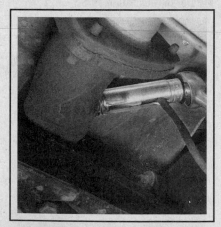

11.9 A special slotted socket, allowing clearance for the wiring harness, may be required for oxygen sensor removal (the tool is available at most auto parts stores)

sensors are equipped with a heating element, powered by fused ignition voltage, to heat the oxygen sensor to operating range as quickly as possible.

4   Proper operation of an oxygen sensor depends on four conditions:

    a)   *Electrical - The low voltages generated by the sensor require good, clean connections which should be checked whenever a sensor problem is suspected or indicated.*

    b)   *Outside air supply - The sensor needs air circulation to the internal portion of the sensor. Whenever the sensor is installed, make sure the air passages are not restricted.*

    c)   *Proper operating temperature - The PCM will not react to the sensor signal until the sensor reaches approximately 600-degrees F. This factor must be considered when evaluating the performance of the sensor.*

    d)   *Unleaded fuel - Unleaded fuel is essential for proper operation of the sensor.*

5   The PCM can detect several different oxygen sensor problems and set diagnostic trouble codes to indicate the specific fault (see Section 2). When an oxygen sensor fault occurs, the PCM will disregard the oxygen sensor signal voltage and revert to open-loop fuel control as described previously.

6   The exhaust pipe contracts when cool, and the oxygen sensor may be hard to loosen when the engine is cold. To make sensor removal easier, start and run the engine for a minute or two; then shut it off. Be careful not to burn yourself during the following procedure. Also observe these guidelines when replacing an oxygen sensor.

    a)   *The sensor has a permanently attached pigtail and electrical connector which should not be removed from the sensor. Damage or removal of the pigtail or electrical connector can harm operation of the sensor.*

    b)   *Keep grease, dirt and other contaminants away from the electrical connector and the louvered end of the sensor.*

    c)   *Do not use cleaning solvents of any kind on the oxygen sensor.*

    d)   *Do not drop or roughly handle the sensor.*

7   If replacing the post-converter oxygen sensor, raise the vehicle and place it securely on jackstands.

8   Disconnect the electrical connector from the sensor.

9   Using a suitable wrench or specialized oxygen sensor socket, unscrew the sensor from the exhaust pipe (see illustration).

10   Anti-seize compound must be used on the threads of the sensor to aid future removal. The threads of most new sensors will be coated with this compound. If not, be sure to apply anti-seize compound before installing the sensor.

11   Install the sensor and tighten it securely.

12   Reconnect the electrical connector to the sensor and lower the vehicle.

12   Knock sensor and module - replacement

♦ **Refer to illustration 12.1a and 12.1b**

※ **WARNING:**

The engine must be completely cool before beginning this procedure.

1   The knock sensor detects abnormal vibration (spark knock or pinging) in the engine (see illustration). The knock control system is designed to reduce spark knock during periods of heavy detonation. This allows the engine to use maximum spark advance to improve driveability. Knock sensors produce AC output voltage which increases with the severity of the knock. The signal is fed into the PCM and the timing is retarded to compensate for the severe detonation. V6 models are equipped with a replaceable knock sensor module in the PCM.

2   Disconnect the cable from the negative battery terminal.

12.1a On V6 models, the knock sensor is threaded into the transmission mounting flange portion of the engine block below the oil pressure sending unit

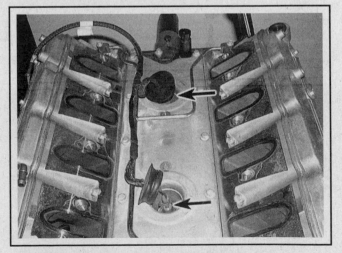

12.1b Knock sensor locations - V8 models

12.12 Remove the screws and the cover to access the knock sensor module

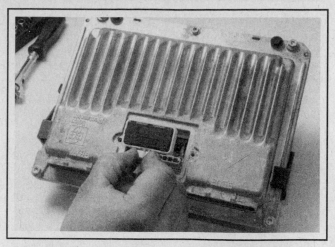

12.13 Pinch the tabs together and pull the knock sensor module straight up

✳✳ **CAUTION:**

On models equipped with the Theftlock audio system, be sure the lockout feature is turned off before performing any procedure which requires disconnecting the battery (see the front of this manual).

KNOCK SENSOR

V6 models

3   Remove the distributor (see Chapter 5).

4   Remove the oil pressure sending unit.

5   Disconnect the electrical connector and remove the knock sensor from the engine block.

6   Installation is the reverse of removal. Be sure to install the distributor in exactly the same position as originally installed (see Chapter 5).

V8 models

7   Remove the intake manifold (see Chapter 2B).

8   Detach the grommets from the valley cover, pull the grommets

up and disconnect the electrical connectors from the knock sensors. Remove the wiring harness.

9   Remove the knock sensors from the engine block.

10 Installation is the reverse of removal.

KNOCK SENSOR MODULE (V6 MODELS)

▶ **Refer to illustrations 12.12 and 12.13**

➥**Note: The knock sensor module may be replaced in the original PCM. If a new PCM is being installed, it must be programmed at a dealer service department (see Section 3).**

11 Remove the PCM (see Section 3).

12 Remove the knock sensor module cover (see illustration).

13 Carefully pinch the retaining tabs and pull the knock sensor straight up (see illustration).

14 To install the knock sensor module, align the tabs on the module with the notches on the socket.

15 Press down on the ends of the knock sensor module until the module is seated in the socket and the retaining tabs click into place.

16 Install the knock sensor module cover.

17 Install the PCM.

13 Vehicle Speed Sensor (VSS) - replacement

▶ **Refer to illustration 13.1**

1   The Vehicle Speed Sensor (VSS) is a permanent magnet generator mounted on the transmission (see illustration). The sensor is triggered by a toothed rotor on the transmission output shaft. As the output shaft rotates, the sensor produces an AC voltage, the frequency of which is proportional to vehicle speed. The PCM uses the sensor input signal for several different engine and transmission control functions. The VSS signal also drives the speedometer on the instrument panel. A defective VSS can cause various driveability and transmission problems.

2   Raise the vehicle and support it securely on jackstands.

3   Disconnect the electrical connector from the VSS.

4   Remove mounting bolt and withdraw the VSS from the transmission case.

5   Replace the sensor O-ring.

6   Installation is the reverse of removal.

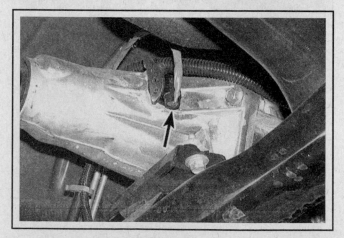

13.1 Vehicle speed sensor location

14 Idle Air Control (IAC) valve - replacement

♦ **Refer to illustrations 14.1a, 14.1b, 14.3 and 14.5**

➡**Note: This actuator is only used on early V8 and all V6 models.**

1   The idle speed is controlled by the Idle Air Control (IAC) valve (see illustrations). The IAC valve regulates the air bypassing the throttle plate by moving the pintle in or out of the air passage. The IAC valve is controlled by the PCM, adjusting the idle speed depending upon the running conditions of the engine (air conditioning system, power steering, cold and warm running etc.). The engine idle speed is not adjustable on these models.

2   On V6 models, remove the air intake duct and resonator (see Chapter 4).

3   Disconnect the electrical connector from the IAC valve. Remove the two mounting screws from the valve and withdraw it from the throttle body (see illustration).

4   Inspect the IAC valve pintle and the air passage and valve seat in the throttle body for heavy carbon deposits. Clean the IAC valve with aerosol carburetor cleaner, a shop towel and a soft brush, if necessary. Do not submerge the IAC valve in any liquid cleaner. If the air passage requires further cleaning, remove the throttle body and clean it thoroughly.

5   If installing a new IAC valve, measure the distance from the tip of the IAC valve pintle to the mounting flange (see illustration). If the distance is greater than 1-1/8 inch, press the pintle in by hand, as necessary.

❊❊ CAUTION:

Do not attempt to press the pintle in on a used IAC valve. The force required to move a pintle shaft with carbon build-up may damage the valve.

6   Install a new O-ring and lubricate it with clean engine oil.

7   Install the IAC valve and tighten the screws securely. Connect the electrical connector.

8   Cycle the ignition key On for ten seconds, then Off for ten seconds to reset the valve. Start the engine, allow it to idle for five minutes, turn the engine off for thirty seconds, then start the engine again and check the idle operation.

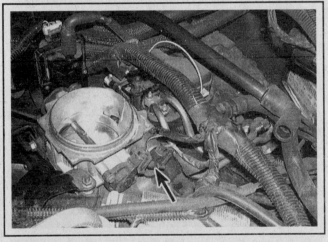

14.1a IAC valve location - V6 models

14.1b IAC valve location - early V8 models

14.3 Remove the screws (arrows) and withdraw the IAC valve from the throttle body

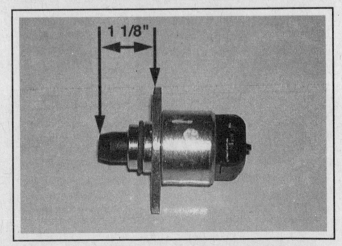

14.5 Before installing a new IAC valve, measure the distance from the tip of the pintle to the mounting flange - press the pintle in until the distance is less than 1-1/8 inch

15 Accelerator Pedal Position (APP) sensor - replacement

➡ **Note: This sensor is only used on later V8 models with electronically-controlled throttles.**

1   The sensor is part of the accelerator pedal assembly.

2   Release the wiring safety clip and disconnect the electrical harness from the sensor.

3   Remove the two bolts and carefully lift the pedal assembly out.

4   Installation is the reverse of removal.

5   The proper operation of the pedal sensor can be checked by a dealer or other qualified repair shop using a diagnostic scan tool. This will verify correct closed-throttle and wide-open settings.

16 Throttle actuator control module - replacement

➡ **Note: This sensor is only used on later V8 models with electronically-controlled throttles.**

1   This module is located on the upper left portion of the firewall.

2   Release the wiring safety clips and disconnect both wiring harnesses from the module.

3   Remove the three retaining nuts and carefully lift the module out.

4   Installation is the reverse of removal.

17 Crankcase ventilation system

♦ **Refer to illustrations 17.2a, 17.2b and 17.2c**

1   When the engine is running, a certain amount of the gasses produced during combustion escape past the piston rings into the crankcase as blow-by gasses. The crankcase ventilation system is designed to reduce the resulting hydrocarbon emissions (HC) by routing the gasses and vapors from the crankcase into the intake manifold and combustion chambers, where they are consumed during engine operation.

2   All models use a Positive Crankcase Ventilation (PCV) system.

The main component of the Positive Crankcase Ventilation (PCV) system is the PCV valve (see illustrations). Fresh air flows from the air intake duct through a vent tube into the engine. Crankcase vapors are drawn from the crankcase by the PCV valve. To maintain idle quality and good driveability, the PCV valve restricts the flow when the intake manifold vacuum is high. When intake manifold vacuum is lower, maximum vapor flow is allowed through the valve (see illustration).

3   Checking and replacement of the PCV valve is covered in Chapter 1.

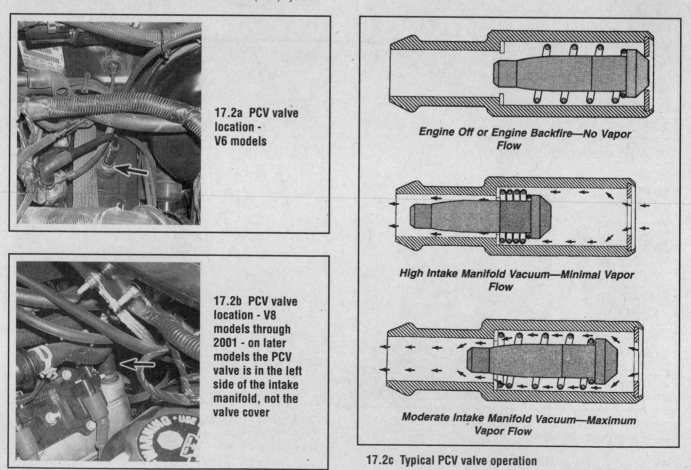

17.2a PCV valve location - V6 models

17.2b PCV valve location - V8 models through 2001 - on later models the PCV valve is in the left side of the intake manifold, not the valve cover

Engine Off or Engine Backfire—No Vapor Flow

High Intake Manifold Vacuum—Minimal Vapor Flow

Moderate Intake Manifold Vacuum—Maximum Vapor Flow

17.2c Typical PCV valve operation

18 Exhaust Gas Recirculation (EGR) system

▶ **Refer to illustrations 18.1a and 18.1b**

1   The Exhaust Gas Recirculation (EGR) system is used to lower NOx (oxides of nitrogen) emission levels caused by high combustion temperatures. The EGR valve (see illustrations) recirculates a small amount of exhaust gases into the intake manifold. The additional mixture lowers the temperature of combustion thereby reducing the formation of NOx compounds.

2   The EGR system consists of an electronic EGR valve and the PCM. The PCM controls the EGR flow rate by energizing the EGR valve solenoid coil, opening or closing the EGR passage in small increments. The PCM monitors the EGR valve pintle position with an EGR position sensor built into the EGR valve. This system allows for precise control of EGR flow, achieving optimum EGR flow depending on engine operating conditions.

REPLACEMENT

▶ **Refer to illustrations 18.5, 18.13a and 18.13b**

EGR valve

3   On V6 models, remove the air intake duct and resonator from the throttle body (see Chapter 4).

4   Disconnect the electrical connector from the EGR valve.

5   Remove the EGR valve mounting bolts (see illustration). Remove the EGR valve and gaskets. Discard the gaskets.

6   Using a gasket scraper, clean the EGR valve gasket surfaces.

7   Installation is the reverse of removal.

EGR pipe

V6 models

8   Remove the EGR pipe bracket bolt.

9   Loosen the fittings at each end of the pipe and remove the pipe.

10 Install the pipe and start the fittings, but do not fully tighten them. Loosely install the bracket bolt.

11 Align the pipe with the adapters and tighten the exhaust manifold fitting, followed by the intake manifold fitting. Tighten the bracket bolt.

V8 models

12 Remove the EGR valve.

13 Remove the EGR pipe-to-intake manifold bolts, followed by the EGR pipe-to exhaust manifold bolts (see illustrations).

14 Remove the EGR pipe-to cylinder head bolt and remove the pipe.

15 Installation is the reverse of removal.

18.1a EGR valve location - V6 models

18.1b EGR valve location - V8 models

18.5 Remove the EGR valve mounting bolts (arrows)

18.13a Remove the EGR pipe-to-intake manifold bolts . . .

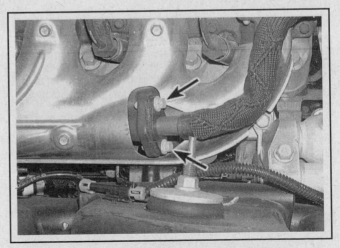

18.13b . . . and the EGR pipe-to-exhaust manifold bolts

19 Evaporative emissions control system

1   The fuel evaporative emissions control (EVAP) system absorbs fuel vapors from the fuel tank and, during engine operation, releases them into the engine intake system where they mix with the incoming air/fuel mixture. The main components of the evaporative emissions system are the canister (filled with activated charcoal to absorb fuel vapors), the purge valve, the vent valve, the fuel tank pressure sensor, the fuel tank and the vapor and purge lines.

2   After passing through a check valve, fuel tank vapor is carried through the vapor hose to the charcoal canister. The activated charcoal in the canister absorbs and stores the vapors. When a programmed set of conditions are met (engine running, warmed to a pre-set temperature, etc.), the PCM opens the purge valve and the vent valve. Fuel vapors from the canister are then drawn through the purge hose by intake manifold vacuum into the intake manifold and combustion chamber where they are consumed during normal engine operation.

3   The PCM regulates the rate of vapor flow from the canister to the intake manifold by controlling the duty cycle of the EVAP purge valve control solenoid. During cold running conditions and hot start time delay, the PCM does not energize the solenoid. After the engine has warmed up to the correct operating temperature, the PCM purges the vapors into the intake manifold according to the running conditions of the engine. The PCM will cycle (ON then OFF) the purge valve control solenoid about 5 to 10 times per second. The flow rate will be controlled by the pulse width, or length of time, the solenoid is allowed to be energized.

4   The system performs a self-diagnostic check when the engine is started cold. When the programmed conditions are met, the PCM opens the EVAP canister purge valve, leaving the vent valve closed. This action allows the engine to draw a vacuum on the entire EVAP system. Once the proper vacuum level is reached, the PCM closes the purge valve, sealing the system. The PCM then monitors the fuel tank pressure sensor voltage and sets a diagnostic code if a leak is detected.

5   The fuel tank pressure sensor operation is similar to the MAP sensor. The PCM supplies a 5-volt reference voltage and ground circuit to the sensor. The sensor returns a signal voltage to the PCM which varies according to the air pressure inside the fuel tank. When the air pressure inside the tank is equal to the outside air pressure (as with the fuel filler cap removed), the sensor output voltage is approximately 1.5 volts. With 14 in-Hg vacuum inside the tank the sensor output voltage is 4.5 volts.

CHECK

→**Note: The evaporative control system, like all emission control systems, is protected by a Federally-mandated warranty (5 years or 50,000 miles at the time this manual was written). The EVAP system probably won't fail during the service life of the vehicle; however, if it does, the hoses or charcoal canister are usually to blame.**

6   Always check the hoses first. A disconnected, damaged or missing hose is the most likely cause of a malfunctioning EVAP system. Refer to the *Vacuum Hose Routing Diagram* (attached to the radiator support) to determine whether the hoses are correctly routed and attached. Repair any damaged hoses or replace any missing hoses as necessary.

7   Check the related fuses and wiring to the purge and vent valves. Refer to the wiring diagrams at the end of Chapter 12, if necessary. The purge and vent valves are normally closed - no vapors will pass

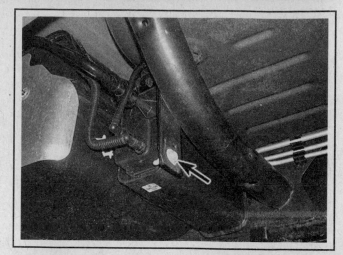

19.12 Remove the EVAP canister bracket mounting bolt (arrow)

through the ports. When the PCM energizes the solenoid (by completing the circuit to ground), the valve opens and vapors flow through.

8   A scan tool is required to thoroughly check the system. If the above checks fail to identify the problem area, have the system diagnosed by a dealer service department or other qualified repair shop.

COMPONENT REPLACEMENT

▶ **Refer to illustrations 19.12, 19.14a, 19.14b, 19.18 and 19.26**

9   All EVAP system hoses are equipped with quick-connect fittings. Before disconnecting a fitting, clean around the fitting and twist the fitting back-and-forth to loosen the seal. To disconnect a large hose fitting, squeeze the retainer tabs together and pull the fitting off the pipe. To disconnect a small hose fitting, push the locking tab in and pull the fitting off the pipe.

EVAP canister

10   The EVAP canister is attached to a bracket near the fuel tank.
11   Raise the vehicle and support it securely on jackstands.
12   Disconnect the hoses from the canister (see Step 9). Remove the bracket mounting bolt and remove the canister (see illustration).
13   Installation is the reverse of removal.

Purge valve

14   The purge valve is mounted on the intake manifold (see illustrations). On V8 models, remove the intake manifold cover.
15   Disconnect the electrical connector. Depress the locking tab and remove the hose from the purge valve (see Step 9).
16   Remove the mounting nuts/bolt. On V6 models, remove the wiring harness retainer from the mounting stud. Remove the purge valve.
17   Installation is the reverse of removal.

Vent valve

18   The vent valve is mounted on a bracket near the fuel tank (see illustration).
19   Raise the vehicle and support it securely on jackstands.
20   Disconnect the electrical connector. Remove the hose from the

19.14a EVAP purge valve/control solenoid location - V6 models

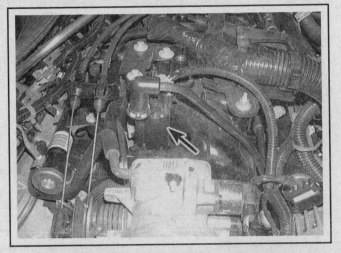

19.14b EVAP purge valve/control solenoid location - V8 models

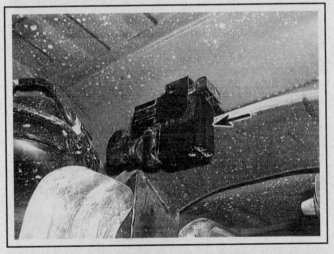

19.18 EVAP vent valve/control solenoid location

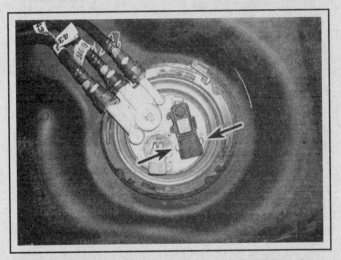

19.26 Pry the retaining clips out (arrows) and withdraw the fuel tank pressure sensor from the fuel pump module

vent valve (see Step 9).

20 Release the retainers and remove the vent valve from the bracket.

21 Installation is the reverse of removal.

Fuel tank pressure sensor

23 The fuel tank pressure sensor is located on the fuel pump module.

24 Remove the fuel tank (see Chapter 4).

25 Disconnect the electrical connector from the fuel tank pressure sensor.

26 Release the retaining clip and remove the sensor from the top of the fuel pump module (see illustration).

27 Installation is the reverse of removal.

20 Secondary Air Injection (AIR) system

1 Some models are equipped with a secondary air injection (AIR) system. The secondary air injection system is used to reduce tailpipe emissions on initial engine start-up. The system uses an electric motor/pump assembly, relay, vacuum valve/solenoid, air shut-off valve, check valves and tubing to inject fresh air directly into the exhaust manifolds. The fresh air (oxygen) reacts with the exhaust gas in the catalytic converter to reduce HC and CO levels. The air pump and solenoid are controlled by the PCM through the AIR relay. During initial start-up, the PCM energizes the AIR relay, the relay supplies battery voltage to the air pump and the vacuum valve/solenoid, engine vacuum is applied to the air shut-off valve which opens and allows air to flow through the tubing into the exhaust manifolds. The PCM will operate the air pump until closed loop operation is reached (or four minutes, maximum). During normal operation, the check valves prevent exhaust backflow into the system.

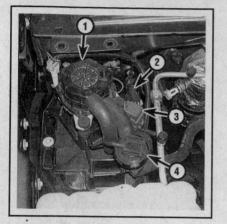

20.2 Secondary air injection component locations

1 Air pump
2 Vacuum valve/solenoid
3 Air pump/solenoid relay
4 Air shut-off valve

20.21 Using hose clamp pliers, squeeze the clamp tangs together, slide the clamp down the hose and remove the hose from the check valve

20.23 Remove the mounting nuts (arrows) and remove the check valve and pipe assembly

CHECK

▶ **Refer to illustration 20.2**

2 Check the air pump hoses and the vacuum hoses (see illustration). Repair any damaged hoses or replace any missing hoses as necessary. Check the vacuum source to the vacuum valve/solenoid. Intake manifold vacuum should be present with the engine running.

3 Check the related fuses, the relay and the wiring to the air pump and vacuum valve/solenoid. Refer to Chapter 12 for the relay check and refer to the wiring diagrams at the end of Chapter 12, if necessary. The vacuum valve/solenoid is normally closed - no vacuum is applied to the air shut-off valve. When the PCM energizes the relay (by completing the circuit to ground), the air pump operates, the vacuum valve opens, vacuum is applied to the air shut-off valve, the shut-off valve opens and air flows through the tubing into the exhaust manifolds.

4 A scan tool is required to thoroughly check the system. If the above checks fail to identify the problem area, have the system diagnosed by a dealer service department or other qualified repair shop.

COMPONENT REPLACEMENT

▶ **Refer to illustrations 20.21 and 20.23**

Air pump

5 Remove the bolts and the fender-to-cowl brace.
6 Disconnect the electrical connector from the air pump motor. Detach the hoses from the air pump.
7 Detach the air pump from the rubber mounting posts and remove the air pump assembly.
8 Installation is the reverse of removal.

Vacuum valve/solenoid

9 Disconnect the electrical connector from the valve/solenoid.
10 Label and disconnect the vacuum hoses from the valve/solenoid.
11 Remove the mounting screw and remove the vacuum valve/solenoid.
12 Installation is the reverse of removal.

Air shut-off valve

13 Detach the vacuum hose from the shut-off valve.
14 Detach the clamp from the assembly base.
15 Loosen the hose clamp and detach the air outlet hose from the shut-off valve.
16 Detach the shut-off valve from the air inlet hose and remove the valve.
17 Installation is the reverse of removal.

Air pump/solenoid relay

18 Disconnect the electrical connector from the relay.
19 Release the retaining tab and remove the relay from the bracket.
20 Installation is the reverse of removal.

Check valve and pipe

✳✳ WARNING:

The engine must be completely cool before beginning this procedure or serious burns may result.

21 Loosen the clamp and remove the air hose from the check valve (see illustration).
22 On V6 models, remove the air pipe-to-exhaust manifold bracket bolt.
23 Remove the mounting bolts/nuts and remove the check valve and pipe assembly (see illustration).
24 To remove the check valve from the pipe, clamp the large nut on the pipe in a vise and remove the check valve with an open-end wrench.
25 Clean the carbon deposits from the pipe flange and the exhaust manifold mounting surface. Remove the carbon deposits from the hole in the manifold, if necessary.
26 Install the check valve on the pipe and install the assembly onto the exhaust manifold with a new gasket. Tighten the fasteners securely.
27 The remainder of installation is the reverse of removal.

21 Catalytic converter

➡**Note: Because of a Federally mandated warranty which covers emissions-related components such as the catalytic converter, check with a dealer service department before replacing the converter at your own expense.**

1 The catalytic converter is an emission control device added to the exhaust system to reduce pollutants from the exhaust gas stream. A three-way (reduction) catalyst design is used. The catalytic coating on the three-way catalyst contains platinum and rhodium, which lowers the levels of oxides of nitrogen (NOx) as well as hydrocarbons (HC) and carbon monoxide (CO).

2 The test equipment for a catalytic converter is expensive and highly sophisticated. If you suspect that the converter on your vehicle is malfunctioning, take it to a dealer or authorized emissions inspection facility for diagnosis and repair.

CHECK

3 Whenever the vehicle is raised for servicing of underbody components, check the converter for leaks, corrosion, dents and other damage. Check the flange bolts that attach the front and rear ends of the converter to the exhaust system. If damage is discovered, the converter should be replaced.

4 A catalytic converter may become plugged. The easiest way to check for a restricted converter is to use a vacuum gauge to diagnose the effect of a blocked exhaust on intake vacuum.

  a) *Connect a vacuum gauge to an intake manifold vacuum source.*
  b) *Warm the engine to operating temperature, place the transmission*
  in Park and apply the parking brake.
  c) *Note and record the vacuum reading at idle.*
  d) *Open the throttle until the engine speed is about 2000 rpm.*
  e) *Release the throttle quickly and record the vacuum reading.*
  f) *Perform the test three more times, recording the reading after each test.*
  g) *If the reading after the fourth test is more than one in-Hg lower than the reading recorded at idle, the catalytic converter, muffler or exhaust pipes may be plugged or restricted.*

REPLACEMENT

▶ **Refer to illustrations 21.7a and 21.7b**

➡**Note: Refer to the exhaust system servicing section in Chapter 4 for additional information.**

5 Raise the vehicle and support it securely on jackstands.
6 Disconnect the electrical connectors from the oxygen sensors.
7 Remove the catalytic converter-to-exhaust pipe flange bolts and separate the exhaust pipe from the catalytic converter (see illustrations). Support the exhaust pipe.
8 Remove the bolts and detach the catalytic converter header pipe from the exhaust manifold (see Chapter 2A or 2B). Remove the catalytic converter and pipe assembly.
9 Clean the carbon deposits from the mounting flanges and install new gaskets.
10 Installation is the reverse of removal.

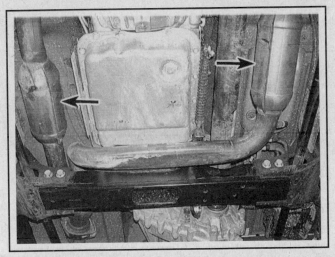

21.7a Catalytic converter locations

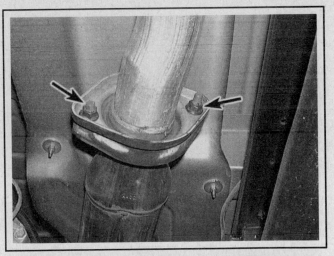

21.7b Remove the catalytic converter-to-exhaust pipe flange bolts (arrows)

Notes

Section

Reference to other Chapters

7A

MANUAL TRANSMISSION

1 General information

The vehicles covered by this manual are equipped with a manual or an automatic transmission. Information on the manual transmission is included in this Part of Chapter 7. Information on the automatic transmission can be found in Part B of this Chapter. Information on the transfer case used on 4WD models can be found in Part C of this Chapter.

Vehicles equipped with a five-speed manual transmission use either an NV 3500 or an NV 4500. Both units are fully synchronized five-speeds with internal shift mechanisms. The NV 3500 transmission is visually identified by its non-removable bellhousing while the NV 4500 transmission has the typical removable bellhousing. Both transmissions are available in two and four wheel drive versions. On

2001 models, there is an optional six-speed manual transmission, the ZF S6-650, which can be identified by its three separate aluminum cases. The front case is the bellhousing, the center houses the shifting mechanism, and the rear case houses the gears. Always refer to the front of this manual to positively identify these transmissions before servicing.

Depending on the cost of having a transmission overhauled, it might be a better idea to replace it with a used or rebuilt unit. Your local dealer or transmission shop should be able to supply information concerning cost, availability and exchange policy. Regardless of how you decide to remedy a transmission problem, you can still save a lot of money by removing and installing the unit yourself.

2 Shift lever and housing - removal and installation

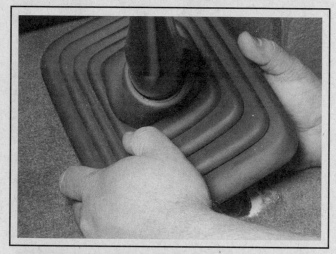

2.4 Remove the retaining screws, then slide the boot and the boot insulator off the shift lever

▶ **Refer to illustrations 2.4, 2.5 and 2.6**

1 Place the shift lever in Third or Fourth gear.

2 Pry out the plastic retaining clips and remove the trim bezel surrounding the shifter boot.

3 Remove the retaining screws securing the shifter boot to the floor pan.

4 Slide the shift lever boot and the boot insulator off the shift lever (see illustration).

5 Loosen the jam-nut at the base of the shift lever several turns, then unscrew the shift lever from the transmission (see illustration)

6 To remove the shift lever housing from the transmission simply detach the outer four bolts securing the housing to the transmission and pull straight up (see illustration).

➡ **Note: The transmission must stay in Third or fourth gear during removal and installation of the shift lever housing. DO NOT remove the shift lever mechanism from the shift lever housing as it may void the manufacturers warranty.**

7 Installation is the reverse of removal. Be sure to tighten the shift lever housing bolts to the torque listed in this Chapter's Specifications.

2.5 Loosen the jam-nut at the base of the lever and unscrew the shift lever from the transmission

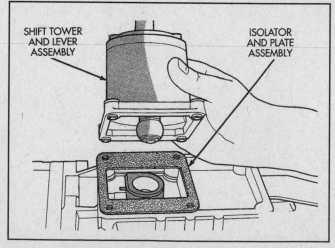

2.6 Pull straight up to remove the shift lever housing

SHIFT TOWER AND LEVER ASSEMBLY

ISOLATOR AND PLATE ASSEMBLY

3 Back-up light switch - check and replacement

♦ Refer to illustrations 3.1a and 3.1b

1   The backup light switch is located on the left side of the transmission case on 3500 and 4500 models (see illustrations). On 2001 and later models with ZF six-speed, the switch is at the rear of the last case, at the top-right.

CHECK

2   Turn the ignition key to the On position and move the shift lever to the Reverse position; the back-up lights should go on.

3   If the lights don't go on, check the back-up light fuse first (see Chapter 12). If the fuse is blown, trace the back-up light circuit for a short-circuit condition.

4   If the fuse is okay, raise the vehicle and support it securely on jackstands. Place the shifter in Reverse.

5   Working under the vehicle, unplug the back-up light switch electrical connector. Using an ohmmeter, check for continuity across the terminals of the switch. Continuity should exist. If not, replace the switch.

6   If the switch has continuity, check for voltage at the electrical connector; one of the two terminals should have battery voltage present with the ignition key in the On position. If no voltage is present, trace the circuit between the fuse block and the electrical connector for an open circuit condition.

7   If voltage is present, trace the back-up light circuit between the electrical connector and the back-up light bulbs for an open circuit condition.

➡Note: Although not very likely, the back-up light bulbs could both be burned out; don't rule out this possibility.

REPLACEMENT

8   Raise the vehicle and support it securely on jackstands, if not already done.

9   Unplug the back-up light switch electrical connector.

10 Unscrew the back-up light switch from the transmission case.

11 Apply RTV sealant or Teflon tape to the threads of the new switch

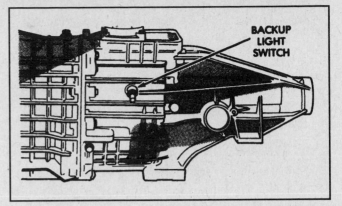

3.1a Location of the back-up light switch (NV 3500 transmission)

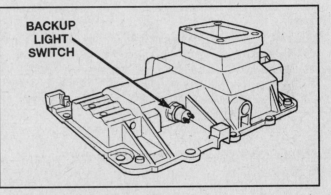

3.1b Location of the back-up light switch (NV 4500 transmission) Specifications

to prevent leakage. Install the switch in the transmission case and tighten it securely. Plug in the electrical connector.

➡Note: The replacement switch may come equipped with thread sealant already applied to the threads. Do not apply RTV sealant or teflon tape to the threads of the new switch if thread sealant has already been applied by the manufacturer.

12 Lower the vehicle and check the operation of the back-up lights.

4 Transmission - removal and installation

REMOVAL

1   Disconnect the cable from the negative terminal of the battery.

✳✳ CAUTION:

On models equipped with the Theftlock audio system, be sure the lockout feature is turned off before performing any procedure which requires disconnecting the battery (see the front of this manual).

2   Shift the transmission into Third or Fourth.

3   Remove the shift lever and housing assembly (see Section 2).

4   Raise the vehicle sufficiently to provide clearance to easily remove the transmission. Support the vehicle securely on jackstands.

5   Disconnect the electrical connector from the back-up light switch

and the vehicle speed sensor. Disengage the wiring harness from the clips on the transmission.

6   Remove the skid plate, if equipped.

7   If the transmission is going to be disassembled, drain the lubricant (see Chapter 1).

8   Remove the driveshaft(s) (see Chapter 8). Use a plastic bag to cover the end of the transmission to prevent fluid loss and contamination.

9   Remove exhaust system components as necessary for clearance (see Chapter 4).

10 On 3500 and 4500 models, Remove the starter motor (see Chapter 5). On ZF six-speed models, unbolt the fuel line brackets at the bellhousing.

11 On 4WD NV 3500 models, remove the transmission-to-transfer case support braces (left and right side) from the transmission and the transfer case. On NV 4500 transmissions remove the flywheel inspec-

tion cover from the lower half of the bellhousing and the transmission support bracket from the right side of the transmission.

12 Remove the plastic bellhousing covers from the left and right side transmission bellhousing if equipped (see illustrations 8.8a and 8.8b in Chapter 7B).

13 Disconnect the clutch hydraulic line from the bellhousing (see Chapter 8).

14 On 4WD models, remove the transfer case shift linkage and the transfer case (see Chapter 7C).

➥**Note: The NV 246 (automatic) transfer case is not equipped with external shift linkage.**

15 Support the engine from above with an engine hoist, or place a jack (with a block of wood as an insulator) under the engine oil pan. The engine must remain supported at all times while the transmission is out of the vehicle.

16 Support the transmission with a jack - preferably a special jack made for this purpose.

➥**Note: These jacks can be obtained at most equipment rental yards.**

Safety chains will help steady the transmission on the jack.

17 Raise the engine slightly and disconnect the transmission mount from the extension housing and the center crossmember (see Chapter 7B).

18 Raise the transmission slightly and remove the bolts and nuts attaching the crossmember to the frame rails.

19 Lower the jacks supporting the transmission and engine assembly.

20 Remove the nuts and bolts attaching the transmission to the engine.

21 Make a final check for any wiring or hoses connected to the transmission, then move the transmission and jack toward the rear of the vehicle until the transmission input shaft clears the splined hub in the clutch disc. Keep the transmission level as this is done.

22 Once the input shaft is clear, lower the transmission slightly and remove it from under the vehicle.

23 While the transmission is removed, be sure to remove and inspect all clutch components (see Chapter 8). In most cases, new clutch components should be routinely installed if the transmission is removed.

INSTALLATION

24 Insert a small amount of multi-purpose grease into the pilot

bearing in the crankshaft and lubricate the inner surface of the bearing. Also apply a light film of grease on the input shaft splines, input shaft bearing retainer and the release lever/bearing contact points (see Chapter 8).

25 Install the clutch components if removed (see Chapter 8).

26 With the transmission secured to the jack as on removal, raise the transmission into position behind the engine and then carefully slide it forward, engaging the input shaft with the clutch plate hub. Do not use excessive force to install the transmission - if the input shaft does not slide into place, readjust the angle of the transmission so it is level and/or turn the input shaft so the splines engage properly with the clutch.

27 Install the transmission-to-engine bolts and tighten them to the torque listed in this Chapter's Specifications.

✸✸ CAUTION:

Don't use the bolts to draw the transmission to the engine. If the transmission doesn't slide forward easily and mate with the engine block, find out why before proceeding.

---

28 Raise the transmission into place, install the crossmember and attach it to the frame rails. Install the transmission mount between the extension housing and the crossmember. Carefully lower the transmission extension housing onto the mount and the crossmember. When everything is properly aligned, tighten all nuts and bolts securely.

29 Remove the jacks supporting the transmission and the engine.

30 On 4WD models, install the transfer case and shift linkage (if equipped) (see Chapter 7C).

31 Install the various items removed previously, referring to Chapter 8 for the installation of the driveshaft(s) and clutch hydraulic line, Chapter 5 for the starter motor, and Chapter 4 for the exhaust system components.

32 Plug in the electrical connector for the vehicle speed sensor and the back-up light switch. Connect any other wiring attached to the transmission or the transfer case.

33 Remove the jackstands and lower the vehicle.

34 Install the shift lever and housing assembly (see Section 2).

35 Fill the transmission with the specified lubricant to the proper level (see Chapter 1).

36 Connect the cable to the negative terminal of the battery.

37 Road test the vehicle for proper operation and check for leakage.

---

5 Transmission overhaul - general information

Overhauling a manual transmission is a difficult job for the do-it-yourselfer. It involves the disassembly and reassembly of many small parts. Numerous clearances must be precisely measured and, if necessary, changed with select fit spacers and snap-rings. As a result, if transmission problems arise, it can be removed and installed by a competent do-it-yourselfer, but overhaul should be left to a transmission repair shop. Rebuilt transmissions may be available - check with your dealer parts department and auto parts stores. At any rate, the time and money involved in an overhaul is almost sure to exceed the cost of a rebuilt unit.

Nevertheless, it's not impossible for an inexperienced mechanic to rebuild a transmission if the special tools are available and the job is done in a deliberate step-by-step manner so nothing is overlooked.

The tools necessary for an overhaul include internal and external

snap-ring pliers, a bearing puller, a slide hammer, a set of pin punches, a dial indicator and possibly a hydraulic press. In addition, a large, sturdy workbench and a vise or transmission stand will be required.

During disassembly of the transmission, make careful notes of how each piece comes off, where it fits in relation to other pieces and what holds it in place. If you note how each part is installed before removing it, getting the transmission back together again will be much easier.

Before taking the transmission apart for repair, it will help if you have some idea what area of the transmission is malfunctioning. Certain problems can be closely tied to specific areas in the transmission, which can make component examination and replacement easier. Refer to the Troubleshooting Section at the front of this manual for information regarding possible sources of trouble.

Specifications

General

Transmission lubricant type	See Chapter 1

Torque specifications	Ft-lbs (unless otherwise indicated)
Back-up light switch	
Through 2000	21
2001 and later	27
Bellhousing cover screws	120 in-lbs
Shift lever jam-nut	35
Shift lever housing-to-transmission bolts	15
Transmission mount-to-transmission bolts	
Through 2000	18
2001 and later	37
Transmission mount-to-crossmember nuts	30
Transmission-to-engine bolts	37

Notes

Section

7B
AUTOMATIC TRANSMISSION

1 General information

All vehicles covered by this manual come equipped with either a five-speed or six-speed manual transmission, or a four-speed automatic transmission. Information on the manual transmission is in Part A of this Chapter. Information on the automatic transmission is included in this Part of Chapter 7. You'll also find certain procedures common to both automatic and manual transmissions - such as oil seal replacement and transmission mount replacement - in this Part of Chapter 7.

The models covered by this manual use either a 4L60-E or a 4L80-E electronic four-speed automatic transmission. They are both similar in design and function, but typically the 4L60-E is used on the 4.3L V6, 4.8L V8 and 5.3L V8 engines. The 4L80-E transmission is typically used on the 6.0L V8 engines. These transmissions are equipped with a torque converter clutch (TCC) that engages in fourth gear, and in third gear when the overdrive switch is turned off. The TCC provides a direct connection between the engine and the drive wheels for improved efficiency and economy. The TCC consists of a solenoid controlled by the Powertrain Control Module (PCM) that locks the converter in third or fourth when the vehicle is cruising on level ground and the engine is fully warmed up. Some models are also equipped with an auxiliary transmission cooler that is mounted in front of the radiator and air conditioning condenser, if equipped.

Due to the complexity of the automatic transmissions covered in this manual and the need for specialized equipment to perform most service operations, this Chapter contains only general diagnosis, routine maintenance, adjustment and removal and installation procedures.

If the transmission requires major repair work, it should be left to a dealer service department or an automotive or transmission repair shop. You can, however, remove and install the transmission yourself and save the expense, even if the repair work is done by a transmission shop.

2 Diagnosis - general

→**Note: Automatic transmission malfunctions may be caused by five general conditions: poor engine performance, improper adjustments, hydraulic malfunctions, mechanical malfunctions or malfunctions in the Powertrain Control Module or its signal network. Diagnosis of these problems should always begin with a check of the easily repaired items: fluid level and condition (see Chapter 1), and shift cable adjustment (see Section 3). Next, perform a road test to determine if the problem has been corrected or if more diagnosis is necessary. Because the transmission relies on many sensors in the engine control system, and since the transmission shift points are controlled by the Powertrain Control Module, you'll also want to check to see if any trouble codes have been stored in the PCM (see Chapter 6 for a list of trouble codes and how to extract them). If the problem persists after the preliminary tests and corrections are completed, additional diagnosis should be done by a dealer service department or transmission repair shop. Refer to the Troubleshooting section at the front of this manual for transmission problem diagnosis.**

PRELIMINARY CHECKS

1 Drive the vehicle to warm the transmission to normal operating temperature.

2 Check the fluid level as described in Chapter 1:

a) *If the fluid level is unusually low, add enough fluid to bring the level within the designated area of the dipstick, then check for external leaks.*

b) *If the fluid level is abnormally high, drain off the excess, then check the drained fluid for contamination by coolant. The presence of engine coolant in the automatic transmission fluid indicates that a failure has occurred in the internal radiator walls that separate the coolant from the transmission fluid (see Chapter 3).*

c) *If the fluid is foaming, drain it and refill the transmission, then check for coolant in the fluid or a high fluid level.*

3 Check the engine idle speed.

→**Note: If the engine is malfunctioning, do not proceed with the preliminary checks until it has been repaired and runs normally.**

4 Inspect the shift control cable (see Section 3). Make sure that it's properly adjusted and that it operates smoothly.

5 Check the Park/Neutral Position (PNP) switch adjustment (see Section 5).

FLUID LEAK DIAGNOSIS

6 Most fluid leaks are easy to locate visually. Repair usually consists of replacing a seal or gasket. If a leak is difficult to find, the following procedure may help.

7 Identify the fluid. Make sure it's transmission fluid and not engine oil or brake fluid (automatic transmission fluid is a deep red color).

8 Try to pinpoint the source of the leak. Drive the vehicle several miles, then park it over a large sheet of cardboard. After a minute or two, you should be able to locate the leak by determining the source of the fluid dripping onto the cardboard.

9 Make a careful visual inspection of the suspected component and the area immediately around it. Pay particular attention to gasket mating surfaces. A mirror is often helpful for finding leaks in areas that are hard to see.

10 If the leak still cannot be found, clean the suspected area thoroughly with a degreaser or solvent, then dry it.

11 Drive the vehicle for several miles at normal operating temperature and varying speeds. After driving the vehicle, visually inspect the suspected component again.

12 Once the leak has been located, the cause must be determined before it can be properly repaired. If a gasket is replaced but the sealing flange is bent, the new gasket will not stop the leak. The bent flange must be straightened.

13 Before attempting to repair a leak, check to make sure that the following conditions are corrected or they may cause another leak.

→**Note: Some of the following conditions cannot be fixed without highly specialized tools and expertise. Such problems must be referred to a transmission shop or a dealer service department.**

Gasket leaks

14 Check the pan periodically. Make sure the bolts are tight, no bolts are missing, the gasket is in good condition and the pan is flat (dents in the pan may indicate damage to the valve body inside).

15 If the pan gasket is leaking, the fluid level or the fluid pressure may be too high, the vent may be plugged, the pan bolts may be too tight, the pan sealing flange may be warped, the sealing surface of the transmission housing may be damaged, the gasket may be damaged or the transmission casting may be cracked or porous. If sealant instead

of gasket material has been used to form a seal between the pan and the transmission housing, it may be the wrong sealant.

Seal leaks

16 If a transmission seal is leaking, the fluid level or pressure may be too high, the vent may be plugged, the seal bore may be damaged, the seal itself may be damaged or improperly installed, the surface of the shaft protruding through the seal may be damaged or a loose bearing may be causing excessive shaft movement.

17 Make sure the dipstick tube seal is in good condition and the tube is properly seated. Periodically check the area around the speedometer gear or vehicle speed sensor for leakage. If transmission fluid is evident, check the O-ring for damage. Also inspect the driveshaft oil seal for leakage.

Case leaks

18 If the case itself appears to be leaking, the casting is porous and will have to be repaired or replaced.

19 Make sure the oil cooler hose fittings are tight and in good condition. The transmission oil cooler lines on these models are equipped with quick connect fittings - always inspect the O-rings if a leak is suspected.

Fluid comes out vent pipe or fill tube

20 If this condition occurs, the transmission is overfilled, there is coolant in the fluid, the case is porous, the dipstick is incorrect, the vent is plugged or the drain back holes are plugged.

3 Shift cable - removal, installation and adjustment

REMOVAL

➡ Note: The shift cable on these models is a two piece design, therefore one end of the cable can be replaced without replacing the other.

1 Disconnect the cable from the negative terminal of the battery.

❋❋ CAUTION:

On models equipped with the Theftlock audio system, be sure the lockout feature is turned off before performing any procedure which requires disconnecting the battery (see the information at the front of this manual).

2 Place the transmission in PARK and apply the parking brake.
3 Block the rear wheels so the vehicle will not accidentally roll in either direction.

Lower cable - transmission end

▶ Refer to illustrations 3.4, 3.5, 3.6, 3.7 and 3.8

4 Disconnect the shift cable from the transmission shift lever (see illustration).
5 Disengage the shift cable from the cable bracket on the transmission (see illustration).

6 Locate the cable connector at the center of the cable. Pull back the white plastic collar to expose the cable connector retaining clip (see illustration).

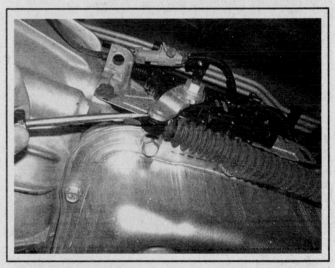

3.4 Use a screwdriver to pry the shift cable off the shift lever at the transmission

3.5 Remove the retaining clip and detach the shift cable from the bracket

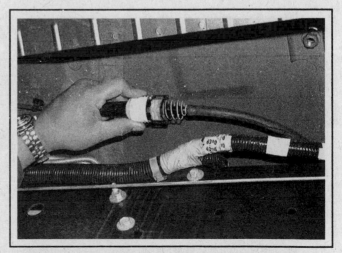

3.6 Pull back the white plastic collar to expose the cable connector retaining clip

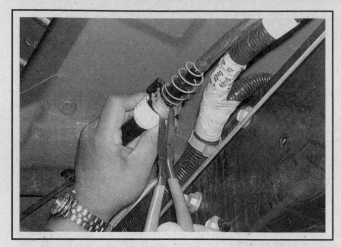

3.7 Pull downward on the center tabs of the connector retaining clip to remove it

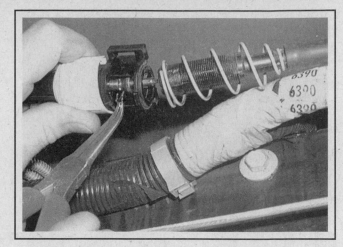

3.8 Detach the cable retaining clip, separate the cable halves and remove the transmission end of the cable from the vehicle

7   Remove the cable connector retaining clip (see illustration).

8   Remove the cable retaining clip (see illustration).

➡**Note: Always replace the cable retaining clip (E-clip) with a new one upon installation.**

9   Separate the cable halves and remove the transmission end of the shift cable from the vehicle.

Upper cable - steering column end

▶ **Refer to illustrations 3.11, 3.12a, 3.12b, 3.13 and 3.16**

10   Remove the steering column trim covers and the knee bolster from below the steering column (see Chapter 11).

➡**Note: It will be easier to access the shift cable and the surrounding components if the drivers seat is also removed, but it's not absolutely necessary.**

11   Pry the shift cable ball socket from the shift lever ball pivot (see illustration).

12   Remove the retaining clip securing the cable to the steering column bracket. Depress the tangs and slide the cable out of the steering column bracket (see illustrations).

13   Working below the steering column, remove the bolt and the cable support wire securing the cable to the lower half of the steering column (see illustration).

14   Working under the vehicle, perform Steps 6 through 8 to separate the upper shift cable from the lower shift cable.

15   Working back inside the passenger compartment, remove the door sill plate and the left kick panel from the vehicle, then peel back the carpeting.

16   Trace the cable to the cable grommet (the point at which it goes through the floor board). Pry out the grommet and pull the upper cable up through the hole in the floor to remove it (see illustration).

INSTALLATION AND ADJUSTMENT

▶ **Refer to illustration 3.20**

17   Installation of the either cable is the reverse of removal with the following exceptions:

18   Make sure the driver's shift lever and the transmission shift lever are in the Park position.

19   Before joining the cable halves together it will be necessary to insert a new cable retaining clip (E-clip) onto the female half of the cable at the cable connector (see illustration 3.8).

20   Using two hands, align the male half of the cable with the female

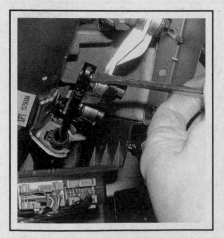

3.11 Pry the end of the shift cable off the shift lever arm

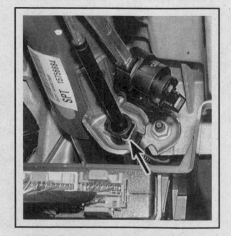

3.12a Detach the cable retaining clip (arrow) . . .

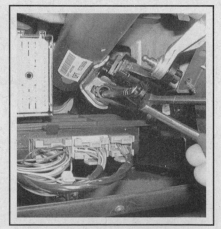

3.12b . . . depress the tangs and push the cable back through the hole in the steering column bracket

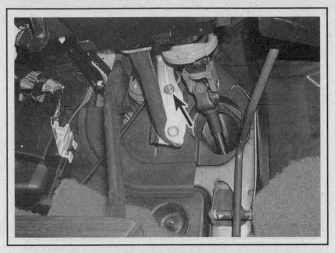

3.13 Unscrew the bolt (arrow) from the rear of the bracket and lift the wire upward until the hook at the other end of the wire disengages from the steering column support bracket

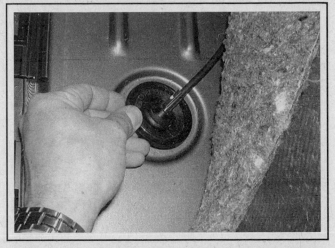

3.16 The cable grommet is located on the floorboard just in front of the drivers seat

half of the cable and push the connector halves together until the blue adjustment spring is fully compressed. This engages the male end of the cable into the E-clip on the female end of the cable and locks the cable together (see illustration).

21 Release the lower (transmission) end of the cable and allow the blue spring to self-adjust the cable. The blue spring must be free standing with no help to properly adjust the cable.

22 Pull back the white plastic collar on the upper (steering column) end of the cable connector and insert the cable connector retaining clip (see illustration 3.6).

23 Verify that the cable connector retaining clip is fully seated and that the white plastic collar slides back over the cable connector retaining clip. Test the vehicle for proper shift operation.

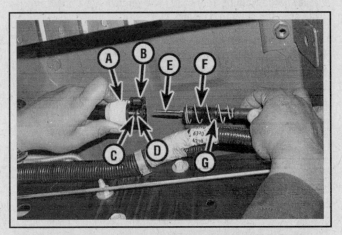

3.20 Shift cable (adjustment) connector installation details

A   White plastic collar
B   Shift cable connector (steering column end)
C   Shift cable retaining clip (E-clip)
D   Shift cable (female half)
E   Shift cable (male half)
F   Shift cable connector (transmission end)
G   Adjustment spring

4   Park/Lock system - description and component replacement

DESCRIPTION

1   The Park/Lock system prevents the shift lever from being moved out of Park unless the brake pedal is depressed simultaneously. It also prevents the ignition key from being removed from the ignition switch unless the shift lever is in the Park position. When the car is started, a solenoid is energized, locking the shift lever in Park; when the brake pedal is depressed, the solenoid is deenergized, unlocking the shift lever so that it can be moved into some other gear.

CABLE REPLACEMENT

▶ Refer to illustration 4.6

2   Remove the steering column covers (see Chapter 11).
3   Place the shift lever in the Park position.
4   Turn the ignition key to the Accessory position.
5   Insert a screwdriver blade into the slot in the lock cylinder housing, depress the cable latch and detach the cable from the lock cylinder housing.

4.6 With the ignition key in the Accessory position and the shifter in Park, depress the cable latch (A) and detach the cable from the lock cylinder housing, then remove the shift lever gate retaining screws (B) and remove the cable from the steering column housing

6   Remove the shift lever gate (see illustration).

7   Slide the opposite end of the cable out of the steering column housing and remove it from the vehicle. Note that the hooked end of the cable was removed from the lock cylinder housing and the round end of the cable was removed from the steering column housing.

8   Make sure the ignition key is in the Accessory position and the shift lever is in the Park position before installing the cable.

9   When installing the steering column end of the cable, insert the cable into the guide in the steering column housing, then align the plastic tab on the cable with the slot in the shift lever gate and install the shift lever gate.

10   When installing the lock cylinder end of the cable, be sure to push the locking tab on the cable connector into the lock cylinder housing until it clicks back into place.

11   Check the operation of the park/lock cable and make sure the ignition key can not be removed without the shift lever in Park.

12   The remainder of the installation is the reverse of removal.

4.15 The Brake/Transmission Shift Interlock (BTSI) solenoid (arrow) is located on the right side of the steering column just above the shift cable

BRAKE/TRANSMISSION SHIFT INTERLOCK (BTSI) SOLENOID REPLACEMENT

◆ **Refer to illustration 4.15**

13   Remove the steering column covers (see Chapter 11).

14   Unplug the electrical connector from the solenoid.

15   Pry off each end of the solenoid from its mounting pins and remove it from the steering column (see illustration).

16   Installation is the reverse of removal.

BTSI ADJUSTMENT

Refer to illustrations 4.19 and 4.20

17   Remove the steering column covers (see Chapter 11).

18   Place the shift lever in the Park position.

19   Disconnect the BTSI solenoid electrical connector from the BTSI solenoid (see illustration).

20   Pull out the tab from the BTSI solenoid block (see illustration).

21   Press the BTSI solenoid block down and simultaneously slide

4.19 Details of the Brake Transmission Shift Interlock (BTSI) solenoid assembly

A	Shift lever	C BTSI solenoid
B	Grommet and mounting pin	

4.20 Pry the BTSI solenoid actuator tab out (A), press the block (B) and slide the block assembly away from the steering column - BTSI assembly removed for clarity

the assembly away from the BTSI solenoid actuator as far as possible.

22 Push the tab in to lock the BTSI solenoid into position. Be sure to push the locking tab into the BTSI solenoid housing until it clicks back into place.

23 Install the electrical connector.

24 Check the operation of the Park/Lock system and make sure the ignition key cannot be removed without the shift lever in Park.

25 The remainder of the installation is the reverse of removal.

5 Park/Neutral Position (PNP) switch/back-up light switch - replacement and adjustment

REPLACEMENT

▶ **Refer to illustrations 5.6, 5.7 and 5.8**

1 Disconnect the cable from the negative terminal of the battery.

❋❋ CAUTION:

On models equipped with the Theftlock audio system, be sure the lockout feature is turned off before performing any procedure which requires disconnecting the battery (see the front of this manual).

2 Apply the parking brake and put the shift lever in Neutral.

3 Locate the Park/Neutral Position (PNP) switch which is mounted on the transmission at the manual lever.

4 Disconnect the shift cable from the manual lever.

5 Unplug the electrical connectors from the PNP switch.

6 Remove the manual lever retaining nut and remove the manual lever.

➡**Note: Be careful not to move the manual lever from the Neutral position while doing this. If the lever moves, insert the manual lever back on the shift shaft loosely and reposition the lever in the Neutral position before removing the PNP switch (see illustration).**

7 Remove the switch retaining bolts and detach the switch from the transmission (see illustration).

8 If you're installing a new switch, align the slots on the switch (where the shaft is inserted) with the notch on the switch body (see illustration). Then install the switch onto the shaft.

9 If you're installing the old switch, simply align the flats of the shift shaft with the flats of the Park/Neutral Position switch and install the switch.

5.6 Transmission manual lever position details

10 Install the switch mounting bolts and tighten them to the torque listed in this Chapter's Specifications.

11 Install the manual lever, tightening the nut to the torque listed in this Chapter's Specifications.

12 Attach the shift cable and reconnect the electrical connectors.

13 The remainder of installation is the reverse of removal.

ADJUSTMENT

14 Verify that the engine will start only in Park or Neutral. If it starts in any other gear, it will be necessary to readjust the switch.

15 To adjust the switch, loosen the switch mounting bolts and turn it slightly one way or the other until the engine now only starts in Park or Neutral. Then tighten the mounting bolts.

5.7 Remove the manual lever retaining nut (A), the manual lever (B) and the switch mounting bolts (C)

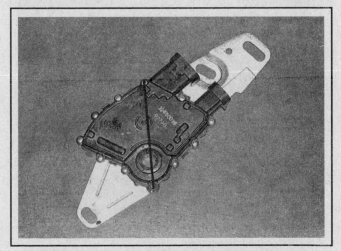

5.8 Before installing the PNP switch, align the tabs on the switch with notch on the switch body - this is the Neutral position

6 Extension housing oil seal (2WD) - replacement

♦ **Refer to illustrations 6.4 and 6.5**

1 Oil leaks frequently occur due to wear of the extension housing oil seal. Replacement of this seal is relatively easy, since it can be performed without removing the transmission from the vehicle.

2 The extension housing oil seal is located at the extreme rear of the transmission, where the driveshaft is attached. If leakage at the seal is suspected, raise the vehicle and support it securely on jackstands. If the seal is leaking, transmission lubricant will be built up on the front of the driveshaft and may be dripping from the rear of the transmission.

3 Remove the driveshaft (see Chapter 8).

4 Using a seal removal tool or a large screwdriver, carefully pry the oil seal out of the rear of the transmission (see illustration). Do not damage the splines on the transmission output shaft.

5 Using a seal driver, a large section of pipe or a very large deep socket as a drift, install the new oil seal (see illustration). Drive it into the bore squarely and make sure it's completely seated.

6 Lubricate the splines of the transmission output shaft and the outside of the driveshaft yoke with lightweight grease, then install the driveshaft (see Chapter 8). Be careful not to damage the lip of the new seal.

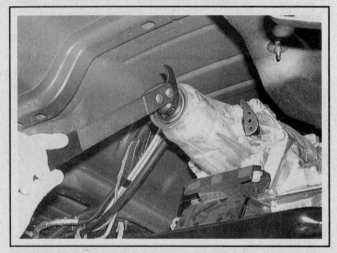

6.4 Carefully pry the old seal out of the extension housing - don't damage the splines on the output shaft

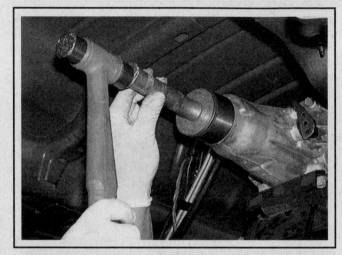

6.5 Drive the new seal into place with a seal driver or a large socket and hammer

7 Transmission mount - check and replacement

7.2 To check the transmission mount, insert a large screwdriver or prybar between the crossmember and the transmission and try to pry the transmission up - it should move very little (2WD model shown)

CHECK

♦ **Refer to illustration 7.2**

1 Raise the vehicle and support it securely on jackstands.

2 Insert a large screwdriver or prybar into the space between the transmission extension housing and the crossmember and try to pry the transmission up slightly (see illustration).

3 The transmission should not move much at all - if the mount is cracked or torn, replace it.

7.4a Transmission mount-to crossmember bolt

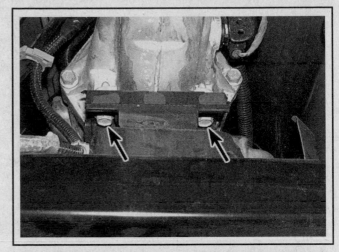

7.4b Transmission mount-to-transmission bolts (arrows)

REPLACEMENT

▶ **Refer to illustrations 7.4a and 7.4b**

4   To replace the mount, remove the bolts or nuts attaching the mount to the crossmember and the bolts attaching the mount to the transmission (see illustrations).

5   Raise the transmission slightly with a jack and remove the mount.

6   Installation is the reverse of the removal procedure. Be sure to tighten all nuts and bolts securely.

8   Automatic transmission - removal and installation

REMOVAL

▶ **Refer to illustrations 8.6, 8.8a, 8.8b, 8.9, 8.11, 8.12, 8.13a, 8.13b, 8.17, 8.18a and 8.18b**

✸ CAUTION:

The transmission and torque converter must be removed as a single assembly. If you try to leave the torque converter attached to the driveplate, the converter driveplate, pump bushing and oil seal will be damaged. The driveplate is not designed to support the load, so none of the weight of the transmission should be allowed to rest on the plate during removal.

1   Disconnect the cable from the negative terminal of the battery.

✸ CAUTION:

On models equipped with the Theftlock audio system, be sure the lockout feature is turned off before performing any procedure which requires disconnecting the battery (see the front of this manual).

2   Raise the vehicle and support it securely on jackstands. Remove the skid plate and skid plate crossmember, if equipped.

3   Remove the transmission oil pan drain plug and drain the transmission fluid (see Chapter 1).

4   Remove all exhaust components which interfere with transmission removal (see Chapter 4).

5   Remove the engine-to-transmission struts, if equipped.

6   Remove the inspection plug at the bottom of the bellhousing and mark the relationship of the torque converter to the driveplate so they can be installed in the same position (see illustration).

7   Remove the starter motor (see Chapter 5).

8.6 Pry off the inspection plug and mark the relationship between the torque converter and the driveplate

8.8a Passenger side bellhousing cover retaining bolt (arrow)

8.8b Driver's side bellhousing cover retaining bolt (arrow)

8.9 With a large screwdriver wedged between the teeth of the driveplate ring gear and the bellhousing, remove the torque converter-to-driveplate bolts - arrow shows one of three bolts

8   Detach the plastic covers on each side of the bellhousing (see illustrations).

9   Remove the torque converter-to-driveplate bolts (see illustration). Turn the crankshaft for access to each bolt. Turn the crankshaft in a clockwise direction only (as viewed from the front).

10   Mark the yokes and remove the driveshaft (see Chapter 8). On 4WD models, remove both driveshafts.

11   Working on the left side of the transmission, disconnect the shift cable from the transmission (see Section 3) and unplug the electrical connectors from the Park/Neutral position switch (see Section 5). Also remove the bolt securing the wiring harness bracket to the left side of the transmission (see illustration). On the 4L60-E models, unbolt the fuel line support bracket from the transmission.

12   Working on the right side of the transmission, remove the heat shield (see illustration). Then unplug the electrical connectors from the transmission solenoid and the vehicle speed sensor (see Chapter 6).

13   Disconnect the transmission cooler lines from the right side of the transmission and the engine (see illustrations). To disconnect the lines from the transmission, simply unsnap the plastic collar from the quick connect fitting, then pry off the quick connect fitting retaining

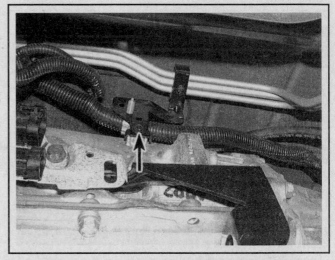

8.11 Remove the bolt (arrow) securing the wiring harness bracket to the left side of the transmission

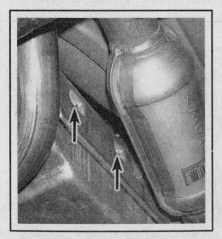

8.12 Remove the heat shield mounting bolts (arrows)

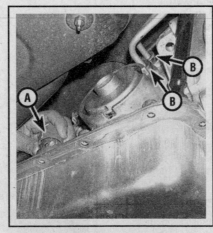

8.13a Working on the passenger side, disconnect the electrical connector from the solenoid (A) and the transmission oil cooler lines (B)

8.13b Also disconnect the bracket (arrow) securing the transmission oil cooler lines to the oil pan

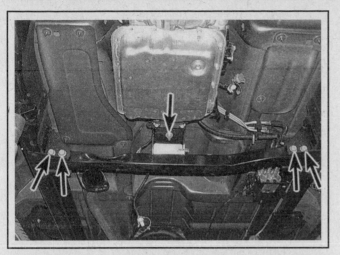

8.17 Transmission crossmember mounting bolts (arrows)

8.18a Driver's side bellhousing bolts (arrows)

clip and remove the lines. Plug the ends of the lines to prevent fluid from leaking out after you disconnect them. Always be sure to inspect the O-rings on the cooler lines before reinstallation.

14 On 4WD models, remove the transfer case (see Chapter 7C).

➡**Note: If you are not planning to replace the transmission, but are removing it in order to gain access to other components such as the torque converter, it isn't really necessary to remove the transfer case. However, the transmission and transfer case are awkward and heavy when removed and installed as a single assembly; they're much easier to maneuver off and on as separate units.**

If you decide to leave the transfer case attached, disconnect the shift rod (manual shift models only) from the transfer case shift lever. Also disconnect the electrical connectors from the transfer case speed sensors and detach the transfer case vent tube (see Chapter 7C).

❋❋ WARNING:

If you decide to leave the transfer case attached to the transmission, be sure to use safety chains to help stabilize the transmission and transfer case assembly and to prevent it from falling off the jack head, which could cause serious damage to the transmission and/or transfer case and serious bodily injury to you.

15 Support the engine with a jack. Use a block of wood under the oil pan to spread the load.

16 Support the transmission with a jack - preferably a jack made for this purpose (available at most tool rental yards). Safety chains will help steady the transmission on the jack.

17 Remove the bolt securing the transmission mount to the crossmember. Then raise the transmission slightly and remove the crossmember (see illustration).

18 Remove the bolts securing the transmission to the engine (see illustrations). A long extension and a U-joint socket will greatly simplify this step.

➡**Note: The upper bolts are easier to remove after the transmission has been lowered (see the next Step).**

19 Lower the engine and transmission slightly and remove the fill/dipstick tube bracket bolt and pull the tube out of the transmission. Don't lose the tube seal (it can be reused if it's still in good shape).

20 Clamp a small pair of locking pliers on the bellhousing case

8.18b Passenger side bellhousing bolts (arrows) - there are three more bolts at the top of the bellhousing that are not visible in this photo

through the lower inspection hole. Clamp the pliers just in front of the torque converter, behind the driveplate. The pliers will prevent the torque converter from falling out while you're removing the transmission. Move the transmission to the rear to disengage it from the engine block dowel pins and make sure the torque converter is detached from the driveplate. Lower the transmission with the jack.

INSTALLATION

21 Prior to installation, make sure the torque converter is securely engaged in the pump. If you've removed the converter, apply a small amount of transmission fluid on the torque converter rear hub, where the transmission front seal rides. Install the torque converter onto the front input shaft of the transmission while rotating the converter back and forth. It should engage into the transmission front pump in stages. To make sure the converter is fully engaged, lay a straightedge across the transmission-to-engine mating surface and make sure the converter lugs are at least 3/4-inch below the straightedge. Reinstall the locking pliers to hold the converter in this position.

22 With the transmission secured to the jack, raise it into position.

23 Turn the torque converter to line up the holes with the holes in

the driveplate. The marks on the torque converter and driveplate made in Step 6 must line up.

24 Move the transmission forward carefully until the dowel pins and the torque converter are engaged. Make sure the transmission mates with the engine with no gap. If there's a gap, make sure there are no wires or other objects pinched between the engine and transmission and also make sure the torque converter is completely engaged in the transmission front pump. Try to rotate the converter - if it doesn't rotate easily, it's probably not fully engaged in the pump. If necessary, lower the transmission and install the converter fully.

25 Install the transmission dipstick tube and seal into the transmission housing, then install the transmission-to-engine bolts and tighten them securely. As you're tightening the bolts, make sure that the engine and transmission mate completely at all points. If not, find out why. Never try to force the engine and transmission together with the bolts or you'll break the transmission case!

26 Raise the rear of the transmission and install the transmission crossmember.

27 Remove the jacks supporting the transmission and the engine.

28 Install the torque converter-to-driveplate bolts. Tighten them to the torque listed in this Chapter's Specifications. Install the plastic bell-housing covers.

29 Install the starter motor (see Chapter 5).

30 Install new retaining rings onto the quick-connect fittings.

➡ **Note: Don't push the retaining rings onto the fittings. Instead, hook one of the ends of the clip into a slot in the fitting, then rotate the other end of the ring into the other slot. If the retaining ring isn't installed like this, it may become spread-out and won't be able to retain the cooler lines securely.**

Connect the transmission fluid cooler lines to the fittings, making sure they click into place, then push the plastic caps onto the fittings.

31 Plug in the transmission electrical connectors and install the heat shield.

32 Connect the shift cable (see Section 3).

33 Install the torque converter inspection cover.

34 On 4WD models, install the transfer case, if removed (see Chapter 7C).

35 Install the driveshaft(s) (see Chapter 8).

36 Adjust the shift cable (see Section 3).

37 Install any exhaust system components that were removed or disconnected (see Chapter 4).

38 Remove the jackstands and lower the vehicle.

39 Fill the transmission with the specified fluid (see Chapter 1), run the engine and check for fluid leaks.

Specifications

General

Transmission fluid type	See Chapter 1

Torque specifications	Ft-lbs (unless otherwise indicated)
Park/Neutral Position (PNP) switch mounting bolts	18
Park/Neutral Position (PNP) switch lever nut	18
Transmission fluid pan bolts	See Chapter 1
Torque converter-to-driveplate bolts	44
Transmission- to engine block bolts	37
Transmission mount bolts	18

Section

7C

TRANSFER
CASE

1 General information

Four-wheel drive (4WD) models are equipped with a transfer case mounted on the rear of the transmission. Drive is transmitted from the engine, through the transmission and the transfer case, to the front and rear axles by driveshafts.

Here is a list of the transfer cases available on the vehicles covered by this manual:

Manual transfer case
New Venture - NVG 261 NP2
Automatic transfer cases
New Venture - NVG 236 NP8
New Venture - NVG 246-NP8
New Venture - NVG 149-NP
New Venture - NVG 149-NP3
New Venture - NVG 263-NP1
New Venture - NVG 261-NP2
Borg Warner - BW 4481-NR3
Borg Warner - BW 4482-NR4

The manual shift transfer case has four gear selections; 2WD High, 4WD High, 4WD Low and Neutral. The automatic shift transfer case has five gear selections, depending on model; 2WD High, 4WD High, 4WD Low, Neutral and automatic four wheel drive (A4WD).

Avalanche models are equipped with selectable 4WD automatic transfer cases. The New Venture Gear (NVG) 246-NP8 is a part-time transfer case with selectable all-wheel drive (Auto 4WD). In this mode, the on-board computer utilizes sensor information to program all-wheel drive response from the transfer case and driveaxles. The Borg Warner (BW) 4481-NR3 is a one-speed all wheel drive transfer case that utilizes a planetary type differential to distribute a 40/60 torque split, front/rear. The BW 4482-NR4 is a two-speed all wheel drive transfer case that utilizes two different sets of planetary gears to distribute the torque to the driveaxles.

The NVG 149-NP3 is a single speed (single mode), all-wheel drive transfer case that is equipped with a viscous coupling. Once the viscous coupling detects wheel speed slipping, silicone fluid inside the viscous coupling heats from the resistance allowing lock-up between the plates. Torque bias is distributed by a planetary differential gear.

We don't recommend trying to rebuild any of these transfer cases at home. They're difficult to overhaul without special tools, and rebuilt units are available for less than it would cost to rebuild your own. However, there are a number of components that you can check, adjust and/or replace - and those are the items covered in this Chapter.

MANUAL SHIFT-ON-THE-FLY (MSOF) SYSTEM

The manual shift-on-the-fly (MSOF) system allows the driver to manually select one of four ranges: 2WD High, 4WD High, 4WD Low or Neutral. The driver can switch between 2WD High and 4WD High at speeds up to 55 mph (up to 45 mph at temperatures below 32 degrees F). 4WD Low or Neutral can only be engaged or disengaged with the vehicle slowed to a roll at a speed of under three mph and shifting the transmission in Neutral or depressing the clutch pedal on manual transmission equipped vehicles, (this is not a synchronized shift).

When shifting from 2WD to 4WD, the 4WD indicator light on the dash is illuminated and the transfer case switch sends a signal to the front axle shift motor to engage the axle and lock the front driveaxles together.

ELECTRONIC SHIFT-ON-THE-FLY (ESOF) SYSTEM

The electronic shift-on-the-fly (ESOF) system allows the driver the same four ranges (2WD High, 4WD High, 4WD Low or Neutral) as the MSOF system with an additional (fifth) 4WD option called, automatic four-wheel-drive (A4WD). The same rules apply for shifting from 2WD High to 4WD High, and for shifting to 4WD Low or Neutral. However, the means by which a shift is initiated is electronic. Shifting into A4WD range requires the same procedure as shifting into 2WD High or 4WD High where the driver can switch the transfer case into A4WD at speeds up to 55 mph (up to 45 mph at temperatures below 32 degrees F). When shifting into 4WD Low the driver must wait until the 4WD Low light stops blinking and becomes fully illuminated before shifting the transmission into gear.

When any range is selected at a switch on the dash, the transfer case shift control module receives a voltage signal commanding it to energize the transfer case shift motor, thus rotating the sector shaft (clockwise or counterclockwise) and shifting the transfer case into the appropriate gear. After the transfer case is positioned in the appropriate gear, the transmission control module will send a signal to engage the front axle. The transfer case encoder is mounted to the shift motor and is used to relay sector shaft position back to the transfer case shift control module. The transfer case also incorporates a motor lock to assure that the transfer case remains in the current gear position. When the A4WD button is depressed the motor lock remains in adaptive mode so it can be applied or released as the transfer case shift control module determines whether the vehicle should be placed in 2WD or 4WD.

The automatic four-wheel-drive (A4WD) feature allows the transfer case to shift from 2WD High to 4WD High under varying road conditions. When the transfer case shift control module receives rotating wheel slip information from speed sensors mounted at the front and rear output shafts of the transfer case, the shift control module will engage the shift control motor to shift the transfer case from 2WD to 4WD. When the shift control module receives information that wheel rotation is the same at both axles, it will send a signal to the shift control motor to shift the transfer case back into 2WD.

A handy feature of the NVG 263-NP1 transfer case is that it has a Neutral position. In this position, the transmission and transfer case are not forced to rotate when the vehicle is being towed, saving wear and tear on these components. To engage Neutral, push both the 4Lo and 2Hi buttons at the same time, and hold for ten seconds. A red Neutral light will come on at the switch panel to the left of the steering wheel.

2 Shift lever (manual-shift models) - removal and installation

1 Raise the front of the vehicle and support it securely on jackstands.

2 Working under the vehicle, detach the shift linkage from the shift control lever. This is accomplished by simply pulling the shift linkage ball socket off the shift lever ball pivot.

3 Working in the passenger compartment of the vehicle, unscrew the shift lever knob.

4 Remove the shift lever bezel retaining screws and remove the bezel.

5 Remove the shift lever retaining bolts and remove the shift lever.

6 Installation is the reverse of removal.

3 Shift linkage (manual-shift models) - adjustment

1 Place the shift lever in the 2WD High position. Have an assistant hold the lever in the indicated position, or tape it in place.
2 Raise the vehicle and support it securely on jackstands.
3 Loosen the adjustment bolt at the center of the shift linkage.
4 Make sure the ball sockets at each end of the shift linkage are securely seated on the ball pivots at the transfer case and the shift lever.
5 Verify that the transfer case range lever is in the 2WD High position.

➡Note: When the transfer case range lever is in the 2WD High position on the NVG 261 transfer case, it will be positioned in the third detent from the rear (two clicks from the rearmost position).

6 Tighten the shift linkage adjustment bolt to the torque listed in this Chapter's Specifications.
7 Lower the vehicle and check the operation of the transfer case.

4 Transfer case control switch (electric-shift models) - replacement

▶ Refer to illustration 4.3

1 Disconnect the cable from the negative terminal of the battery.

✳✳ CAUTION:

On models equipped with the Theftlock audio system, be sure the lockout feature is turned off before performing any procedure which requires disconnecting the battery (see the front of this manual).

2 Remove the instrument cluster bezel (see Chapter 11).
3 Pull out the retaining tabs and remove the transfer case control switch from the instrument panel (see illustration).
4 Unplug the electrical connectors from the rear of the switch and remove the switch from the vehicle.
5 Installation is the reverse of removal.

4.3 Lift up the retaining tabs and pull the transfer case control switch out of the instrument panel, then disconnect the electrical connectors

5 Transfer case shift motor (electric-shift models) - replacement

▶ Refer to illustration 5.5

1 Raise the vehicle and place it securely on jackstands.
2 Remove the stone shields from below the transfer case.
3 Remove the front driveshaft (see Chapter 8).
4 Unplug the shift motor electrical connector.
5 Detach the retaining bolts and remove the electric shift motor and encoder assembly (see illustration).
6 Inspect the rubber gasket for tears and cracks and replace it if necessary. If the gasket is good it can be reused.
7 Position the gasket and the shift motor in place on the transfer case and install the bolts. Tighten the shift motor retaining bolts to the torque listed in this Chapter's Specifications.
8 Installation is the reverse of removal.

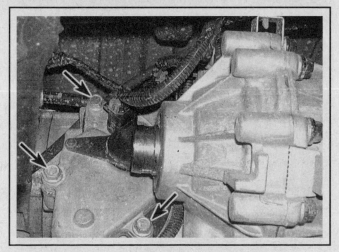

5.5 Disconnect the electrical connector and remove the electric shift motor retaining bolts (arrows)

6 Transfer case speed sensors (electric shift models) - general information

▶ **Refer to illustrations 6.1a and 6.1b**

There are a variety of electric-shift transfer cases on the models covered by this manual and several different combinations of speed sensors available. Early electric-shift transfer cases are equipped with three sensors; input and output shaft speed sensors and a vehicle speed sensor (VSS) (see illustrations). The vehicle speed sensor (VSS) sends information to the PCM for the driveability program and is located at the rear output shaft. Later transfer case technology combines these sensors into one or two sensors for gathering data for the computer. The procedure for checking and replacement of the output shaft speed sensor is essentially the same as the procedure for the vehicle speed sensor (VSS). A scan tool can easily access speed sensor data and trouble codes. Refer to the vehicle speed sensor (VSS) replacement procedure in Chapter 6.

6.1a Location of the transfer case front output shaft speed sensor on an NVG 246 transfer case

6.1b Location of the transfer case rear output shaft speed sensor (A) and the vehicle speed sensor (B) on early 4WD models

7 Transfer case control module (electric-shift models) - replacement

▶ **Refer to illustration 7.1**

1   The transfer case control module is located under the left side of the instrument panel, behind the headlight switch (see illustration).
2   Disconnect the cable from the negative terminal of the battery.

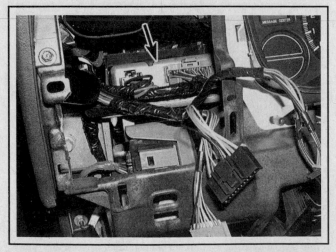

7.1 The transfer case control module (arrow) is located to the left of the instrument cluster behind the headlight switch

✳✳ **CAUTION:**

On models equipped with the Theftlock audio system, be sure the lockout feature is turned off before performing any procedure which requires disconnecting the battery (see the front of this manual).

3   Remove the instrument panel cowl support bracket. Refer to Chapter 11 and read through the entire instrument panel removal procedure before attempting to remove it. The instrument panel removal procedure is quite lengthy and can be particularly difficult for a beginner. Perform only the steps necessary to remove the plastic cowl support bracket surrounding the instrument cluster.

➡**Note: On 2001 and later models, only the instrument cluster bezel needs to be removed to replace the transfer case shift control module.**

4   Once the instrument panel cowl support bracket is removed from the vehicle, disconnect the electrical connectors from the control module.
5   Slide the transfer case control module out of its retaining bracket and remove it from the vehicle.
6   Installation is the reverse of removal.

8   Oil seal - replacement

▶ **Refer to illustrations 8.3a, 8.3b, 8.4a, 8.4b, 8.6a and 8.6b**

➡**Note: This procedure applies to both the front and rear output shaft seals.**

1   Raise the vehicle and support it securely on jackstands.

2   If you're replacing the front seal, remove the front driveshaft; if you're replacing the rear seal, remove the rear driveshaft (see Chapter 8).

3   If you're replacing the front seal it will be necessary to obtain a slide hammer and remove the seal retainer (see illustrations).

4   To remove the either output shaft seal, simply pry the seal out with a screwdriver or a seal removal tool (see illustrations). Don't damage the seal bore.

5   Lubricate the new seal lips with petroleum jelly.

6   Drive the seal into place with a seal driver or a large socket (see illustration). The outside diameter of the socket should be slightly smaller than the outside diameter of the seal. If you replaced the front seal, it will be necessary to drive the front seal retainer back into the transfer case housing in the same manner (see illustration).

7   The remainder of installation is the reverse of removal.

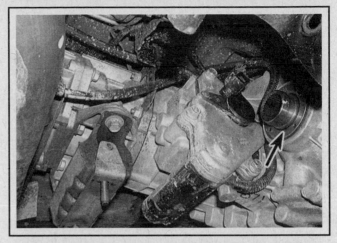

8.3a   When removing the transfer case front oil seal retainer (arrow) it will be necessary to support the transmission with a jack and a block of wood, and remove the transmission crossmember - note the holes on the front of the seal retainer (this is where the hooked end of the slide hammer will be inserted)

8.3b   Using a slide hammer to remove the front seal retainer

8.4a   When removing the front output shaft seal it will be necessary to pierce the seal in order to get behind it and pry the seal out

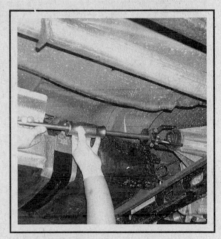

8.4b   The rear output shaft seal can be removed with conventional tools or a slide hammer with a three jaw adapter

8.6a   Drive the new transfer case seals into place with a seal driver, large socket or section of tubing

8.6b   The front oil seal retainer can be driven back into place in the same manner

9 Transfer case - removal and installation

◆ **Refer to illustrations 9.7a, 9.7b, 9.11a and 9.11b**

1 Disconnect the cable from the negative terminal of the battery.

✳✳ CAUTION:

On models equipped with the Theftlock audio system, be sure the lockout feature is turned off before performing any procedure which requires disconnecting the battery (see the front of this manual).

2 On models with a manually shifted transfer case, put the transfer case in 2WD High position.

3 Raise the vehicle and support it securely on jackstands.

4 Remove the stone shields (if equipped).

5 Drain the transfer case lubricant (see Chapter 1).

6 Remove the front and rear driveshafts (see Chapter 8).

7 Unplug all electrical connectors and detach the vent hose from the top of the transfer case (see illustrations).

8 On manually shifted models, disconnect the shift linkage from the transfer case. This is accomplished by simply pulling the shift linkage ball socket off the ball pivot on the transfer case shift lever.

9 Remove any transmission-to-transfer case support braces. Raise the transmission enough to remove the transmission mount (see Chapter 7A or 7B), then support the transmission on a jack or jack-stands.

10 Support the transfer case with a jack - preferably a special jack made for this purpose. Safety chains will help steady the transfer case on the jack.

11 Remove the transmission-to-transfer case nuts (manual transmission) or the adapter-to-transfer case nuts (automatic transmission) (see illustrations). Don't lose the washers.

12 Make a final check that all wires and hoses have been disconnected from the transfer case, then move the transfer case and jack toward the rear of the vehicle until the transfer case is clear of the transmission. Keep the transfer case level as this is done. Once the input shaft is clear, lower the transfer case and remove it from under the vehicle.

13 Installation is the reverse of removal. Be sure to tighten the transmission-to-transfer case nuts to the torque listed in this Chapter's Specifications. On manually shifted models be sure adjust the transfer case shift linkage (see Section 3).

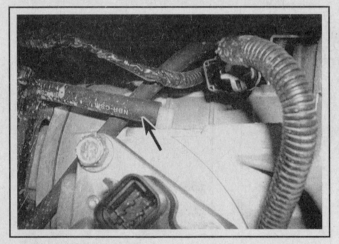

9.7a Detach the vent hose (arrow) from the top of the transfer case and the support bracket

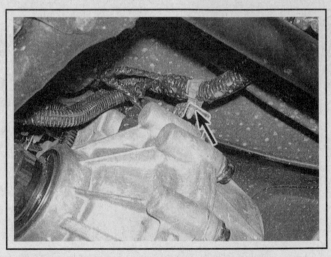

9.7b Also detach any wiring harness retaining clips

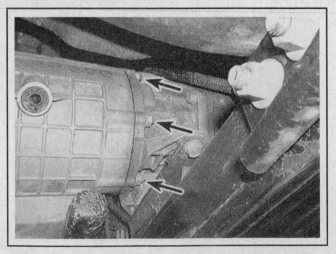

9.11a Passenger side transfer case mounting nuts (arrows) (automatic transmission model shown)

9.11b Driver's side transfer case mounting nuts (arrows) (transmission crossmember removed for clarity)

10 Transfer case overhaul - general information

Overhauling a transfer case is a difficult job for the do-it-yourselfer. It involves the disassembly and reassembly of many small parts. Numerous clearances must be precisely measured and, if necessary, changed with select-fit spacers and snap-rings. As a result, if transfer case problems arise, it can be removed and installed by a competent do-it-yourselfer, but overhaul should be left to a transmission repair shop. Rebuilt transfer cases may be available - check with your dealer parts department and auto parts stores. At any rate, the time and money involved in an overhaul is almost sure to exceed the cost of a rebuilt unit.

Nevertheless, it's not impossible for an inexperienced mechanic to rebuild a transfer case if the special tools are available and the job is done in a deliberate step-by-step manner so nothing is overlooked.

The tools necessary for an overhaul include internal and external snap-ring pliers, a bearing puller, a slide hammer, a set of pin punches, a dial indicator and possibly a hydraulic press. In addition, a large, sturdy workbench and a vise or transmission stand will be required.

During disassembly of the transfer case, make careful notes of how each piece comes off, where it fits in relation to other pieces and what holds it in place. Note how parts are installed when you remove them; this will make it much easier to get the transfer case back together.

Before taking the transfer case apart for repair, it will help if you have some idea what area of the transfer case is malfunctioning. Certain problems can be closely tied to specific areas in the transfer case, which can make component examination and replacement easier. Refer to the Troubleshooting section at the front of this manual for information regarding possible sources of trouble.

Torque specifications

Ft-lbs (unless otherwise indicated)

Shift lever-to-floor pan bolts	108 in-lbs
Shift linkage adjustment bolt	132 in-lbs
Shift motor mounting bolts	18
Transfer case-to-transmission bolts	37
Transfer case-to-transmission support braces	37

8

CLUTCH AND DRIVELINE

1 General information

The information in this Chapter deals with the components from the rear of the engine to the rear wheels, except for the transmission (and transfer case, if equipped), which is dealt with in the previous Chapter. For the purposes of this Chapter, these components are grouped into three categories: clutch, driveshaft and axles. Separate Sections within this Chapter offer general descriptions and checking procedures for components in each of the three groups.

Since nearly all the procedures covered in this Chapter involve working under the vehicle, make sure it's securely supported on sturdy jackstands or on a hoist where the vehicle can be easily raised and lowered.

2 Clutch - description and check

▶ **Refer to illustration 2.1**

1   All models with a manual transmission use a single dry plate, diaphragm spring type clutch (see illustration). The clutch disc has a splined hub which allows it to slide along the splines of the transmission input shaft. The clutch and pressure plate are held in contact by spring pressure exerted by the diaphragm in the pressure plate.

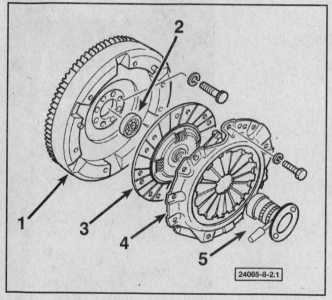

2.1 Exploded view of the clutch components

1	Flywheel	5	Concentric release
2	Pilot bearing		cylinder/release bearing
3	Clutch disc		assembly
4	Pressure plate		

2   The clutch release system is operated by hydraulic pressure. The hydraulic release system consists of the clutch pedal, a master cylinder and fluid reservoir, the hydraulic line, and a concentric release cylinder/release bearing assembly.

3   When pressure is applied to the clutch pedal to release the clutch, hydraulic pressure is generated in the master cylinder and causes the release cylinder/bearing assembly to extend. The release bearing then pushes against the fingers of the diaphragm spring of the pressure plate assembly, which in turn releases the clutch plate.

4   Terminology can be a problem when discussing the clutch components because common names are in some cases different from those used by the manufacturer. For example, the driven plate is also called the clutch plate or disc, the clutch release bearing is sometimes called a throwout bearing, the release cylinder is sometimes called the operating or slave cylinder.

5   Other than to replace components with obvious damage, some preliminary checks should be performed to diagnose clutch problems.

   a) *The first check should be of the fluid level in the clutch master cylinder. If the fluid level is low, add fluid as necessary and inspect the hydraulic system for leaks.*
   b) *To check "clutch spin down time," run the engine at normal idle speed with the transmission in Neutral (clutch pedal up - engaged). Disengage the clutch (pedal down), wait several seconds and shift the transmission into Reverse. No grinding noise should be heard. A grinding noise would most likely indicate a problem in the pressure plate or the clutch disc.*
   c) *To check for complete clutch release, run the engine (with the parking brake applied to prevent movement) and hold the clutch pedal approximately 1/2-inch from the floor. Shift the transmission between First gear and Reverse several times. If the shift is hard or the transmission grinds, component failure is indicated.*
   d) *Visually inspect the pivot bushing at the top of the clutch pedal to make sure there is no binding or excessive play.*

3 Clutch master cylinder - removal and installation

▶ **Refer to illustration 3.4**

✳✳ WARNING:

Wear eye protection when bleeding the brake system. If the fluid comes in contact with your eyes, immediately rinse them with water and seek medical attention.

✳✳ CAUTION:

Brake fluid will damage paint. Cover all body parts and be careful not to spill fluid during this procedure.

1   Disconnect the cable from the negative terminal of the battery.

✳✳ CAUTION:

On models equipped with the "Theftlock" audio system, be sure the lockout feature is turned off before performing any procedure which requires disconnecting the battery (see the information at the front of this manual).

2   Remove the left-side under-dash panel (see Chapter 11) and the heater/air conditioning duct behind it.

3 Disconnect the electrical connector from the clutch pedal position switch. Detach the pushrod from the pedal by pushing the pedal down fully and squeezing the plastic tabs on the bushing to release it.

4 Raise the front of the vehicle and support it securely on jackstands. Disconnect the hydraulic line from the clutch release cylinder where it enters the transmission (see illustration). A special tool, available at most auto parts stores, is required to separate the line fitting.

5 Open the hood and find the clutch master cylinder - it's located on the firewall, to the left of the brake master cylinder. Grasp the body of the master cylinder and twist it 45-degrees counterclockwise to unlock it from the firewall.

6 Detach the hydraulic line from any clips which may be securing it, then remove the master cylinder and line from the vehicle.

7 Installation is the reverse of removal. Check the fluid level in the reservoir, adding as necessary to bring it to the appropriate level. Bleed the system as described in Section 5.

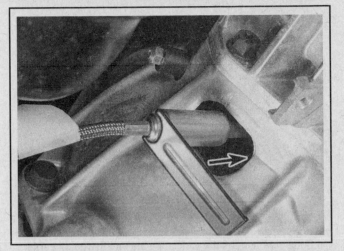

3.4 To disconnect the hydraulic line from the clutch release cylinder, place the special tool against the shoulder of the quick-connect fitting, push in on the fitting and pull the line out

4   Clutch release cylinder and bearing - removal and installation

1 Detach the hydraulic line from the release cylinder (see illustration 3.4).

2 Remove the transmission (see Chapter 7A).

3 Remove the two release cylinder retaining bolts.

4 Slide the release cylinder off the transmission input shaft. Check the operation of the bearing by turning it while applying pressure; if it is rough or noisy, replace it (it can be removed from the release cylinder).

5 While the transmission is removed, inspect the clutch disc and pressure plate assembly (see Section 6) and replace as necessary.

6 Clean off the transmission input shaft and apply a light film of high-temperature grease to it. Slide the new release cylinder into place, install the retaining bolts and tighten them to the torque listed in this Chapter's Specifications.

7 Install the transmission (see Chapter 7A).

8 Connect the hydraulic line to the release cylinder.

9 Fill the clutch fluid reservoir with the recommended fluid (see Chapter 1).

10 Bleed the clutch hydraulic system (see Section 5).

5   Clutch hydraulic system - bleeding

1 The hydraulic system should be bled to remove all air whenever any part of the system has been removed or if the fluid level has been allowed to fall so low that air has been drawn into the master cylinder. The procedure is very similar to bleeding a brake system.

2 Fill the master cylinder with new brake fluid conforming to DOT 3 specifications.

⁂ CAUTION:

Do not re-use any of the fluid coming from the system during the bleeding operation or use fluid which has been inside an open container for an extended period of time.

3 Raise the vehicle and place it securely on jackstands to gain access to the release cylinder bleeder valve, which is located on the left side of the clutch housing.

4 Remove the dust cap which fits over the bleeder valve and push a length of plastic hose over the valve. Place the other end of the hose into a clear container partially filled with clean brake fluid. The hose end must be submerged in the fluid.

5 Have an assistant depress the clutch pedal and hold it. Open the bleeder valve on the release cylinder, allowing fluid to flow through the hose. Close the bleeder valve when the flow of fluid stops. Once closed, have your assistant release the pedal.

6 Continue this process until all air is evacuated from the system, indicated by a solid stream of fluid being ejected from the bleeder valve each time with no air bubbles in the hose or container. Keep a close watch on the fluid level inside the clutch master cylinder reservoir - if the level drops too low, air will be sucked back into the system and the process will have to be started all over again.

7 Install the dust cap and lower the vehicle. Check carefully for proper operation before placing the vehicle in normal service.

6   Clutch components - removal, inspection and installation

⁂ WARNING:

Dust produced by clutch wear and deposited on clutch components is hazardous to your health. DO NOT blow it out with compressed air and DO NOT inhale it. DO NOT use gasoline or petroleum-based solvents to remove the dust. Brake system cleaner should be used to flush the dust into a drain pan. After the clutch components are wiped clean with a rag, dispose of the contaminated rags and cleaner in a covered, marked container.

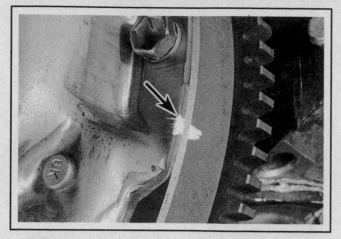

6.5 Be sure to mark the pressure plate and flywheel in order to insure proper alignment during installation (this won't be necessary if a new pressure plate is to be installed)

REMOVAL

▶ **Refer to illustration 6.5**

1   Access to the clutch components is normally accomplished by removing the transmission, leaving the engine in the vehicle. If, of course, the engine is being removed, then check the clutch for wear and replace worn components as necessary. However, the relatively low cost of the clutch components compared to the time and trouble spent gaining access to them warrants their replacement anytime the engine or transmission is removed, unless they are new or in near perfect condition. The following procedures are based on the assumption the engine will stay in place.

2   Referring to Chapter 7 Part A, remove the transmission from the vehicle. Support the engine while the transmission is out. Preferably, an engine hoist or support fixture should be used to support it from above. However, if a jack is used underneath the engine, make sure a piece of wood is positioned between the jack and oil pan to spread the load.

✳✳ CAUTION:

The pickup for the oil pump is very close to the bottom of the oil pan. If the pan is bent or distorted in any way, engine oil starvation could occur.

3   The clutch release bearing assembly can remain attached to the transmission for the time being.

4   To support the clutch disc during removal, install a clutch alignment tool through the clutch disc hub.

5   Carefully inspect the flywheel and pressure plate for indexing marks. The marks are usually an X, an O or a white letter. If they cannot be found, scribe marks yourself so the pressure plate and the flywheel will be in the same alignment during installation (see illustration).

6   Turning each bolt only 1/4-turn at a time, loosen the pressure plate-to-flywheel bolts. Work in a criss-cross pattern until all spring pressure is relieved. Then hold the pressure plate securely and completely remove the bolts, followed by the pressure plate and clutch disc.

INSPECTION

▶ **Refer to illustrations 6.8, 6.10, 6.12a and 6.12b**

7   Ordinarily, when a problem occurs in the clutch, it can be attributed to wear of the clutch driven plate assembly (clutch disc). However,

6.8 Check the flywheel for cracks, hot spots and other obvious defects (slight imperfections can be removed by a machine shop)

all components should be inspected at this time.

8   Inspect the flywheel for cracks, heat checking, grooves and other obvious defects (see illustration). If the imperfections are slight, a machine shop can machine the surface flat and smooth, which is highly recommended regardless of the surface appearance. Refer to Chapter 2 for the flywheel removal and installation procedure.

9   Inspect the pilot bearing (see Section 7).

10   Inspect the lining on the clutch disc. There should be at least 1/16-inch of lining above the rivet heads. Check for loose rivets, distortion, cracks, broken springs and other obvious damage (see illustration). As mentioned above, ordinarily the clutch disc is routinely replaced, so if in doubt about the condition, replace it with a new one.

11   The release bearing should also be replaced along with the clutch disc (see Section 4).

12   Check the machined surfaces and the diaphragm spring fingers of the pressure plate (see illustrations). If the surface is grooved or otherwise damaged, replace the pressure plate. Also check for obvious damage, distortion, cracking, etc. Light glazing can be removed with sandpaper or emery cloth. If a new pressure plate is required, new and factory-rebuilt units are available.

PRESSURE PLATE PRE-ADJUSTING PROCEDURE FOR 6.0L MODELS

▶ **Refer to illustration 6.15**

➡**Note: If installing the original pressure plate on 6.0L engines, before installation, the self adjusting pressure plate must be pre-adjusted. To do so requires a hydraulic press. If you do not have a press, take the flywheel and pressure plate to an automotive machine shop for adjustment.**

13   Place the clutch pressure plate and disc (new) on the hydraulic press with the flange side down.

14   Compress the pressure plate diaphragm spring until the tension is released from the stepped adjusting ring.

15   Using two screwdrivers, place them against two (three total) of the adjusting ring tension spring stops directly in front of the springs (see illustration).

16   Using the screwdrivers, rotate the stepped adjusting rings counterclockwise until the adjusting ring steps are fully adjusted OUT. Do not release the screwdrivers yet.

17   Carefully release the tension on the hydraulic press while holding the ring stops.

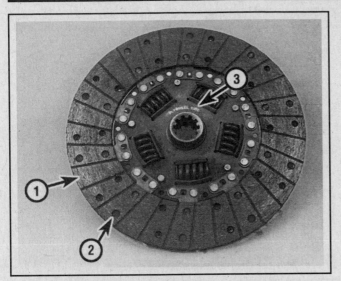

6.10 The clutch plate

1 *Lining* - This will wear down in use
2 *Rivets* - These secure the lining and will damage the flywheel or pressure plate if allowed to contact the surfaces
3 *Markings* - "Flywheel side" or something similar

18 Remove the screwdrivers after the press has been completely released.

INSTALLATION

▶ **Refer to illustration 6.20**

19 Before installation, clean the flywheel and pressure plate machined surfaces with brake system cleaner. It's important that no oil or grease is on these surfaces or the lining of the clutch disc. Handle the parts only with clean hands.

20 Position the clutch disc and pressure plate against the flywheel with the clutch held in place with an alignment tool (see illustration). Make sure it's installed properly (most replacement clutch plates will be marked "flywheel side" or something similar - if not marked, install the clutch disc with the damper springs toward the transmission).

21 Tighten the pressure plate-to-flywheel bolts only finger tight, working around the pressure plate.

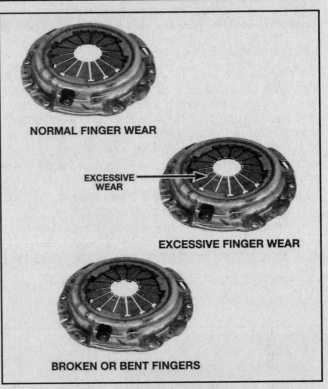

NORMAL FINGER WEAR

EXCESSIVE WEAR

EXCESSIVE FINGER WEAR

BROKEN OR BENT FINGERS

6.12a Replace the pressure plate if excessive wear is noted

22 Center the clutch disc by ensuring the alignment tool extends through the splined hub and into the pilot bearing in the crankshaft. Wiggle the tool up, down or side-to-side as needed to bottom the tool in the pilot bearing. Tighten the pressure plate-to-flywheel bolts a little at a time, working in a criss-cross pattern to prevent distorting the cover. After all of the bolts are snug, tighten them to the torque listed in this Chapter's Specifications. Remove the alignment tool.

23 Using high-temperature grease, lubricate the inner groove of the release bearing. Also place grease on the transmission input shaft bearing retainer.

24 Install the clutch release bearing as described in Section 4.

25 Install the transmission and all components removed previously. Tighten all fasteners to the proper torque specifications.

26 Bleed the clutch hydraulic system (see Section 5).

6.12b Examine the pressure plate friction surface for score marks, cracks and evidence of overheating

6.15 After compressing the diaphragm spring, turn the adjusting ring counterclockwise, then release the press

6.20 Center the clutch disc using a clutch alignment tool

7 Pilot bearing - replacement

♦ **Refer to illustrations 7.5, 7.6a and 7.6b**

1 The clutch pilot bearing is pressed into the rear of the crankshaft. It is greased at the factory and does not require additional lubrication. Its primary purpose is to support the front of the transmission input shaft. The pilot bearing should be inspected whenever the clutch components are removed from the engine. Due to its inaccessibility, if you are in doubt as to its condition, replace it with a new one.

➡**Note: If the engine has been removed from the vehicle, disregard the following steps which do not apply.**

2 Remove the transmission (refer to Chapter 7 Part A).

3 Remove the clutch components (see Section 6).

4 Inspect for any excessive wear, scoring, lack of grease, dryness or obvious damage. If any of these conditions are noted, the bearing should be replaced. A flashlight will be helpful to direct light into the recess.

5 Removal can be accomplished with a slide hammer fitted with a puller attachment (see illustration), which are available at most auto parts stores or equipment rental yards.

6 To install the new bearing, lightly lubricate the outside surface with multi-purpose grease, then drive it into the recess (see illustrations).

❊❊ CAUTION:

Be careful not to let the bearing become cocked in the bore.

a) *If you're working on a V8 engine, drive it in with a hammer and bearing/bushing driver until it is flush with the hole in the crankshaft.*

b) *If you're working on a V6 engine, a socket with an outside diameter slightly smaller than that of the bearing can be used. Drive it in to a depth of 45/64 to 47/64-inch.*

7 Install the clutch components, transmission and all other components removed previously, tightening all fasteners properly.

7.5 A small slide-hammer puller is handy for removing the pilot bearing

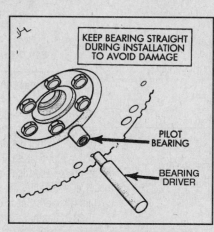

7.6a When installing a pilot bearing into the crankshaft of a V8 engine, use a bearing driver (drive it in until the end of the bearing is flush with the end of the crankshaft)

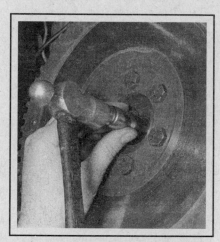

7.6b When installing a pilot bearing into the crankshaft of a V6 engine, a socket can be used (drive it in to the depth listed in the text)

8 Clutch start switch - check and replacement

1 Remove the left side under-dash panel.

CHECK

2 Verify that the engine will not start when the clutch pedal is released. Now, depress the clutch pedal - the engine should start.

3 Locate the switch on the clutch master cylinder pushrod and unplug the electrical connector.

4 Using an ohmmeter, verify that there is continuity between the proper terminals of the clutch start switch when the pedal is depressed (refer to the wiring diagrams at the back of this manual). There should

be no continuity when the pedal is released.

5 If the switch does not work as described, replace it.

REPLACEMENT

6 Unplug the electrical connector from the switch.

7 Pry up the tabs on the plastic retainer that secures the switch to the pushrod, then remove the switch.

8 Installation is the reverse of removal. The switch is self-adjusting, so there's no need for adjustment.

9 Verify that the engine doesn't start when the clutch pedal is released, and does start when the pedal is depressed.

9 Driveshaft and universal joints - general information and inspection

♦ **Refer to illustration 9.1**

GENERAL INFORMATION

1 A driveshaft is a tube, or a pair of tubes, that transmits power between the transmission (or transfer case on 4WD models) and the differential. Universal joints are located at either end of the driveshaft and in the center on two-piece driveshafts (see illustration).

2 Single piece driveshafts employ a splined yoke at the front, which slips into the extension housing of the transmission. This arrangement allows the driveshaft to slide back-and-forth within the transmission during vehicle operation to compensate for changes in length due to suspension movement. An oil seal prevents leakage of fluid at this point and keeps dirt from entering the transmission. If leakage is evident at the front of the driveshaft, replace the oil seal (see Chapter 7, Part B).

3 If a two-piece driveshafts is used, a slip joint is employed on the front of the rear driveshaft section.

4 Two-piece driveshafts also have a center support bearing. The center bearing is a ball-type bearing mounted in a rubber cushion attached to a frame crossmember. The bearing is pre-lubricated and sealed at the factory.

5 On all models, the driveshaft assembly requires very little service. The universal joints are lubricated for life and must be replaced if problems develop. The driveshaft must be removed from the vehicle for this procedure.

6 Since the driveshaft is a balanced unit, it's important that no undercoating, mud, etc. be allowed to stay on it. When the vehicle is raised for service it's a good idea to clean the driveshaft and inspect it for any obvious damage. Also, make sure the small weights used to originally balance the driveshaft are in place and securely attached. Whenever the driveshaft is removed it must be reinstalled in the same relative position to preserve the balance.

7 Problems with the driveshaft are usually indicated by a noise or vibration while driving the vehicle. A road test should verify if the problem is the driveshaft or another vehicle component. Refer to the *Troubleshooting* section at the front of this manual. If you suspect trouble, inspect the driveline.

INSPECTION

8 Raise the rear of the vehicle and support it securely on jackstands. Block the front wheels to keep the vehicle from rolling off the stands.

9 Crawl under the vehicle and visually inspect the driveshaft. Look for any dents or cracks in the tubing. If any are found, the driveshaft must be replaced.

10 Check for oil leakage at the front and rear of the driveshaft. Leakage where the driveshaft enters the transmission or transfer case indicates a defective transmission/transfer case seal (see Chapter 7). Leakage where the driveshaft enters the differential indicates a defective pinion seal (see Section 18).

11 While under the vehicle, have an assistant rotate a rear wheel so the driveshaft will rotate. As it does, make sure the universal joints are operating properly without binding, noise or looseness. Listen for any noise from the center bearing (if equipped), indicating it's worn or damaged. Also check the rubber portion of the center bearing for cracking or separation, which will necessitate replacement.

12 The universal joint can also be checked with the driveshaft motionless, by gripping your hands on either side of the joint and attempting to twist the joint. Any movement at all in the joint is a sign of considerable wear. Lifting up on the shaft will also indicate movement in the universal joints.

13 Finally, check the driveshaft mounting bolts at the ends to make sure they're tight.

14 On 4WD models, the above driveshaft checks should be repeated on the front driveshaft, as well. In addition, check for leakage around the sleeve yoke, indicating failure of the yoke seal.

15 Check for leakage where the driveshafts connect to the transfer

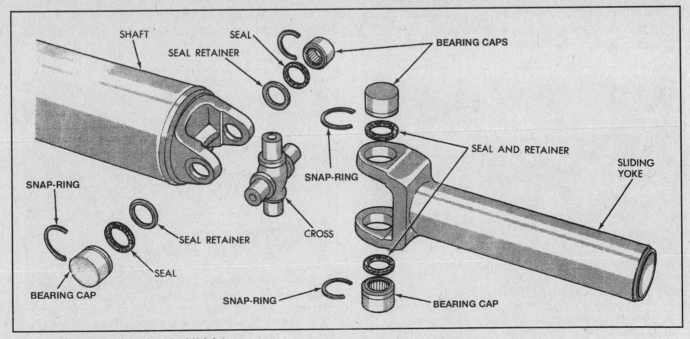

9.1 An exploded view of a typical U-joint

case and front differential. Leakage indicates worn oil seals.

16 At the same time, check for looseness in the joints of the front driveaxles. Also check for grease or oil leakage from around the driveaxles by inspecting the rubber boots and both ends of each axle.

Oil leakage around the axle flanges indicates a defective axleshaft oil seal. Grease leakage at the CV joint boots means a damaged rubber boot. For servicing of these components, see the appropriate Sections.

10 Driveshaft(s) - removal and installation

REAR DRIVESHAFT

▶ **Refer to illustrations 10.2, 10.3 and 10.5**

Removal

1 Raise the vehicle and support it securely on jackstands. Place the transmission in Neutral with the parking brake off. Block the front wheels to prevent the vehicle from rolling.

2 Make reference marks on the driveshaft and the pinion flange in line with each other (see illustration). This is to make sure the driveshaft is reinstalled in the same position to preserve the balance.

3 Remove the rear universal joint bolts and straps. Turn the driveshaft (or wheels) as necessary to bring the bolts into the most accessible position. To prevent the driveshaft from turning when you loosen

the bolts, insert a large screwdriver through the driveshaft yoke (see illustration).

4 If the vehicle is a 4WD model and has a companion flange where the driveshaft connects to the transfer case, mark the relationship of the U-joint yoke to the companion flange, then remove the four bolts, nuts and washers from the flange.

5 On vehicles with a two-piece driveshaft, remove the nuts from the center support bearing (see illustration).

6 On all models, tape the bearing caps to the spider to prevent the caps from coming off during removal.

7 Lower the rear of the driveshaft. Slide the front of the driveshaft out of the transmission or transfer case.

8 Wrap a plastic bag over the transmission or transfer case housing and hold it in place with a rubber band. This will prevent loss of fluid and protect against contamination while the driveshaft is out.

Installation

9 Remove the plastic bag from the transmission or transfer case and wipe the area clean. Inspect the oil seal carefully. Procedures for replacement of this seal can be found in Chapter 7.

10 Slide the front of the driveshaft into the transmission or transfer case or connect the companion flange, installing the fasteners finger-tight.

11 On models with a two-piece driveshaft, raise the center support bearing into position, install the nuts and tighten them to the torque listed in this Chapter's Specifications.

12 Raise the rear of the driveshaft into position, checking to be sure the marks are in alignment. If not, turn the rear wheels to match the pinion flange and the driveshaft.

13 Remove the tape securing the bearing caps and install the straps and bolts. Tighten all bolts to the torque listed in this Chapter's Specifications.

10.2 Mark the relationship of the rear driveshaft to the differential pinion flange

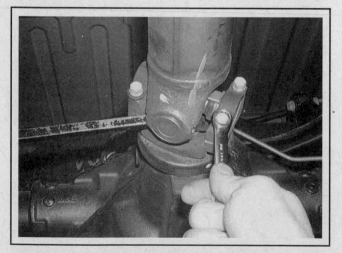

10.3 Insert a screwdriver through the driveshaft yoke to prevent the shaft from turning when you loosen the bolts

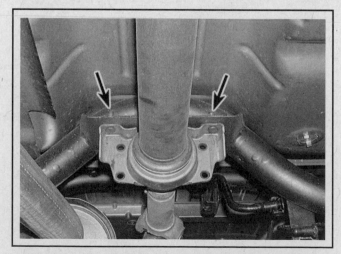

10.5 The center support bearing on two-piece driveshafts is secured by two nuts (arrows)

10.15 Pry up the end of the boot clamp and dislodge the boot from the transfer case output shaft

10.17 Mark the relationship of the front driveshaft to the front differential companion flange, then remove the bolts and straps

FRONT DRIVESHAFT (4WD MODELS)

Removal

▶ **Refer to illustrations 10.15 and 10.17**

14 Raise the front of the vehicle and place it securely on jackstands. Remove the skid plate, if equipped.

15 Pry open the clamp securing the boot at the transfer case output shaft (see illustration). Disengage the boot from the shaft and slide it forward.

16 Mark the relationship of the driveshaft to the front differential companion flange.

17 Remove the bolts and straps from the differential flange (see illustration).

18 Push the driveshaft to the rear far enough to separate it from the differential flange, then lower it and pull the shaft out of the transfer case.

Installation

19 Slide the rear of the driveshaft into the splines in the transfer case output shaft.

20 Attach the front end of the shaft to the differential companion flange (be sure to line up the marks), install the straps and bolts and tighten all of the bolts to the torque listed in this Chapter's Specifications.

21 At the rear end of the shaft, push the boot up over the transfer case output shaft and seat it into its groove. Insert a small screwdriver between the boot and the shaft to equalize pressure inside the boot, then install a new clamp and crimp it into place with a pair of clamp-crimping pliers.

22 Install the skid plate (if equipped).

11 Driveshaft center support bearing - replacement

1 Remove the driveshaft (see Section 10).

2 Mark the relationship of the front portion of the driveshaft to the rear portion of the driveshaft (it's best to make the mark on the slip yoke). Slide the rear shaft off the front shaft.

3 If you have access to a hydraulic press (one tall enough to accommodate the shaft) and the necessary fixtures, press the shaft out of the center support bearing. Reverse this operation to install the new bearing.

4 If you do not have the necessary equipment, take the shaft to an automotive machine shop or other qualified repair facility to have the old bearing pressed off and the new one pressed on.

12 Universal joints - replacement

➡Note: Always purchase a universal joint service kit for your model vehicle before beginning this procedure. Also, read through the entire procedure before beginning work.

1 Remove the driveshaft (Section 10).

OUTER SNAP-RING TYPE

▶ **Refer to illustrations 12.3, 12.4, 12.5 and 12.6**

2 Place the driveshaft on a bench equipped with a vise.

12.3 Use a small pair of pliers to remove the snap-rings from the ends of the universal joint yokes

12.4 To remove the U-joint from the driveshaft, use a vise as a press - the small socket will push the cross and bearing cap into the large socket

12.5 Locking pliers can be used to remove the bearing caps from the yoke

3   Remove the snap-rings with a small pair of pliers (see illustration).

4   Support the cross (also called a spider) on a short piece of pipe or a large socket and use another socket to press out the cross by closing the vise (see illustration).

5   Press the cross through as far as possible, then grip the bearing cap with pliers and remove it (see illustration).

6   A universal joint repair kit will contain a new cross, seals, bearings, caps and snap-rings (see illustration).

7   Inspect the bearing cap bores in the yokes for wear and damage.

8   If the bearing cap bores in the yoke are so worn that the caps are a loose fit, the driveshaft will have to be replaced with a new one.

9   Make sure the dust seals are properly located on the cross.

10 Using a vise, press one bearing cap into the yoke approximately 1/4-inch.

11 Use chassis grease to hold the needle rollers in place in the caps.

12 Insert the cross into the partially installed bearing cap, taking care not to dislodge the needle rollers.

13 Hold the cross in correct alignment and press both caps into place by slowly and carefully closing the jaws of the vise.

14 Use a socket slightly smaller in diameter than the caps to press them into the yoke. Press in one side, install the snap-ring, then press

the other side to shift the cross assembly tight against the installed snap-ring and install the other snap-ring.

15 Repeat the operations for the remaining two bearing caps. Proceed to Step 22.

INJECTED PLASTIC (INNER SNAP-RING) TYPE

▶ **Refer to illustrations 12.16, 12.20 and 12.21**

16 If the joint has been previously rebuilt, remove the snap-rings (bearing retainers) located on the inner part of each bearing cap (see illustration).

17 If this is the first time the joint is being rebuilt it will not be necessary to remove the snap-rings, since there aren't any; the pressing operation will shear the molded plastic retaining material.

➡**Note: It may be necessary to heat the U-joint over 500-degrees (melting the plastic retaining material) before pressing the U-joint apart.**

18 Press out the bearing caps as described in Steps 4 and 5.

19 Remove the cross and clean all plastic material from the yoke. Use a small punch to remove the plastic from the injection holes.

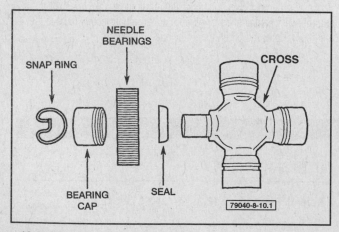

12.6 Outer snap-ring type U-joint

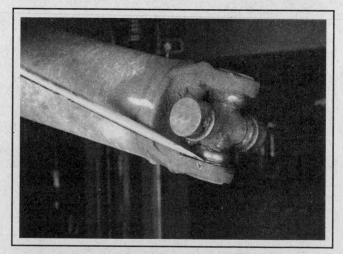

12.16 Remove the inner snap-rings from the U-joint by tapping them off with a screwdriver and hammer

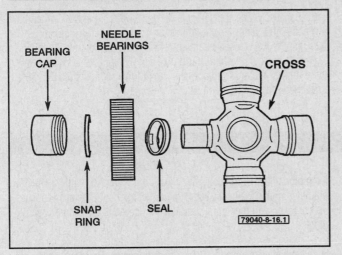

12.20 Inner snap-ring type U-joint

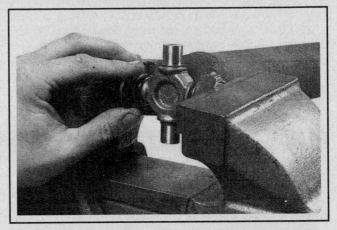

12.21 Installing a snap-ring on an inner snap-ring type U-joint

20 Reassembly is the same as for the outer snap-ring joint described in Steps 9 through 15, except the snap-rings are on the inner part of each bearing cap (see illustration).

21 When installing the bearing cap, press it in until the snap-ring can be installed (see illustration).

ALL MODELS

▶ **Refer to illustration 12.22**

22 If the joint is stiff after assembly, strike the yoke sharply with a hammer (see illustration). This will spring the yoke ears slightly and free up the joint.

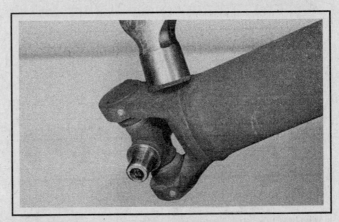

12.22 Strike the yoke sharply with a hammer to "spring" the yoke ears, which will free-up the joint

13 Axles - description and check

DESCRIPTION

1 The rear axle assembly is a hypoid (the centerline of the pinion gear is below the centerline of the ring gear), semi-floating type. When the vehicle goes around a corner, the differential allows the outer rear wheel to turn at a higher speed than the inner tire. The axleshafts are splined to the differential side gears, so when the vehicle goes around a corner, the inner wheel, which turns more slowly than the outer wheel, turns its side gear more slowly than the outer wheel turns its side gear. The differential pinion gears roll around the slower side gear, driving the outer side gear - and tire - more quickly.

2 An optional locking limited-slip rear axle is also available. This differential allows for normal operation until one wheel loses traction. A limited-slip unit is similar in design to a conventional differential, except for the addition of a pair of multi-disc clutch packs which slow the rotation of the differential case when one wheel is on a firm surface and the other on a slippery one. The difference in wheel rotational speed produced by this condition applies additional force to the pinion gears and through the cone, which is splined to the axleshafts, equalizes the rotation speed of the axleshaft driving the wheel with traction.

3 On 4WD models, a fully independent front axle assembly is used. This consists of a differential and a pair of driveaxles. Each driveaxle has an inner and outer constant velocity (CV) joint. Because the differential - like the transfer case - is offset to the left, the distance between the differential and the right front wheel is greater than the distance from the differential to the left wheel. In order to use two equal-length driveaxles, an extension axleshaft is employed on the right side to make up the difference.

CHECK

4 Often, a suspected "axle" problem lies elsewhere. Do a thorough check of other possible causes before assuming the axle is the problem.

5 The following noises are those commonly associated with axle diagnosis procedures:

a) *Road noise is often mistaken for mechanical faults. Driving the vehicle on different surfaces will show whether or not the road surface is the cause of the noise. Road noise will remain the same if the vehicle is under power or coasting.*

b) *Tire noise is sometimes mistaken for mechanical problems. Tires which are worn or low on pressure are particularly susceptible to emitting vibrations and noises. Tire noise will remain about the same during varying driving situations, where axle noise will change during coasting, acceleration, etc.*

c) *Engine and transmission noise can be deceiving because it will travel along the driveline. To isolate engine and transmission noises, make a note of the engine speed at which the noise is most pronounced. Stop the vehicle and place the transmission in Neutral and run the engine to the same speed. If the noise is the same, the axle is not at fault.*

6   Because of the special tools needed, overhauling the differential isn't cost effective for a do-it-yourselfer. The procedures included in this Chapter describe axleshaft removal and installation, axleshaft oil seal replacement, axleshaft bearing replacement and removal of the entire unit for repair or replacement. Any further work should be left to a qualified repair shop.

14 Axleshaft (rear) - removal and installation

SEMI-FLOATING AXLESHAFT

▶ Refer to illustrations 14.3, 14.4, 14.5a and 14.5b

Removal

1   Loosen the rear wheel lug nuts. Raise the rear of the vehicle, support it securely on jackstands and block the front wheels. Remove the wheel and brake disc (see Chapter 9).

2   Remove the differential cover and allow the lubricant to drain into a container (see Chapter 1).

3   Remove the lock screw (see illustration).

4   On models with a conventional differential (non-locking), remove the pinion shaft. On models with a locking differential, withdraw the pinion shaft part way, then rotate the differential until the shaft touches the case, providing enough clearance for access to the C-locks (see illustration).

5   Have an assistant push in on the outer flanged end of the axleshaft while you remove the C-lock from the groove in the inner end of the shaft (see illustration).

➡**Note: On models with a locking differential, use a screwdriver to rotate the C-lock until the open end points in (see illustration).**

6   With the C-lock removed, withdraw the axleshaft, taking care not to damage the oil seal (but note that it is a good idea to replace the seal whenever the axleshaft is removed - see Section 15). Some models have a thrust washer in the differential; make sure it doesn't fall out when the axleshaft is removed.

14.3 Remove the pinion shaft lock bolt

14.4 Withdraw the pinion shaft for access to the C-locks (don't turn the axleshafts after the shaft has been pulled out, or the spider gears may become mispositioned)

14.5a Push the axle flange in, then remove the C-lock from the inner end of the axleshaft

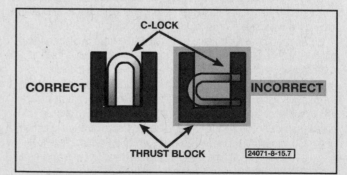

14.5b On models with a locking differential, the C-lock must be positioned as shown before it can be removed

Installation

7   To install, carefully insert the axleshaft into the housing and seat it securely in the differential.

8   Install the C-lock in the axleshaft groove and pull out on the flange to lock it.

9   Insert the pinion shaft, align the hole in the shaft with the lock screw hole and install the lock screw.

➡**Note: Apply a non-hardening, thread-locking compound to the threads of the lock screw before installing it. Tighten the lock screw to the torque listed in this Chapter's Specifications.**

10   Install the cover and fill the differential with the lubricant specified in Chapter 1.

11   Install the brake disc, caliper mounting bracket and caliper, tightening the fasteners to the torque listed in the Chapter 9 Specifications.

Install the wheel and lug nuts, then lower the vehicle. Tighten the lug nuts to the torque listed in the Chapter 1 Specifications.

FULL-FLOATING AXLESHAFT

12   Remove the bolts that attach the axleshaft flange to the hub.

13   Tap the flange with a soft-face hammer to loosen the shaft, then grip the rib in the face of the flange with a pair of locking pliers. Twist the shaft slightly in both directions and withdraw it from the housing. Place a drip pan under the outer end of the axle to catch any lubricant which might leak out while the axle is removed.

14   Installation is the reverse of removal. Be sure to hold the axleshaft level to engage the splines at the inner end with those in the differential side gear. Always use a new gasket on the flange and keep both the flange and hub mating surface free of grease and oil.

---

15 Axleshaft oil seal (rear, semi-floating axle) - replacement

▶ **Refer to illustrations 15.2 and 15.3**

1   Remove the axleshaft (see Section 14).

2   Pry the oil seal out of the end of the axle housing (see illustration).

3   Apply a film of multi-purpose grease to the oil seal recess and tap the new seal evenly into place with a hammer and seal installation tool (see illustration), large socket or piece of pipe so the lips are facing in and the metal face is visible from the end of the axle housing. When correctly installed, the face of the oil seal should be flush with the end of the axle housing.

4   Install the axleshaft (see Section 14).

15.2 Prying out the axleshaft oil seal with a seal removal tool

15.3 Using a seal driver to install the axleshaft oil seal - drive the seal in until it's flush with the bore

---

16 Axleshaft bearing (rear, semi-floating axle) - replacement

▶ **Refer to illustrations 16.2, 16.3 and 16.4**

1   Remove the axleshaft (see Section 14) and the oil seal (see Section 15).

2   A bearing puller which grips the bearing from behind will be required for this job (see illustration).

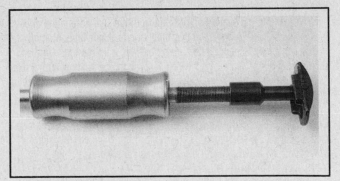

16.2 A typical slide hammer and axleshaft bearing remover attachment

16.3 Removing the axleshaft bearing with a slide hammer

16.4 Use a bearing driver or a large socket to tap the bearing evenly into the axle housing

3   Attach a slide hammer to the puller and extract the bearing from the axle housing (see illustration).

4   Clean out the bearing recess and drive in the new bearing with a bearing installer or a piece of pipe positioned against the outer bearing

race (see illustration). Make sure the bearing is tapped in to the full depth of the recess.

5   Install a new oil seal (see Section 15), then install the axleshaft (see Section 14).

17 Rear hub, wheel bearing and seal (full-floating axle) - removal, bearing/seal replacement and installation

REMOVAL

1   Remove the axleshaft (see Section 14).

2   Loosen the rear wheel lug nuts, raise the rear of the vehicle and support it securely on jackstands. Block the front wheels and remove the rear wheels.

3   Remove the brake disc (see Chapter 9).

4   Remove the retaining ring and key (if equipped) from the end of the axle housing.

5   Remove the adjusting nut, using a special socket available at most auto parts stores.

6   Pull the hub assembly straight off the axle tube.

7   Remove and discard the oil seal from the back of the hub.

8   To further disassemble the hub, use a hammer and a long bar or drift punch to knock out the inner bearing, cup (race) and oil seal.

9   Remove the outer retaining ring, then knock the outer bearing and cup from the hub.

10   Clean the old sealing compound from the seal bore in the hub.

11   Use solvent to clean the bearings, hub and axle tube. A small brush may prove useful; make sure no bristles from the brush embed themselves in the bearing rollers. Now spray the bearings with brake system cleaner, which will remove the solvent and allow the bearings to dry much more rapidly.

12   Carefully inspect the bearings for cracks, wear and damage. Check the axle tube flange, studs and hub splines for damage and corrosion. Check the bearing cups (races) for pitting or scoring. Worn or damaged components must be replaced with new ones.

13   Inspect the brake drum (see Chapter 9).

14   Lubricate the bearings and the axle tube contact areas with wheel

bearing grease. Work the grease completely into the bearings, forcing it between the rollers, cone and cage.

15   Reassemble the hub by reversing the disassembly procedure. Use only the proper size bearing driver when installing the new bearing cups (races).

INSTALLATION

16   Make sure the axle housing oil deflector is in position. Place the hub assembly on the axle tube, taking care not to damage the oil seals.

17   Install the adjusting nut and adjust the bearings as described below.

ADJUSTMENT

18   Rotate the hub, making sure it turns freely.

19   While rotating the hub in the normal direction of rotation (forward), tighten the adjusting nut to 50 ft-lbs with a torque wrench. Again, this will require the special socket, which is available at most auto parts stores.

20   Back the nut off 1/4-turn, then tighten the nut hand-tight with the special socket.

21   Turn the nut to align the closest slot in the nut with the keyway in the spindle, then install the key.

22   Install the retaining ring in the end of the spindle.

23   Wiggle the hub assembly; you shouldn't be able to detect any play, but the hub should turn freely (there shouldn't be any preload on the bearings, but there shouldn't be any freeplay, either).

24   Install the axleshaft (see Section 14) and lower the vehicle.

18 Pinion oil seal - replacement

◆ Refer to illustrations 18.3, 18.4, 18.5, 18.8 and 18.9

➡Note: This procedure applies to the front and rear pinion oil seals.

1 Loosen the wheel lug nuts. Raise the front (for front differential) or rear (for rear differential) of the vehicle and support it securely on jackstands. Block the opposite set of wheels to keep the vehicle from rolling off the stands. Remove the wheels.

2 Disconnect the driveshaft from the differential pinion flange and fasten it out of the way (see Section 10).

3 Rotate the pinion a few times by hand. Use a beam-type or dial-type inch-pound torque wrench to check the torque required to rotate the pinion (see illustration). Record it for use later.

4 Mark the relationship of the pinion flange to the shaft (see illustration), then count and write down the number of exposed threads on the shaft.

5 A special tool, available at most auto parts stores, can be used to keep the companion flange from moving while the self-locking pinion nut is loosened (see illustration). A chain wrench can also be used to immobilize the flange.

6 Remove the pinion nut.

7 Withdraw the flange. It may be necessary to use a two-jaw puller engaged behind the flange to draw it off. Do not attempt to pry or hammer behind the flange or hammer on the end of the pinion shaft.

8 Pry out the old seal and discard it (see illustration).

9 Lubricate the lips of the new seal and fill the space between the seal lips with wheel bearing grease, then tap it evenly into position with a seal installation tool or a large socket (see illustration). Make sure it enters the housing squarely and is tapped in to its full depth.

10 Install the pinion flange, lining up the marks made in Step 4. If necessary, tighten the pinion nut to draw the flange into place. Do not try to hammer the flange into position.

11 Apply a bead of RTV sealant to the ends of the splines visible in the center of the flange so oil will be sealed in.

12 Install the washer and a new pinion nut. Tighten the nut until the number of threads recorded in Step 4 are exposed.

13 Measure the torque required to rotate the pinion and tighten the nut in small increments (no more than 5 ft-lbs) until it matches the figure recorded in Step 3. To compensate for the drag of the new oil seal,

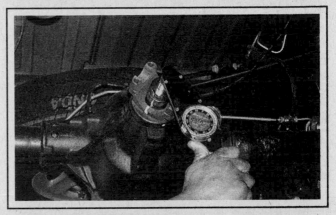

18.3 Use an inch-pound torque wrench to check the torque required to rotate the pinion shaft

18.4 Before removing the nut, mark the position of the flange to the shaft and count the number of exposed threads

the nut should be tightened a little more until the rotational torque of the pinion exceeds the earlier recording by 5 in-lbs.

14 Reinstall all components removed previously by reversing the removal Steps, tightening all fasteners to their specified torque values.

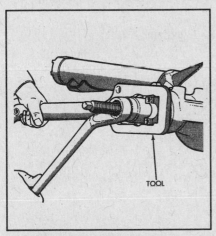

18.5 Hold the pinion flange while removing the nut

18.8 Use a seal removal tool or a large screwdriver to remove the pinion seal (be careful not to disturb the pinion while doing this)

18.9 A large socket with a diameter the same as that of the new pinion seal can be used to drive the seal into the differential housing

19 Axle assembly (rear) - removal and installation

REMOVAL

1 Loosen the rear wheel lug nuts, raise the rear of the vehicle and support it securely on jackstands. Block the front wheels to keep the vehicle from rolling off the stands. Remove the rear wheels.

2 Position a jack under the rear axle differential housing.

3 Disconnect the driveshaft from the rear axle pinion flange (see Section 10). Fasten the driveshaft out of the way with a piece of wire from the underbody.

4 Disconnect the shock absorbers at their lower mounts.

5 Disconnect the vent hose from the fitting on the axle housing and fasten it out of the way.

6 Disconnect the brake hose from the junction block on the axle housing, then plug the hose to prevent fluid leakage.

7 Remove the brake calipers and discs (see Chapter 9).

8 Disconnect the parking brake cables from the actuating levers and the brackets (see Chapter 9).

9 On models with leaf springs, disconnect the spring U-bolts (see Chapter 10). Remove the spring plates.

10 On models with coil springs, remove the stabilizer bar and the coil springs (see Chapter 10).

11 Lower the jack under the differential, then remove the rear axle assembly from under the vehicle.

INSTALLATION

12 Installation is the reverse of removal. Tighten the U-joint strap bolts to the torque listed in this Chapter's Specifications. Tighten all suspension fasteners to the torque values listed in the Chapter 10 Specifications. Tighten the brake fasteners to the torque values listed in the Chapter 9 Specifications.

13 Bleed the brakes (see Chapter 9).

14 Install the wheels and lug nuts to the torque listed in the Chapter 1 Specifications.

20 Driveaxles (4WD models) - general information and inspection

1 Power is transmitted from the front differential/axle to the front wheels through a pair of driveaxles. The inner end of each driveaxle is bolted to an axleshaft connected to the differential side gears; the outer end of each driveaxle has a stub shaft that is splined to the front hub and bearing assembly and locked in place with a large nut.

2 The inner ends of the driveaxles are equipped with sliding constant velocity (CV) joints, which are capable of both angular and axial motion. Each inner CV joint assembly consists of a tripot-type bearing and a housing in which the joint is free to slide in-and-out as the driveaxle moves up-and-down with the wheel.

3 The outer ends of the driveaxles are equipped with "ball-and-cage" type CV joints, which are capable of angular but not axial movement. Each outer CV joint consists of six caged ball bearings running between an inner race and the housing.

4 The boots should be inspected periodically for damage and leak-

ing lubricant. Torn CV joint boots must be replaced immediately or the joints will be damaged. If either boot of a driveaxle is damaged, that driveaxle must be removed in order to replace the boot (see Section 21).

5 Should a boot be damaged, the CV joint can be disassembled and cleaned (see Section 22), but if any parts are damaged, the entire driveaxle assembly must be replaced as a unit.

6 The most common symptom of worn or damaged CV joints, besides lubricant leaks, is a clicking noise in turns, a clunk when accelerating after coasting and vibration at highway speeds. To check for wear in the CV joints and driveaxle shafts, grasp each axle (one at a time) and rotate it in both directions while holding the CV joint housings, feeling for play indicating worn splines or sloppy CV joints. Also check the driveaxle shafts for cracks, dents and distortion.

21 Driveaxle (4WD models) - removal and installation

21.2 A hammer and chisel can be used to knock the cover off the hub

▶ **Refer to illustrations 21.2, 21.3 and 21.5**

REMOVAL

1 Loosen the wheel lug nuts, raise the front of the vehicle and support it securely on jackstands. Remove the wheel.

2 Pry off the hub cover (see illustration).

3 Remove the driveaxle/hub nut. To prevent the hub from rotating, brace a large prybar across two of the wheel studs (see illustration), or insert a long punch or screwdriver through the window in the brake caliper and into the disc cooling vanes.

4 Remove the skid plate, if equipped.

5 Remove the driveaxle-to-axleshaft flange bolts (see illustration). Have an assistant apply the brake as you loosen the bolts to prevent

21.3 A large prybar can be used to immobilize the hub while loosening the nut, or a screwdriver can be inserted through the window in the brake caliper (arrow) and into the disc cooling vanes

21.5 Remove the driveaxle-to-axleshaft flange bolts

the driveaxle from turning. Separate the driveaxle from the axleshaft flange.

6   Lower the inner end of the driveaxle, then pull the stub shaft out of the hub. Carefully guide the driveaxle out from under the vehicle.

➡ **Note 1: It may be necessary to remove the stabilizer bar link to provide clearance for driveaxle removal.**

➡ **Note 2: If the stub shaft sticks in the hub splines, tap on the end of the shaft with a brass punch and a hammer. If that doesn't free the splines, push the driveaxle from the hub with a puller.**

INSTALLATION

7   Installation is the reverse of removal. Before installing the driveaxle, lubricate the splines on the stub shaft with multi-purpose grease. Be sure to tighten the driveaxle/hub nut (new) and the flange bolts to the torque values listed in this Chapter's Specifications. Tighten the wheel lug nuts to the torque listed in the Chapter 1 Specifications.

❋❋ **WARNING:**

The hub nut should not be reused. Install a new hub nut when installing the shaft.

22 Driveaxle boot (4WD models) - replacement

➡ **Note: If the CV joint boots must be replaced, explore all options before beginning the job. Complete rebuilt driveaxles are available on an exchange basis, which eliminates much time and work. Whichever route you choose to take, check on the cost and availability of parts before disassembling the vehicle.**

1   Remove the driveaxle (see Section 21).
2   Place the driveaxle in a vise lined with rags to avoid damage to the axleshaft. Check the CV joint for excessive play in the radial direction, which indicates worn parts. Check for smooth operation throughout the full range of motion for each CV joint. If a boot is torn, disassemble the joint, clean the components and inspect for damage due to loss of lubrication and possible contamination by foreign matter.

➡ **Note: Some models are equipped with a protective cover that clamps around the larger diameter of each boot. Use diagonal cutting pliers to remove the clamps, then slide the cover off for access to the boots.**

INNER CV JOINT

▶ **Refer to illustrations 22.3a through 22.3t**

3   To replace the inner boot, refer to the accompanying illustrations (see illustrations 22.3a through 22.3t).

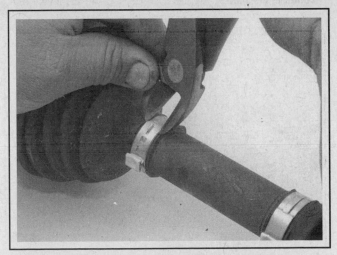

22.3a Cut off the old boot clamps with a pair of diagonal cutting pliers (the larger diameter clamp is actually a "swage ring;" you may have to use a hand-held grinder to cut through it. When reassembling the joint, use a conventional boot clamp, since special tools are required to swage the ring in place)

22.3b Slide the housing off the spider assembly

22.3c Slide the boot towards the center of the driveaxle

22.3d Spread the ends of the stop ring apart and slide it towards the center of the shaft

22.3e Slide the spider assembly back to expose the retaining ring and pry off the ring

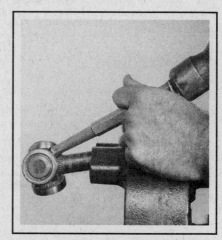

22.3f Carefully tap the spider off the axleshaft with a brass punch (but don't hit it so hard that it flies off, or you'll be picking up needle bearings!)

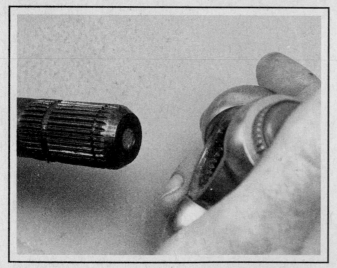

22.3g When you slide the spider off the driveaxle, hold the bearings in place with your hand; even better, use tape or a cloth wrapped around the spider bearing assembly to retain them

22.3h Slide the boot and the stop ring off the axleshaft

22.3i Clean all of the old grease out of the housing and spider assembly, then remove each bearing, one at time

22.3j Carefully disassemble each section of the spider assembly, clean the needle bearings with solvent and Inspect the rollers, spider cross, bearings and housing for scoring, pitting and other signs of abnormal wear

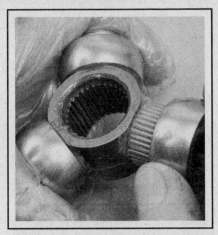

22.3k Apply a coat of CV joint grease to the inner bearing surfaces to hold the needle bearings in place and slide the bearing over them

22.3l Wrap the axleshaft splines with tape to avoid damaging the boot, then slide the small clamp and boot onto the axleshaft

22.3m Slide the spider stop ring onto the axleshaft, past the groove in which it seats

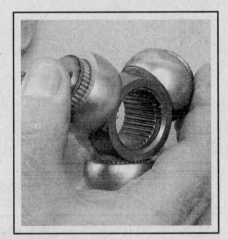

22.3n Install the spider bearing with the recess in the counterbore facing the end of the driveaxle

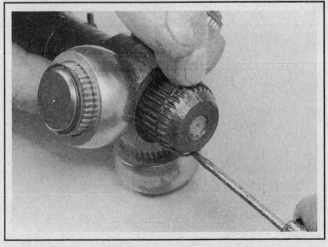

22.3o Install the spider retaining ring, then slide the spider assembly against it and seat the stop ring in its groove

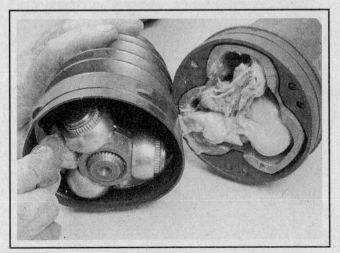

22.3p Pack the housing with half of the grease furnished with the new boot and place the remainder in the boot

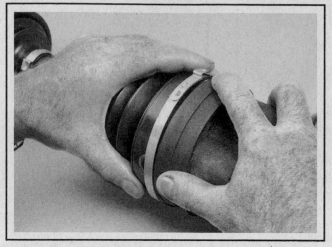

22.3q With the retaining clamps in place (but not tightened), install the tripot housing

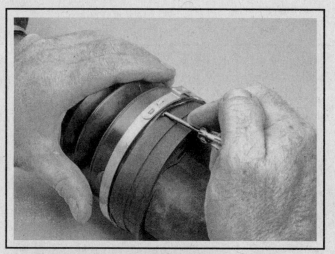

22.3s With the joint set to the proper length, equalize the pressure in the boot by inserting a small screwdriver between the boot and the housing (make sure the boot isn't dimpled, stretched or out of shape) . . .

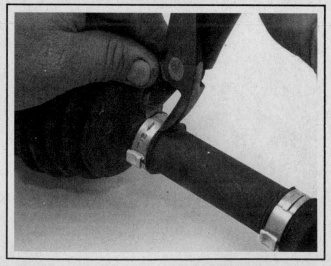

22.4a Cut off the boot retaining clamps with a pair of diagonal cutters

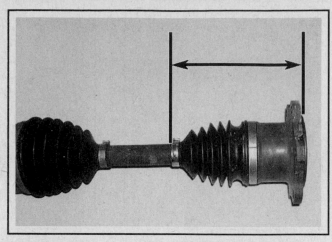

22.3r Seat the boot in the housing and axle seal grooves, then adjust the length of the joint to the dimension listed in this Chapter's Specifications

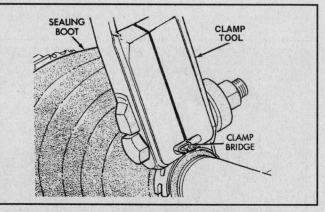

22.3t . . . then secure the boot clamps with a clamp crimping tool (available at auto parts stores)

OUTER CV JOINT

♦ **Refer to illustrations 22.4a through 22.4r**

4   Refer to the accompanying illustrations and perform the outer CV joint boot replacement procedure (see illustrations 22.4a through 22.4r).

22.4b Spread apart the ends of the internal snap-ring, then slide the CV joint off the shaft

22.4c Press down on the inner race far enough to allow a ball bearing to be removed - if it's difficult to tilt, gently tap the cage and inner race with a brass punch and hammer

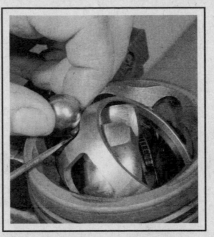

22.4d Pry the balls out of the cage, one at a time

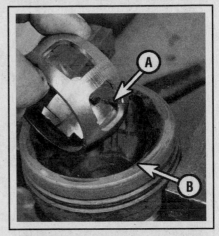

22.4e Tilt the inner race and cage 90-degrees, then align the windows in the cage (A) with the lands of the housing (B) and rotate the inner race and cage up and out of the housing

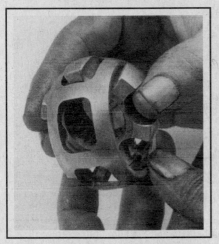

22.4f Align an inner race land with a cage window and rotate the inner race out of the cage

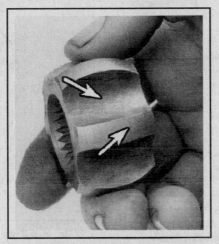

22.4g After cleaning the components with solvent, check the inner race lands and grooves for pitting and score marks

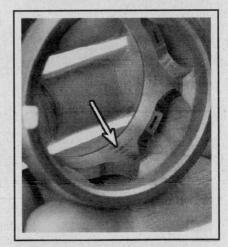

22.4h Check the cage for cracks, pitting and score marks - shiny spots are normal and don't affect operation

22.4i With the race and cage tilted 90-degrees, lower the assembly into the housing

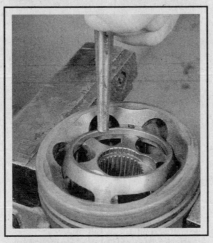

22.4j Rotate the assembly by gently tapping with a hammer and brass punch. . .

22.4k . . . then press the balls into the cage windows, repeating until all of the balls are installed

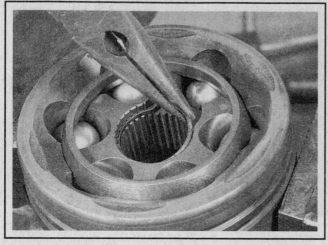

22.4l Use needle-nose pliers to lower a new snap-ring into the groove . . .

22.4m . . . then seat it into the groove with snap-ring pliers

22.4n Apply grease through the splined hole, then insert a wooden dowel (with a diameter slightly less than that of the axle) through the splined hole and push down - the dowel will force the grease into the joint - repeat until the bearing is completely packed

22.4o Install the small clamp and the boot on the driveaxle and apply grease to the inside of the axle boot . . .

22.4p . . . until the level is up to the end of axle

22.4q Position the CV joint assembly on the driveaxle, aligning the splines, then use a soft-face hammer to drive the joint onto the driveaxle until the snap-ring is seated in the groove

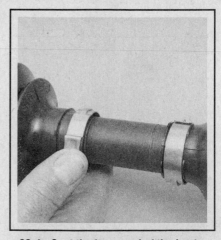

22.4r Seat the inner end of the boot in the groove and install the retaining clamp, then do the same on the other end of the boot - tighten boot clamps with the special tool (see illustration 22.3t)

23 Front axle shift motor (4WD models) - replacement

▶ **Refer to illustrations 23.3**

1   Raise the front of the vehicle and support it securely on jackstands. Remove the splash shield from under the front axle.

2   Disconnect the electrical connector from the shift motor.

3   Unscrew the motor from the axle tube (see illustration).

4   Before installing the motor, coat the threads with RTV sealant. To install the motor, reverse the removal procedure.

23.3 The front axle shift motor simply unscrews from the axle tube

24 Right axleshaft, tube, bearing and shift fork (4WD and AWD models) - removal, component replacement and installation

1   Loosen the wheel lug nuts, raise the vehicle, place it securely on jackstands and remove the right front wheel.

2   Remove the splash shield from under the front axle.

3   Drain the lubricant from the front differential (see Chapter 1).

SELECTABLE 4WD SYSTEMS

▶ **Refer to illustration 24.7**

4   Unbolt the right driveaxle from the axleshaft flange (see Section 21). Support the driveaxle out of the way with a piece of wire - don't let it hang by the outer CV joint.

5   Remove the front axle shift motor (see Section 23).

6   To prevent the differential carrier from cocking when the axle tube is removed, support it with a floor jack and a block of wood.

7   Remove the bolts securing the axle tube to the differential carrier (see illustration).

8   Remove the nuts that attach the tube to its support bracket.

9   Carefully remove the output shaft tube. Make sure you don't allow any of the components to fall out of the tube. Remove the shift sleeve, thrust washer and seal.

10   Mount the tube in a vise, with the jaws clamping on the flange. Remove the damper spring, clip, fork, sleeve, gear, thrust washer and shift shaft.

11   Remove the output shaft from the tube by striking the inside of the flange with a soft-faced hammer while holding the tube.

12   Using a large screwdriver, pry the deflector and seal from the tube.

13   Measure the installed depth of the axleshaft bearing, then remove the bearing using a slide hammer and bearing remover attachment.

14   Install the bearing, with the square shoulder facing in, to the

24.7 Right axleshaft tube details

A	Tube-to-differential mounting bolts	C	Axle tube-to-frame nuts
B	Front axle shift motor	D	Right inner CV joint

original depth using a bearing driver or a socket with an outside diameter slightly smaller than that of the bearing.

15   Install a new seal and deflector. Lubricate the lips of the seal with multi-purpose grease.

16   Install the axleshaft, carefully driving it in with a soft-face hammer.

17 Install the thrust washer, gear, sleeve, shaft, shift fork, clip and spring.

18 Apply a bead of RTV sealant to the tube-to-differential housing mating surface.

19 Apply some grease to the thrust washer and install the washer. Install the gear and shift sleeve.

20 Carefully install the output shaft tube assembly and install the bolts. Tighten the bolts to the torque listed in this Chapter's Specifications.

21 Install the two tube-to-chassis nuts and tighten them to the torque listed in this Chapter's Specifications.

22 Install the driveaxle (see Section 21).

23 Install the front axle shift motor.

24 Fill the differential with the proper lubricant (see Chapter 1).

25 Install the splash shield.

26 Lower the vehicle and check for proper operation.

ALL-WHEEL DRIVE (AWD) SYSTEMS

27 Remove the stabilizer bar link (see Chapter 10).

28 Remove the bolts securing the axle shaft flange to the differential carrier.

29 Separate the axle shaft from the outer wheel drive shaft (see Section 21).

30 Use a brass punch and hammer to tap on the axle shaft and separate it from the differential case side gear.

31 Remove the nuts that attach the axle shaft to its support bracket.

32 Remove the inner axle shaft housing bolts from the differential.

33 Remove the inner axle shaft assembly and the axle shaft from the vehicle.

34 Remove the inner seal and bearing. A special tool is required to pull the bearing from the clutch shaft. Install a new bearing and seal.

35 Apply RTV sealant to the differential sealing surface and Install the inner axle shaft housing assembly. Allow the RTV sealant to set-up, install the bolts and tighten the bolts to the torque listed in this Chapter's Specifications.

36 Install the axle shaft to the support bracket, install the nuts and tighten them to the torque listed in this Chapter's Specifications.

37 Align the splines of the inner axle shaft with the splines on the differential side gear by slowly rotating the inner axle shaft. Tap the inner axle shaft with a mallet until the ring (clip) on the axle shaft is aligned with the groove in the differential case side gear.

38 Install the axle shaft to the inner flange. Install the axle shaft flange bolts and tighten them to the torque listed in this Chapter's Specifications.

39 Install the stabilizer link (see Chapter 10).

40 Fill the differential with the proper lubricant (see Chapter 1).

41 Install the splash shield.

42 Lower the vehicle and check for proper operation.

25 Axleshaft oil seals and bearings (front, 4WD models) - replacement

RIGHT SIDE

1 Refer to Section 24 for the right-side axleshaft seal and bearing replacement procedure.

LEFT SIDE

▶ **Refer to illustration 25.5**

2 Loosen the wheel lug nuts, raise the vehicle, place it securely on jackstands and remove the left front wheel. Remove the splash shield from under the front axle.

3 Remove the left driveaxle (see Section 21).

4 Drain the lubricant from the front differential (see Chapter 1).

5 Pull the left axleshaft out with a slide hammer and adapter (see illustration).

6 Remove the deflector and seal from the differential.

7 Remove the bearing using a slide hammer and bearing remover attachment (see illustration 16.2).

8 Install the bearing, with the square shoulder facing in, using a bearing driver or a socket with an outside diameter slightly smaller than that of the bearing.

9 Install a new seal and deflector. Lubricate the lips of the seal with multi-purpose grease.

25.5 Removing the left front axleshaft with a slide hammer

10 Install the axleshaft, carefully driving it in with a soft-face hammer.

11 Fill the differential with the proper lubricant (see Chapter 1).

12 Install the driveaxle (see Section 21).

13 Install the splash shield.

14 Lower the vehicle and check for proper operation.

26 Front differential carrier - removal and installation

◆ **Refer to illustrations 26.10 and 26.13**

1 Disconnect the cable from the negative terminal of the battery.

❋ CAUTION:

On models equipped with the "Theftlock" audio system, be sure the lockout feature is turned off before performing any procedure which requires disconnecting the battery (see the information at the front of this manual).

2 Loosen the front wheel lug nuts, raise the front of the vehicle and support it securely on jackstands placed under the frame rails. Remove the wheels.

3 Remove the splash shield.

4 Drain the lubricant from the front differential (see Chapter 1).

5 Remove the front driveshaft (see Section 10).

6 Detach the inner ends of the driveaxles from the axleshaft flanges (see Section 21). Suspend the driveaxles with lengths of wire - don't let them hang by the outer CV joints.

7 Disconnect the electrical connector from the shift motor (see illustration 24.7).

8 Detach the vent hose from the differential housing.

9 Disconnect the relay rod from the idler arm and the Pitman arm (see Chapter 10). Move the relay rod forward, out of the way.

10 Remove the carrier rear mounting bolt and nut (see illustration).

11 Support the differential carrier with a floor jack. If a transmission jack adapter is available, use it - it will hold the assembly more securely.

12 Remove the two nuts that attach the axle tube to the chassis (see illustration 24.7).

13 Remove the carrier front mounting bolt and nut (see illustration).

14 Slowly lower the jack and guide the carrier out from under the vehicle.

15 Check the bushings in the front and rear mounting bosses; if they are in need of replacement, take the carrier to an automotive machine shop or other qualified repair facility to have the old bushings pressed out and the new ones pressed in.

16 Installation is the reverse of removal. Tighten all fasteners to the proper torque values. Refill the differential with the proper lubricant (see Chapter 1).

26.10 Remove the nut and bolt (arrow) from the differential carrier rear mount

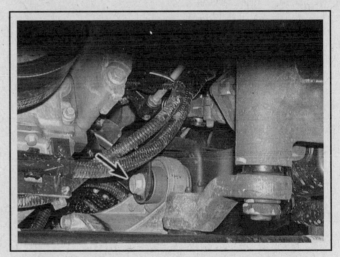

26.13 Remove the nut and bolt (arrow) from the differential carrier front mount

General

Clutch hydraulic fluid type	See Chapter 1
Clutch disc lining thickness	1/16 inch (above rivet)
Inner CV joint length (see illustration 22.3r)	
1500 models	6-11/16 inches
2500 models	7 inches

Torque specifications   Ft-lbs (unless otherwise indicated)

Clutch

Pressure plate-to-flywheel bolts	
V6	30
V8	52
Clutch release cylinder bolts	71 in-lbs

Driveshaft

Front driveshaft U-joint strap bolts	19
Rear driveshaft	
U-joint strap bolts	19
Center support bearing bolts	30

Driveaxles (4WD models)

Driveaxle inner joint-to-axleshaft flange bolts	58
Driveaxle hub nut	177

Rear axle

Pinion shaft lock bolt	
8.6-inch axle	27
9.5-inch axle	37
Differential cover bolts	30
Axleshaft bolts (full-floating axle)	
2001 and earlier models	
10.5-inch axle	110
11-inch axle (hub cover; axle flange	
toothed to hub)	15
2002 and later models	
10.5-inch axle	115
11.5-inch axle	148

Front axle (4WD models)

Right axleshaft tube/shaft-to-chassis nuts	75
Right axleshaft tube/shaft-to differential	
housing bolts	30
Differential housing-to-chassis bolts/nuts	75
Inner axle housing mounting bracket bolts	67
Shift motor	16

Section

Reference to other Chapters

9

BRAKES

1 General information

GENERAL

The vehicles covered by this manual are equipped with hydraulically operated front and rear disc brake systems. Both the front and rear brakes are self adjusting (disc brakes automatically compensate for pad wear).

HYDRAULIC SYSTEM

The hydraulic system consists of two separate circuits, split front-to-rear. The master cylinder has separate reservoirs for the two circuits, and, in the event of a leak or failure in one hydraulic circuit, the other circuit will remain operative and a warning indicator will light up on the instrument panel when a substantial amount of brake fluid is lost, showing that a failure has occurred.

POWER BRAKE BOOSTER

The power brake booster uses either engine manifold vacuum or hydraulic pressure from the power steering pump to provide assistance to the brakes. It is mounted on the firewall in the engine compartment, directly behind the master cylinder.

PARKING BRAKE

The parking brake operates the rear brakes only, through cable

actuation. It's activated by a pedal mounted under the left end of the instrument panel. The parking brake cables actuate a pair of parking brake shoes mounted inside of the drum (hub) portion of each rear brake disc.

SERVICE

After completing any operation involving disassembly of any part of the brake system, always test drive the vehicle to check for proper braking performance before resuming normal driving. When testing the brakes, perform the tests on a clean, dry, flat surface. Conditions other than these can lead to inaccurate test results.

Test the brakes at various speeds with both light and heavy pedal pressure. The vehicle should stop evenly without pulling to one side or the other.

Tires, vehicle load and wheel alignment are factors which also affect braking performance.

✳✳ CAUTION:

On models equipped with the "Theftlock" audio system, be sure the lockout feature is turned off before performing any procedure which requires disconnecting the battery (see the information at the front of this manual).

2 Anti-lock Brake System (ABS) - general information

◆ **Refer to illustration 2.2**

Anti-lock Brake Systems (ABS) maintain vehicle maneuverability, directional stability, and optimum deceleration under severe braking conditions on most road surfaces. It does so by monitoring the rotational speed of the wheels and controlling the brake line pressure to the wheels during braking. This prevents the wheels from locking up on slippery roads or during hard braking.

The ABS system on these vehicles is a three-sensor system; each front wheel is equipped with its own sensor, and the rear wheels share a sensor (mounted in the extension housing of the transmission on 2WD models and in the transfer case on 4WD models). This means that the brake line pressure to the front wheels can be controlled individually, but the two rear brakes are controlled together.

ELECTRO-HYDRAULIC CONTROL UNIT (EHCU)

The Electro-Hydraulic Control Unit (EHCU), mounted on the left-side frame rail underneath the cab, controls hydraulic pressure to the brake calipers by modulating hydraulic pressure to prevent wheel lock-up (see illustration). It is made up of the Brake Pressure Modulator Valve (BPMV) and the Electronic Brake Control Module (EBCM). Basically, the BPMV bleeds off pressure in a brake line when the Electronic Brake Control Module (EBCM) detects an abnormal deceleration in the speed of a wheel (via a wheel speed sensor signal). When the speed of the wheel is restored to normal, the modulator once again allows full

pressure to the brake. This cycle is repeated as many times as necessary, which results in a pulsing of the brake pedal.

➡**Note: The EHCU can't increase brake line pressure above that which is generated by the master cylinder, and it can't apply the brakes by itself.**

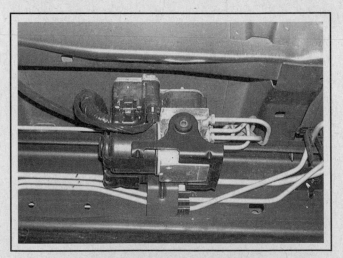

2.2 The ABS Electro-Hydraulic Control Unit (EHCU) is located along the left frame rail, underneath the driver

In addition to sensing and processing information received from the brake switch and wheel speed sensors to control the hydraulic line pressure and avoid wheel lock up, the EBCM also continually monitors the system and stores fault codes which indicate specific problems.

TRACTION CONTROL SYSTEM

Some later models are equipped with the Traction Control System (TCS). When wheel slip is detected, the Electronic Brake Control Module (EBCM) will activate the traction control mode. A signal is sent from the EBCM to the PCM (Powertrain Control Module) commanding less torque to the drive wheels. Torque is reduced by retarding the ignition timing and by controlling the throttle control actuator (TCA).

The Traction Control System (TCS) is deactivated when the transmission shift lever is selected into the LOW position, the driver manually selects OFF on the TCS switch on the dash or the EBCM automatically shuts off the TCS during cruising or non-hazard conditions. The Traction Control System (TCS) can be programmed for the auto-engagement feature. This allows the TCS to activate automatically at start-up.

WHEEL SPEED SENSORS

Each front wheel is equipped with a speed sensor, which is mounted on each front hub and wheel bearing assembly. A toothed sensor ring is integral with the bearing; if it becomes damaged, the entire hub/wheel bearing assembly must be replaced. If the actual sensor which bolts to the hub and bearing assembly malfunctions, it can be replaced separately. The sensors are neither adjustable nor rebuildable.

Rear wheel speed is monitored by the Vehicle Speed Sensor (VSS), which is located in the extension housing on 2WD models and the transfer case on 4WD models. For more information on the VSS, see Chapter 6.

A wheel speed sensor measures wheel speed by monitoring the rotation of a toothed ring. As the teeth of the ring move through the magnetic field of the sensor, an AC voltage signal is generated. This signal frequency increases or decreases in proportion to the speed of the wheel. The EBCM monitors these signals for changes in wheel speed; if it detects the sudden deceleration of a wheel, i.e. wheel lockup, the EBCM activates the ABS system.

WARNING LIGHTS

The ABS system has self-diagnostic capabilities. Each time the vehicle is started, the EBCM runs a self-test. There are two warning lights on the instrument panel, a red BRAKE light and an amber ABS light, each with their own functions. During starting, these lights should come on briefly then go out. If the red BRAKE light stays on, it indicates a problem with the main braking system, such as low fluid level detected or the parking brake is still on. If the light stays on after the parking brake is released, check the brake fluid level in the master cylinder reservoir (see Chapter 1).

The amber ABS light indicates a problem with the ABS system, not the main or basic brake system. If the light stays on, it indicates that there is a problem with the ABS system, but the main system is still working. Take the vehicle to a dealer service department or other qualified repair shop for diagnosis and repair.

CHECKS

Although a special electronic tester is necessary to properly diagnose the system, the home mechanic can perform a few preliminary checks before taking the vehicle to a dealer service department or other repair shop which is equipped with this tester:

 a) *Check the fuses.*
 b) *Check the electrical connectors at the EBCM and the hydraulic modulator/motor pack.*
 c) *Follow the wiring harness to the speed sensors and brake light switch and make sure all connections are secure and the wiring isn't damaged.*
 d) *Make sure the brake lines, calipers and wheel cylinders are in good condition.*
 e) *Check the resistance of the front wheel speed sensors and compare your readings with the values listed in this Chapter's Specifications (see Chapter 6 for the Vehicle Speed Sensor check, which monitors the speed of the rear wheels). If any sensor is out of range, replace it (the sensors are integral with the hub/wheel bearing assemblies).*

If the above preliminary checks don't rectify the problem, the vehicle should be diagnosed by a dealer service department or other qualified repair shop.

---

3   Disc brake pads - replacement

▸ **Refer to illustrations 3.5a through 3.5n**

❋❋ WARNING:

Disc brake pads must be replaced on both front or both rear wheels at the same time - never replace the pads on only one wheel. Also, the dust created by the brake system is harmful to your health. Never blow it out with compressed air and don't inhale any of it. An approved filtering mask should be worn when working on the brakes. Do not, under any circumstances, use petroleum-based solvents to clean brake parts. Use brake system cleaner only!

➥**Note: This procedure applies to the front and rear brake pads.**

1   Remove the cap from the brake fluid reservoir. Remove about two-thirds of the fluid from the reservoir, then reinstall the cap.

❋❋ CAUTION:

Brake fluid will damage paint. If any fluid is spilled, wash it off immediately with plenty of clean, cold water.

2   Loosen the front or rear wheel lug nuts, raise the front or rear of the vehicle and support it securely on jackstands. Block the wheels at the opposite end.

3   Remove the wheels. Work on one brake assembly at a time, using the assembled brake for reference if necessary.

4   Inspect the brake disc carefully as outlined in Section 5. If machining is necessary, follow the information in that Section to remove the disc.

5   Follow the accompanying photo sequence for the actual pad replacement procedure (see illustrations 3.5a through 3.5n). Be sure to

3.5a Before disassembling the brake, wash it thoroughly with brake system cleaner and allow it to dry - position a drain pan under the brake to catch the residue - DO NOT use compressed air to blow off brake dust!

3.5b To make room for the new pads, use a C-clamp to depress the piston(s) into the caliper before removing the caliper and pads - do this a little at a time, keeping an eye on the fluid level in the master cylinder to make sure it doesn't overflow.

➡Note: On ABS models, remove the bleed screw (see illustration 10.8) before compressing the caliper pistons

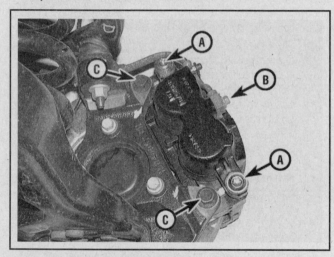

3.5c Front caliper mounting details

A Caliper mounting bolts
B Brake hose inlet fitting bolt
C Caliper mounting bracket bolts

stay in order and read the caption under each illustration.

6   When reinstalling the caliper, be sure to tighten the mounting bolts to the torque listed in this Chapter's Specifications. Tighten the wheel lug nuts to the torque listed in the Chapter 1 Specifications.

7   After the job has been completed, firmly depress the brake pedal a few times to bring the pads into contact with the disc. Check the level of the brake fluid, adding some if necessary (see Chapter 1). Check the operation of the brakes carefully before placing the vehicle into normal service.

3.5d If you're replacing the front brake pads (or, on 2500 models, the rear pads), remove the lower mounting bolt and pivot the caliper up, supporting it in this position

3.5e If you're replacing the rear pads on a 1500 model, hold the caliper slide pin with an open-end wrench, loosen the lower mounting bolt with another wrench, then pivot the caliper up and support it in this position for access to the brake pads

3.5f Remove the inner brake pad

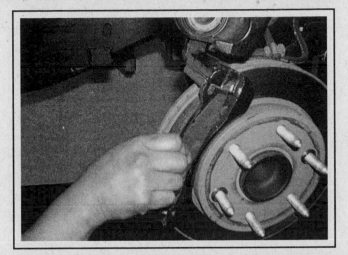

3.5g Remove the outer brake pad

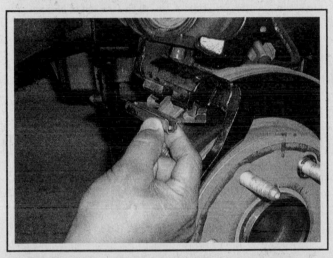

3.5h Remove the upper and lower pad retainers from the caliper mounting bracket; if they are cracked or distorted, replace them

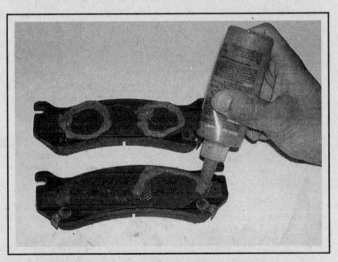

3.5i Apply anti-squeal compound to the back of both pads (let the compound "set up" a few minutes before installing them)

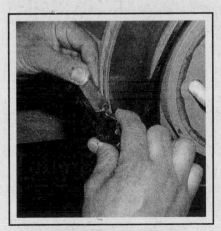

3.5j Install the upper and lower pad retainers on the caliper mounting bracket

3.5k Install the inner brake pad . . .

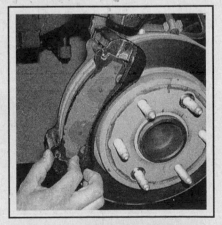

3.5l . . . and the outer brake pad

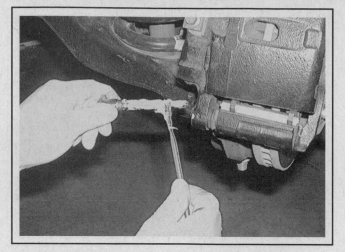

3.5m Inspect the caliper mounting bolt for scoring and corrosion, then lubricate it with high-temperature brake grease. If it was dry, pivot the caliper up again, slide the upper mounting bolt out of the bracket and lubricate it, too.

3.5n Before lowering the rear caliper over the pads, check the condition of the slide pin and the rubber boot, then lubricate the pin with high-temperature brake grease (if it was dry, pivot the caliper up again, pull the upper slide pin and boot out of the bracket and lubricate it, too).

4   Brake caliper - removal and installation

▸ **Refer to illustration 4.2**

✳✳ WARNING:

The dust created by the brake system may contain asbestos, which is harmful to your health. Never blow it out with compressed air and don't inhale any of it. An approved filtering mask should be worn when working on the brakes. Do not, under any circumstances, use petroleum-based solvents to clean brake parts. Use brake system cleaner only!

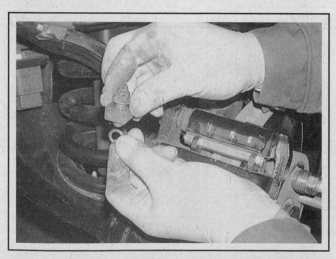

4.2 There is a sealing washer on either side of the brake hose inlet fitting; be sure to replace these with new ones when reconnecting the hose

REMOVAL

1   Loosen the front or rear wheel lug nuts, raise the front or rear of the vehicle and place it securely on jackstands. Block the wheels at the opposite end. Remove the front or rear wheel.

2   Remove the inlet fitting bolt and disconnect the brake hose from the caliper. Discard the old sealing washers (see illustration). Plug the brake hose immediately to keep contaminants and air out of the brake system and to prevent losing any more brake fluid than is necessary.

➡**Note: If you are simply removing the caliper for access to other components, leave the brake hose connected and suspend the caliper with a length of wire - don't let it hang by the hose (see illustration 5.2).**

3   Remove the caliper mounting bolts and detach the caliper from the mounting bracket. When removing a rear caliper on a 1500 model, hold the slide pins with an open-end wrench to prevent them from turning when the mounting bolts are unscrewed (see illustration 3.5e).

INSTALLATION

4   Installation is the reverse of removal. Don't forget to use new sealing washers on each side of the brake hose inlet fitting and be sure to tighten the fitting bolt and the caliper mounting bolts to the torque listed in this Chapter's Specifications.

5   Bleed the brake system (see Section 8).

➡**Note: If the brake hose was not disconnected, bleeding won't be required.**

Make sure there are no leaks from the hose connections. Test the brakes carefully before returning the vehicle to normal service.

5 Brake disc - inspection, removal and installation

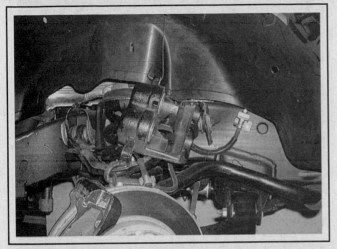

5.2 Hang the caliper out of the way with a piece of wire - don't let it hang by the brake hose!

5.3 The brake pads on this vehicle were obviously neglected, as they wore down completely and cut deep grooves into the disc - wear this severe means the disc must be replaced

INSPECTION

▶ **Refer to illustrations 5.2, 5.3, 5.4a, 5.4b, 5.5a and 5.5b**

1   Loosen the wheel lug nuts, raise the vehicle and support it securely on jackstands. Remove the wheel and install the lug nuts to hold the disc in place.

➡**Note: If the lug nuts don't contact the disc when screwed on all the way, install washers under them.**

2   Remove the brake caliper. It isn't necessary to disconnect the brake hose. After removing the caliper bolts, suspend the caliper out of the way with a piece of wire (see illustration).

3   Visually inspect the disc surface for score marks and other damage. Light scratches and shallow grooves are normal after use and may not always be detrimental to brake operation, but deep scoring requires disc removal and refinishing by an automotive machine shop. Be sure to check both sides of the disc (see illustration). If pulsating has been noticed during application of the brakes, suspect disc runout.

4   To check disc runout, place a dial indicator at a point about 1/2-inch from the outer edge of the disc (see illustration). Set the indicator to zero and turn the disc. The indicator reading should not exceed the specified allowable runout limit. If it does, the disc should be refinished by an automotive machine shop.

➡**Note: When replacing the brake pads, it's a good idea to resurface the discs regardless of the dial indicator reading, as this will impart a smooth finish and ensure a perfectly flat surface, eliminating any brake pedal pulsation or other undesirable symptoms related to questionable discs. At the very least, if you elect not to have the discs resurfaced, remove the glaze from the surface with emery cloth or sandpaper, using a swirling motion (see illustration).**

5   It's absolutely critical that the disc not be machined to a thickness under the specified minimum thickness. The minimum wear (or discard) thickness is cast into the underside of front discs (see illustration) and on the outside of rear discs. The disc thickness can be checked with a micrometer (see illustration).

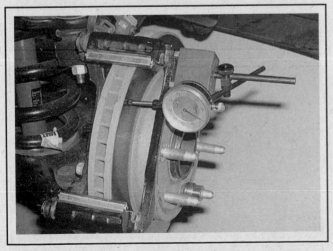

5.4a To check disc runout, mount a dial indicator as shown and rotate the disc

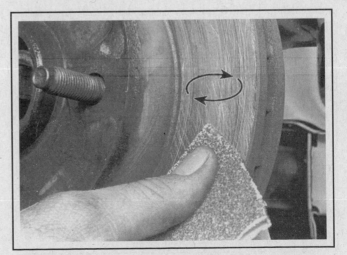

5.4b Using a swirling motion, remove the glaze from the disc with sandpaper or emery cloth

5.5a The minimum thickness is cast into the disc

5.5b Use a micrometer to measure disc thickness

REMOVAL

▶ **Refer to illustrations 5.6a, 5.6b and 5.7**

➡**Note: On 2500 models equipped with dual rear wheels, the wheel hub must be removed (see Chapter 8) and the wheel studs pressed out of the hub/disc assembly.**

6   Remove the two caliper mounting bracket bolts and detach the mounting bracket (see illustrations).

7   Remove the lug nuts which you installed to hold the disc in place and slide the disc off the hub. If pressed-metal retaining clips are present on any of the wheel studs, cut them off (see illustration).

INSTALLATION

8   Place the disc in position over the threaded studs.

9   Install the mounting bracket and tighten the bolts to the torque listed in this Chapter's Specifications. Install the brake pads.

10   Install the caliper onto the mounting bracket, tightening the bolts to the torque listed in this Chapter's Specifications.

11   Install the wheel and lug nuts. Lower the vehicle and tighten the lug nuts to the torque listed in the Chapter 1 Specifications. Depress

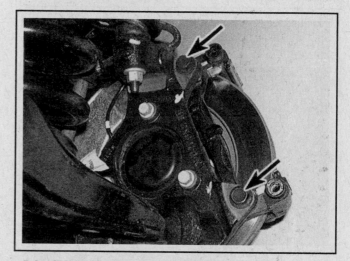

5.6a Caliper mounting bracket bolts - front

the brake pedal a few times to bring the brake pads into contact with the disc. Bleeding won't be necessary unless the brake hose was disconnected from the caliper. Check the operation of the brakes carefully before driving the vehicle.

5.6b Caliper mounting bracket bolts - rear

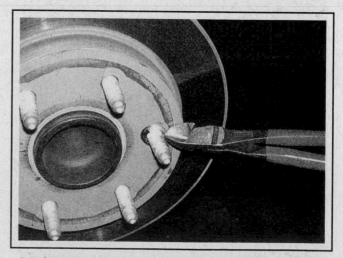

5.7 Cut off and discard the disc retaining washers, if present (it isn't necessary to reinstall them)

6   Drum brake shoes - replacement

▶ **Refer to illustrations 6.2a, 6.2b, 6.3, 6.4, 6.5, 6.9**

✳✳ WARNING:

Drum brake shoes must be replaced on both wheels at the same time - never replace the shoes on only one wheel. Also, the dust created by the brake system is harmful to your health. Never blow it out with compressed air and don't inhale any of it. An approved filtering mask should be worn when working on the brakes. Do not, under any circumstances, use petroleum-based solvents to clean brake parts. Use brake system cleaner only!

1   Loosen the wheel lug nuts, raise the rear of the vehicle and support it securely on jackstands. Block the front wheels to keep the vehicle from rolling. Remove the wheels.

2   Release the parking brake and remove the brake drums (see illustration). If the shoes have worn into the drum, preventing drum removal, remove the access plug from the backing plate, push the lever off the adjuster star wheel with one narrow screwdriver while turning the adjuster star wheel with another narrow screwdriver (or a brake adjusting tool) (see illustration).

3   Before disassembling anything, clean off the brake assembly with brake system cleaner (see illustration).

4   Detach the spring from the adjuster lever (see illustration).

5   Pull the retractor spring out of the hole in each shoe (see illustration).

6   Remove the trailing shoe and adjuster lever, then the adjuster

6.2a If the drum is retained by pressed-metal washers, cut them off and discard them (there is no need to reinstall them)

6.2b If the shoes have worn into the drum, preventing its removal, remove the plug from the backing plate and push the parking brake lever off its stop like this, then insert a brake adjusting tool or another screwdriver and turn the adjuster star wheel upward to retract the shoes

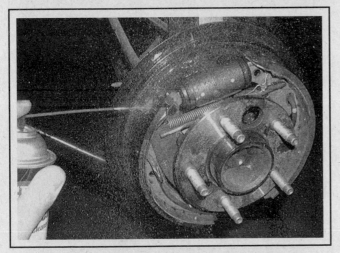

6.3 Before removing any internal drum brake components, wash them off with brake system cleaner and allow them to dry - position a drain pan under the brake to catch the residue - DO NOT USE COMPRESSED AIR TO BLOW THE DUST FROM THE PARTS

6.4 Grip the adjuster spring with a pair of pliers and detach its end from the adjuster lever

6.5 Pull the end of the retractor spring out of the hole in each shoe

6.9 Lubricate the brake shoe contact areas on the backing plate with high-temperature grease

screw assembly.

7 Pull the retractor spring out of the way, then remove the leading shoe.

8 Detach the parking brake lever from the trailing shoe.

9 Clean the backing plate, then lubricate the shoe contact areas with a thin film of high-temperature grease (see illustration).

10 Connect the parking brake lever to the trailing shoe, position the shoe on the backing plate and install the end of the retractor spring in its hole.

11 Clean the adjuster screw assembly, then lubricate the threads and socket end with high-temperature grease (see illustration).

12 Install the adjuster screw assembly, making sure it engages properly with the leading shoe.

13 Lightly lubricate the adjuster lever and install it on the trailing shoe.

14 Position the trailing shoe on the backing plate, making sure it (and the parking brake lever and adjuster lever) engage properly with the adjuster screw assembly, then insert the retractor spring into its hole in the shoe.

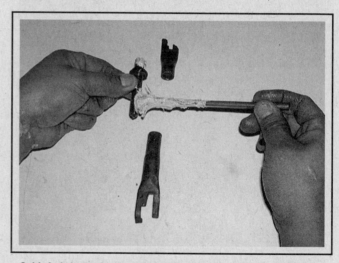

6.11 Lubricate the threads and socket end of the adjuster screw assembly with high-temperature grease

6.16a The maximum permissible diameter is cast into the drum (typical)

6.16b Remove the glaze from the drum surface with sandpaper or emery cloth

15 Insert the actuator spring into its hole in the leading shoe, then stretch it across and connect it to the adjuster lever.

16 Before reinstalling the drum it should be checked for cracks, score marks, deep scratches and hard spots, which will appear as small, discolored areas. If the hard spots cannot be removed with emery cloth or if any of the other conditions listed above exist, the drum must be taken to an automotive machine shop to have it resurfaced.

➡️**Note: Professionals recommend resurfacing the drums whenever a brake job is done. Resurfacing will eliminate the possibility of out-of-round or tapered drums. If the drums are worn so much that they can't be resurfaced without exceeding** the maximum allowable diameter (stamped into the drum) (see illustration), then new ones will be required. At the very least, if you elect not to have the drums resurfaced, remove the glazing from the surface with emery cloth or sandpaper using a swirling motion (see illustration).

17 When installing the drum, adjust the brake shoes by turning the star wheel on the adjuster screw until the drum just slips over the shoes. When turning the drum, the shoes should not rub; if they do, remove the drum and back off the star wheel a little bit so they don't. This adjustment is just to get the shoes close to the drum; the brake shoes will self-adjust after you depress the pedal a few times).

7   Wheel cylinder - removal and installation

REMOVAL

1   Raise the rear of the vehicle and support it securely on jackstands. Block the front wheels to keep the vehicle from rolling.

2   Remove the brake shoe assembly (see Section 6).

3   Remove all dirt and foreign material from around the wheel cylinder.

4   Using a flare-nut wrench, unscrew the brake line fitting from the wheel cylinder. Don't pull the line away from the wheel cylinder (it could get bent).

5   Remove the wheel cylinder mounting bolts and detach the wheel cylinder from the brake backing plate.

INSTALLATION

6   Place the wheel cylinder in position and connect the brake line fitting, being careful not to cross-thread it. Install the mounting bolts, tightening them to the torque listed in this Chapter's Specifications, then tighten the brake line fitting securely.

7   Install the brake shoes (see Section 6).

8   Bleed the brakes (see Section 10).

9   Check the operation of the brakes carefully before driving the vehicle in traffic.

8   Master cylinder - removal, installation and reservoir/O-ring replacement

REMOVAL

▶ **Refer to illustration 8.2**

1   Disconnect the cable from the negative battery terminal.

✳✳ CAUTION:

On models equipped with the "Theftlock" audio system, be sure the lockout feature is turned off before performing any procedure which requires disconnecting the battery (see the information at the front of this manual).

2   Unplug the electrical connector for the fluid level warning switch (see illustration).

3   Remove as much fluid as possible from the reservoir with a suction gun, large syringe or a poultry baster.

✳✳ WARNING:

If a poultry baster is used, never again use it for the preparation of food.

8.2 Master cylinder mounting details

1   *Electrical connector for fluid level sensor*
2   *Brake line fittings*
3   *Mounting nuts*

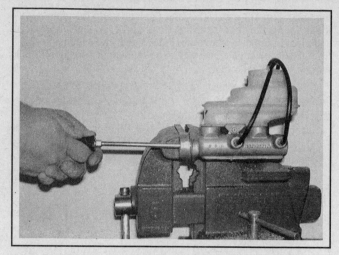

8.8 The best way to bleed air from the master cylinder before installing it on the vehicle is with a pair of bleeder tubes that direct brake fluid into the reservoir during bleeding

4   Place rags under the fittings and prepare caps or plastic bags to cover the ends of the lines once they're disconnected.

✴✴ CAUTION:

Brake fluid will damage paint. Cover all body parts and be careful not to spill fluid during this procedure. Loosen the fittings at the ends of the brake lines where they enter the master cylinder. To prevent rounding off the flats, use a flare-nut wrench, which wraps around the fitting hex.

5   Pull the brake lines away from the master cylinder and plug the ends to prevent contamination.

6   Remove the nuts attaching the master cylinder to the power booster (see illustration 8.2). Pull the master cylinder off the studs to remove it. Again, be careful not to spill the fluid as this is done.

INSTALLATION

▶ **Refer to illustrations 8.8 and 8.16**

7   Bench bleed the new master cylinder before installing it. Mount the master cylinder in a vise, with the jaws of the vise clamping on the mounting flange.

8   Attach a pair of master cylinder bleeder tubes to the outlet ports of the master cylinder (see illustration).

9   Fill the reservoir with brake fluid of the recommended type (see Chapter 1).

10 Slowly push the pistons into the master cylinder (a large Phillips screwdriver can be used for this) - air will be expelled from the pressure chambers and into the reservoir. Because the tubes are submerged in fluid, air can't be drawn back into the master cylinder when you release the pistons.

11 Repeat the procedure until no more air bubbles are present.

12 Remove the bleed tubes, one at a time, and install plugs in the open ports to prevent fluid leakage and air from entering. Install the reservoir cap.

13 Install the master cylinder over the studs on the power brake booster and tighten the attaching nuts only finger tight at this time. Don't forget to use a new gasket.

14 Thread the brake line fittings into the master cylinder. Since

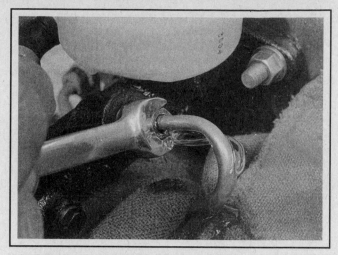

8.16 Have an assistant depress the brake pedal and hold it down, then loosen the fitting nut, allowing air and fluid to escape; repeat this procedure on both fittings until the fluid is clear of air bubbles

the master cylinder is still a bit loose, it can be moved slightly so the fittings thread in easily. Don't strip the threads as the fittings are tightened.

15 Tighten the mounting nuts to the torque listed in this Chapter's Specifications. Tighten the brake line fittings securely.

16 Fill the master cylinder reservoir with fluid, then bleed the lines at the master cylinder, followed by bleeding the remainder of the brake system (see Section 8). To bleed the lines at the master cylinder, have an assistant depress the brake pedal and hold it down. Loosen the fitting to allow air and fluid to escape (see illustration). Tighten the fitting, then allow your assistant to return the pedal to its rest position. Repeat this procedure on both fittings until the fluid is free of air bubbles, then bleed the rest of the system. Check the operation of the brake system carefully before driving the vehicle.

✴✴ WARNING:

If you do not have a firm brake pedal at the end of the bleeding procedure, or have any doubts as to the effectiveness of the brake system, DO NOT drive the vehicle. Have it towed to a dealer service department or other qualified repair shop for diagnosis.

RESERVOIR/O-RING REPLACEMENT

▶ **Refer to illustrations 8.19 and 8.21**

➡**Note: The brake fluid reservoir can be replaced separately from the master cylinder body if it becomes damaged. If there is leakage between the reservoir and the master cylinder body, the O-rings on the reservoir can be replaced.**

17 Remove as much fluid as possible from the reservoir with a suction gun, large syringe or a poultry baster.

✴✴ WARNING:

If a poultry baster is used, never again use it for the preparation of food.

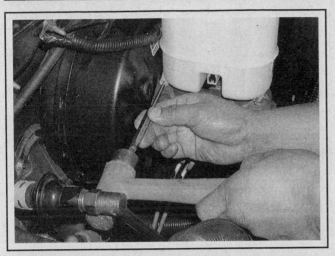

8.19 Driving out the roll pins that retain the master cylinder fluid reservoir

18 Place rags under the master cylinder to absorb any fluid that may spill out once the reservoir is detached from the master cylinder.

✳✳ CAUTION:

Brake fluid will damage paint. Cover all body parts and be careful not to spill fluid during this procedure.

19 Using a hammer and a small punch, drive out the roll pins that retain the reservoir to the master cylinder (see illustration).

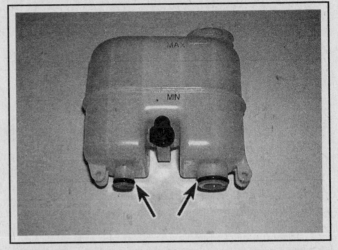

8.21 The reservoir O-rings (arrows) can be replaced if they are leaking

20 Pull the reservoir out of the master cylinder body.
21 If you are simply replacing the O-rings, carefully pry the old O-rings off and install new ones (see illustration).
22 Lubricate the reservoir O-rings with clean brake fluid, then press the reservoir into place on the master cylinder body and secure it with new roll pins.
23 Refill the reservoir with the recommended brake fluid (see Chapter 1) and check for leaks.
24 Bleed the master cylinder (see illustration 8.16).

9   Brake hoses and lines - inspection and replacement

INSPECTION

1   About every six months, with the vehicle raised and supported securely on jackstands, the rubber hoses which connect the steel brake lines with the front and rear brake assemblies should be inspected for cracks, chafing of the outer cover, leaks, blisters and other damage. These are important and vulnerable parts of the brake system and inspection should be complete. A light and mirror will be helpful for a thorough check. If a hose exhibits any of the above conditions, replace it with a new one.

REPLACEMENT

Flexible brake hose

Front

▶ **Refer to illustrations 9.3, 9.4 and 9.6**

2   Loosen the wheel lug nuts, raise the vehicle and support it securely on jackstands. Remove the wheel.
3   At the bracket, unscrew the brake line fitting from the hose (see illustration). Use a flare-nut wrench to prevent rounding off the corners of the fitting nut, and hold the hose end with a wrench to prevent twisting the frame bracket.

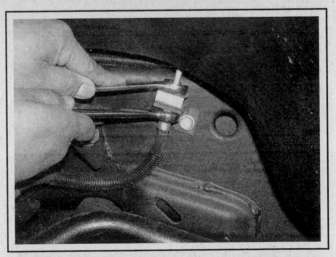

9.3 Using a flare-nut wrench, unscrew the threaded fitting on the brake line, while holding the hose end stationary with an open-end wrench . . .

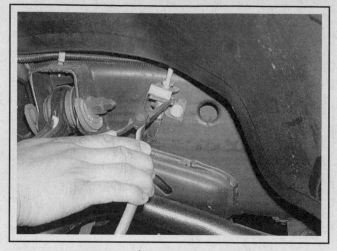

9.4 . . . then remove the U-clip and detach the hose from the bracket

9.6 The brake hose is routed along the top of the steering knuckle and the upper control arm, and is held in place with two brackets

4   Remove the U-clip from the female fitting at the bracket with a pair of pliers, then pass the hose through the bracket (see illustration).

5   At the caliper end of the hose, remove the inlet fitting bolt, then separate the hose from the caliper. Note that there are two copper sealing washers on either side of the inlet fitting (see illustration 4.2) - they should be replaced with new ones during installation.

6   Remove the bolts that secure the hose brackets to the steering knuckle and the upper control arm, then remove the hose (see illustration).

7   To install the hose, connect the fitting to the caliper with the inlet fitting bolt and new sealing washers. Tighten the inlet fitting bolt to the torque listed in this Chapter's Specifications.

8   Route the hose along the top of the steering knuckle, upper control arm and into the frame bracket, making sure it isn't twisted. Tighten the hose bracket bolts securely. Connect the brake line fitting, starting the threads by hand. Install the U-clip, then tighten the fitting securely.

9   Bleed the caliper (see Section 8).

10   Install the wheel and lug nuts, lower the vehicle and tighten the lug nuts to the torque listed in the Chapter 1 Specifications.

Rear

Chassis-to-rear axle

▶ **Refer to illustrations 9.12 and 9.14**

11   Raise the rear of the vehicle and support it securely on jackstands. Block the front wheels to prevent the vehicle from rolling.

12   At the chassis bracket, unscrew the brake line fitting from the hose (see illustration). Use a flare-nut wrench to prevent rounding off the corners of the fitting nut, and hold the hose end with a wrench to prevent twisting the bracket.

13   Remove the U-clip from the female fitting at the bracket with a pair of pliers, then pass the hose through the bracket.

14   At the axle end of the hose, unscrew the two brake line fittings with a flare-nut wrench, unscrew the bolt securing the fitting block to the axle housing, then separate the lines from the fitting block and remove the hose (see illustration).

15   To install the hose, reverse the removal procedure, then bleed both rear calipers (see Section 8).

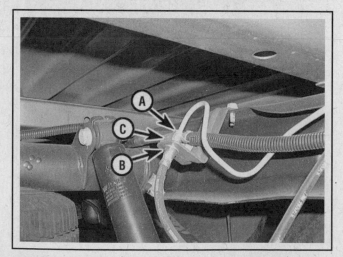

9.12 At the upper end of the chassis-to-rear axle brake hose, unscrew the line fitting (A) with a flare-nut wrench while holding the end of the brake hose (B) with an open-end wrench, then remove the U-clip (C)

9.14 At the lower end of the chassis-to-rear axle brake hose, unscrew the brake line fittings (A) with a flare-nut wrench, then remove the bolt securing the junction block (B)

Rigid line-to-caliper hose

♦ **Refer to illustration 9.17**

16 Loosen the wheel lug nuts, raise the rear of the vehicle and support it securely on jackstands. Block the front wheels to prevent the vehicle from rolling. Remove the wheel.

17 At the bracket, unscrew the brake line fitting from the hose (see illustration). Use a flare-nut wrench to prevent rounding off the corners of the fitting nut, and hold the hose end with a wrench to prevent twisting the bracket.

18 Remove the U-clip from the female fitting at the bracket with a pair of pliers, then pass the hose through the bracket.

19 At the caliper end of the hose, remove the inlet fitting bolt, then separate the hose from the caliper. Note that there are two copper sealing washers on either side of the inlet fitting (see illustration 4.2) - they should be replaced with new ones during installation.

20 To install the hose, connect the fitting to the caliper with the inlet fitting bolt and new sealing washers. Tighten the inlet fitting bolt to the torque listed in this Chapter's Specifications.

21 Route the hose into its bracket, making sure it isn't twisted. Connect the brake line fitting, starting the threads by hand. Install the U-clip, then tighten the fitting securely.

22 Bleed the caliper (see Section 8).

23 Install the wheel and lug nuts, lower the vehicle and tighten the lug nuts to the torque listed in the Chapter 1 Specifications.

Metal brake lines

24 When replacing brake lines, be sure to use the correct parts. Don't use copper tubing for any brake system components. Purchase steel brake lines from a dealer or auto parts store.

25 Prefabricated brake line, with the tube ends already flared and fittings installed, is available at auto parts stores and dealer parts depart-

9.17 Unscrew the rigid line-to-caliper hose fitting with a flare-nut wrench (A), then remove the U-clip (B) and separate the hose from the bracket

ments. These lines must be bent to the proper shapes using a tubing bender.

26 When installing the new line, make sure it's securely supported in the brackets and has plenty of clearance between moving or hot components.

27 After installation, check the master cylinder fluid level and add fluid as necessary. Bleed the brake system (see Section 8) and test the brakes carefully before driving the vehicle in traffic.

10 Brake hydraulic system - bleeding

♦ **Refer to illustration 10.8**

✳✳ WARNING:

Wear eye protection when bleeding the brake system. If the fluid comes in contact with your eyes, immediately rinse them with water and seek medical attention.

➡**Note: Bleeding the hydraulic system is necessary to remove any air that manages to find its way into the system when it's been opened during removal and installation of a hose, line, caliper or master cylinder.**

1 You'll probably have to bleed the system at all four brakes if air has entered it due to low fluid level, or if the brake lines have been disconnected at the master cylinder.

2 If a brake line was disconnected only at a wheel, then only that caliper must be bled.

3 If a brake line is disconnected at a fitting located between the master cylinder and any of the brakes, that part of the system served by the disconnected line must be bled.

4 Remove any residual vacuum (vacuum booster) or pressure (hydraulic booster) from the power brake booster by applying the brake several times with the engine off.

5 Remove the master cylinder reservoir cap and fill the reservoir with brake fluid. Reinstall the cap.

➡**Note: Check the fluid level often during the bleeding operation and add fluid as necessary to prevent the fluid level from falling low enough to allow air bubbles into the master cylinder.**

6 Have an assistant on hand, as well as a supply of new brake fluid, a clear container partially filled with clean brake fluid, a length of clear tubing to fit over the bleeder valve and a wrench to open and close the bleeder valve.

7 Beginning at the right rear wheel, loosen the bleeder valve slightly, then tighten it to a point where it's snug but can still be loosened quickly and easily.

8 Place one end of the tubing over the bleeder valve and submerge

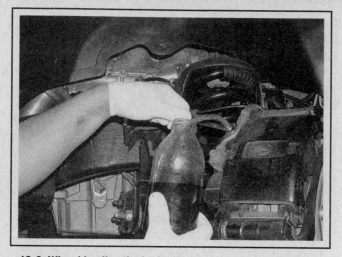

10.8 When bleeding the brakes, a hose is connected to the bleed screw at the caliper and then submerged in brake fluid - air will be seen as bubbles in the tube and container (all air must be expelled before moving to the next wheel)

the other end in brake fluid in the container (see illustration).

9 Have the assistant depress the brake pedal slowly and hold it in the depressed position.

10 While the pedal is held down, open the bleeder valve just enough to allow a flow of fluid to leave the valve. Watch for air bubbles to exit the submerged end of the tube. When the fluid flow slows after a couple of seconds, close the valve and have your assistant release the pedal.

11 Repeat Steps 9 and 10 until no more air is seen leaving the tube,

then tighten the bleeder valve and proceed to the left rear wheel, the right front wheel and the left front wheel, in that order, and perform the same procedure. Be sure to check the fluid in the master cylinder reservoir frequently.

12 Never use old brake fluid. It contains moisture which can cause the fluid to boil, rendering the brake system inoperative.

13 Refill the master cylinder with fluid at the end of the operation.

14 Check the operation of the brakes. The pedal should feel solid when depressed, with no sponginess. If necessary, repeat the entire process.

15 Before driving the vehicle, sit in the driver's seat and:

a) *Take your foot off the brake pedal*

b) *Start the engine and let it run for a minimum of 10 seconds. Watch the amber ABS light on the dash.*

c) *If the light comes on and does not turn off after 10 seconds, have the vehicle towed to a dealer service department or other qualified repair shop. A scan tool will have to be used to diagnose the ABS system.*

d) *If the ABS light goes off after three seconds or so, turn off the ignition.*

e) *Repeat paragraphs a) through d) one more time. If the amber ABS light turns off, test drive the vehicle in an isolated area before returning the vehicle to normal service.*

✳✳ WARNING:

Do not operate the vehicle if you're in doubt about the effectiveness of the brake system.

11 Power brake booster - check, removal and installation

◆ **Refer to illustrations 11.10, 11.14 and 11.15**

✳✳ WARNING:

These models have airbags. Always disable the airbag system before working in the vicinity of any airbag system component to avoid the possibility of accidental deployment of the airbag(s), which could cause personal injury (see Chapter 12).

CHECK

Vacuum booster

Operating check

1 Depress the pedal and start the engine. If the pedal goes down slightly, operation is normal.

2 Depress the brake pedal several times with the engine running and make sure that there is no change in the pedal reserve distance.

Airtightness check

3 Start the engine and turn it off after one or two minutes. Depress

the brake pedal several times slowly. If the pedal goes down farther the first time but gradually rises after the second or third depression, the booster is airtight.

4 Depress the brake pedal while the engine is running, then stop the engine with the pedal depressed. If there is no change in the pedal reserve travel after holding the pedal for 30 seconds, the booster is airtight.

Hydraulic booster

5 Turn the engine off, then depress the brake pedal several times to deplete the pressure in the accumulator.

6 Push down on the brake pedal, exerting approximately 40 pounds of force, then start the engine. If the booster is working properly, the brake pedal will sink towards the floor then rise back up against your foot.

7 If the booster does not work as described, check the fluid level in the power steering reservoir, adding as necessary. Also check the hoses from the power steering pump to the booster for kinks. If everything checks out OK, the booster or power steering pump is defective. Have the power steering pump output pressure checked. If the pump is developing sufficient pressure, replace the booster.

11.10 Pull the vacuum hose fitting straight out of the grommet in the booster

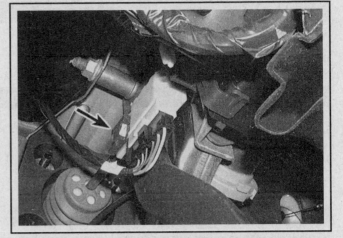

11.14 Pry off the clip retaining the brake light switch and the booster pushrod to the pin on the brake pedal

REMOVAL

8   Disable the airbag system (see Chapter 12). Disconnect the cable from the negative terminal of the battery.

✳✳ CAUTION:

On models equipped with the "Theftlock" audio system, be sure the lockout feature is turned off before performing any procedure which requires disconnecting the battery (see the information at the front of this manual).

9   If you're working on a model with a hydraulic booster, pump the brake pedal several times to deplete the pressure in the accumulator.

10   If you're working on a model with a vacuum booster, detach the vacuum hose from the booster (see illustration).

11   If you're working on a model with a hydraulic booster, detach the pressure and return lines from the booster. Cap the lines to prevent fluid leakage.

12   Remove the master cylinder without detaching the brake lines. Pull it forward and position it aside. Be careful not to bend or kink the brake lines.

13   Remove the left side under-dash panel (see Chapter 11) and the heater duct under the steering column.

14   Remove the pushrod retaining clip (see illustration) and slip the brake light switch and the pushrod off the pin.

15   Remove the four nuts holding the brake booster to the firewall (see illustration).

16   Slide the booster straight out from the firewall until the studs

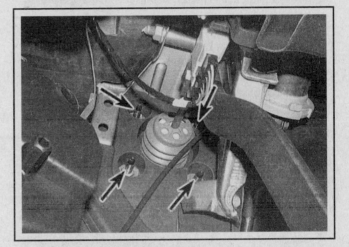

11.15 Unscrew the booster mounting nuts

clear the holes and pull the booster and gasket from the engine compartment.

INSTALLATION

17   Installation is the reverse of removal. Be sure to use a new gasket, and tighten the booster mounting nuts and the master cylinder mounting nuts to the torque values listed in this Chapter's Specifications.

18   If you're working on a model with a hydraulic booster, bleed the power steering system as described in Chapter 10. Check the power steering fluid level and add some, if necessary, to bring it up to the appropriate level.

12 Brake pedal travel - check

1   The brake pedal is not adjustable, but the travel should be checked if the pedal seems low. You'll need a tape measure, yardstick or ruler for this procedure.

2   Depress the pedal a few times to deplete the reserve in the power brake booster.

3   Measure the position of the pedal at rest. You can either measure from the floor to the pedal or from the pedal to the steering wheel.

Record your reading.

4   Now, depress the pedal (exerting approximately 70 lbs. of force) and measure how far the pedal has traveled. Compare your findings with the measurement listed in this Chapter's Specifications.

5   If the pedal travel is excessive, check for air in the system (bleed the brakes - see Section 8). A failed seal in the master cylinder could also cause excessive pedal travel.

13   Parking brake - adjustment

The parking brake cable is self-adjusting, but if the parking brake pedal travel is excessive or won't hold the vehicle on an incline, the parking brake shoes may need to be adjusted or replaced (see Section 15).

14   Parking brake pedal and cables - replacement

PEDAL

▶ **Refer to illustration 14.2**

1   Disconnect the cable from the negative terminal of the battery.

❊❊ **CAUTION:**

On models equipped with the "Theftlock" audio system, be sure the lockout feature is turned off before performing any procedure which requires disconnecting the battery (see the information at the front of this manual). Release the parking brake.

2   From underneath the vehicle, loosen the equalizer nut to relieve tension on the cables (see illustration).

3   Inside the vehicle, remove the left-side under-dash panel and the kick panel.

4   Unplug the electrical connector for the parking brake warning light switch.

5   Unbolt the fuse block and position it aside.

6   Detach the parking brake release cable from the parking brake pedal.

7   Unscrew the nuts securing the parking brake pedal assembly, then pull the assembly off its mounting studs.

8   Detach the cable end from the parking brake lever, then depress the tangs on the cable casing to release the casing from the pedal bracket.

9   Installation is the reverse of removal. Be sure to securely tighten the nut at the equalizer. Depress and release the pedal a few times, which will automatically adjust the cables.

FRONT CABLE

▶ **Refer to illustration 14.12**

10 Disconnect the cable from the negative terminal of the battery.

❊❊ **CAUTION:**

On models equipped with the "Theftlock" audio system, be sure the lockout feature is turned off before performing any procedure which requires disconnecting the battery (see the information at the front of this manual). Release the parking brake.

11 From underneath the vehicle, loosen the equalizer nut (see illustration 14.2).

12 Disconnect the end of the front cable from the connector at the intermediate cable, then, depress the tangs on the cable casing and detach the cable from the bracket (see illustration).

13 Follow the cable towards the front of the vehicle, detaching it from any other brackets that may be present.

14 Remove the parking brake pedal assembly (see Steps 3 through 8).

15 Detach the cable from the pedal assembly.

16 Peel back the carpet, pry the cable grommet out of the floorpan and remove the cable.

17 Installation is the reverse of removal. Be sure to securely tighten the nut at the equalizer. Depress and release the pedal a few times, which will automatically adjust the cables.

INTERMEDIATE CABLE

18 Release the parking brake.

19 From underneath the vehicle, remove the equalizer nut (see illustration 14.2) and separate the intermediate cable from the equalizer.

20 Separate the intermediate cable from the front cable and remove it.

21 Installation is the reverse of removal. Be sure to securely tighten the nut at the equalizer. Depress and release the pedal a few times, which will automatically adjust the cables.

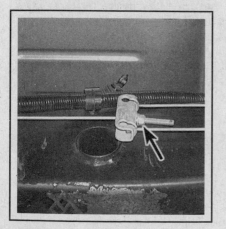

14.2 Loosen the equalizer nut to provide slack in the cables

14.12 Depress the tangs on the cable retainer and pass the cable and casing through the bracket

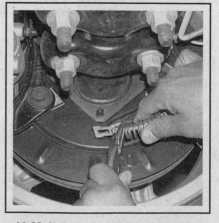

14.26 Unhook the cable end from the parking brake actuator lever

REAR CABLE(S)

▶ **Refer to illustrations 14.26 and 14.27**

22 Raise the rear of the vehicle and support it securely on jack-stands. Block the front wheels to prevent the vehicle from rolling.

23 Loosen the equalizer nut (see illustration 14.2) and detach the rear cable(s) from the equalizer.

24 Detach the cable casing from the bracket on the chassis by depressing the tangs of the retainer and passing the cable through the bracket.

25 Follow the cable and remove any mounting bracket bolts or clips that may be securing the cable.

Disc brake models

26 Detach the end of the cable from the lever on the parking brake actuator (see illustration).

Drum brake models

27 Remove the brake shoes (see Section 6) and disconnect the parking brake cable from the parking brake lever.

28 Depress the tangs on the cable casing retainer and detach the cable casing from the bracket on the backing plate (see illustration). Remove the cable.

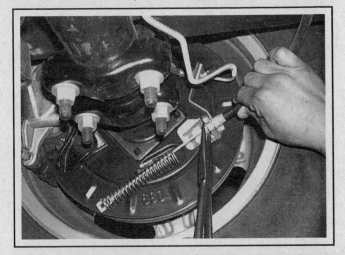

14.27 Depress the tangs on the cable retainer and detach the cable from the bracket on the backing plate

29 Installation is the reverse of removal. Be sure to securely tighten the nut at the equalizer. Depress and release the pedal a few times, which will automatically adjust the cables.

15 Parking brake shoes - replacement

✳✳ WARNING:

The dust created by the brake system is harmful to your health. Never blow it out with compressed air and don't inhale any of it. An approved filtering mask should be worn when working on the brakes. Do not, under any circumstances, use petroleum-based solvents to clean brake parts. Use brake system cleaner only!

➡ **Note: This procedure applies to models with rear disc brakes.**

1 Loosen the rear wheel lug nuts, raise the rear of the vehicle and support it securely on jackstands. Release the parking brake. Block the front wheels to prevent the vehicle from rolling, then remove the rear wheels.

2 Remove the brake caliper (see Section 4), mounting bracket and the brake disc (see Section 5). Loosen the nut on the parking brake equalizer to provide some slack in the cables.

1500 MODELS

▶ **Refer to illustrations 15.3, 15.4 and 15.6**

3 Wash the brake assembly with brake system cleaner. Remove the screw and clip securing the bottom of the shoe (see illustration), then slide the shoe up and off of the actuator.

4 Lift one end of the shoe over the axle flange, then work the shoe over the flange and remove it (see illustration).

15.3 On 1500 models, the parking brake shoe is secured at the bottom by a screw and a clip (arrow)

15.4 Lift one end of the parking brake shoe over the axle flange, then "wind" the rest of the shoe over the flange (1500 models)

15.6 Make sure the ends of the shoe seat in the adjuster screw slot (A) and the tappet slot (B); C is the adjuster screw star wheel (1500 models)

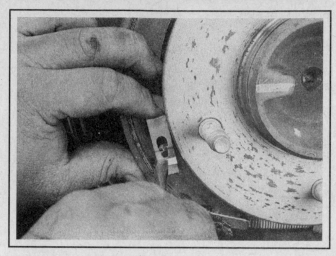

15.9 Push in on the hold-down clip and turn the pin 90-degrees, then remove the clip (2500 models)

5   Before installing the new shoe, turn the adjuster screw star wheel in, then make sure the slots in the adjusting screw and the tappet are parallel with the backing plate.

6   To install the shoe, reverse the removal procedure. Make sure the ends of the shoe seat properly in the slots in the adjuster screw and tappet (see illustration)

7   When installing the new shoe and lining assembly, turn the adjuster screw until the shoe lining just drags on the braking surface inside the disc. Then remove the disc and back-off the adjuster screw until the shoe lining doesn't drag when the disc is installed and turned. The actual clearance between the lining surface of the shoe and the braking surface inside the disc should be 0.026-inch.

8   Installation is otherwise the reverse of the removal procedure. Be sure to tighten the caliper bracket bolts and the caliper mounting bolts to the torque listed in this Chapter's Specifications, and the wheel lug nuts to the torque listed in the Chapter 1 Specifications.

2500 MODELS

▶ **Refer to illustration 15.9**

9   Wash the brake assembly with brake system cleaner, then remove the hold-down clip from each parking brake shoe (see illustration).

10 Unhook the return springs from the top and bottom of each shoe, then remove the shoes from the backing plate.

11 Installation of the new shoes is the reverse of the removal procedure. When installing the new shoes, turn the adjuster screw until the shoe lining just drags on the braking surface inside the disc. Then remove the disc and back-off the adjuster screw until the shoe lining doesn't drag when the disc is installed and turned. The actual clearance between the lining surface of the shoe and the braking surface inside the disc should be 0.026-inch.

12 Be sure to tighten the caliper bracket bolts and the caliper mounting bolts to the torque listed in this Chapter's Specifications, and the wheel lug nuts to the torque listed in the Chapter 1 Specifications.

16   Brake light switch - check, adjustment and replacement

▶ **Refer to illustration 16.1**

CHECK

1   The brake light switch (see illustration) is located on the side of the brake pedal and is retained by the same clip that retains the booster pushrod. The switch activates the brake lights at the rear of the vehicle when the pedal is depressed. To gain access to the switch, remove the left-side under-dash panel and the heater/air conditioning duct.

2   If the brake lights are inoperative, check the fuse first (see Chapter 12).

3   If the fuse is good, check for voltage to the switch on the feed wire (refer to the wiring diagrams at the end of this manual for the proper color wire to check). If no voltage is present, repair the wire between the switch and the fuse box.

4   If voltage is present, depress the brake pedal and check for voltage at the output wire terminal (again, refer to the wiring diagrams). If no voltage is present, replace the switch.

5   If voltage is present, check for power on the brake light wires at

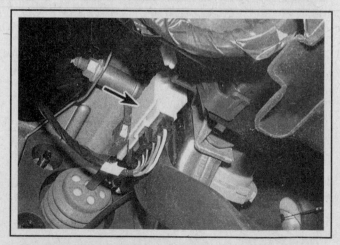

16.1 The brake light switch is mounted on the side of the brake pedal arm

the tail light housings (with the brake pedal depressed). If voltage is not present, repair the circuit between the switch and the brake lights.

6 If voltage is present, check for a bad ground; using a jumper wire connected to a good ground, probe the ground wire terminal at the tail light connector. If the brake lights go on, repair the ground circuit (follow the ground wire from the tail light housing).

7 Keep in mind that the brake light bulbs could be burned out, but the likelihood of all the bulbs being burned out is very slim.

ADJUSTMENT

8 The brake light switch on these vehicles is not adjustable. If it doesn't work as described above, replace it.

REPLACEMENT

9 Remove left-side under-dash panel and the heater/air conditioning duct, if not already done.

10 Unplug the electrical connector from the switch.

11 Remove the clip that retains the switch and pushrod to the pin on the brake pedal arm (see illustration 11.14) and slip the brake light switch off the pin.

12 To install the new switch, reverse the removal procedure. Make sure the retaining clip is properly installed.

Specifications

General

Brake fluid type	See Chapter 1
Front wheel speed sensor resistance	
1999 through 2002	850 to 1230 ohms (at 41 to 116-degrees F)
2003 and later	Not available
Brake pedal travel (maximum)	
With vacuum power brakes	
1999 through 2002	2.75 inches
2003 and later	2.56 inches
With hydraulic power brakes	
1999 through 2002	3.50 inches
2003 and later	3.54 inches

Disc brakes

Minimum pad thickness	See Chapter 1
Brake disc minimum thickness	Cast into disc
Maximum disc runout	0.003 inch
Maximum disc thickness variation	0.001 inch
Drum brakes	
Minimum shoe lining thickness	See Chapter 1
Maximum radial runout	0.0024 inch
Maximum drum diameter	Cast into drum

Torque specifications   Ft-lbs (unless otherwise indicated)

Brake booster mounting nuts (vacuum or hydraulic systems)	
1999 through 2003	27
2004 and later	24
Brake caliper	
Caliper mounting (guide pin) bolts	
Front	
2005 1500 models	74
All others	80
Rear	
1500 models	31
2500 models	80
Caliper mounting bracket bolts	
Front	
1500 models	
1999 through 2004	129
2005	133
2500 models	221
Rear	
1500 models	148
2500 models	
1999 through 2002	128
2003 and later	
JC3/JC5/JH2/JH5	
calipers	148
JH6 calipers	122
JH7 calipers	221
Brake hose-to-caliper inlet fitting bolt	
1999 through 2001	
Front and rear	33
2002 and later	
Front and rear	30
Master cylinder-to-brake booster retaining nuts	27
Parking brake backing plate bolts	
1500	
1999 and 2000	71
2001 and later	100
2500	101
Wheel cylinder bolts	156 in-lbs
Wheel speed sensor (front) mounting screw	156 in-lbs
Wheel lug nuts	See Chapter 1

Section

Reference to other Chapters

10

SUSPENSION AND STEERING SYSTEMS

1 General information

▶ **Refer to illustrations 1.1a, 1.1b, 1.4 and 1.5**

FRONT SUSPENSION

The front suspension (see illustrations) is fully independent. Each wheel is connected to the frame by a steering knuckle, upper and lower balljoints and upper and lower control arms. Coil springs and shock absorbers are used on 2WD pick-up models; 4WD models and 2WD SUV models use shocks and torsion bars. A stabilizer bar connected to the frame and to the two lower control arms reduces body roll during cornering.

REAR SUSPENSION

The rear suspension on pick-up models and 2500 SUV models consists of a pair of multi-leaf springs and two shock absorbers (see illustration). The rear axle assembly is attached to the leaf springs by U-bolts. The front ends of the springs are attached to the frame at the front hangers, through rubber bushings. The rear ends of the springs are attached to the frame by shackles which allow the springs to alter their length as they compress and rebound.

The rear suspension on 1500 SUV models is a five-link design, using coil springs, upper and lower control arms, a lateral link, two shock absorbers and a stabilizer bar (see illustration).

STEERING SYSTEM

The steering system on 2WD 1500 pick-up models consists of a rack-and-pinion steering gear and two adjustable tie-rods. Power assist is standard.

The steering system on other models consists of a recirculating-ball steering gearbox, Pitman arm, idler arm, relay rod, two adjustable tie-rod assemblies (each consisting of an inner tie-rod, adjuster tube and outer tie-rod) and, on some models, a steering damper. When the steering wheel is turned, the gear rotates the Pitman arm which forces the relay rod to one side. The tie-rods, which are connected to the relay rod, transfer steering force to the wheels. The tie-rods are adjustable and are used for toe-in adjustments. The relay rod is supported by the Pitman arm and idler arm. The idler arm pivots on a support attached to the right frame rail. The steering damper, if equipped, is attached to a bracket on the frame and to the relay rod.

An option on 2002 models is a feature called Quadrasteer™, General Motors' name for four-wheel steering. The rear axle on these models is steerable by a rack-and-pinion gear operated by a large electric motor when directed by the rear wheel steering control module, which is mounted above the spare tire. The intent is to improve steerability in low-speed maneuvers, under towing conditions, and provide increased stability at higher speeds. The rather complicated system includes a variety of sensors for yaw/lateral acceleration, steering wheel position, and rear wheel position. A switch on the dash allows the driver to select one of three options: standard two-wheel steering; four-wheel steering; and four-wheel steering for towing situations. In either of the four-wheel steering modes, the module decides which of three steering phases to employ, positive, negative or neutral. In the neutral phase, the rear wheels do not steer, while in the positive phase the rear wheels steer the same direction as the front wheels, and in the negative phase the rear wheels steer in the opposite direction from the front wheels.

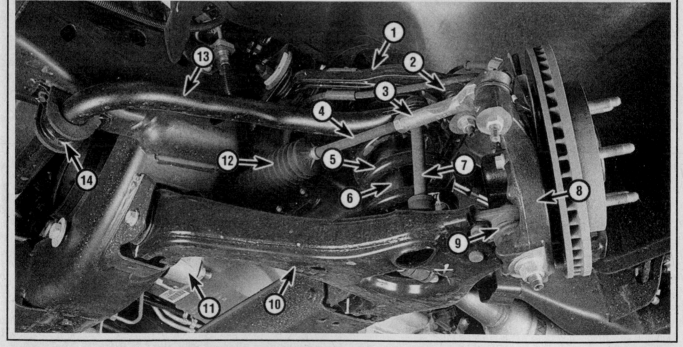

1.1a Front suspension and steering components - 2WD 1500 pick-up

1	Upper control arm	5	Coil spring	8	Steering knuckle	11	Steering gear
2	Upper balljoint	6	Shock absorber	9	Lower balljoint	12	Steering gear boot
3	Tie-rod end	7	Stabilizer bar link	10	Lower control arm	13	Stabilizer bar
4	Tie-rod					14	Stabilizer bar clamp

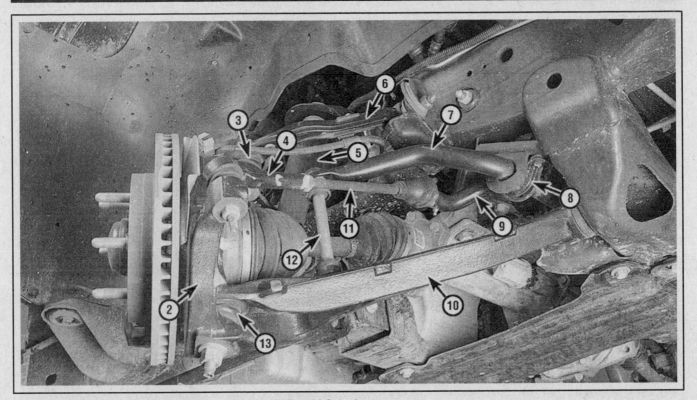

1.1b Front suspension and steering components - 4WD 1500 Suburban

1	Torsion bar	5	Shock absorber	8	Stabilizer bar clamp	11	Tie-rod
2	Steering knuckle	6	Upper control arm	9	Relay rod	12	Stabilizer bar link
3	Upper balljoint	7	Stabilizer bar	10	Lower control arm	13	Lower balljoint
4	Tie-rod end						

1.4 Rear suspension components - 1500 pick-up

1	Leaf spring	3	Spring plate	5	Shock absorber
2	Shackle	4	U-bolt	6	Rear axle

1.5 Rear suspension components - 4WD 1500 Suburban

1	Track bar	4	Trailing arm (lower)	7	Rear axle
2	Stabilizer bar link	5	Stabilizer bar clamp	8	Coil spring
3	Shock absorber	6	Stabilizer bar		

RIDE CONTROL SYSTEMS

Two types of ride control systems are available as an option; the Selectable Ride System and the Real Time Damping/Autoride system, which also incorporates Automatic Leveling Control (ALC). In the Selectable Ride System, the driver can pick between two shock absorber damping levels; normal or firm. This is accomplished through a solenoid inside each shock absorber which changes the size of the damping orifice. In the Real Time Damping/Autoride system, the shock absorber valving is automatically controlled to suit road conditions and driving style. The Automatic Leveling Control keeps the rear of the vehicle at the proper ride height according to the weight of the payload in the vehicle.

PRECAUTIONS

Frequently, when working on the suspension or steering system components, you may come across fasteners which seem impossible to loosen. These fasteners on the underside of the vehicle are continually subjected to water, road grime, mud, etc., and can become rusted or "frozen," making them extremely difficult to remove. In order to unscrew these stubborn fasteners without damaging them (or other components), be sure to use lots of penetrating oil and allow it to soak in for a while. Using a wire brush to clean exposed threads will also ease removal of the nut or bolt and prevent damage to the threads. Sometimes a sharp blow with a hammer and punch is effec-

tive in breaking the bond between a nut and bolt threads, but care must be taken to prevent the punch from slipping off the fastener and ruining the threads. Heating the stuck fastener and surrounding area with a torch sometimes helps too, but isn't recommended because of the obvious dangers associated with fire. Long breaker bars and extension, or "cheater," pipes will increase leverage, but never use an extension pipe on a ratchet - the ratcheting mechanism could be damaged. Sometimes, turning the nut or bolt in the tightening (clockwise) direction first will help to break it loose. Fasteners that require drastic measures to unscrew should always be replaced with new ones.

Since most of the procedures that are dealt with in this Chapter involve jacking up the vehicle and working underneath it, a good pair of jackstands will be needed. A hydraulic floor jack is the preferred type of jack to lift the vehicle, and it can also be used to support certain components during various operations.

✳✳ WARNING:

Never, under any circumstances, rely on a jack to support the vehicle while working on it. Also, whenever any of the suspension or steering fasteners are loosened or removed they must be inspected and, if necessary, replaced with new ones of the same part number or of original equipment quality and design. Torque specifications must be followed for proper reassembly and component retention. Never attempt to heat or straighten suspension or steering components. Instead, replace bent or damaged parts with new ones.

2   Shock absorber (front) - removal and installation

1   Loosen the front wheel lug nuts. Raise the front of the vehicle and support it securely on jackstands, then remove the wheel.

2   Support the outer end of the lower control arm with a floor jack (the shock absorber serves as the down-stop for the suspension). The jack must remain in this position throughout the entire procedure.

3   If equipped with a suspension control system, unlock and unplug the electrical connector from the top of the shock absorber.

2WD MODELS

▶ **Refer to illustrations 2.4 and 2.6**

4   Using a back-up wrench on the stem, remove the shock absorber upper mounting nut (see illustration).

5   Remove the retainer (metal washer) and grommet (rubber washer).

6   Working underneath the vehicle, remove the two bolts that attach the lower end of the shock absorber to the lower control arm (see illustration) and pull the shock out from below.

7   Remove the lower grommet and retainer from the stem.

8   Installation is the reverse of removal. Be sure to tighten the upper mounting nut and the lower mounting bolts to the torque listed in this Chapter's Specifications.

4WD MODELS

▶ **Refer to illustration 2.9**

9   Remove the shock absorber lower mounting nut and bolt (see illustration). Note the direction in which the bolt points.

10   Using a back-up wrench on the stem, remove the shock absorber upper mounting nut (see illustration 2.4).

11   Remove the shock absorber.

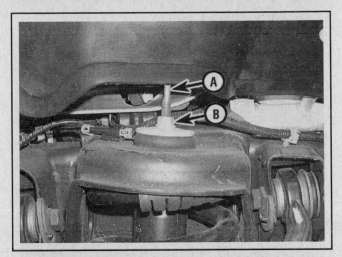

2.4   Hold the shock absorber stem (A) with a wrench to prevent it from turning when the upper mounting nut (B) is loosened (2WD model)

12   Installation is the reverse of removal. Be sure to install the lower mounting bolt so it's pointing in the same direction as it was prior to removal. Tighten all fasteners to the torque listed in this Chapter's Specifications.

ALL MODELS

13   If equipped with a suspension control system, reconnect the electrical connector to the top of the shock absorber.

14   Install the wheels and lug nuts, lower the vehicle and tighten the lug nuts to the torque listed in the Chapter 1 Specifications.

2.6   Shock absorber lower mounting bolts (arrows) - 2WD models

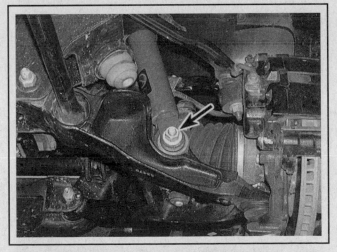

2.9   Shock absorber lower mounting bolt/nut (arrow) - 4WD models

3 Stabilizer bar and bushings (front) - removal and installation

▶ **Refer to illustrations 3.2 and 3.3**

1   Raise the vehicle and support it securely on jackstands. On models so equipped, remove the oil pan skid plate.

2   Remove the nuts from the link bolts and remove the link bolts (see illustration).

➡**Note: Be sure to keep the parts for the left and right sides separate.**

3   Remove the stabilizer bar bracket bolts (see illustration).

4   Remove the stabilizer bar.

5   Remove the rubber bushings.

6   Inspect all parts for wear and damage.

7   When you install the rubber bushings on the stabilizer bar, be sure to position them so the slits face toward the front of the vehicle.

8   Installation is otherwise the reverse of removal. Be sure to tighten all fasteners to the torque listed in this Chapter's Specifications.

3.2 Unscrew the stabilizer bar link bolt while holding the nut with a large wrench

3.3 Remove the stabilizer bar bracket bolts (arrows)

4 Torsion bar - removal and installation

▶ **Refer to illustrations 4.1, 4.2, 4.3, 4.4, 4.5, 4.7a, 4.7b, 4.8 and 4.13**

➡**Note: The torsion bars must be removed as a pair, since the torsion bar crossmember must be removed to provide clearance to slide the bars to the rear.**

1   Raise the front of the vehicle and support it securely on jackstands. Count the number of threads showing on the torsion bar adjuster bolt and mark the relationship of the bolt to the torsion bar adjuster nut (see illustration).

2   In the torsion bar adjuster arm there's a small dimple. Install a puller with its bolt centered on this dimple (see illustration).

4.1 To ensure proper adjustment of the torsion bar upon reassembly, count the number of threads showing on the torsion bar adjuster bolt and mark the relationship of the bolt to the torsion bar adjuster nut as insurance

4.2 Install a two-jaw puller as shown, with the fingers hooked around the flange running along each side of the crossmember; make sure the puller bolt is centered on the dimple in the torsion bar adjuster arm; tighten the puller bolt until all tension is removed from the adjuster bolt

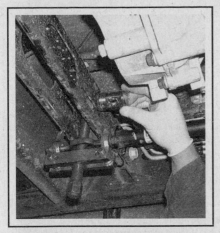

4.3 With tension removed from the adjuster bolt, unscrew the bolt and remove the adjuster nut

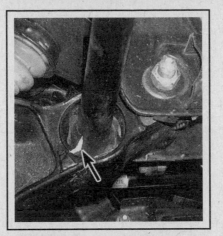

4.4 Mark the relationship of the torsion bar to the lower control arm as shown

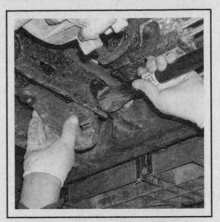

4.5 Slide the torsion bar forward through the lower control arm far enough to pull the rear end of the bar out of the crossmember, then remove the torsion bar adjuster arm

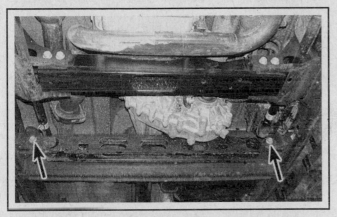

4.7a Remove the torsion bar crossmember mounting bolts from both sides (arrows), then remove the crossmember (1500 model shown)

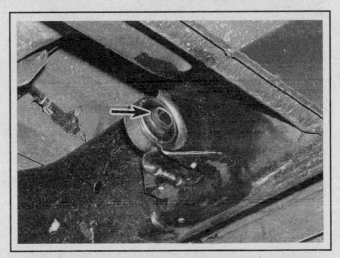

4.7b On 1500 models, the crossmember mounting bushings in the frame are replaceable; they must first be unstaked, then driven out towards the front of the vehicle

3 Turn the puller bolt until all tension is removed from the torsion bar adjuster bolt, then unscrew the torsion bar adjuster bolt and remove the nut (see illustration). Slowly unscrew the puller bolt until the torsion bar unwinds completely and no more tension is on the adjuster arm. Remove the puller.

4 Mark the relationship of the forward end of the torsion bar to the lower control arm (see illustration). Also mark the relationship of the rear end of the torsion bar to the adjuster arm.

5 Push the torsion bar forward, through the lower control arm, until the rear end of the bar clears the crossmember, then remove the torsion bar adjuster arm (see illustration).

6 Repeat Steps 1 through 5 on the other torsion bar.

7 Unbolt the torsion bar crossmember and remove it (see illustration). On 1500 models, inspect the bushings in the frame bosses where the crossmember mounts. If they're worn or otherwise deteriorated they can be replaced. They are staked in place from behind; once unstaked, they can be driven out of their bores toward the front of the vehicle (see illustration). On 2500 models, check the links that secure the torsion bar crossmember. If they're not in good shape, replace them.

8 Slide the torsion bar to the rear, lower the rear end of the bar down and guide it out through the hole in the frame crossmember (see illustration). If the front end of the bar hangs up in the lower control arm, drive it out of the control arm with a brass drift.

4.8 Guide the torsion bar to the rear and down, being careful not to nick it in the process

9 Installation is the reverse of removal, but if both torsion bars were removed, be sure to install them on the proper side of the vehicle (they are marked L and R on the ends). Clean out the hexagonal hole in the lower control arm and lube it with multi-purpose grease before inserting the torsion bar into the arm. Also apply some grease to the hex ends of the torsion bar, to the top of the adjuster arm and to the adjuster bolt. Make sure that the alignment marks you made on the torsion bar and the control arm and adjuster arm line up, and that the torsion bar is completely engaged with the adjuster arm.

10 Tighten the crossmember mounting fasteners to the torque values listed in this Chapter's Specifications.

11 Tighten the torsion bar adjuster bolt until the same number of threads are showing and the marks you made on the adjuster bolt and nut are lined up.

12 Lower the vehicle, jounce the front suspension a couple of times, then roll the vehicle back-and-forth a few feet to settle the suspension.

13 Using a bubble level, measure from the centerline of a pivot bolt for the lower control arm to the level, placed against the bottom of the steering knuckle (just inboard of the lower balljoint stud) (see illustration). This distance is known as the "Z" height, and should be as listed in this Chapter's Specifications. If the "Z" height is not as specified, turn the torsion bar adjusting bolt, in or out as necessary, a little at a time until the dimension is correct. This may take a few tries, and it's important to roll the vehicle back and forth and jounce the front end between adjustments, to settle the suspension and get an accurate reading.

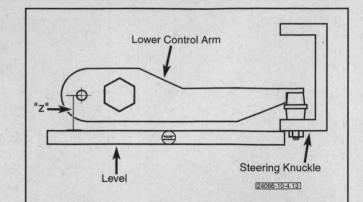

4.13 Place a bubble-type level against the bottom of the steering knuckle, level it, then measure from the level to the centerline of a lower control arm pivot bolt; this distance is called the "Z" height

14 Repeat the Z height check and adjustment procedure on the other lower control arm.

15 Repeat Steps 11 and 12 until both sides of the vehicle are set to the proper ride height.

16 Have the front end alignment checked and, if necessary, adjusted.

5 Coil spring (front) - removal and installation

▶ **Refer to illustration 5.4**

REMOVAL

1 Loosen the wheel lug nuts, raise the vehicle and support it securely on jackstands. Remove the wheel. On models so equipped, remove the oil pan skid plate.

2 Detach the stabilizer bar link from the lower control arm (see Section 3).

3 Support the outer end of the lower control arm with a floor jack,

5.4 Compress the coil spring with an internal-type spring compressor. Warning: *Make sure the tool is rated for the size of coil spring being compressed (diameter, thickness and length of the spring)*

then remove the shock absorber (see Section 2).

4 Install a suitable internal type spring compressor in accordance with the tool manufacturer's instructions (see illustration). Compress the spring enough to relieve all pressure from the spring seats (but don't compress it any more than necessary, or it could be ruined). When you can wiggle the spring, it's compressed enough. (You can buy a suitable spring compressor at most auto parts stores or rent one from a tool rental yard.)

5 Once the spring has been compressed, remove the floor jack, then separate the lower control arm balljoint from the steering knuckle (see Section 7).

6 Pull down on the lower control arm and remove the compressed spring.

7 If the spring is to be replaced, slowly loosen the spring compressor until the spring is fully extended, then install the tool on the new spring.

INSTALLATION

8 Place the insulator on top of the coil spring (the upper end of the spring is the end with the more tightly wound coils).

9 Install the top of the spring into the spring pocket and the bottom in the lower control arm.

10 Connect the lower control arm to the steering knuckle (see Section 7). Support the outer end of the control arm with the floor jack, then remove the spring compressor and install the shock absorber.

11 The remainder of installation is the reverse of removal. Tighten all fasteners to the proper torque values. Tighten the wheel lug nuts to the torque listed in the Chapter 1 Specifications.

12 Have the front end alignment checked and, if necessary, adjusted.

6   Upper control arm - removal and installation

▶ **Refer to illustrations 6.2, 6.3 and 6.5**

REMOVAL

1   Loosen the wheel lug nuts, raise the front of the vehicle and support it securely on jackstands. Remove the wheel. Position a floor jack under the lower control arm in the area underneath the balljoint. Raise the jack slightly to take the spring pressure off the upper control arm.

✷✷ WARNING:

The jack must remain in this position throughout the entire procedure.

6.2 Mark the relationship of the adjusting cams to the frame brackets (arrows)

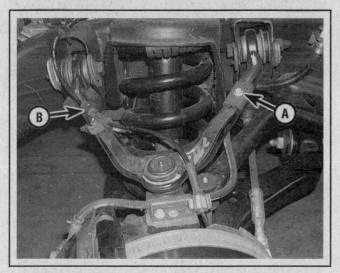

6.3 Unbolt the brake hose bracket from the upper control arm (A), then unclip the wiring harness for the ABS wheel speed sensor (B)

2   Mark the relationship of the adjusting cams to the brackets on the frame (see illustration)

3   Unbolt the brake hose bracket from the upper control arm. Also detach the wheel speed sensor wiring harness from the arm (see illustration).

4   If you're working on a 4WD model, remove the driveaxle (see Chapter 8).

➡**Note: If you use a "picklefork" type balljoint separator it isn't necessary to perform this step.**

5   To disconnect the upper control arm from the steering knuckle, loosen the upper balljoint nut a few turns (don't remove it), install a balljoint remover and break the balljoint loose from the knuckle. Now remove the nut.

➡**Note: If you don't have the proper balljoint removal tool, a "picklefork" type balljoint separator can be used, but keep in mind that this type of tool will probably destroy the balljoint boot (see illustration).**

6   Remove the upper control arm pivot bolts and nuts, noting which way the bolts are installed. Remove the control arm.

INSTALLATION

7   Position the arm in the frame brackets and install the bolts and nuts. Make sure the marks you made prior to disassembly are aligned, then tighten the bolts or nuts to the torque listed in this Chapter's Specifications.

8   Attach the balljoint to the steering knuckle and tighten the ball-stud nut to the torque listed in this Chapter's Specifications.

9   The remainder of installation is the reverse of removal. Tighten the wheel lug nuts to the torque listed in the Chapter 1 Specifications.

10   Have the front end alignment checked and, if necessary, adjusted.

6.5 Separating the upper control arm balljoint from the steering knuckle using a "picklefork" type separator

7   Lower control arm - removal and installation

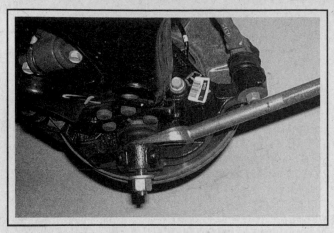

7.7   Separating the lower control arm balljoint with a "picklefork" type balljoint separator

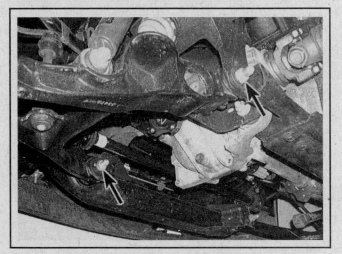

7.8   Remove the lower control arm pivot bolts (arrows) (1500 4WD model)

▶ **Refer to illustrations 7.7 and 7.8**

REMOVAL

1   Loosen the wheel lug nuts, raise the vehicle and support it securely on jackstands placed under the frame rails. Remove the wheel.

2   Remove the stabilizer bar link (see Section 3).

3   If you're working on a 4WD model, remove the driveaxle (see Chapter 8).

4   If you're working on a model with coil spring front suspension, compress the coil spring (see Section 5, Steps 3 and 4).

5   If you're working on a model with torsion bar front suspension, remove the torsion bar (see Section 4).

6   If you're working on a model with torsion bar front suspension, remove the shock absorber lower mounting bolt (see Section 2).

7   To disconnect the lower control arm from the steering knuckle, loosen the balljoint nut a few turns (don't remove it), install a balljoint remover and break the balljoint loose from the knuckle. Now remove the nut.

➡ **Note: If you don't have the proper balljoint removal tool, a "picklefork" type balljoint separator can be used, but keep in mind that this type of tool will probably destroy the balljoint boot (see illustration).**

8   Remove the lower control arm pivot bolts and nuts, noting which way the bolts are installed and, on 4WD models, which way the shoulder on the washers face (they should face the control arm) (see illustration). Pull the lower arm from its frame brackets.

Installation

9   Installation is the reverse of removal. Be sure to tighten all fasteners to the torque values listed in this Chapter's Specifications.

10   Install the wheel and lug nuts. Lower the vehicle and tighten the lug nuts to the torque listed in the Chapter 1 Specifications.

11   If you're working on a model with torsion bar front suspension, be sure to check and adjust the ride ("Z") height (see Section 4).

12   Have the front end alignment checked and, if necessary, adjusted.

8   Balljoints - check and replacement

CHECK

1   Inspect the control arm balljoints for looseness anytime either of them is separated from the steering knuckle. See if you can turn the ballstud in its socket with your fingers. If the balljoint is loose, or if the ballstud can be turned, replace the balljoint. You can also check the balljoints with the suspension assembled as follows.

Upper balljoints

2   Raise the front of the vehicle and support it securely on jackstands placed under the frame rails. Place a floor jack under the lower control arm and raise it slightly.

3   Attach a dial indicator to the upper suspension arm, with the plunger of the indicator touching the steering knuckle, in line with the axle.

4   Grasp the top of the tire and "rock" the tire in-and-out. The dial indicator should indicate no more than 0.030-inch deflection. If the indicated reading exceeds this figure, replace the balljoint.

Lower balljoints

5   Raise the front of the vehicle and support it securely on jackstands placed under the frame rails. Place a floor jack under the lower control arm and raise it slightly.

6   Attach a dial indicator to the lower control arm and position the indicator plunger against the steering knuckle, in-line with the axle.

7   Grasp the bottom of the tire and "rock" the tire in-and-out. The dial indicator should indicate no more than 0.030-inch deflection. If the indicated reading exceeds this figure, replace the balljoint.

REPLACEMENT

Upper balljoint

8   Remove the upper control arm (see Section 6).

9   Take the control arm to an automotive machine shop or other qualified repair facility to have the old balljoint pressed out and the new one pressed in.

10 Install the control arm (see Section 6).

11 Have the front end alignment checked and, if necessary, adjusted.

Lower balljoint

2WD models

12 Remove the lower control arm (see Section 7).

13 Drill out the balljoint rivets as follows: Using a 1/8-inch drill bit, drill a 1/4-inch deep hole in the center of each rivet. Then switch to a 1/2-inch drill bit and finish the job; drill just deep enough to remove the rivet head. Insert a punch through the rivet holes and knock out the rivets.

14 Install the new balljoint on the control arm and secure it with the nuts and bolts supplied with the replacement balljoint. Tighten the nuts to the torque listed in this Chapter's Specifications.

15 Install the control arm (see Section 7).

16 Have the front end alignment checked and, if necessary, adjusted.

4WD models

17 Remove the lower control arm (see Section 7).

18 Take the control arm to an automotive machine shop or other qualified repair facility to have the old balljoint pressed out and the new one pressed in.

19 Install the control arm (see Section 7).

20 Have the front end alignment checked and, if necessary, adjusted.

---

9 Hub and bearing assembly (front) - removal and installation

▶ Refer to illustrations 9.4, 9.5a, 9.5b and 9.6

✳✳ WARNING:

The dust created by the brake system is harmful to your health. Never blow it out with compressed air and don't inhale any of it. Do not, under any circumstances, use petroleum-based solvents to clean brake parts. Use brake system cleaner only.

➡**Note: The hub and bearing assembly is sealed-for-life. If worn or damaged, it must be replaced as a unit.**

REMOVAL

1 Loosen the front wheel lug nuts, raise the vehicle and support it securely on jackstands. Remove the wheel.

2 If you're working on a 4WD model, remove the hub cover, then unscrew the driveaxle/hub nut with a socket and large breaker bar (see Chapter 8). Brace a large prybar across two of the wheel studs or insert a large screwdriver through the center of the brake caliper and into the disc cooling vanes to prevent the hub from turning as the nut is loosened.

3 Remove the brake caliper and hang it out of the way with a piece of wire, then remove the caliper mounting bracket (see Chapter 9). Pull the disc off the hub.

9.4 The ABS wheel speed sensor is retained to the hub by one screw; remove the screw and pull the sensor straight out (don't pry on it)

4 Remove the wheel speed sensor from the hub (see illustration).

5 Working from the back side of the steering knuckle, remove the hub retaining bolts from the steering knuckle (see illustrations).

9.5a The hub and bearing assembly on 1500 models is retained by three bolts - on 2500 models it's retained by four bolts

9.5b On 4WD models there's not much room to get a wrench onto the hub bolt heads, especially when they are backed-out a few turns. So, as the bolts are unscrewed, push in on the driveaxle and pull the hub and bearing out of the knuckle to provide clearance

Remove the disc shield.

6   Remove the hub from the steering knuckle. If you're working on a 4WD model, pull the assembly off the driveaxle splines (see illustration).

※ CAUTION:

Be careful not to pull outward on the driveaxle, as this could separate the inner CV joint components.

9.6 When removing the hub assembly on a 4WD model, don't pull out on the driveaxle; the inner CV joint could become separated

10 Wheel studs - replacement

10.3 Use a small press tool such as this to push the stud out of the flange

11 Steering knuckle - removal and installation

1   Loosen the wheel lug nuts, raise the vehicle and support it securely on jackstands. Remove the wheel.

2   If you're working on a 4WD model, remove the hub cover, then unscrew the driveaxle/hub nut with a socket and large breaker bar (see Chapter 8). Brace a large prybar across two of the wheel studs or insert a large screwdriver through the center of the brake caliper and into the disc cooling vanes to prevent the hub from turning as the nut is loosened.

If the driveaxle splines stick in the hub, attach a two-jaw puller to the hub flange and push the stub axle out of the hub. The hub assembly should come right out of the steering knuckle, but if it doesn't, tap it from side-to-side to free it.

INSTALLATION

7   Clean the mating surfaces on the steering knuckle, bearing flange and knuckle bore. If you're working on a 2500 model, make sure the O-ring came out with the hub assembly, and be sure to install a new O-ring on the back of the hub before fitting the hub to the steering knuckle.

8   Insert the hub and bearing assembly into the steering knuckle and, on 4WD models, onto the end of the driveaxle.

➡Note: On 4WD models, lubricate the splines of the driveaxle with multi-purpose grease before installing the hub. Position the disc shield and install the bolts, tightening them to the torque listed in this Chapter's Specifications.

9   Insert the ABS wheel speed sensor into it's hole in the hub, tightening the bolt to the torque listed in the Chapter 9 Specifications.

10 Install the brake disc, caliper mounting bracket and caliper (see Chapter 9).

11 On 4WD models, install the hub nut and tighten it securely to seat the driveaxle in the hub. Prevent the axle from turning by inserting a screwdriver through the caliper and into a disc cooling vane.

12 Install the wheel, lower the vehicle and tighten the lug nuts to the torque listed in the Chapter 1 Specifications.

13 If you're working on a 4WD model, tighten the driveaxle/hub nut to the torque listed in the Chapter 8 Specifications.

▶ Refer to illustration 10.3

➡Note: This procedure applies to both the front and rear wheel studs.

1   Loosen the wheel lug nuts, raise the vehicle and support it securely on jackstands. Remove the wheel.

2   Remove the brake disc (see Chapter 9).

3   Push the stud out of the hub flange with a press tool (see illustration).

4   Insert the new stud into the hub flange from the back side and install some flat washers and a lug nut on the stud.

5   Tighten the lug nut until the stud is seated in the flange.

6   Reinstall the disc and caliper (see Chapter 9). Install the wheel and lug nuts. Lower the vehicle and tighten the lug nuts to the torque listed in the Chapter 1 Specifications.

3   Support the lower control arm with a floor jack. Raise the jack slightly.

※ WARNING:

The jack must remain in this position throughout the entire procedure.

4   Remove the brake caliper and brake disc (see Chapter 9). Hang the caliper out of the way on a piece of wire (don't disconnect the brake hose).

5   Remove the hub and bearing assembly (see Section 9).

6   Remove the disc splash shield from the steering knuckle.

7   Unbolt the brake hose bracket from the top of the steering knuckle.

8   Disconnect the tie-rod end from the steering knuckle (see Section 20).

9   Disconnect the balljoints from the steering knuckle (see Sec-tions 6 and 7).

10 Remove the steering knuckle.

11 Installation is the reverse of removal. Be sure to tighten the balljoint and tie-rod end fasteners to the torque values listed in this Chapter's Specifications. Tighten the caliper mounting bolts to the torque values listed in the Chapter 9 Specifications. Tighten the driveaxle/hub nut to the torque listed in the Chapter 8 Specifications (4WD models). Tighten the wheel lug nuts to the torque listed in the Chapter 1 Specifications.

12   Shock absorber (rear) - removal and installation

▶ **Refer to illustrations 12.4a and 12.4b**

1   Raise the rear of the vehicle and support it securely on jack-stands placed underneath the frame rails. Block the front wheels so the vehicle doesn't roll off the stands.

➡**Note: It isn't necessary to remove the rear wheels, but doing so will improve access to the shock absorbers.**

2   If the vehicle is equipped with Real Time Damping or Selectable Ride system, disconnect the electrical connector and the air line, if equipped, from the shock absorber.

3   Support the rear axle with a floor jack placed under the axle tube closest to the shock absorber being removed.

4   Remove the shock absorber upper and lower mounting fasteners (see illustrations).

5   Remove the shock absorber.

6   Installation is the reverse of removal. Tighten all fasteners to the torque values listed in this Chapter's Specifications.

12.4a Rear shock absorber upper mounting nut/bolt

12.4b Rear shock absorber lower mounting nut/bolt

13   Stabilizer bar and bushings (rear) - removal and installation

▶ **Refer to illustrations 13.2 and 13.4**

1   Loosen the rear wheel lug nuts, raise the rear of the vehicle and support it securely on jackstands. Block the front wheels to keep the vehicle from rolling off the stands. Remove the rear wheels.

2   Remove the stabilizer bar link-to-frame nuts/bolts (see illustration).

3   Remove the nuts from the lower ends of the links, then separate the link from the bar.

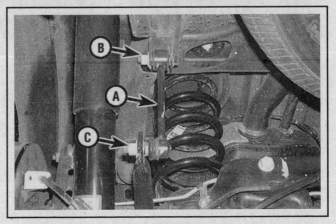

13.2 Stabilizer bar link mounting details

A   Link
B   Link-to-frame bolt/nut
C   Link-to-stabilizer bar nut

13.4 Remove the stabilizer bar clamp bolts from the axle housing

4 Remove the stabilizer bar clamp bolts (see illustration) and remove the stabilizer bar assembly.

5 Inspect the stabilizer bar bushings and link bushings for cracks, tears and other signs of deterioration. Replace as necessary.

6 Installation is the reverse of removal. Be sure to tighten all fasteners to the torque listed in this Chapter's Specifications.

14 Leaf spring - removal and installation

▶ Refer to illustrations 14.7, 14.8 and 14.9

REMOVAL

1 If you're removing the left leaf spring, relieve the fuel system pressure (see Chapter 4).

2 Loosen the rear wheel lug nuts, raise the rear of the vehicle and support it securely on jackstands placed underneath the frame rails. Block the front wheels to keep the vehicle from rolling off the stands. Remove the rear wheels.

3 Remove the trailer hitch, if so equipped.

4 If you're removing the left leaf spring, remove the fuel tank (see Chapter 4).

5 If you're removing the right leaf spring, unbolt the rear portion of the exhaust system from the collector flange, then detach the system from its rubber hangers to position it toward the center of the vehicle (this is to provide clearance for the front mounting bolt removal).

6 Support the axle with a floor jack placed under the axle tube and raise it slightly to take the weight of the axle.

7 Remove the four U-bolt nuts and washers (see illustration), the spring plate and the two U-bolts. Discard the U-bolts (the manufacturer recommends using new ones during installation).

8 At the front end of the spring, remove the nut and bolt from the spring-to-front bracket (see illustration).

9 At the rear end of the spring, remove the spring shackle-to-frame nut and bolt (see illustration).

10 Lower the jack slightly and remove the spring assembly. If necessary, remove the shackle from the spring.

11 If the bushings at the ends of the spring are worn or deteriorated, an automotive machine shop or dealer service department can press the old ones out and press new ones in.

INSTALLATION

12 If removed, install the shackle to the spring, but don't tighten the nut yet.

13 Place the spring in position and install the forward mounting bolt and nut, but don't tighten the nut yet.

14 Raise the axle on the jack until it mates properly with the spring. Install the spring plate and new U-bolts, then install the nuts and washers. Tighten the U-bolt nuts to the torque listed in this Chapter's

14.7 Remove the four U-bolt nuts and washers, then remove the spring plate and the two U-bolts

14.8 At the front end of the leaf spring, remove the nut and bolt that attach the spring to the frame bracket

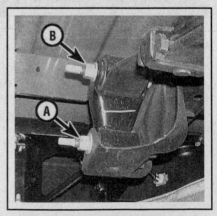

14.9 At the rear end of the spring, remove the spring shackle-to-frame nut and bolt (A); the shackle-to-spring nut and bolt (B) can't be removed until the spring and shackle are removed from the vehicle

Specifications.

15 Tighten the front mounting bolt/nut, the shackle-to-frame bolt/nut and the spring-to-shackle bolt/nut to the torque values listed in this Chapter's Specifications.

16 The remainder of installation is the reverse of the removal procedure.

17 Install the wheel and lug nuts. Lower the vehicle and tighten the lug nuts to the torque listed in the Chapter 1 Specifications.

15 Coil spring (rear) - removal and installation

REMOVAL

1 Loosen the rear wheel lug nuts. Raise the rear of the vehicle and support it securely on jackstands placed underneath the frame rails. Block the front wheels to prevent the vehicle from rolling. Remove the rear wheels.

2 If equipped with Real Time Damping, disconnect the sensor link.

3 Support the rear axle housing with a floor jack placed underneath the differential.

4 Disconnect the rigid brake lines from the junction block on the rear brake hose, then unbolt the junction block from the axle housing (see Chapter 9). Plug the hose fitting to prevent excessive fluid loss and the entry of air and contamination.

5 Detach the rear axle vent hose.

6 Unbolt the track bar from the bracket on the rear axle housing (see Section 16).

7 Disconnect the lower ends of the shock absorbers from the axle housing (see Sec-tion 12).

8 Slowly lower the floor jack until the coil springs are fully extended, then remove the springs and insulators.

9 Check the condition of the insulators. If they're cracked, hardened or otherwise deteriorated, replace them.

INSTALLATION

10 Place the springs and insulators in position on the axle and raise the axle until the ends of the springs engage properly with their upper mounts (an assistant would be helpful).

11 Continue to raise the axle until the shock absorbers can be connected to the axle housing. Install the bolts and nuts, tightening them to the torque listed in this Chapter's Specifications.

12 Connect the track bar to the axle, tightening the bolt to the torque listed in this Chapter's Specifications.

13 Reattach the vent hose.

14 Reconnect the brake lines to the brake hose, then connect the hose to the axle housing. Bleed the rear brakes (see Chapter 9).

15 If equipped with Real Time Damping, reconnect the sensor link.

16 Install the wheels and lug nuts. Lower the vehicle and tighten the lug nuts to the torque listed in the Chapter 1 Specifications.

16 Suspension arms (rear) - removal and installation

➡Note: This procedure applies to models with coil spring rear suspension only.

TRAILING ARMS

▶ Refer to illustrations 16.2 and 16.2b

❋ WARNING:

Remove and install only one arm at a time. This will prevent the axle housing from shifting on the jack.

1 Loosen the rear wheel lug nuts. Raise the rear of the vehicle and support it securely on jackstands placed underneath the frame rails. Block the front wheels to prevent the vehicle from rolling. Remove the wheel(s).

2 Support the rear axle with a floor jack, then remove the nuts, washers and bolts from each end of the trailing arm (see illustrations)

3 Remove the arm. Check the bushings in the arm for cracking, hardness or other signs of deterioration. If the bushings are in need of replacement, check with your local auto parts store or dealer parts department regarding the availability of replacement bushings. If replacement bushings are available, take the arm and the bushings to an automotive machine shop or other qualified repair facility to have

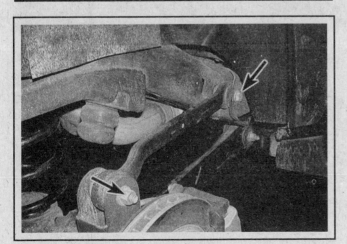

16.2a Upper trailing arm mounting details

16.2b Lower trailing arm mounting details

the old ones pressed out and the new ones pressed in.

4   Installation is the reverse of removal. Before tightening the bolts/nuts, raise the rear axle with a floor jack to simulate normal ride height, then tighten the fasteners to the torque listed in this Chapter's Specifications.

TRACK BAR

▶ **Refer to illustration 16.7**

5   Raise the rear of the vehicle and support it securely on jackstands placed underneath the frame rails. Block the front wheels to prevent the vehicle from rolling.

6   Detach the parking brake cable from the clips on the arm.

7   Remove the nuts/bolts from each end of the bar (see illustration).

8   Remove the bar. Check the bushings in the bar for cracking, hardness or other signs of deterioration. If the bushings are in need of replacement, check with your local auto parts store or dealer parts department regarding the availability of replacement bushings. If replacement bushings are available, take the bar and the bushings to an automotive machine shop or other qualified repair facility to have the old ones pressed out and the new ones pressed in.

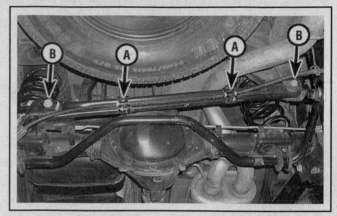

16.7 Track bar mounting details

A   Parking brake cable clip   *B   Mounting bolt*

9   Installation is the reverse of removal. Before tightening the bolts/nuts, raise the rear axle with a floor jack to simulate normal ride height, then tighten the fasteners to the torque listed in this Chapter's Specifications.

---

17 Steering wheel - removal and installation

※※ **WARNING:**

These models are equipped with airbags. Always disable the airbag system (see Chapter 12) before working in the vicinity of any airbag system component to avoid the possibility of accidental deployment of the airbag, which could cause personal injury.

REMOVAL

▶ **Refer to illustrations 17.3a, 17.3b, 17.4, 17.6, 17.7 and 17.8**

1   Park the vehicle with the wheels pointing straight ahead. Disconnect the cable from the negative terminal of the battery.

※※ **CAUTION:**

On models equipped with the "Theftlock" audio system, be sure the lockout feature is turned off before performing any procedure which requires disconnecting the battery (see the information at the front of this manual).

2   Refer to Chapter 12 and disable the airbag system.

3   Turn the steering wheel 90-degrees to gain access to the hole in the backside (the side facing the dash) of the steering wheel. Insert a screwdriver into the hole for the spring clip that retains the airbag module (see illustrations) and push the spring aside to release the pin. Now turn the steering wheel 180-degrees in the other direction and do the same thing to release the other pin.

17.3a To release the pins that secure the airbag module to the steering wheel, insert a screwdriver into the holes in the back side of the steering wheel . . .

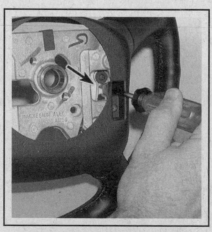

17.3b . . . and pry each spring clip (arrow) aside to clear the pin (there are two pins; one on each side of the steering wheel) - steering wheel removed for clarity

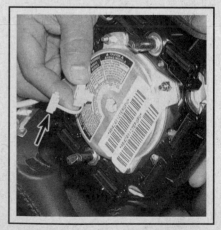

17.4 Pry up the connector lock (arrow), then pull the connector out of the airbag module

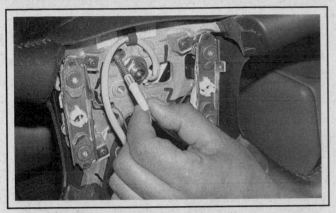

17.6 To unplug the electrical connector for the horn, push it in and turn it counterclockwise to release it

4   Pry up the connector lock and unplug the yellow electrical connector from the module (see illustration). Set the module aside in a safe, isolated area, with the airbag side of the module facing UP.

✳✳ WARNING:

When carrying the airbag module, keep the driver's (trim) side of it away from your body, and when you set it down, make sure the driver's side is facing up.

5   Center the steering wheel.
6   Unplug the electrical connector for the horn (see illustration).
7   Remove the steering wheel retaining nut and mark the position of the steering wheel to the shaft, if marks don't already exist or don't line up (see illustration).
8   Use a puller to detach the steering wheel from the shaft (see illustration).

✳✳ WARNING:

Do not hammer on the shaft or the puller in an attempt to loosen the wheel from the shaft.

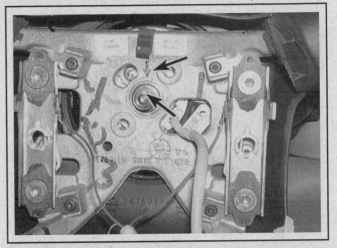

17.7 Check to see if there are alignment marks on the steering wheel and the steering shaft; if there are none, make your own

9   Lift the steering wheel from the shaft.

✳✳ WARNING:

Don't allow the steering shaft to turn with the steering wheel removed. If the shaft turns, the airbag clockspring will become uncentered, which may cause the wire inside to break when the vehicle is returned to service.

INSTALLATION

▶ **Refer to illustrations 17.10, 17.11, 17.12a and 17.12b**

10   Before installing the steering wheel, make sure the airbag clockspring is centered (see illustration).

11   If the airbag system clockspring is not centered, remove the steering column covers (see Chapter 11). Remove the snap-ring (see illustration) and lift the clockspring off the steering column. You may have to cut a plastic wire-tie securing the clockspring harness to the steering column.

17.8 Remove the steering wheel with a puller that bolts to the hub of the wheel - do not try to hammer the steering wheel off or you will damage the column

17.10 When the clockspring is centered, the arrow on the housing will be aligned with the arrow on the hub

17.11 The clockspring is retained to the steering shaft with a snap-ring

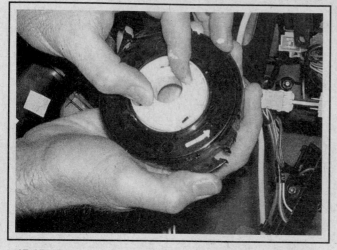

17.12a To center the clockspring, hold it with its underside facing up, depress the spring lock and rotate the hub in the direction of the arrow until it stops, then turn it in the opposite direction 2-1/2 turns

17.12b On clocksprings with a centering window, the clockspring is centered when the window (A) appears yellow and the two arrows (B) are aligned

12 Center the clockspring:

➡**Note: There are two types of clocksprings, alignment window type and windowless type. Each type is equipped with either a lock spring or without a lock spring on the back of the assembly. Follow the directions carefully depending on the type.**

a) *If your clockspring does not have a window on the front, turn it over and depress the spring lock (if equipped) on the back, then rotate the hub in the direction of the arrow on the housing until it stops (don't apply too much force). Now turn the hub 2-1/2 turns in the opposite direction until the arrows on the front are aligned (see illustration 17.10), release the spring lock tab. Proceed to the next Step.*

b) *If your clockspring has a window on the front, turn it over and depress the spring lock (if equipped) on the back, hold it face up and turn the hub clockwise until it stops (don't apply excessive force). Now slowly turn the hub counterclockwise at least two*

turns until the window turns yellow and the arrows on the hub and the housing are in alignment (see illustrations). Proceed to the next step.

13 Install the clockspring and snap-ring. Secure the wiring harness with a new wire-tie, making sure the harness isn't kinked. Install the steering column covers. Install the wheel on the steering shaft, aligning the marks.

14 Install the steering wheel nut and tighten it to the torque listed in this Chapter's Specifications.

15 Plug in the horn wire, push down and twist it clockwise to lock it in place.

16 Connect the airbag connector to the back of the airbag module. Make sure the connector lock is securely engaged.

17 Position the airbag module on the steering wheel and push it in until the pins on the module engage with the spring clips.

18 Refer to Chapter 12 for the procedure to enable the airbag system.

18 Steering column - removal and installation

▶ **Refer to illustrations 18.6, 18.7, 18.8a and 18.8b**

❋❋ **WARNING:**

The models covered by this manual are equipped with airbags. Always disable the airbag system when working in the vicinity of airbag system components (see Chapter 12).

REMOVAL

1 Park the vehicle with the wheels pointing straight ahead. Disconnect the cable from the negative terminal of the battery. Disable the airbag system (see Chapter 12).

2 Remove the steering wheel (see Section 17), then turn the ignition key to the LOCK position to prevent the steering shaft from turning.

❋❋ **CAUTION:**

If this is not done, the airbag clockspring could be damaged.

3 Remove the knee bolster and the reinforcement behind it (see Chapter 11). On models with a column-mounted shifter, detach the shift cable from the shift lever on the column (see Chapter 7B).

4 If the vehicle is equipped with a tilt column, unscrew the tilt lever.

5 Remove the steering column shrouds (see Chapter 11).

6 Disconnect the electrical connectors for the steering column harness and pry out the retaining clip securing the harness to the column.

18.6　Body Control Module (BCM) mounting screws (arrows)

18.7　Upper intermediate shaft-to-steering column shaft bolt and nut; don't attempt to unscrew the bolt, since it's staked to an anti-rotation bracket. Unscrew the nut (arrow) then pull the bolt out

Remove the Body Control Module (BCM) and bracket from below the steering column (see illustration). Follow the yellow wiring harness from the airbag clockspring and disconnect it from the BCM.

　7　Remove the shaft coupler nut and remove the bolt securing the steering shaft to the upper intermediate shaft (see illustration).

➡**Note: Unscrew the nut, not the bolt.**

Mark the relationship of the intermediate shaft to the steering column shaft.

　8　Remove the steering column mounting nuts (see illustrations), lower the column and pull it to the rear, making sure nothing is still connected. Separate the intermediate shaft from the steering shaft and remove the column.

INSTALLATION

➡**Note: If a new column is being installed, check to see if a shipping lock pin is present. If so, remove it.**

　9　Guide the steering column into position, connect the intermediate shaft, then install the mounting nuts, but don't tighten them yet.

　10　Install the coupler bolt and nut, then tighten the nut to the torque listed in this Chapter's Specifications.

　11　Tighten the column mounting nuts to the torque listed in this Chapter's Specifications.

　12　The remainder of installation is the reverse of removal. Adjust the shift cable following the procedures described in Chapter 7B.

18.8a　Remove the steering column lower mounting nuts (arrows)

18.8b　Remove the steering column upper mounting nuts (arrows)

19 Intermediate shaft - removal and installation

▶ **Refer to illustration 19.3**

1   Park the vehicle with the wheels pointing straight ahead. Disconnect the cable from the negative terminal of the battery. Disable the airbag system (see Chapter 12).

2   Turn the ignition key to the LOCK position to prevent the steering shaft from turning.

✳✳ CAUTION:

If this is not done, the airbag clockspring could be damaged.

3   Working under the hood, mark the relationship of the upper intermediate shaft to the lower intermediate shaft (see illustration). Remove the shaft coupler nut and remove the bolt securing the lower intermediate shaft to the upper intermediate shaft.

4   Mark the relationship of the lower intermediate shaft to the steering gear input shaft, then remove the intermediate shaft-to-steering gear pinch bolt (see Section 23).

5   Slide the lower portion of the intermediate shaft downwards and off the upper intermediate shaft, the remove the lower shaft from the steering gear.

6   If it is necessary to remove the upper portion of the intermediate shaft, refer to Section 18, Step 7.

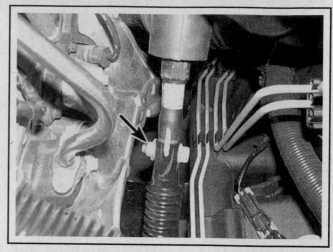

19.3 Mark the relationship of the upper and lower halves of the intermediate shaft, then remove the coupler nut and bolt

7   Installation is the reverse of removal. Be sure to align the matchmarks and tighten the coupler bolt/nut and the shaft-to-steering gear pinch bolt to the torque listed in this Chapter's Specifications.

20 Tie-rod ends - removal and installation

▶ **Refer to illustrations 20.2, 20.3a and 20.3b**

➡**Note: This procedure applies to 2WD and 4WD models.**

REMOVAL

1   Loosen the wheel lug nuts, raise the front of the vehicle and support it securely on jackstands. Apply the parking brake and block the rear wheels to keep the vehicle from rolling off the jackstands. Remove the wheel.

2   Break loose the tie-rod end jam nut (see illustration). Don't back the nut off; once it has just been loosened, it will serve as the point to which the tie-rod end will be threaded. If you are removing the tie-rod end to replace the steering gear boot on a model with rack-and-pinion steering, mark the threads of the tie-rod on the inner side of the nut.

3   Loosen (but don't remove) the nut on the tie-rod end ballstud and disconnect the tie-rod end from the steering knuckle arm with a puller (see illustrations).

4   Unscrew the tie-rod end from the tie-rod.

20.2 Hold the tie-rod end with a wrench while loosening the jam nut

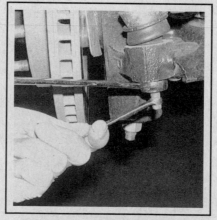

20.3a If the ballstud turns while attempting to loosen the nut, hold it stationary with a small wrench

20.3b Back-off the ballstud nut a few turns, then separate the tie-rod end from the steering knuckle with a puller (leaving the nut on the ballstud will prevent the tie-rod end from separating violently)

INSTALLATION

5   If the jam nut was removed, thread it onto the tie-rod until it meets the mark applied in Step 2. Thread the tie-rod end onto the tie-rod until it contacts the jam nut, then connect the tie-rod end to the steering arm. Install the ballstud nut and tighten it to the torque listed in this Chapter's Specifications.

6   Tighten the jam nut securely and install the wheel. Lower the vehicle and tighten the lug nuts to the torque listed in the Chapter 1 Specifications.

7   Have the front end alignment checked and, if necessary, adjusted.

21   Steering gear boots - replacement

▶ **Refer to illustration 21.4**

➡ **Note: This procedure applies to models with rack-and-pinion steering only.**

1   Loosen the wheel lug nuts, raise the front of the vehicle and support it securely on jackstands. Remove the wheels.
2   Remove the tie-rod ends from the tie-rods (see Section 20).
3   Remove the tie-rod end jam nuts.

✳✳ WARNING:

The manufacturer recommends replacing the jam nuts with new ones whenever they are removed.

4   Remove the outer boot clamps with a pair of pliers, then cut off the inner boot clamps and discard them (see illustration).
5   Mark the location of the breather tube (if used) in relation to the rack assembly, then remove the boots and the tube. Apply some grease to the exposed ends of the toothed rack before installing new boots.
6   Install a new clamp on the inner end of the boot.
7   Apply multi-purpose grease to groove on the tie-rod (where the outer end of the boot will ride) and the mounting grooves on the steering gear (where the inner boot end will be clamped).
8   Line up the breather tube with the marks made during removal and slide the new boot onto the steering gear housing.

21.4 The outer clamp (A) on the steering gear boot can be squeezed and removed with a pair of pliers; the inner clamp (B) must be cut off

9   Make sure the boot isn't twisted, then tighten the new inner clamp.
10 Install the outer clamps and tie-rod end jam nuts.
11 Install the tie-rod ends (see Section 20).
12 Have the front-end alignment checked and, if necessary, adjusted.

22   Steering linkage - inspection, removal and installation

➡ **Note: This Section applies to all models except those with rack-and-pinion steering.**

INSPECTION

▶ **Refer to Illustration 22.4**

1   The steering linkage (see illustration 1.1b) connects the steering gear to the front wheels and keeps the wheels in proper relation to each other. The linkage consists of the Pitman arm, the idler arm, the relay rod, two adjustable tie-rods and, on some models, a steering damper. The Pitman arm, which is fastened to the steering gear shaft, moves the relay rod back-and-forth. The relay rod is supported on the other end by a frame-mounted idler arm. The back-and-forth motion of the relay rod is transmitted to the steering knuckles through a pair of tie-rod assemblies.
2   Unlock the steering wheel.
3   Raise the front of the vehicle and support it securely with jackstands placed underneath the frame rails.
4   Grasp the relay rod and the tie-rod and try to push them together

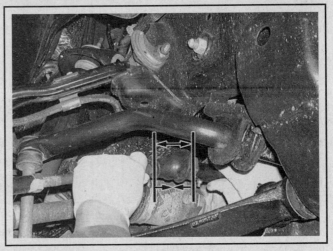

22.4 Try to move the tie-rod in-and-out of the relay rod - if there is more than 1/32-inch of play between the tie-rod and relay rod, replace the relay rod assembly

and pull them apart (see illustration). If there is more than 1/32-inch of play, replace the relay rod/tie-rod assembly. Now push up and pull down on the tie-rod end; if it moves more than 1/8-inch, replace the tie-rod end.

5   Push up, then pull down on the relay rod end of the idler arm, exerting a force of approximately 25 pounds each way. Measure the total distance the end of the arm travels. If the play is greater than 5/64-inch, replace the idler arm.

6   Check for torn ballstud boots and bent or damaged linkage components.

REMOVAL AND INSTALLATION

Tie-rod end

7   Refer to Section 20 for the tie-rod end replacement procedure.

Tie-rod

8   The tie-rods are an integral part of the relay rod and cannot be replaced separately.

Relay rod

9   Raise the vehicle and support it securely on jackstands. Apply the parking brake.

10   Detach the tie-rod ends from the steering knuckle arms, then remove the tie-rod ends from the tie-rods (see Section 20).

11   If equipped with a steering damper, separate the damper from the relay rod.

12   Separate the relay rod from the Pitman arm.

13   Separate the relay rod from the idler arm.

14   Installation is the reverse of the removal procedure. Use new nuts on all of the ballstuds. If the ballstuds spin when attempting to tighten the nuts, force them into the tapered holes with a large pair of pliers. Be sure to tighten all of the nuts to the torque listed in this Chapter's Specifications.

Idler arm

▶ **Refer to illustration 22.16**

15   Raise the vehicle and support it securely on jackstands. Apply the parking brake.

16   Loosen but do not remove the idler arm-to-relay rod nut (see illustration).

17   Separate the idler arm from the relay rod with a two jaw puller. Remove the nut. Discard the nut - don't reuse it.

18   Remove the idler arm-to-frame bolts (see illustration 22.16).

19   To install the idler arm, position it on the frame and install the bolts, tightening them to the torque listed in this Chapter's Specifications.

20   Insert the idler arm ballstud into the relay rod and install a new nut. Tighten the nut to the torque listed in this Chapter's Specifications. If the ballstud spins when attempting to tighten the nut, force it into the tapered hole with a large pair of pliers.

Pitman arm

▶ **Refer to illustrations 22.25 and 22.26**

21   Raise the vehicle and support it securely on jackstands.

22   Remove the relay rod nut from the Pitman arm ballstud. Discard the nut - don't reuse it.

23   Using a puller, separate the relay rod from the Pitman arm ballstud.

24   Remove the steering gear (see Section 23).

25   Remove the Pitman arm nut and washer and discard the nut - use a new one during installation (see illustration). Mark the Pitman arm and the steering gear shaft to ensure proper alignment at reassembly time (only if the same Pitman arm is going to be used).

26   Remove the Pitman arm with a Pitman arm puller or a two-jaw puller (see illustration).

27   Inspect the ballstud threads for damage. Inspect the ballstud seal for excessive wear. Clean the threads on the ballstud.

28   Installation is the reverse of removal. Make sure the marks you made on the Pitman arm and Pitman shaft are aligned, and be sure to use a new nut.

STEERING DAMPER

29   Inspect the steering damper for fluid leakage. A slight film of fluid near the shaft seal is normal, but if there's excessive fluid present and

22.16 Remove the idler arm ballstud nut (A) and separate the ballstud from the relay rod with a puller, then remove the idler arm mounting nuts and bolts (B)

22.25 With the steering gear secured in a vise, use a prybar to hold the Pitman arm and break loose the Pitman arm nut. Be sure to mark the relationship of the Pitman arm to the steering gear shaft before pulling it off

22.26 Remove the Pitman arm with a Pitman arm puller (shown here) or a heavy-duty two-jaw puller

it's obviously coming from the steering damper, replace the damper.

30 Inspect the steering damper bushing for excessive wear. If it's in bad shape, replace the damper.

31 To test the damper itself, disconnect it from the relay rod. Using as much travel as possible, extend and compress the damper. The resistance should be smooth and constant for each stroke. If any binding, dead spots or unusual noises are present, replace the damper.

32 Remove the damper ballstud-to-relay rod nut. Separate the damper from the relay rod using a small puller.

33 Remove the steering damper mounting bolt and nut, then remove

the damper.

34 Installation is the reverse of removal.

✳✳ WARNING:

The manufacturer recommends using new nuts on the ballstuds during installation.

Tighten the fasteners to the torque values listed in this Chapter's Specifications.

23 Steering gear - removal and installation

✳✳ WARNING:

DO NOT allow the steering column shaft to rotate with the steering gear removed or damage to the airbag system could occur. As a method of preventing the shaft from turning, wrap the seat belt around the rim of the steering wheel and buckle the belt in place.

MODELS WITH RACK-AND-PINION STEERING GEAR

▶ **Refer to illustrations 23.3, 23.5 and 23.6**

1 Loosen the front wheel lug nuts, raise the front of the vehicle and support it securely on jackstands. Apply the parking brake. Remove the wheels.

2 Remove the under-vehicle splash shield. Also remove the skid plate bolts and the skid plate, if equipped. Refer to Section 3 and remove the stabilizer bar.

3 Mark the relationship of the intermediate shaft coupler to the steering gear input shaft and remove the pinch bolt (see illustration).

4 Detach the tie-rod ends from the steering knuckles (see Section 20).

5 Position a drain pan under the steering gear. Using a flare-nut wrench, if available, unscrew the power steering pressure and return lines from the steering gear (see illustration). Cap the lines to prevent leakage.

6 Unscrew the mounting nuts, remove the washers and slide the

23.3 Remove the pinch bolt from the lower end of the intermediate shaft

bolts forward into the frame. Lower the steering gear from the vehicle (see illustration).

7 Installation is the reverse of removal. Be sure to tighten all fasteners to the torque values listed in this Chapter's Specifications. Tighten the wheel lug nuts to the torque listed in the Chapter 1 Specifications. Check the power steering fluid level and add some, if necessary (see Chapter 1), then bleed the system as described in Section 25.

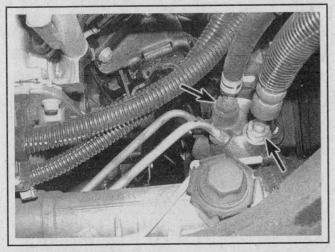

23.5 Unscrew the pressure and return line fittings from the power steering gear

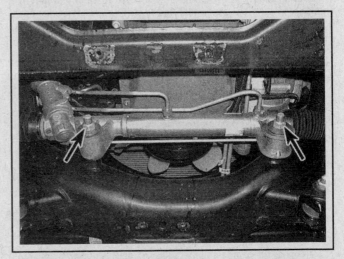

23.6 Rack-and-pinion steering gear mounting nuts/bolts

MODELS WITH RECIRCULATING BALL STEERING GEAR

8   Raise the front of the vehicle and support it securely on jackstands. Apply the parking brake.

9   Remove the under-vehicle splash shield. Also remove the skid plate bolts and the skid plate, if equipped.

10 Mark the relationship of the intermediate shaft coupler to the steering gear input shaft, then remove the pinch bolt from the coupler.

11 Position a drain pan under the steering gear, then unscrew the power steering lines from the steering gear. Use a flare-nut wrench, if available, to prevent rounding-off the fittings.

12 Separate the relay rod from the Pitman arm.

13 Remove the steering gear retaining bolts from the frame rail, then detach the steering gear from the frame and remove it.

14 If you're installing a new steering gear or a new Pitman arm, remove the Pitman arm from the steering gear sector shaft (see Section 22).

15 Installation is the reverse of removal. Be sure to tighten all fasteners to the torque values listed in this Chapter's Specifications. Check the power steering fluid level and add some, if necessary (see Chapter 1), then bleed the system as described in Section 25.

24 Power steering pump - removal and installation

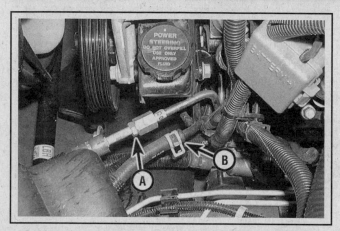

24.5 Detach the power steering pressure line (A) and return hose (B) from the lines coming out of the pump

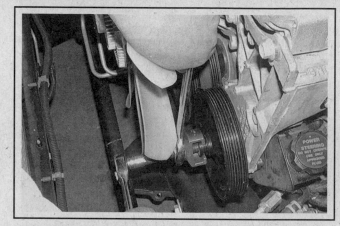

24.6 Remove the pulley from the power steering pump with a pulley removal tool

REMOVAL

▶ **Refer to illustrations 24.5, 24.6 and 24.9**

1   Disconnect the cable from the negative terminal of the battery.

✳✳ CAUTION:

On models equipped with the "Theftlock" audio system, be sure the lockout feature is turned off before performing any procedure which requires disconnecting the battery (see the information at the front of this manual).

2   Remove the radiator upper fan shroud (see Chapter 3) and the serpentine drivebelt (see Chapter 1).

3   Raise the vehicle and support it securely on jackstands.

4   Remove the skid plate, if equipped.

5   Position a drain pan under the power steering pump. Disconnect the pressure and return hoses from the hard lines coming out of the pump (see illustration). Plug the hoses to prevent contaminants from entering.

6   Using a special power steering pump pulley remover, remove the pulley from the pump (see illustration).

7   Remove the pinch bolt and detach the lower intermediate shaft from the power steering gear (see illustration 23.3).

8   Working on the backside of the pump, remove the bolt retaining the rear bracket to the engine.

9   Remove the pump mounting fasteners (see illustration) and lift the pump from the vehicle, taking care not to spill fluid on the painted surfaces.

INSTALLATION

▶ **Refer to illustrations 24.13a and 24.13b**

10 Position the pump in the mounting bracket and install the mounting bolts or nuts. Tighten the fasteners to the torque listed in this Chapter's Specifications.

11 Connect the hoses to the pump. Tighten the fittings securely.

24.9 The power steering pump on models with V8 engines is retained by four bolts (the bolt on the back of the pump securing the bracket to the engine is not visible in this photo); on V6 models it's retained by two nuts, both accessed from the back of the pump

24.13a Press the pulley onto the shaft using a pulley installation tool - don't attempt to drive it on with a hammer or push it on with a traditional press!

24.13b An alternative to the special pulley installer tool can be fabricated from a long bolt with the same thread pitch as the internal threads of the pump shaft, a nut, washer and a

12 Connect the intermediate shaft to the steering gear and tighten the pinch bolt to the torque listed in this Chapter's Specifications.

13 Press the pulley onto the shaft using a special pulley installer tool (see illustrations). An alternative tool can be fabricated from a long bolt, nut, washer and a socket of the same diameter as the pulley hub. Push the pulley onto the shaft until the front of the hub is flush with the shaft, but no further.

14 Install the drivebelt and fan shroud.

15 Fill the power steering reservoir with the recommended fluid (see Chapter 1) and bleed the system following the procedure described in the next Section.

25 Power steering system - bleeding

1 Following any operation in which the power steering fluid lines have been disconnected, the power steering system must be bled to remove all air and obtain proper steering performance.

2 With the front wheels in the straight ahead position, check the power steering fluid level and, if low, add fluid until it reaches the Cold mark on the dipstick.

3 Start the engine and allow it to run at fast idle. Recheck the fluid level and add more if necessary to reach the Cold mark on the dipstick.

4 Bleed the system by turning the wheels from side-to-side, without hitting the stops. This will work the air out of the system. Keep the reservoir full of fluid as this is done.

5 When the air is worked out of the system, return the wheels to the straight ahead position and leave the vehicle running for several more minutes before shutting it off. Recheck the fluid level.

6 Road test the vehicle to be sure the steering system is functioning normally and noise free.

7 Recheck the fluid level to be sure it's up to the Hot mark on the dipstick while the engine is at normal operating temperature. Add fluid if necessary (see Chapter 1).

26 Wheels and tires - general information

▶ **Refer to illustration 26.1**

Most vehicles covered by this manual are equipped with metric-size fiberglass or steel belted radial tires (see illustration), or inch-pattern light truck tires. Use of other size or type of tires may affect the ride and handling of the vehicle. Don't mix different types of tires, such as radials and bias belted, on the same vehicle as handling may be seriously affected. It's recommended that tires be replaced in pairs on the same axle, but if only one tire is being replaced, be sure it's the same size, structure and tread design as the other.

Because tire pressure has a substantial effect on handling and wear, the pressure on all tires should be checked at least once a month or before any extended trips (see Chapter 1).

Wheels must be replaced if they're bent, dented, leak air, have elongated bolt holes, are heavily rusted, out of vertical symmetry or if the lug nuts won't stay tight. Wheel repairs that use welding or peening are not recommended.

Tire and wheel balance is important to the overall handling, braking and performance of the vehicle. Unbalanced wheels can adversely affect handling and ride characteristics as well as tire life. Whenever a tire is installed on a wheel, the tire and wheel should be balanced by a shop with the proper equipment.

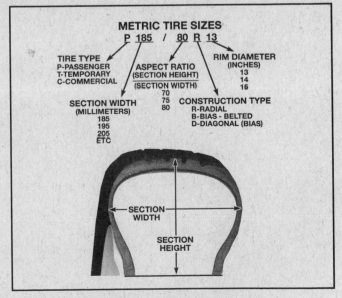

socket that's the same diameter as the pulley hub

27 Front end alignment - general information

▶ **Refer to illustration 27.1**

➡**Note: On models equipped with the Quadrasteer™ option, the vehicle should always have a "four-wheel" alignment at a qualified shop whenever an alignment is done.**

A front end alignment (see illustration) refers to the adjustments made to the front wheels so they're in proper angular relationship to the suspension and the ground. Front wheels that are out of proper alignment not only affect steering control, but also increase tire wear.

Getting the proper front wheel alignment is a very exacting process, one in which complicated and expensive machines are necessary to perform the job properly. Because of this, you should have a technician with the proper equipment perform these tasks. We will, however, use this space to give you a basic idea of what is involved with front end alignment so you can better understand the process and deal intelligently with the shop that does the work.

Toe-in is the turning in of the front wheels. The purpose of a toe specification is to ensure parallel rolling of the front wheels. In a vehicle with zero toe-in, the distance between the front edges of the wheels will be the same as the distance between the rear edges of the wheels. The actual amount of toe-in is normally only a fraction of an inch. Toe-in is adjusted by turning the tie-rod in the tie-rod end to lengthen or shorten the tie-rod. Incorrect toe-in will cause the tires to wear improperly by making them scrub against the road surface.

Camber is the tilting of the front wheels from vertical when viewed from the front of the vehicle. When the wheels tilt out at the top, the camber is said to be positive (+). When the wheels tilt in at the top the camber is negative (-). The amount of tilt is measured in degrees from the vertical and this measurement is called the camber angle. This angle affects the amount of tire tread which contacts the road and compensates for changes in the suspension geometry when the vehicle is cornering or traveling over an undulating surface. Camber is adjusted by turning the upper control arm pivot bolts, one way or the other, in equal amounts.

Caster is the tilting of the top of the front steering axis from vertical. A tilt toward the rear is positive caster and a tilt toward the front is negative caster. Caster is adjusted by turning the upper control arm pivot bolts, one way or the other, in opposite directions.

When making adjustments to the front end alignment, the caster is set first, then the camber, then the toe-in.

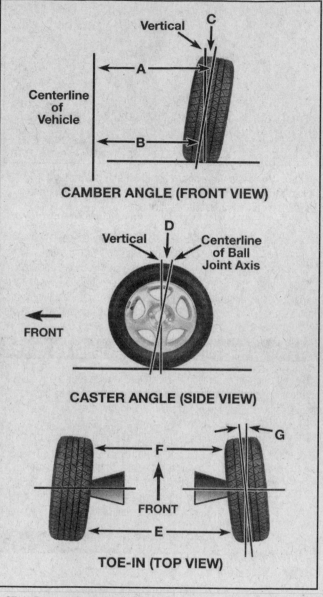

CAMBER ANGLE (FRONT VIEW)

CASTER ANGLE (SIDE VIEW)

TOE-IN (TOP VIEW)

27.1 Front end alignment details

A minus B = C (degrees camber)
D = degrees caster
E minus F = toe-in (measured in inches)
G = toe-in (expressed in degrees)

Specifications

General

Power steering fluid type	See Chapter 1
Front suspension "Z" height (models with torsion bars) (see illustration 4.13)	
SS models	3.5 to 4 inches
All others	4.7 inches

Torque specifications   Ft-lbs (unless otherwise indicated)

Front suspension

Shock absorber	
Upper mounting nut	15
Lower mounting bolts (2WD models)	19
Lower mounting bolt/nut (4WD models)	59
Upper control arm pivot bolt nuts	140
Lower control arm pivot bolt nuts	
1999 through 2002	110
2003	
2WD	107
4WD	110
2004 and later	129
Balljoint-to-steering knuckle nut	
1999 and 2000	
Upper	37
Lower	74
2001	
Upper	74
Lower	101
2002 and later	
Upper	37
Lower	74
Balljoint (replacement)-to-lower control arm nuts	52
Stabilizer bar	
Link nut	89 in-lbs
Clamp bolts	
1999 through 2004	
1500 models	24
2500 models	39
2005	37
Hub/bearing assembly-to-steering knuckle bolts	133
Torsion bar crossmember-to-frame bolts/nuts	70

Rear suspension

Shock absorber	
Upper bolt/nut	
1999 through 2004	70
2005 and later	15

Torque specifications (continued) Ft-lbs (unless otherwise indicated)

Lower bolt/nut	
1999 through 2004	70
2005 and later	
2WD	18
4WD	59
Stabilizer bar	
Link nuts	48
Clamp bolts	24
Leaf spring	
1999 through 2002	
U-bolt nuts	
14 mm U-bolts	59
16 mm U-bolts	89
Spring-to-frame (front hanger) bolt/nut	92
Rear shackle bolts/nuts	70
2003 and later	
U-bolt nuts	
1500	53
2500	110
Spring-to-frame (front hanger) bolt/nut	110
Rear shackle bolts/nuts	70
Trailing arm bolts/nuts	
Upper	77
Lower	89
Track bar bolts/nuts	77

Steering

Steering gear-to-frame bolts/nuts (rack-and-pinion)	
1999 and 2000	92
2001 and later	136
Steering gear-to-frame bolts (recirculating ball)	110
Intermediate shaft pinch bolt	33
Tie-rod end-to-steering knuckle nut	
1999 through 2001	33
2002	
Avalanche	33
All others	48
2003 and 2004	48
2005 and later	
1500	37
2500	48
Steering linkage (non rack-and-pinion)	
Pitman shaft nut	184
Pitman arm-to-relay rod nut	46
Idler arm mounting bolts/nuts	73
Idler arm ballstud nut	46
Steering damper-to-relay rod nut	
1999 through 2002	
except 2002 Silverado	46
2002 Silverado and all 2003 and later	30
Steering damper-to-frame bolt/nut	30

Torque specifications (continued)   Ft-lbs (unless otherwise indicated)

Steering column

Steering wheel nut	29
Steering column bracket bolts/nuts	
1999 through 2003	22
2004 and later	156 in-lbs
Shaft coupler bolt	35
Power steering pump	
Mounting nuts (V6 engines)	37
Mounting bolts (V8 engines)	37

Wheel lug nuts   See Chapter 1

Notes

Section

11

BODY

1 General information

❋❋ WARNING:

The models covered by this manual are equipped with Supplemental Restraint Systems (SRS), more commonly known as airbags. Always disable the airbag system before working in the vicinity of any airbag system components to avoid the possibility of accidental deployment of the airbags, which could cause personal injury (see Chapter 12).

The vehicles covered by this manual are built with body-on-frame construction. The frame is a hydroformed, ladder-type, consisting of C-shaped center rails welded to boxed front and rear sections, with both welded-in and bolt-in crossmembers.

The Pick-up body is in two separate sections, the cab and the bed, while the SUV body incorporates the cab, back-seat area and cargo compartment in one unitized structure.

Certain components are particularly vulnerable to accident damage and can be unbolted and repaired or replaced. Among these parts are the hood, doors, seats, tailgate, liftgate, bumpers and front fenders.

Only general body maintenance practices and body panel repair procedures within the scope of the do-it-yourselfer are included in this Chapter.

2 Body - maintenance

1   The condition of your vehicle's body is very important, because the resale value depends a great deal on it. It's much more difficult to repair a neglected or damaged body than it is to repair mechanical components. The hidden areas of the body, such as the wheel wells, the frame and the engine compartment, are equally important, although they don't require as frequent attention as the rest of the body.

2   Once a year, or every 12,000 miles, it's a good idea to have the underside of the body steam cleaned. All traces of dirt and oil will be removed and the area can then be inspected carefully for rust, damaged brake lines, frayed electrical wires, damaged cables and other problems. The front suspension components should be greased after completion of this job.

3   At the same time, clean the engine and the engine compartment with a steam cleaner or water-soluble degreaser.

4   The wheel wells should be given close attention, since undercoating can peel away and stones and dirt thrown up by the tires can cause the paint to chip and flake, allowing rust to set in. If rust is found, clean down to the bare metal and apply an anti-rust paint.

5   The body should be washed about once a week. Wet the vehicle thoroughly to soften the dirt, then wash it down with a soft sponge and plenty of clean, soapy water. If the surplus dirt is not washed off very carefully, it can wear down the paint.

6   Spots of tar or asphalt thrown up from the road should be removed with a cloth soaked in tar remover or kerosene lamp oil.

7   Once every six months, wax the body and chrome trim. If a chrome cleaner is used to remove rust from any of the vehicle's plated parts, remember that the cleaner also removes part of the chrome, so use it sparingly.

3 Vinyl trim - maintenance

Don't clean vinyl trim with detergents, caustic soap or petroleum-based cleaners. Plain soap and water works just fine, with a soft brush to clean dirt that may be ingrained. Wash the vinyl as frequently as the rest of the vehicle. After cleaning, application of a high-quality rubber and vinyl protectant will help prevent oxidation and cracks. The protectant can also be applied to weather-stripping, vacuum lines and rubber hoses, which often fail as a result of chemical degradation, and to the tires.

4 Upholstery and carpets - maintenance

1   Every three months remove the floormats and clean the interior of the vehicle (more frequently if necessary). Use a stiff whiskbroom to brush the carpeting and loosen dirt and dust, then vacuum the upholstery and carpets thoroughly, especially along seams and crevices.

2   Dirt and stains can be removed from carpeting with basic household or automotive carpet shampoos available in spray cans. Follow the directions and vacuum again, then use a stiff brush to bring back the "nap" of the carpet.

3   Most interiors have cloth or vinyl upholstery, either of which can be cleaned and maintained with a number of material-specific cleaners or shampoos available in auto supply stores. Follow the directions on the product for usage, and always spot-test any upholstery cleaner on an inconspicuous area (bottom edge of a backseat cushion) to ensure that it doesn't cause a color shift in the material.

4   After cleaning, vinyl upholstery should be treated with a protectant.

➡Note: Make sure the protectant container indicates the product can be used on seats - some products may make a seat too slippery.

❋❋ CAUTION:

Do not use protectant on vinyl-covered steering wheels.

5   Leather upholstery requires special care. It should be cleaned regularly with saddlesoap or leather cleaner. Never use alcohol, gasoline, nail polish remover or thinner to clean leather upholstery.

6   After cleaning, regularly treat leather upholstery with a leather conditioner, rubbed in with a soft cotton cloth. Never use car wax on leather upholstery.

7   In areas where the interior of the vehicle is subject to bright sunlight, cover leather seating areas of the seats with a sheet if the vehicle is to be left out for any length of time.

5 Body repair - minor damage

PLASTIC BODY PANELS

The following repair procedures are for minor scratches and gouges. Repair of more serious damage should be left to a dealer service department or qualified auto body shop. Below is a list of the equipment and materials necessary to perform the following repair procedures on plastic body panels.

Wax, grease and silicone removing solvent
Cloth-backed body tape
Sanding discs
Drill motor with three-inch disc holder
Hand sanding block
Rubber squeegees
Sandpaper
Non-porous mixing palette
Wood paddle or putty knife
Curved-tooth body file
Flexible parts repair material

Flexible panels (front and rear bumper trim)

1 Remove the damaged panel, if necessary or desirable. In most cases, repairs can be carried out with the panel installed.

2 Clean the area(s) to be repaired with a wax, grease and silicone removing solvent applied with a water-dampened cloth.

3 If the damage is structural, that is, if it extends through the panel, clean the backside of the panel area to be repaired as well. Wipe dry.

4 Sand the rear surface about 1-1/2 inches beyond the break.

5 Cut two pieces of fiberglass cloth large enough to overlap the break by about 1-1/2 inches. Cut only to the required length.

6 Mix the adhesive from the repair kit according to the instructions included with the kit, and apply a layer of the mixture approximately 1/8-inch thick on the backside of the panel. Overlap the break by at least 1-1/2 inches.

7 Apply one piece of fiberglass cloth to the adhesive and cover the cloth with additional adhesive. Apply a second piece of fiberglass cloth to the adhesive and immediately cover the cloth with additional adhesive in sufficient quantity to fill the weave.

8 Allow the repair to cure for 20 to 30 minutes at 60-degrees to 80-degrees F.

9 If necessary, trim the excess repair material at the edge.

10 Remove all of the paint film over and around the area(s) to be repaired. The repair material should not overlap the painted surface.

11 With a drill motor and a sanding disc (or a rotary file), cut a "V" along the break line approximately 1/2-inch wide. Remove all dust and loose particles from the repair area.

12 Mix and apply the repair material. Apply a light coat first over the damaged area; then continue applying material until it reaches a level slightly higher than the surrounding finish.

13 Cure the mixture for 20 to 30 minutes at 60-degrees to 80-degrees F.

14 Roughly establish the contour of the area being repaired with a body file. If low areas or pits remain, mix and apply additional adhesive.

15 Block sand the damaged area with sandpaper to establish the actual contour of the surrounding surface.

16 If desired, the repaired area can be temporarily protected with several light coats of primer. Because of the special paints and techniques required for flexible body panels, it is recommended that the vehicle be taken to a paint shop for completion of the body repair.

STEEL BODY PANELS

See photo sequence

Repair of minor scratches

17 If the scratch is superficial and does not penetrate to the metal of the body, repair is very simple. Lightly rub the scratched area with a fine rubbing compound to remove loose paint, then use a wax-and-grease remover (available at auto parts stores) to clean the area. Rinse the area with clean water.

18 Apply touch-up paint to the scratch, using a small brush. Continue to apply thin layers of paint until the surface of the paint in the scratch is level with the surrounding paint. Allow the new paint at least two weeks to harden, then blend it into the surrounding paint by rubbing with a very fine rubbing compound. Finally, apply a coat of wax to the scratch area.

19 If the scratch has penetrated the paint and exposed the metal of the body, causing the metal to rust, a different repair technique is required. Remove all loose rust from the bottom of the scratch with a pocketknife, then apply rust inhibiting paint to prevent the formation of rust in the future. Using a rubber or nylon applicator, coat the scratched area with glaze-type filler. If required, the filler can be mixed with thinner to provide a very thin paste, which is ideal for filling narrow scratches. Before the glaze filler in the scratch hardens, wrap a piece of smooth cotton cloth around the tip of a finger. Dip the cloth in thinner and then quickly wipe it along the surface of the scratch. This will ensure that the surface of the filler is slightly hollow. The scratch can now be painted over as described earlier in this Section.

Repair of dents

20 When repairing dents, the first job is to pull the dent out until the affected area is as close as possible to its original shape. There is no point in trying to restore the original shape completely as the metal in the damaged area will have stretched on impact and cannot be restored to its original contours. It is better to bring the level of the dent up to a point that is about 1/8-inch below the level of the surrounding metal. In cases where the dent is very shallow, it is not worth trying to pull it out at all.

21 If the backside of the dent is accessible, it can be hammered out gently from behind using a soft-face hammer. While doing this, hold a block of wood firmly against the opposite side of the metal to absorb the hammer blows and prevent the metal from being stretched.

22 If the dent is in a section of the body which has double layers, or some other factor makes it inaccessible from behind, a different technique is required. Drill several small holes through the metal inside the damaged area, particularly in the deeper sections. Screw long, self-tapping screws into the holes just enough for them to get a good grip in the metal. Now pulling on the protruding heads of the screws with locking pliers can pull out the dent.

23 The next stage of repair is the removal of paint from the damaged area and from an inch or so of the surrounding metal. This is easily done with a wire brush or sanding disk in a drill motor, although it can be done just as effectively by hand with sandpaper. To complete the preparation for filling, score the surface of the bare metal with a screwdriver or the tang of a file or drill small holes in the affected area. This will provide a good grip for the filler material. To complete the repair, see the Section on filling and painting.

These photos illustrate a method of repairing simple dents. They are intended to supplement Body repair - minor damage in this Chapter and should not be used as the sole instructions for body repair on these vehicles.

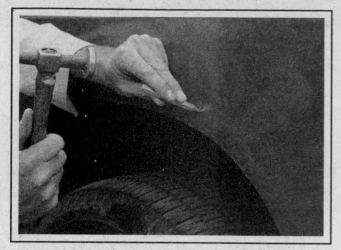

1   If you can't access the backside of the body panel to hammer out the dent, pull it out with a slide-hammer-type dent puller. In the deepest portion of the dent or along the crease line, drill or punch hole(s) at least one inch apart . . .

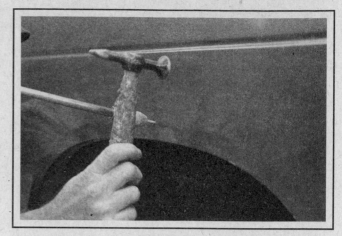

2   . . . then screw the slide-hammer into the hole and operate it. Tap with a hammer near the edge of the dent to help 'pop' the metal back to its original shape. When you're finished, the dent area should be close to its original contour and about 1/8-inch below the surface of the surrounding metal

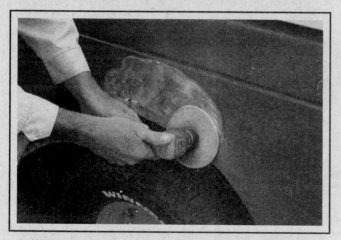

3   Using coarse-grit sandpaper, remove the paint down to the bare metal. Hand sanding works fine, but the disc sander shown here makes the job faster. Use finer (about 320-grit) sandpaper to feather-edge the paint at least one inch around the dent area

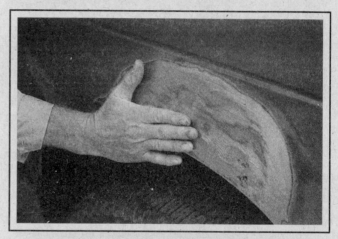

4   When the paint is removed, touch will probably be more helpful than sight for telling if the metal is straight. Hammer down the high spots or raise the low spots as necessary. Clean the repair area with wax/silicone remover

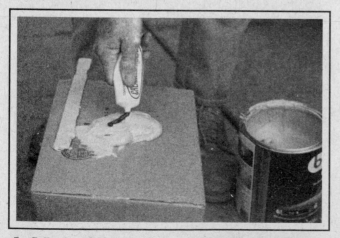

5   Following label instructions, mix up a batch of plastic filler and hardener. The ratio of filler to hardener is critical, and, if you mix it incorrectly, it will either not cure properly or cure too quickly (you won't have time to file and sand it into shape)

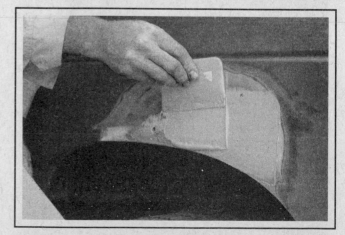

6   Working quickly so the filler doesn't harden, use a plastic applicator to press the body filler firmly into the metal, assuring it bonds completely. Work the filler until it matches the original contour and is slightly above the surrounding metal

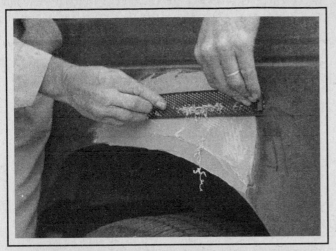

7 Let the filler harden until you can just dent it with your fingernail. Use a body file or Surform tool (shown here) to rough-shape the filler

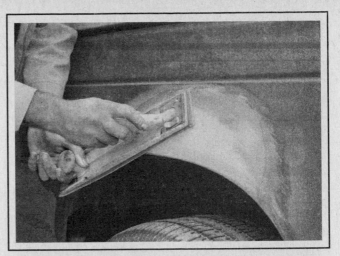

8 Use coarse-grit sandpaper and a sanding board or block to work the filler down until it's smooth and even. Work down to finer grits of sandpaper - always using a board or block - ending up with 360 or 400 grit

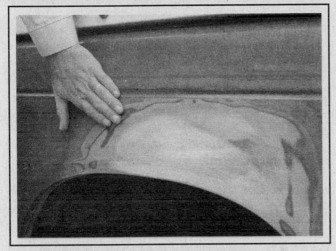

9 You shouldn't be able to feel any ridge at the transition from the filler to the bare metal or from the bare metal to the old paint. As soon as the repair is flat and uniform, remove the dust and mask off the adjacent panels or trim pieces

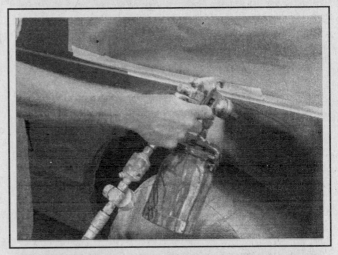

10 Apply several layers of primer to the area. Don't spray the primer on too heavy, so it sags or runs, and make sure each coat is dry before you spray on the next one. A professional-type spray gun is being used here, but aerosol spray primer is available inexpensively from auto parts stores

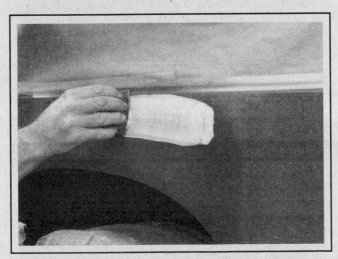

11 The primer will help reveal imperfections or scratches. Fill these with glazing compound. Follow the label instructions and sand it with 360 or 400-grit sandpaper until it's smooth. Repeat the glazing, sanding and respraying until the primer reveals a perfectly smooth surface

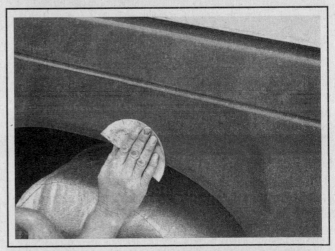

12 Finish sand the primer with very fine sandpaper (400 or 600-grit) to remove the primer overspray. Clean the area with water and allow it to dry. Use a tack rag to remove any dust, then apply the finish coat. Don't attempt to rub out or wax the repair area until the paint has dried completely (at least two weeks)

Repair of rust holes or gashes

24 Remove all paint from the affected area and from an inch or so of the surrounding metal using a sanding disk or wire brush mounted in a drill motor. If these are not available, a few sheets of sandpaper will do the job just as effectively.

25 With the paint removed, you will be able to determine the severity of the corrosion and decide whether to replace the whole panel, if possible, or repair the affected area. New body panels are not as expensive as most people think and it is often quicker to install a new panel than to repair large areas of rust.

26 Remove all trim pieces from the affected area except those which will act as a guide to the original shape of the damaged body, such as headlight shells, etc. Using metal snips or a hacksaw blade, remove all loose metal and any other metal that is badly affected by rust. Hammer the edges of the hole in to create a slight depression for the filler material.

27 Wire-brush the affected area to remove the powdery rust from the surface of the metal. If the back of the rusted area is accessible, treat it with rust inhibiting paint.

28 Before filling is done, block the hole in some way. This can be done with sheet metal riveted or screwed into place, or by stuffing the hole with wire mesh.

29 Once the hole is blocked off, the affected area can be filled and painted. See the following subsection on filling and painting.

Filling and painting

30 Many types of body fillers are available, but generally speaking, body repair kits which contain filler paste and a tube of resin hardener are best for this type of repair work. A wide, flexible plastic or nylon applicator will be necessary for imparting a smooth and contoured finish to the surface of the filler material. Mix up a small amount of filler on a clean piece of wood or cardboard (use the hardener sparingly). Follow the manufacturer's instructions on the package, otherwise the filler will set incorrectly.

31 Using the applicator, apply the filler paste to the prepared area. Draw the applicator across the surface of the filler to achieve the desired contour and to level the filler surface. As soon as a contour that approximates the original one is achieved, stop working the paste. If you continue, the paste will begin to stick to the applicator. Continue to add thin layers of paste at 20-minute intervals until the level of the filler is just above the surrounding metal.

32 Once the filler has hardened, the excess can be removed with a body file. From then on, progressively finer grades of sandpaper should be used, starting with a 180-grit paper and finishing with 600-grit wet-or-dry paper. Always wrap the sandpaper around a flat rubber or wooden block, otherwise the surface of the filler will not be completely flat. During the sanding of the filler surface, the wet-or-dry paper should be periodically rinsed in water. This will ensure that a very smooth finish is produced in the final stage.

33 At this point, the repair area should be surrounded by a ring of bare metal, which in turn should be encircled by the finely feathered edge of good paint. Rinse the repair area with clean water until all of the dust produced by the sanding operation is gone.

34 Spray the entire area with a light coat of primer. This will reveal any imperfections in the surface of the filler. Repair the imperfections with fresh filler paste or glaze filler and once more smooth the surface with sandpaper. Repeat this spray-and-repair procedure until you are satisfied that the surface of the filler and the feathered edge of the paint are perfect. Rinse the area with clean water and allow it to dry completely.

35 The repair area is now ready for painting. Spray painting must be carried out in a warm, dry, windless and dust free atmosphere. These conditions can be created if you have access to a large indoor work area, but if you are forced to work in the open, you will have to pick the day very carefully. If you are working indoors, dousing the floor in the work area with water will help settle the dust that would otherwise be in the air. If the repair area is confined to one body panel, mask off the surrounding panels. This will help minimize the effects of a slight mismatch in paint color. Trim pieces such as chrome strips, door handles, etc., will also need to be masked off or removed. Use masking tape and several thickness of newspaper for the masking operations.

36 Before spraying, shake the paint can thoroughly, then spray a test area until the spray painting technique is mastered. Cover the repair area with a thick coat of primer. The thickness should be built up using several thin layers of primer rather than one thick one. Using 600-grit wet-or-dry sandpaper, rub down the surface of the primer until it is very smooth. While doing this, the work area should be thoroughly rinsed with water and the wet-or-dry sandpaper periodically rinsed as well. Allow the primer to dry before spraying additional coats.

37 Spray on the top coat, again building up the thickness by using several thin layers of paint. Begin spraying in the center of the repair area and then, using a circular motion, work out until the whole repair area and about two inches of the surrounding original paint is covered. Remove all masking material 10 to 15 minutes after spraying on the final coat of paint. Allow the new paint at least two weeks to harden, then use a very fine rubbing compound to blend the edges of the new paint into the existing paint. Finally, apply a coat of wax.

6 Body repair - major damage

1 Major damage must be repaired by an auto body shop specifically equipped to perform body and frame repairs. These shops have the specialized equipment required to do the job properly.

2 If the damage is extensive, the body must be checked for proper alignment or the vehicle's handling characteristics may be adversely affected and other components may wear at an accelerated rate.

3 Due to the fact that all of the major body components (hood, fenders, etc.) are separate and replaceable units, any seriously damaged components should be replaced rather than repaired. Sometimes the components can be found in a wrecking yard that specializes in used vehicle components, often at considerable savings over the cost of new parts.

7   Hinges and locks - maintenance

Once every 3000 miles, or every three months, the hinges and latch assemblies on the doors, hood and trunk should be given a few drops of light oil or lock lubricant. The door latch strikers should also be lubricated with a thin coat of grease to reduce wear and ensure free movement. Lubricate the door and trunk locks with spray-on graphite lubricant.

8   Windshield and fixed glass - replacement

Replacement of the windshield and fixed glass requires the use of special fast-setting adhesive/caulk materials and some specialized tools and techniques. These operations should be left to a dealer service department or a shop specializing in glasswork. On SUV models, the fixed glass also includes the quarter windows.

9   Radiator grille - removal and installation

▶ **Refer to illustrations 9.1, 9.2 and 9.4**

1   Open the hood and remove the plastic panel over the radiator (see illustration).

2   Remove the mounting screw at the hood latch, then at either side of the bottom of the grille, use a Phillips screwdriver to turn the fasteners a quarter-turn, releasing the fasteners from the radiator support (see illustration).

3   Refer to Chapter 12 and remove the headlight housings.

4   At each end of the grille, pull forward sharply to disengage the large clip at the left and right ends of the grille (see illustration). Lift out the grille.

5   Installation is the reverse of removal. Next to each of the quarter-turn fasteners are plastic alignment pins that should be started in their holes in the radiator support before twisting the fasteners.

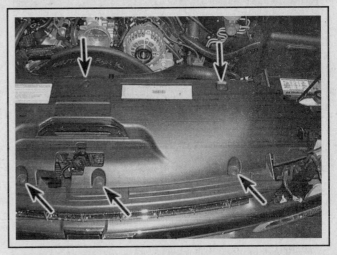

9.1 Remove the plastic pushpins (arrows) and lift off the radiator panel

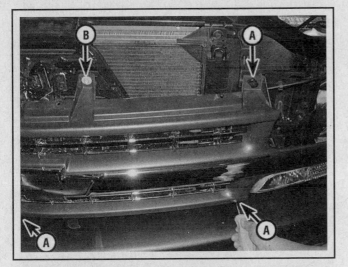

9.2 Twist the quarter-turn fasteners (A) with a screwdriver, then remove the screw (B) securing the top of the grille to the hood latch mechanism

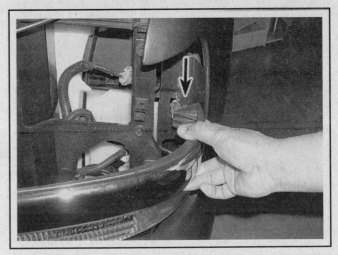

9.4 With the headlight housings removed, squeeze the large grille-to-body clip (arrow) on each end and withdraw the grille

10 Hood - removal, installation and adjustment

♦ Refer to illustrations 10.2, 10.10 and 10.11

➡Note: The hood is heavy and somewhat awkward to remove and install - at least two people should perform this procedure.

REMOVAL AND INSTALLATION

1 Use blankets or pads to cover the cowl area of the body and the fenders. This will protect the body and paint as the hood is lifted off.

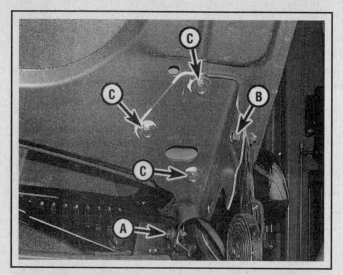

10.2 With the help of an assistant to hold the hood, remove the rear retaining bolt (A), and the hinge spring bolt (B) from each hinge plate and lift off the hood/hinges - only remove the hinge-to-hood bolts (C) if the hood or hinges are to be replaced (and, if you do that, be sure to mark the relationship of the hinges to the hood)

2 Scribe alignment marks around the hinge flanges to insure proper alignment during installation (paint or a permanent-type felt-tip marker also will work for this) (see illustration).

3 Disconnect the electrical connector at the underhood light, and the ground wire lug attached to the rear of the hood.

4 Have an assistant support the weight of the hood. Remove the hinge-to-hood bolts.

➡Note: Unless the hood or hinges are to be replaced, only remove the one bolt at the rear of each hinge and the hinge-to-hinge bracket bolt, not the hinge bracket-to-hood bolts. Hood realignment will be much easier because the original hinge-to-hood relationship is maintained.

5 Lift off the hood.

6 Installation is the reverse of removal.

ADJUSTMENT

7 Fore-and-aft and side-to-side adjustment of the hood is done by moving the hood in relation to the hinge flanges after loosening the bolts.

8 Scribe or trace a line around the entire hinge plate so you can judge the amount of movement.

9 Loosen the nuts and move the hood into correct alignment. Move it only a little at a time. Tighten the hinge nuts and carefully lower the hood to check the alignment.

10 Remove the plastic radiator cover (see Section 9), and adjust the hood latch so the hood closes securely (see illustration).

11 Adjust the hood bumpers on the radiator support so the hood is flush with the fenders when closed (see illustration).

12 The safety catch assembly on the hood itself can also be adjusted fore-and-aft and side-to-side after loosening the bolts.

13 The hood latch assembly, as well as the hinges, should be periodically lubricated with white lithium-base grease to prevent sticking and wear.

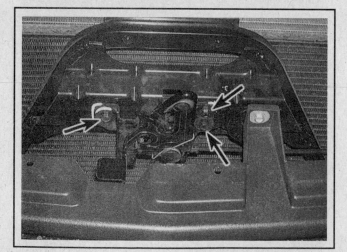

10.10 Loosen the hood latch bolts (arrows), then move the latch as necessary to adjust the hood-closed position

10.11 Twist the rubber bumpers in-or-out to make fine adjustments to the hood closed height

11 Hood latch and release cable - removal and installation

LATCH

▶ **Refer to illustration 11.1**

1 Remove the bolts and detach the latch assembly (see illustration 10.10). Unhook the spring and use pliers to detach the cable end from the latch (see illustration).

2 Installation is the reverse of removal. Adjust the latch so the hood engages securely when closed and the hood bumpers are slightly compressed (see Section 10).

RELEASE CABLE

▶ **Refer to illustrations 11.5a, 11.5b and 11.6**

3 Disconnect the release cable from the hood latch assembly as described in Step 1.

4 Unclip the release cable from the engine wiring harness. Attach a length of wire to the cable to assist with the installation of the new cable.

5 Working in the passenger compartment, remove the driver's kick panel to expose the hood latch release cable and handle (see illustrations).

➡**Note: On late models, it will be necessary to remove the electrical center to gain access to the release cable. Remove the center cover by removing the center bolt and releasing the side bails (clips). Remove the side clips on each side of the electrical center and slide the assembly out of the retaining grooves. Position the electrical center off to the side.**

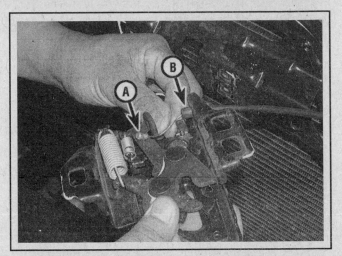

11.1 To disconnect the cable from the hood latch mechanism, pry the cable ferrule (A) out of the latch assembly and use pliers to disengage the cable housing end (B) from its slot in the latch

6 Use pliers to pull the cable housing end from the tab on the handle frame (see illustration).

➡**Note: If the handle assembly itself must be replaced, remove the one mounting bolt and remove the handle from the cowl.**

7 Trace the cable forward to the grommet where the cable goes through the firewall and pry the grommet out of the firewall. Pull the handle and cable rearward into the passenger compartment.

8 Disconnect the guide wire from the old cable and fasten it to the new cable.

9 With the new cable attached to the wire, pull the wire back through the firewall until the new cable reaches the latch assembly. Make sure that the grommet is properly seated on both sides of the hole in the firewall. Push on the grommet with your fingers from the passenger compartment side to seat the grommet in the firewall correctly.

10 The remainder of installation is the reverse of removal.

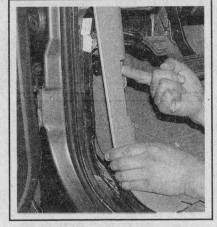

11.5a Firmly grasp the door sill trim and pull it up

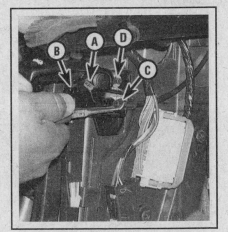

11.5b Pull out the driver's kick panel while guiding the release handle through the opening

11.6 Work the cable housing end (A) out of the notch (B), then use pliers to twist the housing end (C) out of the bracket - to detach the hood latch release cable handle, remove the retaining nut (D)

12 Bumpers - removal and installation

⁂ WARNING:

The models covered by this manual are equipped with Supplemental Restraint Systems (SRS), more commonly known as airbags. Always disable the airbag system before working in the vicinity of any airbag system components to avoid the possibility of accidental deployment of the airbags, which could cause personal injury (see Chapter 12).

1 Bumpers on all models are chrome-plated steel, with black or color-coded plastic upper and lower trim panels.

FRONT BUMPER

▶ **Refer to illustrations 12.4a and 12.4b**

2 Support the bumper with a jack or jackstand. Disconnect the electrical connectors at the fog lights, if equipped.

3 Refer to Section 9 and remove the radiator grille.

4 With an assistant supporting the bumper, remove the bolts/nuts retaining the bumper to the frame (see illustrations).

5 Disconnect any wiring harnesses or any other components that would interfere with bumper removal and detach the bumper.

6 Installation is the reverse of removal. Tighten the retaining bolts to 63 ft-lbs.

REAR BUMPER

▶ **Refer to illustrations 12.9a and 12.9b**

7 Support the bumper with a jack or jackstand.

8 Disconnect the license plate light.

9 With an assistant supporting the bumper, remove the bolts, nuts and stud plates retaining the bumper to the frame (see illustrations).

➡**Note: On models with a locking access hole for the spare-tire-lowering handle, pull the bumper straight back until the plastic tube on the back of the bumper clears the metal tube.**

10 Installation is the reverse of removal. Tighten the plate nuts to 66 ft. lbs, the lower frame rail bolts to 74 ft. lbs, and side frame rail bolt to 30 ft. lbs.

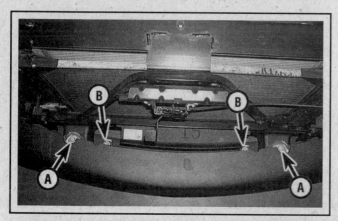

12.4a With the grille removed, there is access to the upper bumper mounting bolts (A) - also remove these two lower bolts (B)

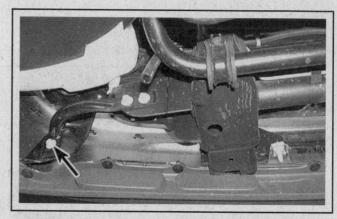

12.4b From below, remove the one bolt (arrow) on each side at the bumper brace

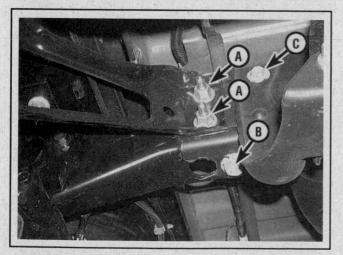

12.9a Remove these bolts and nuts (arrows, right side shown) to remove the rear bumper with its brackets attached - A are the plate nuts, B is the lower frame rail bolt and C is the side frame rail bolt

12.9b If the bumper alone is to be removed, remove these nuts (arrows)

13 Front fender - removal and installation

▶ Refer to illustrations 13.5, 13.6a, 13.6b, 13.7, 13.8 and 13.10

❉❉ WARNING:

The models covered by this manual are equipped with Supplemental Restraint Systems (SRS), more commonly known as airbags. Always disable the airbag system before working in the vicinity of any airbag system components to avoid the possibility of accidental deployment of the airbags, which could cause personal injury (see Chapter 12).

1 Disconnect the negative cable from the battery.

❉❉ CAUTION:

On models equipped with the Theftlock audio system, be sure the lockout feature is turned off before performing any procedure which requires disconnecting the battery (see the front of this manual).

Loosen the wheel lug nuts, raise the vehicle, support it securely on jackstands and remove the front wheel.

2 Refer to Section 9 and remove the radiator grille.

3 Refer to Section 10 and remove the hood. Remove the hood spring from the side of the vehicle from which you are removing the fender.

4 Refer to Section 14 and remove the side panel of the cowl cover, on the side from which you are removing the fender.

5 Pry out the plastic rivets, remove the screws and remove the inner fenderwell liner (see illustration).

6 From below, remove the fender bolt at the front of the fender opening and the bolt at the rocker panel (see illustrations).

7 Open the door and remove the fender-to-cowl bolts in the door-jamb (see illustration).

8 If removing the left fender, remove the battery and battery tray (see Chapter 5), and remove the bolts securing the Power Distribution Center (PDC). Set the PDC aside without disconnecting the electrical cables. Also remove the pencil brace at the front (see illustration). Also disconnect the hood release cable from the clips on the fender, and disconnect the windshield washer hose.

13.5 Remove the plastic pins (arrows) and the fenderwell liner

13.6a With the fender liner removed, remove this bolt at the front (arrow) . . .

13.6b . . . and the lower bolt (arrow) securing the bottom-rear of the fender to the rocker panel

13.7 Remove these fender bolts (arrows) in the door jamb

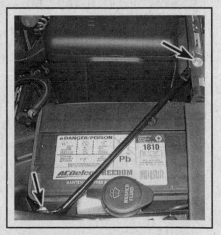

13.8 Unbolt the pencil brace bolts (arrows) at the front of the left fender

9 If removing the right fender, unbolt and set aside the air filter box and the radiator surge tank (see Chapter 3).

10 Remove the upper fender mounting bolts (see illustration).

11 Detach the fender. It's a good idea to have an assistant support the fender while it's being moved away from the vehicle to prevent damage to the surrounding body panels.

12 Installation is the reverse of the removal procedure. Tighten all nuts, bolts and screws securely.

13.10 At the top of each fender, remove the brace bolts (A), the upper cowl-to-fender bolt (B), and the fender-to-body bolts (C)

14 Cowl cover - removal and installation

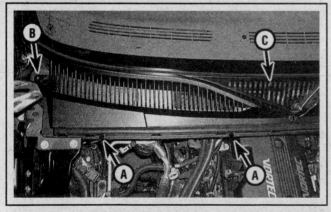

14.3 The end sections of the cowl cover snap in place without fasteners

▶ **Refer to illustrations 14.3, 14.4a and 14.4b**

1 Mark the position of the windshield wiper blades on the windshield with a wax marking pencil.

2 Remove the wiper arms (see Chapter 12).

3 At each side of the cowl, pull the side plates of the cowl cover up and off (see illustration).

4 Remove the cowl grille retainers, disconnect the windshield washer hoses and detach the cowl grille from the vehicle (see illustrations).

5 Installation is the reverse of removal. Make sure to align the wiper blades with the marks made during removal.

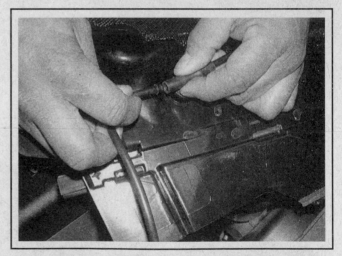

14.4a Remove the plastic clips (A, right side of cowl shown), the Torx screw (B), and the plastic pushpin (C)

14.4b Once the cowl cover is raised, disconnect and plug the hose from the windshield washer reservoir (attached to bottom of cowl cover)

15 Door trim panels - removal and installation

CONVENTIONAL DOORS (PICK-UP AND SUV)

♦ Refer to illustrations 15.2a, 15.2b, 15.3a, 15.3b, 15.3c, 15.3d, 15.5 and 15.6

1   On models with power door locks and/or power windows, disconnect the cable from the negative terminal of the battery (see Chapter 1).

※ CAUTION:

On models equipped with the Theftlock audio system, be sure the lockout feature is turned off before performing any procedure which requires disconnecting the battery (see the front of this manual).

2   On manual window models, remove the window crank (see illustration). On power-window models, pry the power switch assembly out of the door panel with a flat-bladed trim tool (see illustration).

3   Remove all door trim panel retaining screws and door pull/armrest assemblies (see illustrations).

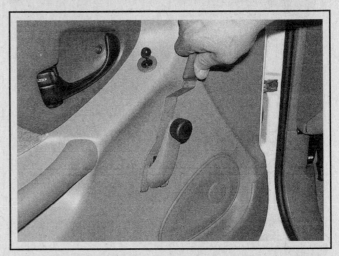

15.2a Use a hooked tool or a special window crank removal tool like this one to remove the retaining clip, then detach the window crank handle

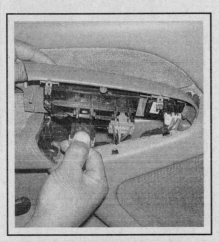

15.2b Pry up the power window switch assembly and disconnect the electrical connectors

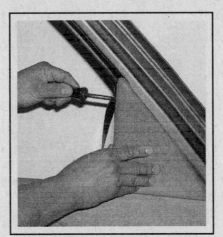

15.3a Use a trim tool to pry out the trim panel covering the outside mirror mount

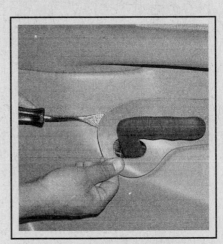

15.3b Use a trim tool to carefully pry out the trim around the inside door handle

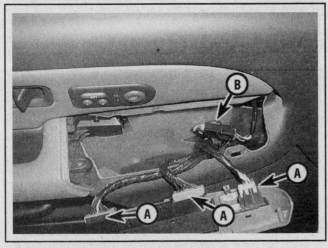

15.3c Disconnect the electrical connectors at the window switch panel (A) and for the seat heater switch (B)

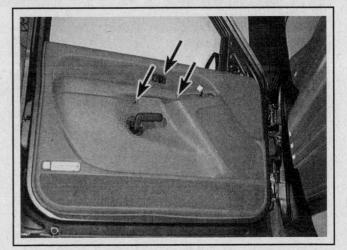

15.3d Remove the mounting screws (arrows), then lift the door panel straight up and off

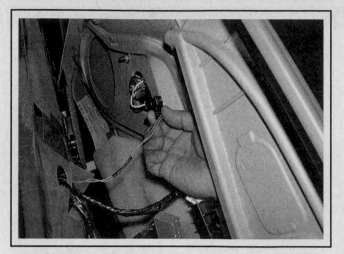

15.5 Pull the panel up and away from the door and unplug the electrical connectors

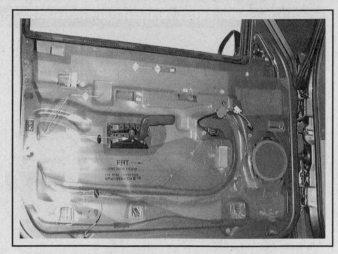

15.6 Peel the water deflector carefully away from the door, taking care not to tear it

15.10 Remove the door panel screws (arrows) in the pick-up third door

15.11 Carefully pry the trim from around the inner door handle

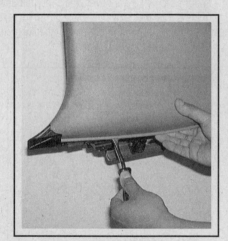

15.12 Release the clips at the bottom of the door, then lift the panel straight up

➡**Note: Some models are equipped with more than two door panel retaining screws. Locate the caps that cover the screws and remove all the door panel retaining screws before removing the door panel.**

4   Pull upward and outward at the same time to release the door panel from the clips on the door.

5   Once all of the clips are disengaged, raise the trim panel up and off the door. Disconnect any wiring harness connectors and remove the trim panel from the vehicle (see illustration). Most models have courtesy lights to disconnect (see Chapter 12), while some have optional heated-seat switches that have to be pried out with a trim tool.

6   For access to the inner door, carefully peel back the plastic watershield (see illustration).

7   Prior to installation of the door panel, be sure to reinstall any clips in the panel which may have come out during the removal procedure and remain in the door itself.

8   Connect the wiring harness connectors and place the panel in position on the door. Press the trim panel straight against the door (slightly higher than the final position) until the clips on the trim panel

align with all the holes in the door, then push down on the panel until the clips are seated.

9   Install the armrest/door pulls, screws and the window crank. Connect the negative battery cable.

THIRD AND FOURTH DOORS (EXTENDED-CAB PICK-UPS)

▶ **Refer to illustrations 15.10, 15.11 and 15.12**

10   In the door pull and cupholder cavities, remove the two door panel screws (see illustration).

11   Use a flat-bladed trim tool to pry out the plastic trim panel around the inside door handle for the third (or optional fourth) door (see illustration).

12   Use the trim tool to work all around the lower portion of the door panel, to release the clips (see illustration).

13   Pull straight up and out on the door panel to release its inner tabs from the slots in the door.

14   Installation is the reverse of the removal procedure.

16 Door - removal and installation

▶ **Refer to illustrations 16.3a, 16.3b and 16.6**

1   Remove the door trim panel (see Section 15). Disconnect any electrical connectors and push them through the door opening so they won't interfere with door removal. Leave the wiring harness boot attached to the door but disconnected from the body.

2   Place a jack under the door or have an assistant on hand to support it when the hinge bolts are removed.

➡**Note: If a jack is used, place a rag between it and the door to protect the door's painted surfaces.**

3   Remove the fasteners and carefully lift off the door (see illustrations).

➡**Note: The hinges separate into two halves. Each hinge half is welded to the door or the cowl, and they are not adjustable. If a** hinge needs to be replaced, the work should be performed at a body shop.

4   Installation is the reverse of removal.

5   Rear doors on SUV models are removed and installed as described above for front doors, except that the door is attached to the body "B" pillar and the pillar trim must be removed before removing the door.

6   On pick-up models with the right-rear access door (or optional left-rear access door), the door hinges do not have bolts, but rather two pins. To remove the door, follow the Steps above, but remove the clips on the upper door hinge pins, the move the door straight up until the door half of the hinges clear the body (see illustration). Installation is the reverse of the removal procedure. After lowering the door hinges back onto the pins, replace the clips on the top pins.

16.3a Remove the Torx door retaining strap bolt (arrow)

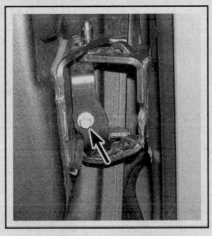

16.3b With the door supported, remove the two hinge bolts (arrow indicates bolt in lower hinge) and lift the door off

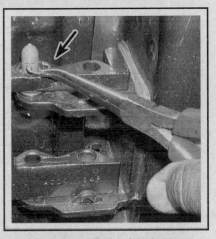

16.6 On pick-up third or fourth doors, the hinges pivot on pins, remove the C-clip (arrow) at each hinge and lift the door straight up off the pins

17 Door latch, lock cylinder and handles - removal and installation

LATCH

Standard doors (pick-up and SUV)

▶ **Refer to illustrations 17.2 and 17.3**

1   Raise the window completely and remove the door trim panel and watershield (see Section 15).

2   Rotate the plastic retaining clips off, then detach the latch rods from the lock cylinder, outside handle and inside handle (see illustration).

➡**Note: It may be easier to reach the lock cylinder rod clip when the rubber access plug is removed from the door (see below for outside handle).**

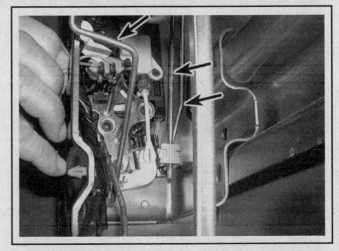

17.2 Detach the latch rods (arrows) at the latch, working through the opening in the door

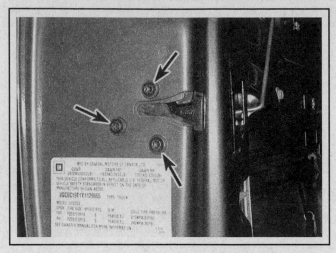

17.3 Door latch mounting screws (arrows) are Torx-head fasteners

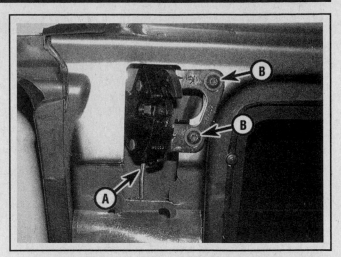

17.7a Disconnect the linkage rod (A), then remove the bolts (B) to remove the upper latch

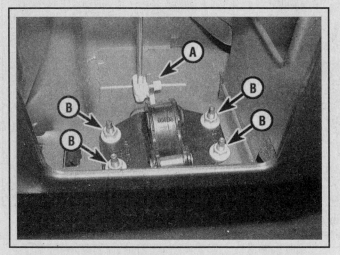

17.7b Disconnect the linkage rod (A), then remove the nuts (B) to remove the lower latch

17.9 Pry off the lock cylinder retaining clip (A) and slip the cylinder out of the back of the handle assembly, then disconnect the rod (B) - C indicates the handle retaining nuts (this view is looking up inside door)

3 Remove the three Torx-head mounting screws (it may be necessary to use an impact-type screwdriver to loosen them), then remove the latch from the door (see illustration). If possible, disconnect the rods while the latch is in the door, if not, pull the latch out with the rods attached, then disconnect the rods and electrical connectors.

4 Installation is the reverse of the removal procedure. Check the door to make sure it latches and unlatches properly.

Third and fourth doors (extended-cab pick-ups)

▶ **Refer to illustrations 17.7a and 17.7b**

5 The third (rear) door on the right side of extended-cab pick-ups (and the optional fourth door on the driver's side) has two latches, one at the top and one at the bottom. The door handles attach to a central mechanism that has rods going to both latches.

6 To remove either of the latches, see Section 16 for removal of the door panel and plastic weathershield.

7 Disconnect the rods at each latch, then remove the latch mounting bolts (see illustrations).

8 Installation is the reverse of the removal procedure.

LOCK CYLINDER

▶ **Refer to illustration 17.9**

9 Remove the outside door handle (see below). Disconnect the link, use a screwdriver to push the key lock cylinder retainer off and withdraw the lock cylinder from the door handle (see illustration).

10 Installation is the reverse of removal.

OUTSIDE HANDLE

▶ **Refer to illustrations 17.11 and 17.12**

11 Disconnect the outside handle link from the latch, remove the mounting nuts and detach the handle from the door (see illustration 17.9). One nut can only be reached by removing a rubber plug in the rear jamb of the door (see illustration).

12 On third and fourth doors, remove the handle mounting screws in the front jamb of the door and pull the handle assembly out (see illustration).

13 Place the handle in position, attach the link and install the nuts. Tighten the nuts securely.

17.11 Remove the plug to gain access to the upper mounting nut of the outside door handle through this hole (arrow)

17.12 On third and fourth pickup doors, remove the two screws (arrows) and pull out the "outside" handle

17.15 Release the lock rod clip (A), then remove the inside handle mounting bolt (B)

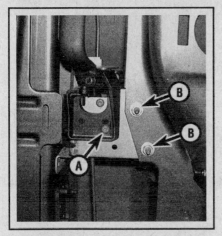

17.16 The third door inside handle is retained by one bolt (A) - the nuts (B) secure the handle bracket

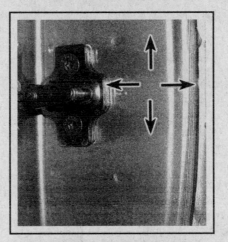

17.17 The latch striker on the door jamb can be adjusted slightly up/down or in/out

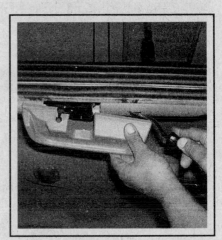

17.19a Use a trim tool to remove this panel . . .

INSIDE HANDLE

▶ **Refer to illustrations 17.15 and 17.16**

14 Follow the Steps in Section 16 to remove the door trim panel.

15 On standard doors, disconnect the latch rod from the handle assembly, then remove the mounting bolt (see illustration).

16 On third and fourth doors (extended-cab pick-ups), remove the one mounting bolt and take out the handle assembly (see illustration).

LATCH STRIKERS

▶ **Refer to illustrations 17.17, 17.19a and 17.19b**

17 To make minor door adjustments for latch alignment, the bolts on the latch striker (which is mounted opposite the latch) can be loosened and the striker moved slightly (see illustration). Retighten the striker mounting bolts and check for proper latch operation.

➡**Note: The striker can be moved up-and-down, or left-and-right to make adjustments.**

18 The third and fourth doors on extended-cab pick-ups have two latches, and thus two strikers, one above and one below the door. The bottom striker is in the rocker panel.

19 The striker for the upper latch is attached to the vehicle's roof. To access it for removal or adjustment, remove the trim piece around it (see illustrations).

17.19b . . . to access the upper striker for third and fourth pick-up doors

18 Door window glass - removal and installation

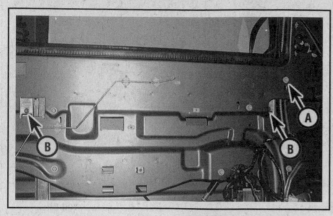

18.4 Remove the run channel bolt (A), then align the window so that the bolts (B) at the glass track can be loosened

▶ Refer to illustration 18.4

1   Remove the door trim panel and watershield (see Section 15). Removal and installation of the window glass is essentially the same for front and rear (SUV) doors.

2   Lower the glass until the glass track bolts are visible in the door openings.

3   Remove the bolt from the front window glass channel, to allow the channel to move away from the glass.

4   Loosen the two bolts retaining the glass to the window regulator track (see illustration).

5   Lift the glass up and out of the door through the glass opening.

6   To install, lower the glass into the door, slide it into position and tighten the nuts.

7   The remainder of installation is the reverse of removal.

19 Door window glass regulator - removal and installation

▶ Refer to illustration 19.3

✳✳ WARNING:

Do not remove the electric motor from the regulator assembly. The motor is available only as an integral unit with a new regulator.

1   Remove the door trim panel and watershield.

➡ **Note: The procedure is the same for both front and rear (SUV) door regulators.**

2   Remove the door window glass (see Section 18).

3   The window regulator assembly consists of two guides and cables. Remove the window regulator mounting bolts (see illustration). When withdrawing the assembly from the door, push the two guides toward each other to "collapse" the assembly for easier removal. The rear door regulator on SUV models is removed in much the same manner as for the front door regulator.

4   On power window equipped models, unplug the electrical connector.

5   Remove the regulator from the door.

6   Installation is the reverse of removal.

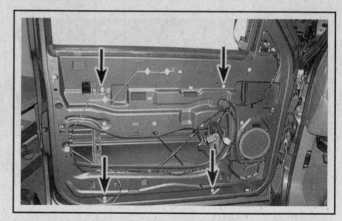

19.3 Door window regulator mounting bolt locations (arrows)

20 Mirrors - removal and installation

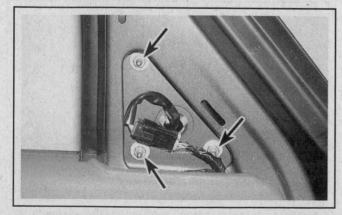

20.3 Remove the three outside mirror mounting nuts (arrows); on power models (shown), disconnect the electrical connector

▶ Refer to illustrations 20.3 and 20.6

OUTSIDE MIRRORS

1   Remove the upper corner interior trim panel by pulling it straight off until the clips release from the door (see illustration 15.3a).

2   On power mirrors, unplug the electrical connector.

3   Remove the nuts and detach the mirror from the door (see illustration).

4   Installation is the reverse of removal.

INSIDE MIRROR

5 Remove the setscrew, then slide the mirror up off the support base on the windshield (see illustration).

6 Installation is the reverse of removal.

7 If the support base for the mirror has come off the windshield, it can be reattached with a special mirror adhesive kit available at auto parts stores. Clean the glass and support base thoroughly and follow the directions on the adhesive package, allowing the base to bond overnight before attaching the mirror.

20.5 Remove the setscrew and slide the inside mirror from the support base

21 Tailgate (pick-up models) - removal and installation

▶ **Refer to illustrations 21.1, 21.2 and 21.4**

1 Open the tailgate and detach the retaining cables (see illustration). On 2001 and later models, remove the bolt at the lower right tailgate hinge.

2 Lower the tailgate until the flat on the right side hinge-pin aligns with the slot in the hinge pocket. Lift the tailgate out of the pocket (see illustration). With the help of an assistant to support the weight, withdraw the left hinge pin from the body and remove the tailgate from the vehicle.

3 Installation is the reverse of removal.

➡**Note: Apply some white grease to the mating parts of the tailgate hinge assembly before installation.**

4 If alignment is necessary, the latches (one on each side) can be loosened and moved (see Section 22), and/or the latch striker pins can be moved slightly for best tailgate fit (see illustration).

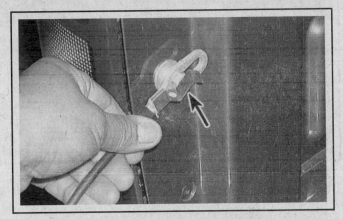

21.1 Lift the spring retainer (arrow) up and slide the cable end off the pin

21.2 Lower the tailgate enough to align the open area (arrow) on the right side hinge pin pocket with the straight sides of the pin, then lift the tailgate and slide it to the right and off the vehicle

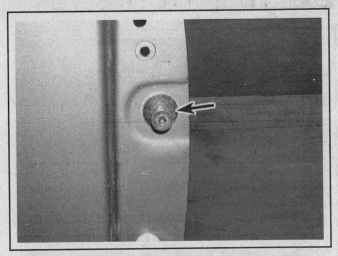

21.4 The tailgate latch strikers (right side shown) can be loosened with a male Torx bit to adjust their position slightly

22 Tailgate latch and handle (pick-up models) - removal and installation

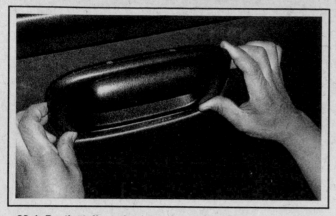

22.1 Pry the tailgate latch bezel out and down

▶ **Refer to illustrations 22.1, 22.2, 22.3 and 22.4**

1 Use a small screwdriver or trim tool to pry off the handle escutcheon. Once the bottom is pried out, pull the escutcheon down and away from the tailgate (see illustration). If a screwdriver is used, cover the tip with electrical tape to prevent scratching the paint.
2 From the bed side of the tailgate, remove the handle mounting bolts (see illustration).
3 Rotate the plastic retaining clips off the control rods and detach the rods from the handle (see illustration).
4 Remove the bolts and withdraw the latch from the end of the tailgate (see illustration).
5 Installation is the reverse of removal. Tighten all fasteners securely.

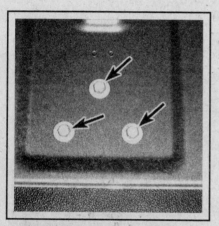

22.2 Tailgate handle mounting bolts (arrows)

22.3 Rotate the plastic retaining clips (arrows) off the control rods and detach the rods from the handle

22.4 Remove the tailgate latch mounting bolts (arrows) and withdraw it with the control rod

23 Liftgate and liftgate glass (SUV models) - removal and installation

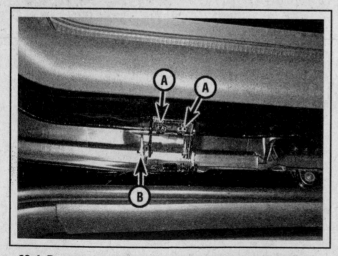

23.4 Remove the liftgate hinge-to-body mounting bolts (A, left side shown) - B indicates the C-clip securing the liftgate glass hinge

LIFTGATE

▶ **Refer to illustration 23.4**

✳✳ WARNING:

The liftgate is heavy and awkward to hold. At least two people should perform this procedure.

1 Open the liftgate and support it fully in this position. Use a trim tool to remove the interior molding above the liftgate.
2 Disconnect the electrical connectors for the liftgate and disconnect the washer fluid hose.
3 Detach the support struts at the liftgate (see Section 24).
4 Remove the liftgate hinge-to-body mounting bolts (see illustration). Remove the bolts while at least one assistant, preferably two, helps you hold the liftgate.
5 Installation is the reverse of the removal procedure.

LIFTGATE GLASS

6   Disconnect the electrical connector for the rear window defogger.

7   Open the liftgate and remove the C-clip at the left end of each liftgate hinge (see illustration 23.4).

8   Now close the liftgate. With an assistant to help, open the liftgate glass and slide it to the left, until the glass hinge slides off the pins on the liftgate hinges. The liftgate glass hinges are part of the rear glass assembly.

9   Installation is the reverse of the removal procedure. Make sure the C-clips snap firmly into place in the grooves in the hinge pins.

24 Liftgate panels, lock cylinder, latch and support struts (SUV models) - removal and installation

INTERIOR TRIM PANELS

▶ **Refer to illustrations 24.1, 24.2a, 24.2b and 24.2c**

1   Open the liftgate glass, then remove the plastic pushpins securing the trim panel to the liftgate glass latch (see illustration).

2   Remove the assist strap, then use a trim tool to pry out the plastic fasteners on the trim panel (see illustrations). The upper trim panel must be removed first for access to the lower (larger) liftgate trim panel.

3   The lower panel must be pulled straight up (towards the liftgate glass) until it is free of the tabs on the liftgate. Do not pull outward, or the plastic clips on the back of the panel may break.

4   Installation is the reverse of the removal procedure.

LOCK CYLINDER

▶ **Refer to illustrations 24.6, 24.7 and 24.8**

5   Remove the trim panels from the liftgate (Steps 1 through 3).

6   Where the lock cylinder extends through the latch assembly, remove the C-clip and the lock cylinder lever (see illustration).

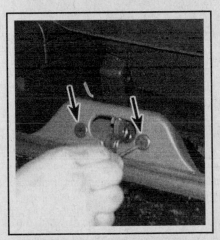

24.1 Remove the two pushpins (arrows) at the liftgate glass latch - pry up the center pins at each fastener to remove them

24.2a Pry with a trim tool around the edges of the upper liftgate trim panel until it can be removed

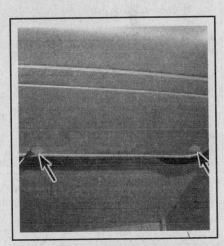

24.2b Pry out the plastic fasteners around the lower liftgate trim panel

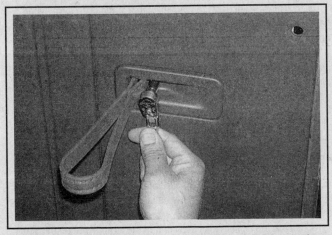

24.2c Remove the Torx screw securing the assist strap in the center of the lower trim panel

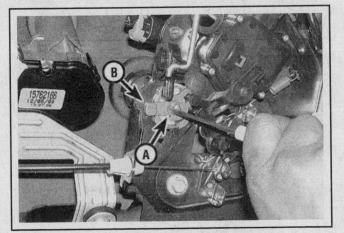

24.6 Pry out the C-clip (A) at the latch end of the lock cylinder, then remove the lock cylinder lever (B)

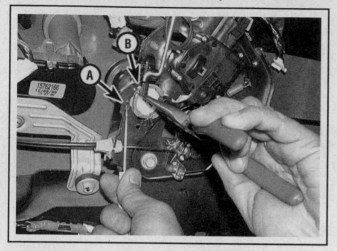

24.7 Use an awl to depress the spring-loaded pin (A) while using pliers to twist the lock cylinder until the tabs (B indicates one) align with the notches in the latch plate

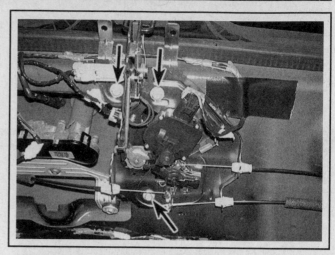

24.8 Remove the three bolts (arrows) to pull the latch operating assembly away from the liftgate

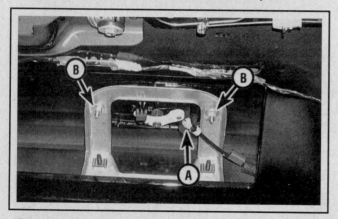

24.11 Disconnect the cable end (A) from the handle assembly, then remove the two mounting nuts (B)

24.14 Remove the two bolts from below (arrows) to remove a liftgate latch

7   Twist the lock cylinder at the interior end until its tabs align with the notches in the latch plate (see illustration).

8   Remove the three bolts securing the latch assembly to the liftgate (see illustration). Pull the latch away from the liftgate enough to reach behind and extract the lock cylinder.

➡ **Note: None of the rods or cables attached to the latch assembly need to be disconnected to extract the lock cylinder.**

9   Installation is the reverse of the removal procedure.

OUTSIDE HANDLE

▶ **Refer to illustration 24.11**

10   Remove the trim panels (see Steps 1 through 3).

11   Remove the handle-to-latch cable, then the mounting nuts (see illustration).

12   Installation is the reverse of the removal procedure.

LATCHES

▶ **Refer to illustration 24.14**

13   Remove the interior liftgate panels (see Steps 1 through 3). The

latching system for the liftgate is somewhat complex. There are two latches, mounted to the bottom edge of the liftgate, where it meets the body sill. At the middle of the liftgate is the latch operating assembly, which is connected by one cable to the outside handle. When that handle is pulled, the single cable pulls the central mechanism via cables to each of the two latches.

14   To remove a latch, disconnect the cable to the latch from inside the liftgate. From the bottom of the liftgate, remove the two latch mounting bolts (see illustration).

15   To remove the latch operating assembly, mark and disconnect the three cables and the electrical connector, then refer to Steps 5 through 8 to remove the assembly from the liftgate (see illustration 24.8).

16   Installation is the reverse of the removal procedure.

SUPPORT STRUTS

▶ **Refer to illustration 24.18**

17   There are two support struts for the liftgate, and two separate struts to support the glass. Open the liftgate (or liftgate glass) and prop it securely in the full open position.

18   Release the small clip at each end of the strut, then pull the strut from the mounting ball (see illustration).

19   Installation is the reverse of the removal procedure.

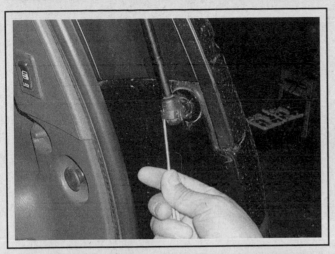

24.18 Detach either end of the liftgate support strut by pulling out the retainer clip with a small screwdriver, then pull the strut from the ball-stud (liftgate strut shown, liftgate glass strut similar)

STRIKER

▶ Refer to illustration 24.21 and 24.22

20 The closing position of the liftgate can be adjusted slightly by moving either or both of the liftgate strikers.

21 To access the strikers, use a trim tool to pry beneath the edge of the sill trim plate (see illustration).

22 Loosen the striker mounting bolts, move the striker slightly, retighten the bolts and check the liftgate closing (see illustration).

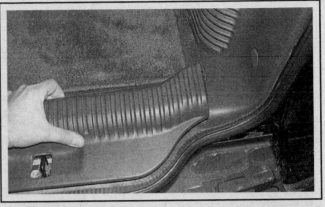

24.21 Pry up and then pull up the liftgate sill trim plate to access the strikers

24.22 Striker mounting bolts (arrows, left striker shown) - make a reference mark around the edges of the striker before repositioning it for adjustment

---

25 Center console - removal and installation

✳✳ WARNING:

The models covered by this manual are equipped with Supplemental Restraint Systems (SRS), more commonly known as airbags. Always disable the airbag system before working in the vicinity of any airbag system components to avoid the possibility of accidental deployment of the airbags, which could cause personal injury (see Chapter 12).

CENTER FLOOR CONSOLE

▶ Refer to illustrations 25.1, 25.2a, 25.2b, 25.2c, 25.3, 25.4a and 25.4b

1 On all models, open the console lid and remove the bolts securing the console to the floor bracket (see illustration).

➡Note: If the console bracket must be removed, or you are working on a model with the deluxe console, the front seats will have to be removed first for access.

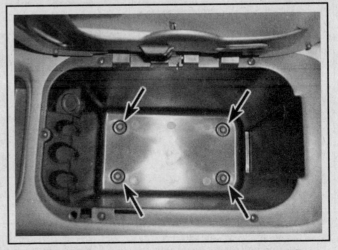

25.1 Remove the four screws (arrows) in the bottom of the console storage area

25.2a Pull up the cupholder insert, then remove these two screws (arrows)

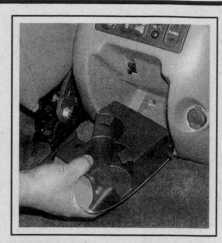

25.2b On SUV models, tilt the cupholder at the rear of the console down and lift the lower corners free of the console . . .

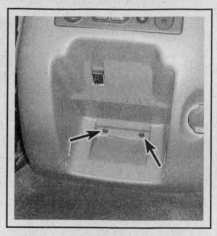

25.2c . . . to expose the two console mounting screws (arrows)

2   Remove the front cupholder and the screws in the cavity (see illustration). At this point, the main portion of the console can be removed on pick-up models. On SUV models, radio controls are mounted at the rear of the console, and the rear portion of the console must be unbolted (see illustrations). Disconnect the electrical connectors from the radio control and power-point socket (see Chapter 12).

3   To remove the trim bezel between the front console extension and the instrument panel, remove the screws and pry out the upper part of the bezel (see illustration).

✳✳ CAUTION:

When pulling on the bezel, do not grip it by the CD compartment door. It can break off.

➡Note: On Denali models, pull of the bezel at the front of the console. Remove the screws and the Driver's Information Center and CD player, if applicable. This gives access to the console-to-dash extension fasteners.

4   With the bezel off, remove the storage bin, then the screws holding the console extension to the instrument panel (see illustrations).

5   Unplug any electrical connectors and remove the console from the vehicle.

6   Installation is the reverse of removal.

OVERHEAD CONSOLE

▸ **Refer to illustration 25.8**

7   Disconnect the negative battery cable (see Chapter 1).

✳✳ CAUTION:

On models equipped with the Theftlock audio system, be sure the lockout feature is turned off before performing any procedure which requires disconnecting the battery (see the front of this manual).

25.3 Remove the two screws (arrows) and pull up the bezel with the CD compartment - don't pull on the CD compartment door

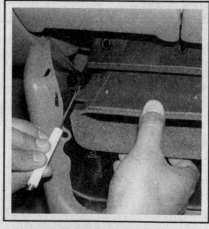

25.4a Pull backward on the storage bin, while using a small screwdriver to depress the clips on each side of the bin

25.4b With the bin removed, you can access the two extension-to-dash screws (arrows), using a long 1/4-in-drive extension and a "flex" socket

8   Remove the retaining screw at the front, pull the front of the console down and then toward the rear to detach the rear clips. On models with a full-length, one-piece overhead console, remove the screw at the front, lower the front down and move the console toward the windshield to release the clip at the rear. Unplug the electrical connector and lower the console (see illustration). SUV models may have rear HVAC controls in the overhead console. If so, disconnect those connectors as well.

9   SUV models may have a second overhead console over the second set of seats. This console is removed in the same manner as the front overhead console.

10   Installation is the reverse of removal.

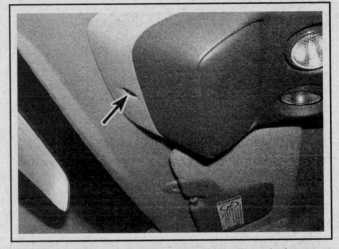

25.8 After removing the front bolt (arrow), pull evenly down on both sides at the front of the overhead console, then slide it rearward to disengage from the clips in the roof - do not pull the whole console straight down or the rear clips could be broken

26 Dashboard trim panels - removal and installation

✳ WARNING:

The models covered by this manual are equipped with Supplemental Restraint Systems (SRS), more commonly known as airbags. Always disable the airbag system before working in the vicinity of any airbag system components to avoid the possibility of accidental deployment of the airbags, which could cause personal injury (see Chapter 12).

INSTRUMENT CLUSTER BEZEL

▶ **Refer to illustration 26.3**

1   With the wheels blocked, apply the parking brake and lower the shift lever as far as possible.

2   On models equipped with tilt steering columns, tilt the steering wheel down as far as possible.

3   Grasp the bezel securely and pull out gently to detach the retaining clips from the instrument panel (see illustration).

4   Installation is the reverse of removal.

KNEE BOLSTER

▶ **Refer to illustrations 26.7 and 26.8**

5   Remove the cover over the fuse/relay box at the left end of the dash.

6   Refer to Steps 1 through 3 and remove the instrument cluster trim bezel.

7   Remove the screws securing the driver's knee bolster and pull it outward away from the dash (see illustration).

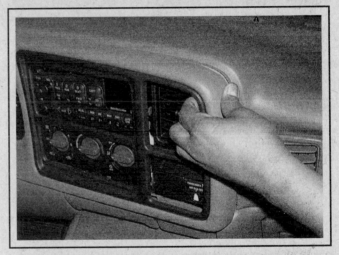

26.3 Grasp the cluster bezel securely and pull out gently to detach the clips

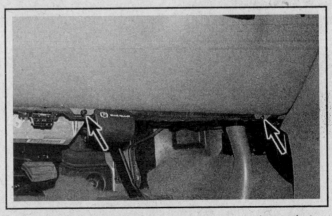

26.7 The knee bolster is held in place by screws (arrows) at the bottom, and clips at the top

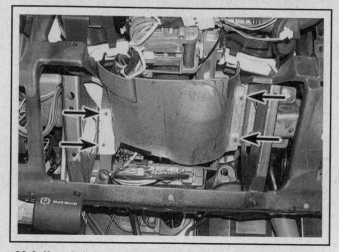

26.8 Knee bolster reinforcement plate mounting nuts (arrows)

8   If the knee bolster reinforcement panel needs to be removed for any reason, remove the four nuts and take down the panel (see illustration).

9   Installation is the reverse of removal.

CENTER AND RIGHT-SIDE AIR OUTLETS

10   Push the swivel part of the outlet as far to the left as possible, then push the whole outlet to the left and pull out from the dash to release it from the clips.

11   Installation is the reverse of removal.

GLOVE BOX

▶ **Refer to illustration 26.14**

12   Open the glove box door.

13   Squeeze the two sides of the glove compartment bin together and pull the door down until the bumpers on the bin have cleared the stops.

14   Remove the screws along the bottom hinge of the glove box door and remove the glove box (see illustration).

➡**Note: If the glove compartment is to be replaced, rivets will have to be drilled out along the hinge, since the glove box is part of the lower instrument panel cover. If the glove box is being removed for access behind it, just remove the whole lower trim panel with the glove box (see Section 28), without removing the rivets.**

15   Installation is the reverse of removal.

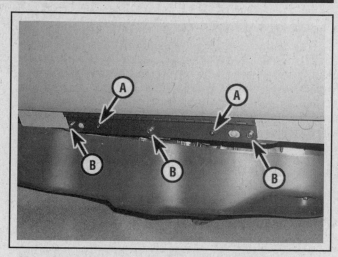

26.14 Drill out the two rivets (A), then remove the sorews (B) along the bottom of the glove box hinge

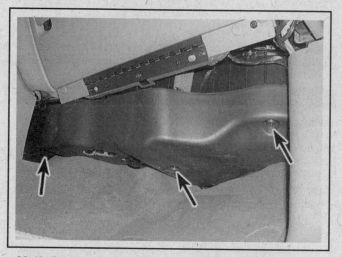

26.16 Remove the three screws (arrows) to drop the lower right sound insulator panel

LOWER RIGHT SOUND INSULATOR PANEL

▶ **Refer to illustration 26.16**

16   To access components under the right side of the instrument panel, remove the three screws and remove the lower sound panel from the vehicle (see illustration).

27 Steering column covers - removal and installation

▶ **Refer to illustration 27.2**

1   If equipped with a tilt-column, remove the tilt lever by pulling it sharply straight out from the column. It's held in by prongs.
2   Remove the screws and detach the lower half of the steering column cover (see illustration).

➡**Note: Some 2002 models have screws retaining the column covers, others are retained only by clips. Always check for the presence of clips before pulling the covers off.**

3   Pull the upper column cover straight up and off.
4   Installation is the reverse of removal.

27.2 With the tilt lever removed, remove these screws (arrows) and pull down the lower steering column cover

28 Instrument panel and cowl support structure - removal and installation

➡**Note: This procedure is lengthy and difficult, even for an experienced mechanic. Due to the number of electrical connections, fasteners used, and the various safety systems involved, we don't recommend instrument panel removal for the home mechanic.**

1   Turn the front wheels to the straight-ahead position and lock the steering column, then disconnect the negative battery cable (see Chapter 1).

2   Disable the airbag system (see Chapter 12).

INSTRUMENT PANEL TRIM PADS

▶ **Refer to illustrations 28.9a, 28.9b, 28.9c, 28.10, 28.12a, 28.12b and 28.12c**

3   Remove the dashboard trim panels (see Section 26).

4   Remove the heater and air conditioning control assembly (see Chapter 3).
5   Refer to Chapter 12 and remove the stereo, instrument cluster, both switch modules, and disconnect the electrical connectors from the fuse box at the left end, and the electrical junction box on the right end of the instrument panel.
6   Refer to Chapter 10 and remove the steering wheel and column.
7   Remove the center console (see Section 25).
8   Open the glove compartment, then push in the sides to release the tabs, allowing the glove box to hang straight down on its hinge.
9   Remove the screws, then remove the glove box and lower dash trim panel as one unit (see illustrations).

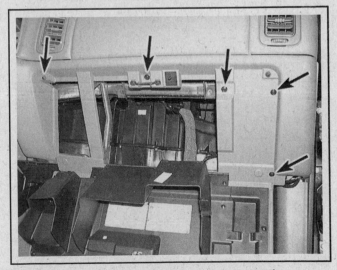

28.9a With the glove compartment down, remove these screws (arrows) from the lower dash trim panel . . .

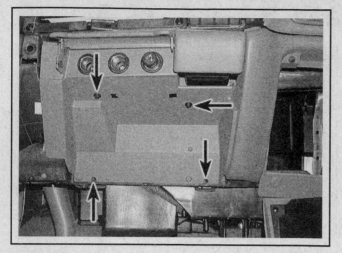

28.9b . . . and these screws (arrows) at the center of the dash

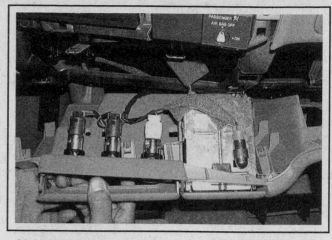

28.9c With the lower dash trim panel pulled away, disconnect the electrical connectors

28.10 Through the air duct holes, use a pry tool to push out the ends of the dashboard grab bar

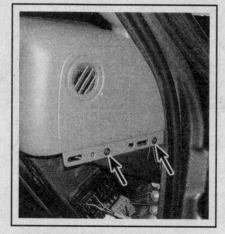

28.12a Remove the trim pad screws (arrows, right-side shown) at each end of the instrument panel

28.12b Remove the screws (arrows) in the duct openings

10 Twist the center and right-side air ducts to the side, then pull them out of the dash. Through the holes left by the air ducts, push in the clips at each end of the dashboard grab bar and remove the bar (see illustration).

11 Use a trim tool to remove the windshield post interior trim strips.

12 Remove the upper instrument panel trim pad retaining screws (see illustrations).

13 When lifting off the top trim pad, disconnect any electrical connectors.

14 Installation is the reverse of removal.

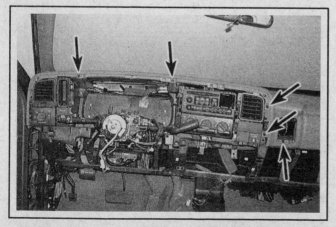

28.12c Remove these screws (arrows) around the instrument cluster area

28.16 Pull the air duct module (left side shown) out of the instrument panel framework

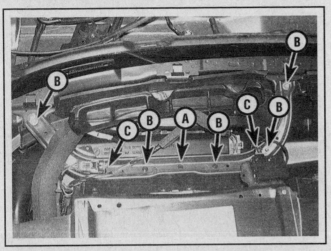

28.17a At the left upper instrument panel bracket (A), remove the bolts (B) and disconnect the electrical connectors (C) - this view is looking down on the dash through the windshield

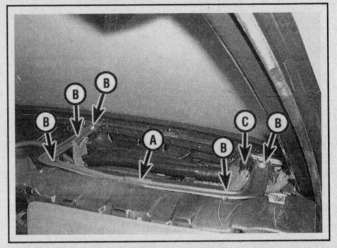

28.17b To remove the right upper bracket (A), remove the bolts (B) and disconnect the electrical connectors (C)

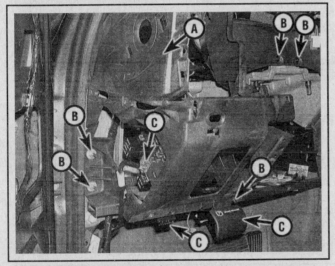

28.19a Instrument panel framework (A) fasteners at the left end - B are the nuts/bolts, C are components to be removed

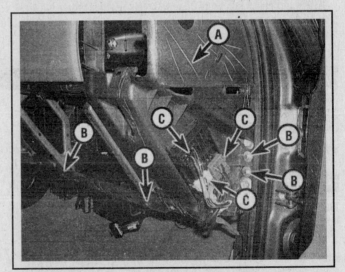

28.19b Instrument panel framework (A) fasteners at the right end - B are the nuts/bolts, C are electrical connectors to be disconnected

COWL SUPPORT STRUCTURE

♦ Refer to illustrations 28.16, 28.17a, 28.17b, 28.19a, 28.19b, 28.19c, 28.19d and 28.20

15 Behind the Instrument panel trim pads is a complicated, unitized structure that supports the body's cowl, the steering, the heating/air conditioning modules and other components. Refer to Chapter 3 and disconnect the coolant and refrigerant lines from the evaporator and heater core.

16 Refer to Chapter 12 and remove the passenger-side airbag. Remove the vents and any switch assemblies still attached (see illustration).

17 Remove the bolts at the two upper instrument panel brackets (see illustrations).

18 Remove the parking brake release handle from under the dash, and mark and disconnect any electrical connectors not yet disconnected.

19 Remove the fasteners holding the instrument panel framework to the cowl support (see illustrations).

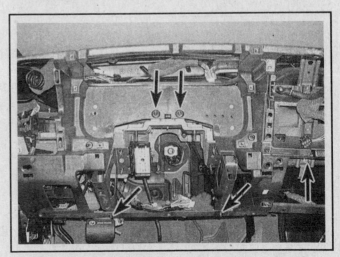

28.19c At the driver's side, remove these screws (arrows) and remove the framework

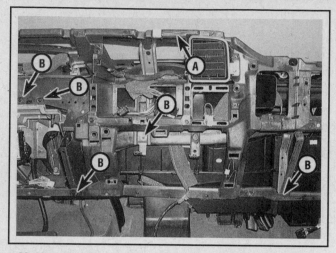

28.19d At the center of the instrument panel framework (A), remove these screws (B)

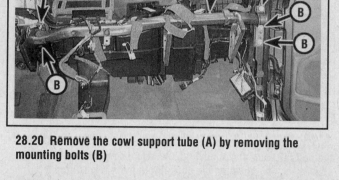

28.20 Remove the cowl support tube (A) by removing the mounting bolts (B)

20 Remove the support tube-to-cowl bolts at each side (see illustration).

21 Installation is the reverse of the removal procedure. Do not reconnect electrical power until you are certain that no harnesses have been pinched, all fasteners are tight and no connectors have been overlooked.

29 Seats - removal and installation

FRONT BUCKET SEAT (ALL MODELS)

▶ **Refer to illustrations 29.2a and 29.2b**

> ❋❋ **WARNING:**
>
> The models covered by this manual are equipped with Supplemental Restraint Systems (SRS), more commonly known as airbags. Always disable the airbag system before working in the vicinity of any airbag system components to avoid the possibility of accidental deployment of the airbags, which could cause personal injury (see Chapter 12).

1 Buckets seats are offered on all models, with an option of a center bucket seat when a floor console is not installed. On SUV models, the second row of seats may be a "60/40" bench-type or a pair of buckets seats with armrests. The second-row bucket seats are removed in the same manner as described here for the front bucket seats.

2 Remove the seat track-to-floor bolts and remove the front seats (see illustrations).

3 If the center front bucket seat is to be removed, its mounting bolts are accessible only when the other two bucket seats are removed first.

BENCH REAR SEAT (PICK-UP MODELS)

▶ **Refer to illustration 29.5**

4 The seat back and seat bottom on pick-up rear seats are part of

29.2a With the seat moved forward, remove the rear mounting bolts (arrows)

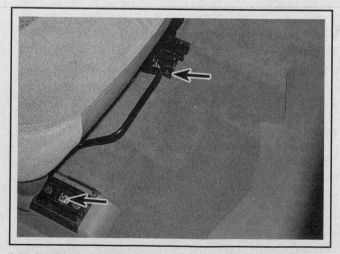

29.2b Remove the front bolt (arrows) from the front seat

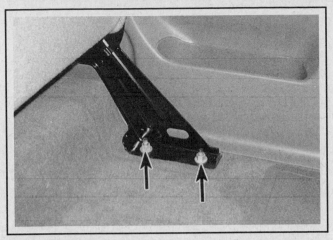

29.5 On pick-up models, remove the nuts (arrows) securing the rear seat assembly brackets to the floor (left side bracket shown here)

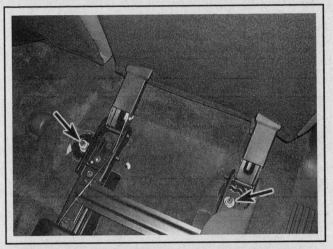

29.7a Flip the right-side seat bottom forward on the SUV second seat, then remove these front mounting nuts (arrows)

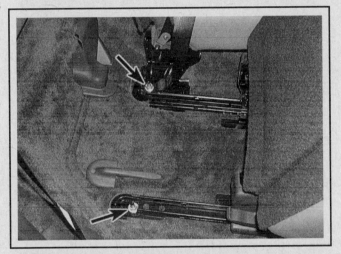

29.7b Slide the right seat forward, then remove these rear mounting nuts (arrows)

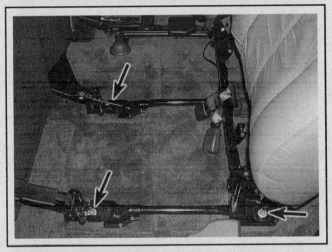

29.8 With the left side flipped forward, remove these mounting nuts (arrows) and remove the middle seat as a unit

an assembly that is removed or installed intact.

5 Remove the lower seat bracket-to-floor bolts and lift the rear seat assembly up and out (see illustration).

➡**Note: This is an awkward procedure, have an assistant help you.**

6 Installation is the reverse of the removal procedure.

2ND SEAT (SUV MODELS)

▶ **Refer to illustrations 29.7a, 29.7b and 29.8**

7 Fold the right-side middle seat forward, then remove the mounting bolts (see illustrations).

8 Fold the left-side seat bottom forward to access the remaining mounting nuts (see illustration).

9 Remove the seat assembly as a unit.

➡**Note: This is a job for two people.**

10 Installation is the reverse of removal.

3RD SEAT (SUV MODELS)

▶ **Refer to illustrations 29.11a and 29.11b**

11 Pull up the lever (arrow) marked "1", then the lever marked "2"

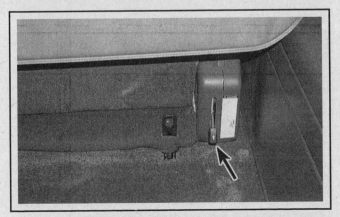

29.11a Pull up lever "1" (arrow) at the right side of the third seat to flip the seatback down

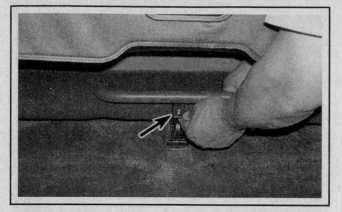

29.11b Pull lever "2" (arrow) at the center of the seat to flip the folded seat forward

(see illustrations).

12 With the seat folded and flipped up, pull the lever marked "3" at the lower center of the folded seat, then have an assistant help you remove the third seat assembly.

13 Installation is the reverse of removal. Once the seat is set in position in the vehicle, roll the seat into the floor pockets, pull lever "3" to set the latch, then flip the seat down and tilt up the seat back.

Section

12

CHASSIS ELECTRICAL SYSTEM

1 General information

Refer to the Warning and Caution in Chapter 5, Section 1 under "Battery disconnection."

The electrical system is a 12-volt, negative ground type. Power for the lights and all electrical accessories is supplied by a lead/acid-type battery that is charged by the alternator.

This Chapter covers repair and service procedures for the various electrical components not associated with the engine. Information on the battery, alternator, distributor and starter motor can be found in Chapter 5.

It should be noted that when portions of the electrical system are serviced, the negative cable should be disconnected from the battery to prevent electrical shorts and/or fires.

✳✳ **CAUTION:**

On models equipped with the Theftlock audio system, be sure the lockout feature is turned off before performing any procedure which requires disconnecting the battery (see the front of this manual).

2 Electrical troubleshooting - general information

▶ **Refer to illustrations 2.5a, 2.5b, 2.6, 2.9 and 2.15**

A typical electrical circuit consists of an electrical component, any switches, relays, motors, fuses, fusible links or circuit breakers related to that component and the wiring and connectors that link the component to both the battery and the chassis. To help you pinpoint an electrical circuit problem, wiring diagrams are included at the end of this Chapter.

Before tackling any troublesome electrical circuit, first study the appropriate wiring diagrams to get a complete understanding of what makes up that individual circuit. Trouble spots, for instance, can often be narrowed down by noting if other components related to the circuit are operating properly. If several components or circuits fail at one time, chances are the problem is in a fuse or ground connection, because several circuits are often routed through the same fuse and ground connections.

Electrical problems usually stem from simple causes, such as loose or corroded connections, a blown fuse, a melted fusible link or a failed relay. Visually inspect the condition of all fuses, wires and connections in a problem circuit before troubleshooting the circuit.

If test equipment and instruments are going to be utilized, use the diagrams to plan ahead of time where you will make the necessary connections in order to accurately pinpoint the trouble spot.

The basic tools needed for electrical troubleshooting include a circuit tester or voltmeter (a 12-volt bulb with a set of test leads can also be used), a continuity tester, which includes a bulb, battery and set of test leads, and a jumper wire, preferably with a circuit breaker incorporated, which can be used to bypass electrical components (see illustrations). Before attempting to locate a problem with test instruments, use the wiring diagram(s) to decide where to make the connections.

VOLTAGE CHECKS

Voltage checks should be performed if a circuit is not functioning properly. Connect one lead of a circuit tester to either the negative battery terminal or a known good ground. Connect the other lead to a

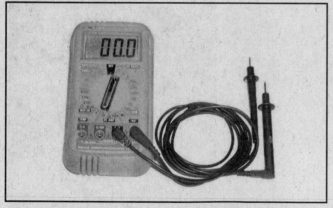

2.5a The most useful tool for electrical troubleshooting is a digital multimeter that can check volts, amps, and test continuity

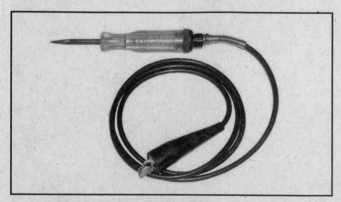

2.5b A test light is a very handy tool for checking voltage

2.6 In use, a basic test light's lead is clipped to a known good ground, then the pointed probe can test connectors, wires or electrical sockets - if the bulb lights, the part being tested has battery voltage

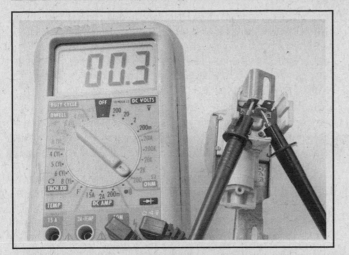

2.9 With a multimeter set to the ohms scale, resistance can be checked across two terminals - when checking for continuity, a low reading indicates continuity, a high reading indicates lack of continuity

2.15 To backprobe a connector, insert a small, sharp probe (such as a straight-pin) into the back of the connector alongside the desired wire until it contacts the metal terminal inside; connect your meter leads to the probes - this allows you to test a functioning circuit

connector in the circuit being tested, preferably nearest to the battery or fuse (see illustration). If the bulb of the tester lights, voltage is present, which means that the part of the circuit between the connector and the battery Is problem free. Continue checking the rest of the circuit In the same fashion. When you reach a point at which no voltage is present, the problem lies between that point and the last test point with voltage. Most of the time the problem can be traced to a loose connection.

➡Note: Keep in mind that some circuits receive voltage only when the ignition key is in the Accessory or Run position.

FINDING A SHORT

One method of finding shorts in a circuit is to remove the fuse and connect a test light or voltmeter in place of the fuse terminals. There should be no voltage present in the circuit. Move the wiring harness from side-to-side while watching the test light. If the bulb goes on, there is a short to ground somewhere in that area, probably where the insulation has rubbed through. The same test can be performed on each component in the circuit, even a switch.

GROUND CHECK

Perform a ground test to check whether a component is properly grounded. Disconnect the battery and connect one lead of a continuity tester or multlmeter (set to the ohms scale), to a known good ground. Connect the other lead to the wire or ground connection being tested. If the resistance is low (less than 5 ohms), the ground is good. If the bulb on a self-powered test light does not go on, the ground is not good.

CONTINUITY CHECK

A continuity check is done to determine if there are any breaks in a circuit - if it is passing electricity properly. With the circuit off (no power in the circuit), a self-powered continuity tester or multimeter can be used to check the circuit. Connect the test leads to both ends of the circuit (or to the "power" end and a good ground), and if the test light comes on the circuit is passing current properly (see illustration). If the

resistance is low (less than 5 ohms), there is continuity; if the reading is 10,000 ohms or higher, there is a break somewhere in the circuit. The same procedure can be used to test a switch, by connecting the continuity tester to the switch terminals. With the switch turned On, the test light should come on (or low resistance should be indicated on a meter).

FINDING AN OPEN CIRCUIT

When diagnosing for possible open circuits, it is often difficult to locate them by sight because the connectors hide oxidation or terminal misalignment. Merely wiggling a connector on a sensor or in the wiring harness may correct the open circuit condition. Remember this when an open circuit is indicated when troubleshooting a circuit. Intermittent problems may also be caused by oxidized or loose connections.

Electrical troubleshooting is simple If you keep in mind that all electrical circuits are basically electricity running from the battery, through the wires, switches, relays, fuses and fusible links to each electrical component (light bulb, motor, etc.) and to ground, from which it is passed back to the battery. Any electrical problem is an interruption in the flow of electricity to and from the battery.

CONNECTORS

Most electrical connections on these vehicles are made with multiwire plastic connectors. The mating halves of many connectors are secured with locking clips molded into the plastic connector shells. The mating halves of large connectors, such as some of those under the instrument panel, are held together by a bolt through the center of the connector.

To separate a connector with locking clips, use a small screwdriver to pry the clips apart carefully, then separate the connector halves. Pull only on the shell, never pull on the wiring harness as you may damage the individual wires and terminals inside the connectors. Look at the connector closely before trying to separate the halves. Often the locking clips are engaged in a way that is not immediately clear. Additionally, many connectors have more than one set of clips.

Each pair of connector terminals has a male half and a female half. When you look at the end view of a connector in a diagram, be sure to understand whether the view shows the harness side or the component side of the connector. Connector halves are mirror images of each other, and a terminal shown on the right side end-view of one half will be on the left side end-view of the other half.

It is often necessary to take circuit voltage measurements with a connector connected. Whenever possible, carefully insert a small straight pin (not your meter probe) into the rear of the connector shell to contact the terminal inside, then clip your meter lead to the pin. This kind of connection is called "backprobing" (see illustration). When inserting a test probe into a terminal, be careful not to distort the terminal opening. Doing so can lead to a poor connection and corrosion at that terminal later. Using the small straight pin instead of a meter probe results in less chance of deforming the terminal connector.

3   Fuses and fusible links - general information

FUSES

▶ **Refer to illustrations 3.1a, 3.1b, 3.3a and 3.3b**

The electrical circuits of the vehicle are protected by a combination of fuses, circuit breakers and fusible links. The interior fuse/relay panel is located at the left end of the instrument panel, while the main fuse-relay panel is in the engine compartment (see illustrations).

Each of the fuses is designed to protect a specific circuit, and the various circuits are identified on the fuse panel itself.

Several sizes of fuses are employed in the fuse blocks. There are small, medium and large sizes of the same design, all with the same blade terminal design. The medium and large fuses can be removed with your fingers, but the small fuses require the use of pliers or the small plastic fuse-puller tool found in most fuse boxes. If an electrical component fails, always check the fuse first. The best way to check the fuses is with a test light. Check for power at the exposed terminal tips of each fuse (see illustration). If power is present at one side of the fuse but not the other, the fuse is blown. A blown fuse can also be identified by visually inspecting it (see illustration).

Be sure to replace blown fuses with the correct type. Fuses (of the same physical size) of different ratings may be physically interchangeable, but only fuses of the proper rating should be used. Replacing a fuse with one of a higher or lower value than specified is not recommended. Each electrical circuit needs a specific amount of protection. The amperage value of each fuse is molded into the top of the fuse body.

3.1a The main fuse/relay box is in the engine compartment - the inside of the cover has a legend to identify the fuses and relays

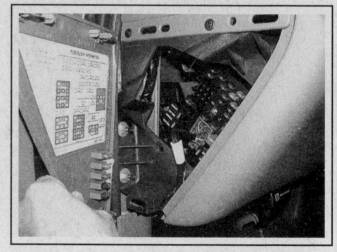

3.1b The interior fuse/relay panel is located at the left end of the instrument panel under a cover - the inside of the instrument panel end cap has the identification legends

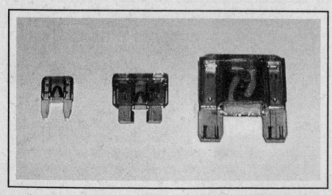

3.3a All three of these fuses are of 30-amp rating, yet are different sizes - make sure you get the right amperage and size when purchasing replacement fuses

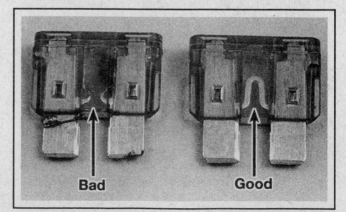

3.3b When a fuse blows, the element between the terminals melts - the fuse on the left is blown, the one on the right is good

If the replacement fuse immediately fails, don't replace it again until the cause of the problem is isolated and corrected. In most cases, this will be a short circuit in the wiring caused by a broken or deteriorated wire.

FUSIBLE LINKS

▶ **Refer to illustrations 3.7 and 3.9**

Some circuits are protected by fusible links. The links are used in circuits that are not ordinarily fused, such as the alternator circuit.

The fusible link for the alternator circuit is located on the front side of the engine, and is easily identified (see illustration). The link is a short length of heavy wire that is marked "fusible link" on the outer cover.

To replace a fusible link, first disconnect the negative battery cable.

❄❄ **CAUTION:**

On models equipped with the Theftlock audio system, be sure the lockout feature is turned off before performing any procedure which requires disconnecting the battery (see the front of this manual).

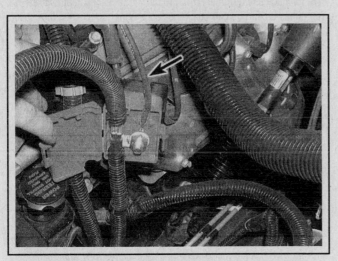

3.7 This cable (arrow) from the alternator to the battery cable jumper terminal is the fusible link

Although the fusible links appear to be a heavier gauge than the wires they're protecting, the appearance is due to the thick insulation. All fusible links are several wire gauges smaller than the wire they're designed to protect. Fusible links can't be repaired, but a new link of the same size wire can be installed. The procedure is as follows:

a) Cut the damaged fusible link out of the wire just behind the connector.

b) Strip the insulation back approximately 1-inch.

c) Spread the strands of the exposed wire apart, push them together and twist them in place (see illustration).

d) Use rosin core solder and solder the wires together to obtain a good connection.

e) Use plenty of electrical tape around the soldered joint. No wires should be exposed.

f) Connect the negative battery cable. Test the circuit for proper operation.

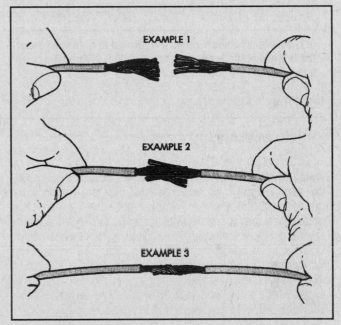

3.9 To repair a fusible link, cut out the damaged section, then join a new section by stripping the wire and twisting it together, as shown here - when securely joined, solder the connections and wrap them with electrical tape

---

4   Circuit breakers - general information and check

Circuit breakers protect certain circuits, such as the power windows and power seats. Depending on the vehicle's accessories, there may be two 25-amp circuit breakers, located in the interior fuse/relay box at the left end of the dashboard.

Because the circuit breakers reset automatically, an electrical overload in a circuit-breaker-protected system will cause the circuit to fail momentarily, then come back on. If the circuit does not come back on, check it immediately.

For a basic check, pull the circuit breaker up out of its socket on the fuse panel, but just far enough to probe with a voltmeter. The breaker should still contact the sockets.

With the voltmeter negative lead on a good chassis ground, touch each end prong of the circuit breaker with the positive meter probe. There should be battery voltage at each end. If there is battery voltage only at one end, the circuit breaker must be replaced.

5 Relays - general information and testing

5.1 Several additional relays are located here (arrow) under the left end of the instrument panel, with a cover retained by a twist-off plastic nut

GENERAL INFORMATION

▶ **Refer to illustration 5.1**

1   Several electrical accessories in the vehicle, such as the fuel injection system, horns, starter, and fog lamps use relays to transmit the electrical signal to the component. Relays use a low-current circuit (the control circuit) to open and close a high-current circuit (the power circuit). If the relay is defective, that component will not operate properly. Most relays are mounted in the engine compartment and interior fuse/relay boxes (see illustrations 3.1a and 3.1b). The electrical center located below the left end of the instrument panel, also contains several relays (see illustration). If a faulty relay is suspected, it can be removed and tested using the procedure below or by a dealer service department or a repair shop. Defective relays must be replaced as a unit.

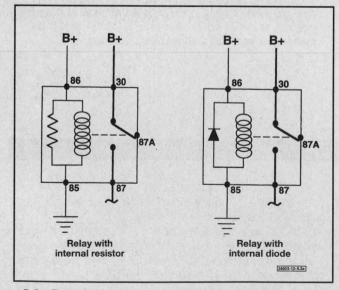

5.2a Typical ISO relay designs, terminal numbering and circuit connections

TESTING

▶ **Refer to illustrations 5.2a and 5.2b**

2   Most of the relays used in these vehicles are of a type often called "ISO" relays, which refers to the International Standards Organization. The terminals of ISO relays are numbered to indicate their usual circuit connections and functions. There are two basic layouts of terminals on the relays used in the covered vehicles (see illustrations).

3   Refer to the wiring diagram for the circuit to determine the proper connections for the relay you're testing. If you can't determine the correct connection from the wiring diagrams, however, you may be able to determine the test connections from the information that follows.

4   Two of the terminals are the relay control circuit and connect to the relay coil. The other relay terminals are the power circuit. When the relay is energized, the coil creates a magnetic field that closes the larger contacts of the power circuit to provide power to the circuit loads.

5   Terminals 85 and 86 are normally the control circuit. If the relay contains a diode, terminal 86 must be connected to battery positive (B+) voltage and terminal 85 to ground. If the relay contains a resistor, terminals 85 and 86 can be connected in either direction with respect to B+ and ground.

6   Terminal 30 is normally connected to the battery voltage (B+) source for the circuit loads. Terminal 87 is connected to the ground side of the circuit, either directly or through a load. If the relay has several alternate terminals for load or ground connections, they usually are numbered 87A, 87B, 87C, and so on.

7   Use an ohmmeter to check continuity through the relay control coil.

   a) *Connect the meter according to the polarity shown in the illustration for one check; then reverse the ohmmeter leads and check continuity in the other direction.*

   b) *If the relay contains a resistor, resistance should be indicated on the meter, and should be the same value with the ohmmeter in either direction.*

   c) *If the relay contains a diode, resistance should be higher with the ohmmeter in the forward polarity direction than with the meter leads reversed.*

   d) *If the ohmmeter shows infinite resistance in both directions, replace the relay.*

8   Remove the relay from the vehicle and use the ohmmeter to

5.2b Most relays are marked on the outside to easily identify the control circuit and power circuit - this one is of the four-terminal type

check for continuity between the relay power circuit terminals. There should be no continuity between terminal 30 and 87 with the relay de-energized.

9   Connect a fused jumper wire to terminal 86 and the positive battery terminal. Connect another jumper wire between terminal 85 and ground. When the connections are made, the relay should click.

10 With the jumper wires connected, check for continuity between the power circuit terminals. Now, there should be continuity between terminals 30 and 87.

11 If the relay fails any of the above tests, replace it.

6   Turn signal and hazard flashers - check and replacement

▶ **Refer to illustration 6.5**

1   The "combination" flasher, located on the back of the interior fuse/relay box, flashes the turn signals when the turn signal switch is operated, and all four signals when the emergency flasher switch on top of the steering column is On.

2   When the flasher unit is functioning properly, an audible click can be heard during its operation. If the turn signal indicator on one side of the vehicle flashes much more rapidly than normal, a faulty turn signal bulb is indicated.

3   If both turn signals fail to blink, the problem may be due to a blown fuse, a faulty flasher unit, a broken switch or a loose or open connection. If a quick check of the fuse box indicates that the turn signal fuse has blown, check the wiring for a short before installing a new fuse.

4   The type of combination flasher unit used on the covered models has complex internal circuitry, and can't be tested using standard electrical test equipment. Refer to the wiring diagrams at the end of this Chapter and test the circuitry before replacing the flasher with a known-good unit.

5   To remove the flasher, reach up under the left end of the instrument panel and pull it out of the fuse block (see illustration).

➡**Note: It will be easier to access if the driver's knee bolster is removed first (see Chapter 11).**

6.5 The turn signal/hazard flasher (arrow) is located on the backside of the left instrument panel fuse/relay box (shown with driver's knee bolster removed for clarity)

6   Make sure that the replacement unit is identical to the original. Compare the old one to the new one before installing it.

7   Installation is the reverse of removal.

8   If the flasher unit is not the problem, refer to Section 7 and test the turn signal/hazard portion of the multi-function switch.

7   Steering column switches - replacement

▶ **Refer to illustrations 7.3 and 7.4**

❋❋ WARNING:

The models covered by this manual are equipped with Supplemental Restraint Systems (SRS), more commonly known as airbags. Always disable the airbag system before working in the vicinity of any airbag system components to avoid the possibility of accidental deployment of the airbags, which could cause personal injury (see Section 28).

1   The multi-function switch is located on the left side of the steering column. It incorporates into one switch the turn signal, headlight dimmer, windshield wiper/washer and, if equipped, cruise control functions.

2   Remove the steering column covers and driver's knee bolster (see Chapter 11).

3   Remove the Torx-head multi-function switch screws, then detach the switch from the steering column (see illustration).

7.3 Remove the screws (arrows) with a Torx bit

7.4 The two multi-function switch harness connectors (arrows) are plugged into this larger connector next to the steering column

4   Trace the multi-function switch wires down to the large connector, and unplug the connectors from the larger connector (see illustration).

5   Unplug the two, two-wire connectors from the multi-function switch and snip the wire ties that bundle the multi-function switch harness to the other harnesses at the large connector. Remove the harness with the multi-function switch.

6   Installation is the reverse of removal.

---

8   Ignition switch and key lock cylinder - replacement

▶ **Refer to illustrations 8.4a, 8.4b, 8.4c and 8.5**

✷ WARNING:

The models covered by this manual are equipped with Supplemental Restraint Systems (SRS), more commonly known as airbags. Always disable the airbag system before working in the vicinity of any airbag system components to avoid the possibility of accidental deployment of the airbags, which could cause personal injury (see Section 28).

1   The ignition switch, located on the right side of the steering column, is comprised of a cast-metal housing, an ignition lock cylinder and an electrical component, the switch device.

2   Disconnect the negative battery cable.

✷ CAUTION:

On models equipped with the Theftlock audio system, be sure the lockout feature is turned off before performing any procedure which requires disconnecting the battery (see the front of this manual).

3   Remove the steering column covers and driver's knee bolster (see Chapter 11). On models with automatic transmissions, the shift linkage must be in Park before removing/installing the ignition switch.

4   The ignition switch must be replaced with its electrical harness and end connectors where the harness joins with the vehicle electrical system. Disconnect the electrical connectors at the switch and the ignition switch harness ends, then remove the switch (see illustrations). Refer to Section 7 and remove the two multi-function switch connec-

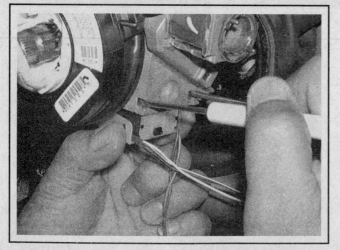

8.4a Remove the electrical portion of the ignition switch (arrow) by prying down with two screwdrivers

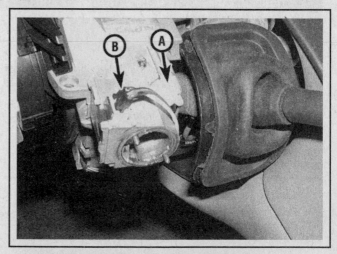

8.4b With the switch pulled away from the column, disconnect these two connectors - twist connector A clockwise and pull out, then pull up on connector B (key cylinder must be removed first as shown)

8.4c Remove this connector (A) from the back of the left-hand fuse/relay panel, and remove the main steering column connector (B) with the ignition switch harness (multi-function switch connectors removed from main connector)

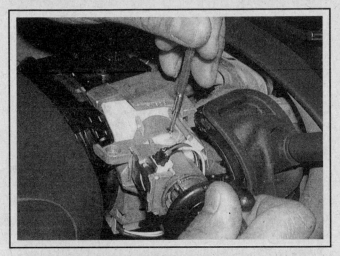

8.5 Push the retaining pin (arrow) in to unseat the lock cylinder, then withdraw the key and cylinder

tors from the larger steering column connector.

➡**Note: The key lock cylinder must be removed first, see below.**

5   To remove the key lock cylinder, place the key in the lock and rotate clockwise to the Start (1999 through 2002) or Run (2003 and

later) position. Push in the retainer pin and pull the key and lock cylinder from the ignition switch (see illustration).

6   When installing the cylinder, align the retainer with the retainer slot in the housing, then push the cylinder in until it snaps in position.

7   The remainder of installation is the reverse of removal.

| 9 | Instrument panel switches - replacement |

❈❈ WARNING:

The models covered by this manual are equipped with Supplemental Restraint Systems (SRS), more commonly known as airbags. Always disable the airbag system before working in the vicinity of any airbag system components to avoid the possibility of accidental deployment of the airbags, which could cause personal injury (see Section 28).

HEADLIGHT SWITCH

▸ **Refer to illustration 9.3**

1   Disconnect the negative cable at the battery (see Chapter 1).

❈❈ CAUTION:

On models equipped with the Theftlock audio system, be sure the lockout feature is turned off before performing any procedure which requires disconnecting the battery (see the front of this manual).

2   Remove the instrument cluster bezel (see Chapter 11).

3   Use a small screwdriver to pry the two plastic clips, then pull the

headlight/panel dimmer switch out of the left electrical pod (see illustration).

4   Disconnect the electrical connector on the back of the switch.

5   Installation is the reverse of removal.

9.3 Pry the clips with a small screwdriver to remove the headlight switch

ON/OFF SWITCHES

▶ **Refer to illustration 9.7**

6   Depending on the options of the vehicle, there may be one or more switches on the instrument panel, including fog lights, overhead beacon, cargo lamp or selectable ride control. In addition, all models have a passenger airbag On/Off switch that allows you to disengage the passenger airbag if a child is riding in the right-front passenger seat.

7   All of the above-mentioned switches are accessible when the instrument cluster bezel is removed (see Chapter 11), and are removed by prying clips with a small screwdriver and pulling the switch out (see illustration).

✳✳ CAUTION:

Before removing the airbag On/Off switch, disable the airbag system (see Section 28).

8   With simple on/off switches, use an ohmmeter or self-powered continuity tester, check the switch for proper continuity between the terminals. There should be continuity between terminals only when the switch is engaged. If the switch fails the test, replace the switch.

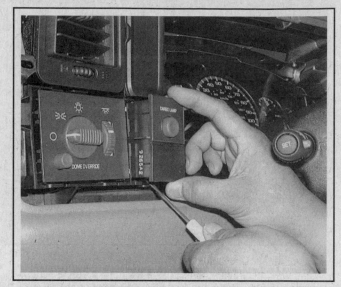

9.7 Remove on/off type switches (cargo lamp switch shown) by depressing the clips (arrows) and pulling the switch out of the instrument panel

10 Fuel, temperature and oil pressure gauges - check

✳✳ WARNING:

The models covered by this manual are equipped with Supplemental Restraint Systems (SRS), more commonly known as airbags. Always disable the airbag system before working in the vicinity of any airbag system components to avoid the possibility of accidental deployment of the airbags, which could cause personal injury (see Section 28).

➡Note: **This procedure applies to conventional analog type gauges (NON-digital) only.**

1   All tests below require the ignition switch to be turned to the Off position before testing.

2   If the gauge pointer does not move from the empty or cold positions, check the fuse. If the fuse is OK, locate the particular sending

unit for the circuit you're working on (see Chapter 4 for fuel sending unit location, Chapter 3 for the temperature gauge sending unit location, Chapter 2 for the oil pressure sending unit location). Connect the sending unit connector to ground with a jumper wire.

3   Turn the ignition key to On momentarily. If the pointer goes to the full or hot position replace the sending unit.

➡Note: **Turn the key Off right away, because grounding the sending unit for too long could damage the gauge.**

If the pointer stays in same position, use a jumper wire to ground the sending unit terminal on the back of the gauge. If necessary, refer to the wiring diagrams at the end of this Chapter. If the pointer moves, the problem lies in the wiring between the gauge and the sending unit. If the pointer does not move with the sending unit terminal on the back of the gauge grounded, check for voltage at the other terminal of the gauge. There should not be voltage.

11 Instrument cluster - removal and installation

▶ **Refer to illustrations 11.4 and 11.5**

✳✳ WARNING:

The models covered by this manual are equipped with Supplemental Restraint Systems (SRS), more commonly known as airbags. Always disable the airbag system before working in the vicinity of any airbag system components to avoid the possibility of accidental deployment of the airbags, which could cause personal injury (see Section 28).

1   Disconnect the negative cable from the battery (see Chapter 1).

✳✳ CAUTION:

On models equipped with the Theftlock audio system, be sure the lockout feature is turned off before performing any procedure which requires disconnecting the battery (see the front of this manual).

2   Remove the instrument cluster bezel (see Chapter 11).

3   On models with tilt steering columns, lower the column as far as

11.4 Remove the instrument cluster mounting screws (arrows)

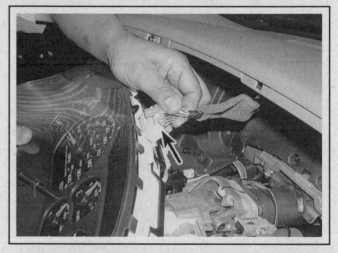

11.5 Pull the cluster out enough to disconnect the electrical connector (arrow)

it will go, and on models with column shift, apply the parking brake and lower the shift lever as far as possible.

4   Remove the screws securing the cluster to the instrument panel (see illustration).

5   Pull the cluster forward enough to disengage the single, large electrical connector at the back, then pull the cluster out, tilting the bottom out first (see illustration).

6   Installation is the reverse of removal.

12 Radio and speakers - removal and installation

✳ WARNING:

The models covered by this manual are equipped with Supplemental Restraint Systems (SRS), more commonly known as airbags. Always disable the airbag system before working in the vicinity of any airbag system components to avoid the possibility of accidental deployment of the airbags, which could cause personal injury (see Section 28).

RADIO

▶ **Refer to illustrations 12.3a and 12.3b**

1   Refer to Chapter 1 and disconnect the negative battery cable, then remove the instrument cluster bezel (see Chapter 11).

✳ CAUTION:

On models equipped with the Theftlock audio system, be sure the lockout feature is turned off before performing any procedure which requires disconnecting the battery (see the front of this manual).

2   Refer to Chapter 11 and remove the instrument cluster bezel.

3   Squeeze the mounting clips, pull the radio out of the instrument panel, disconnect the connectors, then remove it from the vehicle (see illustrations).

4   Installation is the reverse of removal.

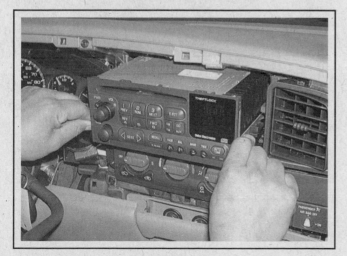

12.3a Depress the clips (arrows) and pull the radio out

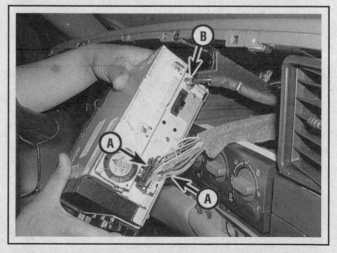

12.3b Disconnect the two connectors (A) from the back of the radio, then disconnect the ground wire and the antenna cable (B)

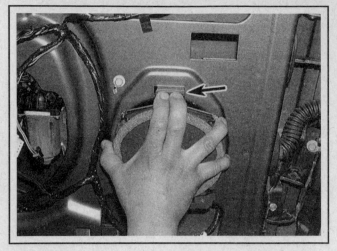

12.6a Push down on the door speaker mounting tab (arrow), then tilt the top out and pull up to clear the lower tabs

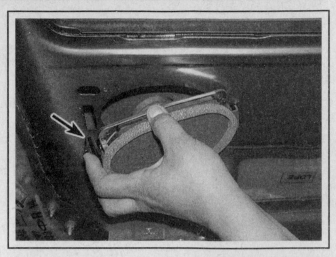

12.6b On rear speakers in pick-ups, depress the clip (arrow) at the rear of the speaker

SPEAKERS

▶ **Refer to illustrations 12.6a and 12.6b**

5   Remove the door trim panel (see Chapter 11).

➡**Note: SUV models have as many as nine door speakers, with a separate subwoofer in the rear. Standard pick-up models have one speaker in each door and one rear speaker on each side mounted in the rear corner trim panel. All are mounted in a similar fashion. Pick-ups with higher-level sound systems have more speakers.**

6   Push down on the plastic tab at the top of the speaker and lean the top of the speaker out, then lift the speaker up off the lower tabs (see illustrations). Pull the speaker out of the door, disconnect the electrical connector and remove the speaker from the vehicle.

➡**Note: On some speaker installations, the speaker mounting tabs are at the left and right sides, rather than top and bottom.**

REAR SEAT AUDIO CONTROLS (SUV MODELS)

▶ **Refer to illustrations 12.9 and 12.10**

7   Audio controls for the middle seat passengers in SUV models are located at the rear of the center console.

8   To access these controls, remove the upper cover of the console (see Chapter 11).

9   Pull up the clips at the top of the console rear panel, and tilt it back to access the radio controls (see illustration).

10 Disconnect the electrical connectors, then squeeze the clips in and push the radio controls out of the console (see illustration).

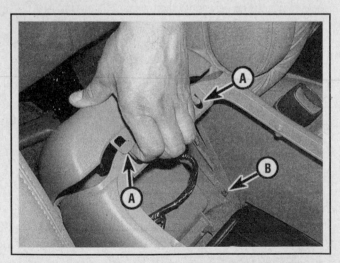

12.9 Pull up the clips (A) and tilt the console rear panel back, pivoting on the metal clips (B) at the bottom

12.10 Disconnect the electrical connectors, then squeeze in the clips (arrows) and push the radio controls out of the panel

13 Antenna - removal and installation

▶ **Refer to illustrations 13.1 and 13.4**

1   Use a small open-end wrench to unscrew the antenna mast (see illustration). Be very careful - the tool could slip and scratch the body. It's a good idea to surround the base of the antenna with masking tape to prevent scratching.

2   If the cable itself must be replaced, refer to Chapter 11 and remove the instrument panel upper trim pad.

3   With the trim pad removed, disconnect the antenna mast cable from the radio cable where they join in a connector at the far right end of the instrument panel. If the entire cable must be replaced, Refer to Section 12 and remove the radio, then release the cable from the clips along the top edge of the instrument panel.

4   Attach a "fish" wire to the end of the cable, then remove the antenna mast base mounting screws and pull up the base and its cable (see illustration).

5   Attach the new cable to the fish wire and pull the wire back slowly and carefully into the body, routing it over the instrument panel as the original cable had been.

6   Installation of the antenna base and mast is the reverse of the removal procedure.

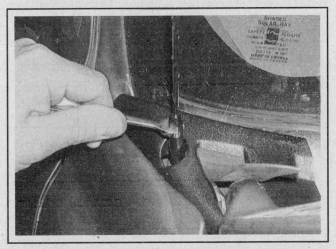

13.1 Use a small wrench to remove the antenna mast

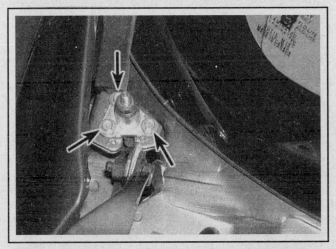

13.4 To remove the antenna base and cable, remove the base mounting screws (arrows) in the right cowl/fender area

14 Headlight bulb - replacement

▶ **Refer to illustration 14.2**

✳✳ WARNING:

Halogen bulbs are gas-filled and under pressure and may shatter if the surface is scratched or the bulb is dropped. Wear eye protection and handle the bulbs carefully, grasping only the base whenever possible. Don't touch the surface of the bulb with your fingers because the oil from your skin could cause it to overheat and fail prematurely. If you do touch the bulb surface, clean it with rubbing alcohol.

1   Refer to Section 16 and remove the headlight housing.

2   Turn the headlight bulb holder counterclockwise and withdraw the bulb holder (see illustration).

3   Remove the old bulb from the bulb-holder. Handling the new bulb only with gloves or a clean rag, insert the new bulb in the holder.

4   Installation is the reverse of the removal procedure.

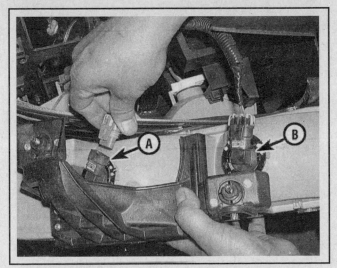

14.2 Disconnect the electrical connector from the headlight housing and pull the bulb holder out, then replace the bulb - A is the low-beam bulb, B is the high-beam bulb

15 Headlights and fog lights - adjustment

⁂ WARNING:

The headlights must be aimed correctly. If adjusted incorrectly, they could temporarily blind the driver of an oncoming vehicle and cause an accident or seriously reduce your ability to see the road. The headlights should be checked for proper aim every 12 months and any time a new headlight is installed or front-end bodywork is performed. The following procedure is only an interim step to provide temporary adjustment until the headlights can be adjusted by a properly equipped shop.

HEADLIGHTS

▶ **Refer to illustrations 15.1 and 15.2**

➡**Note: It is important that the headlights are aimed correctly. If adjusted incorrectly they could blind the driver of an oncoming vehicle and cause a serious accident or seriously reduce your ability to see the road. The headlights should be checked for proper aim every 12 months and any time a new headlight is installed or front end body work is performed. It should be emphasized that the following procedure is only an interim step that will provide temporary adjustment until the headlights can be adjusted by a properly equipped shop.**

1   Some models are equipped with composite headlights with two adjustment screws, one controlling left-and-right movement and one for up-and-down movement (see illustration). Later models have only one adjustment screw, controlling up-and-down movement.

2   There are several methods of adjusting the headlights. The simplest method requires a blank wall 25 feet in front of the vehicle and a level floor (see illustration).

3   Position masking tape vertically on the wall in reference to the vehicle centerline and the centerlines of both headlights.

4   Position a horizontal tape line in reference to the centerline of all the headlights.

➡**Note: It may be easier to position the tape on the wall with the vehicle parked only a few inches away.**

5   Adjustment should be made with the vehicle sitting level, the gas tank half-full and no unusually heavy load in the vehicle.

6   Starting with the low beam adjustment, position the high intensity zone so it is two inches below the horizontal line and two inches to the side of the vertical headlight line, away from oncoming traffic. Twist the adjustment screws until the desired level has been achieved.

7   With the high beams on, the high intensity zone should be vertically centered with the exact center just below the horizontal line.

➡**Note: It may not be possible to position the headlight aim exactly for both high and low beams. If a compromise must be made, keep in mind that the low beams are the most used and have the greatest effect on driver safety.**

8   Have the headlights adjusted by a dealer service department at the earliest opportunity.

FOG LIGHTS

▶ **Refer to illustration 15.11**

9   Some models have optional fog lights that can be aimed just like headlights.

10 Position tape on a wall 25 feet in front of the vehicle (see illustra-

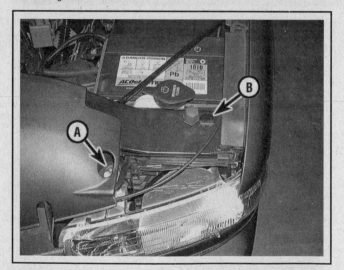

15.1 Open the hood and adjust the headlight alignment with the screws (arrows indicate the access holes) - use a T15 Torx screwdriver

A = Side-to-side adjustment   *B = Up-and-down adjustment*

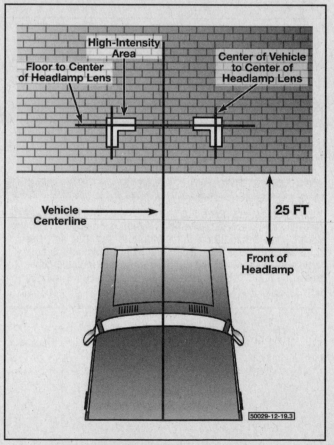

15.2 Headlight adjustment details

tion 15.2). Tape a horizontal line on the wall that represents the height of the fog lamps, and another tape line four inches below that line.

11 Using the adjusting screws on the fog lamps, adjust the pattern on the wall so that the top of the fog lamp beam meets the lower line on the wall, and that the beam is centered horizontally in front of the fog lamps (see illustration).

15.11 Twist the thumbscrew (arrow) to adjust the aim of optional fog lights (seen here from behind the bumper)

16 Headlight housing - replacement

▶ **Refer to illustration 16.1**

1 Open the hood, swing the headlight housing retaining rod(s) forward and pull them up (see illustration).

➡**Note: Some models have two rods, others have only one.**

2 Pull the housing forward, out of the body.
3 Disconnect the electrical connectors.
4 Installation is the reverse of removal.

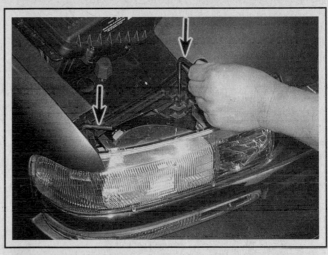

16.1 Twist the headlight housing mounting rod(s) (arrows) out of their clips and pull them straight up to disengage the housings from the vehicle

17 Bulb replacement

⁂ WARNING:

Bulbs can remain hot for up to twenty minutes after they're turned off. Be sure bulbs are off and cool before you touch them.

TURN SIGNAL/SIDE-MARKER/DAYTIME RUNNING LIGHTS

▶ **Refer to illustrations 17.2, 17.4a and 17.4b**

1 Refer to Section 16 and remove the headlight housing.
2 Push in on the spring clip securing one end of the turn-signal housing, then swing the housing out away from the vehicle (see illustration).
3 Disconnect the electrical connectors.

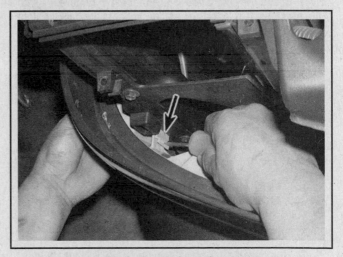

17.2 Push in on the plastic clip (arrow) and swing the turn signal housing out away from the vehicle

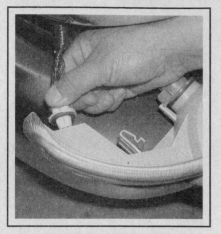

17.4a Pull out the bulb holder for the sidemarker lamp and replace the bulb

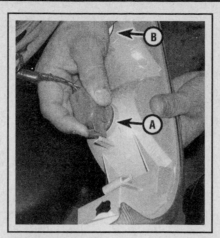

17.4b Twist out the bulb holder for the turn signal light (A). The Daytime Running Light bulb (B) is replaced in the same manner

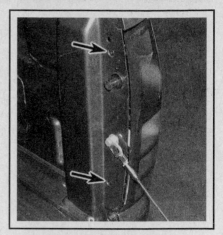

17.6 Remove the taillight housing screws (arrows, pick-up model shown)

4 Each bulb is replaced in the same manner, by twisting the bulb holder out (see illustrations). The bulbs pull straight out of their holder.

5 Installation is the reverse of removal.

17.7 Rotate the bulb holder and pull it out to remove it - A is the brake light, B is the turn signal, and C is the back-up light

TAIL/STOP/TURN/BACK-UP LIGHT

▶ **Refer to illustrations 17.6 and 17.7**

6 On all models, these rear lights are all in one housing. On pick-up models, lower the tailgate and remove the screws (see illustration). Rotate the housing out to disengage the hooks from in the body. On SUV models, open the liftgate or optional rear doors and remove the screws, then rotate the housing so the hooks will clear the holes in the body.

7 On all models, rotate the bulb holders 1/4-turn counterclockwise and pull them from the housing. Replace the bulb, by pulling it straight out of the holder and pushing the new one in, then insert the holder into the housing and rotate 1/4-turn clockwise to lock (see illustration).

8 Installation is the reverse of removal.

CENTER HIGH-MOUNTED STOP LIGHT (CHMSL)/ CARGO LAMP

▶ **Refer to illustrations 17.9a, 17.9b and 17.12**

Pick-up models

9 Standing in the truck bed, remove the two Phillips-head screws

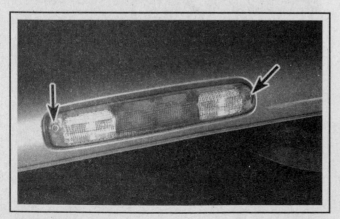

17.9a Remove the screws and pull the CHMSL/cargo light housing out (pick-up models)

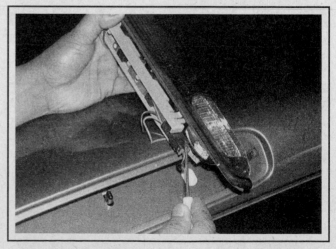

17.9b Release these tabs (arrows) to pull off the bulb holder plate

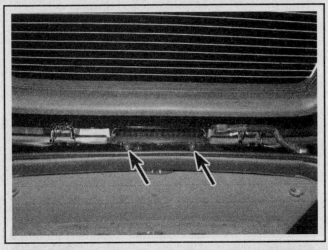

17.12 On SUV models, the CHMSL light assembly comes off once the screws (arrows) are removed

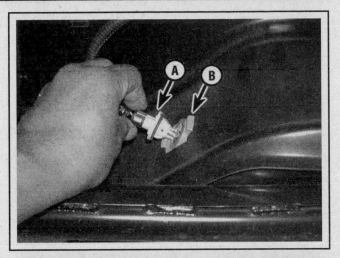

17.15 Reach up behind the bumper to rotate and remove the bulb holder (A) - if the light housing must be replaced, squeeze in the clips (B) and push the light to the outside of the bumper

and withdraw the CHMSL/cargo lamp housing from the cab (see illustration). Release the tabs at each end of the plate behind the four bulbs (see illustration).

10 Pull the bulb assembly away from the housing. The two outer bulbs are cargo lights and are removed by twisting a quarter-turn. The two center bulbs are the CHMSL bulbs and are pulled straight out of their holders.

11 Installation is the reverse of the removal procedure. Make sure the gasket on the back of the housing is intact, or a water leak could develop in the cab.

Suburban/Yukon models

12 On SUV models, raise the liftgate and remove the screws to access the bulb holders (see illustration).

13 On all models, rotate the bulb holder 1/4-turn clockwise and withdraw it, then replace the bulb by pulling it straight from the holder.

14 Installation is the reverse of removal.

LICENSE PLATE BULB

▶ **Refer to illustration 17.15**

15 The license plate lamp is attached to the rear bumper, but the bulb holder can be removed by reaching up behind the bumper (see illustration). The bulb is pulled straight out of the holder.

16 Installation is the reverse of removal.

INSTRUMENT CLUSTER LIGHTS

▶ **Refer to illustrations 17.17 and 17.18**

17 To gain access to the instrument cluster illumination lights, the instrument cluster will have to be removed (see Section 11). The bulbs can then be removed and replaced from the rear of the cluster, after removing a cover panel (see illustration).

18 Rotate the bulb counterclockwise to remove it (see illustration).

19 Installation is the reverse of removal.

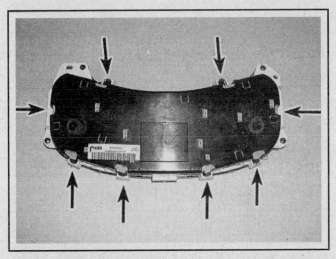

17.17 Release the clips (arrows) and remove the cover from the rear of the instrument cluster

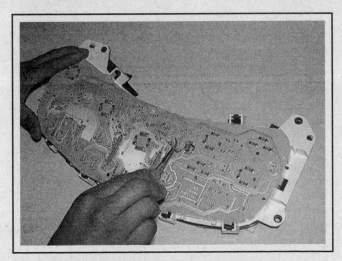

17.18 Use pliers or tweezers to rotate and remove the individual cluster lights

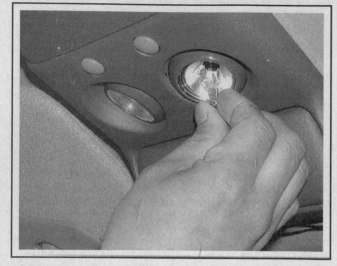

17.21 Remove the map light lens, then pull out the bulb (2000 model shown)

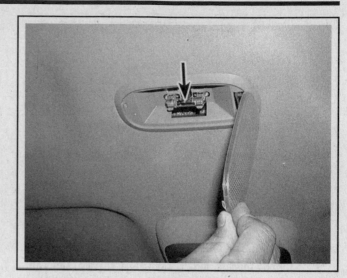

17.23a Pull the dome light bulb (arrow) straight down, out of its sockets (pick-up models)

INTERIOR LIGHTS

Overhead console reading lights

▶ Refer to illustration 17.21

20 On 1999 models, push up on the reading light and twist counter-clockwise, then pull the light out and replace the bulb from behind it.

21 On 2000 models, use a small screwdriver to pry off the reading light lens, then remove the bulb (see illustration).

22 Installation is the reverse of removal.

Dome light

▶ Refer to illustrations 17.23a and 17.23b

23 Pry the dome light lens off, then replace the bulb by pulling it straight out (see illustrations).

24 Installation is the reverse of removal.

Door courtesy lights

▶ Refer to illustration 17.25

25 Pry the light out of the door panel and replace the bulb from the rear (see illustration).

26 Installation is the reverse of removal.

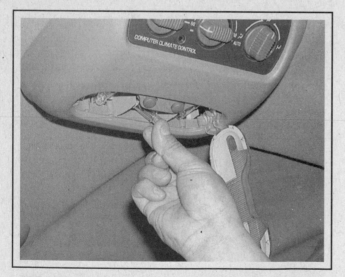

17.23b On SUV models, the dome light is in the middle overhead console - pry down the lens (from the left side) and pull out the tubular bulb

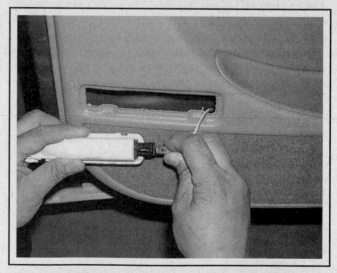

17.25 Pry the courtesy light out of the door panel, then remove the bulb holder from the end of the light housing

18 Wiper motor - check and replacement

FRONT

▶ **Refer to illustrations 18.2, 18.4 and 18.5**

1   Disconnect the negative cable from the battery (see Chapter 1).

✳✳ CAUTION:

On models equipped with the Theftlock audio system, be sure the lockout feature is turned off before performing any procedure which requires disconnecting the battery (see the front of this manual).

2   Mark the positions of the wiper arms on the windshield, then remove the wiper arms (see illustration).

➡ **Note: Disconnect the washer hose from the wiper arm.**

3   Remove the cowl grille (see Chapter 11). Remove the four bolts and the reinforcement panel above the wiper assembly.

4   Disconnect the electrical connector at the wiper motor, then remove the wiper motor/linkage mounting bolts (see illustration).

5   Remove the assembly and unbolt the motor from the linkage (see illustration). Pry the link from the wiper motor arm.

6   Installation is the reverse of removal.

REAR (SUV MODELS)

▶ **Refer to illustrations 18.8 and 18.10**

7   Disconnect the negative cable from the battery (see Chapter 1).

✳✳ CAUTION:

On models equipped with the Theftlock audio system, be sure the lockout feature is turned off before performing any procedure which requires disconnecting the battery (see the front of this manual).

8   Mark the positions of the wiper arm on the liftgate glass, then remove the wiper arm cover and nut at the outside of the liftgate, then the bezel (see illustration). Be careful not to scratch the paint on the liftgate.

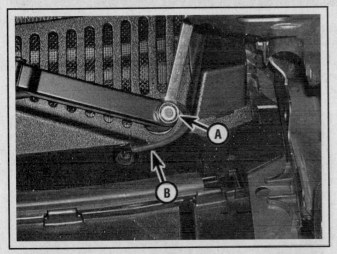

18.2 Lift the cover, use a wrench to remove the nut (A) on the wiper shaft, then grasp the wiper arm and use a rocking motion to detach it from the shaft - disconnect the washer hose (B)

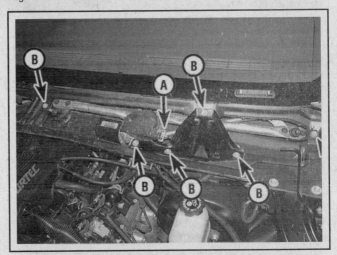

18.4 Wiper motor electrical connector (A) and wiper assembly mounting bolts (B) (later models have only two bolts)

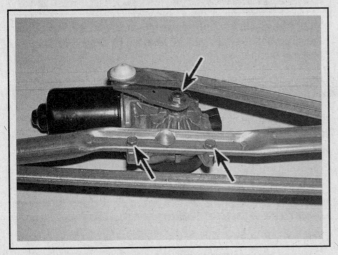

18.5 Remove the bolts (arrows) to separate the wiper motor from the linkage assembly

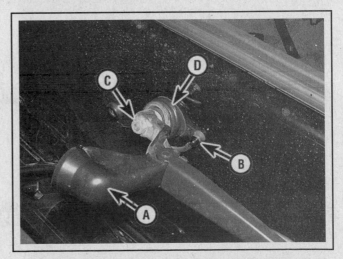

18.8 At the liftgate on SUV models, lift the cover (A), disconnect the washer hose (B), remove the nut (C), arm and bezel (D)

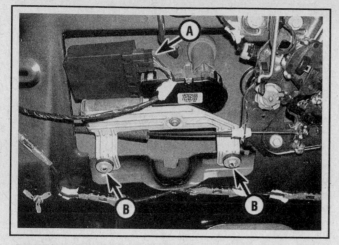

18.10 On SUV models, disconnect the electrical connector (A) at the rear wiper motor, then remove the two mounting bolts (B)

9   Refer to Chapter 11 and remove the upper and lower liftgate interior trim panels.

10 Disconnect the electrical connector at the rear wiper motor, then remove the two mounting bolts (see illustration).

✳ CAUTION:

Support the motor while removing the bolts.

11 Installation is the reverse of removal.

19 Horn - check and replacement

CHECK

▶ **Refer to illustration 19.2**

1   Remove the cover from the underhood fuse/relay box (see illustration 3.1a) and check the horn fuse and relay, replacing any faulty components.

2   Disconnect the electrical connectors from the horns (see illustration). There are two horns, one at each lower corner of the radiator support.

3   Have an assistant press the horn button and use a voltmeter to make sure there is battery voltage at the supply wire terminal (see the wiring diagrams at the end of this Chapter)..If the relay is good and there's no voltage at the horn, the wire (which leads to the relay) has a fault.

4   Use an ohmmeter to measure the resistance between the wiring connector black wire and a good ground. There should be zero ohms. If not, repair the fault in the ground circuit.

5   If there's voltage at the horn and the wiring circuits are good, the horn is faulty and must be replaced.

REPLACEMENT

6   Disconnect the electrical connectors, remove the mounting bolts and detach the horns (see illustration 19.2).

7   Installation is the reverse of removal.

19.2 Disconnect the horn connector (A) and remove the mounting bolt (B) - shown here from below and behind the front bumper

20 Daytime Running Lights (DRL) - general information

The Daytime Running Lights (DRL) system used on all models illuminates the running lights, located in the front turn signal housings, whenever the ignition is On. The only exception is with the engine running and the parking brake engaged (standard-shift models) or with the shift lever in Park (automatic-transmission models). Once the parking brake is released or the shift lever is moved, the lights will remain on as long as the ignition switch is on.

21 Rear window defogger (SUV models) - check and repair

1   The rear window defogger consists of a number of horizontal heating elements baked onto the inside surface of the glass. Power is supplied through a large fuse from the underhood fuse/relay box in the engine compartment. The heater is controlled by the instrument panel switch.

2   Small breaks in the element can be repaired without removing the rear window.

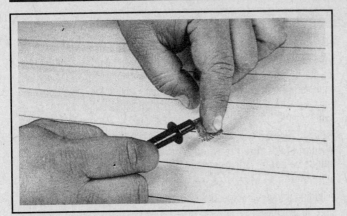

21.5 When measuring the voltage at the rear window defogger grid, wrap a piece of aluminum foil around the positive probe of the voltmeter and press the foil against the wire with your finger

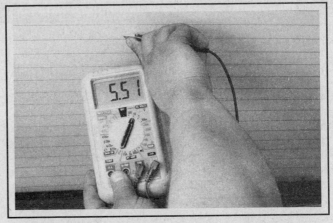

21.6 To determine if a heating element has broken, check the voltage at the center of each element - if the voltage is 6-volts, the element is unbroken

21.8 To find the break, place the voltmeter negative lead against the defogger ground terminal, place the voltmeter positive lead with the foil strip against the heat wire at the positive terminal end and slide it toward the negative terminal end - the point at which the voltmeter deflects from several volts to zero volts is the point at which the wire is broken

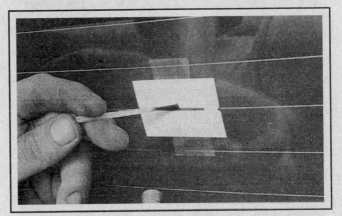

21.14 To use a defogger repair kit, apply masking tape to the inside of the window at the damaged area, then brush on the special conductive coating

CHECK

▸ **Refer to illustrations 21.5, 21.6 and 21.8**

3   Turn the ignition switch and defogger switch to the ON position.

4   Using a voltmeter, place the positive probe against the defogger grid positive terminal and the negative probe against the ground terminal. If battery voltage is not indicated, check the fuse, defogger switch, defogger relay and related wiring. If voltage is indicated, but all or part of the defogger doesn't heat, proceed with the following tests.

5   When measuring voltage during the next two tests, wrap a piece of aluminum foil around the tip of the voltmeter positive probe and press the foil against the heating element with your finger (see illustration). Place the negative probe on the defogger grid ground terminal.

6   Check the voltage at the center of each heating element (see illustration). If the voltage is 5 to 6 volts, the element is okay (there is no break). If the voltage is 0 volts, the element is broken between the center of the element and the positive end. If the voltage is 10 to 12 volts the element is broken between the center of the element and the ground side. Check each heating element.

7   If none of the elements are broken, connect the negative probe to a good chassis ground. The voltage reading should stay the same; if it

doesn't, the ground connection is bad.

8   To find the break, place the voltmeter negative probe against the defogger ground terminal. Place the voltmeter positive probe with the foil strip against the heating element at the positive side and slide it toward the negative side. The point at which the voltmeter deflects from several volts to zero is the point where the heating element is broken (see illustration).

REPAIR

▸ **Refer to illustration 21.14**

9   Repair the break in the element using a repair kit specifically for this purpose, such as Dupont paste No. 4817 (or equivalent). The kit includes conductive plastic epoxy.

10   Before repairing a break, turn off the system and allow it to cool for a few minutes.

11   Lightly buff the element area with fine steel wool; then clean it thoroughly with rubbing alcohol.

12   Use masking tape to mask off the area being repaired.

13   Thoroughly mix the epoxy, following the kit instructions.

14   Apply the epoxy material to the slit in the masking tape, overlapping the undamaged area about 3/4-inch on either end (see illustration).

15   Allow the repair to cure for 24 hours before removing the tape and using the system.

22 Cruise control system - description and check

♦ **Refer to illustrations 22.5a, 22.5b and 22.7**

MODELS WITHOUT ELECTRONIC THROTTLE CONTROL

1   The cruise control system maintains vehicle speed with a servo motor (located on the left side of the firewall) that is connected to the throttle linkage by a cable. The system consists of the servo motor, brake switch, cable, control switches, relay and associated wiring. Some features of the system require special testers and diagnostic procedures that are beyond the scope of the home mechanic. Listed below are some general procedures that may be used to locate common problems.

2   Check the cruise control fuse in the interior fuse/relay box at the left-hand end of the instrument panel (see Section 3).

3   The brake pedal position (BPP) switch (or brake light switch) deactivates the cruise control system. Have an assistant press the brake pedal while you check the brake light operation.

4   If the brake lights do not operate properly, correct the problem and retest the cruise control.

5   Check the control cable between the cruise control servo/amplifier and the throttle linkage and replace as necessary (see illustrations). To adjust the cable at the throttle end, some models have a screw-

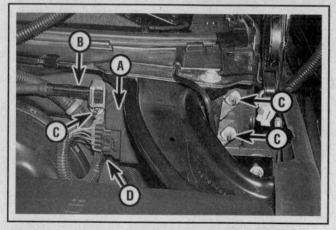

22.5a The cruise control servo (A) is located at the left end of the firewall - make sure the cruise control cable (B) is not damaged and that it operates smoothly when the throttle is opened. C indicates the servo mounting nuts, and D is the electrical connector

22.5b Adjust the cruise control cable by turning the thumbscrew (arrow) to remove slack (not all models)

thread adjuster, and others have a clip-type. On the screw-threaded type, make sure the throttle is in the fully-closed position and adjust the plastic screw until slack is removed in the cruise cable. On models equipped with the clip-type, release the lock-clip at the cable housing end (at the throttle linkage) by squeezing the sides of the clip together until the clip can be pulled out of the adjuster. Now move the cable by hand to remove any slack, then push the lock-clip back in.

➥**Note: Make sure the white mark on the side of the clip can no longer be seen. This ensures that the clip is fully seated.**

6   The cruise control system uses information from the PCM, including the Vehicle Speed Sensor, which is located in the transmission. To test the speed sensor, see Chapter 6.

7   Some tests of the servo can be made by the home mechanic. Turn the ignition key to On (engine not running). Disconnect the electrical connector at the servo and use a grounded test light to check for battery power at terminal F on the harness side (see illustration). If power isn't there, refer to the wiring diagrams at the end of this Chapter and check the circuit.

8   With the cruise control switch in the On position, there should be battery voltage present in terminal A, and at terminal B in the Set/Coast position.

9   Test-drive the vehicle to determine if the cruise control is now working. If it isn't, take it to a dealer service department or an automotive electrical specialist for further diagnosis.

MODELS WITH ELECTRONIC THROTTLE CONTROL

10 From inside the vehicle, the cruise control system on models with Electronic Throttle Control seems identical to the system used on models without Electronic Throttle Control, with the same indicators on the cluster, the same cruise control switch on the steering wheel, same brake and clutch pedal position switches, etc. However, there is no cruise control servo motor or cable. Instead, the cruise control system is under the direct control of the Powertrain Control Module (PCM). Under the hood, there is no servo, nor servo cable, because these models have an electronically-controlled throttle body (no accelerator cable). When you select the speed that you want to maintain, the PCM controls vehicle speed by opening and closing the throttle plate by means of a computer-controlled solenoid (motor) inside the throttle body.

11 The diagnostic procedures for troubleshooting the cruise control system are beyond the scope of this manual, but if the system can't be set, or the set speed doesn't cancel when the brake pedal is depressed, check the fuses.

12 Other than checking the fuses, the diagnostic procedures for troubleshooting the cruise control system on models with Electronic Throttle Control are beyond the scope of this manual. A dealer service department or other qualified repair shop should handle any further testing.

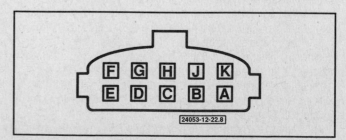

22.7 Pin identification for the cruise control servo connector

23 Power window system - description and check

▶ **Refer to illustrations 23.12a and 23.12b**

1   The power window system operates electric motors, mounted in the doors, which lower and raise the windows. The system consists of the control switches, the motors, regulators, glass mechanisms and associated wiring.

2   The power windows can be lowered and raised from the master control switch by the driver or by remote switches located at the individual windows. Each window has a separate motor that is reversible. The position of the control switch determines the polarity and therefore the direction of operation.

3   The circuit is protected by a fuse and a circuit breaker. Each motor is also equipped with an internal circuit breaker; this prevents one stuck window from disabling the whole system.

4   The power window system will only operate when the ignition switch is ON. In addition, many models have a window lockout switch at the master control switch which, when activated, disables the switches at the rear windows and, sometimes, the switch at the passenger's window also. Always check these items before troubleshooting a window problem.

5   These procedures are general in nature, so if you can't find the problem using them, take the vehicle to a dealer service department or other properly equipped repair facility.

6   If the power windows won't operate, always check the fuse and circuit breaker first.

7   If only the rear windows are inoperative (SUV), or if the windows only operate from the master control switch, check the rear window lockout switch for continuity in the unlocked position. Replace it if it doesn't have continuity.

8   Check the wiring between the switches and fuse panel for continuity. Repair the wiring, if necessary.

9   If only one window is inoperative from the master control switch, try the other control switch at the window.

▶**Note: This doesn't apply to the driver's door window.**

10 If the same window works from one switch, but not the other, check the switch for continuity.

11 If the switch tests OK, check for a short or open in the circuit between the affected switch and the window motor.

12 If one window is inoperative from both switches, Use a flat-bladed trim tool to pry up and remove the switch panel from the affected door. Check for voltage at the switch (see illustrations) and at the motor (refer to Chapter 11 for door panel removal) while the switch is operated.

13 If voltage is reaching the motor, disconnect the glass from the regulator (see Chapter 11). Move the window up and down by hand while checking for binding and damage. Also check for binding and damage to the regulator. If the regulator is not damaged and the window moves up and down smoothly, replace the motor. If there's binding or damage, lubricate, repair or replace parts, as necessary.

14 If voltage isn't reaching the motor, check the wiring in the circuit for continuity between the switches and motors. You'll need to consult the wiring diagram at the end of this Chapter. If the circuit is equipped with a relay, check that the relay is grounded properly and receiving voltage.

15 Test the windows after you are done to confirm proper repairs.

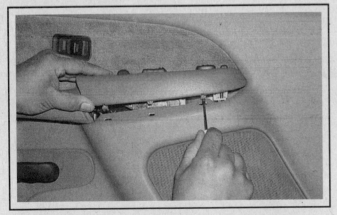

23.12a Pry up the driver's door switch assembly from the door panel

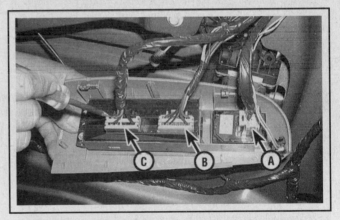

23.12b There are several switch connectors in the driver's door module: the mirror switch (A), and the window/door connectors (B and C) - disconnect the electrical connector at the switch, then squeeze the clips to remove a switch

24 Power door lock and keyless entry system - description and check

▶ **Refer to illustration 24.10**

1   The power door lock system operates the door lock actuators mounted in each door. The system consists of the switches, actuators, relays and associated wiring. Diagnosis can usually be limited to simple checks of the wiring connections and actuators for minor faults that can be easily repaired.

2   Power door lock systems are operated by bi-directional solenoids located in the doors. The lock switches have two operating positions: Lock and Unlock. These switches activate a relay, which in turn connects voltage to the door lock solenoids. Depending on which way the relay is activated, it reverses polarity, allowing the two sides of the circuit to be used alternately as the feed (positive) and ground side.

3   Some vehicles may have keyless entry, electronic control modules and anti-theft systems incorporated into the power locks. If you are unable to locate the trouble using the following general steps, consult your dealer service department.

▶**Note: Some vehicles also have control switches connected to the key locks in the doors, which unlock all the doors when one is unlocked.**

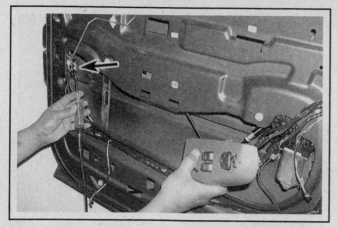

24.10 To test a door lock solenoid, check that power is getting to the solenoid connector (arrow) while the switch is operated

4   Always check the circuit protection first. Some vehicles use a combination of circuit breakers and fuses. Refer to the wiring diagrams at the end of this Chapter.

5   Operate the door lock switches in both directions (Lock and Unlock) with the engine off. Listen for the faint click of the relay operating.

6   If there's no click, check for voltage at the switches. If no voltage is present, check the wiring between the fuse panel and the switches for shorts and opens.

7   If voltage is present but no click is heard, test the switch for continuity. Replace it if there's not continuity in both switch positions. To remove the switch, use a flat-bladed trim tool to pry out the door/window switch assembly (see Chapter 11).

8   If the switch has continuity but the relay doesn't click, check the wiring between the switch and relay for continuity. Repair the wiring if

there's no continuity.

9   If the relay is receiving voltage from the switch but is not sending voltage to the solenoids, check for a bad ground at the relay case. If the relay case is grounding properly, replace the relay. Relay tests are described in Section 5.

10 If all but one lock solenoids operate, remove the trim panel from the affected door (see Chapter 11) and check for voltage at the solenoid while the lock switch is operated (see illustration). One of the wires should have voltage in the Lock position; the other should have voltage in the Unlock position.

11 If the inoperative solenoid is receiving voltage, replace the solenoid.

12 If the inoperative solenoid isn't receiving voltage, check for an open or short in the wire between the lock solenoid and the relay.

➡**Note: It's common for wires to break in the portion of the harness between the body and door (opening and closing the door fatigues and eventually breaks the wires).**

13 On the models covered by this manual, power door lock system communication goes through the Body Control Module. If the above tests do not pinpoint a problem, take the vehicle to a dealer or qualified shop with the proper scan tool to retrieve trouble codes from the BCM.

KEYLESS ENTRY SYSTEM

14 The keyless entry system consists of a remote control transmitter that sends a coded infrared signal to a receiver, which then operates the door-lock system.

15 Replace the battery when the transmitter doesn't operate the locks at a distance of 10 feet. Normal range should be about 30 feet.

16 Use a small screwdriver to carefully separate the case halves.

17 Replace the three-volt, CR2032 lithium battery.

18 Snap the case halves together.

25 Electric side view mirrors - description and check

SIDE MIRROR

1   The electric rear view mirrors use two motors to move the glass; one for up and down adjustments and one for left-right adjustments.

2   The control switch has a selector portion which sends voltage to the left or right side mirror. With the ignition in the ACC position and the engine OFF, roll down the windows and operate the mirror control switch through all functions (left-right and up-down) for both the left and right side mirrors.

3   Listen carefully for the sound of the electric motors running in the mirrors.

4   If the motors can be heard but the mirror glass doesn't move, there's probably a problem with the drive mechanism inside the mirror. Power mirrors have no user-serviceable parts inside - a defective mirror must be replaced as a unit (see Chapter 11).

5   If the mirrors don't operate and no sound comes from the mirrors, check the Mirr/Lock fuse in the fuse block located in interior fuse/relay box, and the Htd/Mirr fuse in the underhood fuse/relay box (see Section 3).

6   If the fuses are OK, remove the switch panel for access to the back of the mirror control switch without disconnecting the wires attached to it (see illustration 23.12b). Turn the ignition ON and check for voltage at the switch. There should be voltage at one terminal. If

there's no voltage at the switch, check for an open or short in the wiring between the fuse panel and the switch.

7   If there's voltage at the switch, disconnect it. Check the switch for continuity in all its operating positions. If the switch does not have continuity, replace it.

8   Locate the wire going from the switch to ground. Leaving the switch connected, connect a jumper wire between this wire and ground. If the mirror works normally with this wire in place, repair the faulty ground connection.

9   If the mirror still doesn't work, remove the mirror and check the wires at the mirror for voltage. Check with ignition ON and the mirror selector switch on the appropriate side. Operate the mirror switch in all its positions. There should be voltage at one of the switch-to-mirror wires in each switch position (except the neutral "off" position).

10 If voltage is absent in each switch position, check the wiring between the mirror and control switch for opens and shorts.

11 If there's voltage, remove the mirror and test it off the vehicle with jumper wires. Replace the mirror if it fails this test.

AUTOMATIC/DAY NIGHT MIRROR

12 To reduce glare, the automatic day/night mirror adjusts the amount of light reflected according to conditions. This is achieved with two photocell sensors, one facing forward and one facing rearward, that

darken or lighten the thin layer of electrochromic material incorporated into the mirror glass. On some models, the mirror also incorporates a display, turned on by switches at the bottom of the mirror, that shows an illuminated compass or a thermometer. The display is in the upper right corner of the mirror.

13 If the mirror is not operating, check the IGN 1 fuse in the interior fuse/relay box (see Section 3).

14 Disconnect the electrical connector from the front side of the mirror. With the ignition On, the connector cavity with the pink wire should have battery voltage.

15 With the ignition Off, the cavity with the black wire should have continuity to ground. If not, there is a loose ground connection in the circuit.

16 With the connector in place and the ignition On, cover the forward facing sensor, shine a light into the rear facing sensor, make sure the glass darkens, then shift the transmission into reverse and make sure it lightens. If it doesn't, replace the mirror (see Chapter 11). The automatic mirror function is wired into the back-up switch, to lighten the mirror for safety when backing up.

26 Power seats - description and check

1 Power seats allow you to adjust the position of the seat with little effort. These models feature a six-way seat that goes forward and backward, up and down and tilts forward and backward. The seats are powered by three reversible motors, mounted in one housing, that are controlled by switches on the side of the seat. Each switch changes the direction of seat travel by reversing polarity to the drive motor.

2 Diagnosis is a simple matter, using the following procedures.

3 Look under the seat for any object which may be preventing the seat from moving.

4 If the seat won't work at all, check the 25-amp Seats circuit breaker in the left-side interior fuse/relay box. See Section 4 for circuit breaker testing.

5 With the engine off to reduce the noise level, operate the seat controls in all directions and listen for sound coming from the seat motors.

6 If the motors make noise or don't work, check for voltage at the motors while an assistant operates the switch. With the door open, try the seat switch again. If the dome light dims while trying to operate the seat, this indicates something may be jammed in the seat tracks.

7 If the motor is getting voltage but doesn't run, test it off the vehicle with jumper wires. If it still doesn't work, replace it.

8 If the motor isn't getting voltage, remove the switch and check for voltage. If there's no voltage to the switch (orange wire), check the wiring between the fuse block and the switch. If there's battery voltage at the switch, check the other terminals for voltage while moving the switch around. If the switch is OK, check for a short or open in the wiring between the switch and motor.

9 Test the completed repairs.

27 Data Link Communication system - description

1 The vehicles covered by this manual have a complex electrical system, encompassing many power accessories, and a number of separate electronic modules.

2 The Powertrain Control Module (PCM) is mainly responsible for engine and transaxle control, but also communicates with other modules around the vehicle through a Data Link Communication system, which sends serial port data very quickly between the various modules. Many of the computer functions involved in the operation of body systems are routed through the Body Control Module (BCM), which communicates with the PCM.

3 Among the modules in the Data Link system besides the BCM and PCM are the Sensing Diagnostic Module (airbag system), the Electronic Brake Control Module, Vehicle Control Module and the instrument panel cluster. The BCM further communicates with various body subsystems.

4 All of the modules in the vehicle have associated trouble codes. When other troubleshooting procedures fail to pinpoint the problem, check the wiring diagrams at the end of this Chapter to see if the BCM or PCM are involved in the circuit. If so, bring your vehicle to a dealer with the factory diagnostic tools to extract the trouble codes.

28 Airbag system - general information

▶ **Refer to illustrations 28.1, 28.8, 28.13 and 28.15**

1 These models are equipped with a Supplemental Restraint System (SRS), more commonly known as airbags, designed to protect the driver and front seat passenger from serious injury in the event of a head-on or frontal collision. All models have a sensing/diagnostic control unit, located under the driver's seat, below the carpeting (see illustration).

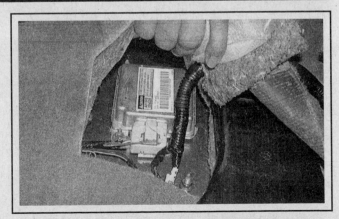

28.1 The airbag control module is located under the driver's seat - do not tamper with the yellow connectors attached to it

AIRBAG MODULES

2   The airbag modules consist of a housing incorporating the cushion (airbag) and inflator unit. The inflator assembly is mounted on the back of the housing over a hole through which gas is expelled, inflating the bag almost instantaneously when an electrical signal is sent from the system. The specially wound wire on the driver's side that carries this signal to the driver's module is called a clockspring. The clockspring is a flat, ribbon-like electrically conductive tape that is wound many times so that it can transmit an electrical signal regardless of steering wheel position. Airbag modules are located in the steering wheel, on the passenger side above the glove box, and on some 2000 and later SUV models, at the upper side of each front seat (side-impact airbags).

SENSING/DIAGNOSTIC CONTROL UNIT AND SENSORS

3   The sensing/diagnostic control unit contains an on-board microprocessor which monitors the operation of the system, and also contains a crash sensor. It checks this system every time the vehicle is started, causing the "AIRBAG" light to flash seven times then go off, if the system is operating properly. If there is a fault in the system, the light may not come on at all, or the light will go on and continue, either illuminated steadily or blinking, and the unit will store fault codes indicating the nature of the fault.

4   Another impact-activated sensor, called the discriminating sensor is mounted to the underside of the radiator support.

OPERATION

5   For the airbag(s) to deploy, the discriminating sensor and the impact sensor in the sensing/diagnostic control unit must be activated. When this condition occurs, the circuit to the airbag inflator is closed and the airbag inflates. If the battery is destroyed by the impact, or is too low to power the inflator, a back-up power unit inside the SRS system provides power.

SELF-DIAGNOSIS SYSTEM

6   A self-diagnosis circuit in the SRS unit displays a light on the instrument panel when the ignition switch is turned to the On position. If the system is operating normally, the light should go out after about seven blinks. If the light doesn't come on, or doesn't go out after a short time, or if it comes on while you're driving the vehicle, or if it blinks at any time, there's a malfunction in the SRS system. Have it inspected and repaired as soon as possible. Do not attempt to troubleshoot or service the SRS system yourself. Even a small mistake could cause the SRS system to malfunction when you need it.

SERVICING COMPONENTS NEAR THE SRS SYSTEM

7   Nevertheless, there are times when you need to remove the steering wheel, radio or service other components on or near the dash-

28.8 Disconnect the passenger airbag connector (arrow) behind the glove box area

board. At these times, you'll be working around components and wire harnesses for the SRS system. Do not use electrical test equipment on airbag system wires; it could cause the airbag(s) to deploy. **ALWAYS DISABLE THE SRS SYSTEM BEFORE WORKING NEAR THE SRS SYSTEM COMPONENTS OR RELATED WIRING.**

DISABLING THE SRS SYSTEM

8   To disable the airbag system, perform the following steps:

a) *Turn the steering wheel to the straight-ahead position and turn the ignition switch to the Lock position, then remove the key.*

b) *Remove the airbag fuse located in the interior fuse/relay box at the left end of the instrument panel (1999 through 2002 models) or in the engine compartment fuse/relay box (2003 and later models).*

c) *Wait at least two minutes for the back up power supply to be depleted before beginning work.*

d) *Remove the driver's knee bolster (see Chapter 11) and disconnect the driver's airbag connector at the steering column (see Chapter 10).*

e) *Open and drop the glove box door (see Chapter 11) and disconnect the connector to the passenger airbag (see illustration).*

ENABLING THE SYSTEM

9   To enable the airbag system, perform the following steps:

a) *Turn the ignition switch to the Lock position and remove the key.*

b) *Reconnect the passenger and driver's airbag connectors, making sure the CPA (Connector Position Assurance) clips are in place so the connectors can't accidentally disengage.*

c) *Reinsert the airbag fuse.*

d) *Turn the ignition switch to the On position. Confirm that the airbag warning light glows for 6 to 8 seconds, then goes out, indicating the system is functioning properly.*

28.13 Remove the passenger airbag module mounting bolts (arrows) and lift the module out of the instrument panel

28.16 The passenger airbag On/Off switch (arrow) is mounted at the center of the instrument panel

REMOVAL AND INSTALLATION

Driver's airbag

10 Disable the airbag system (see Step 8). Refer to Chapter 10, Section 17 for removal and installation of the driver's side airbag.

Passenger airbag

11 Disable the airbag system (see Step 8).

12 Remove the glove box and the air outlets on either side of the airbag module (see Chapter 11).

13 Remove the screws and gently pry the airbag unit from the back of the dashboard (see illustration).

✴✴ CAUTION:

The airbag assembly is heavier than it looks, use both hands when removing it from the dash.

14 Installation is the reverse of the removal procedure.

Side-impact airbags

15 Some SUV models have side-impact airbags located in the edge of the seatback facing the door. To disable these airbags (after following Steps 8A through 8E), disconnect the yellow two-wire connectors under the driver and passenger seats.

PASSENGER AIRBAG ON/OFF SWITCH

16 The models covered by this manual have a switch at the center of the instrument panel that can turn the passenger airbag module Off (see illustration). If an infant in a car seat, a child under 12 or a person with special medical conditions must ride in the front passenger seat, the driver can turn the passenger airbag Off. Read your owner's manual for more information on risk groups for the passenger airbag.

17 Inserting the vehicle key, push in the switch and turn to either the On or Off position, then remove the key. Once that passenger is no longer using the right front seat, you should turn the airbag back On again to provide maximum crash protection for adult passengers.

✴✴ WARNING:

The key should never be left in the switch.

29 Wiring diagrams - general information

Since it isn't possible to include all wiring diagrams for every year and model covered by this manual, the following diagrams are those that are typical and most commonly needed.

Prior to troubleshooting any circuits, check the fuse and circuit breakers (if equipped) to make sure they're in good condition. Make sure the battery is properly charged and check the cable connections (see Chapter 1).

When checking a circuit, make sure that all connectors are clean, with no broken or loose terminals. When disconnecting a connector, do not pull on the wires. Pull only on the connector housings themselves.

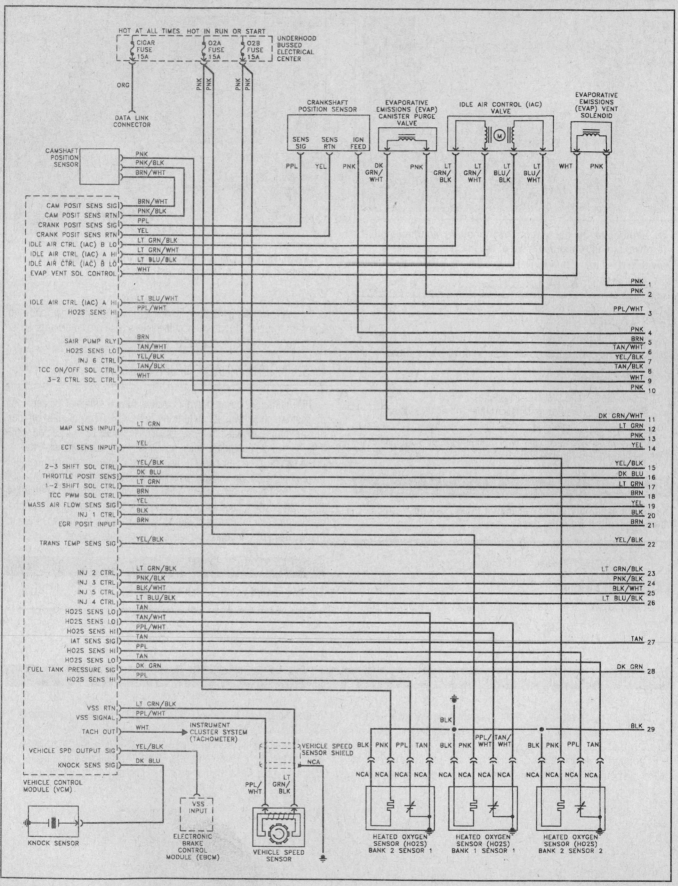

Engine control system – typical V6 (part 1 of 4)

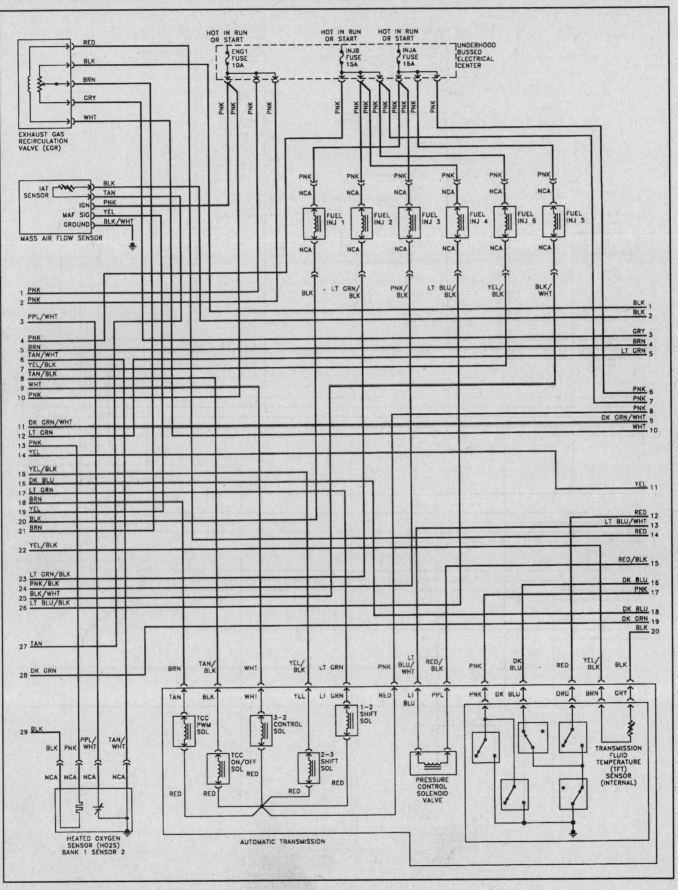

Engine control system – typical V6 (part 2 of 4)

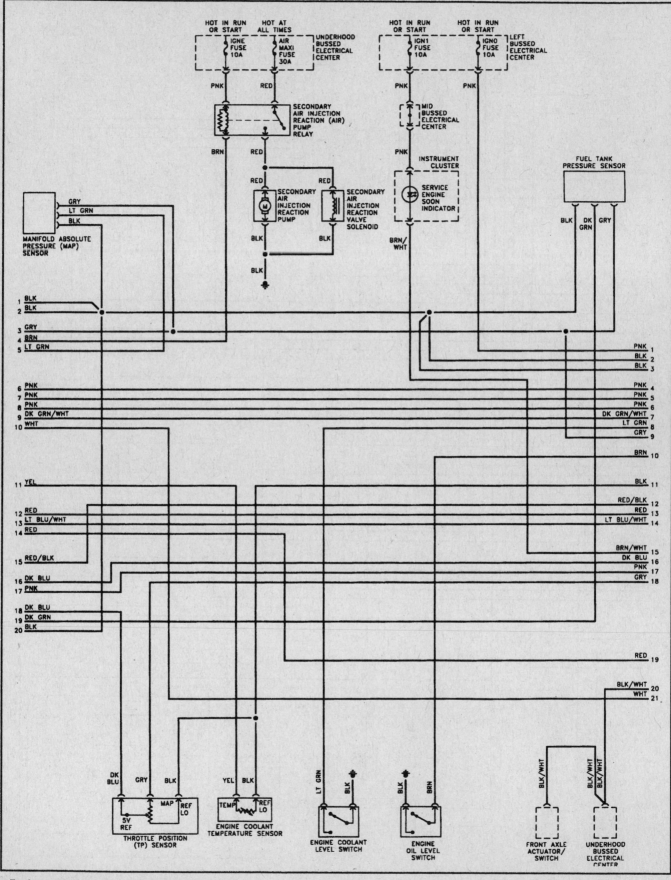

Engine control system – typical V6 (part 3 of 4)

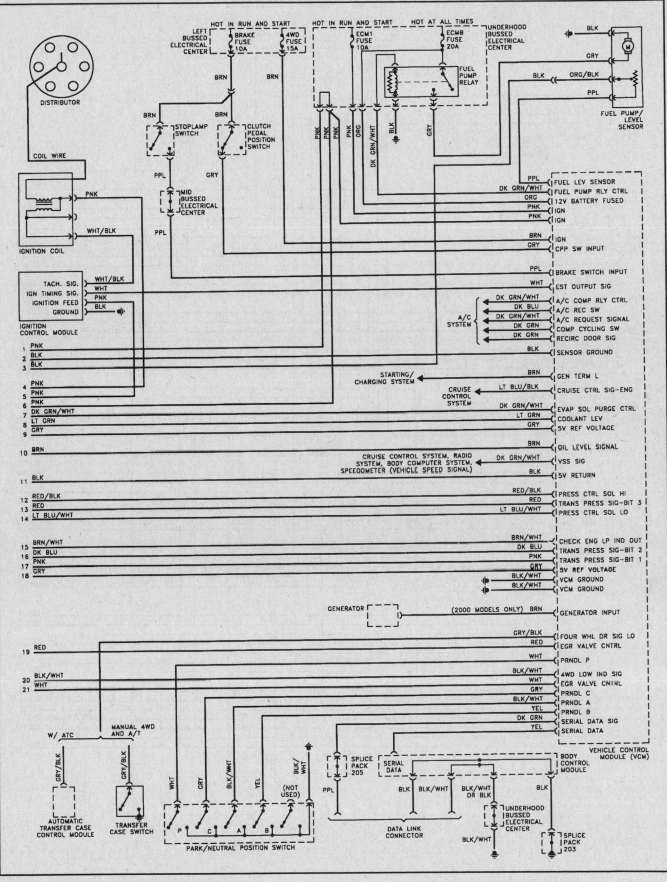

Engine control system – typical V6 (part 4 of 4)

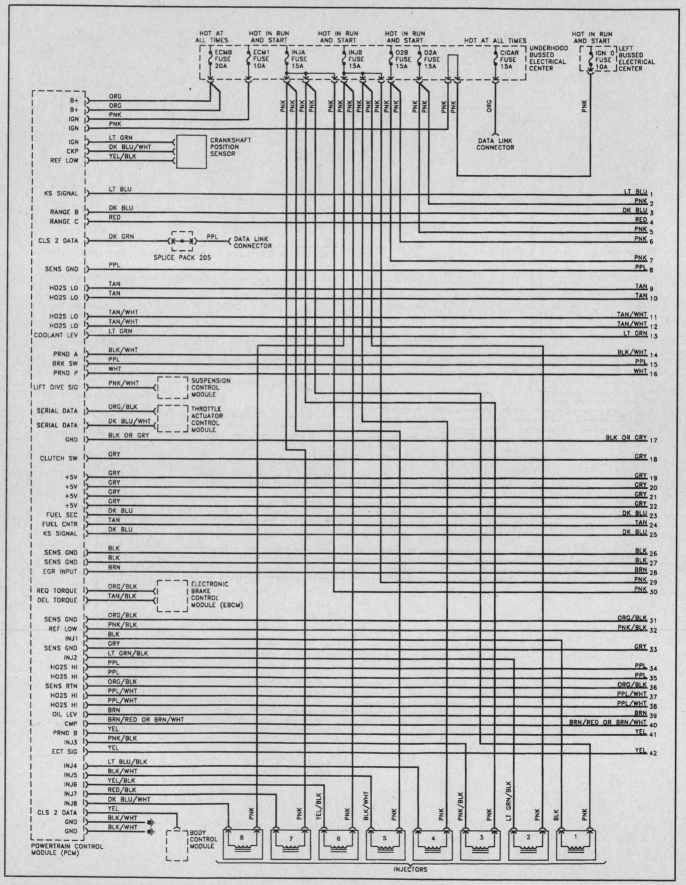

Engine control system – typical V8 (part 1 of 4)

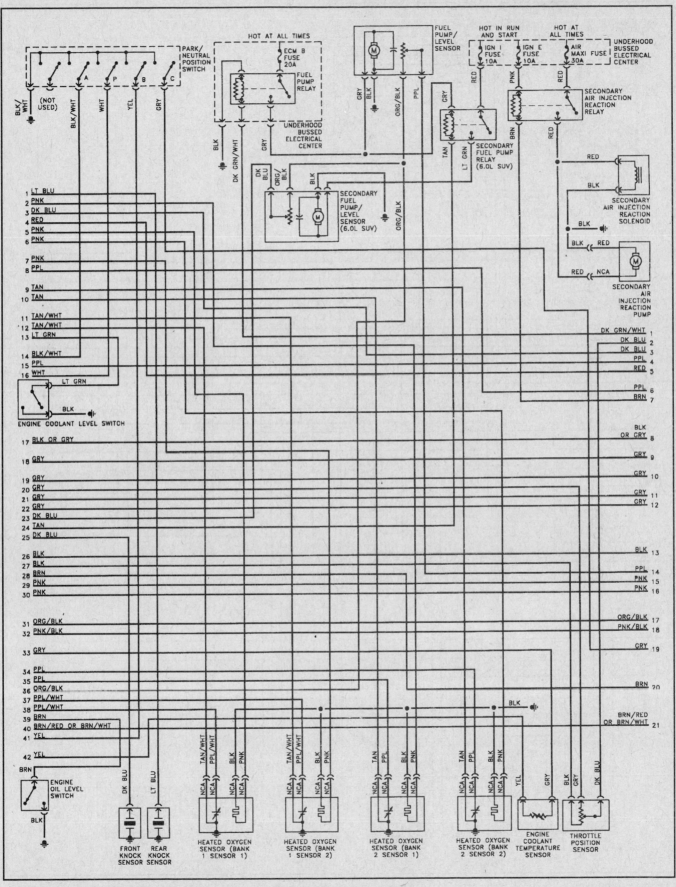

Engine control system – typical V8 (part 2 of 4, without Electronic Throttle Control)

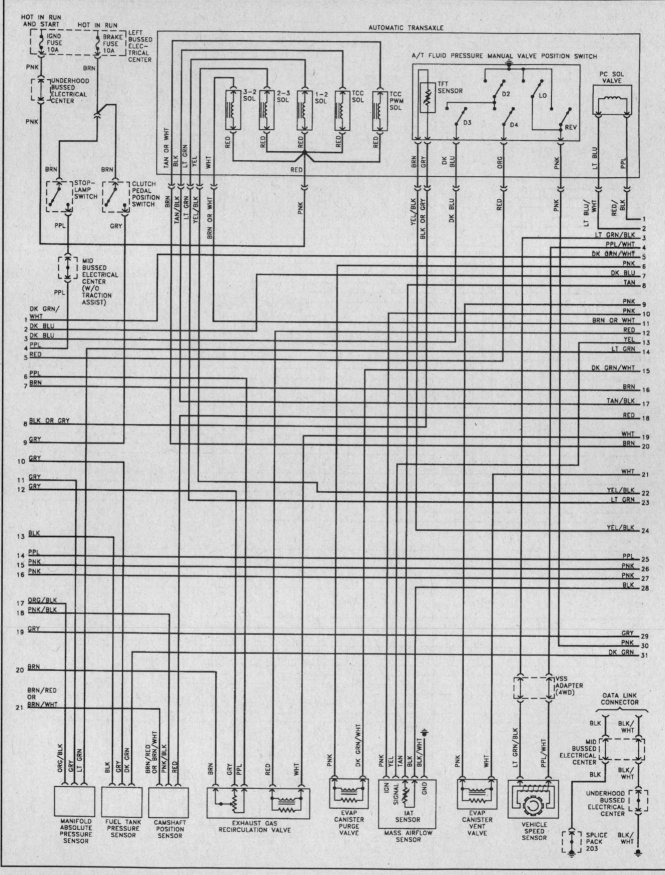

Engine control system – typical V8 (part 3 of 4)

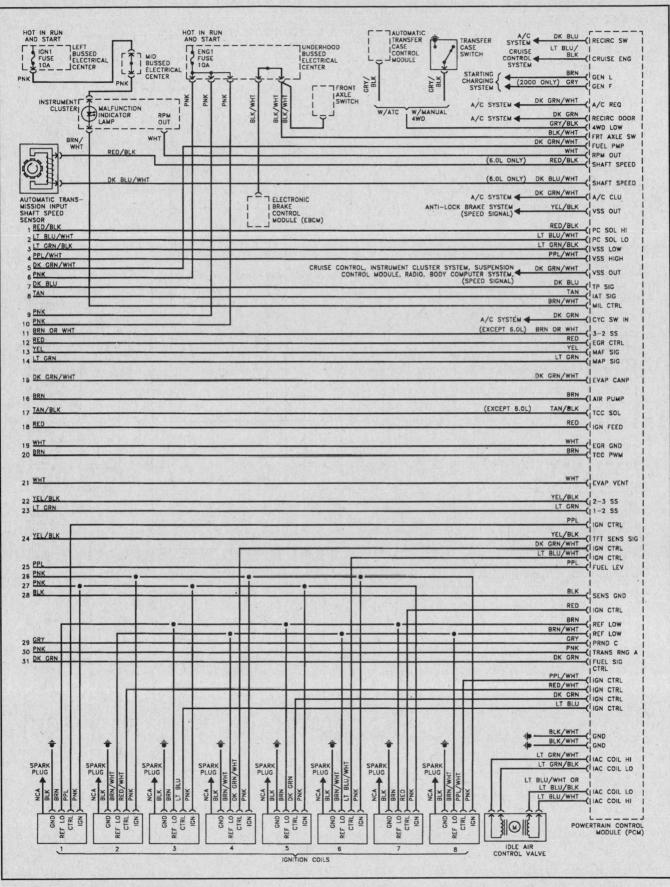

Engine control system – typical V8 (part 4 of 4)

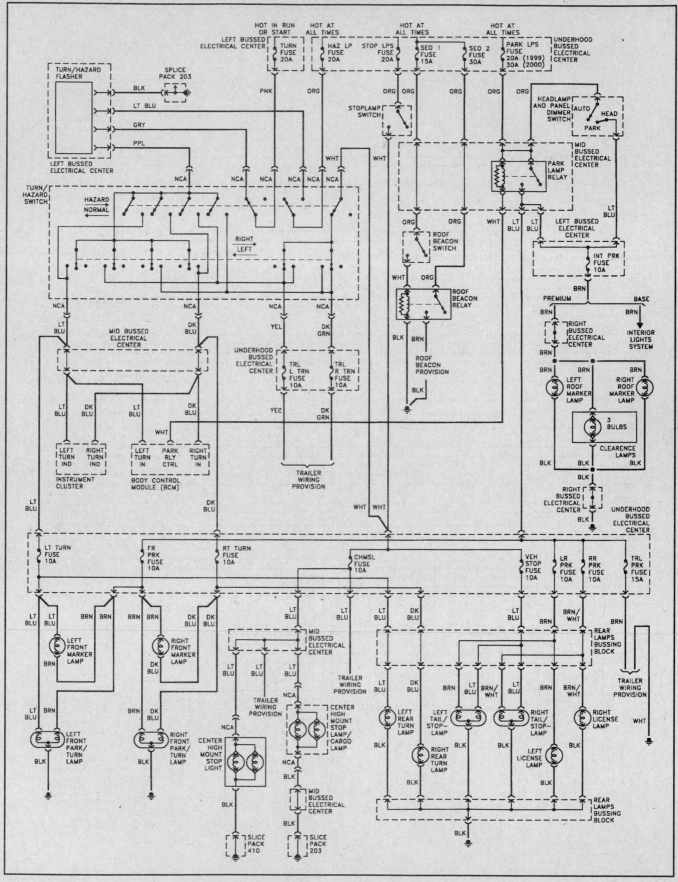

Exterior lighting system – typical pickup models (part 1 of 2)

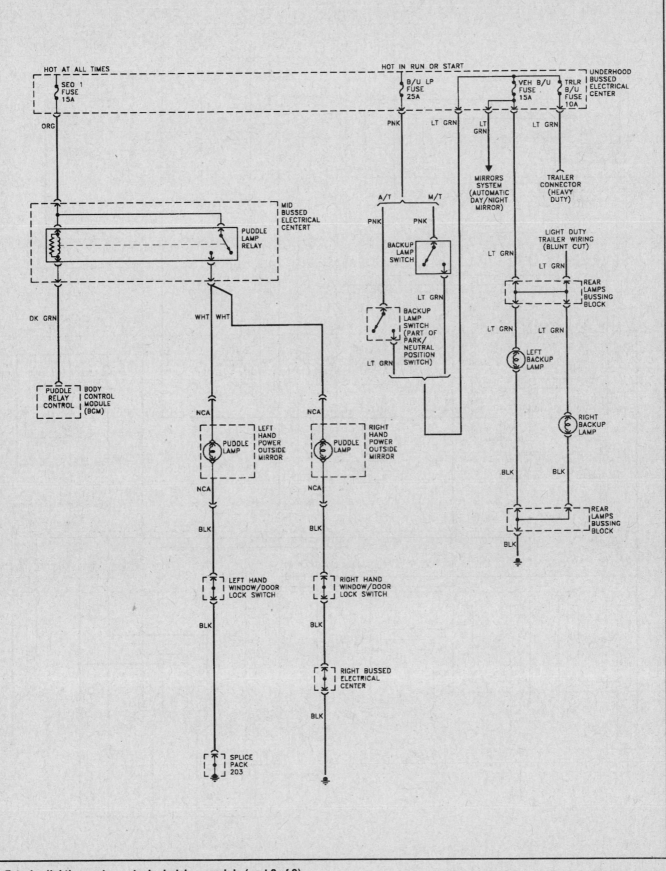

Exterior lighting system – typical pickup models (part 2 of 2)

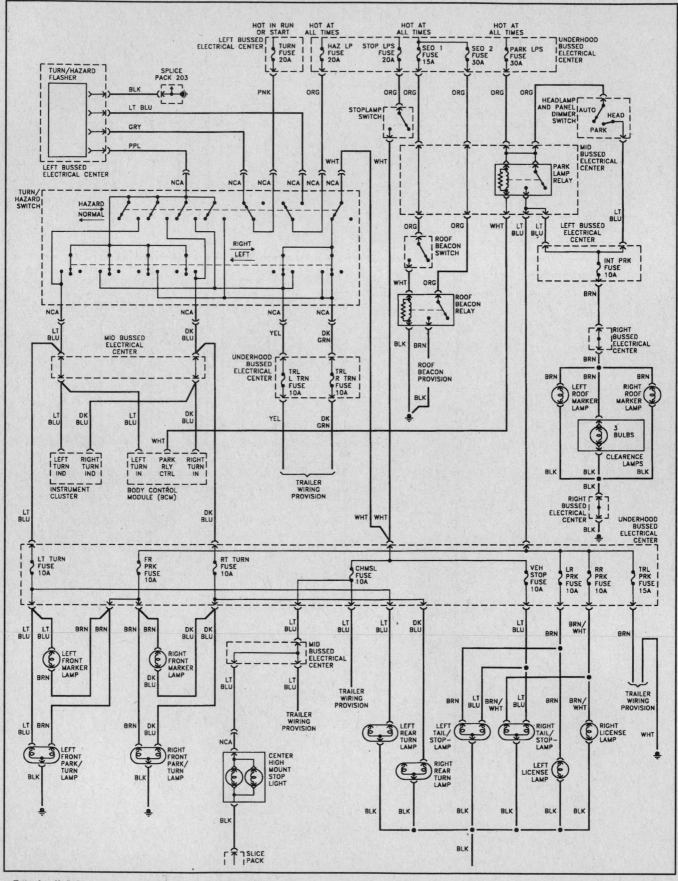

Exterior lighting system – typical SUV models (part 1 of 2)

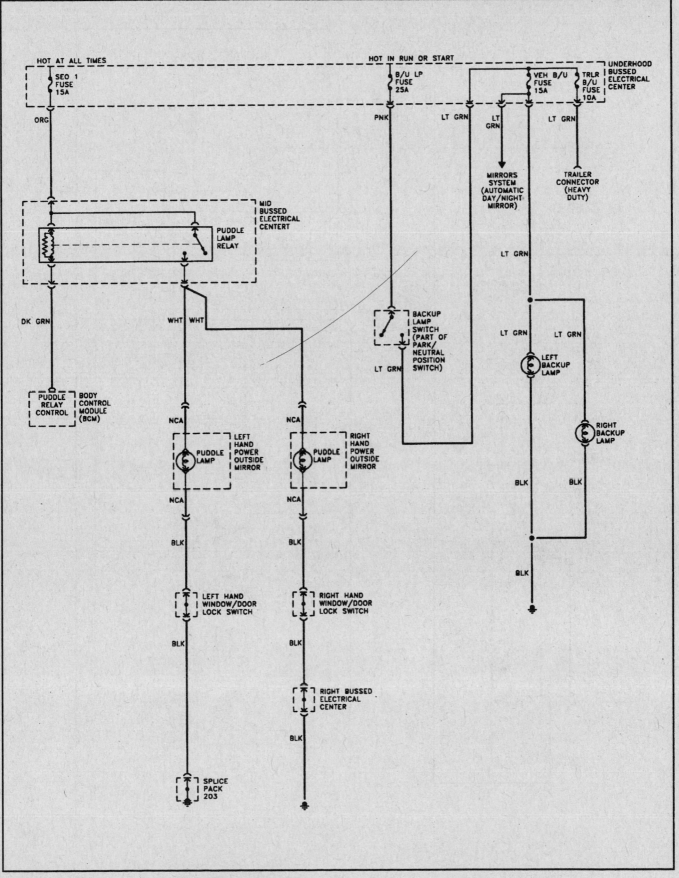

Exterior lighting system – typical SUV models (part 2 of 2)

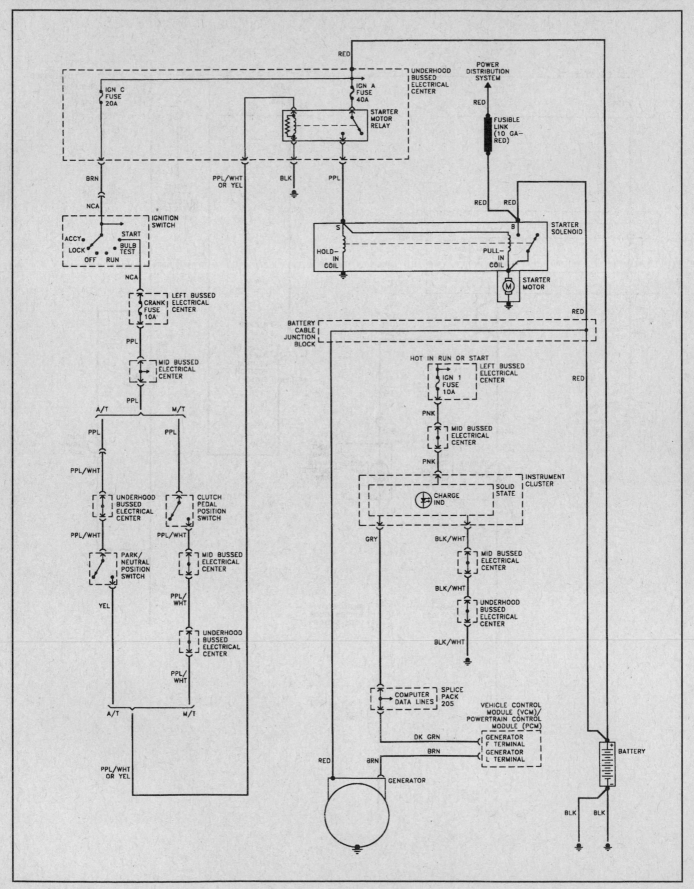

Starting and charging systems – typical

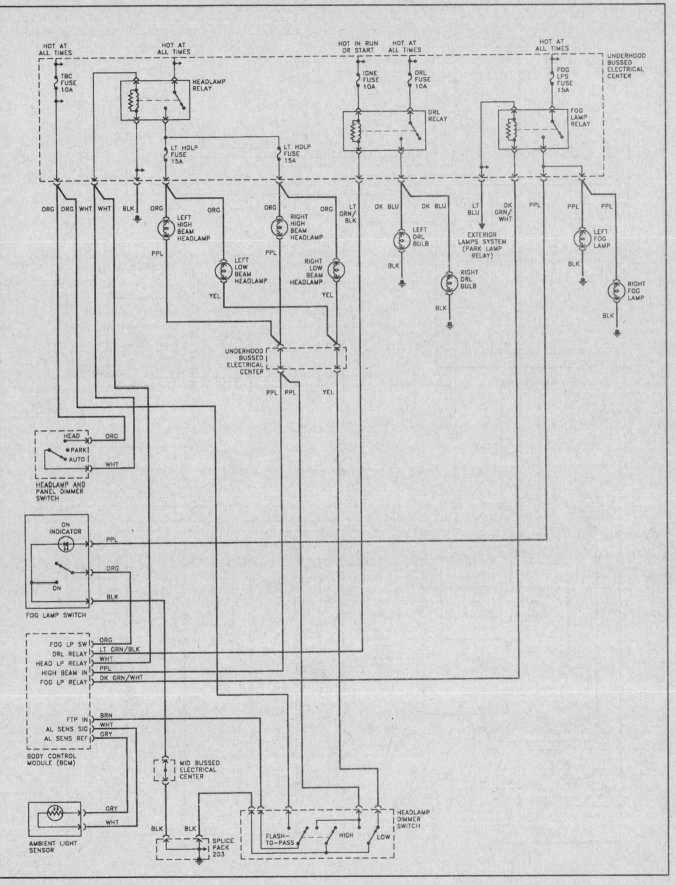

Headlight system – typical

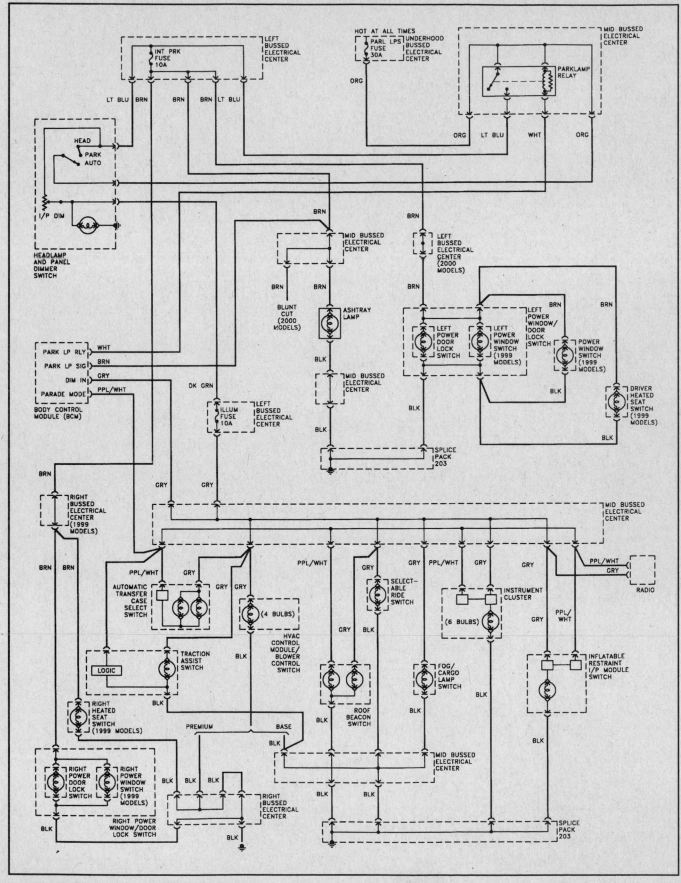

Interior lighting system – typical pickup models

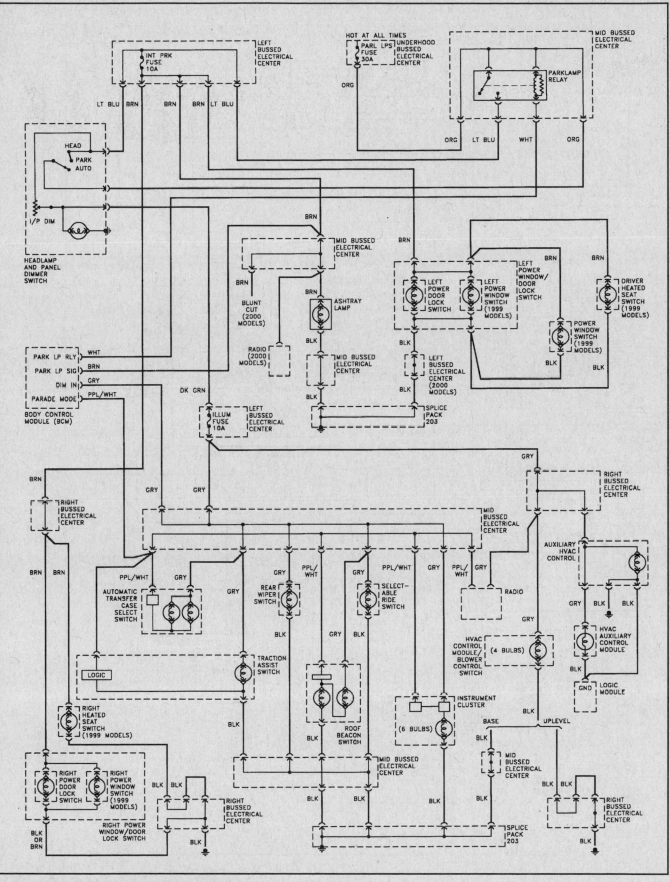

Interior lighting system – typical SUV models

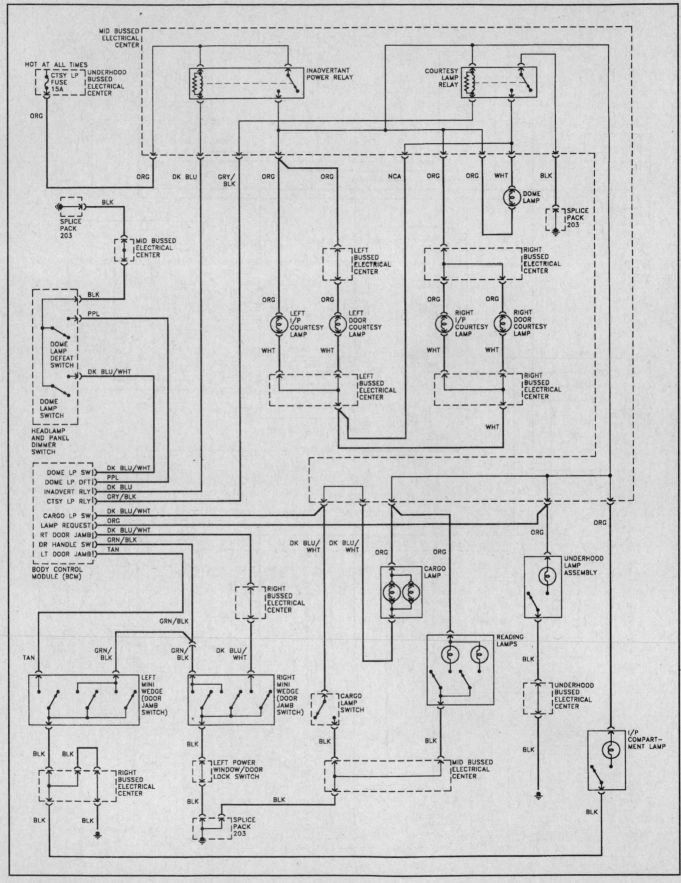

Courtesy lighting system – typical 1999 models

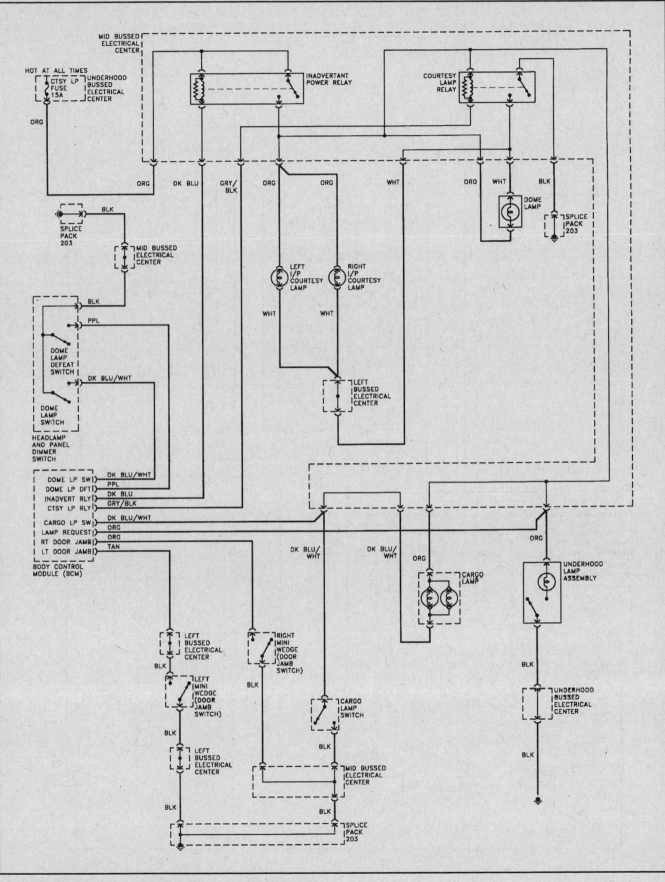

Courtesy lighting system – typical 2000 and later pickup models

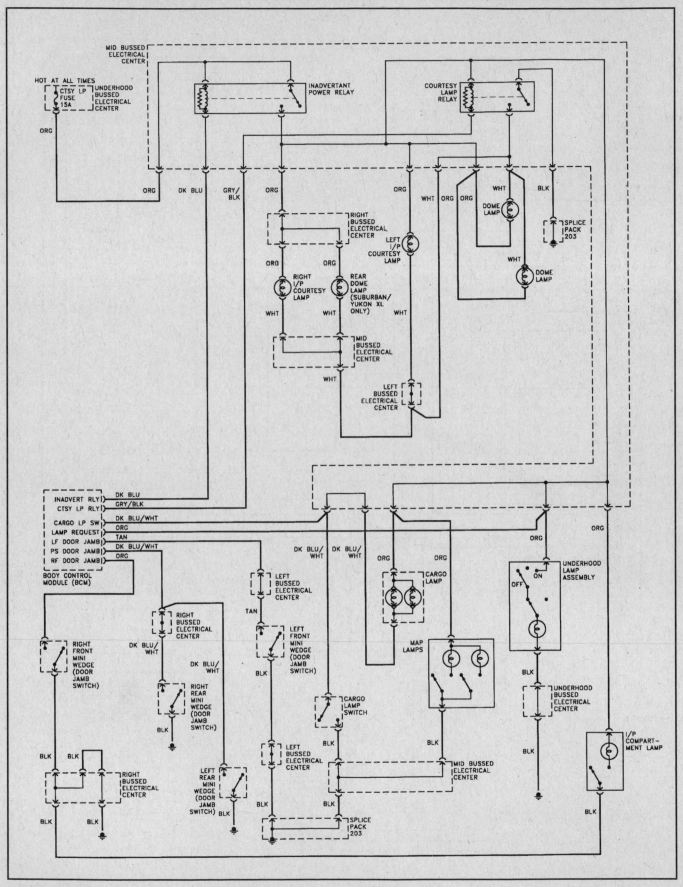

Courtesy lighting system – typical 2000 and later SUV models

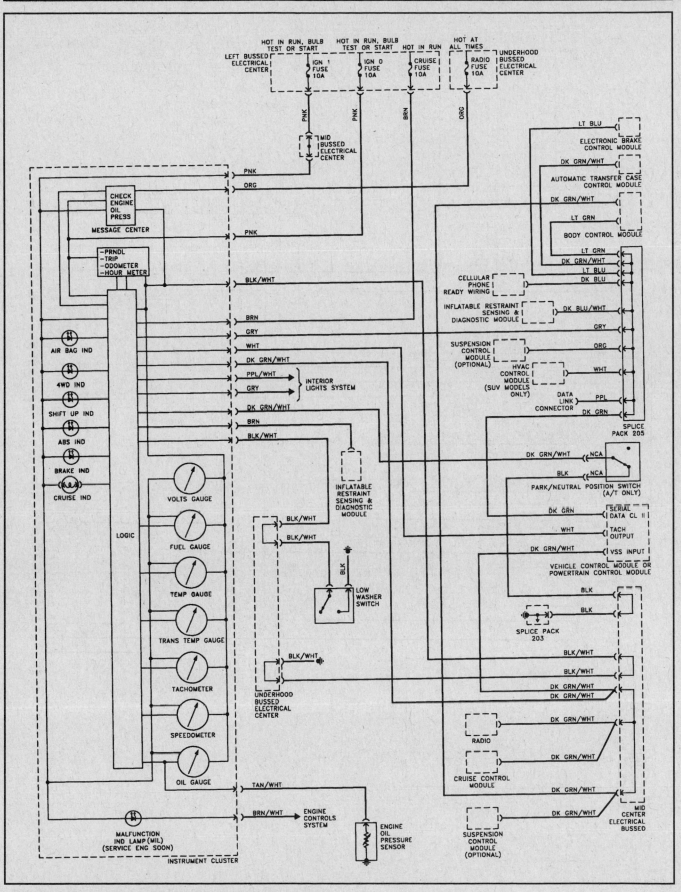

Warning lighting system – typical (without side-impact airbags)

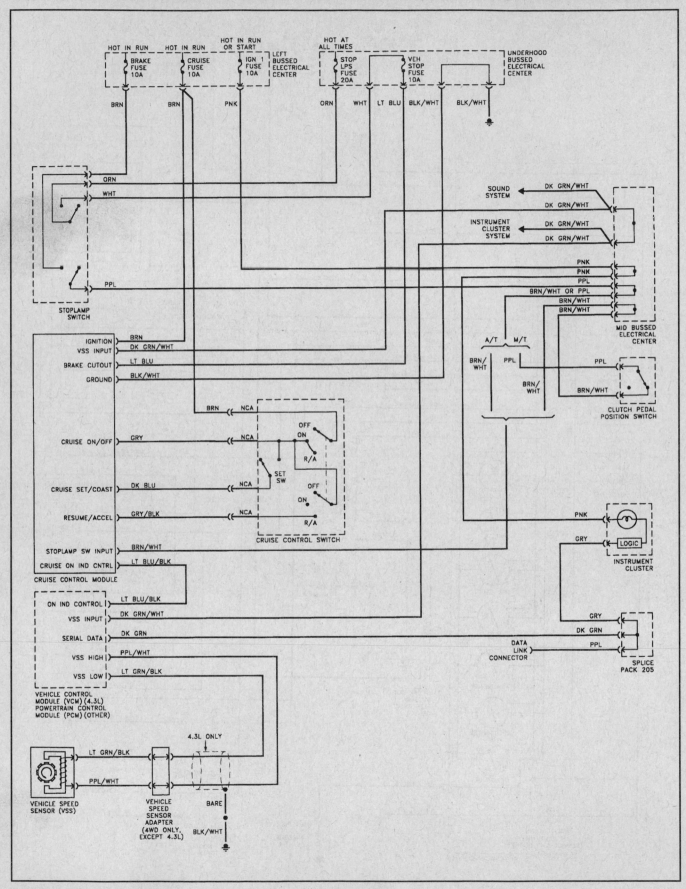

Cruise control system – typical

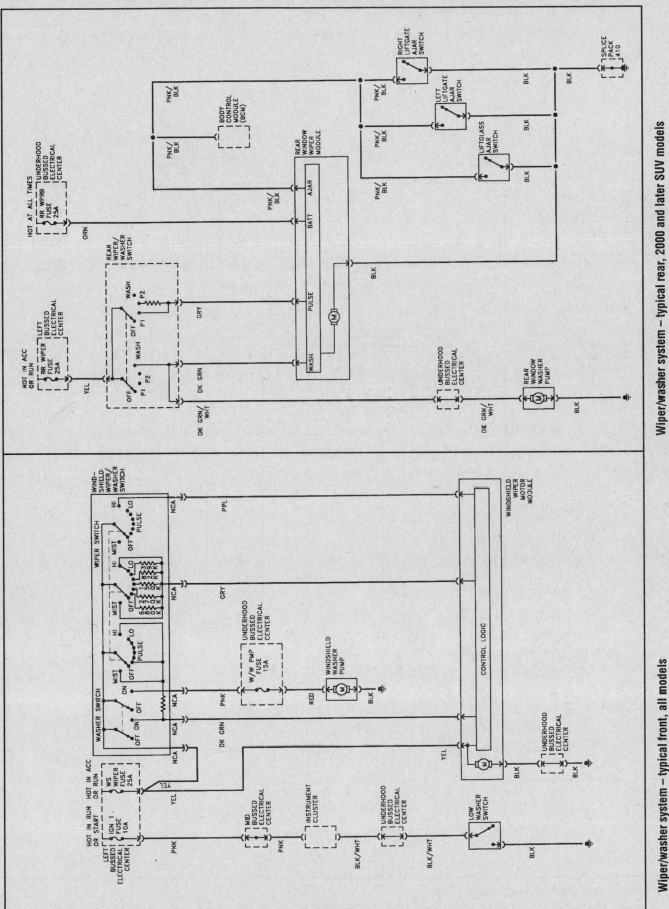

Wiper/washer system – typical rear, 2000 and later SUV models

Wiper/washer system – typical front, all models

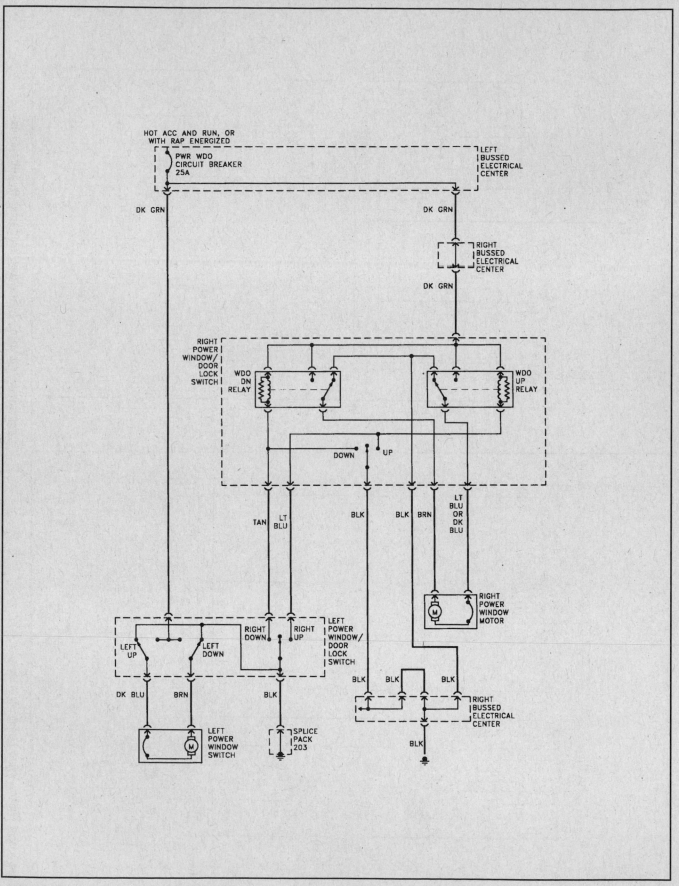

Power window system – typical pickup models

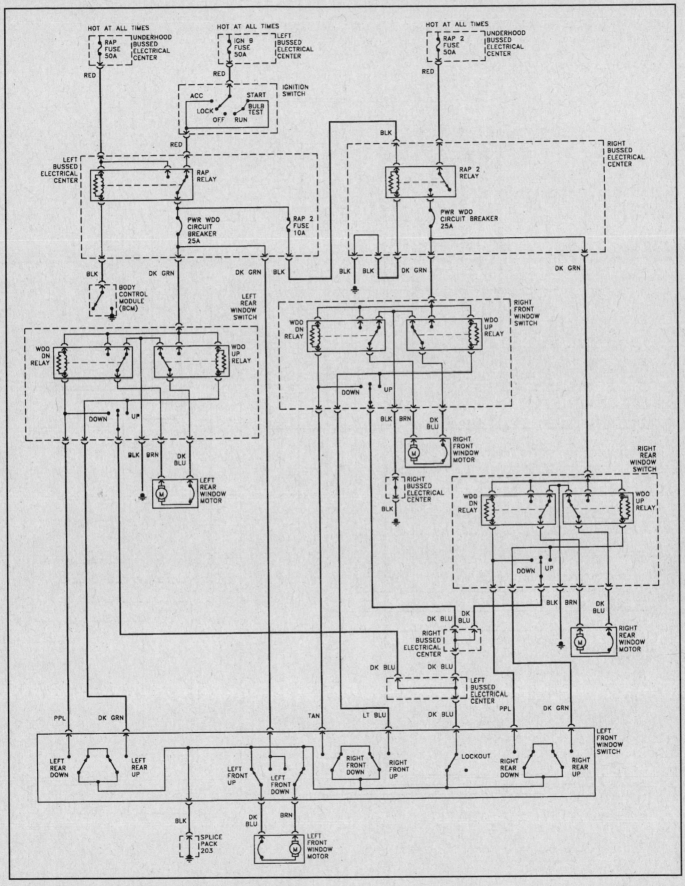

Power window system – typical 2000 and later SUV models

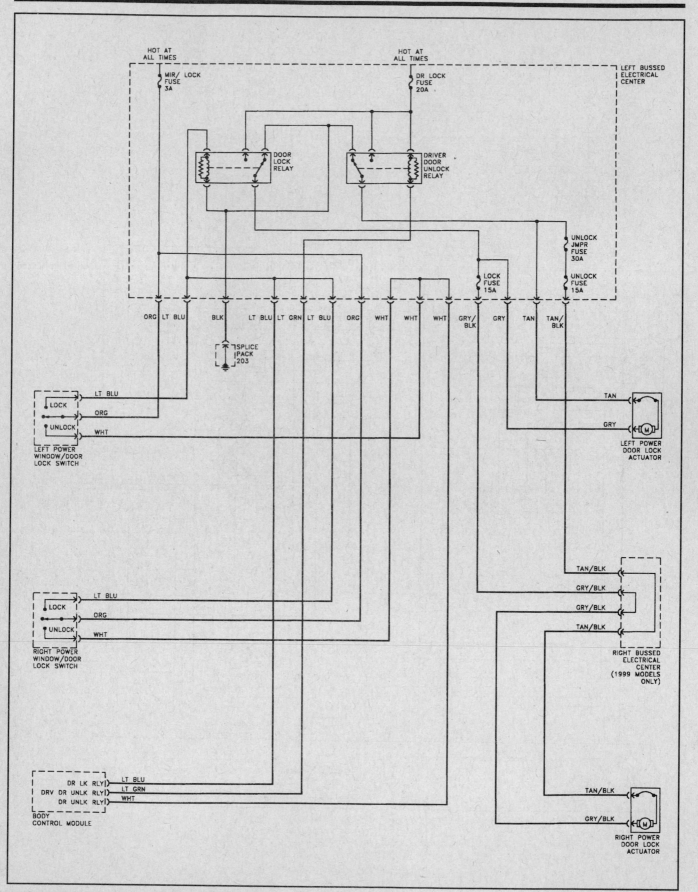

Power door lock system – typical base pickup models

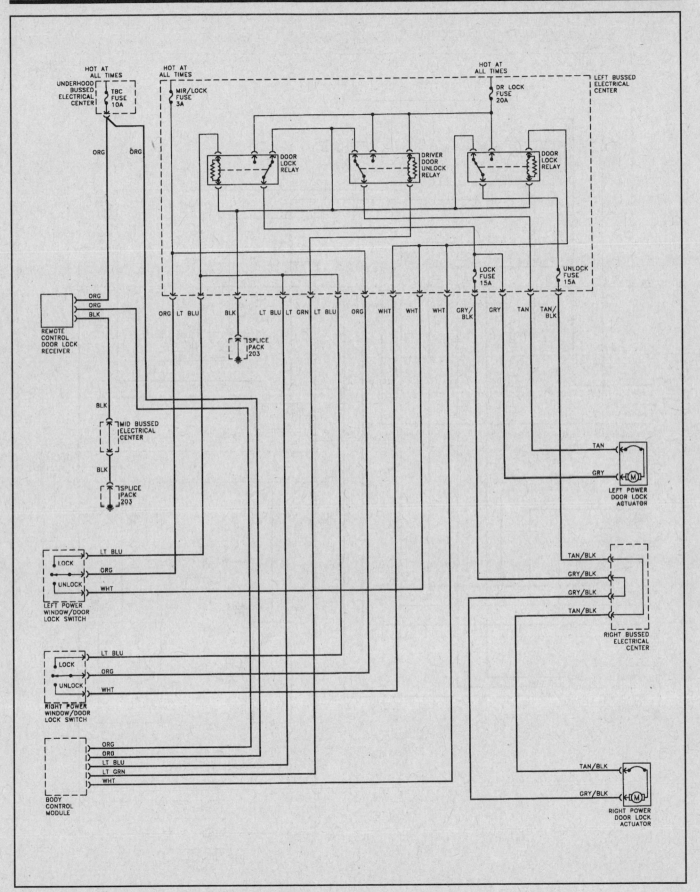

Power door lock system – typical premium pickup models

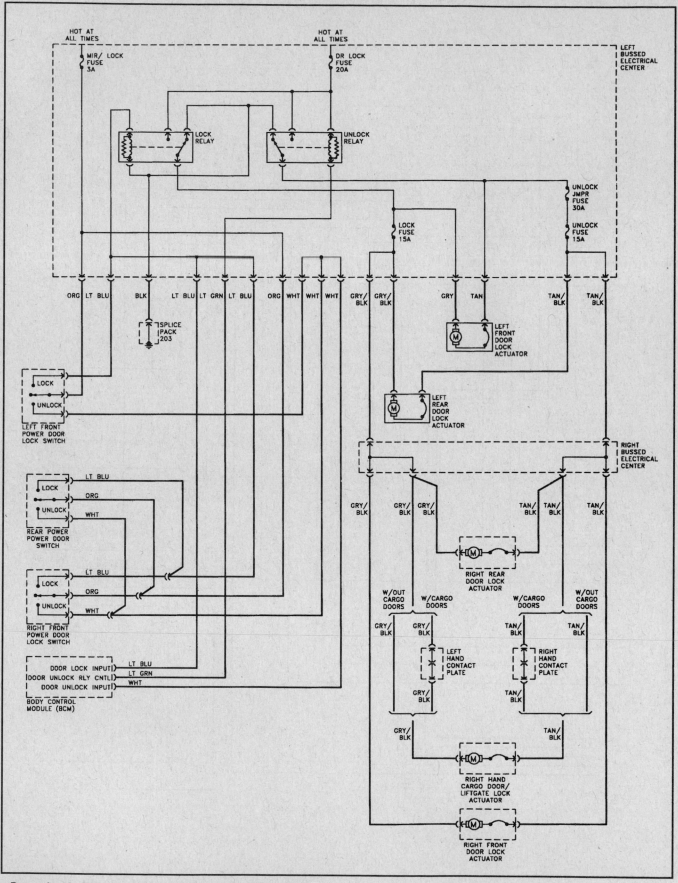

Power door lock system – typical 2000 and later SUV models

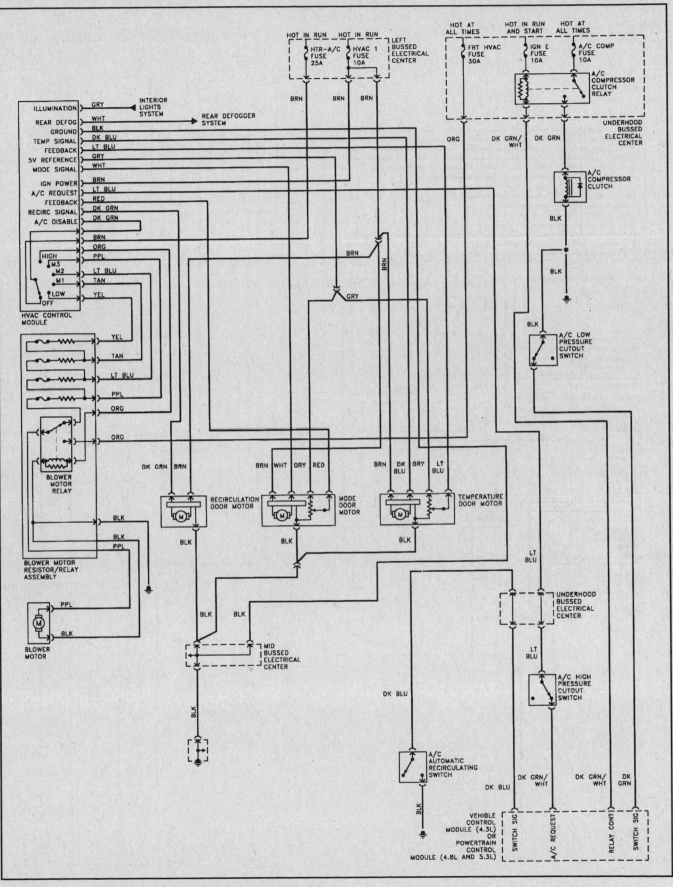

Heating and air-conditioning system – typical 1999 base models

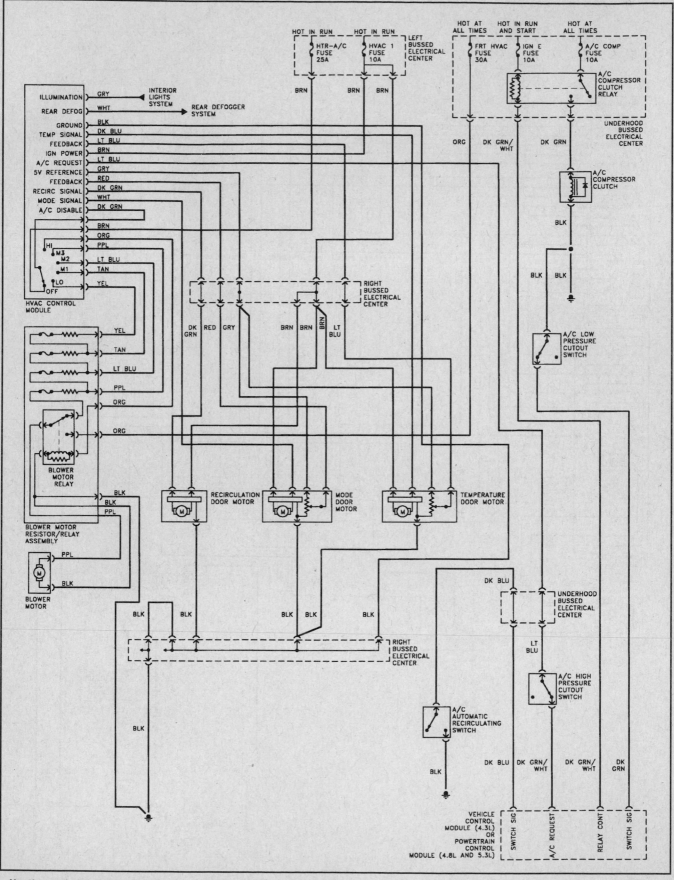

Heating and air-conditioning system – typical 1999 premium models

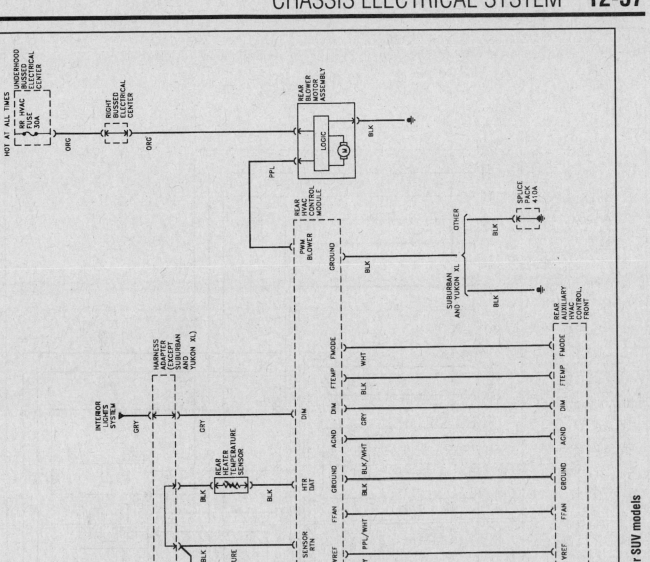

Heating and air-conditioning system – typical rear circuit, 2000 and later SUV models

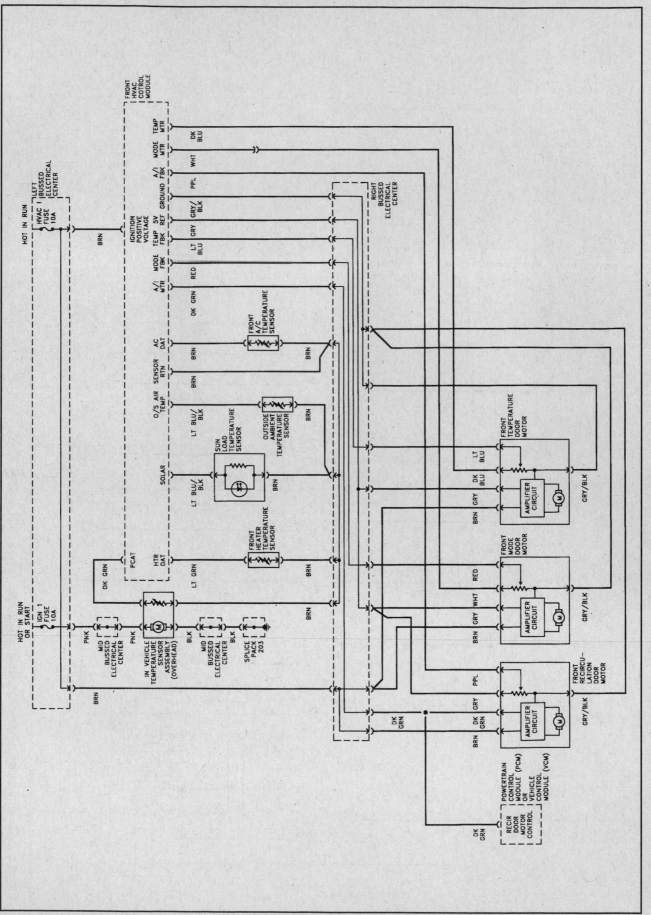

Heating and air-conditioning system – typical 2000 and later front circuit (part 1 of 2)

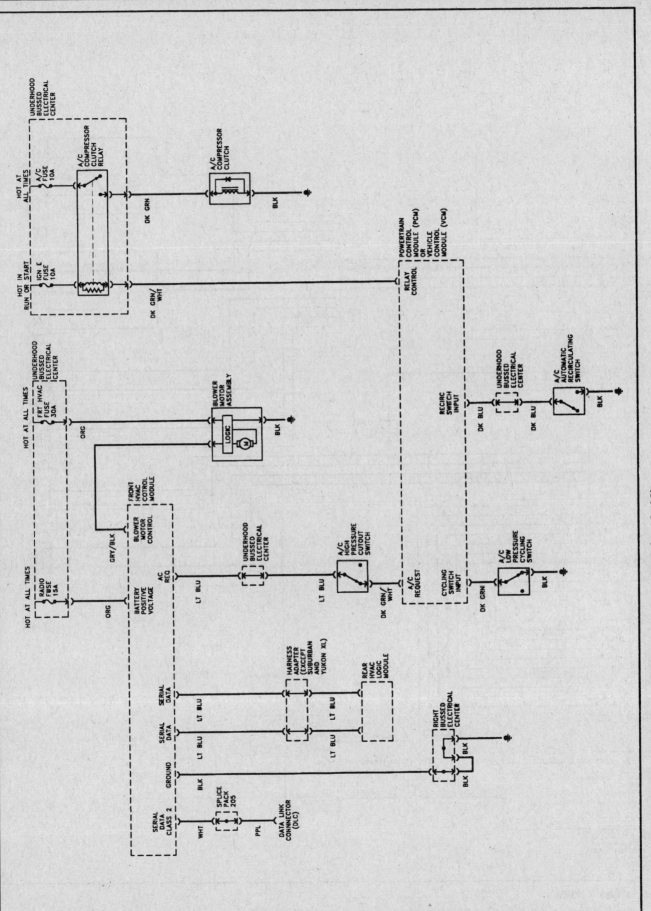

Heating and air-conditioning system – typical 2000 and later front circuit (part 2 of 2)

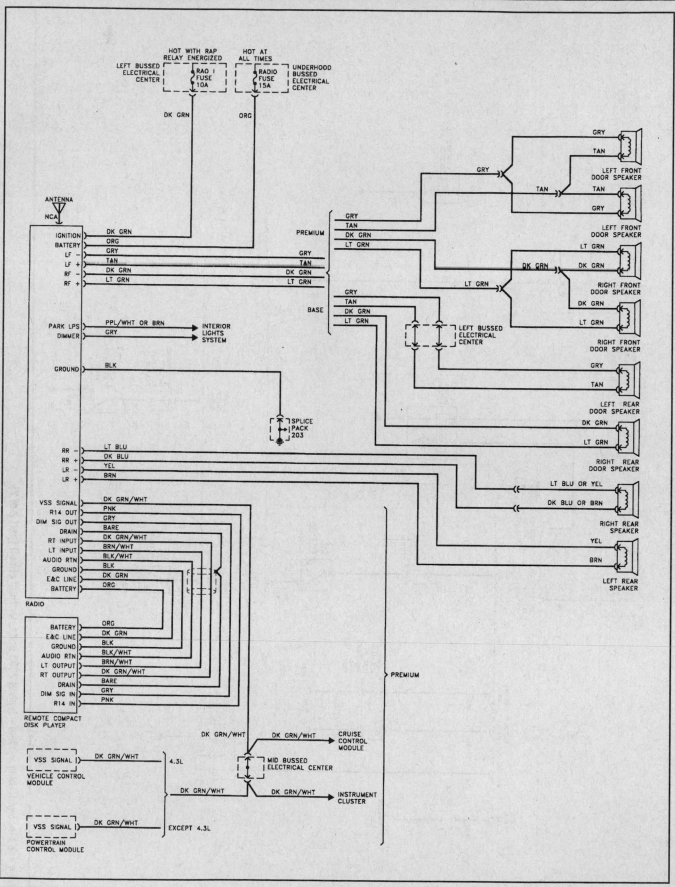

Audio system - typical

1999 AND LATER V6 SENSORS

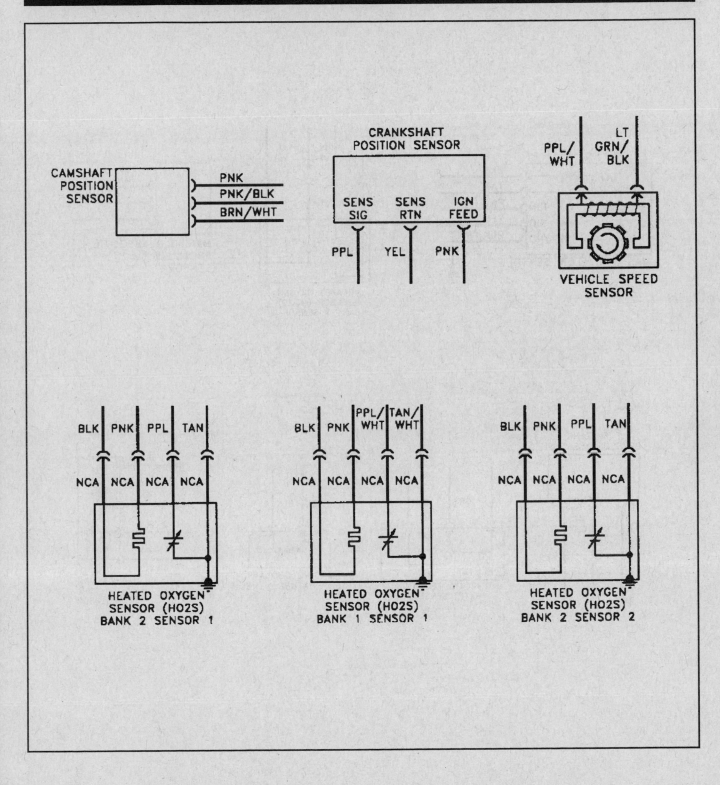

CAMSHAFT POSITION SENSOR

PNK
PNK/BLK
BRN/WHT

CRANKSHAFT POSITION SENSOR

SENS SIG
SENS RTN
IGN FEED

PPL
YEL
PNK

PPL/WHT
LT GRN/BLK

VEHICLE SPEED SENSOR

BLK PNK PPL TAN

NCA NCA NCA NCA

HEATED OXYGEN SENSOR (HO2S) BANK 2 SENSOR 1

BLK PNK PPL/WHT TAN/WHT

NCA NCA NCA NCA

HEATED OXYGEN SENSOR (HO2S) BANK 1 SENSOR 1

BLK PNK PPL TAN

NCA NCA NCA NCA

HEATED OXYGEN SENSOR (HO2S) BANK 2 SENSOR 2

SENSORS 1999 AND LATER V6

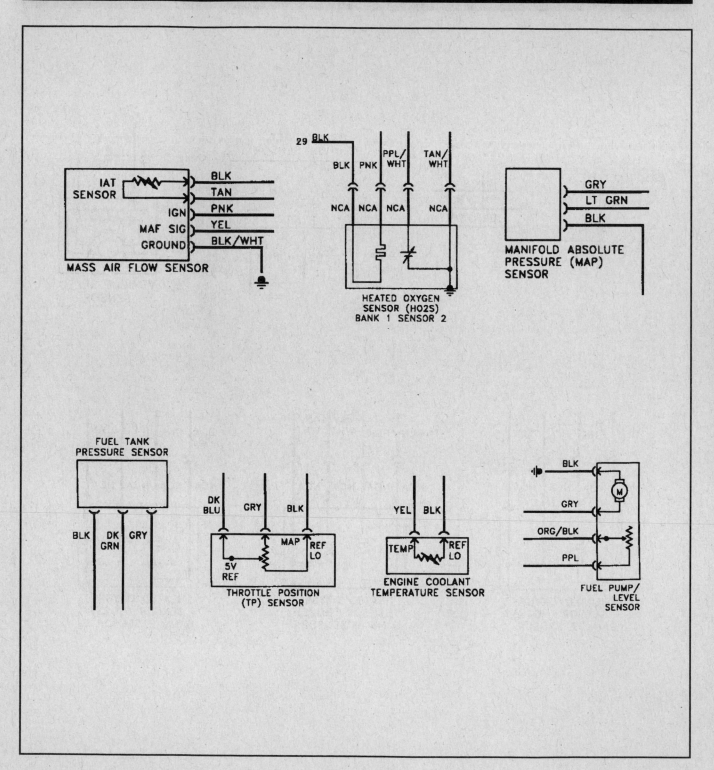

1999 AND LATER V8 SENSORS

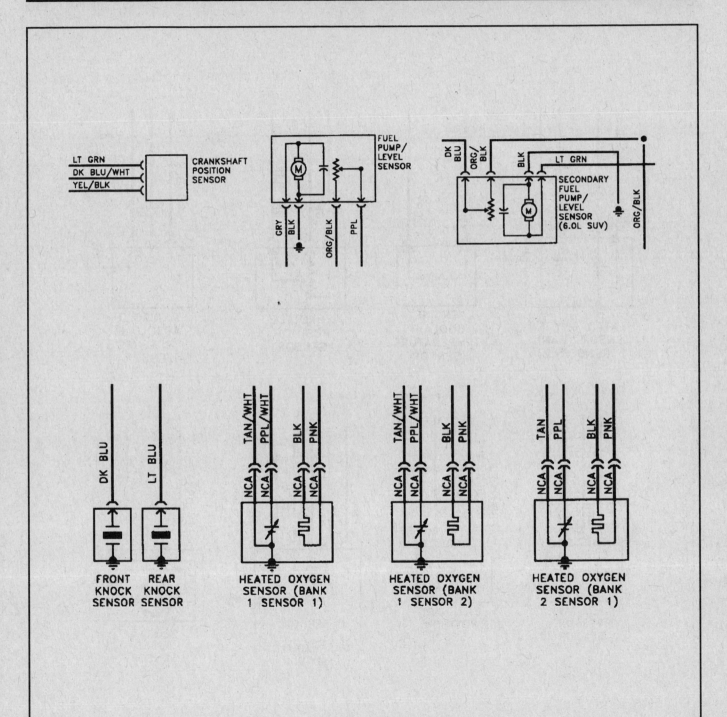

SENSORS 1999 AND LATER V8

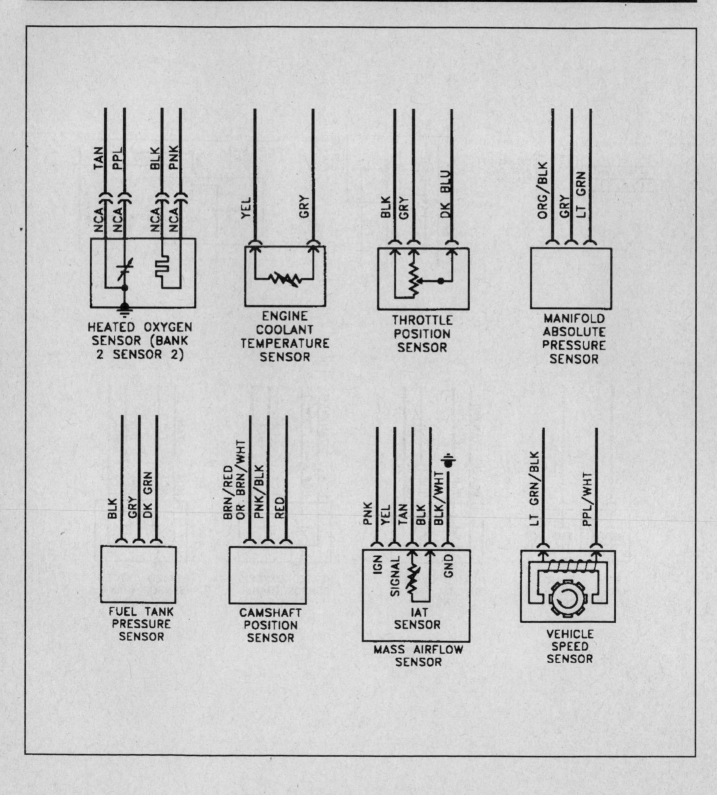

1999 AND LATER V6 SWITCHES

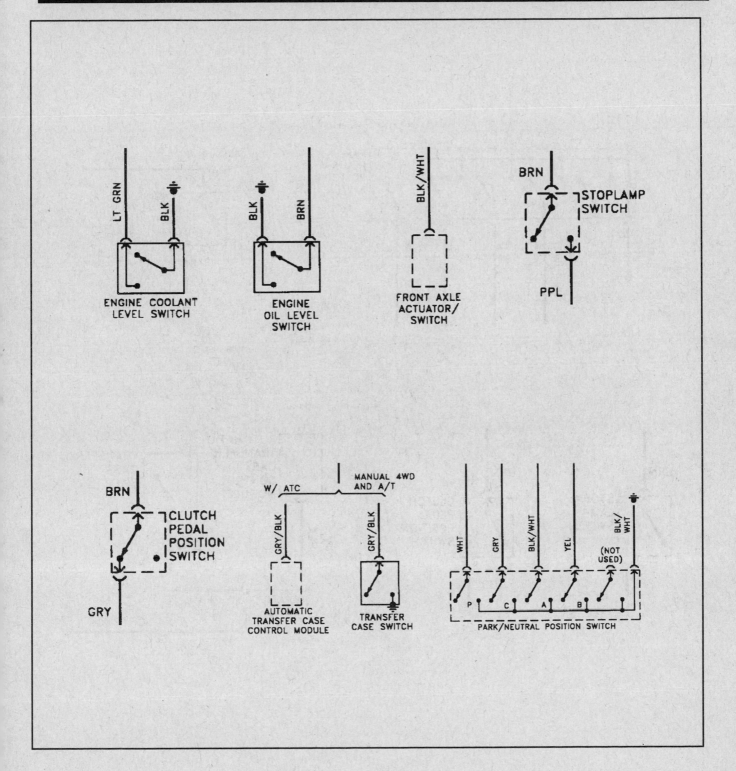

ENGINE COOLANT LEVEL SWITCH

ENGINE OIL LEVEL SWITCH

FRONT AXLE ACTUATOR/ SWITCH

STOPLAMP SWITCH

CLUTCH PEDAL POSITION SWITCH

AUTOMATIC TRANSFER CASE CONTROL MODULE

TRANSFER CASE SWITCH

PARK/NEUTRAL POSITION SWITCH

SWITCHES 1999 AND LATER V8

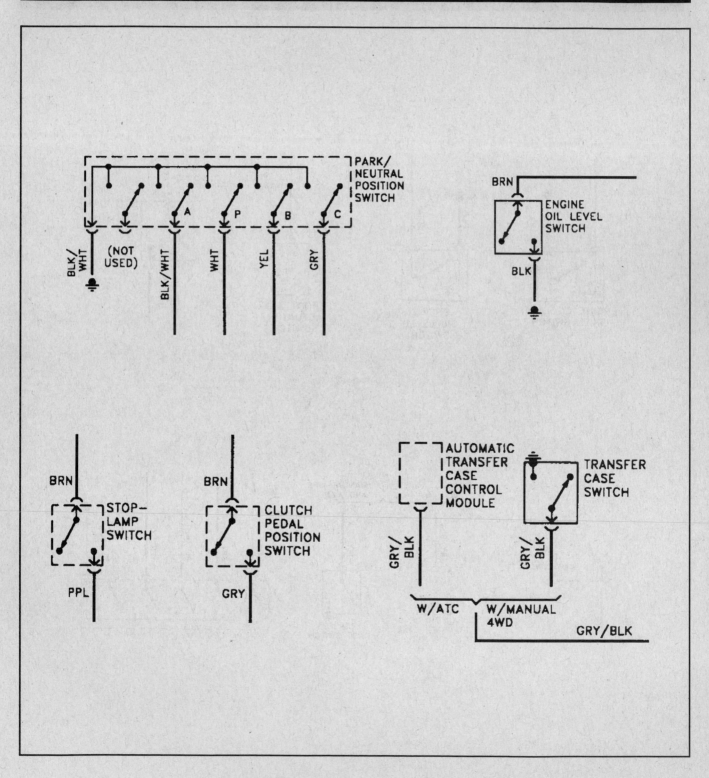

PICK-UP MODELS **SWITCHES**

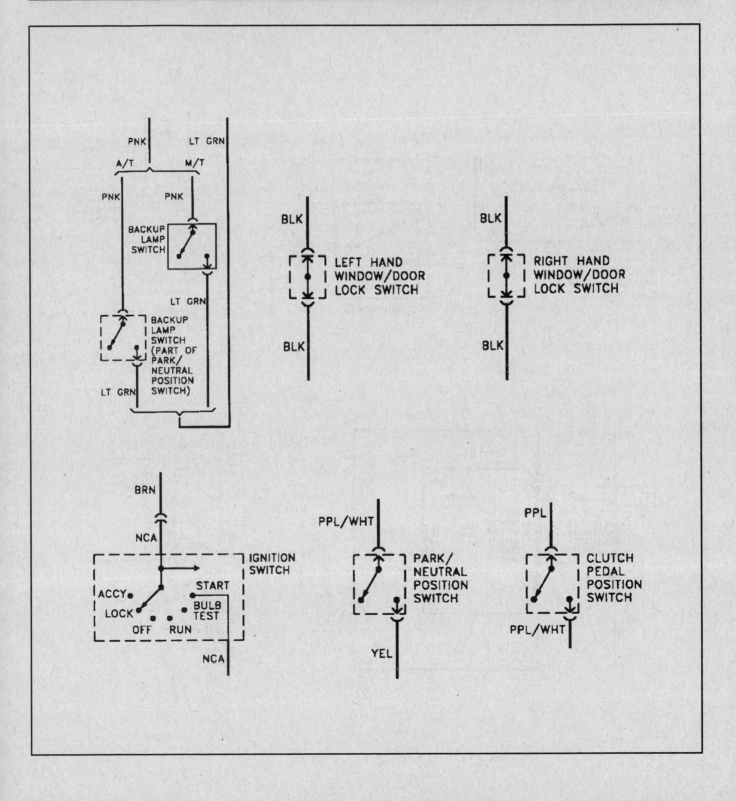

SWITCHES PICK-UP MODELS

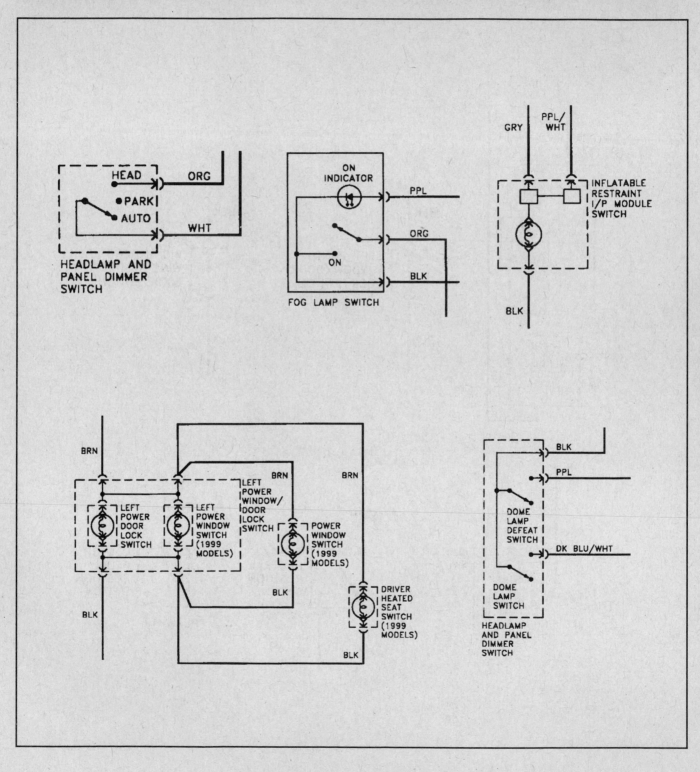

PICK-UP MODELS **SWITCHES**

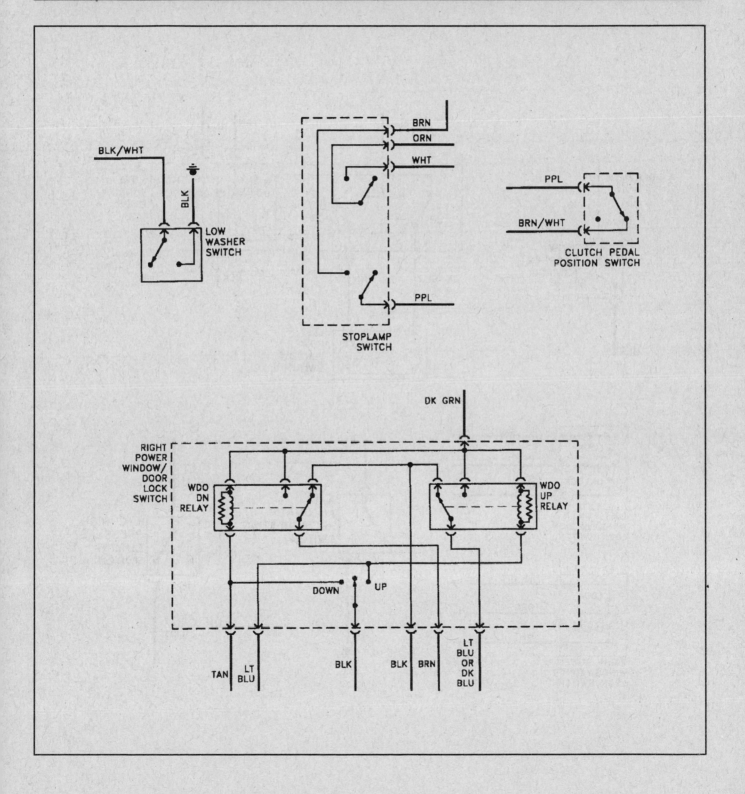

SWITCHES PICK-UP MODELS

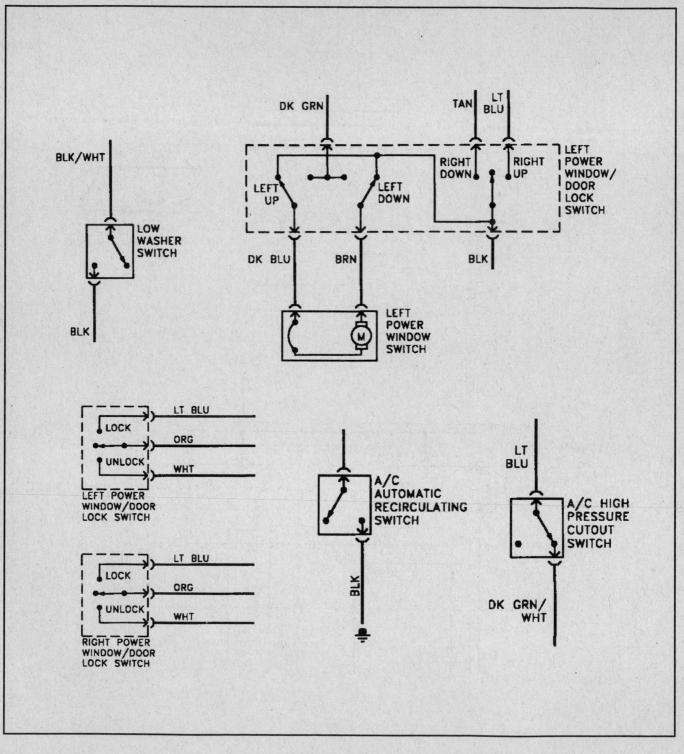

SUV MODELS **SWITCHES**

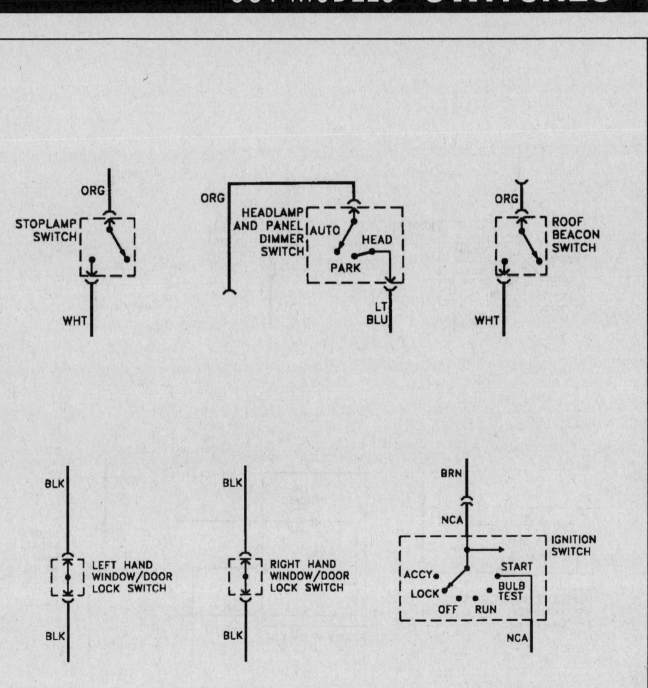

SWITCHES SUV MODELS

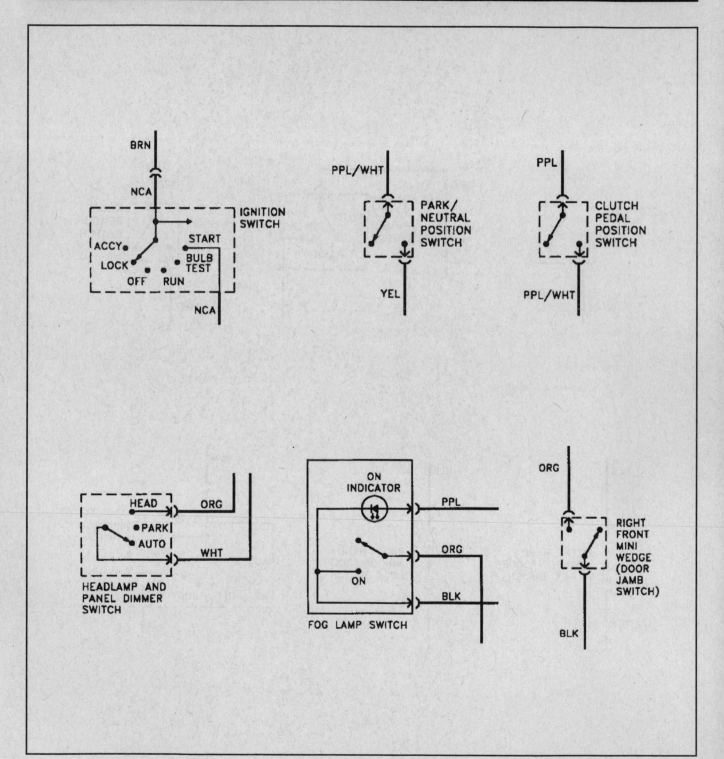

SUV MODELS **SWITCHES**

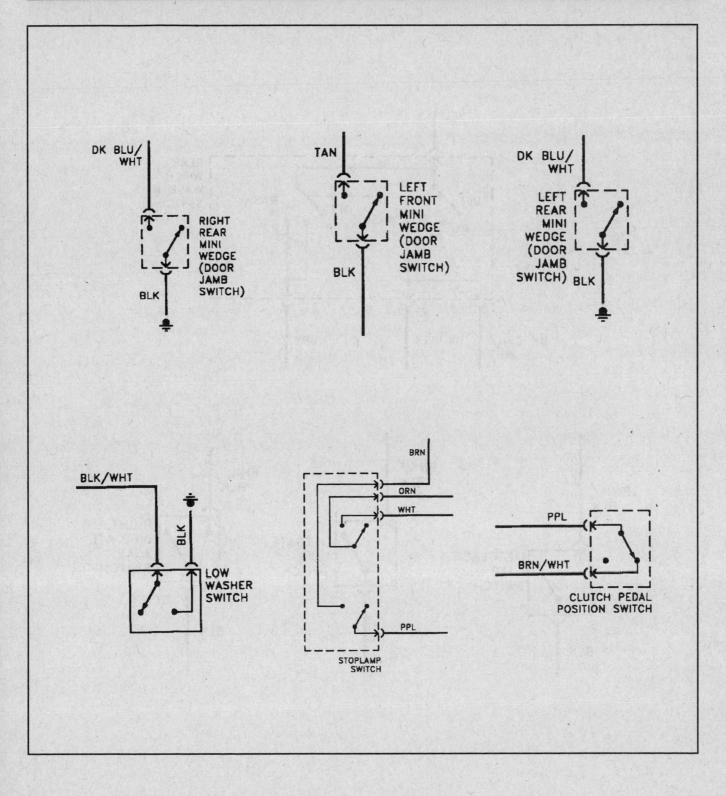

SWITCHES SUV MODELS

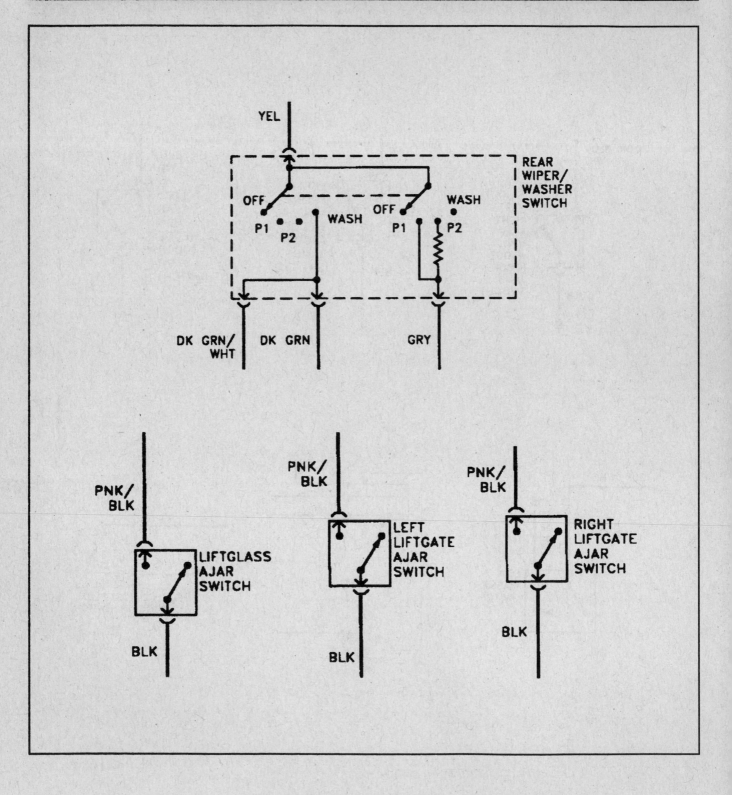

SUV MODELS **SWITCHES**

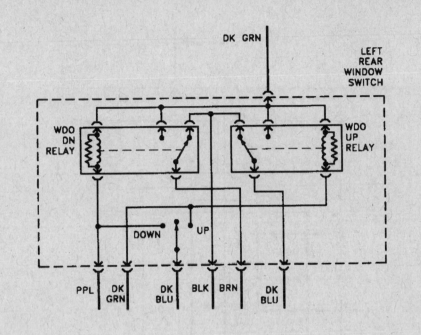

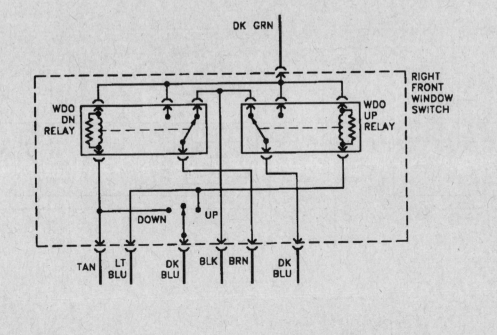

SWITCHES SUV MODELS

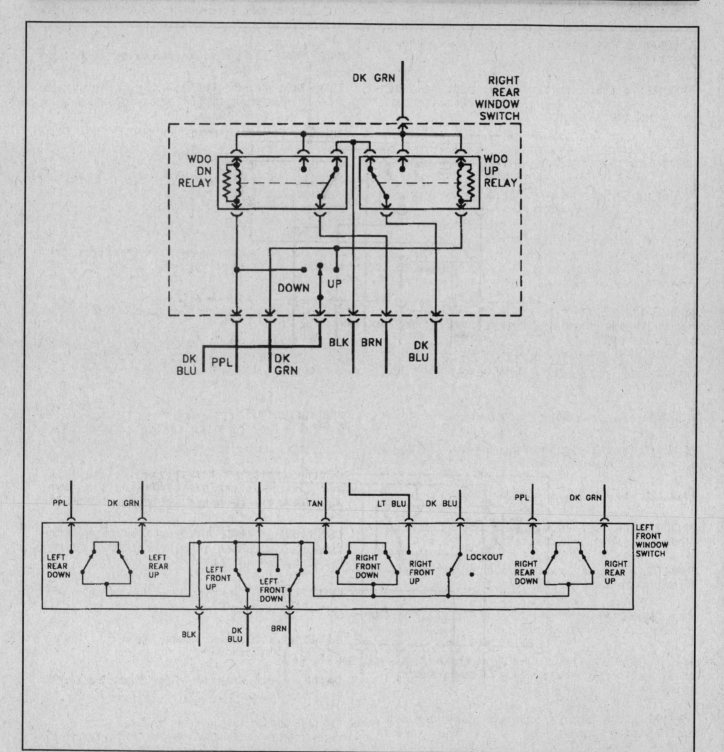

GLOSSARY

AIR/FUEL RATIO: The ratio of air-to-gasoline by weight in the fuel mixture drawn into the engine.

AIR INJECTION: One method of reducing harmful exhaust emissions by injecting air into each of the exhaust ports of an engine. The fresh air entering the hot exhaust manifold causes any remaining fuel to be burned before it can exit the tailpipe.

ALTERNATOR: A device used for converting mechanical energy into electrical energy.

AMMETER: An instrument, calibrated in amperes, used to measure the flow of an electrical current in a circuit. Ammeters are always connected in series with the circuit being tested.

AMPERE: The rate of flow of electrical current present when one volt of electrical pressure is applied against one ohm of electrical resistance.

ANALOG COMPUTER: Any microprocessor that uses similar (analogous) electrical signals to make its calculations.

ARMATURE: A laminated, soft iron core wrapped by a wire that converts electrical energy to mechanical energy as in a motor or relay. When rotated in a magnetic field, it changes mechanical energy into electrical energy as in a generator.

ATMOSPHERIC PRESSURE: The pressure on the Earth's surface caused by the weight of the air in the atmosphere. At sea level, this pressure is 14.7 psi at 32°F (101 kPa at 0°C).

ATOMIZATION: The breaking down of a liquid into a fine mist that can be suspended in air.

AXIAL PLAY: Movement parallel to a shaft or bearing bore.

BACKFIRE: The sudden combustion of gases in the intake or exhaust system that results in a loud explosion.

BACKLASH: The clearance or play between two parts, such as meshed gears.

BACKPRESSURE: Restrictions in the exhaust system that slow the exit of exhaust gases from the combustion chamber.

BAKELITE: A heat resistant, plastic insulator material commonly used In printed circuit boards and transistorized components.

BALL BEARING: A bearing made up of hardened inner and outer races between which hardened steel balls roll.

BALLAST RESISTOR: A resistor in the primary ignition circuit that lowers voltage after the engine is started to reduce wear on ignition components.

BEARING: A friction reducing, supportive device usually located between a stationary part and a moving part.

BIMETAL TEMPERATURE SENSOR: Any sensor or switch made of two dissimilar types of metal that bend when heated or cooled due to the different expansion rates of the alloys. These types of sensors usually function as an on/off switch.

BLOWBY: Combustion gases, composed of water vapor and unburned fuel, that leak past the piston rings into the crankcase during normal engine operation. These gases are removed by the PCV system to prevent the buildup of harmful acids in the crankcase.

BRAKE PAD: A brake shoe and lining assembly used with disc brakes.

BRAKE SHOE: The backing for the brake lining. The term is, however, usually applied to the assembly of the brake backing and lining.

BUSHING: A liner, usually removable, for a bearing; an anti-friction liner used in place of a bearing.

CALIPER: A hydraulically activated device in a disc brake system, which is mounted straddling the brake rotor (disc). The caliper contains at least one piston and two brake pads. Hydraulic pressure on the piston(s) forces the pads against the rotor.

CAMSHAFT: A shaft In the engine on which are the lobes (cams) which operate the valves. The camshaft is driven by the crankshaft, via a belt, chain or gears, at one half the crankshaft speed.

CAPACITOR: A device which stores an electrical charge.

CARBON MONOXIDE (CO): A colorless, odorless gas given off as a normal byproduct of combustion. It is poisonous and extremely dangerous in confined areas, building up slowly to toxic levels without warning If adequate ventilation is not available.

CARBURETOR: A device, usually mounted on the intake manifold of an engine, which mixes the air and fuel in the proper proportion to allow even combustion.

CATALYTIC CONVERTER: A device installed in the exhaust system, like a muffler, that converts harmful byproducts of combustion into carbon dioxide and water vapor by means of a heat-producing chemical reaction.

CENTRIFUGAL ADVANCE: A mechanical method of advancing the spark timing by using flyweights in the distributor that react to centrifugal force generated by the distributor shaft rotation.

CHECK VALVE: Any one-way valve installed to permit the flow of air, fuel or vacuum in one direction only.

CHOKE: A device, usually a moveable valve, placed in the intake path of a carburetor to restrict the flow of air.

CIRCUIT: Any unbroken path through which an electrical current can flow. Also used to describe fuel flow in some instances.

CIRCUIT BREAKER: A switch which protects an electrical circuit from overload by opening the circuit when the current flow exceeds a predetermined level. Some circuit breakers must be reset manually, while most reset automatically.

COIL (IGNITION): A transformer in the ignition circuit which steps up the voltage provided to the spark plugs.

COMBINATION MANIFOLD: An assembly which includes both the intake and exhaust manifolds in one casting.

COMBINATION VALVE: A device used in some fuel systems that routes fuel vapors to a charcoal storage canister instead of venting them into the atmosphere. The valve relieves fuel tank pressure and allows fresh air into the tank as the fuel level drops to prevent a vapor lock situation.

COMPRESSION RATIO: The comparison of the total volume of the cylinder and combustion chamber with the piston at BDC and the piston at TDC.

CONDENSER: 1. An electrical device which acts to store an electrical charge, preventing voltage surges. 2. A radiator-like device in the air conditioning system in which refrigerant gas condenses into a liquid, giving off heat.

CONDUCTOR: Any material through which an electrical current can be transmitted easily.

CONTINUITY: Continuous or complete circuit. Can be checked with an ohmmeter.

COUNTERSHAFT: An intermediate shaft which is rotated by a mainshaft and transmits, in turn, that rotation to a working part.

CRANKCASE: The lower part of an engine in which the crankshaft and related parts operate.

CRANKSHAFT: The main driving shaft of an engine which receives reciprocating motion from the pistons and converts it to rotary motion.

CYLINDER: In an engine, the round hole in the engine block in which the piston(s) ride.

CYLINDER BLOCK: The main structural member of an engine in which is found the cylinders, crankshaft and other principal parts.

CYLINDER HEAD: The detachable portion of the engine, usually fastened to the top of the cylinder block and containing all or most of the combustion chambers. On overhead valve engines, it contains the valves and their operating parts. On overhead cam engines, it contains the camshaft as well.

DEAD CENTER: The extreme top or bottom of the piston stroke.

DETONATION: An unwanted explosion of the air/fuel mixture in the combustion chamber caused by excess heat and compression, advanced timing, or an overly lean mixture. Also referred to as "ping".

DIAPHRAGM: A thin, flexible wall separating two cavities, such as in a vacuum advance unit.

DIESELING: A condition in which hot spots in the combustion chamber cause the engine to run on after the key is turned off.

DIFFERENTIAL: A geared assembly which allows the transmission of motion between drive axles, giving one axle the ability to turn faster than the other.

DIODE: An electrical device that will allow current to flow in one direction only.

DISC BRAKE: A hydraulic braking assembly consisting of a brake disc, or rotor, mounted on an axle, and a caliper assembly containing, usually two brake pads which are activated by hydraulic pressure. The pads are forced against the sides of the disc, creating friction which slows the vehicle.

DISTRIBUTOR: A mechanically driven device on an engine which is responsible for electrically firing the spark plug at a predetermined point of the piston stroke.

DOWEL PIN: A pin, inserted in mating holes in two different parts allowing those parts to maintain a fixed relationship.

DRUM BRAKE: A braking system which consists of two brake shoes and one or two wheel cylinders, mounted on a fixed backing plate, and a brake drum, mounted on an axle, which revolves around the assembly.

DWELL: The rate, measured in degrees of shaft rotation, at which an electrical circuit cycles on and off.

ELECTRONIC CONTROL UNIT (ECU): Ignition module, module, amplifier or igniter. See Module for definition.

ELECTRONIC IGNITION: A system in which the timing and firing of the spark plugs is controlled by an electronic control unit, usually called a module. These systems have no points or condenser.

END-PLAY: The measured amount of axial movement in a shaft.

ENGINE: A device that converts heat into mechanical energy.

EXHAUST MANIFOLD: A set of cast passages or pipes which conduct exhaust gases from the engine.

FEELER GAUGE: A blade, usually metal, of precisely predetermined thickness, used to measure the clearance between two parts.

FIRING ORDER: The order in which combustion occurs in the cylinders of an engine. Also the order in which spark is distributed to the plugs by the distributor.

FLOODING: The presence of too much fuel in the intake manifold and combustion chamber which prevents the air/fuel mixture from firing, thereby causing a no-start situation.

FLYWHEEL: A disc shaped part bolted to the rear end of the crankshaft. Around the outer perimeter is affixed the ring gear. The starter drive engages the ring gear, turning the flywheel, which rotates the crankshaft, imparting the initial starting motion to the engine.

FOOT POUND (ft. lbs. or sometimes, ft.lb.): The amount of energy or work needed to raise an item weighing one pound, a distance of one foot.

FUSE: A protective device in a circuit which prevents circuit overload by breaking the circuit when a specific amperage is present. The device is constructed around a strip or wire of a lower amperage rating than the circuit it is designed to protect. When an amperage higher than that stamped on the fuse is present in the circuit, the strip or wire melts, opening the circuit.

GEAR RATIO: The ratio between the number of teeth on meshing gears.

GENERATOR: A device which converts mechanical energy into electrical energy.

HEAT RANGE: The measure of a spark plug's ability to dissipate heat from its firing end. The higher the heat range, the hotter the plug fires.

HUB: The center part of a wheel or gear.

HYDROCARBON (HC): Any chemical compound made up of hydrogen and carbon. A major pollutant formed by the engine as a byproduct of combustion.

HYDROMETER: An instrument used to measure the specific gravity of a solution.

INCH POUND (inch lbs.; sometimes in.lb. or in. lbs.): One twelfth of a foot pound.

INDUCTION: A means of transferring electrical energy in the form of a magnetic field. Principle used in the ignition coil to increase voltage.

INJECTOR: A device which receives metered fuel under relatively low pressure and is activated to inject the fuel into the engine under relatively high pressure at a predetermined time.

INPUT SHAFT: The shaft to which torque is applied, usually carrying the driving gear or gears.

INTAKE MANIFOLD: A casting of passages or pipes used to conduct air or a fuel/air mixture to the cylinders.

JOURNAL: The bearing surface within which a shaft operates.

KEY: A small block usually fitted in a notch between a shaft and a hub to prevent slippage of the two parts.

MANIFOLD: A casting of passages or set of pipes which connect the cylinders to an inlet or outlet source.

MANIFOLD VACUUM: Low pressure in an engine intake manifold formed just below the throttle plates. Manifold vacuum is highest at idle and drops under acceleration.

MASTER CYLINDER: The primary fluid pressurizing device in a hydraulic system. In automotive use, it is found in brake and hydraulic clutch systems and is pedal activated, either directly or, in a power brake system, through the power booster.

MODULE: Electronic control unit, amplifier or igniter of solid state or integrated design which controls the current flow in the ignition primary circuit based on input from the pick-up coil. When the module opens the primary circuit, high secondary voltage is induced in the coil.

NEEDLE BEARING: A bearing which consists of a number (usually a large number) of long, thin rollers.

OHM: (Ω) The unit used to measure the resistance of conductor-to-electrical flow. One ohm is the amount of resistance that limits current flow to one ampere in a circuit with one volt of pressure.

OHMMETER: An instrument used for measuring the resistance, in ohms, in an electrical circuit.

OUTPUT SHAFT: The shaft which transmits torque from a device, such as a transmission.

OVERDRIVE: A gear assembly which produces more shaft revolutions than that transmitted to it.

OVERHEAD CAMSHAFT (OHC): An engine configuration in which the camshaft is mounted on top of the cylinder head and operates the valve either directly or by means of rocker arms.

OVERHEAD VALVE (OHV): An engine configuration in which all of the valves are located in the cylinder head and the camshaft is located in the cylinder block. The camshaft operates the valves via lifters and pushrods.

OXIDES OF NITROGEN (NOx): Chemical compounds of nitrogen produced as a byproduct of combustion. They combine with hydrocarbons to produce smog.

OXYGEN SENSOR: Use with the feedback system to sense the presence of oxygen in the exhaust gas and signal the computer which can reference the voltage signal to an air/fuel ratio.

PINION: The smaller of two meshing gears.

PISTON RING: An open-ended ring with fits into a groove on the outer diameter of the piston. Its chief function is to form a seal between the piston and cylinder wall. Most automotive pistons have three rings: two for compression sealing; one for oil sealing.

PRELOAD: A predetermined load placed on a bearing during assembly or by adjustment.

PRIMARY CIRCUIT: the low voltage side of the ignition system which consists of the ignition switch, ballast resistor or resistance wire, bypass, coil, electronic control unit and pick-up coil as well as the connecting wires and harnesses.

PRESS FIT: The mating of two parts under pressure, due to the inner diameter of one being smaller than the outer diameter of the other, or vice versa; an interference fit.

RACE: The surface on the inner or outer ring of a bearing on which the balls, needles or rollers move.

REGULATOR: A device which maintains the amperage and/or voltage levels of a circuit at predetermined values.

RELAY: A switch which automatically opens and/or closes a circuit.

RESISTANCE: The opposition to the flow of current through a circuit or electrical device, and is measured in ohms. Resistance is equal to the voltage divided by the amperage.

RESISTOR: A device, usually made of wire, which offers a preset amount of resistance in an electrical circuit.

RING GEAR: The name given to a ring-shaped gear attached to a differential case, or affixed to a flywheel or as part of a planetary gear set.

ROLLER BEARING: A bearing made up of hardened inner and outer races between which hardened steel rollers move.

ROTOR: 1. The disc-shaped part of a disc brake assembly, upon which the brake pads bear; also called, brake disc. 2. The device mounted atop the distributor shaft, which passes current to the distributor cap tower contacts.

SECONDARY CIRCUIT: The high voltage side of the ignition system, usually above 20,000 volts. The secondary includes the ignition coil, coil wire, distributor cap and rotor, spark plug wires and spark plugs.

SENDING UNIT: A mechanical, electrical, hydraulic or electro-magnetic device which transmits information to a gauge.

SENSOR: Any device designed to measure engine operating conditions or ambient pressures and temperatures. Usually electronic in nature and designed to send a voltage signal to an on-board computer, some sensors may operate as a simple on/off switch or they may provide a variable voltage signal (like a potentiometer) as conditions or measured parameters change.

SHIM: Spacers of precise, predetermined thickness used between parts to establish a proper working relationship.

SLAVE CYLINDER: In automotive use, a device in the hydraulic clutch system which is activated by hydraulic force, disengaging the clutch.

SOLENOID: A coil used to produce a magnetic field, the effect of which is to produce work.

SPARK PLUG: A device screwed into the combustion chamber of a spark ignition engine. The basic construction is a conductive core inside of a ceramic insulator, mounted in an outer conductive base. An electrical charge from the spark plug wire travels along the conductive core and jumps a preset air gap to a grounding point or points at the end of the conductive base. The resultant spark ignites the fuel/air mixture in the combustion chamber.

SPLINES: Ridges machined or cast onto the outer diameter of a shaft or inner diameter of a bore to enable parts to mate without rotation.

TACHOMETER: A device used to measure the rotary speed of an engine, shaft, gear, etc., usually in rotations per minute.

THERMOSTAT: A valve, located in the cooling system of an engine, which is closed when cold and opens gradually in response to engine heating, controlling the temperature of the coolant and rate of coolant flow.

TOP DEAD CENTER (TDC): The point at which the piston reaches the top of its travel on the compression stroke.

TORQUE: The twisting force applied to an object.

TORQUE CONVERTER: A turbine used to transmit power from a driving member to a driven member via hydraulic action, providing changes in drive ratio and torque. In automotive use, it links the driveplate at the rear of the engine to the automatic transmission.

TRANSDUCER: A device used to change a force into an electrical signal.

TRANSISTOR: A semi-conductor component which can be actuated by a small voltage to perform an electrical switching function.

TUNE-UP: A regular maintenance function, usually associated with the replacement and adjustment of parts and components in the electrical and fuel systems of a vehicle for the purpose of attaining optimum performance.

TURBOCHARGER: An exhaust driven pump which compresses intake air and forces it into the combustion chambers at higher than atmospheric pressures. The increased air pressure allows more fuel to be burned and results in increased horsepower being produced.

VACUUM ADVANCE: A device which advances the ignition timing in response to increased engine vacuum.

VACUUM GAUGE: An instrument used to measure the presence of vacuum in a chamber.

VALVE: A device which control the pressure, direction of flow or rate of flow of a liquid or gas.

VALVE CLEARANCE: The measured gap between the end of the valve stem and the rocker arm, cam lobe or follower that activates the valve.

VISCOSITY: The rating of a liquid's internal resistance to flow.

VOLTMETER: An instrument used for measuring electrical force in units called volts. Voltmeters are always connected parallel with the circuit being tested.

WHEEL CYLINDER: Found in the automotive drum brake assembly, it is a device, actuated by hydraulic pressure, which, through internal pistons, pushes the brake shoes outward against the drums.

A

B

MASTER INDEX